THE
KINGDOM
OF THE
CULTS

THE KINGDOM OF THE CULTS

Walter Martin

Limited Edition

BETHANY HOUSE PUBLISHERS
MINNEAPOLIS, MINNESOTA 55438

Limited paperback edition.
Forty-sixth printing—April 1992

Copyright © 1965, 1977, 1985
Walter Martin
All Rights Reserved

Published by Bethany House Publishers
A Division of Bethany Fellowship, Inc.
6820 Auto Club Road, Minneapolis, Minnesota 55438

Printed in the United States of America

Library of Congress Cataloging in Publication Data

Martin, Walter Ralston, 1928–1989
    The kingdom of the cults.

    Bibliography: p.
    Includes index.
    1. Religions. 2. Cults—United States.
3. Christian sects—United States. 4. United States—Religion.
I. Title.
BL80.2.M289   1985   291.9   85–7410
ISBN 0–87123–796–2

In Memory of
Peter de Visser

my friend and brother in the common faith. His help and encouragement made this volume possible. If you seek his monument, consult the libraries of the informed.

ABOUT THE AUTHOR

WALTER MARTIN held four earned degrees, having received his doctorate from California Coast University in the field of Comparative Religions. Author of a dozen books and a half-dozen booklets and many articles, he was nationally known as "The Bible Answer Man," host of a popular syndicated radio call-in program which was heard across the country. He was founder and director of the Christian Research Institute, located in Irvine, California. A few months after finishing *The New Age Cult*, Dr. Martin went to be with the Lord.

ACKNOWLEDGMENTS

I wish to express my deep gratitude to Pierson Curtis, former senior master of the Stony Brook School, who helped edit and correct the original manuscript; the Rev. Anthony Collarile, Messrs. Herbert Jacobsen, Robert Smith and John Carter, who offered valuable insights and research data; Mr. Walter Bjorck, Jr., of the American Tract Society, who made many helpful manuscript suggestions which were adopted in a number of instances, editor-researcher Gretchen Passantino, who revised the majority of this present edition, and associate Clark F. Hyman, who also contributed significantly to the revision of this present edition.

OTHER BOOKS BY WALTER MARTIN . . .

The Christian and the Cults
The Christian Science Myth
Esssential Christianity
Jehovah of the Watchtower
The Maze of Mormonism
The New Age Cult
The New Cults
Screwtape Writes Again
The Truth About Seventh-Day Adventism
Walter Martin's Cults Reference Bible
Walter Martin Speaks Out on the Cults

BOOKLETS

Abortion: Is It Always Murder?
Christian Science
Herbert W. Armstrong and the Worldwide Church of God
Jehovah's Witnesses
Mormonism
The Riddle of Reincarnation
Unity

CONTENTS

Chapter 1

THE KINGDOM OF THE CULTS

It has been said of the United States that it is "the great melting pot" for the people of the world. And the contents of that pot would not be complete unless it also included the religions of those masses that now make up the populace of America. This writer has spent the last thirty-one years of his life in research and field work among the religions of America, and this volume, limited as it is by the vastness and complexity of the problem itself, constitutes his evaluation of that vibrant brand of religion which has come to be recognized by many as the "Kingdom of the Cults."

In his study of modern American cults and minority religious movements as found in his text, *These Also Believe*, Dr. Charles Braden, emeritus professor at Northwestern University (1954), and John C. Schaffer, lecturer (1955), and visiting professor at Scripps College (1954 to 1956), made a number of observations with which this writer agrees. In regard to the term "cult," for instance, Dr. Braden states:

"By the term cult I mean nothing derogatory to any group so classified. A cult, as I define it, is any religious group which differs significantly in some one or more respects as to belief or practice from those religious groups which are regarded as the normative expressions of religion in our total culture" (Preface, xii). I may add to this that a cult might also be defined as a group of people gathered about a specific person or person's mis-interpretation of the Bible. For example, Jehovah's Witnesses are, for the most part, followers of the interpretations of Charles T. Russell and J. F. Rutherford. The Christian Scientist of today is a disciple of Mary Baker Eddy and her interpretations of Scripture. The Mormons, by their own admission, adhere to those interpretations found in the writings of Joseph Smith and Brigham Young. It would be possible to go on citing many others, such as the Unity School of Christianity, which follows the theology of Charles and Myrtle Fillmore. From a theological viewpoint, the cults contain many major deviations from historic Christianity. Yet paradoxically, they continue to insist that they are entitled to be classified as Christians.

It is my conviction that the reader is entitled to know the theological position from which this volume is written so that there will be no misconceptions as to the ground for my evaluation. I am a Baptist minister, an evangelical holding to the inerrancy of Scripture, and teach in the fields of Biblical Theology, Comparative Religion, and Apologetics, and am currently Director of the M.A. program at the Simon Greenleaf School of Law (Orange, Calif.). It is impossible for me to agree with Dr. Braden, "an unrepentant liberal" (p. xi), or to agree that I "hold no brief for any particular cult, nor . . . violently opposed to any" (p. xi). While I am in agreement that "in

11

general the cults represent the earnest attempt of millions of people to find the fulfillment of deep and legitimate needs of the human spirit, which most of them seem not to have found in the established churches" (p. xi), I feel there is still much more to be said. It has been wisely observed by someone that "a man who will not stand for something is quite likely to fall for almost anything." So I have elected to stand on the ramparts of Biblical Christianity as taught by the apostles, defended by the church fathers, rediscovered by the reformers, and embodied in what is sometimes called Reformed Theology.

It is the purpose of this book then, to evaluate the so-called cults and –isms which today are found in abundance in America and, in quite a number of cases, on the great mission fields of the world. My approach to the subject then is threefold: (1) historical analysis of the salient facts connected with the rise of the cult systems; (2) the theological evaluation of the major teachings of those systems; and (3) an apologetic contrast from the viewpoint of Biblical theology, with an emphasis upon exegesis and doctrine.

It is not my desire in any sense to make fun of adherents of cult systems, the large majority of whom are sincere, though I am not adverse to humor when it can underscore a point. A study of the cults is a serious business. They constitute a growing trend in America—a trend which is away from the established Christian churches and the historic teachings of the Bible— an emphasis upon autosoteric efforts, or the desire to save one's self apart from Biblical revelation.

It is most significant that those who have written on the cults have only recently stressed the authority of the Scriptures as a criterion for measuring either the truth or falsity of cultic claims. When this book first appeared in 1965, it was the first to make such a stress on such a large scale. Since then my example has been followed and the Christian is now in a position to readily find the Scripture's verdict on the cults. Dr. Marcus Bach, who has written extensively from a liberal viewpoint on the cults, summed up this attitude of tolerance apart from Scriptural authority when he wrote:

> Somehow I felt I must become a representative of the average church-goer everywhere in America, whose heart was with me in my seeking. If the Jehovah's Witnesses have some heavenly tip-off that the world is coming to an end in 1973,[1] we want to tell our friends about it in plenty of time! If Father Divine is really God, we want to know about it! If Unity is building a new city down in Missouri, we Americans want to get in on the ground floor! If that man in Moscow, Idaho, talked with God, actually and literally, we have a right to know how it's done! Certainly these modern movements suggest that there was a vital, if not always coherent, moving force back of them, giving luster and drive to their beliefs. I decided that I would not concern myself so much with the rivalry among groups as with their realization. I would devote myself more to the *way* than to the *why* of their doctrine. Let others turn ecclesiastical microscopes on them, or weigh them in the sensitive scale of final truth; I would content myself with the age-old verdict of Gamaliel: "If this work be of men, it will come to naught; but if

---

[1]They most recently decided on September of 1975, to their later dismay. This new false prophecy cost them thousands of members.

it be of God, we cannot overthrow it."

I decided to set forth on my own, with no strings attached, and no stipend from any university, no commission from any church, no obligation to any individual or group, no bias, no preconceived judgment, no illusions.

"All roads that lead to God are good." As I began my adventure the fervor of this naive and youthful conviction rushed over me once more. (*They Have Found a Faith*, pages 19, 20, 21).

Dr. Bach admits more in this statement than perhaps he intended, for though it is a laudable aim to become "representative of the average church-goer everywhere in America," the use of the word "if" in the reference to the teachings of the cults indicates that the final truth, grounded in the authority of Scripture and the revelation of Jesus Christ, has not been obtained by the Christian Church, and that other sources must be investigated in order to ascertain the whole truth of the Christian message. We are in full agreement that "these modern movements suggest that there was a vital, if not always coherent, moving force back of them, giving luster and drive to their beliefs." But since most, if not all the cult systems vigorously oppose the Christian Church, particularly in the realm of Christology and soteriology, perhaps it is not at all out of order to suggest that "that force" is the same as that which opposed our Lord and the apostles, and has consistently opposed the efforts of the Christian Church, the force described by our Lord as "the god of this world."

Liberal scholars, then, have devoted themselves more to "the way" than to "the why" of the doctrines of the cults, and they have adopted the statement of Gamaliel as their creed. It will be remembered that Gamaliel counseled the Jews not to oppose the Christians for "if this counsel or this work be of men, it will come to nought: But if it be of God, ye cannot overthrow it" (Acts 5:38–39).

Let it not be forgotten that Gamaliel's advice is not Biblical theology; and if it were followed in the practical realm of experience as steadfastly as it is urged, then we would have to recognize Islam as "of God," because of its rapid growth and reproductive virility throughout the world. We would have to acknowledge Mormonism (six people in 1830 to over 5 million in 1982) in the same category as Islam, something which most liberals are unwilling to do, though some have not hesitated to so declare themselves. We do not suggest that we "turn ecclesiastical microscopes" on the cults, but rather, that they be viewed in the light of what we know to be divine revelation, the Word of God, which itself weighs them, "in the sensitive scale of final truth," for it was our Lord who taught, "If you believe not that I AM, you will die in your sins." And the final criterion today as always, must remain, "What think ye of Christ, whose son is He?"

I must dissent from the view that "all roads that lead to God are good" and believe instead the words of our Lord, "I am the way, the truth, and the life: no man cometh unto the Father, but by me" (John 14:6). It should be carefully noted that Jesus did not say "I am one of many equally good ways," or, "I am a better way than the others, I am an aspect of truth; I am a fragment of the life." Instead, His claim was absolute, and allegiance to Him, as the Savior of the world, was to take precedence over all the claims of men and religions.

I should like to make it clear that in advancing criticism of some of the views of liberal scholars in the field of cults and –isms, I do not discount their many valuable contributions. And no one study, regardless of the time involved and the thoroughness of the investigation, can review all the data and evaluate all the facts necessary to completely understand the origin and development of cultism. My approach is quite honestly theological in its orientation, with the aim of contrast and reaffirmation in view. Dr. Van Baalen is correct when he says that "the cults are the unpaid bills of the church" (*Chaos of Cults*, p. 14). They are this and more, for they are a challenge to the Church to affirm once again the great principles and foundations of the Gospel of Christ, and to make them meaningful to the present generation. There can be no doubt that the great trend in religion is synchretistic, or a type of homogenization of religions, such as the great historian Arnold Toynbee has more than once suggested.

We are consistently being told in books, articles, council pronouncements and ecumenical conclaves, that we must "play down the things that divide us and emphasize those things which make for unity." This is all well and good, if we are speaking about a firm foundation of doctrinal, as well as of moral and ethical truth, and if we are speaking about true unity within the body of Christ. But if, as some suggest, this be broadened to include those who are not in agreement with the essentials of Biblical Christianity, we must resolutely oppose it. It is most interesting to note that the National Council of Churches and the World Council of Churches, which constitute the spearhead of the ecumenical movement throughout the world, have consistently denied membership to the cults under study in this volume on the ground that they do not recognize or worship Jesus Christ as God and Savior. In 1957 *The Christian Century* printed a series of articles on four prominent cults which were written by Dr. Marcus Bach. Dr. Bach's presentation was so sympathetic that the then editors of *The Christian Century* were compelled to write an editorial, pointing out the differences between the cults and Christianity. Editor Harold Fey and Managing Editor Theodore Gill wrote that the promises of the cults were empty and could not satisfy as Christianity could (p. 551). We can sympathize with Fey and Gill's concerns, since any series of articles which presents the cults in such a favorable light, though appearing to be objective, does little or nothing for Christianity, except to encourage weaker Christians to dabble in what is a dangerous hobby.

Biblical Perspectives

The age which saw the advent of Jesus Christ was an age rich in religion, stretching from the crass animism and sex worship of the great majority of the world, to the Roman pantheon of gods and the Greek mystery religions. One need only pursue Gibbon's *Decline and Fall of the Roman Empire* to become acutely aware of the multiplicity of gods and goddesses, as well as of philosophical and ethical systems which pervaded the religious horizon in that era of history. Judaism had withdrawn itself from any extensive missionary activity, burdened as the Jews were by the iron rule of an unsympathetic Roman paganism. The law of God had been interpreted and reinterpreted through commentaries and rabbinical emendations to the place where our Lord had to say to the religious leaders of His day: "Why do ye also transgress the commandment of God by your tradition? . . . Ye made the commandment of God of none effect by your tradition" (Matthew 15:3, 6).

Into this whirlpool of stagnant human philosophy and perverted revelation, came the Son of God who, through His teachings and example, revealed that there was such a thing as divine humanity, and through His miraculous powers, vicarious death and bodily Resurrection, cut across the maze of human doubts and fears, and was lifted up, to draw all men unto Him. It has been wisely observed that men are at liberty to reject Jesus Christ and the Bible as the Word of God; they are at liberty to oppose Him; they are at liberty to challenge it. But they are not at liberty to alter the essential message of the Scriptures, which is the good news that God does care for the lost souls of His children, and so loved us as to send His only Son that we might live through Him.

In keeping with this gospel of God's grace, our Lord not only announced it, but He prophesied the trials and tribulations which would encompass His followers, both within the Church and without, and one of the greatest of all these trials would, our Lord taught, be the challenge of false prophets and false christs, who would come in His name and deceive many (Matthew 24:5). So concerned was Christ in this area that He at one time declared:

> Beware of false prophets, which come to you in sheep's clothing, but inwardly they are ravening wolves. Ye shall know them by their fruits. Do men gather grapes of thorns, or figs of thistles? Even so every good tree bringeth forth good fruit; but a corrupt tree bringeth forth evil fruit. A good tree cannot bring forth evil fruit, neither can a corrupt tree bring forth good fruit. Every tree that bringeth not forth good fruit is hewn down, and cast into the fire. Wherefore by their fruits ye shall know them. Not every one that saith unto me, Lord, Lord, shall enter into the kingdom of heaven; but he that doeth the will of my Father which is in heaven. Many will say to me in that day, Lord, Lord, have we not prophesied in thy name? and in thy name have cast out devils? and in thy name done many wonderful works? And then will I profess unto them, I never knew you: depart from me, ye that work iniquity (Matthew 7:15–23).

[margin note: False prophets]

Christ pointed out that the false prophets would come. There was not a doubt in the mind of the Son of God that this would take place, and the history of the heresies of the first five centuries of the Christian Church bear out the accuracy of His predictions. Christ further taught that the fruits of the false prophets would also be apparent, and that the Church would be able to detect them readily. Let us never forget that "fruits" from a corrupt tree can also be doctrinal, as well as ethical and moral. A person may be ethically and morally "good" by human standards, but if he sets his face against Jesus Christ as Lord and Savior, and rejects Him, his fruit is corrupt and he is to be rejected as counterfeit. The Apostle John understood this when he wrote: "They went out from us, but they were not of us; for if they had been of us, they would no doubt have continued with us: but they went out, that they might be made manifest that they were not all of us" (1 John 2:19).

The Bible, then, does speak of false prophets, false christs, false apostles and "Deceitful workers, transforming themselves into the apostles of Christ. And no marvel; for Satan himself is transformed into an angel of light. Therefore it is no great thing if his ministers also be transformed as the ministers of righteousness; whose end shall be according to their works" (2 Corinthians 11:13–15).

We cannot afford then, to have any concept of the purveyors of erroneous doctrines different from that held by our Lord and the apostles, and agree with the Apostle Paul that we must "abhor that which is evil; cleave to that which is good" (Romans 12:9). In the light of Paul's teaching, it is extremely difficult for this writer to understand how it is possible to cleave to that which is good, without an abhorrence of that which is evil.

The Biblical perspective then, where false teachers and false teachings are concerned, is that we are to have compassion and love for those who are enmeshed in the teachings of the false prophets, but we are to vigorously oppose the teachings, with our primary objective the winning of the soul, and not so much the argument. It must never be forgotten that cultists are souls for whom Jesus Christ died, for "he is the propitiation for our sins: and not for ours only, but also for the sins of the whole world" (1 John 2:2).

Today, the kingdom of the cults stretches throughout the world, its membership in the millions, with over 20 million cult members in the United States alone. The Church of Jesus Christ has badly neglected both the evangelizing and refuting of the various cult systems, although there is cause for some optimism.

But the problem faces us all the same and continues to grow: The kingdom of the cults is expanding, and when it is remembered that the rate of growth for the Mormon Church in the United States is greater than that of all of the Protestant denominations and the Roman Catholic Church together, the issue comes clearly into focus.

Our purpose in this volume is to further awaken interest to this tremendously important field of Christian missionary effort among the cults, to point out the flaws in the various cult systems, and to provide the information which will enable Christians both to answer cultists and to present effectively to them the claims of the Gospel of Christ, with a deep concern for the redemption of their souls. It is also the aim of this book to so familiarize the reader with the refreshing truths of the Gospel of Christ, that he may see the great heritage which is ours in the Christian faith, and be challenged more effectively to both live and to witness for the Savior.

The American Banking Association has a training program which exemplifies this aim of the author. Each year it sends hundreds of bank tellers to Washington in order to teach them to detect counterfeit money, which is a great source of a loss of revenue to the Treasury Department. It is most interesting that during the entire two-week training program, no teller touches counterfeit money. Only the original passes through his hands. The reason for this is that the American Banking Association is convinced that if a man is thoroughly familiar with the original, he will not be deceived by the counterfeit bill, no matter how much like the original it appears. It is the contention of this writer that if the average Christian would become familiar once again with the great foundations of his faith, he would be able to detect those counterfeit elements so apparent in the cult systems, which set them apart from Biblical Christianity.

Charles W. Ferguson, in his provocative volume, *The New Books of Revelation*, describes the advent of modern cult systems as "the modern Babel," then goes on to state that:

> It should be obvious to any man who is not one himself, that the land is overrun with messiahs. I refer not to those political quacks, who promise in one election to rid the land of evil, but rather, to those inspired fakirs who promise to reduce the diaphragm, or orient the soul through the machinery of a cult religion. Each of these has made himself the center of a new theophany, has surrounded himself with a band of zealous apostles, has hired a hall for a shrine and then set about busily to rescue truth from the scaffold, and put it on the throne (page 1).

Ferguson did the Christian Church a great service in the late 1920's by focusing attention upon the rise of the cults. His observations were pithy and to-the-point, and though they cannot always be endorsed from a Biblical standpoint, there can be little doubt that he put his finger upon the cults as a vital emergent force in American Protestantism, with which the Church of Jesus Christ must reckon. It is with this force that we now come to deal, confident that, on the authority of the Scriptures, the Christian Church has the answers, and in the Gospel of Christ, the Savior who can provide the cultist with something no cult system has ever been able to originate—peace with God and fellowship with the Father and with His Son, Jesus Christ. The cults have capitalized upon the failure of the Christian Church to understand their teachings and to develop a workable methodology both to evangelize and to refute cult adherents. Within the theological structure of the cults there is considerable truth, all of which, it might be added, is drawn from Biblical sources, but so diluted with human error as to be more deadly than complete falsehood. The cults have also emphasized the things which the Church has forgotten, such as divine healing (Christian Science, Unity, New Thought), prophecy (Jehovah's Witnesses and Mormonism), and a great many other things which in the course of our study we will have opportunity to observe. But let it never be forgotten that where the Gospel of Jesus Christ is proclaimed in power and with what Dr. Frank E. Gaebelein has called "a compelling relevancy," cults have made little or no headway. This has led Dr. Lee Belford, Professor of Comparative Religions at New York University, to state,

> The problem is essentially theological where the cults are concerned. The answer of the Church must be theological and doctrinal. No sociological or cultural evaluation will do. Such works may be helpful, but they will not answer the Jehovah's Witness or Mormon, who is seeking Biblical authority for either the acceptance or rejection of his beliefs.

The problem, then, is complex. There is no simple panacea, but it constitutes a real challenge to Christianity which cannot be ignored nor neglected any longer. For the challenge is here, and the time is now.

Chapter 2

SCALING THE LANGUAGE BARRIER

The scientific age in which we live has, in the very real sense of the term, given rise to a new vocabulary, which, unless it is understood, can create enormous problems in the realm of communication. The revolutions in culture which have taken place in the vocabularies of technology, psychology, medicine and politics have not left untouched the religions of the world in general, and the theology of Christianity in particular. Writing in *Eternity* magazine, the noted theologian Dr. Bernard Ramm calls attention to this particular fact, when evaluating the theological system of the late Dr. Tillich, leading theological luminary of our day and former Professor of Theology at the University of Chicago's Divinity School. Dr. Ramm charges that Tillich has so radically redefined standard theological terms that the effect upon Christian theology is nothing short of cataclysmic. ". . . Such Biblical notions of sin, guilt, damnation, justification, regeneration, etc., all come out retranslated into a language that is foreign to the meaning of these concepts in the Scriptures themselves."[1]

Dr. Ramm is quite right in his observations, for any student of Paul Tillich's theology, and, for that matter, the theology of contemporary Neoliberalism and Neo-orthodoxy, will concede immediately that, in the theological framework of these two systems of thought, the vocabulary of what has been rightly termed by Dr. Edward Carnell "classical orthodoxy," undergoes what can only be termed radical redefinition. Just how this is effected is worthy of another chapter, but no one informed on the subject seriously questions that this is what has occurred.

It is therefore possible for the modern theologians to use the terminology of the Bible and historic theology, but in an entirely different sense from that intended by the writers of Scripture.

Before attempting to examine the non-Christian cult systems contained in this volume, one must face the fact that the originators and promulgators of cult theology have done exactly the same thing to the semantic structure of Christian theology as did the modern theologians. So it is possible for a Jehovah's Witness, a Christian Scientist or a Mormon, for example, to utilize the terminology of Biblical Christianity with absolute freedom, having already redesigned these terms in a theological framework of his own making and to his own liking, but almost always at direct variance with the historically accepted meanings of the terms.

The student of cultism, then, must be prepared to scale the language barrier of terminology. First, he must recognize that it does exist, and second, he must acknowledge the very real fact that unless terms are defined when

---

[1]November 1963, page 33.

one is either speaking or reading cult theology, the semantic jungle which the cults have created will envelop him, making difficult, if not impossible, a proper contrast between the teachings of the cults and those of orthodox Christianity.

On countless occasions, the author has been asked, "Why is it, that when I am talking with a cultist, he seems to be in full agreement with what I am saying; but, when we have finished talking, I am aware of a definite lack of communication, almost as though we were not talking the same language?"

The answer to this question is, of course, that we have not been communicating, because the vocabulary of the cults is not the vocabulary of the Bible by definition. Only the Lord knows how many fruitless hours have been spent attempting to confront cultists with the claim of the Gospel, when five short minutes of insistence upon definitions of the terms employed in conversation, (particularly concerning the nature of God and the Person, nature and work of Jesus Christ), would have stripped the cult theology of one of its most potent tools, that of theological term-switching. Through the manipulation of terminology, it is therefore obvious that the cultist has the Christian at a distinct disadvantage, particularly in the realm of the great fundamental doctrines of Biblical theology. The question then is, how can the interested Christian solve that problem, if indeed it can be solved at all? In short, is there some common denominator that one can use when faced with a cultist of any particular variety, and, if so, how does one put this principle into practice?

The cults capitalize on the almost total inability of the average Christian to understand the subtle art of redefinition in the realm of Biblical theology. Human nature being what it is, it is only natural that Christian ministers as well as laymen should desire a panacea to the irritating and, at times, frustrating problem of cult terminology. Unfortunately, however, no such panacea exists. But lest we become discouraged with the prospect of facing the ever-multiplying bodies of non-Christian cults unprepared for this conflict, (and make no mistake, this *is* spiritual conflict), proper usage of definitions as a practical tool will rob the cultist of at least two of his advantages: surprise and confusion.

The Riddle of Semantics

The problem of semantics has always played an important part in human affairs, for by its use, or abuse, whichever the case may be, entire churches, thrones and even governments for that matter, have been erected, sustained or overthrown. The late George Orwell's stirring novel, *1984*, in which he points out that the redefinition of common political terms can lead to slavery when it is allowed to pass unchallenged by a lethargic populace, is a classic illustration of the dangers of perverted semantics. It should be of no particular surprise to any student of world history that trick terminology is a powerful propaganda weapon. The communist dictatorship of China, which even the Russian theorists have rejected as incalculably brutal and inept, dares to call itself the Peoples Republic of China. As history testifies, the people have very little, if any, say in the actual operation of communism, and if democracy is to be understood as the rule of the people, the Chinese communists have canonized the greatest misnomer of all time!

Both the Chinese communists and the Russians have paid a terrible price for not defining terminology, and for listening to the siren song of Marxism without carefully studying and analyzing the atheistic collectivism through which the music came.

Applying this analogy to the field of cults, it is at once evident that a distinct parallel exists between the two systems. For cultism, like communism, plays a type of hypnotic music upon a semantic harp of terminological deception. And there are many who historically have followed these strains down the broad road to spiritual eternal judgment. There is a common denominator then, and it is inextricably connected with language and the precise definition of terminology. It is what we might call the key to understanding cultism.

Precisely how to utilize the key which will help unlock the jargon of cult semantics is best illustrated by the following facts, drawn from over thirty years of research and practical field work with cultists of every variety.

The average non-Christian cult owes its very existence to the fact that it has utilized the terminology of Christianity, has borrowed liberally from the Bible, almost always out of context, and sprinkled its format with evangelical clichés and terms wherever possible or advantageous. Up to now this has been a highly successful attempt to represent their respective systems of thought as "Christian."

On encountering a cultist then, always remember that you are dealing with a person who is familiar with Christian terminology, and who has carefully redefined it to fit the system of thought he or she now embraces.

A concrete example of a redefinition of terms can be illustrated in the case of almost any of the Gnostic cult systems which emphasize healing, and hold in common a pantheistic concept of God (example: Christian Science, New Thought, Unity, Christ Unity Science, Metaphysics, Religious Science, Divine Science, etc.).

In the course of numerous contacts with this type of cultist, the author has had many opportunities to see the semantic maze in full operation, and it is awesome to behold. Such a cult adherent will begin talking at length about God and Christ. He will speak especially about love, tolerance, forgiveness, the Sermon on the Mount and, as always, the out-of-context perversion of James' "faith without works is dead."

It should be noted that hardly ever in their discourses will such cultists discuss the essential problem of evil, the existence of personal sin, or the necessity of the substitutionary atonement of Christ as the sole means of salvation from sin, through the agency of divine grace and the exercise of faith. In fact, they conscientiously avoid such distasteful subjects like the proverbial plague, and discuss them only with great reluctance. Of course, there are exceptions to this rule, but on the average, it is safe to assume that reticence will characterize any exploration of these touchy issues. Both Christian Science and Unity talk of God as Trinity; but their real concept of God is a pantheistic abstraction (Life, Truth and Love constitute the Triune divine principles—Christian Science).

The historic doctrine of the Trinity is seldom, if ever, considered without careful redefinition. If the reader consults the *Metaphysical Bible Dictionary*, published by the Unity School of Christianity, he will see the masterpiece of redefinition for himself. For in this particular volume, Unity has redefined exhaustively many of the cardinal terms of Biblical theology, much as Mrs. Eddy did, in her Glossary of Terms in the book, *Science and Health with Key to the Scriptures*. The reader will be positively amazed to find what has happened to Biblical history, the person of Adam, the concept of human sin, spiritual depravity and eternal judgment. One thing, however, will emerge very clearly from this study, and that is the fact that Unity may *use* the terminology of the Bible, but by no stretch of the imagination can the redefinition be equated with the thing itself.

Another confusing aspect of non-Christian cultists' approach to semantics is the manner in which they will surprise the Christian with voluminous quotations from no less authority than the Bible, and give the appearance of agreeing with nearly every statement the Christan makes in attempting to evangelize the cultist. Such stock phrases as, "We believe that way too; we agree on this point," or the more familiar, Mrs. Eddy or Mr. or Mrs. Fillmore, Mr. Evans, Dr. Buchman, Joseph Smith or Brigham Young, etc. "says exactly the same thing; we are completely in agreement." All such tactics based upon the juggling of terms usually have the effect of frustrating the average Christian, for he is unable to put his finger upon what he knows is error, and is repeatedly tantalized by seeming agreement which, as he knows, does not exist. He is therefore often forced into silence because he is unaware of what the cultist is actually doing. Often, even though he may be aware of this, in a limited sense, he hesitates to plunge into a discussion for fear of ridicule because of an inadequate background or a lack of Biblical information.

The solution to this perplexing problem is far from simple. The Christian must realize that for every Biblical or doctrinal term *he* mentions, a redefinition light flashes on in the mind of the cultist, and a lightning-fast redefinition is accomplished. Realizing that the cultist will apparently agree with the doctrine under discussion, while firmly disagreeing in reality with the historical and Biblical concept, the Christian is on his way to dealing effectively with cult terminology. This amazing operation of terminological redefinition works very much like a word-association test in psychology.

It is simple for a cultist to spiritualize and redefine the clear meaning of Biblical texts and teachings so as to be in apparent harmony with the historic Christian faith. However, such a harmony is at best a surface agreement, based upon double meanings of words which cannot stand the test of Biblical context, grammar, or sound exegesis. Language is, to be sure, a complex subject; all are agreed on this. But one thing is beyond dispute, and that is that in context, words mean just what they say. Either we admit this, or we must be prepared to surrender all the accomplishments of grammar and scholastic progress, and return to writing on cave walls with charcoal sticks in the tradition of our alleged stone-age ancestors. To illustrate this point more sharply, the experience of everyday life points out the absurdity of terminological redefinitions in every way of life.

An attorney who is retained by his client must know the laws which govern trial procedure, cross-examination and evidence. But above all else he must believe in the innocency of his client. A client who tells his attorney that he is guilty of a misdemeanor but not a felony is using the vocabulary of law. But if his attorney finds out that his client has perverted that vocabulary, so that the terms are interchangeable, he will either refuse to defend him or will clarify the terminology before the court, because by definition, a misdemeanor is a misdemeanor and a felony is a felony. A man who says he stole only ninety dollars (petty theft), but who really means that it was ninety dollars more or less, and in reality knows that it was in excess of five hundred dollars (grand theft), is playing a game that the law will not tolerate. He will most certainly be punished for such perversions of standard legal terms. In the realm of medicine, a doctor who announces that he will perform an open-heart operation, then proceeds in the presence of his colleagues to remove the gall bladder, and then attempts to defend his action by the claim that open-heart surgery actually means removal of the gall bladder in his vocabulary, could not practice medicine for long! Open-heart surgery is delicate repair of the heart muscle. Removal of the gall bladder is, by definition, surgery of another type. In law and in medicine therefore, terms are what they are by definition. On the business and professional level also, this holds, true. But to the cultists, words do not always mean what they have always meant by definition in specific context. And just as the American Bar Association will not tolerate confusion of terminology in the trial of cases, and as the American Medical Association will not tolerate redefinition of terminology in diagnostic and surgical medicine, so also the Church of Jesus Christ has every right not to tolerate the gross perversions and redefinitions of historical, Biblical terminology, simply to accommodate a culture and a society which cannot tolerate an absolute standard or criterion of truth, even if it be revealed by God in His Word and through the true witness of His Spirit.

The major cult systems, then, change the definition of historic terms without a quibble. They answer the objections of Christian theologians with the meaningless phrase, "You interpret it your way, I'll interpret it in mine. Let's be broad-minded. After all, one interpretation is as good as another."

Is it any wonder then, that orthodox Christians feel called upon to openly denounce such perversions of clearly defined and historically accepted Biblical terminology, and claim that the cults have no rights—scholastically, Biblically or linguistically—to redefine Biblical terms as they do?

We ought never to forget for one moment that things are what they are by definition. Any geometric figure whose circumference is $2 \pi r$ is by definition circular. Any two figures whose congruency can be determined by the application of angle-side-angle, side-angle-side, or side-side-side is, by definition, a triangle. To expand this, we might point out that any formula which expresses hydrogen to be in two parts and oxygen to be in one, is water, and hydrogen to be in two parts, sulfur in one part and oxygen in four parts is sulfuric acid. H_2O can never be H_2SO_4. Nor can atonement become at-one-ment, as the theology of the Gnostic cults (Christian Science, Unity, New Thought, etc.) explains it. It simply cannot be, if language means anything.

To spiritualize texts and doctrines, or attempt to explain them away on the basis of the nebulous phrase "interpretation," is scholastic dishonesty, and it is not uncommonly found in leading cult literature. Cultists are destined to find out that the power of Christianity is not in its terminology, but in the relationship of the individual to the historic Christ of revelation. The divine-human encounter must take place. One must become a new creation in Christ Jesus, and the emptying of Christian terminology of all its historic meanings serves only the purpose of confusion and can never vitiate the force of the Gospel, which is the Person of the Savior performing the historic function of redeeming the sinner by grace.

The Christ of Scripture is an eternal, divine personality who cannot be dismissed by a flip of the cultist's redefinition switch, regardless of how deftly it is done. The average Christian will do well to remember the basic conflict of terminology which he is certain to encounter when dealing with cultists of practically every variety.

Summary

Whenever a Christian encounters a cultist then, certain primary thoughts must be paramount in his mind: (1) he must strive to direct the conversation to the problem of terminology and maneuver the cult adherent into a position where he must define his usage of terms and his authority, if any, for drastic, un-Biblical redefinitions, which are certain to emerge; (2) the Christian must then compare these "definitions" with the various contexts of the verses upon which the cultist draws for support of his doctrinal interpretations; (3) he must define the words "interpretation," "historic orthodoxy," and standard doctrinal phrases, such as "the new birth," "atonement," "context," "exegesis," "eternal judgment," etc., so that no misunderstanding will exist when these things come under discussion as they inevitably will; (4) the Christian must attempt to lead the cultist to a review of the importance of properly defining terms for all important doctrines involved, particularly the doctrine of personal redemption from sin, which most cult systems define in a markedly un-Biblical manner; (5) it is the responsibility of the Christian to present a clear testimony of his own regenerative experience with Jesus Christ, in terminology which has been carefully clarified regarding the necessity of such regeneration on the part of the cultist in the light of the certain reality of God's inevitable justice. It may be necessary also, in the course of discussing terminology and its dishonest recasting by cult systems, to resort to occasional polemic utterances. In such cases, the Christian should be certain that they are tempered with patience and love, so that the cultist appreciates that such tactics are motivated by one's personal concern for his eternal welfare, and not just to "win the argument."

Let it never be forgotten that cultists are experts at lifting texts out of their respective contexts, without proper concern for the laws of language or the established principles of Biblical interpretation. There are those of whom Peter warns us, who "wrest scriptures, unto their own destruction" (2 Peter 3:16). This is an accurate picture of the kingdom of the cults in the realm of terminology.

Looking back over the picture of cult semantics, the following facts emerge:

1. The average cultist knows his own terminology very thoroughly. He also has a historic knowledge of Christian usage, and is therefore prepared to discuss many areas of Christian theology intelligently.

2. The well-trained cultist will carefully avoid definition of terms concerning cardinal doctrines such as the Trinity, the Deity of Christ, the Atonement, the Bodily Resurrection of our Lord, the process of salvation by grace and justification by faith. If pressed in these areas, he will redefine the terms to fit the semantic framework of orthodoxy, unless he is forced to define his terms explicitly.

3. The informed Christian must seek for a point of departure, preferably the authority of the Scriptures, which can become a powerful and useful tool in the hands of the Christian, if properly exercised.

4. The concerned Christian worker must familiarize himself to some extent with the terminology of the major cult systems if he is to enjoy any measure of success in understanding the cultist's mind when bearing a witness for Christ.

We have stressed heavily the issue of terminology and a proper definition of terms throughout this entire chapter. It will not have been wasted effort if the reader has come to realize its importance, and will be guided accordingly when approaching the language barrier, which is an extremely formidable obstacle both to evangelizing cultists and to giving a systematic and effective defense of the Christian faith against their perversions.

Chapter 3

THE PSYCHOLOGICAL STRUCTURE OF CULTISM

It is extremely difficult, when approaching the study of the field of non-Christian cults, to accurately appraise such groups without some knowledge of the psychological factors involved in both their formation and growth.

Each cult has what might be called its own "belief system" which follows a distinct pattern and, allowing for obvious differences of personality which exist in any group, can be analyzed and understood in relation to its particular theological structure. Since until recently very little, if anything, has been written on the subject relative to the cults, considerable research was necessary in order to bring this matter under discussion. That it must be discussed and understood as an integral part of the whole complex of the development of American cult systems, no thorough student will deny.

In the course of working with cultists it has been the observation of this writer that each cultist, though different as an individual, does share certain psychological traits in common with his fellow members, and a careful study of these similarities has revealed some interesting trends.

It is not possible in one chapter to cover all of the cult systems so we have limited our observations to Jehovah's Witnesses, Mormonism and Christian Science. The Jehovah's Witnesses represent those cult systems which put strong emphasis upon eschatology and prophecy, the Mormons those which emphasize priestly authority, secret rituals and symbols, and Christian Science, the gnostic cults which ground their experience in metaphysical pantheism and physical healing (a fact which contains within itself enough material to merit an entire book on the problem of psychosomatic medicine and healing).

Dr. Milton Rokeach in his illuminating book, *The Open and Closed Mind,* notes that there are three regions or levels that psychologists generally recognize in any belief or disbelief system. The first or central region is that which encompasses the individual's basic primitive outlook on the world in which he lives and asks such questions as, "Is the world a threatening place, or is it an accepting place?"

The second or intermediate region is the area of authority. In other words, whose authority is a person willing to accept in matters pertaining to the functions of life?

Finally, there is the peripheral region which penetrates into the details of the structure of living. The details may vary or change according to the specific content which the authority, once accepted, may invoke.

There is no doubt in my mind that the belief systems of the cults share much in common, and that some of these common factors are worth noting.

First and foremost, the belief systems of the cults are characterized by closed-mindedness. They are not interested in a rational cognitive evaluation of the facts. The organizational structure interprets the facts to the cultist, generally invoking the Bible and/or its respective founder as the ultimate source of its pronouncements. Such belief systems are in isolation; they never shift to logical consistency. They exist in what we might describe as separate compartments in the cultist's mind, and are almost incapable of penetration or disruption if the individual cultist is completely committed to the authority pattern of his organization.

Secondly, cultic belief systems are characterized by genuine antagonism on a personal level since the cultist almost always identifies his dislike of the Christian message with the messenger who holds such opposing beliefs.

The identification of opposing beliefs with the individual in the framework of antagonism leads the cultist almost always to reject the individual as well as the belief, a problem closely linked with closed-mindedness and one that is extremely difficult to deal with in general dialogue with cultists.

Theoretically speaking, if one could drive a wedge between the individual (or the personality of the individual toward whom the cultist is antagonistic) and the theology (which is the real source of the antagonism) it would be possible to deal with the individual cultist by becoming in his or her eyes a neutral objective source of data. The Christian would then become a person who maintains a system of theology opposed to theirs but not necessarily involved on a level of personal antagonism toward the cultist. Experience has shown me that when this is accomplished it is the first step in a systematic under-cutting of one of the basic problems all cultists face in interpersonal contact, the problem of hostility toward those who reject their interpretations.

Such a procedure can go a long way toward allaying hostility, for once a cultist, who has been thoroughly "brainwashed" psychologically by his own authority system (The Watchtower Society, Mrs. Eddy's books, the writings of Joseph Smith and Brigham Young, etc.), is confronted by a Christian whom he can learn to accept on a personal basis apart from differences of theological opinion, the possibility of communication improves markedly.

In effect, the cultist is faced with a dilemma, "How can this person (the Christian) be such an acceptable personality yet not share his (the cultist's) theology?"

The cultist, then, quite often begins to wonder how it is possible for the Christian to accept him as a person and yet not accept his beliefs. This can be the beginning of rapport in the realm of personal evangelism.

Since almost all systems of authority in cult organizations indoctrinate their disciples to believe that anyone who opposes their beliefs cannot be motivated by anything other than satanic force or blind prejudice and ignorance, a cultist's encounter with Christains who do not fit this pattern can produce startling results. A discerning Christian who gives every indication of being unprejudiced, reasonably learned and possessed of a genuine love for the welfare of the cultist himself (which is easily detectable in the Christian's concern for his soul and spiritual well-being generally) can have a devastating effect upon the conditioning apparatus of any cult system.

Above all else, Christians must learn that most cults consider that they have freed their adherents from religious exploitation which they almost always accuse historic Christianity of practicing. In this connection it becomes a vital necessity to demonstrate genuine interest in the cultist as a person for the sake of himself and his personal redemption, rather than as a possible statistic for any given denomination.

The prime task of Christians who would be effective witnesses for Christ in the midst of the kingdom of the cults is that they be free from all appearance of guile and ulterior motivation, remembering that our main task is to communicate to those who are by their very adherence to cultic systems of belief in virtual isolation from the Christian message.

This isolationism, which can be extreme, must be considered in preparing one's presentation of the gospel to a cultist. It is a very real mental and emotional chain which has a strong hold on the cultist's ability to discern truth from error, light from darkness. If the tragedy of Jonestown on November 18, 1978, when over 900 cult followers of "Rev." Jim Jones committed forced suicide, has taught us anything, it has taught us the despair and isolationism of cultists. The following quote from *People's Temple—People's Tomb* (Phil Kerns with Doug Wead, Plainfield, NJ: Logos International, 1979, p. 205) illustrates this graphically:

> A sealed note found on the cult commander's body, apparently written by a follower just prior to the ritual suicide, gave additional credence to this theory. "Dad," the note said, "I see no way out—I agree with your decision— I fear only that without you the world may not make it to communism. For my part I am more than tired of this wretched, merciless planet and the hell it holds for so many masses of beautiful people—thank you for the ONLY life I've known."

While this volume deals primarily with traditional American cults and therefore will not treat Jim Jones' People's Temple cult in a separate chapter, it is important for us to remember that the cultic psychological patterns evidenced in manic proportions at Jonestown are present to some degree in each and every cult.

Thirdly, almost without exception, all cultic belief systems manifest a type of institutional dogmatism and a pronounced intolerance for any position but their own. This no doubt stems from the fact that in the case of non-Christian cult systems which wish to be identified with Christianity the ground for their claims is almost always supernatural.

We do not wish to imply that there is no such thing as an authoritative dogmatism which is valid and true (such as the teachings of Jesus Christ), but rather that cult systems tend to invest with the authority of the supernatural whatever pronouncements are deemed necessary to condition and control the minds of their followers.

Thus it is that when Joseph Smith, Jr., the Mormon prophet, and his successor, Brigham Young, wished to implement doctrines or changes of practice in the Mormon Church, they prefaced their remarks with proclamations that God had revealed to them the necessity of such doctrines or practices among the "saints."

An example of this was Charles Taze Russell's bold claim that his writings were indispensable to the study of the Bible for Jehovah's Witnesses, and that to study the Bible apart from his inspired comments was to go into spiritual darkness. Russell also taught that concentration upon his writings even at the expense of studying the Bible would most certainly lead one into deeper spiritual illumination within two years.

Mary Baker Eddy also conformed to this pattern by requiring her followers to regard her book *Science and Health with Key to the Scriptures* as a divine revelation, and her religion as a "higher, clearer, and more permanent revelation than before."[1] Mrs. Eddy did not hesitate to state that she would blush to write of "Science and Health with Key to the Scriptures" as she did if she apart from God were its author.[2]

The history of cultism generally begins with an authoritarian pronouncement on the part of the founder or founders. This in turn is institutionalized during their lifetime or after their death into a dogmatic system which requires absolute faith in the supernatural authority of those who received the initial revelation and whose writings and pronouncements are alleged to have transmitted it.

Some interesting studies of institutional dogmatism can be found in such books as George Orwell's *1984*, Eric Hoffer's *The True Believer* and Crossman's volume *The God That Failed*.

The problem of intolerance is closely linked to institutional dogmatism or authoritarianism, and those systems which embody this line of reasoning are resistant to change and penetration since the cults thrive on conformity, ambiguity and extremeness of belief.

The fourth and final point in any analysis of the belief system of cults is the factor of isolation.

Within the structure of non-Christian cult systems one can observe the peaceful coexistence of beliefs that are beyond a question of a doubt logically contradictory and which in terms of psychological analysis would come under the heading of "compartmentalization." In his classic book, *1984*, George Orwell describes this as "double think." Rokeach commenting on this illustrates the point admirably:

> In everyday life we note many examples of double "think"; expressing an abhorrence of violence and at the same time believing it is justifiable under certain conditions; affirming a faith in the common man and at the same time believing that the masses are stupid; being for democracy but also advocating a government run by an intellectual elite; believing in freedom for all but also believing that certain groups should be restricted; believing that science makes no value judgments but also knowing a good theory from a bad theory and a good experiment from a bad experiment. Such expressions of clearly contradictory beliefs will be taken as one indication of isolation in the belief system . . . a final indicator of isolation is the outright denial of contradiction. Contradictory facts can be denied in several

---

[1]From a personal letter to a student by Mrs. Eddy. Quoted in Georgine Milnine, *The Life of Mary Baker G. Eddy and the History of Christian Science* (Grand Rapids: Baker Book House, 1909, 1937).
[2]Mary Baker Eddy, *The First Church of Christ, Scientist, and Miscellany* [Boston: Trustees under the Will of Mary Baker Eddy, 1941 (first pub. in 1913)], p. 115.

ways: on grounds of face absurdity ("it is absurd on the face of it"), "chance," "the exception that proves the rule," "the true facts are not accessible, and the only available sources of information are biased."[3]

Relating this to the belief system of cults, I do not believe it could be stated with greater clarity. Dr. Rokeach has hit the proverbial nail squarely on the head. Jehovah's Witnesses are well aware of the fact that the Watchtower organization under the leadership of Judge Rutherford maintained that Abraham, Isaac and Jacob would return to earth before the close of the 1920's, and even bought a home for the patriarchs to dwell in (San Diego, California, Beth Sarim, "the house of princes"). At the same time Jehovah's Witnesses are fully aware of the fact that the patriarchs did not materialize on schedule, yet they cling tenaciously to the same principles of prophetic interpretation which conceived and brought forth the now defunct interpretations of previous Watchtower leaders. How tenaciously they do cling is evident from their latest fiasco, a prediction that the Battle of Armaggedon would occur in 1975. It obviously hasn't occurred yet, but faithful Jehovah's Witnesses are still pounding on the doors of America, telling of the "light" they receive through Jehovah's organization.

Well-informed Mormon historians and theologians are equally aware that the first edition of *The Book of Mormon* and the present edition of *The Book of Mormon* are quite different in 3,913 separate instances (over 25,000 including punctuation changes), the first edition having been revised and corrected by Joseph Smith and his successors over the last one hundred and fifty years. Yet both the errors and the revisions of *The Book of Mormon* are heralded as divine revelation by Mormons. This is another example of the peaceful coexistence of logical contradiction within the belief system of Mormonism which permits the isolation or compartmentalization of conflicting evidence or concepts.

Still another example of contradiction is the fact that the Christian Science Church has known for many years that though Mary Baker Eddy spoke vigorously against doctors and drugs as well as vigorously affirming the unreality of pain, suffering and disease, she herself was frequently attended in her declining years by doctors, received injections of morphine for the alleviation of pain, wore glasses, and had her teeth removed when they became diseased. However, despite this the Christian Science Church insists upon the validity of Mrs. Eddy's teachings which deny the very practices Mrs. Eddy herself exemplified. Here is a classic example of isolation which might justly come under the heading of "physician heal thyself!"

It would be possible to point out many other instances of psychological aberration in the belief systems of the major cults, but it is apparent that we are confronted with those whom the Apostle Paul described as victims of the master psychologist and propagandist of the ages, described by our Lord as "the prince of this world" and by the Apostle Paul as "the god of this age"—the one who by the sheer force of his antagonism to the truth of divine revelation in the person of Jesus Christ has psychologically "blinded the minds" of those who believe not the Gospel, "lest the light of the glorious

---

[3]*The Open and Closed Mind*, pages 36 and 37.

gospel of Christ, who is the image of God, should shine unto them" (2 Corinthians 4:4).

This, of course, is not only a psychological blindness but a spiritual blindness brought about by the isolation of man from God through the rebellion of human nature and the repeated violation of divine law. These are factors which cannot be ignored for they are a direct reflection of the forces which from "the heavenlies" dominate the world in which we live (Ephesians 6:10–12).

The Psychological Conditioning Process

To conclude our observations in this seldom considered area of cultic analysis let us consider examples of just how the cult systems of Jehovah's Witnesses, Mormonism, and Christian Science condition their adherents to respond to the "outside world" of unbelievers.

In the case of Jehovah's Witnesses, the literature of the Watchtower is replete with examples of a psychological conditioning which elicits a definite pattern of religious reflexes in response to a given stimuli. As Pavlov's dog salivated at the sound of a bell which represented food, so a true Jehovah's Witness will spiritually and emotionally salivate whenever the Watchtower rings the conditioning bell of Russellite theology. The example which I believe best demonstrates this is taken in context from Watchtower publications and speaks for itself.

> . . . In Christendom as surprising as it may seem to some the false religious teachings create traditions, and commands of men are both directly and indirectly responsible for the physical and spiritual miseries of the poor, notwithstanding Christendom's showy display of charity.[4]

> . . . Christendom's pretended interest in the poor is sheer hypocrisy . . . her priests have done violence to my law and have profaned my holy things . . . her princes in the midst thereof are like wolves ravening the prey to shed blood and to destroy souls that they may get dishonest gain . . . and her prophets have daubed them with untempered mortar seeing false visions in divining lies unto them saying thus says Jehovah when Jehovah hath not spoken . . . the people of the land have used oppression and exercised robbery, yea they have vexed the poor and needy and have oppressed the sojourners wrongfully . . . oh wicked Christendom why have you forsaken God's clean worship? Why have you joined forces and become part of Satan's wicked organization that oppresses the people? Why have you failed to show concern for the poor as Jehovah commands?[5]

> The little charitable help the poor get from Christendom is like the crumbs that beggar Lazarus picked up from the rich man's table while the dog licked his ulcerous sores. Neither the crumbs nor the licking remedied the beggarly condition. Only Jehovah can effect a rescue. How comforting then for the dejected, down-trodden people of the earth to learn that there is One higher than the highest of Christendom's moguls . . . yes, Jehovah

---

[4]*The Watchtower*, December 1, 1951, page 731.
[5]*Ibid.*, page 732 and 733.

the Almighty hears the cries of the half dead ones and in hearing He answers their prayers and sends His good samaritans to the rescue even the witnesses who are despised by Christendom.[6]

Haters of God and His people are to be hated, but this does not mean that we will take any opportunity of bringing physical hurt to them in the spirit of malice or spite, for both malice and spite belong to the devil, whereas, pure hatred does not.

We must hate in the truest sense which is to regard with extreme and active aversion, to consider as loathsome, odious, filthy, to detest. Surely any haters of God are not fit to live on His beautiful earth. The earth will be rid of the wicked and we shall not need to lift a finger to cause physical harm to come to them, for God will attend to that, but we must have a proper perspective of these enemies. His name signifies recompense to the enemies.

Jehovah's enemies are recognized by their intense dislike for His people and the work these are doing. For they would break it down and have all of Jehovah's Witnesses sentenced to jail or concentration camps if they could. Not because they have anything against the Witnesses personally but on account of their work. They publish blasphemous lies and reproach the holy name Jehovah. Do we not hate those who hate God? We cannot love those hateful enemies for they are fit only for destruction. We utter the prayer of the Psalmist, "How long, oh God, shall the adversary reproach, shall the enemy blaspheme thy name forever? Why drawest thou back thy hand, even thy right hand? Pluck it out of thy bosom and consume them" (Psalm 74:10, 11).

We pray with intensity and cry out this prayer for Jehovah to delay no longer and plead that His anger be made manifest, oh Jehovah, God of hosts . . . be not merciful to any wicked transgressors. . . . Consume them in wrath, consume them so that they shall be no more (Psalm 59:4–6, 11–13). These are the true sentiments, desires and prayers of the righteous ones today. Are they yours . . . how we despise the workers of iniquity and those who would tear down God's organization! ". . . Oh, Jehovah. Let them be put to shame and dismayed forever, yea, let them be confounded and perish that they may know that Thou alone whose name is Jehovah art the most high over all the earth" (Psalm 83:9–18).

. . . The near neighbors of Judah . . . have been the opposers of the Israelites right from the time when refusal was given by them to supply provisions to Israel as they journeyed to the promised land. Moab hired Baalam to curse Israel . . . they had much contempt for Jehovah's people and prided themselves in their own lofty city, her counterpart today being that rich, lofty city, the mighty religious organization standing for the whole of Satan's organization. The modern-day Moabites are the professing Christians whose words and actions are as far removed from Christianity and true worship of Jehovah as Moab was removed from true worship in the covenant of Jehovah. Jehovah had warned Moab of His proposed punishment for her iniquity and opposition.

The modern-day Moabites have opposed Jehovah's Witnesses with a hatred not born of righteousness but from the devil and against all righteousness. Their hatred for God's true people increases as they see upon us the very plain evidence of Jehovah's favor in the obvious disfavor they

---

[6]*Ibid.*, page 733.

themselves are in. They put forth every effort to prevent the people of goodwill from entering the new world. They are richer than Jehovah's Witnesses in material things and with it they have much pride and arrogance. . .

The modern-day Moabites will be brought low for Jehovah has completely finished with them. Hear just a part of the punishment:

"For in this mountain will the hand of Jehovah rest and Moab shall be trodden down in his place, even as straw is trodden down in the water of the dung hill. He shall spread forth his hands in the midst thereof as he that swimmeth spreadeth forth his hands to win, but Jehovah will lay low his pride together with the craft of his hands."

It is a sure thing that one cannot have much pride left when one is being pressed down into a manure pile, showing the utter contempt Jehovah has for modern-day Moab, keeping her wallowing in the mire of shame.

"For thou has made of a city a heap of a fortified city a ruin a palace of strangers to be no city; it shall never be built."

He hath put down them that dwell on high the lofty city, he layeth it low, he layeth it low even to the ground, he bringeth it even to the dust. The foot shall tread it down, even the feet of the poor and the steps of the needy . . .

When this happens what a tremendous change will take place, the tables will be turned! Brought down will be the lofty from dwelling on high as the great, high influential ones of this world to the lowest possible place imaginable, so low and degraded they can only be compared to being trampled under foot by the poor like straw in a manure heap. Christendom's lofty looks, boastful words, bragging tongue are superior attitude toward the holy Word of God, her trust in idols, men and riches such as belong to this world will not provide her with security or any safety from Jehovah's storm and blast. They have no defense nor disgrace . . .

Christendom's defenses are of no value but Jehovah's Witnesses have a strong city and this is something to sing about. There are millions who want a safe place and are in need of security, let them know we have a strong city! "Thou shalt call thy wall salvation and thy gates praise" (Isaiah 60:18). Only God's Kingdom offers such protection and salvation for inside the city one is safe. Those desiring salvation must make for God's organization and find entrance into it and remain there permanently.[7]

God has been grossly misrepresented by the clergy. If this statement is true, then that alone is proof conclusive that the clergy do not in fact represent God and Christ but do represent God's enemy, the Devil. . . . If the Bible plainly proves that the doctrines they teach are wrong and their course of action is wrong, then the most that can be said in extenuation of their wrongful teachings and their wrongful course of action is that they have been misled by the evil and seductive influence of Satan, the enemy of God. If the doctrines taught and the course taken by the clergy differ from that which is declared in the Word of God, then the clergy are in no wise safe guides for the people and should no longer be followed by the people.[8]

These doctrines originated with the Devil. They have long been taught by his representatives. . . . The clergy have been his instruments freely used to instill these false doctrines into the minds of men. Whether the clergy have willingly done so or not does not alter the fact. If they have now learned

---

[7]*Ibid.*, page 734.
[8]Judge J. F. Rutherford, *Reconciliation* (Brooklyn, NY: Watchtower Bible and Tract Society, 1928), p. 85.

that they are wrong they should be eager to get that false thought out of the minds of the people. They do not take such course.[9]

The clergy have at all times posed as the representatives of God on earth. Satan overreached the minds of these clergymen and injected into their minds doctrines, which doctrines the clergy have taught the people concerning Jesus and His sacrifice. These doctrines have brought great confusion. The apostles taught the truth, but it was not long after their death until the Devil found some clergyman wise in his own conceit who thought he could teach more than the inspired apostles.[10]

(The clergy) are willingly or unwillingly the instruments in the hands of the god of this world, Satan the Devil, who has used them to blind the minds of the people, to prevent the people from understanding God's great plan of salvation and reconciliation.[11]

The clergy of Christendom are obviously the villains and are the object of "pure hatred." Just how pure hatred differs from good old-fashioned hatred the Watchtower never gets around to explaining, but it is clear that Christendom (all historic communions) led by the allegedly corrupt clergy has foisted the "satanically conceived" Trinity doctrine, and the doctrines of hell and eternal punishment upon the unsuspecting masses of mankind. Clergymen are therefore always suspect and their theology is to be regarded as untrustworthy and inspired by Satan.

Is it any wonder that the usually calm and detached Stanley High writing in *The Reader's Digest* of June, 1940, could state:

"Jehovah's Witnesses hate everybody and try to make it mutual . . . Jehovah's Witnesses make hate a religion."

The doctrines of hell and eternal punishment which stimulate fear of judgment are "unreasonable" and not in accord with the Watchtower concept of the character of God; therefore, it and the doctrine of the Trinity are satanic in origin and all must be rejected and hated as false.

What the Watchtower does in essence is attach polemic significance to certain common theological terms (Holy Trinity, Deity of Christ, Hell, Eternal Punishment, Christendom, immortal soul, etc.), thus every time these terms are mentioned by anyone the reflex action on the part of the Jehovah's Witnesses is instantaneous and hostile.

If we couple this with the Watchtower's heavy emphasis upon the fulfillment of prophecy and a distorted eschatology, the sense of urgency they radiate about Armageddon (which they believe will solve all these problems by annihilating the clergy and all organized religion), then begins to make sense and the reason for their actions becomes clear.

When dealing with the average Jehovah's Witness this entire pattern of preconditioning must be understood so that the Christian can avoid, where possible, direct usage of terms that will almost certainly evoke a theologically conditioned reflex and sever the lines of communication.

Another important point where Jehovah's Witnesses are concerned is the fact that an intricate part of their belief system is the conviction that

[9]*Ibid.*, p. 91.
[10]*Ibid.*, p. 100.
[11]*Ibid.*, p. 125.

Christians will always attack Jehovah's Witnesses on a personal as well as a religious level, hence the Witnesses readily assume a martyr or persecution complex the moment any antagonism is manifested toward Russell, Rutherford, their theology, the Watchtower or themselves. It is apparently a comfortable, somewhat heroic feeling to believe that you are standing alone against the massed forces of "the devil's organization" (a Watchtower synonym for Christendom!), and this illusion is made to seem all the more real when unthinking Christians unfortunately accommodate the Witnesses by appearing overly aggressive toward the Watchtower theology or the Witnesses personally.

In the light of Jehovah's Witnesses' insistence upon "pure hatred" one wonders how they live with their own New World Translation of Matthew 5:43, 44, which read:

> You heard that it was said you must love your neighbor and hate your enemy. However, I say to you: continue to love your enemies and pray for those persecuting you; that you may prove yourselves sons of your Father who is in the heavens.

The Watchtower then does not hesitate to accuse the clergy and Christendom of provoking all kinds of evil; in fact, they have not hesitated to suggest that Christendom encouraged and did nothing to prevent the two great world wars:

"Had Christendom chosen to do so she could easily have prevented World Wars 1 and 2."[12]

Some of the basic motivations of the Watchtower are clearly seen in stark contrast with the teachings of Holy Scripture and reveal that there is more than a spiritual disorder involved. Indeed there exist deep psychological overtones which cannot be considered healthy in any sense of the term.

Whereas Jehovah's Witnesses are occupied with Armageddon, the theocracy, the end of the ages, and "pure hatred," the Mormons have quite different psychological and theological emphases.

At the very core of Mormon theology there is a tremendous emphasis upon authority as it is invested in the priesthood, rituals and symbols presided over by the hierarchy of the Mormon Church. Mormons are taught from their earliest days that the priesthood has the key to authority, and that one of the marks which identifies the "restoration" of the true church of Jesus Christ on earth is the fact that this priesthood exists and perpetuates that authority.

A devout Mormon will wear symbolic underclothing which perpetually reminds him of his responsibility and duties as a Mormon. When this is coupled with Mormonism's tremendous emphasis upon baptism for the remission of sins, tithing and voluntary missionary service, it is seen to bind its followers into a tight, homogeneous circle, escape from which, apart from severe spiritual as well as economic penalties, is virtually impossible.

Every Mormon is indoctrinated with the concept that his is the true Christian religion or to use their terms, "the restoration of Christianity to earth." The secret rites in the Mormon temples, the rituals connected with

---

[12]*The Watchtower*, December 1, 1951, page 731.

baptism for the dead, and the secret handshakes, signs and symbols bind the average Mormon and his family into what might be called in psychological terms the "in group." Apart from acceptance by this group the average Mormon can find no peace, or for that matter, community status or prestige.

Instances of discrimination against Mormons who have experienced true Christian conversion are not infrequent in Mormon dominated areas where a man can lose his business very easily by incurring the disfavor of the Mormon Church.

The social welfare program of the Mormons is another excellent inducement to Mormons to remain faithful, since if the "bread winner" of the family is injured, loses his job, or dies, the church undertakes the care and support of his family. So effective is this work that during the Great Depression of the 1930's no Mormon families went hungry and no soup kitchens or bread lines disfigured the domain of Mormondom.

The Mormons also conscientiously invoke the Biblical principle of helping each other. They lend to each other, work for each other, and cooperate toward the common goal of bringing "restored Christianity" to the masses of mankind. These and other forces make Mormonism a family-centered religion which ties the faith of the church to the indissoluble bonds of family unity and loyalty. This forges an incredibly complex system of pressures and intertwining values over which is superimposed the theological structure of the Mormon Church, which stands between the *average* Mormon and the attainment of "exaltation" or progression to godhood. (See chapter on Mormonism for a discussion of this.)

With such great psychological, economic and religious forces concentrated upon him, it is a courageous person indeed who shakes off these varied yokes and steps into the freedom of a genuine experience with the Son of God. But a growing number are doing just this as the Spirit of God continues to call out the Church which is Christ's Body.

Christian Science, unlike the two other cults we have considered, is neither interested in bestowing godhood (Mormonism) on its adherents nor pushing the eschatological panic button of Armageddon (Jehovah's Witnesses).

Christian Science is an ingenious mixture of first century gnostic theology, eighteenth century Hegelian philosophy, and nineteenth century idealism woven into a redefined framework of Christian theology with an emphasis upon the healing of the body by the highly questionable practice of denying its objective material reality!

In Christian Science there is a complete separation between the objective world of physical reality (matter) and the spiritual world of supernatural existence (mind). Mrs. Eddy taught that "man as God's idea is already saved with an everlasting salvation."[13]

Hence it is unnecessary for Christian Scientists to think of themselves as sinners in need of a salvation they believe is already theirs by virtue of the fact that "man is already saved" because he is a reflection of the divine mind.

---

[13]Mary Baker Eddy, *Miscellaneous Writings* [Boston: Trustees under the Will of Mary Baker Eddy, 1924 (first pub. 1896)], p. 261.

However, in Christian Science there are disturbing psychological aberrations. Mrs. Eddy demanded of her followers that they abstain from any critical contact with the non-spiritual elements of the illusory material world. She forbade the reading of "obnoxious literature" lest Christian Scientists become convinced that the physical body and its diseases, suffering and inevitable death were real.

There is in Christian Science a subconscious repression, a conscious putting out of one's mind certain things which are disconcerting to the entire configuration of psychological patterns of conditioning. Christian Scientists are conditioned to believe in the non-existence of the material world even though their senses testify to its objective reality. They continually affirm that matter has no true existence, and thus, in a very real sense, entertain a type of religious schizophrenia. One side of their personality testifies to the reality of the material world and its inexorable decay, while the conditioning process of Christian Science theology hammers relentlessly to suppress this testimony and affirm that the only true reality is spiritual or mental.

In Margaret Mitchell's classic novel, *Gone With the Wind*, Scarlet O'Hara, the heroine, when confronted with the harsh realities of life in the wake of the Civil War repeatedly states, "I'll think about that tomorrow," as if not thinking about it today would eliminate the reality of its claim at that moment.

When working with sensory data Christian Scientists totally disassociate their religious convictions, for, if they did not, they would not continue to feed, clothe or house their bodies. But in still another sense, they attempt to master the all too obvious frailties of the body by the application of a religion which denies the material reality of that body. A psychologist of the behaviorist school in one sense does the same thing. In the office he may talk about "conditioning" and may associate everything, including his home, with mechanistic psychology; however, at home he still loves his wife and children, and doesn't respond in that same manner. This is one of the chief reasons why Christian Scientists sometimes appear to be almost immune to the conviction of personal guilt as a result of sin. Guilt implies the threat of judgment and a standard which is the basis of that judgment; hence the reality of the concept of sin which is transgression of the law of God. Christian Scientists desperately want only a "good" world, a pleasant place full of happiness, life, love and security. This they can have only if they deny the empirical evidence of the opposites of those concepts. In effect they affirm the reality of "good" at the expense of the antithesis of "good," as if by denying the existence of evil one had annihilated evil!

There can be no doubt that there is "selective perception" in the mind of the Christian Scientist which enables him to select those things which are of a metaphysical nature, disassociate them from the sense perception of the physical world, and still maintain his idealistic philosophy and gnostic theology. This he accomplishes by repressing or suppressing any evidence to the contrary.

By following Mrs. Eddy's advice and avoiding what she would call "obnoxious literature," i.e., evidence which controverts the idealism of Christian Science philosophy, Christian Scientists avoid facing the damaging data of physical reality. It is in effect an act of unconscious suppression utilized in order to escape the data. Concluding our thoughts in this area we might say that in the kingdom of the cults we are actually seeing a mosaic of abnormal conditioned behavior patterns that express themselves in a theological framework, utilizing Christian terms perverted by redefinition and represented as "new insight" when in truth they are only old errors with new faces. The defense mechanisms on a psychological level are apparent when one considers the background and vocabulary of the cult systems. There exists, beyond a question of a doubt, an abnormal behavior syndrome operating in the mentality of most cultists, which causes the cultist (in the case of Christian Scientists) to build his theological system upon a preconditioned and artificially induced criterion of evaluation, i.e., the divine mission and inspiration of Mary Baker Eddy. In the case of other cultists, the names Joseph Smith, "Pastor" Russell, Brigham Young, or any other cult authority figure could be supplied and the conditioned reflex would be virtually the same.

There are many more observations which could be made but space will not permit. It is my hope that in observing and analyzing the facets of cult behavior patterns already discussed, the reader may obtain a deeper insight and appreciation of the psychological structure of cultism as it continues to influence a growing segment of professing Christendom which is ill prepared for the subtleties and dangers of such psychological and theological deviations

Chapter 4

JEHOVAH'S WITNESSES AND THE WATCH-TOWER BIBLE AND TRACT SOCIETY

A Brief History

Charles Taze Russell was the founder of what is now Jehovah's Witnesses and the energetic administrator that brought about its far-flung organization. The name Jehovah's Witnesses, incidentally, was taken at Columbus, Ohio, in 1931, to differentiate between the Watchtower and the true followers of Russell as represented by The Dawn Bible Students and the Laymen's Home Missionary Movement. C. T. Russell was born on February 16, 1852, the son of Joseph L. and Anna Eliza Russell, and spent most of his early years in Pittsburgh and Allegheny, Pennsylvania, where at the age of 25 he was known to be manager of several men's furnishings stores. At an early age he rejected the doctrine of eternal torment, probably because of the severe indoctrination he had received as a Congregationalist, and as a result of this act entered upon a long and varied career of denunciation aimed at "Organized Religions." In 1870, at the age of 18, Russell organized a Bible class in Pittsburgh which in 1876 elected him "Pastor" of the group. From 1876 to 1878 the "Pastor" was assistant editor of a small Rochester, New York, monthly magazine, but resigned when a controversy arose over Russell's counter arguments on "the atonement" of Christ.

Shortly after leaving his position, Russell founded *The Herald of the Morning* (1879) which developed into today's *The Watchtower Announcing Jehovah's Kingdom*. From 6,000 initial issues the publication has grown to 17.8 million copies per month in 106 languages. The other Watchtower periodical, *Awake!*, has a circulation of 15.6 million per month in 34 languages. It is true that this magazine has grown until it has surpassed even Russell's fondest dreams. In the year 1884 "Pastor" Russell incorporated "Zion's Watch Tower Tract Society" at Pittsburgh, Pennsylvania, which in 1886 published the first in a series of seven books (Russell wrote six by himself), now entitled *Studies in the Scriptures* and originally published as *The Millennial Dawn*. The seventh volume was edited from his writings after his death and published in 1917. This seventh volume, *The Finished Mystery*, caused a split in the organization, which culminated in a clean division, the larger group following J. F. Rutherford, the smaller remaining by itself. This group subsequently became "The Dawn Bible Students Association." Meanwhile, under Rutherford's leadership, the "Society" became known by its present name "Jehovah's Witnesses."

According to Watchtower statistics, in January of 1981, the Watchtower Bible and Tract Society (founded 1896), which is the focal point of the organization, had known branches in more than 100 lands, and missionary works and Kingdom preaching in over 250. Its literature is distributed in 110 languages, and the Society's volunteers (called "publishers") numbered 563,453. The Society has become a great disseminator of propaganda and a challenge to the zeal of every Christian.

In the year 1908 the headquarters of the movement was transferred to Brooklyn, New York, where property was purchased (17 Hicks Street) and became known as "The Brooklyn Tabernacle." Large tracts of property were purchased by the Society on Columbia Heights, as it grew and prospered, until today whole blocks are in their possession. Among the other things the Society owns are: a large up-to-date printing plant which has produced billions of pieces of literature since its inauguration in 1928 and expansions in 1949 and 1957; a modern apartment building and office quarters; one "Kingdom Farm," which supplies food, wood for furniture, etc.; a Bible school, "Gilead"; and many more enterprises of like character. All employees in the factory are allowed a nominal sum, receive room and board, and work for nothing—no salaries are paid.

Russell continued his teachings until his death on October 31, 1916, aboard a transcontinental train in Texas. The former pastor had a remarkable life highly colored with legal entanglements, but not without success in his chosen field. In fairness to the reader and in the interest of truth, the following account is quoted from *The Brooklyn Daily Eagle*, November 1, 1916 (Obit. Column), and has been inserted at this point to authenticate beyond doubt the true history of Russell so that even his most devoted followers may realize the character of the man to whose teachings they have entrusted their eternal destiny.

A year after this publication, *The Watch Tower*, had been established Russell married Maria Ackley in Pittsburgh. She had become interested in him through his teachings, and she helped him in running the Watch Tower.

Two years later, in 1881, came "The Watch Tower Bible and Tract Society," the agency through which in later years "Pastor" Russell's sermons were published (as advertisements) in newspapers throughout the world. This Society progressed amazingly under the joint administration of husband and wife, but in 1897 Mrs. Russell left her husband. Six years later, in 1903, she sued for separation. The decree was secured in 1906 following sensational testimony and "Pastor" Russell was scored by the courts.

There was much litigation then that was quite undesirable from the "Pastor's" point of view regarding alimony for his wife, but it was settled in 1909 by the payment of $6,036 to Mrs. Russell. The litigation revealed that "Pastor" Russell's activities in the religious field were carried on through several subsidiary societies and that all of the wealth which flowed into him through these societies was under the control of a holding company in which the "Pastor" held $990 of the $1,000 capital and two of his followers the other $10.

Thus Russell apparently controlled the entire financial power of the Society and was not accountable to anyone.

The *Eagle* column goes on to say:

After the "work" had been well started here, "Pastor" Russell's Watch Tower publication advertised wheat seed for sale at $1.00 a pound. It was styled "Miracle Wheat," and it was asserted that it would grow five times as much as any other brand of wheat. There were other claims made for the wheat seed, and the followers were advised to purchase it, the proceeds to go to the Watch Tower and be used in publishing the "Pastor's" sermons.

The *Eagle* first made public the facts about this new venture of the Russellites and it published a cartoon picturing the "Pastor" and his "Miracle Wheat" in such a way that "Pastor" Russell brought suit for libel, asking $100,000 damages. Government departments investigated the wheat for which $1.00 a pound was asked, and agents of the Government were important witnesses at the trial of the libel suit in January, 1913. The "Miracle Wheat" was low in the Government tests, they said. The *Eagle* won the suit.

Prior to entering court the *Eagle* had said,

The *Eagle* goes even further and declares that at the trial it will show that "Pastor" Russell's religious cult is nothing more than a money-making scheme.

The court's decision vindicated the *Eagle's* statement and proved its reliability.

All during this time the "Pastor's" sermons were being printed in newspapers throughout the world, notably when he made a tour of the world in 1912 and caused accounts to be published in his advertised sermons telling of enthusiastic greetings at the various places he visited. It was shown in many cases that the sermons were never delivered in the places that were claimed.

For the benefit of any naïve Jehovah's Witness who may think that the "Miracle Wheat" fraud is an invention of the "jealous religionists" who are trying to defame the "Pastor's" memory, we document the scandal, trial, and verdict as follows:

From originals (now microfilmed in New York) of *The Brooklyn Daily Eagle*, the following dates and articles—

(1) January 1, 1913, pages 1, 2. Miracle Wheat Scandal.
(2) January 22, 1913, page 2. Testimony of Russellite beliefs.
(3) January 23, 24, 1913, page 3. Testimony on wheat.
(4) January 25, 1913, page 16. Financial statements proving Russell's absolute control, made by Secretary-Treasurer Van Amberg.
(5) *Van Amberg's statement:*
   ". . . We are not responsible to anyone for our expenditures. We are responsible only to God."
(6) January 27, 1913, page 3. Government experts testify on "Miracle Wheat" and ascertain beyond doubt that it is not miraculous or overly excellent.
(7) January 28, 1913, page 2. Prosecution and Defense sum-up. Russell assailed, but not present to hear it.
(8) January 29, 1913, page 16. Russell loses libel suit.

In recent years the Watchtower Society has maintained that Russell never made money on the "Miracle Wheat," and that proceeds from its sale were "contributions" to the organization. They fail to note that Russell controlled the Watchtower Society, owning 990 of the 1,000 shares of its stock. Any

so called miracle wheat seed [handwritten marginal note]

contributions to it were also to Russell!

The Brooklyn *Eagle* led the fight to expose the hypocrisy of "Pastor" Russell and nothing could be more appropriate than their on-the-spot testimony as to his many fraudulent claims. The following documentary evidence is taken from *The Brooklyn Daily Eagle*, page 18, February 19, 1912, and is titled "Pastor Russell's Imaginary Sermons—Printed Reports of Addresses in Foreign Lands that He Never Made—One at Hawaii, a Sample." These excerpts concern the Pastor's "World Tour" and are very enlightening with respect to his reliability and truthfulness.

"Pastor" Russell, who has found the atmosphere of Brooklyn uncongenial ever since the *Eagle* published the facts concerning his methods and morals, is making some new records in the far parts of the world. He is delivering sermons to imaginary audiences on tropical islands and completing "searching investigations" into the missions of China and Japan by spending a few hours in each country.

Following the *Eagle's* exposing "Pastor" Russell's "Miracle Wheat" enterprise and the publication of the testimony on the basis of which Mrs. Russell obtained a separation and alimony, the "Pastor" developed the "world tour" idea. He set his printing plant to work to get out advance literature, huge bundles of which were sent to every place where he intended to appear. Then he contracted for advertising space in many American newspapers to print his imaginary sermons.

His first stop after sailing from the Pacific Coast was Honolulu. And Presto!—the newspapers in which advertising space had been engaged printed long cable dispatches which presented the "Pastor's" discourses. In one paper which printed the advertisement the opening sentences read "Honolulu Hawaiian Islands:

"The International Bible Students Committee of Foreign Mission investigation stopped at Honolulu and made observations. Pastor Russell, Chairman of the Committee, delivered a public address. He had a large audience and attentive hearing."

Then follows the sermon, full of local color and allusions to the "Paradise of the Pacific":

"I can now well understand [the printed report makes the 'Pastor' say] why your beautiful island is 'The Paradise of the Pacific.' I note your wonderful climate and everything which contributes to bring about this Paradise likeness."

And so on for two columns.

It has long been known that "Pastor" Russell has a strong imagination, but now it appears that he is even capable of delivering imaginary sermons. *Pastor Russell never spoke in Honolulu during the few hours that his ship stopped there to take on coal.* In the hope of securing an accurate report of his sermon, the *Eagle* wrote to the editor of the *Hawaiian Star*, which is published in Honolulu.

The following reply was shortly thereafter received:

"In answer to your inquiry of December 19th concerning Pastor Russell, I would say that he was here for a few hours with a Bible students' committee of foreign mission investigation, but did not make a public address as was anticipated." Walter G. Smith, Editor, *Star*.

That this was an isolated occurrence is refuted in other documentation.

The following evidence is taken from *The Brooklyn Daily Eagle,* January 11, 1913.

> *Tour of Orient branded huge advertising scheme.*
>
> As to the "Pastor's" methods of carrying Russellism to the heathen and the speed with which his searching investigations into the missions of the world are being conducted, the *Japan Weekly Chronicle* of January 11 supplies some interesting information. After explaining how the office of the paper had for weeks been bombarded with Russell literature and advance agents with contracts "just as if the reverend gentleman were an unregenerated theatrical company" the *Chronicle* says:
>
> "These gentlemen arrived in Japan on Saturday the 30th December. On the following day 'Pastor' Russell delivered a sermon in Tokyo entitled 'Where are the Dead?' which, though the title is a little ambiguous, does not seem to have any special connection with the mission work. On Monday it is assumed that the mission work in Japan was begun and finished, for the next day seems to have been devoted to traveling, and on Wednesday 'Pastor' Russell and his coadjutors left Kobe for China in the same vessel in which they had arrived in Yokohama . . . the truth is that the whole expedition is merely a huge advertising scheme!"

Russell carried on many such advertising stunts, and despite his protestations about earthly governments and laws being organizations of the devil, he was always the first to claim their protection when it was convenient for him to do so.

To mention one instance in addition to the *Eagle* suit, Russell brought suit for "defamatory libel" against the Reverend J. J. Ross, pastor of the James Street Baptist Church of Hamilton, Ontario, when the fearless minister wrote a blistering pamphlet denouncing Russell's theology and personal life. Russell lost this attempt (see *The Brooklyn Daily Eagle,* January 11, 1913) with J. F. Rutherford as his attorney. For the benefit of the interested reader, at this time we recount the facts concerning the libel suit as it actually occurred.

In June, 1912, the Reverend J. J. Ross, pastor of the James Street Baptist Church, Hamilton, Ontario, published a pamphlet entitled, "Some facts about the Self-Styled 'Pastor' Charles T. Russell" which minced no words in its denunciation of Russell, his qualifications as a minister, or his moral example as a "Pastor." Russell promptly sued Ross for "defamatory libel" in an effort to silence the courageous minister before the pamphlet could gain wide circulation and expose his true character and the errors of his theology. Mr. Ross, however, was unimpressed by Russell's action and eagerly seized upon the opportunity as a means of exposing Russell for the fraud he was. In his pamphlet, Ross assailed Russell's teachings as revealed in "Studies in the Scriptures" as "the destructive doctrines of one man who is neither a scholar nor a theologian" (page 7). Mr. Ross scathingly denounced Russell's whole system as "anti-rational, anti-scientific, anti-Biblical, anti-Christian, and a deplorable perversion of the gospel of God's Dear Son" (page 7).

Continuing his charges in the pamphlet, Ross exposed Russell as a pseudo-scholar and philosopher who "never attended the higher schools of learning; knows comparatively nothing of philosophy, systematic or historical theology, and is totally ignorant of the dead languages" (pages 3, 4). It must be clearly understood at this point by the reader that in a libel suit of the type pursued by Russell, the plantiff (Russell) had to *prove* that the charges lodged against him by the defendant (Ross) were not true. It is significant to note that Russell lost his suit against Ross when the High Court of Ontario, in session March, 1913, ruled that there were no grounds for libel; and "the case was thrown out of Court by the evidence furnished by 'Pastor' Russell himself" (page 15).[1]

"Pastor" Russell refused to give any evidence to substantiate his "case" and the only evidence offered was Russell's own statements, made under oath and during cross-examination by Ross's lawyer, Counselor Staunton. By denying Ross's charges, Russell automatically claimed high scholastic ascendancy, recognized theological training (systematic and historical), working knowledge of the dead languages (Greek, Hebrew, etc.), and valid ordination by a recognized body.[2] To each part of Mr. Ross's pamphlet (and all was read) Russell entered vigorous denials, with the exception of the "Miracle Wheat Scandal" which he affirmed as having "a grain of truth in a sense" to it.[3] "Pastor" Russell had at last made a serious mistake. He had testified under oath before Almighty God, and had sworn to tell "the truth, the whole truth, and nothing but the truth." He was soon to regret his testimony and stand in jeopardy as a perjurer, an unpleasant experience for the "Pastor" which more than explains his aversion to the witness chair.

Jehovah's Witnesses cannot deny this documentary evidence; it is too well substantiated. This is no "religionist scheme" to "smear" the "Pastor's" memory; I offer it as open proof of their founder's inherent dishonesty and lack of morals, that they may see the type of man to whose doctrines they have committed their eternal souls.

The following reference quotations are taken in part from Mr. Ross's second pamphlet entitled *Some Facts and More Facts About the Self-Styled Pastor—Charles T. Russell:*

> But now what are the facts as they were brought out by the examination on March 17, 1913? As to his scholastic standing he (Russell) had sworn that what was said about it was not true. Under the examination, he admitted that at most he had attended school only seven years of his life at the public school, and that he had left school when he was about fourteen years of age . . .

The cross examination of Russell continued for five hours. Here is a sample of how the "Pastor" answered.

The following reproduction of the *Russell* v. *Ross* transcript relative to the perjury charge made against Russell is taken from a copy on file in the headquarters of the cult in Brooklyn and is presented in the interests of thorough investigation.

Question: (Attorney Staunton)—"Do you know the Greek alphabet?"
Answer: (Russell)—"Oh yes."

---

[1]*Some Facts and More Facts About the Self-Styled Pastor—Charles T. Russell.* Mr. Ross's second pamphlet.
[2]*Ibid*, p.18.
[3]*Ibid*, p.17.

Question: (Staunton)—"Can you tell me the correct letters if you see them?"

Answer: (Russell)—"Some of them, I might make a mistake on some of them."

Question: (Staunton)—"Would you tell me the names of those on top of the page, page 447 I have got here?"

Answer: (Russell)—"Well, I don't know that I would be able to."

Question: (Staunton)—"You can't tell what those letters are, look at them and see if you know?"

Answer: (Russell)—"My way . . ." [he was interrupted at this point and not allowed to explain]

Question: (Staunton)—"Are you familiar with the Greek language?"

Answer: (Russell)—"No."

It should be noted from this record of the testimony that Russell frequently contradicted himself, claiming first to "know" the Greek alphabet, then claiming under pressure that he might make mistakes in identifying the letters, and then finally admitting that he couldn't read the alphabet at all when confronted with a copy of it.

From this it is easy to see that Russell did not "know" the Greek alphabet in any proper sense of the term, since it is assumed that when we say we "know" the English alphabet, for example, we shall be able upon request to name the letters by their correct titles.

"Pastor" Russell in failing to name the letters of the Greek alphabet, therefore, proved himself a perjurer, for he had previously stated that he "knew" them, thereby implying the ability to recite them, which he could *not* do.

It makes very little difference, therefore, whether the Watchtower wants to admit Russell's guilt or not since their own transcript shows that Russell said he "knew" what was later proved he did not know.

Here is conclusive evidence; the "Pastor" under oath perjured himself beyond question. Can one sincerely trust the teachings of a man who thought nothing of such evidence?

This, however, was not all of Russell's testimony, and as Counselor Staunton pressed him further the "Pastor" admitted that he knew *nothing* about Latin and Hebrew, and that he had never taken a course in philosophy or systematic theology, much less attended schools of higher learning. Bear in mind now that Russell a short time before had sworn he *did* have such knowledge by denying Mr. Ross's allegations. But there was no way out now; the "Pastor" was caught in a bold-faced fabrication and he knew it. However, all was not over yet. It will be remembered that Russell claimed "ordination" and equal if not superior status to ordained and accredited ministers. Counselor Staunton next smashed this illusion by demanding that Russell answer "Yes" or "No" to the following questions:

Question: (Ross' lawyer)—"Is it true you were never ordained?"

Answer: (Russell)—"It is not true."

It was necessary at this point for Counselor Staunton to appeal to the magistrate in order to make Russell answer the question directly. The magistrate presiding ruled that Russell must answer the questions put to him. Here is the result of the cross-examination.

Question: (Counselor Staunton)—"Now, you never were ordained by a bishop, clergyman, presbytery, council, or any body of men living?"
Answer: (Russell, after a long pause)—"I never was."

Once again Russell's "unswerving" honesty received a rude blow; the situation was out of his hands and Russell stood helpless as Counselor Staunton wrung statement after statement from him which established him beyond doubt as a premeditated perjurer. Russell further swore that his wife had not divorced him, and that the Court had not granted alimony from him, a statement he soon regretted when Counselor Staunton forced him to admit that the Court did divorce[4] him from his wife, and did award his wife alimony. The evidence was in; the case was clear. Russell was branded a perjurer by the Court's verdict "No Bill." As a result of the Court's action Mr. Ross's charges were proven true and the real character of Russell was revealed, that of a man who had no scruples about lying under oath and whose doctrines were admittedly based on no sound educational knowledge of the subject in question. Much evidence is available concerning Russell's moral life, but I see no reason to inject lewdness into the text. The character of the man is evident for all to see.

The easily offended "Pastor" might have practiced what he preached for once and heeded Christ's injunction concerning the patient enduring of "reviling and persecution" (Matthew 5:11, 12), but in Russell's case it is not at all applicable. However, Russell took every opportunity to make money, and legal clashes were frequent as a result. He maneuvered masterfully just one jump ahead of the law, and had it not been for Rutherford, who was a clever lawyer, the "Pastor" might not have been so fortunate. Russell hid, whenever cornered, behind the veil of a martyr for religious toleration, and despite the denunciation of churches and ministers he somehow succeeded in escaping the effects of damaging publicity. The Christian Church fought him openly but without the unified effort needed to squelch his bold approach. Some churches and pastors were united (see *The Brooklyn Daily Eagle*, January 2, 1913, page 18) and called for Russell's silencing as a menace. The "Pastor" was also deported from Canada because he hindered mobilization (see *The Daily Standard Union*, November 1, 1916), and in the early stages of World War I he was a prominent conscientious objector as all of his followers (Jehovah's Witnesses) still are today.

As a speaker, Russell swayed many; as a theologian, he impressed no one competent; as a man, he failed before the true God. Russell traveled extensively, spoke incessantly, and campaigned with much energy for "a great awakening" among the people of the world. In the course of his writings and lectures Russell denied many of the cardinal doctrines of the Bible—the Trinity, the Deity of Christ, the physical Resurrection and Return of Christ, eternal punishment, the reality of Hell, the eternal existence of the soul and the validity of the infinite Atonement, to state a few. The honest fact is that Russell had no training or education to justify his interpretation of Scripture. By this it is not meant that great education is a necessary qualification for exegesis, but when a man contradicts practically every major doctrine of the

---

[4]Neither party, however, obtained an absolute decree.

Bible he ought to have the education needed to defend (if that is possible) his arguments. "Pastor" Russell did not have that knowledge, or even the qualifications for ordination by any recognized body. The title "Pastor" was assumed, not earned, and to document this fact we quote from the November 1, 1916, edition of *The Brooklyn Daily Eagle*. "Although he styled himself a 'pastor' and was so addressed by thousands of followers all over the world, he had never been ordained and had no ministerial standing in any other religious sect than his own."

Psychologically, the man was an egotist whose imagination knew no bounds and who is classed (by his followers) along with St. Paul, Wycliffe and Luther as a great expounder of the Gospel. These are trite words for a man who proffered his writings as necessary for a clear understanding of the Scriptures and who once declared that it would be better to leave the Scriptures unread and read his books, rather than to read the Scriptures and neglect his books.

For the benefit of those so naïve as to believe that the "Pastor" did not make such a claim, we document the above assertion from *The Watchtower*, September 15, 1910, page 298, where the "Pastor" makes the following statement concerning his "Studies in the Scriptures" and their "indispensable" value when examining the Bible.

> If the six volumes of SCRIPTURE STUDIES are practically the Bible, topically arranged with Bible proof texts given, we might not improperly name the volumes THE BIBLE IN AN ARRANGED FORM. That is to say, they are not mere comments on the Bible, but *they are practically the Bible itself*, ...
>
> Furthermore, not only do we find that *people cannot see the divine plan in studying the Bible by itself*, but we see, also, that if anyone lays the SCRIPTURE STUDIES aside, even after he has used them, after he has become familiar with them, after he has read them for ten years—if he then lays them aside and ignores them and goes to the Bible alone, though he has understood his Bible for ten years, our experience shows that within two years *he goes into darkness*. On the other hand, if he had merely read the SCRIPTURE STUDIES with their references, and *had not read a page of the Bible, as such*, he would be in the *light* at the end of two years, because he would have the light of the Scriptures.[5]

Nowhere was Russell's egotism or boldness better revealed than in that statement. Think of it—according to the "Pastor" it is impossible to understand God's plan of salvation independent of Russellite theology, and to relegate one's study to the Bible alone void of Russell's interpretations is to walk in darkness at the end of two years. But there is a ray of hope for all those foolish enough to study God's Word alone. If all will adopt Russellism as a guide in Biblical interpretation, mankind will enter into a "new" Kingdom Age; for then, by virtue of the "Pastor's" expositions, true understanding of the Bible's basic doctrines will have been arrived at. To quote Mr. Ross: "This inspiration has its origin in the pit" (page 42).

Jehovah's Witnesses pursue this same line of theological interpretation today. Russellism did not die with Charles Taze Russell; it lives under the

---

[5]Emphasis is ours.

title *The Watchtower Announcing Jehovah's Kingdom.* The "Pastor's" dream has survived its author and remains today a living challenge to all Christians everywhere. Let us recognize it for what it is and unmask the unsound principles upon which it stands.

Upon Russell's death the helm of leadership was manned by Judge Joseph Franklin Rutherford, who acquitted himself nobly in the eyes of the Society by attacking the doctrines of "organized religion" with unparalleled vigor, and whose radio talks, phonograph recordings, numerous books, and resounding blasts against Christendom reverberated down the annals of the organization until his death on January 8, 1942, from cancer, at his palatial mansion, "Beth Sarim," in San Diego, California. He was 72. Rutherford's career was no less amazing than Russell's, for the Judge was an adversary of no mean proportions, whether in action against "organized religion" which he termed "rackets" or against those who questioned his decisions in the Society.

Throughout the years following Russell's death, Rutherford rose in power and popularity among the "Russellites" and to oppose him was tantamount to questioning the authority of Jehovah Himself. An example of this one-man sovereignty concerns the friction that occurred in the movement when Rutherford denounced Russell's pyramid prophecies scheme as an attempt to find God's will outside the Scriptures (1929). Many followers of Russell's theory left the Society as a result of this action by Rutherford, only to be witheringly blasted by the vituperative Judge, who threatened that they would "suffer destruction" if they did not repent and recognize Jehovah's will as expressed through the Society.

Rutherford also approached at times the inflated egotism of his predecessor Russell, and especially when, in his pamphlet *Why Serve Jehovah?*, he declared in effect that he was the mouthpiece of Jehovah for this age and that God had designated His words as the expression of divine mandate. It is indeed profitable to observe that Rutherford, as do all would-be "incarnations of infallibility," manifested unfathomable ignorance of God's express injunctions, especially against the preaching of "any other gospel" (Galatians 1:8, 9).

Fear of retaliation or rebuke was never characteristic of Judge Rutherford, and quite often he displayed complete contempt for all "religions" and their leaders. Lashing out against the persecution of the Witnesses in 1933, Judge Rutherford challenged all of Christendom, especially the Roman Catholic Church, to answer his charges of religious intolerance. Needless to say, he was ignored. Rutherford also battled against the Federal Council of the Churches of Christ in the U.S.A. and even offered to pay half the time cost for a radio debate on the subject of persecution. When ignored, Rutherford abated for a time. Few things, however, were allowed to dampen the Judge's vociferous thunderings and even a term in Atlanta Federal Penitentiary, for violation of the "Espionage Act" in 1918, failed to silence the Judge's attacks. Rutherford was released from Atlanta in March, 1919, and returned to the Witnesses' fold a martyr-hero, a complex readily appropriated by all Witnesses upon the slightest pretext. Indeed they enjoy greatly playing the role of persecuted saints. One only regrets that some of our less prudent administrators have so obligingly accommodated them.

The person of J. F. Rutherford, then, in the light of these facts, cannot be ignored in any true evaluation which seeks valid data concerning the Society's history. The great personal magnetism and the air of mystery which surround the man account most probably for his success as a leader, for he was almost a legendary figure even during his lifetime. The Judge shunned photographs, although he was most photogenic and presented both an imposing and impressive figure when attired in his familiar wing collar, bow tie and black suit. Reading glasses, which hung on a string across his honor's portly profile, accentuated the illusion of dignified importance, along with the title of Judge, which, contrary to popular opinion, he did hold from the days of his early legal career, when he was a special judge of the Eighth Judicial Circuit Court of Boonville, Missouri. Rutherford also possessed a deep, powerful voice which was capable of holding large audiences with its crescendo-like effect—but he seldom appeared in public and lived a closely guarded private life. Toward the end of his life, Rutherford's reign was not overly smooth, notably when the deposed head of the Witnesses' legal staff, Mr. Olin Moyle, sued Rutherford and several members of the Watchtower's Board of Directors in 1939 for libel and won his case, a judgment of $25,000, in 1944, two years after Rutherford's demise.

In comparing Russell and Rutherford it must be noted that the former was a literary pygmy compared to his successor. Russell's writings (approximation) were distributed, some fifteen or twenty million copies of them, over a period of sixty years, but Rutherford's in half that time were many times that amount. The prolific Judge wrote over one hundred books and pamphlets, and his works as of 1941 had been translated into eighty languages. This, then, was the Society's second great champion, who, regardless of his many failings, was truly an unusual man by any standards. Russell and Rutherford are the two key figures in the Society's history, and without them no doubt the organization would never have come into existence. But conjecture never eliminated a problem, and Jehovah's Witnesses are now a problem with which every intelligent Christian must cope.

The next president of the combined organization was Nathan Homer Knorr, who was elected president immediately after Rutherford's death. Mr. Knorr was responsible for the Gilead Missionary Training School in South Lansing, New York. Mr. Knorr followed diligently in the footsteps of Russell and Rutherford, and under his tutelage Christianity saw much opposition. Knorr died in June of 1977 and Frederick W. Franz, a longtime leader and then vice-president of the Society, was elected president and continues to pilot the Watchtower in the pattern of his predecessors. With each succeeding president, the control of the Society grows stronger.

One of the most distressing traits manifested in the literature and teachings of Jehovah's Witnesses is their seemingly complete disregard for historical facts and dependable literary consistency. At the same time, however, they condemn all religious opponents as "enemies of God"[6] and perpetrators of what they term "a racket."[7]

---

[6]J. F. Rutherford, *Deliverance* (Brooklyn: Watchtower Bible and Tract Society, 1926), p. 91.
[7]*Religion*, pp. 88, 104, 133, 137; 140, 141, etc.

For some time now the author has been considerably disturbed by Jehovah's Witnesses' constant denial of any theological connection whatsoever with "Pastor" Charles T. Russell, their admitted founder and first president of The Watchtower Bible and Tract Society. Since Russell was long ago proven to be a perjurer under oath, a sworn adversary of historic Christianity, and a scholastic fraud, it is obvious why the Witnesses seek to avoid his influence and memory whenever possible. However, some light should be thrown on the repeated self-contradictions which are committed by the Witnesses in their zeal to justify their position and the ever-wavering doctrines to which they hold. It is my contention that they are following the basic teachings of Charles T. Russell in relation to many Biblical doctrines which he denied, and from their own publications I shall document this accusation.

In their eagerness to repudiate the charge of "Russellism," the Witnesses dogmatically say: ". . . but who is preaching the teachings of Pastor Russell? *Certainly not* Jehovah's Witnesses! They cannot be accused of following him, for they *neither quote him as an authority nor publish nor distribute his writings*."[8] This is the statement of the Witnesses' magazine. Now let us compare this with history, and the truth will be plainly revealed.

Historically, Jehovah's Witnesses have quoted "Pastor" Russell numerous times since his death in 1916. The following is a token sample of what we can produce as concrete evidence. In 1923, seven years after the "Pastor's" demise, Judge J. F. Rutherford, then heir apparent to the Russellite throne, wrote a booklet some fifty-odd pages in length, entitled *World Distress—Why and the Remedy*. In this informative treatise, the new president of The Watchtower Bible and Tract Society and the International Bible Students quoted "Pastor" Russell no fewer than *sixteen* separate times; referred to his books, *Studies in the Scriptures* over *twelve* times; and devoted *six* pages at the end of the booklet to advertising these same volumes. Further than this, in a fifty-seven-page pamphlet published in 1925 and entitled *Comfort for the People*, by the same Rutherford, "his honor," in true Russellite character, defines clergymen as "dumb dogs (D.D.)," proceeds to quote "Pastor" Russell's prophetical chronology (1914 A.D.),[9] and then sums up his tirade against Christendom universal by recommending Russell's writing in *four* pages of advertisements at the rear of the book.

The dark specter of historical facts thus begins to creep across the previously happy picture of a "Russell-free"[10] movement. But let us further consult history. In the year 1927, The Watchtower Bible and Tract Society published Judge Rutherford's "great" literary effort entitled *Creation*, which was circulated into the millions of copies, and in which this statement appeared concerning "Pastor" Russell:

---

[8]*Awake*, May 8, 1951, page 26.

[9]Jehovah's Witnesses still hold to it today and teach it as dogma.

[10]In recent years, Jehovah's Witnesses have been forced openly to acknowledge Russell owing to the effect of my book *Jehovah of the Watchtower*, which gave the true history of Russell's infamous doings, thus necessitating an answer from the Witnesses, even if it was an unreliable one in many respects and highly colored. The historical series was run in *The Watchtower* for some months and was entitled "A Modern History of Jehovah's Witnesses." It was a very weak apologetic. Another history, *Jehovah's Witnesses in the Divine Purpose*, was published still later and gave high praise to Russell as well.

The second presence of Christ dates from about 1874.

From that time forward many of the truths long obscured by the enemy began to be restored to the honest Christian.

As William Tyndale was used to bring the Bible to the attention of the people, so the Lord used Charles T. Russell to bring to the attention of the people an understanding of the Bible, particularly of those truths that had been taken away by the machinations of the Devil and his agencies. Because it was the Lord's due time to restore these truths, he used Charles T. Russell to write and publish books known as *Studies in the Scriptures* by which the great fundamental truths of the divine plan are clarified. Satan has done his best to destroy these books because they *explain* the Scriptures. Even as Tyndale's Version of the Bible was destroyed by the clergy, so the clergy in various parts of the earth have gathered together thousands of volumes of *Studies in the Scriptures* and burned them publicly. But such wickedness has only served to advertise the truth of the divine plan.

Please consider, if you will, this statement by the then president of the Jehovah's Witnesses organization. Rutherford plainly quotes Russell and his writings as authoritative material, yet *The Watchtower* today claims *that Jehovah's Witnesses are free* from the taint of "Russellism"!

Concluding this brief historical synopsis of the Watchtower Society's past, we quote the grand finale of J. F. Rutherford's funeral oration over the prostrate remains of "dear brother Russell" who, according to the floral sign by his casket, remained "faithful unto death." Said the Judge: "Our brother sleeps not in death, but was instantly changed from the human to the divine nature, and is now forever with the Lord." This episode in Jehovah's Witnesses' history is cited for its uniqueness, to show the adoration in which Russell was once held by the theological ancestors of those who deny his influence today.

Leaving the past history of the Witnesses, I shall now answer those who say: "The Society may have quoted him in the past, but that was before Judge Rutherford's death. We do not do it now, and after all, didn't we say 'neither quote . . . publish . . . nor distribute his writings'? This is in the *present* tense, not the past." This would, we agree, be a splendid refutation of our claims if it were true, but as we shall now conclusively prove, it is not! Not only did Jehovah's Witnesses quote the "Pastor" as an authority in the past, before Rutherford's death in 1942, but they have done it many times up through the present.

In the July 15, 1950, edition of *The Watchtower* (page 216), the Witnesses quoted "Pastor" Russell as an authority regarding his chronology on the 2,520-year-reign of the Gentiles, which reign allegedly ended, according to his calculations (and Jehovah's Witnesses), in A.D. 1914. To make it an even more hopeless contradiction, they listed as their source, *The Watchtower* of 1880, of which "Pastor" Russell was editor-in-chief! Now if they "do not consider his writings authoritative and do not circulate them," why (1) publish his chronology, (2) quote his publication as evidence and (3) admit his teachings on this vital point in their theology?

To shatter any misconception as to their literary shortcomings, I refer the interested reader to a pamphlet published by the Watchtower, entitled *Jehovah's Witnesses, Communists or Christians?* (1953). Throughout the major content of this propaganda, Jehovah's Witnesses defend the thesis that they are not communists (which they are not), but, in their zeal to prove "their skirts clean," they quote "Pastor" Russell's writings no less than *five times*, refer to them with apparent pride *twice* (pages 4, 5), and even mention *two* of his best-known works, *The Plan of the Ages* (1886) and *The Battle of Armageddon* (1897). Further than this, *The Watchtower* of October 1, 1953, quoted "Pastor" Russell's *Studies in the Scriptures* (Vol. IV, page 554) (and Judge Rutherford's *Vindication* [Vol. II, page 311])—convincing evidence indeed that the Watchtower still follows the Russellite theology of its much denied founder. All this despite the fact that they say, in their own words, "Jehovah's Witnesses . . . neither quote him [Russell] as an authority nor publish nor distribute his writings." *Jehovah's Witnesses in the Divine Purpose*, a Society history published in 1959, devoted almost fifty pages to Russell and his invaluable contributions to the Society and its doctrines. More recently, the 1973 Watchtower publication, *God's Kingdom of a Thousand Years Has Approached*, based its assertion of the end of the "Gentile Times" on the studies and declarations of Russell (p. 188).

Through a careful perusal of these facts, it is a simple matter to determine that Jehovah's Witnesses have never stopped being "Russellites," no matter how loudly they proclaim the opposite. To those who are enmeshed in the Watchtower's web, we can only say that you are *not* following a "new" theocratic organization; you are following the old teachings of Charles Taze Russell, a bitter antagonist of historic Christianity, who has bequeathed to you a gospel of spiritual confusion. Those who are contemplating becoming members of the Watchtower Society, we ask to weigh the evidence found here and elsewhere[11] and to judge for yourselves whether it is wiser to trust the plain teachings of the Scripture and the guidance of the Holy Spirit and the Christian Church or to cast your lot with a group of zealous but misled people who are "blindly leading the blind down the broad way which leads to destruction." These persons, it should be remembered, have abandoned practically every cardinal doctrine of Biblical Christianity for the dogmatic doctrinal deviations of Charles Taze Russell and J. F. Rutherford. In the light of Holy Scripture, however, Russellism is shown to be a snare from whose grip only Jesus Christ can deliver.

This, then, is the history of Jehovah's Witnesses, the product of Charles Taze Russell, who, because he would not seek instruction in the Word of God, dedicated his unschooled talents to a lone vain search without the guidance of the Holy Spirit. This attempt has produced a cult of determined people who are persuaded in their own minds and who boldly attempt to persuade all others that the Kingdom of God is "present," and that they are Jehovah's Witnesses, the only *true* servants of the living God.

Some of the Doctrines of Jehovah's Witnesses

I. There is one solitary being from all eternity, Jehovah God, the Creator and Preserver of the Universe and of all things visible and invisible.

---

[11]Walter Martin, *Jehovah of the Watchtower* (Minneapolis, MN: Bethany House Publishers, 1975), chapter 1.

II. The Word or Logos is "a god," a mighty god, the "beginning of the Creation" of Jehovah, and His active agent in the creation of all things. The Logos was made human as the man Jesus and suffered death to produce the ransom or redemptive price for obedient men.

III. The Bible is the inerrant, infallible, inspired Word of God as it was originally given, and has been preserved by Him as the revealer of His purposes.

IV. Satan was a great angel who rebelled against Jehovah and challenged His Sovereignty. Through Satan, sin and death came upon man. His destiny is annihilation with all his followers.

V. Man was created in the image of Jehovah but willfully sinned, hence all men are born sinners and are "of the earth." Those who follow Jesus Christ faithful to the death will inherit the heavenly Kingdom with Him. Men of good will who accept Jehovah and His Theocratic Rule will enjoy the "new earth"; all others who reject Jehovah will be annihilated.

VI. The atonement is a ransom paid to Jehovah God by Christ Jesus and is applicable to all who accept it in righteousness. In brief, the death of Jesus removed the effects of Adam's sin on his offspring and laid the foundation of the New World of righteousness including the Millennium of Christ's reign.

VII. The man Christ Jesus was resurrected a divine spirit creature after offering the ransom for obedient man.

VIII. The soul of man is not eternal but mortal, and it can die. Animals likewise have souls, though man has the pre-eminence by Special creation.

IX. Hell, meaning a place of "fiery torment" where sinners remain after death until the resurrection, does not exist. This is a doctrine of "Organized Religion," not the Bible. Hell is the common grave of mankind, literally *sheol* (Hebrew), "a place of rest in hope" where the departed sleep until the resurrection by Jehovah God.

X. Eternal Punishment is a punishment or penalty of which there is no end. It does not mean "eternal torment" of living souls. Annihilation, the second death, is the lot of all those who reject Jehovah God and it is eternal.

XI. Jesus Christ has returned to earth A.D. 1914, has expelled Satan from Heaven and is proceeding to overthrow Satan's organization, establish the Theocratic Millennial Kingdom, and vindicate the name of Jehovah God. He did not return in a physical form and is invisible as the Logos.

XII. The Kingdom of Jehovah is Supreme, and as such cannot be compatible with present Human Government ("Devil's Visible Organization") and any allegiance to them in any way which violates the allegiance owed to Him, is a violation of the Scripture.

The Holy Trinity

1. "The doctrine, in brief, is that there are three gods in one: 'God the Father, God the Son, and God the Holy Ghost,' all three equal in power, substance and eternity" (*Let God be True*, Brooklyn: Watchtower Bible and Tract Society, 1946 ed., p. 100).

2. "The obvious conclusion is, therefore, that Satan is the originator of the trinity doctrine" (*Ibid.*, p. 101).

3. "... sincere persons who want to know the true God and serve Him find it a bit difficult to love and worship a complicated, freakish-looking, three-headed God" (*Ibid.*, p. 102).

4. "The trinity doctrine was not conceived by Jesus or the early Christians" (*Ibid.*, p. 111).

5. "The plain truth is that this is another of Satan's attempts to keep God-fearing persons from learning the truth of Jehovah and his Son, Christ Jesus. No, there is no trinity" (*Ibid.*, p. 111).

6. "Any trying to reason out the Trinity teaching leads to confusion of mind. So the Trinity teaching confuses the meaning of John 1:1, 2; it does not simplify it or make it clear or easily understandable" (*"The Word" Who Is He? According to John*, p. 7).

Deity of Christ

1. "... the true Scriptures speak of God's Son, the Word, as 'a god.' He is a 'mighty god,' but not the Almighty God, who is Jehovah" (*The Truth Shall Make You Free*, Brooklyn: Watchtower Bible and Tract Society, 1943, p. 47).

2. "In other words, he was the first and direct creation of Jehovah God" (*The Kingdom Is at Hand*, Brooklyn: Watchtower Bible and Tract Society, 1944, pp. 46, 47, 49).

3. "... the Bible shows that there is only one God. . . . 'greater than His Son.' . . . And that the Son, as the First-born, Only-begotten and 'the creation by God,' had a beginning. That the Father is greater and older than the Son is reasonable, easy to understand and is what the Bible teaches" (*From Paradise Lost to Paradise Regained*, Brooklyn: Watchtower Bible and Tract Society, 1958, p. 164).

4. "... Jesus was 'the Son of God.' Not God himself!" (*"The Word" Who Is He?*, p. 20).

5. "The very fact that he was sent proves he was not equal with God but was less than God his Father" (*Ibid.*, p. 41).

6. "Certainly the apostle John was not so unreasonable as to say that someone ('the Word') was with some other individual ('God') and at the same time was that other individual ('God')" (*Ibid.*, p. 53).

The Holy Spirit

1. "... The holy spirit is the invisible active force of Almighty God that moves his servants to do his will" (*Let God Be True*, p. 108).

2. "As for the 'Holy Spirit,' the so-called 'third Person of the Trinity,' we have already seen that it is, not a person, but God's active force" (*The Truth That Leads to Eternal Life*, Brooklyn: Watchtower Bible and Tract Society, 1968, p. 24).

3. "The Scriptures themselves unite to show that God's holy spirit is not a person but is God's *active force* by which he accomplishes his purpose and executes his will" (*Aid to Bible Understanding*, Brooklyn: Watchtower Bible and Tract Society, 1969, 1971, p. 1543).

The Virgin Birth

1. "Mary was a virgin. . . .
"... when Joseph learned that Mary was going to have a child, he did

not want to take her as his wife. But God's angel . . . said: '. . . that which has been begotten in her is by holy spirit . . .' . . . He took Mary his wife home. 'But he had no relations with her until she gave birth to a son.'—Matthew 1:20–25" (*From Paradise Lost to Paradise Regained*, pp. 122, 123).

2. ". . . Jesus was conceived by a sinless, perfect Father, Jehovah God . . .

". . . The perfect child Jesus did not get human life from the sinner Adam, but received only a human body through Adam's descendant, Mary. Jesus' life came from Jehovah God, the Holy One.

". . . Jehovah took the perfect life of his only-begotten Son and transferred it from heaven to . . . the womb of the unmarried girl Mary . . . Thus God's Son was conceived or given a start as a human creature. It was a miracle. Under Jehovah's holy power the child Jesus, conceived in this way, grew in Mary's womb to the point of birth" (*Ibid.*, pp. 126, 127).

3. ". . . Jesus' birth on earth was not an incarnation . . . He emptied himself of all things heavenly and spiritual, and God's almighty spirit transferred his Son's life down to the womb of the Jewish virgin of David's descent. By this miracle he was born a man . . . He was not a spirit-human hybrid, a man and at the same time a spirit person. . . . He *was* flesh" (*What Has Religion Done for Mankind?* p. 231).

The Atonement

1. "That which is redeemed or bought back is what was lost, namely, perfect human life, with its rights and earthly prospects" (*Let God Be True*, p. 114).

2. ". . . Jesus as the glorified High Priest, by presenting in heaven this redemptive price, is in position to relieve the believing ones of Adam's descendants from the inherited disability under which all are born" (*Ibid.*, pp. 118, 119).

3. "The human life that Jesus Christ laid down in sacrifice must be exactly equal to that life which Adam forfeited for all his offspring: it must be a perfect human life, no more, no less. . . . This is just what Jesus gave . . . for men of all kinds" (*You May Survive Armageddon into God's New World*, Brooklyn: Watchtower Bible and Tract Society, 1955, p. 39).

Salvation by Grace

1. "Immortality is a reward for faithfulness. It does not come automatically to a human at birth" (*Let God Be True*, p. 74).

2. "Those people of good will today who avail themselves of the provision and who steadfastly abide in this confidence will find Christ Jesus to be their 'everlasting Father' " (Isaiah 9:6) (*Ibid.*, p. 121).

3. "We have learned that a person could fall away and be judged unfavorably either now or at Armageddon, or during the thousand years of Christ's reign, or at the end of the final test . . . into everlasting destruction" (*From Paradise Lost to Paradise Regained*, p. 241).

The Resurrection of Christ

1. "This firstborn from the dead was raised from the grave, not a human creature, but a spirit" (*Let God Be True*, p. 276).

2. ". . . Jehovah God raised him from the dead, not as a human Son, but as a mighty immortal spirit Son. . . . For forty days after that he mater-

ialized, as angels before him had done, to show himself alive to his disciples . . ." (*Ibid.*, p. 40).

3. ". . . Jesus did not take his human body to heaven to be forever a man in heaven. Had he done so, that would have left him ever lower than the angels. . . . God did not purpose for Jesus to be humiliated thus forever by being a fleshly man forever. No, but after he had sacrificed his perfect manhood, God raised him to deathless life as a glorious spirit creature" (*Ibid.*, p. 41).

4. "Usually they could not at first tell it was Jesus, for he appeared in different bodies. He appeared and disappeared just as angels had done, because he was resurrected as a spirit creature. Only because Thomas would not believe did Jesus appear in a body like that in which he had died . . ." (*From Paradise Lost to Paradise Regained*, p. 144).

The Return of Christ and Human Government

1. "Christ Jesus returns, not again as a human, but as a glorious spirit person" (*Let God be True*, p. 196).

2. "Some wrongfully expect a literal fulfillment of the symbolic statements of the Bible. Such hope to see the glorified Jesus coming seated on a white cloud where every human eye will see him . . . Since no earthly men have ever seen the Father . . . neither will they see the glorified Son" (*Ibid.*, p. 186).

3. "It does not mean that he [Christ][12] is on the way or has promised to come, but that he has already arrived and is here" (*Ibid.*, p. 198).

4. "Any national flag is a symbol or image of the sovereign power of its nation" (*Ibid.*, p. 242).

5. "All such likenesses [symbols of a national power, eagle, sun, lion, etc.] are forbidden by Exodus 20:2–6 [the commandment of idolatry]" (*Ibid.*, p. 242).

6. ". . . hence no witness of Jehovah, who ascribes salvation *only* to Him, may salute any national emblem without violating Jehovah's commandment against idolatry as stated in His Word" (*Ibid.*, p. 243).

The Existence of Hell and Eternal Punishment

1. ". . . those who have been taught by Christendom to believe the God-dishonoring doctrine of a fiery hell for tormenting conscious human souls eternally" (*Let God Be True*, p. 88).

2. "It is so plain that the Bible hell is mankind's common grave that even an honest little child can understand it, but not the religious theologians" (*Ibid.*, p. 92).

3. "Who is responsible for this God-defaming doctrine of a hell of torment? The promulgator of it is Satan himself. His purpose in introducing it has been to frighten the people away from studying the Bible and to make them hate God" (*Ibid.*, p. 98).

4. "Imperfect man does not torture even a mad dog, but kills it. And yet the clergymen attribute to God, who is love, the wicked crime of torturing human creatures merely because they had the misfortune to be born sinners. . ." (*Ibid.*, p. 99).

5. "The doctrine of a burning hell where the wicked are tortured

---

[12]All emphases and brackets on this page are the author's.

eternally after death cannot be true, mainly for four reasons: (1) Because it is wholly unscriptural; (2) it is unreasonable; (3) it is contrary to God's love; and (4) it is repugnant to justice" (*Ibid.*, p. 99).

Man the Soul, His Nature and Destiny

1. ". . . man is a combination of two things, namely, the 'dust of the ground' and 'the breath of life.' The combining of these two things (or factors) produced a living soul or creature called man" (*Ibid.*, p. 68).

2. "So we see that the claim of religionists that man has an immortal soul and therefore differs from the beast is not Scriptural" (*Ibid.*, p. 68).

3. "The fact that the human soul is mortal can be amply proved by a careful study of the Holy Scriptures. An immortal soul can not die, but God's Word, at Ezekiel 18:4, says concerning humans: 'Behold all souls are mine; . . . the soul that sinneth it shall die' " (*Ibid.*, pp. 69, 70).

4. ". . . it is clearly seen that even the man Christ Jesus was mortal. He did not have an immortal soul: Jesus, the human soul, died" (*Ibid.*, p. 71).

5. "Thus it is seen that the serpent (the Devil) is the one that originated the doctrine of the inherent immortality of human souls" (*Ibid.*, pp. 74, 75).

6. "The Scriptures show that the destiny of the sinful man is death" (*Ibid.*, p. 75).

7. ". . . the Holy Scriptures alone offer real hope for those who do seek Jehovah God and strive to follow his ways" (*Ibid.*, p. 75).

The Kingdom of Heaven (a Heavenly One)

1. "Who and how many are able to enter it [the Kingdom]? The Revelation limits to 144,000 the number that become a part of the Kingdom and stand on heavenly Mount Zion . . ." (*Ibid.*, p. 136).

2. "In the capacity of priests and kings of God they reign a thousand years with Christ Jesus" (*Ibid.*, p. 137).

3. "He [Christ] went to prepare a heavenly place for his associate heirs, 'Christ's body,' for they too will be invisible spirit creatures" (*Ibid.*, p. 138).

4. "If it is to be a heavenly kingdom, who will be the subject of its rule? In the invisible realm angelic hosts, myriads of them, will serve as faithful messengers of the King. And on earth the faithful children of the King Christ Jesus, including faithful forefathers of his then resurrected, will be 'princes in all the earth'. . . . Then, too, the 'great crowd' of his 'other sheep' . . . will continue to 'serve him day and night,' and many of them will also be 'princes'. . . . they will 'multiply and fill the earth' in righteousness, and their children will become obedient subjects of the King Christ Jesus. And finally the 'unrighteous' ones that are to be resurrected then, to prove their integrity, must joyfully submit themselves to theocratic rule. . . . Those who prove rebellious or who turn unfaithful during the loosing of Satan at the end of Christ's thousand-year reign will be annihilated with Satan the Devil" (*Ibid.*, pp. 318, 319).

5. ". . . the Creator loved the new world so much that he gave his only-begotten Son to be its King" (*Ibid.*, p. 143).

6. "The undefeatable purpose of Jehovah God to establish a righteous kingdom in these last days was fulfilled A.D. 1914" (*Ibid.*, p. 143).

7. "Obey the King Christ Jesus and flee, while there is still time, to the Kingdom heights. . . . Time left is short, for 'the kingdom of the heavens has drawn near' " (*Ibid.*, p. 144).

Jehovah's Witnesses become intensely disturbed whenever they are referred to as "Russellites" or their theology as "Russellism." After a thorough examination of the doctrines of the Society and a lengthy comparison with the teachings of "Pastor" Russell its founder, the author is convinced that the two systems are basically the same, and whatever differences do exist are minute and affect in no major way the cardinal beliefs of the organization. I believe, however, that in any research project substantiating evidence should be produced for verification whenever possible. I have attempted to do this and as a result have listed below five of the major doctrines of Jehovah's Witnesses paralleled with the teachings of Charles Taze Russell their late great "Pastor." I am sure that the interested reader will recognize the obvious relationship between the two systems for it is inescapably evident that Russell is the author of both.

The Teachings of Charles Taze Russell or "Russellism"

The Doctrines of Jehovah's Witnesses

I. Triune Godhead

1. "This view [the Trinity][13] suited well 'the dark ages' it helped to produce" (*Studies in the Scriptures*, Vol. V, p. 166).

(Speaking of John 1:1–3)
1. "Does this mean that Jehovah God (Elohim) and the . . . Son are two persons but at the same time one God and members of a so called 'trinity' or 'triune god'? When religion so teaches it violates the Word of God, wrests the Scriptures to the destruction of those who are misled, and insults God-given intelligence and reason" (*The Truth Shall Make You Free*, p. 45).

2. ". . . this theory . . . is as unscriptural as it is unreasonable" (*Ibid.*, Vol. V, p. 166).

2. "The confusion is caused by the improper translation of John 1:1–3 . . ., such translation being made by religionists who tried to manufacture proof for their teaching of a 'trinity' " (*Ibid.*, pp. 45, 46).

3. ". . . if it were not for the fact that this trinitarian nonsense was drilled into us from earliest infancy, and the fact that it is so soberly taught in Theological Seminaries by gray haired professors, . . . nobody would give it a moment's serious consideration" (*Ibid.*, Vol. V, p. 166).

3. "The obvious conclusion is, therefore, that Satan is the originator of the 'trinity doctrine" (*Let God Be True*, p. 101).

4. "How the great Adversary [Satan] ever succeeded in foisting it

---
[13]Brackets are ours.

[The Triune Godhead] upon the Lord's people to bewilder and mystify them, and render much of the Word of God of none effect, is the real mystery. . ." (*Ibid.*, Vol. V, p. 166).

II. The Deity of Jesus Christ

1. ". . . our Lord Jesus Christ is *a* God . . . still the united voice of the Scriptures most emphatically asserts that there is but one Almighty God, the Father of all" (*Studies in the Scriptures*, Vol. V, p. 55).

2. "Our Redeemer existed as a spirit being before he was made flesh and dwelt amongst men.

At that time, as well as subsequently, he was properly known as 'a god'—a mighty one" (*Ibid.*, Vol. V, p. 84).

3. ". . . the Logos [Christ] himself was 'the beginning of the creation of God' " (*Ibid.*, Vol. V, p. 86).

4. "As chief of the angels and next to the Father, he [Christ] was known as the Archangel (highest angel or messenger), whose name, Michael, signifies, 'Who as God' or God's Representative" (*Ibid.*, Vol. V. p. 84).

1. ". . . the true Scriptures speak of God's Son, the Word, as 'a god.' He is a 'mighty god,' but not the Almighty God, who is Jehovah—Isaiah 9:6" (*The Truth Shall Make You Free*, p. 47).

2. "At the time of his beginning of life he was created by the everlasting God, Jehovah, without the aid or instrumentality of any mother. In other words, he was the first and direct creation of Jehovah God . . . He was the start of God's creative work. . . . He was not an incarnation in flesh but was flesh, a human Son of God, a perfect man, no longer a spirit, although having a spiritual or heavenly past and background" (*The Kingdom Is at Hand*, pp. 46, 47, 49).

3. "This One was not Jehovah God, but was 'existing in God's form. . . .' He was a spirit person . . . he was a mighty one, although not Almighty as Jehovah God is . . . he was a God, but not the Almighty God, who is Jehovah" (*Let God Be True*, pp. 32, 33).

4. "Being the only begotten Son of God, . . . the Word would be a prince among all other creatures. In this office he [Christ] bore another name in heaven, which name is 'Michael'. . . . Other names were given to the Son in course of time" (*The Truth Shall Make You Free*, p. 49).

III. The Resurrection of Christ

1. ". . . our Lord was put to death

1. ". . . In his resurrection he was

in *flesh*, but was made alive *in spirit*; he was put to death *a man*, but was raised from the dead *a spirit being* of the highest order of the divine nature. . ." (*Studies in the Scriptures*, Vol. V, p. 453).

2. ". . . it could not be that the man Jesus is the Second Adam, the *new* father of the race instead of Adam; for the *man* Jesus is dead, forever dead" (*Ibid.*, Vol. V, p. 454).

3. ". . . he [Christ] instantly created and assumed such a body of flesh and such clothing as he saw fit for the purpose intended" (*Ibid.*, Vol. II, p. 127).

4. "Our Lord's human body. . . . did not decay or corrupt. . . . Whether it was dissolved into gases or whether it is still preserved somewhere . . . no one knows" (*Ibid.*, Vol. II, p. 129).

no more human. He was raised as a spirit creature, . . ." (*The Kingdom Is at Hand*, p. 258).

2. ". . . Jehovah God raised him from the dead, not as a human Son, but as a mighty immortal spirit Son" (*Let God Be True*, p. 40).

. . . So the King Christ Jesus was put to death in the flesh and was resurrected an invisible spirit creature" (*Ibid.*, p. 138).

3. "Therefore the bodies in which Jesus manifested himself to his disciples after his return to life were not the body in which he was nailed to the tree. They were merely materialized for the occasion, resembling on one or two occasions the body in which he died. . ." (*The Kingdom Is at Hand*, p. 259).

4. "This firstborn from the dead was raised from the grave not a human creature, but a spirit" (*Let God Be True*, p. 276).

IV. The Physical Return of Christ

1. "And in *like manner* as he went away (quietly, secretly, so far as the world was concerned, and unknown except to his followers), *so*, in this manner, he comes again" (*Studies in the Scriptures*. Vol. II, p. 154).

2. [Russell's idea of what Christ is saying, and his teaching on the matter.] ". . . he comes to us in the early dawn of the Millennial Day, [Jesus] seems to say . . . Learn that I am a spirit being no longer visible to human sight" (*Ibid.*, Vol. II, p. 191).

1. "Christ Jesus comes, not again as a human, but as a glorious spirit person" (*Let God Be True*, page 196).

2. "Since no earthly men have ever seen or can see the Father, they will be unable to see the glorified Son" (*Ibid.*, p. 197).

3. "He [Christ] does not come in the body of his humiliation, a human body, which he took for the suffering of death, . . . but in his glorious spiritual body. . ." (*Ibid.*, Vol. II, p. 108).

3. "It is a settled Scriptural truth, therefore, that human eyes will not see him at his second coming, neither will he come in a fleshy body" (*The Truth Shall Make You Free*, p. 295).

4. ". . . Christ Jesus came to the Kingdom in A.D. 1914, but unseen to men" (*Ibid.*, p. 300).

V. The Existence of Hell or a Place of Conscious Torment After Death

1. "Many have imbibed the erroneous idea that God placed our race on trial for life with the alternative of *eternal torture*, whereas nothing of the kind is even hinted at in the penalty" (*Studies in the Scriptures*, Vol. I, p. 127).

2. "Eternal torture is nowhere suggested in the Old Testament Scriptures, and only a few statements in the New Testament can be so misconstrued as to appear to teach it . . ." (*Ibid.*, Vol. I, p. 128).

1. ". . . the Bible hell is mankind's common grave . . ." (*Let God Be True*, p. 92).

2. ". . . God-defaming doctrine . . ." (*Ibid.*, p. 98).

3. "The doctrine of a burning hell where the wicked are tortured eternally after death cannot be true. . ." (*Ibid.*, p. 99).

In concluding this comparison it is worthwhile to note that as far as the facts are concerned, "Jehovah's Witnesses" is simply a pseudonym for "Russellism" or "Millennial Dawnism." The similarity of the two systems is more than coincidental or accidental regardless of the Witnesses' loud shouts to the contrary. The facts speak for themselves. Inquisitive persons may ask at this point why the organization assumed the name of "Jehovah's Witnesses." The answer is more than understandable.

After Russell's death Judge Rutherford, the newly elected president of the Society, saw the danger of remaining Russellites and over a period of fifteen years he labored to cover up the "Pastor's" unpleasant past, which did much to hinder the organization's progress. In 1931 Rutherford managed to appropriate the name "Jehovah's Witnesses" from Isaiah 43:10, thus escaping the damaging title "Russellites." Rutherford thus managed to hide the unsavory background of Russellistic theology and delude millions of people into believing that Jehovah's Witnesses was a "different" organization. Rutherford's strategy has worked well for the Russellites, and as a result today those trusting souls and millions like them everywhere sincerely believe that they are members of a "New Kingdom Order" under Jehovah God, when in reality they are deluded believers in the theology of *one* man, Charles

Taze Russell, who was proven to be neither a Christian nor a qualified Bible student. Jehovah's Witnesses who have not been in the movement any great period of time deny publicly and privately that they are Russellites; and since few of the old-time members of "Pastor" Russell's personal flock are still alive, the Society in safety vehemently denounces any accusations which tend to prove that Russell's theology is the basis of the entire Watchtower system. Proof of this is found in a personal letter from the Society to the author dated February 9, 1951, wherein, in answer to my question concerning Russell's influence, they stated—"We are not 'Russellites' for we are not following Charles T. Russell or any other imperfect man. Honest examination of our literature today would quickly reveal that it differs widely from that of Russell's, even though he was the first President of our Society."

Further than this, the Society, in another letter dated November 6, 1950, and signed by Nathan H. Knorr, then its legal President, declared that "the latest publications of The Watchtower Bible and Tract Society set out the doctrinal views of this organization, and I think any information you want in that regard you can find yourself without an interview." So then it is evident from these two official letters that we must judge the faith of the Jehovah's Witnesses by their literature.

A Refutation of Watchtower Theology

The Triune Deity.[14]

One of the greatest doctrines of the Scriptures is that of the Triune Godhead (les theotetos) or the nature of God Himself. To say that this doctrine is a "mystery" is indeed inconclusive and no informed minister would explain the implications of the doctrine in such abstract terms. Jehovah's Witnesses accuse "The Clergy" of doing just that, however, and it is unfortunate to note that they are, as usual, guilty of misstatement in the presentation of the facts, and even in their definition of what Christian clergymen believe the Deity to be.

First of all, Christian ministers and Christians as a whole do not believe that there are "three gods in one" (Let God Be True, p. 100), but do believe that there are three Persons all of the same Substance, co-equal, co-existent and co-eternal. There is ample ground for this belief in the Scriptures, where plurality in the Godhead is very strongly intimated if not expressly declared. Let us consider just a few of these references.

In Genesis 1:26 Jehovah is speaking of creation and He speaks in the plural number, "Let us create man in our image after our likeness." Now it

---

[14]Jehovah's Witnesses take great delight in pointing out that the word "Trinity" does not appear as such in the Bible. They further state that since it is not a part of Scripture, it must be of pagan origin and should be discounted entirely. What the Witnesses fail to understand is that the very word "Jehovah," which they maintain is the only true name for God, also does not appear as such in the Bible, but is an interpolation of the Hebrew consonants YHWH or JHVH, any vowels added being arbitrary. Thus it is seen that the very name by which they call themselves is just as unbiblical as they suppose the Trinity to be.

is obvious that God would not create man in His image and the angels' images if He were talking to them, so He must have been addressing someone else and who, but His *Son* and the Holy Spirit who are equal in Substance could He address in such familiar terms? Since there is no other god but Jehovah (Isaiah 43:10, 11), not even "a lesser mighty god" as Jehovah's Witnesses affirm Christ to be, there must be a unity in plurality and Substance or the passage is not meaningful. The same is true of Genesis 11:7, at the tower of Babel, when God said, "Let *us* go down," and also of Isaiah 6:8, "who will go for *us* . . ." These instances of plurality indicate something deeper than an interpersonal relationship; they strongly suggest what the New Testament fully develops, namely, a Tri-Unity in the One God. The claim of Jehovah's Witnesses that Tertullian and Theophilus propagated and introduced the threefold unity of God into Christianity is ridiculous and hardly worth refuting. Any unbiased study of the facts will convince the impartial student that before Tertullian or Theophilus lived the doctrine was under study and considered sound. No one doubts that among the heathens (Babylonians and Egyptians) demon gods were worshiped, but to call the Triune Godhead a doctrine of the devil (*Let God Be True*, p. 101), as Jehovah's Witnesses do, is blasphemy and the product of untutored and darkened souls.

In the entire chapter "Is there a Trinity?" (*Let God Be True*, pp. 100, 101), the whole problem as to why the Trinity doctrine is "confusing" to Jehovah's Witnesses lies in their interpretation of "death" as it is used in the Bible. To Jehovah's Witnesses death is the cessation of consciousness, or *destruction*. However, no single or collective rendering of Greek or Hebrew words in any reputable lexicon or dictionary will substantiate their view. Death in the Scriptures is "separation" from the body as in the case of the first death (physical), and separation from God for eternity as in the second death (the lake of fire, Revelation 20). Death never means annihilation and Jehovah's Witnesses cannot bring in one word in context in the original languages to prove it does. A wealth of evidence has been amassed to prove it does not. I welcome comparisons on this point.

The rest of the chapter is taken up with childish questions—some of which are painful to record. "Who ran the universe the three days Jesus was dead and in the grave?" (death again portrayed as extinction of consciousness) is a sample of the nonsense perpetrated on gullible people. "Religionists" is the label placed on all who disagree with the organization's views regardless of the validity of the criticism. Christians do not believe that the Trinity was incarnate in Christ and that they were "three in one" during Christ's ministry. Christ voluntarily limited Himself in His earthly body, but heaven was always open to Him. At His baptism the Holy Spirit descended like a dove, the Father spoke and the Son was baptized. What further proof is needed to show a threefold unity? Compare the baptism of Christ (Matthew 3:16, 17) with the commission to preach in the threefold Name of God (Matthew 28:19) and the evidence is clear and undeniable. Even in the incarnation itself (Luke 1:35) the Trinity appears (see also John 14:16 and 15:26). Of course it is not possible to fathom this great revelation completely but this we do know: there is a unity of Substance, not three gods, and that unity is One in every sense, which no reasonable person can doubt after surveying the evidence. When Jesus said, "My Father is greater than I," He spoke the truth, for in the form of a servant (Philippians 2:7) and as a man, the Son was subject to the Father willingly; but upon His Resurrection and in the radiance of His glory taken again from whence He veiled it (verses 7, 8), He showed forth His Deity when He declared, "All authority is surrendered to me in heaven and earth" (Matthew 28:18); proof positive of His intrinsic Nature and Unity of Substance. It is evident then that the Lord Jesus Christ was never inferior, speaking of His nature, to His Father during His sojourn on earth.

Jehovah's Witnesses vs. the Scriptures, Reason, and the Trinity

Every major cult and non-Christian religion which seeks to deride orthodox theology continually attacks the doctrine of the Trinity. Jehovah's Witnesses (the Russellites of today) are the most vehement in this endeavor, and because they couch their clever misuse of terminology in Scriptural contexts, they are also the most dangerous. Throughout the whole length and breadth of the Watchtower's turbulent history, one "criterion" has been used in every era to measure the credibility of any Biblical doctrine. This "criterion" is *reason*. During the era of "Pastor" Russell and right through until today, *reason* has always been "the great god" before whom all followers of the Millennial Dawn[15] movement allegedly bow with unmatched reverence. In fact the "great paraphraser," as Russell was once dubbed, even went so far as to claim that reason, or the ability to think and draw conclusions, opened up to the intellect of man the very character of God Himself! Think of it, according to the "Pastor," God's nature is actually openly accessible to our feeble and erring reasoning powers. In the first volume of the *Millennial Dawn* series (later titled *Studies in the Scriptures*) (p. 41), "Pastor" Russell makes God subject to our powers of reasoning. Wrote the "Pastor": ". . . let us examine the character of the writings claimed as inspired (The Bible), to see whether their teachings correspond with the character we have *reasonably* imputed to God." Here it is plain to see that for Russell man's understanding of God's character lies, not in God's revelation of Himself to be taken by faith, but in our ability to reason out that character subject to the laws of our reasoning processes. Russell obviously never considered Jehovah's Word as recorded in the fifty-fifth chapter of Isaiah the Prophet, which discourse clearly negates man's powers of reasoning in relation to the divine character and nature of his Creator.

"For my thoughts are not your thoughts, neither are your ways my ways, saith the Lord. For as the heavens are higher than the earth, so are my ways higher than your ways, and my thoughts than your thoughts" (Isaiah 55:8, 9). By this statement God certainly did not say reason and thought should be abandoned in the process of inquiry, but merely that no one can know the mind, nature, or thoughts of God in all their fullness, seeing that man is finite and He is infinite. The term "reason" and derivatives of it (reasonable, reasoning, reasoned, etc.) are used eighty-eight times in the English Bible,

---

[15]Name originally given to the movement by Russell in 1886.

and only *once* in all these usages (Isaiah 1:18) does God address man. Jehovah's Witnesses maintain that since God said, "Come now and let us reason together . . ." that He therefore gave reason a high place, even using it Himself to commune with His creatures. While this is true, it is only so in a limited sense at best. God never said, "Reason out the construction of my Spiritual Substance and Nature," or "limit my character to your reasoning powers." Nevertheless, Jehovah's Witnesses, by making Christ (The Logos, John 1:1) "a god" or "a mighty god," but not "Jehovah God," have done just these things. In the reference quoted above (Isaiah 1:18), Jehovah showed man the way of salvation and invited him to be redeemed from sin. God never invited him to explore His deity or probe into His mind. The Apostle Paul says, "For who hath known the mind of the Lord? or who hath been his counselor? or who hath first given to him, and it shall be recompensed unto him again? For of him, and through him, and to him, are all things: to whom be glory for ever" (Romans 11:34–36).

But now let us examine this typical propaganda from the Watchtower's arsenal and see if they really do follow "Pastor" Russell and his theory of reason. In this article (*The Watchtower*, January 1, 1973), "The Scriptures, Reason, and the Trinity," the Witnesses constantly appeal to *reason* as the standard for determining what God thinks. The following are quotations which we believe illustrate this point beyond doubt.

1. "To hold that Jehovah God the Father and Christ Jesus His Son are co-eternal is to fly in the face of reason" (page 22). Notice that reason is used as the "yardstick" to determine the validity of a Scriptural doctrine.

2. "Jehovah God says: 'Come now, and let us reason together' (Isaiah 1:18). The advocates of the Trinity admit that it is not subject to *reason* or logic, and so they resort to terming it a 'mystery.' *But the Bible contains no divine mysteries.* It contains 'sacred secrets.' Every use of the word 'mystery' and 'mysteries' in the *King James Version* comes from the same Greek root word meaning 'to shut the mouth,' that is to keep secret. *There is a vast difference between a secret and a mystery. A secret is merely that which has not been made known, but a mystery is that which cannot be understood.*"[16]

Once again the interested reader must pay close attention to the Witnesses' favorite game of term-switching. *The Watchtower* makes a clever distinction between the term "mystery" and the term "secret" and declares that ". . . the Bible contains no divine mysteries." It is affirmed that "a secret is merely that which has not been made known, but a mystery is that which cannot be understood." In view of the seriousness of this Watchtower exercise in semantics, we feel obliged to destroy their *manufactured* distinction between "secret" and "mystery," by the simple process of consulting the dictionary. "Mystery" is defined as: "1. Secret, something that is hidden or unknown." "Secret" is defined as: "1. Something secret or hidden; mystery." Surely this is proof conclusive that the Bible contains "divine mysteries" as far as the meaning of the term is understood. It must also be equally apparent that Jehovah's Witnesses obviously have no ground for rejecting the word "mystery" where either the Bible or the dictionary are concerned. We fail to note

---

[16]Emphasis is this author's.

any "vast difference" between the two words, and so does the dictionary. The truth is that the Watchtower rejects the Trinity doctrine and other cardinal doctrines of historic Christianity, not because they are mysterious, but because Jehovah's Witnesses are determined to reduce Jesus, the Son of God, to a creature or "a second god," all Biblical evidence notwithstanding. They still follow in "Pastor" Russell's footsteps, and one needs no dictionary to substantiate that.

3. "Jehovah God by His Word furnishes us with ample *reasons* and logical bases for all regarding which he expects us to exercise faith. . . . We can make sure of what is right *only* by a process of *reasoning* on God's Word" (p. 24).

Here indeed is a prime example of what Jehovah's Witnesses continually represent as sound thinking. They cannot produce even one shred of evidence to bolster up their unscriptural claim that God always gives us reason for those things in which He wants us to "exercise faith." Biblical students (even "International"[17] ones) really grasp at theological straws in the wind when they attempt to prove so dogmatic and inconclusive a statement. A moment of reflection on the Scriptures will show, we believe, that this attempt to overemphasize *reason* is a false one.

First, does God give us a reason for creating Lucifer and allowing him to rebel against the Almighty? Is such a reason found in the Scripture? It is not, and yet we must believe that he exists, that he opposes God and that all references in the Scripture to Satan are authoritative. God demands that we exercise faith in their objective truth, yet He *never* gives us a reason for it.

Second, does God anywhere give to man a "reasonable" explanation of how it is possible that He exists in Trinity—as three persons while at the same time retaining oneness of nature and essence? No. Never in Scripture is this explained. Here we see a gross inconsistency of Watchtower reliance upon reason in their rejection of the Trinity. When compared to their acceptance of the miracles of Jesus, one wonders what they consider "reasonable." If they can believe that Jesus raised Lazarus from the dead, changed the water into wine, and fed five thousand with only two fishes and five loaves, *without* a "reasonable" explanation as to "how" He did this, should the "how" of the Trinity be of more difficulty in "reasonableness"? Surely the former is every much as mysterious as the latter!

Third, does God anywhere give the grieving parent who has just lost a child a "reasonable" explanation as to the "why"? That certain physical catastrophies can be traced to the results of sin upon mankind, no one will argue. But is God under any obligation to furnish the parent with a "reason" as to why his child *in particular* was taken? No. Never do the Scriptures address the issue. Yet, through it all God asks us to believe that these seemingly indescribable evils will ultimately work out His divine plan, and He asks us at times to believe in Him *against reason* and with the eyes of faith.

Much, much more could be said along the same lines, but enough has been shown to refute adequately the contention of Jehovah's Witnesses that

---

[17]International Bible students is one of the other names for Russellism.

God *always* gives us "reasons and logical bases" for all regarding which He expects us to exercise faith.

Let us also remember the falsity of their other claim in the same paragraph: "We can make sure of what is right only by a process of reasoning on God's Word." But Jesus said: "The Comforter, which is the Holy Ghost, whom the Father will send in my name, he shall teach you all things, and bring all things to your remembrance, whatsoever I have said unto you" (John 14:26). Now if only by a process of reasoning on God's Word we can make sure of what is right, as Jehovah's Witnesses contend, then Jesus and they are at direct variance, for they do not have the guidance of the Holy Spirit, since they deny His person and deity. In a controversy of this nature we prefer to choose God and His Word to the Watchtower's jumbled Russellism.

Fourth, "God, through His Word, appeals to our reason. The Trinity doctrine is a negation of both the Scriptures and reason." Like so many other of the Watchtower's clever examples of phraseology, this statement contains a mixture of truth and error, with just enough of the former to make good sense, and just enough of the latter to confuse the gullible reader. It is unquestionably true that God through His Word appeals to our reason; were it not so we could not understand His desires. But by the same token, God does not invite our inquiry into His nature or character. Jehovah's Witnesses, however, if their views are rightly understood, assume that human *reason* is capable of doing just that.

The Watchtower has never failed to echo the old Arian heresy. This was a theory popularized by Arius of Alexandria (in Egypt) in the fourth century A.D., which taught that Jesus was the first creature, a second and created god, inferior to Jehovah, the Father. It is upon this theological myth, banished from the Church in 326 A.D. with Arius, that Jehovah's Witnesses unsteadily base their whole system.

Jehovah's Witnesses know beyond doubt that if Jesus is Jehovah God then every one of them is going to a flaming hereafter; and hell they fear above all else. This no doubt explains a great deal of their antagonism to the doctrines of the Trinity and Hell. The Witnesses, it must be remembered, consistently berate the Trinity doctrine as of the devil, and never tire proclaiming that the Bible hell is the grave. The thought of being punished in unquenchable fire for their disobedience to God is probably the strongest bond that binds the Watchtower's flimsy covers together.

Let us further pursue the Watchtower's logic. In *The Watchtower*'s various articles, two other terms are repeated constantly by Jehovah's Witnesses. These terms are "equal" and "co-eternal." The terms are used some six times in this particular article and each time it is denied that Jesus Christ is either equal to or co-eternal with God His Father. Says *The Watchtower*:

"We see God in heaven as the Superior One. . . . We see his Son on earth expressing delight to do his Father's will; clearly two separate and distinct personalities and *not* at all equal. Nothing here (Matthew 28:18–20) to indicate that it (The Holy Spirit) is a person, let alone that it is equal with Jehovah God [p. 21]. The very fact that the Son received his life from the Father proves that *he could not be co-eternal with him.* (John 1:18; 6:57) . . . Nor can it be argued that God was superior to Jesus only because of Jesus' then being a human, for *Paul makes clear that Christ Jesus in his pre-human form was not equal with his father.* In Philippians 2:1–11 (NWT)[18] he counsels Christians not to be motivated by egotism but to have lowliness of mind, even as Christ Jesus had, who, although existing in God's form before coming to earth was not *ambitious* to become equal with his Father [p. 22] . . . Jesus did not claim to be *The God*, but *only* God's Son. That Jesus is inferior to his Father, is also apparent . . . etc. [p. 23] . . . The 'Holy Ghost' or Holy Spirit is God's active force . . . There is no basis for concluding that the Holy Spirit is a Person . . . Yes, the Trinity finds its origin in the pagan concept of a multiplicity, plurality, or pantheon of Gods. The law Jehovah God gave to the Jews stated diametrically the opposite. 'Jehovah our God is *one* Jehovah' (Deuteronomy 6:4) [p. 24]."

Briefly let us examine these statements of Jehovah's Witnesses and see if they have any rational content where the Bible is concerned. The Watchtower maintains that Christ and His Father are "not at all equal," which has been their boldest insult to Christianity since Russell and Rutherford concocted and promoted the whole Watchtower nightmare. This type of unbelief where Christ's true deity is concerned has gladdened the hearts of nonintellectuals the country over, who find it easier to mock the Trinity than to trust God's Word and His Son. Concerning His relationship with the Father, the Apostle John in the fifth chapter of his gospel, the eighteenth verse, when speaking of Jesus and the Jews said, "Therefore the Jews sought the more to kill him, because he not only had broken the sabbath, but said also God was his Father, making himself *equal* with God" (A.V.). The Greek word for equal is *ison*, which according to *Thayer's Greek Lexicon* (p. 307), an acknowledged authority, means "equal in quality as in quantity, to claim for one's self the *Nature*, rank, authority, which belong to God" (John 5:18). Dr. Thayer, Jehovah's Witnesses might take notice, was a Unitarian who denied Christ's Deity even as they themselves do; yet, being honest, he gave the true meaning of the Biblical terms even though they contradicted his views. Thus God's Word directly contradicts Jehovah's Witnesses and this they dare not deny.

The Watchtower further contends that since Christ received life from His Father—"I live by the Father" (John 6:57)—He could not be co-eternal with Him. At first glance this seems plausible, especially when coupled with John 5:26: "As the Father hath life in himself; so hath he given to the Son to have life in himself." Taking this text in its context we readily see that it cannot mean that Christ derived "eternal existence" from the Father. John 1:1 bears witness that "the Word was God," therefore eternity was inherent in His makeup by Nature. The logical conclusion must be that the indwelling "Life" of "God The Word" entered time in the form of "the Son of Man" and by this operation the Father through the agency of the Holy Spirit gave the "Son of Man" to have "Life in himself," the same Life that was eternally His as the eternal Word. But it takes more than a glance to support this

---

[18]NWT stands for the *New World Translation of the Holy Scriptures* (Brooklyn: Watchtower Bible and Tract Society, 1961).

garbled Watchtower polytheism as we shall soon see. Unwittingly, Jehovah's Witnesses answer their own Scriptural doubletalk when they quote Philippians 2:5–11 on page 22 of their article. In this passage of Scripture Paul claims full Deity for Christ and maintains that in His pre-incarnate life He "existed in the form of God" and "thought it not something to be grasped at to be *equal* with God, but took upon Himself the *form* of a servant and was made in the likeness of men." The term *equal* here is another form of *ison*, namely *isa*, which again denotes *absolute sameness of Nature*, thus confirming Christ's true Deity. Further, this context reveals beyond reasonable doubt that *all* reference to Christ's being subject to His Father (John 5:26; 6:57) pertain to His earthly existence, during which "he emptied Himself" to become as one of us. This in no way affected His true Deity or unity with the Father, for Jesus claimed Jehovahistic identity (John 8:58) when He announced Himself to the unbelieving Jews as The "I Am" of Exodus 3:14. Twice, then, in the same terms Jehovah's Witnesses deny what the Scriptures specifically testify, that Christ *is equal* with God in Essence, Character, and Nature, which truths the Watchtower's term-switching campaigns can never change. I should also like to call attention to an extremely bold example of misquoting so commonly found in Watchtower propaganda. On page 22 the Russellite oracle declares, ". . . *Paul makes clear that Christ Jesus in his pre-human form was not equal to his father.* In Philippians 2:1–11 (NWT) he counsels Christians not to be motivated by egotism but to have lowliness of mind even as Christ Jesus had, who, although existing in God's form before coming to earth *was not ambitious to become equal with his Father.*"

Now as far as the original Greek text of Philippians 2:1–11 is concerned, this is an absurd and plainly dishonest statement. Paul never even mentions Christ's being ambitious to attain anything at all or even his lack of ambition, since no Greek term there can be translated "ambition." Jehovah's Witnesses themselves do not use the word ambition in their own New World Translation, nor does any other translator that we know of. Despite this, however, they introduce the term which clouds the real meaning of the Greek terms. Further than this, and worse, the Watchtower plainly attempts to use Paul's declaration of Christ's Deity as a means of confusing the issue. They maintain that Paul here taught that Jesus was inferior in Nature to His Father, when in reality Paul's entire system of theology says the opposite. If we are to believe the Greek text, Paul declares that Jesus did *not* consider equality with God something "to be grasped after, or robbed" (Greek *arpazo*) since He previously existed as the eternal Word of God (John 1:1) prior to His incarnation (John 1:14), and as such shared the Father's prerogatives and attributes. Hence He had no desire to strive for what was His by Nature and inheritance. Paul elsewhere calls Christ "all the fullness of the Deity in the flesh" (Colossians 2:9), "The great God and our Savior" (Titus 2:13), and "God" (Hebrews 1:3, 8). These are just a few of the references; there are at least twenty-five more which could be cited from his writings and over seventy-five from the balance of the New Testament. Contrary to the Watchtower, then, Paul never wrote their Russellite interpretational paraphrase as recorded on page twenty-two, since even the Greek text bears witness against them.

Jehovah's Witnesses sum up their latest blast at the Trinity doctrine by informing us that John 1:1 should be rendered, "In the beginning was the Word, and the Word was with God, and the Word was *a god*." This is another example of the depths to which the Watchtower will descend to make Jesus "*a second god*" and thus introduce polytheism into Christianity. Needless to say, no recognized translators in the history of Greek exegesis have ever sanctioned such a grammatical travesty as the Watchtower translation and the Watchtower translators know it. Such a rendition is an indication of markedly inferior scholarship and finds no basis whatsoever in New Testament Greek grammar. Both James Moffatt and Edgar Goodspeed, liberal translators, render John 1:1: ". . . the Word was Divine"; but Mantey translates it "The Word was Deity," as does every acknowledged authority. Moffatt and Goodspeed, however, admit that Scripture teaches the full and *equal* Deity of Jesus Christ, something Jehovah's Witnesses vehemently deny. Beyond doubt the Watchtower of Jehovah's Witnesses presents a strange dilemma, "ever learning, and never able to come to a knowledge of the truth." The Russellite movements (there are other small branches) all cry loudly the old Jewish Scripture, "Hear, O Israel, the Lord our God is *one Lord*" (or, "The Lord is One"), and attempt to use it against the doctrine of the Trinity. But once again language betrays the shallowness of their resources. The term *Echod*, "One" in Hebrew, does *not* denote *absolute* unity in many places throughout the Old Testament, and often it definitely denotes *Composite Unity*, which argues for the Trinity of the Deity (Jehovah). In the second chapter and the twenty-fourth verse of Genesis, the Lord tells us that "a man leaves his father and his mother and cleaves to his wife, and they become one flesh" (in Hebrew, *Bosor Echod*). Certainly this does not mean that in marriage a man and his wife become one *person*, but that they become *one* in the unity of their substance and are considered as *one* person in the eyes of God. Please note, this is true unity; yet *not solitary*, but *composite unity*. Let us further consider composite unity. Moses sent twelve spies into Canaan (Numbers 13:23) and when they returned they brought with them a great cluster of grapes (in Hebrew *Eschol Echod*). Now since there were hundreds of grapes on this one stem, it could hardly be absolute or solitary unity, yet again *Echod* (one) is used to describe the cluster. This shows conclusively that the grapes were considered one in the sense of their being of the same origin, hence *composite unity* is again demonstrated. Jehovah's Witnesses continually ask, "If Jesus when on the cross was truly an incarnation of Jehovah, then who was in heaven?" This is a logical question to which the eighteenth chapter of Genesis gives fourteen answers, each reaffirming the other. As recorded in the eighteenth chapter of Genesis, Abraham had three visitors. Two of them were angels (Genesis 19:1), but the third he addressed as *Jehovah God, fourteen times!* Abraham's third visitor stayed and conversed with him and then departed, saying concerning Sodom, "I will go down and see whether they have done altogether according to the outcry which has come to me, and if not, I will know" (18:21). And so, "The Lord went his way when he had finished speaking to Abraham, and Abraham returned to his place" (verse 33). Now if John is to be believed without question, and Jehovah's Witnesses agree that he must be, then "No man hath seen God [the Father] at any time; the only begotten Son [Jesus Christ] who is in the bosom of the Father, he hath revealed him" (John 1:18). To further confuse the Witnesses' peculiar view of God as a *solitary unit,* Jesus Himself said concerning His Father, ". . . you have not at any time either heard his voice *or* seen his form . . . for God is a Spirit, and they that worship him must worship him in Spirit and in truth" (John 4:24; 5:37). Now, then, here is the evidence. Moses declares that God spoke face to face with Abraham (Genesis 18:26), and Jesus and John say, "No man hath seen God at any time." But Jesus makes it clear that He is referring to *the Father,* and so does John. The nineteenth chapter of Genesis, the twenty-fourth verse, solves then this problem for us once and for all, as even Jehovah's Witnesses will eventually be forced to admit. Moses here reveals a glimpse of the *composite unity* in the Triune God. "Then Jehovah rained on Sodom and Gomorrah brimstone and fire *from Jehovah* out of heaven." This unquestionably is the only solution to this dilemma. God the Father rained fire on Sodom and Gomorrah, and God the Son spoke and ate with Abraham and Sarah. Two persons (the third Person of the Trinity is revealed more fully in the New Testament: John 14:26; 16:7–14; etc.) are both called Jehovah (Genesis 18:21; 19:24; cf. Isaiah 9:6; Micah 5:2), and both are *One (Echod)* with the Holy Spirit in *composite unity* (Deuteronomy 6:4). God the Father was in heaven, God the Son died on the cross, God the Holy Spirit comforts the Church till Jesus shall come again. This is the Triune God whom Jehovah's Witnesses are committed to ridicule, berate, and blaspheme in the name of "human reason." God said in Genesis 1:26, "Let us make man in *our* image after *our* likeness," not in *my* image, after *my* likeness. Here plurality is seen, obviously, God speaking to His co-eternal Son (Christ) and addressing *Him* as an *equal.* Genesis 11:7, 9 with reference to the Tower of Babel, also lends strong support to the Triune God Doctrine, where God, speaking as an *equal* to His Son, declares, "Let *us* go down and there confound their language"—again plurality and *equal* discourse. In the face of all these texts, the Watchtower is strangely silent. They, however, rally afresh to the attack on page 23 of their article and declare that "there is no basis for concluding that the Holy Spirit is a person." This is so immature and unskilled an attack that it hardly justifies an effort to refute it. The fact that the Holy Spirit is referred to as a Person in the masculine gender throughout the New Testament, that He also is described as possessing an active *will* ("If I go not away, he will not come to you," John 16:7), which is the most concrete trait of a distinct personality, and that He is said to exercise the characteristics of a *teacher* (John 16:8), apparently all falls on deaf ears where the Watchtower is concerned. The literature of Jehovah's Witnesses is also consistently filled with nonsensical questions such as, "How could the one hundred and twenty persons at Pentecost be baptized with a Person," etc.? (Acts 1:5, 2:1–4). In answer to this, it evidently escapes the ever-zealous Russellites that the fulfillment of Jesus' prophecy as recorded in Acts 1:5 was explained in chapter two, verse four. Luke here says, "And they were all filled (Greek *eplesthesan*) with the Holy Spirit," etc. Jesus all too obviously did not mean that the apostles would be "immersed" in a Person, but filled with and immersed in the power of His Presence as symbolized in the tongues like unto fire. If Jehovah's Witnesses ever studied the Scriptures in the open with good scholars and stopped masquerading as Biblical authorities, which they are not, it might be interesting to see the results. Of course, great scholarship is not necessary to obtain a saving knowledge of Jesus Christ from God's Word; but when people deny the historic Christian faith and berate those who profess it, they ought to have some scholastic support, and Jehovah's Witnesses have none. The Watchtower widely cries that they will meet all persons with an open Bible, but to this date not one of their alleged authorities has materialized despite our numerous invitations. We of orthodox Christianity do not desire maliciously to attack any one's faith for the "joy" of doing it; but we must be faithful to our Lord's command to "preach the word and contend for the faith." As long as the Watchtower continues to masquerade as a Christian movement and attack without Biblical provocation or cause orthodox Christian theology with such articles as "The Scripture, Reason, and the Trinity," etc., so long will our voice be raised in answer to their consistent misrepresentations. God granting us the grace, we can do no other but be faithful to Him "who is the faithful and true witness, the *source* through whom God's creation came" (Revelation 3:14, Knox Version), His eternal Word and beloved Son, Jesus Christ our Lord.

Jehovah's Witnesses and the Holy Spirit

Though it is rudimentary to any study of the Bible, the Personality and Deity of the Holy Spirit must constantly be defended against the attacks of the Watchtower.

The Watchtower, as has been seen, denies His Personality and Deity, but the following references, a few of many in Scripture, refute their stand completely:

(1) Acts 5:3, 4—In verse 3 Peter accuses Ananias of lying *to* the Holy Spirit, and in verse 4 he declares the Holy Spirit to be God, an equation hard for the Watchtower to explain, much less deny. Who else but a Person can be lied to?

(2) Acts 13:2, 4—In the context the Holy Spirit speaks and sends, as He does in 21:10, 11, where He prophesies Paul's imprisonment. Only a Personality can do these things, *not* "an invisible active force," as the Jehovah's Witnesses describe Him.

(3) Finally, such references as John 14:16, 17, 26 and 16:7–14 need no comment. *He* is a divine Person and He is God (Genesis 1:2).

The New World Translation of the Bible

In any dealings one may have with the Watchtower or its numerous representatives, it is a virtual certainty that sooner or later in the course of events the Watchtower's "translation" of the Bible will confront the average prospective convert. This translation of the entire Bible is called the *New World Translation of the Holy Scriptures* (Brooklyn: Watchtower Bible and Tract Society, rev. ed. 1961). It is usually abbreviated as NWT.

First published in part in 1950 and later revised in 1951 and 1961, the New Testament version of this "translation" sold over 480,000 copies before its initial revision, and has now sold between 5 and 10 million copies. This version possesses a thin veneer of scholarship which proclaims the Society's daring and boldness in a field that all informed scholars know Jehovah's Witnesses are almost totally unprepared to venture into.

The "translation" exists and has had wide distribution both in the continental United States, Canada and all of the six continents. Jehovah's Witnesses boast that their "translation" is "the work of competent scholars" and further that it gives a clarity to the Scriptures that other translations have somehow failed to supply. Such stupendous claims by the Watchtower involves the necessity of a careful examination of their translation so that it may be weighed by the standards of sound Biblical scholarship. An exhaustive analysis of this work is impossible in this limited space, but we have selected some of the outstanding examples of fraud and deceit from the *New World Translation*. These examples should discourage any fair-minded individual from placing much value upon the Jehovah's Witnesses' Bible.

In their foreword to the *New World Translation of the Christian Greek Scriptures* (published before the whole Bible in 1950) the translation committee of the Watchtower cleverly claims for itself and its translation a peculiar freedom from what they define as "the misleading influence of religious traditions which have their roots in paganism" (p. 7). This "influence," the Watchtower insists, has colored the inspired Word of God, so it is necessary for them, Jehovah's chosen theocratic representatives, to set aright the numerous alleged examples of "human traditionalism" (p. 6) evidenced in all translations from John Wycliffe to the Revised Standard Version. Should anyone question that this arrogant attitude is the true Watchtower position regarding other translations, the following quote from this Foreword will dismiss all doubt:

> But honesty compels us to remark that, while each of them has its points of merit, they have fallen victim to the power of human traditionalism in varying degrees. Consequently, religious traditions, hoary with age, have been taken for granted and gone unchallenged and uninvestigated. These have been interwoven into the translations to color the thought. In support of a preferred religious view, an inconsistency and unreasonableness have been insinuated into the teachings of the inspired writings.
>
> The Son of God taught that the traditions of creed-bound men made the commandments and teachings of God of no power and effect. The endeavor of the New World Bible Translation Committee has been to avoid this snare of religious traditionalism (p. 6).

From this pompous pronouncement it is only too evident that the Watchtower considers its "scholars" the superiors of such great scholars as Wycliffe and Tyndale, not to mention the hundreds of brilliant, consecrated Christian men who produced the King James, American Standard, and Revised Standard Versions of the Bible. Such a pretext is of course too absurd to merit refutation, but let it be remembered that the New World Bible Translation Committee had no known translators with recognized degrees in Greek or Hebrew exegesis or translation. In fact, Frederick W. Franz, then representing the translation committee and now the Watchtower Society's fourth president, admitted under oath that he could not translate Genesis 2:4 from the Hebrew.

From the Pursuer's Proof of the cross-examination held on Wednesday, November 24, 1954, p. 7, paragraphs A-B, Examining Fred W. Franz, vice-president of the Watchtower Bible and Tract Society and sent as representative of the Society and the Translation Communications:

Q: Have you also made yourself familiar with Hebrew?
A: (Franz) Yes.
Q: So that you have a substantial linguistic apparatus at your command?
A: Yes, for use in my biblical work.
Q: I think you are able to read and follow the Bible in Hebrew, Greek, Latin, Spanish, Portuguese, German, and French?
A: Yes.

Later, during the same cross-examination:

Q: You, yourself, read and speak Hebrew, do you?
A: I do not speak Hebrew.
Q: You do not?
A: No.
Q: Can you, yourself, translate that into Hebrew?
A: Which?
Q: That fourth verse of the second chapter of Genesis?
A: You mean here?
Q: Yes.
A: No.

We asked a Hebrew teacher at Biola University/Talbot Theological Seminary if the fourth verse of the second chapter of Genesis was a particularly difficult verse to translate. After all, the pursuer's question would hardly have been fair if it were the hardest verse in the Old Testament to translate. The professor said that he would never pass a first year Hebrew student who could not translate that verse. This is an example of the "scholarship" backing the NWT.

However, the Watchtower translation speaks for itself and shows more clearly than pen can, the scholastic dishonesty and lack of scholarship so rampant within its covers. In order to point out these glaring inconsistencies, the author has listed five prime examples of the Watchtower's inaccuracies in translating the New Testament.

(1) The first major perversion that Jehovah's Witnesses attempt to foist upon the minds of the average reader is that it has remained for them as God's true Witnesses to restore the divine name "Jehovah" to the text of the New Testament. But let us observe this pretext as they stated it in their own words.

The evidence is, therefore, that the original text of the Christian Greek Scriptures has been tampered with, the same as the text of the LXX [the Septuagint—a Greek translation of the Old Testament] has been. And, at least from the 3rd century A.D. onward, the divine name in tetragrammaton [the Hebrew consonants YHWH, usually rendered "Jehovah"] form has been eliminated from the text by copyists. . . . In place of it they substituted the words *kyrios* (usually translated "the Lord") and *theos*, meaning "God" (p. 18).

The "evidence" that the Witnesses refer to is a papyrus roll of the LXX which contains the second half of the book of Deuteronomy and which does have the tetragrammaton throughout. Further than this, the Witnesses refer to Aquila (A.D. 128) and Origen, who both utilized the tetragrammaton in their respective Version and Hexapla. Jerome in the fourth century also mentioned the tetragrammaton as appearing in certain Greek volumes even in his day. On the basis of this small collection of fragmentary "evidence" Jehovah's Witnesses conclude their argument thusly:

> It proves that the original LXX did contain the divine name wherever it occurred in the Hebrew original. Considering it a sacrilege to use some substitute such as *kyrios* or *theos*, the scribes inserted the tetragrammaton at its proper place in the Greek version text (p. 12).

The whole case the Witnesses try to prove is that the original LXX and the New Testament autographs all used the tetragrammaton (p. 18) but owing to "tampering" all these were changed; hence their responsibility to restore the divine name. Such is the argument, and a seemingly plausible one to those not familiar with the history of manuscripts and the Witnesses' subtle use of terms.

To explode this latest Watchtower pretension of scholarship completely is indeed an elementary task. It can be shown from literally thousands of copies of the Greek New Testament that not *once* does the tetragrammaton appear, not even in Matthew, possibly written in Hebrew or Aramaic originally, and therefore more prone than all the rest to have traces of the divine name in it, yet it does not! Beyond this, the roll of papyrus (LXX) which contains the latter part of Deuteronomy and the divine name only proves that one copy did have the divine name (YHWH), whereas all other existing copies use *kyrios* and *theos*, which the Witnesses claim are "substitutes." The testimonies of Aquila, Origen and Jerome, in turn, only show that *sometimes* the divine name was used, but the general truth, upheld by all scholars, is that the Septuagint with minor exceptions always uses *kyrios* and *theos* in place of the tetragrammaton, and the New Testament never uses it at all. Relative to the nineteen "sources" the Watchtower uses (pp. 30–33) for restoring the tetragrammaton to the New Testament, it should be noted that they are all translations from Greek (which uses *kyrios* and *theos*, not the tetragrammaton) back into Hebrew, the earliest of which is A.D. 1385, and therefore they are of no value as evidence.

These cold logical facts unmask once and for all the shallow scholarship of Jehovah's Witnesses, whose arrogant pretension that they have a sound basis for restoring the divine name (Jehovah) to the Scriptures, while inferring that orthodoxy suppressed it centuries ago, is revealed to be a hollow scholastic fraud.

No reasonable scholar, of course, objects to the use of the term Jehovah in the Bible. But since only the Hebrew consonants YHWH appear without vowels, pronounciation is at best uncertain, and dogmatically to settle on *Jehovah* is straining at the bounds of good linguistics. When the Witnesses arrogantly claim then to have "restored" the divine name (Jehovah), it is almost pathetic. All students of Hebrew know that any vowel can be inserted between the consonants (YHWH or JHVH) so that theoretically the divine name could be any combination from JoHeVaH to JiHiViH without doing violence to the grammar of the language in the slightest degree. So much then for this, another empty claim of the Watchtower's pseudo-scholars.

(2) *Colossians 1:16*—"by means of him all [other][19] things were created in the heavens and upon the earth, the things visible and the things invisible, no matter whether they are thrones or lordships or governments or authorities" (NWT).

In this particular rendering, Jehovah's Witnesses attempt one of the most clever perversions of the New Testament texts that the author has ever seen. Knowing full well that the word *other* does not occur in this text, or for that matter in any of the three verses (16, 17, 19) where it has been added, albeit in brackets, the Witnesses deliberately insert it into the translation in a vain attempt to make Christ a creature and one of the "things" He is spoken of as having created.

Attempting to justify this unheard of travesty upon the Greek language and simple honesty, the New World Bible Translation Committee enclosed each added "other" in brackets, which are said by them to "enclose words inserted to complete or clarify the sense in the English text" (*New World Translation of the Christian Greek Scriptures*, op. cit., "Foreword," p. 6). Far from *clarifying* God's Word here, these unwarranted additions serve only to further the erroneous presupposition of the Watchtower that our Lord Jesus Christ is a creature rather than the Eternal Creator.

The entire context of Colossians 1:15–22 is filled with superlatives in its description of the Lord Jesus as the "image of the invisible God, the first-begetter [or 'original bringer forth'—Erasmus] of every creature." The Apostle Paul lauds the Son of God as *creator* of all things (verse 16) and describes Him as existing "before all things" and "holding together all things" (verse 17). This is in perfect harmony with the entire picture Scripture paints of the eternal Word of God (John 1:1) who was made flesh (John 1:14) and of whom it was written: "All things were made by him, and without him was nothing made that was made" (John 1:3). The writer of the book of Hebrews also pointed out that God's Son "upholds all things by the word of his power" (Hebrews 1:3) and that He is Deity in all its fullness, even as Paul wrote to the Colossians: "For . . . in him should all the fullness [of God] dwell" (Colossians 1:19, A.S.V.).

The Scriptures, therefore, bear unmistakable testimony to the creative activity of God's Son, distinguishing Him from among the "things" created, as *the* Creator and Sustainer of "all things."

Jehovah's Witnesses have no conceivable ground, then, for this dishonest rendering of Colossians 1:16, 17 and 19 by the insertion of the word "other" since they are supported by no grammatical authorities, nor do they dare dispute their perversions with competent scholars lest they further parade their obvious ignorance of Greek exegesis.

---

[19]Brackets are part of the NWT text itself.

(3) *Matthew 27:50*—"Again Jesus cried out with a loud voice, and yielded up his breath" (NWT).

Luke 23:46—"And Jesus called with a loud voice and said: 'Father, into your hands I entrust my spirit" (NWT).

For many years the Watchtower has been fighting a vain battle to redefine Biblical terms to suit their own peculiar theological interpretations. They have had some measure of success in this attempt in that they have taught the rank and file a new meaning for tried and true Biblical terms, and it is this trait of their deceptive system that we analyze now in connection with the above quoted verses.

The interested student of Scripture will note from Matthew 27:50 and Luke 23:46 that they are parallel passages describing the same event, namely the crucifixion of Jesus Christ. In Matthew's account, the Witnesses had no difficulty substituting the word "breath" for the Greek "spirit" (*pneuma*), for in their vocabulary this word has many meanings, none of them having any bearing upon the general usage of the term Biblically, i.e., that of an immaterial cognizant nature, inherent in man by definition and descriptive of angels through creation. Jehovah's Witnesses reject this immaterial nature in man and call it "breath," "life," "mental disposition" or "something windlike." In fact they will call it anything but what God's Word says it is, an invisible nature, eternal by creation, a spirit, made in the image of God (Genesis 1:27). Sometimes and in various contexts, spirit (*pneuma*) can mean some of the things the Witnesses hold, but context determines translation, along with grammar, and their translations quite often do not remain true to either.

Having forced the word "breath" into Matthew's account of the crucifixion, to make it appear that Jesus only stopped breathing and did not yield up His invisible nature upon dying, the Witnesses plod on to Luke's account, only to be caught in their own trap. Luke, learned scholar and master of Greek that he was, forces the Witnesses to render his account of Christ's words using the correct term "spirit" (*pneuma*), instead of "breath" as in Matthew 27:50. Thus in one fell swoop the entire Watchtower fabric of manufactured terminology collapses, because Jesus would hardly have said: "Father, into thy hands I commit my *breath*"—yet if the Witnesses are consistent, which they seldom are, why did they not render the identical Greek term (*pneuma*) as "breath" both times, for it is a parallel account of the same scene!

The solution to this question is quite elementary as all can clearly see. The Witnesses could not render it "breath" in Luke and get away with it, so they used it where they could and hoped nobody would notice it, or the different rendering in Matthew. The very fact that Christ dismissed His spirit proves the survival of the human spirit beyond the grave, or as Solomon so wisely put it: "Then shall the dust return to the earth as it was: and the spirit [*pneuma*—LXX] shall return unto God who gave it" (Ecclesiastes 12:7).

(4) *Philippians 1:21–23*—"For in my case to live is Christ, and to die, gain. Now if it be to live on in the flesh, this is a fruitage of my work—and yet which thing to select I do not know. I am under pressure from these two things; but what I do desire is the releasing and the being with Christ, for this, to be sure, is far better" (NWT).

In common with other cults that teach soul-sleep after the death of the body, Jehovah's Witnesses translate texts contradicting this view to suit their own ends, a prime example of which is their rendering of Philippians 1:21–23. To anyone possessing even a cursory knowledge of Greek grammar the translation "but what I do desire is the releasing. . . ." (verse 23) signifies either a woeful ignorance of the rudiments of the language or a deliberate, calculated perversion of terminology for a purpose or purposes most questionable.

It is no coincidence that this text is a great "proof" passage for the expectation of every true Christian who after death goes to be with the Lord (2 Corinthians 5:8). Jehovah's Witnesses realize that if this text goes unchanged or unchallenged it destroys utterly their Russellite teaching that the soul becomes extinct at the death of the body. This being the case, and since they could not challenge the text without exploding the myth of their acceptance of the Bible as the final authority, the Watchtower committee chose to alter the passage in question, give it a new interpretation, and remove this threat to their theology.

The rendering, "but what I do desire is the releasing. . . ," particularly the last word, is a gross imposition upon the principles of Greek exegesis because the untutored Russellites have rendered the first aorist active infinitive of the verb *analuo* (*analusai*) as a substantive ("the releasing"), which in this context is unscholarly and atrocious Greek. In order to translate it "the releasing," the form would have to be the participle construction (*analusas*), which when used with the word "wish" or "desire" denotes "a great longing" or "purpose" and must be rendered "to depart" or "to unloose." (See Thayer, Liddell and Scott, Strong, Young and A. T. Robertson.)

Quite frankly, it may appear that I have gone to a great deal of trouble just to refute the wrong usage of a Greek form, but in truth this simple switching of terms is used by the Witnesses in an attempt to teach that Paul meant something entirely different than what he wrote to the Philippians. To see just how the Watchtower manages this, I quote from their own appendix to the *New World Translation of the Christian Greek Scriptures* (op. cit., pp. 780, 781):

> The verb *a-na-ly'sai* is used as a verbal noun here. It occurs only once more in the Christian Greek Scriptures, and that is at Luke 12:36, where it refers to Christ's return. The related noun (*a-na'-ly-sis*) occurs but once, at 2 Timothy 4:6, where the apostle says: "The due time for my releasing is imminent." . . . But here at Philippians 1:23 we have not rendered the verb as "returning" or "departing," but as "releasing." The reason is, that the word may convey two thoughts, the apostle's own releasing to be with Christ at his return and also the Lord's releasing himself from the heavenly restraints and returning as he promised.
>
> In no way is the apostle here saying that immediately at his death he would be changed into spirit and would be with Christ forever. . . . It is to this return of Christ and the apostle's releasing to be always with the Lord that Paul refers at Philippians 1:23. He says there that two things are immediately possible for him, namely, (1) to live on in the flesh and (2) to die. Because of the circumstances to be considered, he expressed himself as being under pressure from these two things, not knowing which thing to

choose as proper. Then he suggests a third thing, and this thing he really desires. There is no question about his desire for this thing as preferable, namely, the releasing, for it means his being with Christ.

The expression *tou a-na-ly'-sai*, or *the releasing* cannot therefore be applied to the apostle's death as a human creature and his departing thus from this life. It must refer to the events at the time of Christ's return and second presence, that is to say, his second coming and the rising of all those dead in Christ to be with him forevermore.

Here, after much grammatical intrigue, we have the key as to why the Witnesses went to so much trouble to render "depart" as "releasing." By slipping in this grammatical error, the Watchtower hoped to "prove" that Paul wasn't really discussing his impending death and subsequent reunion with Christ at all (a fact every major Biblical scholar and translator in history has held), but a *third* thing, namely, "the events at the time of Christ's return and second presence." With breathtaking dogmatism, the Witnesses claim that *the releasing* cannot therefore be applied to the apostle's death. . . . It must refer to the events at the time of Christ's return. . . ."

Words fail the trained mind when confronted with this classic example of unparalleled deceit, which finds no support in any Greek text or exegetical grammatical authority. Contrary to the Watchtower's statement that "the word may convey two thoughts, the apostle's own releasing to be with Christ at his return and also the Lord's releasing himself from the heavenly restraints and returning as he promised," as a matter of plain exegetical fact, Christ's return is not even the subject of discussion—rather it is the Apostle's death and his concern for the Philippians that is here portrayed. That Paul never expected to "sleep" in his grave until the resurrection as Jehovah's Witnesses maintain is evident by the twenty-first verse of the chapter, literally—"For me to live is Christ, and to die is gain." There would be no gain in dying if men slept till the resurrection, for "God is not the God of the dead but of the living" (Mark 12:27). Clearly then, Paul was speaking of but two things: his possible death and subsequent presence with the Lord (2 Corinthians 5:8), and also the possibility of his continuing on in the body, the latter being "more needful" for the Philippian Christians. His choice in his own words was between these two (verse 23), and Jehovah's Witnesses have gone to great trouble for nothing; the Greek text still records faithfully what the inspired Apostle said—not what the Watchtower maintains he said, all their deliberate trickery to the contrary.

Concluding our comments upon these verses in Philippians, we feel constrained to point out a final example of Watchtower dishonesty relative to Greek translation.

On page 781 of the *New World Translation of the Christian Greek Scriptures*, it will be recalled that the Committee wrote: "The expression *tou a-na-ly'-sai* or *the releasing* cannot therefore be applied to the apostle's death as a human creature and his departing thus from this life."

If the interested reader will turn to page 626 of the same Watchtower translation, he will observe that in 2 Timothy 4:6 the Witnesses once more use the term "releasing" (*analuseos*), where all translators are agreed that it refers to Paul's impending *death*. The Revised Standard Version, often appealed to by Jehovah's Witnesses, puts it this way:

"For I am already on the point of being sacrificed, the time of my departure has come." (See also—*An American Translation* [Goodspeed], *Authorized Version*, J. N. Darby's Version, James Moffatt's Version, J. B. Rotherham's Version, Douay Version [Roman Catholic], etc.).

Jehovah's Witnesses themselves render the text: "For I am already being poured out like a drink offering, and the due time for my *releasing* is imminent" (2 Timothy 4:6, NWT).

Now since it is admitted by the Witnesses under the pressure of every translator's rendering of his text, that it refers to Paul's death, and further, since the noun form of the Greek word (*analuseos*) is here used and translated "releasing," why is it that they claim on page 781 that this expression "*the releasing*" (*analusai*—Philippians 1:23) ". . . cannot therefore be applied to the apostle's death as a human creature and his departing thus from this life"? The question becomes more embarrassing when it is realized that Jehovah's Witnesses themselves admit that these two forms (*analusai* and *analuseos*) are "related" (p. 781). Hence they have no excuse for maintaining in one place (Philippians 1:23) that "the releasing" cannot refer to the Apostle's death, and in another place (2 Timothy 4:6) using a form of the same word, and allowing that it does refer to his death. This one illustration alone should serve to warn all honest people of the blatant deception employed in the Watchtower's "translations," a name not worthy of application in many, many places.

(5) *Matthew 24:3*—"While he was sitting upon the mount of Olives, the disciples approached him privately, saying: 'Tell us, When will these things be, and what will be the sign of your presence and of the conclusion of the system of things?" (NWT).

Since the days of "Pastor" Russell and Judge Rutherford, one of the favorite dogmas of the Watchtower has been that of the *parousia*, the second coming or "presence" of the Lord Jesus Christ. Jehovah's Witnesses, loyal Russellites that they are, have tenaciously clung to the "Pastor's" theology in this respect and maintain that in the year 1914 when the "times of the Gentiles" ended (according to Russell), the "second presence" of Christ began. (See *Make Sure of All Things*, p. 319—Watchtower Bible and Tract Society.)

From the year 1914 onward, the Witnesses maintain,

> Christ has turned his attention toward earth's affairs and is dividing the peoples and educating the true Christians in preparation for their survival during the great storm of Armageddon, when all unfaithful mankind will be destroyed from the face of the earth (*op. cit.*, p. 319).

For Jehovah's Witnesses, then, Christ is not coming; He is here! (A.D. 1914)—only invisibly—and He is directing His activities through His theocratic organization in Brooklyn, New York. In view of this claim, it might be well to hearken unto the voice of Matthew who wrote:

> Then if any man shall say unto you, Lo, here is Christ, or there; believe it not. For there shall arise false Christs, and false prophets, and shall shew great signs and wonders; insomuch that, if it were possible, they shall deceive the very elect. Behold, I have told you before. Wherefore if they shall

say unto you, Behold, he is in the desert; go not forth: behold, he is in the secret chambers; believe it not. For as the lightning cometh out of the east, and shineth even unto the west; so shall also the coming of the Son of man be (Matthew 24:23–27).

Jehovah's Witnesses in their *New World Translation of the Christian Greek Scriptures* on page 780 list the twenty-four occurrences of the Greek word *parousia*, which they translate each time as "presence." They give the following defense found on page 779:

> The tendency of many translators is to render it here "coming" or "arrival." But throughout the 24 occurrences of the Greek word *parousia* . . . we have consistently rendered it "presence." From the comparison of the *parousia* of the Son of man with the days of Noah at Matthew 24:37– 39, it is very evident that the meaning of the word is as we have rendered it. And from the contrast that is made between the presence and the absence of the apostle both at 2 Corinthians 10:10, 11 and at Philippians 2:12, the meaning of *parousia* is so plain that it is beyond dispute by other translators.

Following this gigantic claim, namely, that their translation of the word *parousia* is "beyond dispute by other translators," the theocratic authorities proceed to list the verses in question.

Now the main issue is not the translation of *parousia* by "presence" because in some contexts it is certainly allowable (see 1 Corinthians 16:16; 2 Corinthians 7:6, 7; 10:10 and Philippians 1:26; 2:12). But there are other contexts where it cannot be allowed in the way Jehovah's Witnesses use it, because it not only violates the contextual meaning of the word, but the entire meaning of the passages as always held by the Christian Church.

Jehovah's Witnesses claim scholarship for this blanket translation of *parousia*, yet not one great scholar in the history of Greek exegesis and translation has ever held this view. Since 1871, when "Pastor" Russell produced this concept, it has been denounced by every competent scholar upon examination.

The reason this Russellite rendering is so dangerous is that it attempts to prove that *parousia* in regard to Christ's second advent really means that His return or "presence" was to be invisible and unknown to all but "the faithful" (Russellites, of course). (See *Make Sure of All things*, op. cit., pp. 319, 320–323.)

The New World Translators, therefore, on the basis of those texts where it is acceptable to render *parousia* "presence," conclude that it must be acceptable in all texts. But while it appears to be acceptable grammatically, no one but Jehovah's Witnesses or their sympathizers accept the New World Translation blanket use of "presence," be the translators Christian or not. It simply is not good grammar, and it will not stand up under comparative exegesis as will be shown. To conclude that "presence" necessarily implies invisibility is also another flaw in the Watchtower's argument, for in numerous places where they render *parousia* "presence" the persons spoken of were hardly invisible. (See 1 Corinthians 16:17; 2 Corinthians 7:6 and 10:10, also Philippians 1:26 and 2:12.)

If the Watchtower were to admit for one moment that *parousia* can be translated "coming" or "arrival," in the passages which speak of Christ's return the way all scholarly translators render it, then "Pastor" Russell's "invisible presence" of Christ would explode in their faces. Hence their determination to deny what all recognized Greek authorities have established.

The late Dr. Joseph F. Thayer, a Unitarian scholar, author of one of the best lexicons of the Greek New Testament (who, incidentally, denied the visible second coming of Christ), said on page 490 of that work, when speaking of *parousia*: ". . . a return (Philippians 1:26) . . . In the New Testament especially of the Advent, i.e., the future visible return from heaven of Jesus, the Messiah, to raise the dead, hold the last judgment, and set up formally and gloriously the Kingdom of God." (For further references, see Liddell and Scott, Strong and any other reputable authority.)

Dr. Thayer, it might be mentioned, was honest enough to say what the New Testament Greek taught, even though he didn't believe it. One could wish that Jehovah's Witnesses were at least that honest, but they are not!

In concluding this discussion of the misuse of *parousia* we shall discuss the verses Jehovah's Witnesses use to "prove" that Christ's return was to be an invisible "presence" instead of a visible glorious, verifiable event.

The following references and their headings were taken from the book, *Make Sure of All Things*, published by the Watchtower as an official guide to their doctrine.

(1) "Angels Testified at Jesus' Ascension as a Spirit that Christ Would Return in Like Manner, Quiet, Unobserved by the Public" (p. 320).

> And after he had said these things while they [only the disciples] were looking on, he was lifted up and a cloud caught him up from their vision. . . . "Men of Galilee, why do you stand looking into the sky? This Jesus who was received up from you into the sky will come thus in the same manner as you have beheld him going into the sky" (Acts 1:9, 11, NWT).

It is quite unnecessary to refute in detail this open perversion of a clear Biblical teaching because as John 20:27 clearly shows, Christ was not a spirit, and did not ascend as one. The very text they quote shows that the disciples were "looking on" and saw him "lifted up and a cloud caught him up from their vision" (verse 9). They could hardly have been looking at a spirit, which by definition is incorporeal,* not with human eyes at least, and Christ had told them once before, "Behold my hands and my feet, that it is I myself: handle me, and see; for a spirit hath not flesh and bones, as ye see me have" (Luke 24:39).

So it remains for Christ Himself to denounce the Russellite error that He "ascended as a spirit." Moreover, since He left the earth visibly from the Mount of Olives it is certain that He will return visibly even as the Scriptures teach (see Matthew 26:63, 64; Daniel 7:13, 14; Revelation 1:7, 8; Matthew 24:7, 8, 30).

(2) "Christ's Return Invisible, as He Testified that Man Would Not See Him Again in Human Form" (p. 321).

> A little longer and the world will behold me no more (John 14:19, NWT).
>
> For I say to you, You will by no means see me from henceforth until

---

*Even angels have to take a human form in order to be seen (Genesis 19:1, 2).

you say, "Blessed is he that comes in Jehovah's name!" (Matthew 23:39, NWT).

These two passages in their respective contexts give no support to the Russellite doctrine of an invisible "presence" of Christ for two very excellent reasons:

(a) John 14:19 refers to Christ's anticipated death and resurrection—the "little longer" He made reference to could only have referred to His resurrection and subsequent ascension (Acts 1:9, 11), before which time and during the period following His resurrection He appeared only to believers, not the world (or unbelievers), hence the clear meaning of His words. Jesus never said that *no* one would ever "see Him Again in Human Form" as the Watchtower likes to make out. Rather in the same chapter He promised to "*come again*, and receive you unto myself; that where I am, there ye may be also" (verse 3). The Bible also is quite clear in telling us that one day by His grace alone "we shall be like him, for we shall *see* him as he is" (1 John 3:2). So the Watchtower once more is forced to silence by the voice of the Holy Spirit.

(b) This second text, Matthew 23:39, really proves nothing at all for the Watchtower's faltering arguments except that Jerusalem will never see Christ again until it blesses Him in repentance as the anointed of God. Actually the text hurts the Russellite position, for it teaches that Christ will be *visible* at His coming, else they could not see Him to bless Him in the name of the Lord. Christ also qualified the statement with the word "until," a definite reference to His visible second advent (Matthew 24:30).

(3) "Early Christians Expected Christ's Return to Be Invisible. Paul Argued There Was Insufficient Evidence in Their Day" (p. 321).

> However, brothers, respecting the presence of our Lord Jesus Christ and our being gathered together to him, we request of you not to be quickly shaken from your reason nor to be excited either through an inspired expression or through a verbal message or through a letter as though from us, to the effect that the day of Jehovah is here. Let no one seduce you in any manner, because it will not come unless the apostasy comes first and the man of lawlessness gets revealed, the son of destruction (2 Thessalonians 2:1–3, NWT).

This final example from 2 Thessalonians most vividly portrays the Witnesses at their crafty best, as they desperately attempt to make Paul teach what in all his writings he most emphatically denied, namely that Christ would come invisibly for His saints.

In his epistle to Titus, Paul stressed the importance of "looking for that blessed hope, and the glorious appearing of the great God and our Savior Jesus Christ" (2:13), something he would not have been looking for if it was to be a secret, invisible *parousia* or "presence."

Paul, contrary to Jehovah's Witnesses, never believed in an invisible return, nor did any bona fide member of the Christian Church up until the fantasies of Charles Taze Russell and his *parousia* nightmare, as a careful look at Paul's first epistle to the Thessalonians plainly reveals. Said the inspired Apostle:

For this we say unto you by the word of the Lord, that we which are alive and remain unto the *coming* of the Lord shall not prevent them which are asleep.

For the Lord himself shall *descend* from heaven [visible] with a shout [audible], with the voice of the archangel, and with the trump of God: and the dead in Christ shall rise first (4:15, 16).

Here we see that in perfect accord with Matthew 26 and Revelation 1, Christ is pictured as *coming* visibly, and in this context no reputable Greek scholar alive will allow the use of "presence"; it must be "coming." (See also 2 Thessalonians 2:8.)

For further information relative to this subject, consult any standard concordance or Greek lexicon available, and trace Paul's use of the word "*coming*," etc. This will convince any fair-minded person that Paul never entertained the Watchtower's fantastic view of Christ's return.

These things being clearly understood, the interested reader should give careful attention to those verses in the New Testament which do not use the word *parousia* but are instead forms of the verb *elthon* and related to the word *erchomai* (see Thayer, pp. 250ff) and which refer to the Lord's coming as a visible manifestation. These various texts cannot be twisted to fit the Russellite pattern of "presence," since *erchomai* means "to come," "to appear," "to arrive," etc., in the most definite sense of the term. (For reference, check Matthew 24:30 in conjunction with Matthew 26:64—*erchomenon*; also John 14:3—*echomai*; and Revelation 1:7—*erchetai*.)

Once it is perceived that Jehovah's Witnesses are only interested in what they can make the Scriptures say, and not in what the Holy Spirit has already perfectly revealed, then the careful student will reject entirely Jehovah's Witnesses and their Watchtower translation. These are as "blind leaders of the blind" (Matthew 15:14) who have "turned the grace of God into lasciviousness, and denied our only Master and Lord Jesus Christ" (Jude 4). Further, that they "wrest the scriptures to their own destruction" (2 Peter 3:16), the foregoing evidence has thoroughly revealed for all to judge.

The Deity of Jesus Christ

Throughout the entire content of inspired Scripture the fact of Christ's identity is clearly taught. He is revealed as Jehovah God in human form (Isaiah 9:6; Micah 5:2; Isaiah 7:14; John 1:1; 8:58; 17:5; cf. Exodus 3:14; and Hebrews 1:3; Philippians 2:11; Colossians 2:9; and Revelation 1:8, 17, 18; etc.). The Deity of Jesus Christ is one of the cornerstones of Christianity, and as such has been attacked more vigorously throughout the ages than any other single doctrine of the Christian faith. Adhering to the old Arian heresy, which Athanasius the great Church Father refuted in his famous essay "On the Incarnation of the Word," many individuals and all cults steadfastly deny the equality of Jesus Christ with God the Father, and hence the Triune Deity. Jehovah's Witnesses, as has been observed, are no exception to this infamous rule. However, the testimony of the Scriptures stand sure and the above mentioned references alone put to silence forever this blasphemous heresy, which in the power of Satan himself deceives many with its "deceitful handling of the Word of God."

The Deity of Christ then is a prime answer to Jehovah's Witnesses, for if the Trinity is a reality, which it is, if Jesus and Jehovah are "one" and the Same, then the whole framework of the cult collapses into a heap of shattered disconnected doctrines incapable of even a semblance of congruity. We will now consider the verses in question, and their bearing on the matter.

1. (a) Isaiah 7:14—"Therefore the Lord [Jehovah] himself shall give you a sign; Behold, a virgin shall conceive, and bear a son, and shall call his name Immanuel" (lit., God or Jehovah with us, since Jehovah is the *only* God).

   (b) Isaiah 9:6—"For unto us a child is born, unto us a son is given: and the government shall be upon his shoulder: and his name shall be called Wonderful, Counselor, The mighty God, The everlasting Father, The Prince of Peace."

   (c) Micah 5:2—"But thou, Bethlehem Ephratah, though thou be little among the thousands of Judah, yet out of thee shall he come forth unto me that is to be ruler in Israel; whose goings forth have been from of old, from everlasting."

Within the realm of Old Testament Scripture Jehovah, the Lord of Hosts, has revealed His plan to appear in human form and has fulfilled the several prophecies concerning this miracle in the Person of Jesus Christ. Examination of the above listed texts will more than convince the unbiased student of Scripture that Jehovah has kept His promises and did become man, literally "God with us" (Matthew 1:23; Luke 1:32, 33; John 1:14).

The key to Isaiah 7:14 is the Divine Name "Immanuel," which can only be rightly rendered "God with us"; and since there is no other God but Jehovah by His own declaration (Isaiah 43:10, 11), therefore Jesus Christ and Jehovah God are of the same Substance in power and eternity, hence equal. This prophecy was fulfilled in Matthew 1:22, 23; thus there can be no doubt that Jesus Christ is the "son of the virgin" so distinctly portrayed in Isaiah 7:14. Jehovah's Witnesses can present no argument to refute this plain declaration of Scripture, namely that Jehovah and Christ are "One" and the Same, since the very term "Immanuel" (God or Jehovah with us) belies any other interpretation.

Isaiah 9:6 in the Hebrew Bible is one of the most powerful verses in the Old Testament in proving the Deity of Christ, and incontestably declares that Jehovah Himself planned to appear in human form. The verse clearly states that all government will rest upon the "Child born" and the "Son given" whose identity is revealed in the very terms used to describe His attributes. Isaiah under the inspiration of the Holy Spirit describes Christ as "Wonderful, Counselor, The mighty God, The everlasting Father, The Prince of Peace," all attributes of God alone. The term "mighty God" is in itself indicative of Jehovah since not only is He the only God (Isaiah 43:10, 11), but the term "mighty" is applied to Him alone in relation to His Deity. Jehovah's Witnesses dodge this verse by claiming that Christ is a mighty god, but not the Almighty God (Jehovah). This argument is ridiculous on the face of the matter. However, Jehovah's Witnesses argue that since there is no article in the Hebrew text, "mighty," therefore, does not mean Jehovah. The question then arises, are there two "mighty Gods"? This we know is absurd; yet Jehovah's Witnesses persist in the fallacy, despite Isaiah 10:21, where Isaiah (without the article) declares that "Jacob shall return" unto the "mighty God," and we know that Jehovah is by His own word to Moses "the God of Jacob" (Exodus 3:6). In Jeremiah 32:18 (with the article) the prophet declares that He (Jehovah) is "the great, and the Mighty God" (two forms of saying the same thing). (Cf. Isaiah 9:6; 10:21; Jeremiah 32:18.) If we are to accept Jehovah's Witnesses' view, there must be two "Mighty Gods"; and that is impossible, for there is only One True and Mighty God (Isaiah 45:22).

The prophet Micah, writing in Micah 5:2, recording Jehovah's words, gives not only the birthplace of Christ (which the Jews affirmed as being the City of David, Bethlehem), but he gives a clue as to His identity—namely God in human form. The term "goings forth" can be rendered *origin* (reference—Brown, Driver and Briggs, *Hebrew Lexicon of the Old Testament*, 426 [a] Item [2]), and we know that the only one who fits this description, whose origin is "from everlasting" must be God Himself, since He alone is "the eternally existing One" (Isaiah 44:6, 8). The overwhelming testimony of these verses alone ascertains beyond reasonable doubt the Deity of the Lord Jesus Christ, who became man, identified Himself with us in that incarnation, and offered Himself "once for all" a ransom for many, the eternal sacrifice who is able to save to the uttermost whoever will appropriate His cleansing power.

> 2. John 1:1—"In the beginning [or 'origin,' Greek, *Arche*] was the Word [*Logos*] and the Word was with God [*Ton Theon*] and the Word was God [*Theos*]."

Contrary to the translations of *The Emphatic Diaglott* and the *New World Translation of the Holy Scriptures*, the Greek grammatical construction leaves no doubt whatsoever that this is the only possible rendering of the text. The subject of the sentence is *Word (Logos)*, the verb, *was*. There can be no direct object following *was* since according to grammatical usage intransitive verbs take no objects but take instead predicate nominatives which refer back to the subject, in this case, *Word (Logos)*. In fact, the late New Testament Greek scholar, Colwell, formulated a rule which clearly states that a definite predicate nominative (in this case, *theos*—God) never takes an article when it precedes the verb (was) as we find in John 1:1. It is therefore easy to see that no article is needed for *Theos* (God) and to translate it "a god" is both incorrect grammar and poor Greek since *Theos* is the predicate nominative of *was* in the third sentence-clause of the verse and must refer back to the subject, *Word (Logos)*. Christ, then, if He is the Word "made flesh" (John 1:14) can be no one else except God unless the Greek text and consequently God's Word be denied.

Jehovah's Witnesses in their *New World Translation of the Christian Greek Scriptures*, on the appendix pages 773–77, attempt to discredit the Greek text on this point, for they realize that if Jesus and Jehovah are "One" in nature, their theology cannot stand since they deny that unity of nature. The refutation of their arguments on this point is conclusive.

The claim is that since the definite article is used with *Theon* in John 1:1c and not with *Theos* in John 1:1d, therefore the omission is designed to show a difference; the alleged difference being that in the first case the One True God (Jehovah) is meant, while in the second "a god," other than, and inferior to, the first is meant, this latter "god" being Jesus Christ.

On page 776b the claim is made that the rendering "a god" is correct because ". . . all the doctrine of sacred Scriptures bears out the correctness of this rendering." This remark focuses attention on the fact that the whole problem involved goes far beyond this text. Scripture does in fact teach the full and equal Deity of Christ. Why then is so much made of this one verse? It is probably because of the surprise effect derived from the show of pseudo-scholarship in the use of a familiar text. Omission of the article with *Theos* does not mean that "a god" other than the one true God is meant. Let one examine these passages where the article is not used with *Theos* and see if the rendering "a god" makes sense: Matthew 5:9; 6:24; Luke 1:35, 78; 2:40; John 1:6, 12, 13, 18; 3:2, 21; 9:16, 33; Romans 1:7, 17, 18; 1 Corinthians 1:30; 15:10; Philippians 2:11, 13; Titus 1:1 and many, many more. The "a god" contention proves too weak and is inconsistent. To be consistent in this rendering of "a god," Jehovah's Witnesses would have to translate every instance where the article is absent as "a god (nominative), of a god (genitive), to or for a god (dative)," etc. This they do not do in Matthew 5:9; 6:24; Luke 1:35, 78; John 1:6, 12, 13, 18; Romans 1:7, 17, etc. (See the *New World Translation of the Holy Scriptures* and *The Emphatic Diaglott* at above mentioned references.)

You cannot honestly render *theos* "a god" in John 1:1, and then *theou* "of God" (Jehovah), in Matthew 5:9, Luke 1:35, 78; John 1:6, etc., when *theou* is the genitive case of the *same* noun (second declension), *without* an article and *must* be rendered (following Jehovah's Witnesses' argument) "of a god" not "of God" as both *The Emphatic Diaglott* and *New World Translation of the Holy Scriptures* put it. We could list at great length, but suggest consultation of the Greek New Testament by either D. Erwin Nestle or Westcott & Hort, in conjunction with *The Elements of Greek* by Francis Kingsley Ball (New York: Macmillan, 1948, pp. 7, 14) on noun endings, etc. So then if Jehovah's Witnesses must persist in this fallacious "a god" rendition they can at least be consistent, which *they are not*, and render every instance where the article is absent in the same manner. The truth of the matter is this, that Jehovah's Witnesses use and remove the articular emphasis whenever and *wherever* it suits their fancy regardless of grammatical laws to the contrary. In a translation as important as God's Word, every law must be observed. Jehovah's Witnesses have not been consistent in their observances of those laws.

The writers of the claim have exhibited another trait common to Jehovah's Witnesses, that of half quoting or misquoting a recognized authority to bolster their ungrammatical renditions. On page 776 of the appendix to the *New World Translation of the Christian Greek Scriptures* when quoting Dr. Robertson's words, "among the ancient writers *ho theos* was used of the god of absolute religion in distinction from the mythological gods," they fail to note that in the second sentence following, Dr. Robertson says, "In the New Testament, however, while we have *pros ton theon* (John 1:1, 2) it is far more common to find simply *theos*, especially in the Epistles."

In other words, the writers of the New Testament frequently do not use the article with *theos* and yet the meaning is perfectly clear in the context, namely that the One True God is intended. Let one examine the following references where in successive verses and even in the same sentence the article is used with *one* occurrence of *theos* and *not* with another form, and it will be absolutely clear that no such drastic inferences can be drawn from John's usage in John 1:1, 2 (Matthew 4:3, 4; 12:28; 28:43; Luke 20:37, 38; John 3:2; 13:3; Acts 5:29, 30; Romans 1:7, 8, 17–19; 2:16, 17; 3:5, 22, 23; 4:2, 3, etc.).

The doctrine of the article is important in Greek; it is *not* used indiscriminately. But we are *not* qualified to be sure in *all* cases what is intended. Dr. Robertson is careful to note that "it is only of recent years that a really scientific study of the article has been made" (p. 755, A. T. Robertson). The facts are not all known and no such drastic conclusion, as the writers of the appendix note, should be dogmatically affirmed.

It is nonsense to say that a simple noun can be rendered "divine," and that one without the article conveys merely the idea of quality (pp. 773, 774, appendix to the *New World Translation of the Christian Greek Scriptures*). The authors of this note themselves later render the same noun *theos* as "a god" not as "a quality." This is a self-contradiction in the context.

In conclusion, the position of the writers of this note is made clear at page 774 of the appendix to the *New World Translation of the Christian Greek Scriptures;* according to them it is "unreasonable" that the Word (Christ) should be the God with whom He was (John 1:1). Their own manifestly erring reason is made the criterion for determining Scriptural truth. One need only note the obvious misuse in their quotation from Dana and Mantey (the *New World Translation of the Christian Greek Scriptures*, pp. 774, 775). Mantey clearly means that the "Word was Deity" in accord with the overwhelming testimony of Scripture, but the writers have dragged in the interpretation "a god" to suit their own purpose, which purpose is the denial of Christ's Deity, and as a result a denial of the Word of God. The late Dr. Mantey publicly stated that he was quoted out of context and he personally wrote the Watchtower, declaring "there is no statement in our grammar that was ever meant to imply that 'a god' was a permissible translation in John 1 :1" and "it is neither scholarly nor reasonable to translate John 1:1 'The Word was a god' " (Michael Van Buskirk, *The Scholastic Dishonesty of the Watchtower*, P.O. Box 2067, Costa Mesa, CA 92626: CARIS, 1976, p. 11).

3. John 8:58—"Jesus said unto them . . . before Abraham was [born], *I am*."

In comparing this with the Septuagint translation of Exodus 3:14 and Isaiah 43:10–13, we find that the translation is identical. In Exodus 3:14, Jehovah, speaking to Moses, said "*I am*," which any intelligent scholar recognizes as synonymous with God. Jesus literally said to them, "*I am* Jehovah" (*I am*), and it is clear that they understood Him to mean just that, for they attempted, as the next verse reveals, to stone Him. Hebrew law on this point states five cases in which stoning was legal—and bear in mind that the Jews were legalists. Those cases were: (1) Familiar spirits, Leviticus 20:27; (2) Cursing (blasphemy), Leviticus 24:10–23; (3) False prophets who lead to idolatry, Deuteronomy 13:5–10; (4) Stubborn son, Deuteronomy 21:18–21;

and (5) Adultery and rape, Deuteronomy 22:21–24 and Leviticus 20:10. Now any honest Biblical student must admit that the only legal ground the Jews had for stoning Christ (and actually they had none at all) was the second violation—namely, blasphemy. Many zealous Jehovah's Witnesses maintain that the Jews were going to stone Him because He called them children of the devil (John 8:44). But if this were true, why did they not try to stone Him on other occasions (Matthew 1:34; 23:33; etc.) when He called them sons of vipers? The answer is very simple. They could not stone Christ on that ground because they were bound by the law which gives only five cases, and would have condemned them on their own grounds had they used "insult" as a basis for stoning. This is not all, however, for in John 10:33, the Jews again attempted to stone Christ and accused Him of making Himself God (not *a god*, which subject has already been treated at length).[20] Let us be logical then; if the Jews observed the laws of stoning on other occasions when they might have been insulted, why would they violate the law as they would have had to do if Jehovah's Witnesses are right in John 8:58? Little more need be said. The argument is ridiculous in its context; there is only *one "I am"* in the Scriptures (Isaiah 48:12; 44:6; Revelation 1:8, 17), and Jesus laid claim to that Identity for which the Jews, misinterpreting the law, set about to stone Him.

Jehovah's Witnesses (p. 312 of the *New World Translation of the Christian Greek Scriptures*, footnote C) declare that the Greek rendering of *Ego Eimi (I am)* in John 8:58 is "properly rendered in the 'perfect indefinite tense' (I have been), not 'I am.' To unmask this bold perversion of the Greek text we shall now examine it grammatically to see if it has any valid grounds for being so translated.

It is difficult to know what the author of the note on page 312 means since he *does not* use standard grammatical terminology, nor is his argument documented from standard grammars. The aorist infinitive as such does *not* form a clause. It is the adverb *Prin* which is significant here, so that the construction should be called a *Prin* clause. The term "perfect indefinite" is not a standard grammatical term and its use here has been invented by the authors of the note, so it is impossible to know what is meant. The real problem in the verse is the verb *"Ego Eimi."* Dr. Robertson, who is quoted as authoritative by the NWT translators, states (p. 880) that *Eimi* is "absolute." This usage occurs four times (in John 8:24; 8:58; 13:19; 18:5). In these places the term is the same used by the Septuagint at Deuteronomy 32:39; Isaiah 43:10; 46:4; etc., to render the Hebrew phrase "I (am) He." The phrase occurs *only* where Jehovah's Lordship is reiterated. The phrase then is a claim to full and equal Deity. The incorrect and rude rendering of the NWT only serves to illustrate the difficulty of evading the meaning of the phrase and the context.

The meaning of the phrase in the sense of full Deity is especially clear at John 13:19 where Jesus says that He has told them things before they

---

[20]Jehovah's Witnesses point to the *New English Bible*'s rendering of this as "a god" as proof of the validity of their translation. The fact is, however, that the *NEB* mistranslated this passage and no reputable translation would support the Watchtower idea that this passage could mean that Jesus Christ was only claiming to be "a god."

came to pass, that when they do come to pass the disciples may believe that *Ego Eimi (I am)*. Jehovah is the only One who knows the future as a present fact. Jesus is telling them beforehand that when it does come to pass in the future, they may know that "*I am*" (Ego Eimi), i.e., that *He is Jehovah!*

In conclusion, the facts are self-evident and undeniably clear—the Greek allows no such impositions as "I have been." The Watchtower's contention on this point is that the phrase in question is a "historical present" used in reference to Abraham, hence permissible. This is a classic example of Watchtower double talk. The passage is not a narrative, but a direct quote of Jesus' argument. Standard grammars reserve the use of "historical present" to narratives alone. The term is translated here correctly only as "*I am*" and since Jehovah is the only "*I am*" (Exodus 3:14; Isaiah 44:6), He and Christ are "One" in Nature, truly the fullness of the "Deity" in the flesh.

The Septuagint translation of Exodus 3:14 from the Hebrew *ehyeh* utilizes *ego eimi* as the equivalent of "*I am*," Jehovah, and Jesus quoted the Septuagint to the Jews frequently, hence their known familiarity with it, and their anger at His claim (8:59).

> 4. Hebrews 1:3—"He is the reflection of [his] glory and the exact representation of his very being, and he sustains all things by the word of his power . . ." (NWT).

This passage of Scripture, I believe, clarifies beyond doubt the Deity of Jesus Christ. It would be illogical, and unreasonable, to suppose that Christ, who is the image imprinted by Jehovah's *Substance*, is not *of* the Substance of Jehovah and hence God, or the second Person of the Triune Deity. No creation is ever declared to be of God's very "Substance" or "Essence" (Greek *upostaseos*); therefore the eternal Word, who is "the fullness of the Godhead [Deity] bodily" (Colossians 2:9), cannot be a creation, or a created being. The writer of the book of Hebrews clearly intended to portray Christ as Jehovah, or he never would have used such explicit language as "the image imprinted by His Substance," and as Isaiah 7:14 clearly states, the Messiah was to be Immanuel, literally "God with us." Jehovah's Witnesses attempt the articular fallacy of "a god" instead of God, in reference to Immanuel; but if there has been "no god formed before or after Me" (Jehovah speaking in Isaiah 43:10), then it is impossible on that ground alone, namely God's declaration, for any other god ("a God" included) to exist. Their argument, based on a grammatical abstraction, fails to stand here; and the Deity of the Lord Jesus, as always, remains unscathed.

> 5. Philippians 2:11—". . . And every tongue should confess that Jesus Christ is Lord, to the glory of God the Father."

If we compare this verse of Scripture with Colossians 2:9 and Isaiah 45:23, we cannot help but see the full Deity of the Lord Jesus in its true light.

Jehovah spoke in Isaiah 45:23 and said, "I have sworn by myself, the word is gone out of my mouth in righteousness, and shall not return, that unto *me* every knee shall bow, every tongue shall swear." In Colossians 2:9 the Apostle Paul writing under the inspiration of the Holy Spirit declares, "For in Him [Christ] dwelleth all the fullness of the Godhead bodily." The literal translation of the Greek word *theotetos* (Godhead) is *Deity*, so in Christ all the fullness (*pleroma*) of the Deity resides in the flesh (*somatikos*).

In Thayer's *Greek-English Lexicon of the New Testament*, which is referred to as being "comprehensive" by the Watchtower, a complete analysis of *theotetos* (Godhead, Deity) is given, especially its interpretation in the context of Colossians 2:9. Jehovah's Witnesses will do well to remember that Thayer was a Unitarian (one who denies the Deity of Christ), therefore more prone to accept their interpretations than those of evangelical Christianity. But despite his theological views, Thayer was a Greek scholar whose integrity in the presentation of honest facts, despite their disagreement with his beliefs, is the trait exemplified in all good critics and honest scholars. On page 288 of the edition of 1886, Thayer states that *theotetos* [Godhead, Deity] is a form of *theot* [Deity] or in his own words "i.e., the state of Being God, Godhead" (Colossians 2:9)! In other words Christ was the fullness of "The Deity" (Jehovah) in the flesh! *The Emphatic Diaglott* correctly translates *theotetos* "Deity"; but the NWT erroneously renders it "the divine quality," which robs Christ of His Deity. Jehovah's Witnesses arrive at this inaccurate translation by substituting the word *theiotes*, a form of *theiot* (divinity) and thus escaping the condemning evidence of "The Deity" (Jehovah) *tes theotetos*. However, documentary evidence reveals that they cannot rightfully do this for in Thayer's own words (p. 288), "*theot* (Deity) *differs* from *theiot* (divinity) as essence differs from quality or attribute." This fact again exposes the deception employed by Jehovah's Witnesses to lead the unwary Bible student astray into the paths of blasphemy against the Lord Jesus. It is improper, it *cannot* be so translated, the substitution of one word for another in translation is pure scholastic dishonesty and Jehovah's Witnesses can produce no authority for this bold mistranslation of the Greek text. Jesus Christ, according to the words themselves, is the same *essence* and *substance* as Jehovah, and as the essence (Deity) differs from the *quality* (divinity), so He is God—*tes theotetos* (The Deity)— Jehovah manifest in the flesh.

That Jesus and Jehovah are "One" in nature dare not be questioned from these verses which so clearly reveal the plan and purpose of God. Paul sustains this argument in his epistle to the Philippians (before quoted) when he ascribes to the Lord Jesus the identity of Jehovah as revealed in Isaiah 45:23. Paul proclaims boldly, "That at the name of *Jesus* every knee should bow . . . and every tongue confess that Jesus Christ is Lord to the glory of God the Father." It is a well-known Biblical fact that the highest glory one can give to God is to acknowledge and worship Him in the Person of His Son, and as Jesus Himself said, "No man cometh unto the Father, but by *Me*" (John 14:6) and "all men should honor the Son even as they honor the Father" (John 5:23).

It is therefore clear from the context that the wonder of the Godhead is specifically revealed in Jesus Christ to the fullest extent, and it is expedient for all men to realize the consequences to be met if any refuse the injunctions of God's Word and openly deny the Deity of His Son, who is "the true God and eternal life" (1 John 5:20).

6. Revelation 1:8—" 'I am the Alpha and the Omega,' says Jehovah God, 'the One who is and who was and who is coming, the Almighty' " (NWT) cf. Rev. 1:7, 8, 17, 18; 2:8; 22:13; Matt. 24:30; Isaiah 44:6.

In the seventh, eighth, seventeenth and eighteenth verses of the first chapter of Revelation a unique and wonderful truth is again affirmed—namely, that Jesus Christ and Jehovah God are of the same *substance*, hence co-equal, co-existent and co-eternal, in short, *one nature* in its fullest sense. We shall pursue that line of thought at length in substantiating this doctrine of Scripture.

Comparing Matthew 24:30 with Revelation 1:7, it is inescapably evident that Jesus Christ is the "One coming with clouds" in both the references mentioned.

> And then shall appear the sign of the Son of man in heaven: and then shall all the tribes of the earth mourn, and they shall *see* the Son of man coming *in the clouds of heaven with power* and great glory (Matthew 24:30).
>
> *Behold, he cometh with clouds;* and every eye shall see him, and they also which pierced him: and all kindreds of the earth shall wail because of him. Even so, Amen (Revelation 1:7).

Following this train of thought, we find that Jehovah declares in Isaiah 44:6 that He alone is the First and the Last and the *only* God, which eliminates forever any confusion as to their being *two* Firsts and Lasts. Since Jehovah is the only God, then how can the *Logos* be "a god," a lesser god than Jehovah, as Jehovah's Witnesses declare in John 1:1? (*The Emphatic Diaglott* and *New World Translation.*) Many times Jehovah declares His existence as the "Only" God and Savior (Isaiah 41:4; 43:11–13; 44:6; 45:5; 48:12; etc.). This is indeed irrefutable proof, since Christ could not be our Savior or Redeemer if He were not Jehovah, for Jehovah is the only Savior (Isaiah 43:11). However, despite the testimony of Scripture that ". . . before me there was no God formed, neither shall there be after me" (Isaiah 43:10), the "a god" fallacy is pursued and taught by Jehovah's Witnesses in direct contradiction to God's Word. In 1 Corinthians 8:4–6 Paul points out that an idol or false god is nothing and, even though men may worship many things as gods, there is only one true and living God (cf. Acts 5:3, 4 and John 1:1 for the other persons of the Trinity).

Revelation 1:17, 18 and 2:8 add further weight to the Deity of Christ, for they reveal Him as the First and the Last, who became dead and lives forever. Now since Jehovah is the only First and Last (cf. Isaiah references), either He and Christ are "One," or to claim otherwise Jehovah's Witnesses must deny the authority of Scripture.

In order to be consistent we must answer the arguments advanced by Jehovah's Witnesses concerning the use of First and Last (Greek, *protos*) in Revelation 1:17 and 2:8.

By suggesting the translation of *prototokos* (First Born) instead of *protos* (First) in these passages (see the footnotes to the passages in the *New World Translation of the Christian Greek Scriptures* and *The Emphatic Diaglott*), Jehovah's Witnesses attempt to rob Christ of His Deity and make Him a created being with "a beginning" (*Let God Be True*, p. 107). When approached on this point they quickly refer you to Colossians 1:15 and Revelation 3:14 "proving" that the Logos had "a beginning" (see John 1:1, *The Emphatic Diaglott* and the NWT). To any informed Bible student this argument is fallacious. A *Greek-Lexicon of the New Testament* by J. H. Thayer, edition of 1886, states that the only correct rendering of *protos* is "First" and in Thayer's own words *"The Eternal One"* [Jehovah] (Revelation 1:17). Here again the Deity of Christ is vindicated.

Further proof of this synthesis is the fact that the best and most authoritative manuscripts (Sinaiticus, Vaticanus, etc.) have *protos* "First." The Alexandrinian Manuscript, since it possesses no accent marks, should be translated "Original Bringer Forth"[21] (Erasmus) in keeping with the laws of textual criticism (Colossians 1:15). In short, the whole problem is one of accentuation. Since there are no marks of punctuation or accent in the Alexandrinian Manuscript wording of Revelation 1:17; 2:8; etc., and since all the other manuscripts have *protos* "First," it is a contradiction to accentuate *prototokos* so as to make Christ a created being instead of the Creator. The correct accentuation of *prototokos* agrees with all the other manuscripts in portraying Christ as "The pre-eminent one" which is as it should be. These truths coupled with the fact that all reliable translations and translators bear out the rendering "First" in preference to "First Born" expose one more of the many clever attempts to pervert the Word of God by mistranslations and linguistic manipulation.

Jesus said: "I am Alpha and Omega, the First and the Last, the Origin and the End" (Revelation 22:13), and not only this but it is He who is revealing the mysteries to John (Revelation 1:1 and 22:16) and declaring Himself to be the "Faithful Witness" (Revelation 1:5) who testifies "I come quickly" (Revelation 22:20). It is evident then that Jesus is the One testifying and the "One" coming (Revelation 1:2, 7) throughout the book of Revelation since it is by His command (Revelation 22:16) that John records everything. So in honesty we must acknowledge His Sovereignty as the "First and Last" (Isaiah 48:12, Revelation 1:17 and 22:13), the Lord of all and the Eternal Word of God incarnate (John 1:1).

Revelation 3:14 asserts that Christ is the "beginning of the creation of God" and Colossians 1:15 states that Christ is "Firstborn of all creation." These verses in no sense indicate that Christ was a created being. The Greek word *arche* (Revelation 3:14) can be correctly rendered "origin" and is so translated in John 1:1 of the Jehovah's Witnesses' own 1951 edition of the *New World Translation of the Christian Greek Scriptures*. Revelation 3:14 then declares that Christ is the faithful and true witness, the "origin" or "source" of the creation of God. This corroborates Hebrews 1:2 and Colossians 1:16, 17 in establishing Christ as the Creator of all things and hence God (Genesis 1:1). Christ is the Firstborn of all creation since He is the new Creation, conceived without sin (Luke 1:35), the second Adam (1 Corinthians 15:45 and 47) who is the fulfillment of the divine Promise of the God-man (Isaiah 7:14; 9:6; Micah 5:2) and the Redeemer of the world (Colossians 1:14). John 3:13 states that no one has ascended into heaven but Christ who came down; Philippians 2:11 declares that He is Lord (Greek, *kurios*), and as such is "The Lord from heaven" of 1 Corinthians 15:47, hence God, and not a created being or "a god."

The Lord Jesus is also the "First Born" of the dead (Revelation 1:5)—

---

[21]Or more literally, "First Begetter"—See Hebrews 1:2.

that is, the First one to rise in a glorified body (*not* a spirit form—see Luke 24:39, 40), which type of body Christians will someday possess as in the words of the Apostle John, ". . . it does not yet appear what we shall be [but] we know that when He shall appear we shall be like [similar to] Him for we shall see Him as He is" (1 John 3:2). We know that these promises are sure, for He is faithful who promised (Hebrews 10:23), and all who deny the Deity of Christ might well take cognizance of His warning and injunction when He said,

> For I testify unto every man that heareth the words of the prophecy of this book, If any man shall add unto these things, God shall add unto him the plagues that are written in this book: And if any man shall take away from the words of the book of this prophecy, God shall take away his part out of the book of life, and out of the holy city, and from the things which are written in this book (Revelation 22:18, 19).

7. John 17:5—And now, O Father, glorify thou me with thine own self *with the glory which I had with thee before the world was* (Jesus Christ).

This passage of Scripture in cross reference with Isaiah 42:8 and 48:11 proves conclusively the identity of the Lord Jesus, and is a fitting testimony to the Deity of Christ.

In Isaiah 42:8 Jehovah Himself is speaking and He emphatically declares "I am the Lord: that is my name: and my glory will I not give to another, neither my praise, to graven images." Again in Isaiah 48:11 Jehovah is speaking and He declares "For mine own sake, even for mine own sake, will I do it: for how should my name be polluted? *and I will not give my glory unto another.*"

It is plain to see from these references in Isaiah that Jehovah has irrevocably declared that His divinely inherent glory, which is of His own Nature, cannot and will not be given to any person other than Himself. There is *no* argument Jehovah's Witnesses can erect to combat the truth of God as revealed in these passages of Scripture. The inherent glory of God belongs to God alone and by His own mouth He has so ordained it to be. God, however, bestowed upon the incarnate Word a certain glory manifested in the presence of the Holy Spirit through whose power and agency Christ worked while in the flesh and Jesus in turn bestowed this upon his followers (John 17:22). But it was *not* the glory of God's nature, but instead the abiding presence of His Spirit. The two quite different types of glory should not be confused. Jesus prayed to receive *back* again the glory He had with the Father "before the world was" (John 17:5) and it was *not* the glory given to Him as the Messiah, which glory Christ promised to share with His disciples (verse 22). Nowhere in Scripture are the two types of glory equated.

The Lord Jesus Christ, when He prayed in John 17:5, likewise irrevocably revealed that He would be glorified with *the glory of the Father* and that the glory of the Father (Jehovah) was not new to Him, since He affirmed that He possessed it, *with* (Greek, *para*) the Father (". . . the glory which I *had with* thee") even before the world came into existence. Jehovah's Witnesses attempt to answer this by saying that if He were God, where was His glory while He walked the earth?

In answer to this question the Scriptures list at least four separate instances where Christ manifested His glory and revealed His power and Deity. On the Mount of Transfiguration (Matthew 17:2) Christ shone with the inherent glory of God, which glory continued undiminished when in John 18:6 the Lord applied to Himself the "*I am*" of Jehovahistic identity that radiated glory enough to render His captors powerless at His will. The seventeenth chapter of John, the twenty-second verse, also confirms the manifestation of Jehovah's glory when Jesus, looking forward to the cross, prays for His disciples and affirms the origin of His glory as being the Substance of God. The resurrection glory of Christ also serves to illustrate His Deity and reveal it as of God Himself.

So it is plain to see that the argument Jehovah's Witnesses advance, to the effect that Christ did not manifest the glory of Himself, is invalid and finds no basis in the Scriptures. The truth of the whole matter is that the Lord Jesus did reveal the true glory of His Nature in the very works He performed, and as John says (1:14): "And the Word was made flesh, and dwelt among us, (and we beheld his glory, the glory as of the only begotten of the Father,) full of grace and truth."

St. Paul in the second chapter of Philippians removes all doubt on this question when he writes, guided by the Holy Spirit, that Christ never ceased to be Jehovah even during His earthly incarnation. It is interesting to note that the Greek term *uparchon*, translated "being" in Philippians 2:6, literally means "remaining or not ceasing to be" (see also 1 Corinthians 11:7), hence in the context Christ never ceased to be God, and "remained" in His basic Substance; He was truly "God manifest in the flesh."

An average Jehovah's Witness interviewed recently, in attempting to escape the obvious declaration of Christ's Deity as revealed in this text, reverted to the old Greek term-switching routine of the Society and asserted that the word "with" (Greek, *para*) in John 17:5, really means "through," and therefore the glory that is spoken of is not proof of Christ's Deity since the glory is Jehovah's and is merely shining "through" the Son; it is not His own but a manifestation of Jehovah's glory.

Once again we are confronted with the problem of illogical exegesis, the answer to which must be found in the Greek text itself. We must believe that the grammar of the Bible is inspired by God if we believe that God inspired the writers, or how else could He have conveyed His thoughts without error? Would God commit His inspired words to the failing grammatical powers of man to record? No! He could not do this without risking corruption of His message; therefore, as the wise and prudent Lord that He is, He most certainly inspired the grammar of His servants that their words might transmit His thoughts without error, immutable and wholly dependable. With this thought in mind, let us consider the wording and construction of the verse.

The Greek word *para* (with) is used in the dative case in John 17:5 and is not translated "through" (Greek *dia*) but is correctly rendered according to Thayer's *Lexicon* as "with," and Thayer quotes John 17:5, the very verse in question, as his example of how *para* (with) should be translated.

Never let it be said that *para* in this context indicates anything less than possessive equality—"the glory which I had *with* thee before the world was."

The Lord Jesus Christ clearly meant that He as God the Son was the possessor of divine glory along with the Father and the Holy Spirit before the world was even formed. Christ also declared that He intended to appropriate that glory in all its divine power once again, pending the resurrection of His earthly temple, which by necessity, since it was finite, veiled as a voluntary act His eternal power and Deity (Philippians 2:5–8). The glory He spoke of did not only shine through the Father; it was eternally inherent in the Son, and since John, led by the Holy Spirit, deliberately chose *para* (literally "with") in preference to *dia* (through), the argument that Jehovah's Witnesses advance cannot stand up. The Lord Jesus claimed the same glory of the Father as His own, and since Jehovah has said that He will not give His inherent glory to another (Isaiah 42:9), the unity of Substance between Him and Christ is undeniable; they are One in all its wonderful and mysterious implications which, though we cannot understand them fully, we gladly accept, and in so doing remain faithful to God's Word.

   8. John 20:28—Thomas answered and said unto him, My Lord and my
      God!

No treatment of the Deity of Christ would be complete without mentioning the greatest single testimony recorded in the Scriptures. John 20:28 presents that testimony.

Beginning at verse 24 the disciple Thomas is portrayed as being a thorough-going skeptic in that he refused to believe that Christ had risen and appeared physically in the *same* form which had been crucified on the cross. In verse 25 Thomas stubbornly declares that "Except I shall see in his hands the print of the nails, and put my finger into the print of the nails, and thrust my hand into his side I will not believe." Following through the sequence of events in verses 26 and 27, we learn that the Lord appeared to Thomas together with the other disciples and presented His body bearing the wounds of Calvary to Thomas for his inspection. This was no spirit or phantom, no "form" assumed for the occasion as Jehovah's Witnesses maintain. This was the very body of Christ which bore the horrible imprints of excruciating torture and the pangs of an ignominious death. Here displayed before the eyes of the unbelieving disciple was the evidence which compelled him by the sheer power of its existence to adore the One who manifested the Essence of Deity. "Thomas answered and said to him, My Lord and my God." This was the only answer Thomas could honestly give; Christ had proved His identity; He was truly "The Lord God." Let us substantiate this beyond doubt.

Jehovah's Witnesses have vainly striven to elude this text in the Greek (*The Emphatic Diaglott* and the *New World Translation of the Holy Scriptures*), but they have unknowingly corroborated its authority beyond refutation as a brief survey of their sources will reveal.

In *The Emphatic Diaglott* (John 20:28, page 396) *o theos mou*, literally "The God of me, or my God," signifies Jehovahistic identity, and since it is in possession *of the definite article*, to use Jehovah's Witnesses' own argument, it must therefore mean "the only true God" (Jehovah), not "a god." On page 776 of the appendix to the *New World Translation of the Christian Greek Scriptures* the note states, "So, too, John 1:1, 2 uses *o theos* to distinguish Jehovah

God from the Word (Logos) as a god, the only begotten god as John 1:18 calls him." Now let us reflect as sober individuals. If Thomas called the risen Christ, Jehovah (definite article) (*o kurios mou kai o theos mou*), and Christ did not deny it but confirmed it by saying (verse 29), "Because thou hast seen me, thou hast believed; Blessed are they not having seen yet having believed," then no juggling of the text in context can offset the basic thought—namely, that Jesus Christ is Jehovah God!

The *New World Translation of the Christian Greek Scriptures* carefully evades any explanation of the Greek text on the aforementioned point, but just as carefully inserts in the margin (page 350) six references to Christ as "a god," which they attempt to slip by the unwary Bible student. These references as usual are used abstractly and four of them (Isaiah 9:6; John 1:1; 1:18; and 10:35) have been mentioned already in previous points. The question then is, is there any other god beside Jehovah which Jehovah's Witnesses affirm to be true by their reference to Christ as "a god" (John 1:1; Isaiah 9:6)? The Scriptures give but one answer: Emphatically *NO!* There is no god but Jehovah. (See Isaiah 45:21–23; 44:68; 37:16, 20; etc.).

To be sure, there are many so-called gods in the Scriptures, but they are not gods by identity and self-existence, but by human acclamation and adoration. Satan also falls into this category since he is the "god of this world," who holds that position only because unregenerate and ungodly men have accorded to him service and worship belonging to God.

The Apostle Paul seals this truth with his clear-cut analysis of idolatry and false gods in 1 Corinthians 8:4–6, where he declares that an idol is nothing in itself and there is no god but Jehovah in heaven or earth regardless of the inventions of man.

The picture then is clear. Thomas adored Christ as the risen incarnation of the Deity (Jehovah); John declared that Deity from all eternity (John 1:1); and Christ affirmed it irrefutably—"If ye believe not that I Am [Jehovah] ye shall die in your sins" (John 8:24; cf. Exodus 3:14). All of the pseudo-scholastic and elusive tactics ever utilized can never change the plain declarations of God's Word. Jesus Christ is Lord of all; and like it or not, Jehovah's Witnesses will never destroy or remove that truth. Regardless of what is done to God's Word on earth, it remains eternal in the glory, as it is written, "For ever, O Lord, thy word is settled in heaven" (Psalm 119:89).

9. John 5:18—He said that God was his Father, making himself equal with God.

Concluding our chapter on this vital topic is this verse that is self-explanatory. The Greek term "equal" (*ison*) cannot be debated; nor is it contextually or grammatically allowable that John is here recording *what the Jews said about Jesus*, as Jehovah's Witnesses lamely argue. The sentence structure clearly shows that *John said it* under the inspiration of the Holy Spirit, and *not* the Jews! Anyone so inclined can diagram the sentence and see this for himself. No serious scholar or commentator has ever questioned it. In the Jewish mind, for Jesus to claim to be God's Son was a claim to equality with God, a fact Jehovah's Witnesses might profitably consider!

We see, then, that our Lord was equal with God the Father and the Holy

Spirit in His divine nature, though inferior (as a man) by choice in His human nature as the last Adam (John 14:28; 1 Corinthians 15:45–47). This text alone is of enormous value and argues powerfully for our Lord's Deity.

The Resurrection of Christ

Jehovah's Witnesses, as has been observed, deny the bodily resurrection of the Lord Jesus Christ and claim instead that He was raised a "divine spirit being," or as an "invisible spirit creature." They answer the objection that He appeared in human form by asserting that He simply took human forms as He needed them, which enabled Him to be seen, for as the Logos He would have been invisible to the human eye. In short, Jesus did not appear in the "*same*" form which hung upon the cross since that body either "dissolved into gases or . . . is preserved somewhere as the grand memorial of God's love" (Charles Russell, *Studies in the Scriptures*, op. cit., Vol. V, p. 454). This, in spite of Paul's direct refutation in 1 Timothy 2:5, where he calls "the *man* Christ Jesus" our only mediator—some thirty years after the resurrection!

The Scriptures, however, tell a completely different story, as will be evident when their testimony is considered. Christ Himself prophesied His own bodily resurrection, and John tells us "He spoke of the temple of His body" (John 2:21).

In John 20:25, 26, the disciple Thomas doubted the literal physical resurrection of Christ only to bitterly repent (verse 28) after Jesus (verse 27) offered His body, the same one that was crucified and still bore the prints and spear wound, to Thomas for his examination. No reasonable person will say that the body the Lord Jesus displayed was not His crucifixion body, unless he either ignorantly or willfully denies the Word of God. It was no other body "assumed" for the time by a spiritual Christ; it was the identical form that hung on the tree—the Lord Himself; He was alive and undeniably tangible, not a "divine spirit creature." The Lord foresaw the unbelief of men in His bodily resurrection and made an explicit point of saying that He was not a spirit but flesh and bones (Luke 24:39–44), and He even went so far as to eat human food to prove that He was identified with humanity as well as Deity. Christ rebuked the disciples for their unbelief in His physical resurrection (Luke 24:25) and it was the physical resurrection that confirmed His Deity, since only God could voluntarily lay down and take up life at will (John 10:18). We must not forget that Christ prophesied not only His resurrection but also the nature of that resurrection, which He said would be bodily (John 2:19–21). He said He would raise up "the temple" in three days (verse 19) and John tells us "He spoke of the temple of His *body*" (verse 21).

Jehovah's Witnesses utilize, among other unconnected verses, 1 Peter 3:18, as a defense for their spiritual resurrection doctrine. Peter declares that Christ was "put to death in the flesh, made alive by the Spirit." Obviously He was made alive in the Spirit and by the Spirit of God, for the Spirit of God, the Substance of God Himself, raised up Jesus from the dead, as it is written, "But if the Spirit of him that has raised up Jesus from the dead dwell in you . . ." (Romans 8:11). The meaning of the verse then is quite clear. God did not raise Jesus a spirit but raised Him by His Spirit, which follows perfectly John 20:27 and Luke 24:39–44, in establishing the physical resurrection of the Lord.

The Watchtower quotes Mark 16:12 and John 20:14–16 as proof that Jesus has "other bodies" after His resurrection. Unfortunately for them the reference in Mark is a questionable source. A doctrine should not be built around one questionable verse. The reason that Mary and the Emmaus disciples (Luke 24) did not recognize Him is explained in Luke 24:16 (RSV): "Their eyes were kept from recognizing him," but it was Jesus Himself (verse 15).

Jehovah's Witnesses also try to undermine our Lord's bodily resurrection by pointing out that "the doors were shut" (John 20:26) when Jesus appeared in the upper room. However, Christ had a "spiritual body" (1 Corinthians 15:50, 53) in His glorified state, identical in form to his earthly body, but immortal, and thus capable of entering either the dimension of earth or heaven with no violation to the laws of either one.

St. Paul states in Romans 4:24; 6:4; 1 Corinthians 15:15; etc., that Christ is raised from the dead; and Paul preached the physical resurrection and return of the God-man, not a "divine spirit being" without a tangible form. Paul also warned that if Christ is not risen then our faith is vain; to us who believe God's Word there is a Man in the Glory who showed His wounds as a token of His reality and whose question we ask Jehovah's Witnesses—"Has a spirit flesh and bones as you see me have?"

The Atonement of Christ

The infinite atonement of the Lord Jesus Christ is one of the most important doctrines of the Bible since it is the guarantee of eternal life through the complete forgiveness of sins to whoever appropriates its cleansing power. The Old Testament clearly teaches that, "it is the *blood* that makes an atonement for the soul." Leviticus 17:11 and Hebrews 9:22 corroborate this beyond doubt, for in truth "without shedding of blood is no remission." The Lord Jesus Christ became the one blood sacrifice for sin that insures everlasting life, as John said upon seeing Jesus—"Behold the Lamb of God, which taketh away the sin of the world" (John 1:29). The Apostle John writing in Revelation 13:8 declares that the Lamb (Christ) slain from the foundation of the world is God's own eternal sacrifice that cleanses from all sin and provides redemption for lost souls who trust in its efficacy. The writer of the epistle to the Hebrews goes to great length to show that the sacrifices of the Old Testament were types designed to show forth the coming sacrifices of Christ on Calvary (Hebrews 9 and 10). The Hebrew term *kaphar* (covering) and the Greek term *katallage*, which literally means reconciliation, are used in reference to payment of an obligation or exchange. The picture then portrays Christ as bearing our sins in His own body on the tree (1 Peter 2:24) and giving us peace with God through the *blood* of His cross (Colossians 1:20), which blood is the everlasting covenant that is able to make us perfect, in that God through it empowers us to do His will (Hebrews 13:20, 21). The Scriptures give vast testimony to the redeeming power of the Lamb's blood

(Romans 3:25; 5:9; Colossians 1:14; Hebrews 9:22; 1 Peter 1:19; 1 John 1:7; Revelation 5:9; 12:11) which *alone* can save and cleanse (Hebrews 9:22).

Charles Taze Russell resigned from a position he once held as assistant editor of a Rochester, New York, newspaper because he disagreed with the editor's view of the Atonement. Whether Russell was right in that disputation or wrong we do not know, but his doctrine of the Atonement and Jehovah's Witnesses' doctrine we do have knowledge of and know it to be completely unscriptural. Jehovah's Witnesses argue that the Atonement is not wholly of God, despite 2 Corinthians 5:20, but rather half of God and half of man. Jesus, according to their argument, removed the effects of Adam's sin by His sacrifice on Calvary, but the work will not be fully completed until the survivors of Armageddon return to God through free will and become subject to the Theocratic rule of Jehovah. For Jehovah's Witnesses the full realization of the matter is reconciliation with God, which will be completed in relation to the Millennial Kingdom. This utterly unreasonable and illogical interpretation of Scripture does away with the validity of the "infinite Atonement" unconditionally administered by God and through God for man. Russell and Jehovah's Witnesses have detracted from the blood of Christ by allowing it only partial cleansing power, but the truth still stands; it is either all-sufficient or insufficient; and if the latter be the case, man is hopelessly lost in an unconnected maze of irrelevant doctrines which postulate a finite sacrifice and, by necessity, a finite god.

The Physical Return of Christ

Jehovah's Witnesses declare that Christ returned to the temple in 1914 and cleansed it by 1918 for judgment upon sinful men and Satan's organizations. They affirm that since He did not rise physically, neither will He return physically (*The Truth Shall Make You Free*, op. cit., p. 295).

The first claim is that Jesus said ". . . the world seeth me no more" (John 14:19); therefore, no mortal eye shall see Him. The second claim is the intimation that *parousia* (Greek for presence, coming, advent, etc.) in Matthew 24:26–28, can only be rendered "exactly" as *presence*; therefore, Christ is now present, not coming.

These arguments are another example of the half-truths used by Jehovah's Witnesses to lead people astray. To begin with, Thayer, who is esteemed reliable in the field of scholarship, clearly states on page 490 of his *Greek-English Lexicon of the New Testament* that *parousia*, especially in the New Testament, refers to the second coming of Christ in *visible* form to raise the dead, hold the last judgment and set up the Kingdom of God. Christ is present; His "Presence" is always near ("I will never leave you . . ." Hebrews 13:5. ". . . I am with you always . . . to the consummation of the age," Matthew 28:20) for as God He is omnipresent, everywhere. But that does not mean He is here physically as the Scriptures attest He will be at the Second Advent. The physical return of Christ is the "Blessed Hope" of Christendom (Titus 2:13) and the language used to portray its visible certainty is most explicit. In Titus 2:13 the Greek word *epiphaneia* ("Appearing") is more correctly translated "Manifestation" or "Visible" from *phanero*, "to make manifest, or visible, or known" (Thayer's *Greek-English Lexicon of the New Testament*, p. 648). The language is self-explanatory. When the Lord returns with His saints "every eye shall see Him" (Matthew 24:30, cf. Revelation 1:7). How then can Jehovah's Witnesses claim that He has already returned but is invisible? The answer is they cannot and still remain honest Scripturally. To further establish these great truths the Apostle Paul writing to Timothy in 1 Timothy 6:14 clearly states that the Lord Jesus will appear physically by using *epiphaneia*, another form of *phanero* which also denotes visibility or manifestations. In 1 Thessalonians 4:16, 17 the Lord's return is revealed as being visible and audible, not invisible as Jehovah's Witnesses affirm contrary to Scripture.

The Old Testament bears out the physical return of the Messiah, also a wonderful testimony to the consistency of God's Word. Comparing Zechariah 12:10; 14:4 with Revelation 1:7; Matthew 24:30; and Acts 1:9-12, it is obvious that the Lord's ascension was visible, for the disciples *saw* Him rise, and in like fashion (Greek, *tropos*) the angels declared He would return. Zechariah 12:10 quotes Jehovah (further proof of Christ's Deity), "And they shall look upon *me* whom they have pierced." Revelation 1:7 states that Christ is the One pierced, and *visible* to human eyes. Zechariah 14:4 reveals Christ as touching the Mount of Olives at His visible return, and the Scriptures teach that this literally corroborates the angelic proclamation of Acts 1:9–12 even to the Lord's return to the exact location of His ascension, the Mount of Olives (verse 12). The doctrine of the physical return of Christ cannot be denied in the Scriptures unless a denial of God's Word also be entered which would exhibit unfathomable ignorance.

Jehovah's Witnesses and Human Government

Jehovah's Witnesses refuse to pay homage in any way to the flag of any nation or even to defend their own individual nation from assault by an enemy. Patriotism as displayed in bearing arms is not one of their beliefs since they claim to be ambassadors of Jehovah and as such deem themselves independent of allegiance to any government other than His. In this age of uncertainty, sincerity is a priceless gem and no doubt Jehovah's Witnesses believe themselves sincere, but all their arguments avail nothing when in Romans 13:1–7 St. Paul clearly outlines the case for human government as instituted by God. Paul goes to great length to stress that the "Higher Powers" (human governmental rules) are allowed and sanctioned by God. As supposed followers of His Word the Witnesses ought to heed both Christ and Paul and "render unto Caesar what is Caesar's," which in the context of Romans 13:1–7 clearly means subjugation to governmental rule. Paul settles the question decisively and in conclusion we quote his teaching:

> Let every soul be subject unto the higher powers. For there is no power but of God: the powers that be are ordained of God. Whosoever therefore resisteth the power, resisteth the ordinance of God: and they that resist shall receive to themselves damnation. For rulers are not a terror to good works, but to the evil. Wilt thou then not be afraid of the power? do that which is good, and thou shalt have praise of the same: For he is the minister of God to thee for good. But if thou do that which is evil, be afraid; for he beareth

not the sword in vain: for he is the minister of God, a revenger to execute wrath upon him that doeth evil. Wherefore ye must needs be subject, not only for wrath, but also for conscience sake. For for this cause pay ye tribute also: for they are God's ministers, attending continually upon this very thing. Render therefore to all their dues: tribute to whom tribute is due; custom to whom custom; fear to whom fear; honour to whom honour (Romans 13:1–7).

The Existence of Hell and Eternal Punishment

The question of the existence of hell and eternal punishment presents no problem to any Biblical student who is willing to practice honest exegesis unhindered by the teachings of any organizations of man. Jehovah's Witnesses use emotionally loaded words such as "hell fire screechers" and "religionists," etc., to describe the theological views of anyone who disagrees with their philosophy. In order to understand their views it must first be established that their beliefs are based upon no sound or valid knowledge of the original languages, and it should be remembered that this one factor influences practically every major phase of semantic study. However, we will now consider this problem in its context, and contrast it with Jehovah's Witnesses' interpretation which professes to have solved the problem, though on what grounds it is difficult to ascertain.

1. To begin with, Jehovah's Witnesses use poor reasoning in their construction of grammar, and from the evidence seldom check the original scripts beyond the dictionary and lexicon stage. I document to prove the point and reveal this shortcoming. On pages 69 and 70 of *Let God Be True* (ed. 1946) the following statement appears:

> If you were to translate a book from a foreign language into English and there you found the foreign word for bread 65 times, would you translate it 31 times bread, 31 times fish, and 3 times meat? Of course not. Why? Because if you did your translation would not be correct. For what is bread cannot at the same time be fish or meat and vice versa. The same holds true with the word sheol. If sheol is the grave, it is impossible at the same time to be a place of fiery torture and at the same time a pit.

It is most interesting to note in passing that in the Watchtower revision of *Let God Be True* in 1951, this paragraph was carefully omitted.

To the average Jehovah's Witness then, Hell (sheol) is literally "the grave," the place where mortals wait the resurrection. Their chief argument is that a Greek or Hebrew word means one thing and has no contextual connotation. This is a typical Jehovah's Witness approach and again reveals the linguistic failings of the organization. First of all, the very example the author of the chapter uses concerning bread, fish and meat, etc., is a reality in the text of the Bible, and unless one recognizes the varieties of meanings of words in different contexts, he is unable to understand the plain meaning of Scripture. A little research would have revealed this truth. In the Hebrew text, the word *lechem* is translated bread 238 times, one time as "feast," 21 times as "food," one time as "fruit," 5 times as "loaf," 18 times as "meat," one time as "provision," twice as "victuals," and once as "eat." It is clear that sheol has a difference of meaning which must be decided from the context, not by conjectures of misinformed authors.

2. In the second place, Jehovah's Witnesses have conceived of death as being unconsciousness or extinction, which definition cannot be found in the Bible. Death in the Biblical sense never means extinction or annihilation, and not one word, Greek or Hebrew, in either Testament will be found to say that it does. Death in the Bible is portrayed as separation. "The soul that sinneth . . . it shall be *separated*" (Ezekiel 18:4) is a better rendition in the sense that the word conveys. When Adam sinned, his soul became separated from God in the sense of fellowship—and consequently, as a result of sin, all men die or are separated from God by Adam's as well as their own sins. But God has provided a reconciliation for us in the person of His Son and we are "born again," regenerated and reconciled to God by the sacrifice of His Son "in whom we have redemption through his blood even the forgiveness of sins" (cf. John 3:3–7, 15, 16; 2 Corinthians 5:17–21; Colossians 1:14). So then we see that death in reality is not extinction but conscious existence, as was demonstrated in Matthew 17:1–3, when Moses and Elijah talked with Christ. Moses' body was dead—no one will deny; his soul was also dead according to Jehovah's Witnesses. Then what or who was it talking to Christ? The answer is simple. Moses as a living soul spoke to Christ, and he was alive and conscious! Substantiating all this is Christ's own declaration, "I am the resurrection, and the life; he that believeth in me, though he were dead, yet shall he live: And whosoever liveth and believeth in me shall never die" (John 11:25). Therefore, death is only the separation between, not the extinction of personalities (Isaiah 59:1, 2; see also 2 Corinthians 5:8 and Philippians 1:21–23).

3. Jehovah's Witnesses claim on page 96 of *Let God Be True* that—"In all places where hell is translated from the Greek word *Gehenna* it means everlasting destruction."

This is indeed a bold-faced misrepresentation of the Greek language and certainly ranks next to the "a god" fallacy of John 1:1 as an outstanding example of complete falsehood. There is no evidence that Gehenna ever means annihilation in the New Testament but rather abundant evidence to the contrary. In Matthew 5:22 Gehenna is portrayed as literally "The Hell of fire," in 10:28 coupled with *apolesai* "to be delivered up to eternal misery" (see Thayer, page 64). It indicates everlasting misery, and in Matthew 18:9 the same words corroborate 5:22, "The Hell of fire." If we are to follow through with Jehovah's Witnesses' argument, then Gehenna simply means the smoldering furnaces of Hinnon. But is that fire everlasting? No! For today the valley of Hinnon is not burning, so unless Jesus meant the example for just those living at that time, and this not even Jehovah's Witnesses will affirm, then Gehenna must be what it is, the symbol of eternal separation in conscious torment by a flame which is unquenchable (Isaiah 66:24).

4. It is fruitless to pursue this analysis of the Greek any further for it must be clear from the contexts that more than the grave or extinction is portrayed in Sheol, Hades and Gehenna. Without benefit of any complicated textual exegesis we shall let God's Word speak its own message and commit to the honest reader the decision as to whether or not eternal punishment,

rather than annihilation, is Scriptural doctrine. The following verses collectively refer to a place of everlasting conscious torment where Satan and his followers must remain in future everlasting wounding or misery, separated from God's Presence and "the glory of His power" (2 Thessalonians 1:9; cf. Thayer, page 443a on *olethros* and the Latin *vulnus—to wound*).

1. And I say unto you, that many shall come from the east and the west, and shall sit down with Abraham, and Isaac, and Jacob, in the kingdom of heaven. But the children of the kingdom shall be cast out into outer darkness: there shall be weeping and gnashing of teeth (Matthew 8:11, 12).
2. And shall cast them into the furnace of fire: there shall be wailing and gnashing of teeth (Matthew 13:42, 50).
3. Then said the king to the servants, Bind him hand and foot, and take him away, and cast him into outer darkness; there shall be weeping and gnashing of teeth (Matthew 22:13).
4. Strive to enter in at the strait gate: for many, I say unto you, will seek to enter in, and shall not be able. When once the master of the house is risen up, and hath shut to the door, and ye begin to stand without, and to knock at the door saying, Lord, Lord, open unto us; and he shall answer and say unto you, I know you not whence ye are· Then shall ye begin to say, We have eaten and drunk in thy presence, and thou hast taught in our streets. But he shall say, I tell you, I know you not whence ye are; depart from me, all ye workers of iniquity. There shall be weeping and gnashing of teeth, when ye shall see Abraham, and Isaac, and Jacob, and all the prophets, in the kingdom of God, and you yourselves thrust out (Luke 13:24–28).
5. These are wells without water, clouds that are carried with a tempest; to whom the mist of darkness is reserved for ever (2 Peter 2:17).
6. Raging waves of the sea, foaming out their own shame; wandering stars, to whom is reserved the blackness of darkness for ever (Jude 13).
7. And the third angel followed them, saying with a loud voice, if any man worship the beast and his image, and receive his mark in his forehead, or in his hand, the same shall drink of the wine of the wrath of God, which is poured out without mixture into the cup of his indignation; and he shall be tormented with fire and brimstone in the presence of the holy angels, and in the presence of the Lamb: And the smoke of their torment ascendeth up for ever and ever: and they have no rest day nor night, who worship the beast and his image, and whosoever receiveth the mark of his name (Revelation 14:9–11).
8. And the beast was taken, and with him the false prophet that wrought miracles before him, with which he deceived them that had received the mark of the beast, and them that worshipped his image. These both were cast alive into a lake of fire burning with brimstone (Revelation 19:20).

These verses are conclusive proof that everlasting conscious separation from God and real torment exist, and no possible confusion of terminology can change their meaning in context. Revelation 20:10 is perhaps the most descriptive of all the verses in the Greek. John positively states that "the devil who deceived them was cast into the lake of fire and brimstone where the beast and the false prophet are and they will be tormented (*basanisthesontai*) day and night into the everlasting (*aionas*) of the everlasting." The Greek word *basanizo* literally means "to torment," "to be harassed," "to torture," or "to vex with grievous pains" (Thayer, page 96b), and is used throughout the New Testament to denote great pain and conscious misery, not annihilation, cessation of consciousness, or extinction. Further proof of the reality of conscious torment, not annihilation, is found in the following verses where *basanizo* is utilized to exhibit the truth of God's eternal justice.

1. Matthew 8:6—The one tormented (suffering) with palsy (*basanizomenos*).
2. Matthew 8:29—The demons addressing Jesus admit the certainty of future torment (*basanisai*). "Art thou come here before (the) time to *torment* us?"
3. Mark 5:7—Again the demon cries out, "Torment (*basanisas*) me not." He obviously feared conscious pain, not extinction.
4. Luke 8:28—A demon once more reveals his knowledge of coming torment (*basanisas*): "do not torment me" is his supplication to Christ.
5. Revelation 14:10, 11—"He (the believer in the beast) shall be tormented (*basanistheasetai*) with fire and brimstone, in the presence of the holy angels, and in the presence of the Lamb. And the smoke of their torment rises up into the everlasting of the everlasting; and they have no intermission, cessation or relief (*anapausis*—Thayer, page 40b, also Liddell and Scott) day and night who worship the Beast and his image and if any one receive the mark of his name."

The Scriptures, then, clearly teach eternal conscious punishment and torment for those who reject Christ as Lord, and the language of the texts leaves no room for doubt that the apostles intended that confirmation. Jehovah's Witnesses think God a "Fiend" because He executes eternal righteous judgment. They make much to-do about God being Love but forget that because He is Love, He is also Justice and must require infinite vengeance from anyone who treads underfoot the precious blood of Christ, who is the Lamb slain for lost sinners from the foundation of the world. Death is not extinction, hell is not an illusion, and everlasting conscious punishment is a terrifying reality of God's infinite justice upon the souls of unbelieving men. The Apostle Paul summed up this certainty in Romans 2:8, 9, when he declared that God's indignation (*thumos*) and wrath (*orges*) are upon all who work unrighteousness. These two words have identical usage in Revelation 14:10, where John speaks of the eternal torment of those who serve the beast, ". . . that wine of the wrath (*orges*) of God, which is mingled undiluted in the cup of His indignation (*thumou*) . . . " So then the picture is clear. God is both Love and Justice and it is not He who condemns man, but man who condemns himself. As it is written—"For by thy words wilt thou be justified and by thy words wilt thou be condemned" (Matthew 12:37).

5. In *Let God Be True*, p. 93, Jehovah's Witnesses again exhibit their lack of knowledge as to what fundamental Christians believe, where, when speaking of the "religious theologians" they declare—"But are not Satan the Devil and his demons down in hell keeping the fires and making it hard for those who are in it? This is what is taught by Christendom's clergy . . ." It is nonsense to suppose that the Devil and his demons "are in hell keeping up the fires" and no responsible clergyman or Christian would make so childish a statement. Jehovah's Witnesses attribute to Christianity the same caliber of

reasoning that appeals to their untutored minds and to claim that "religionists" teach such doctrines is to reveal ignorance of the facts, a symptom not at all healthy in the processes of logical analysis. Further comment is not justified. Further examination is superfluous.

6. Luke 16:19–31 is claimed to be a parable in the text, by Jehovah's Witnesses, but nowhere is this substantiated in Luke's account. It is pure conjecture. Jehovah's Witnesses claim that the "parable" portrays a coming event which was fulfilled in A.D. 1918. The rich man represents the clergy and Lazarus the "faithful body of Christ." The clergy is constantly tormented by the truth proclaimed through the faithful remnant (*Let God Be True*, p. 98). Comment on this interpretational travesty is senseless since Jehovah's Witnesses twist the Scriptures to suit their own ends regardless of the textual background. The Lord Jesus in this account portrayed the condition of a lost soul (the rich man) who rejected God, and the beggar who partook of the Lord's mercy. The rich man went into conscious torment after physical death (Greek, *basanois*), verse 24, and even proclaimed his spiritual conscious anguish (Greek *odunomai*), "I am being tormented" (see Thayer, page 438b). There can be no doubt; he was suffering and knew it. Jehovah's Witnesses believe that in order to suffer you must exist physically, but this is naïve to say the least since souls suffer, as is demonstrated in this account. It must also be remembered that Christ, in parables, never used personal names, such as *Lazarus*. The language, although literal, is forceful in depicting spiritual suffering.

We must conclude then that Luke's account is a record of an actual case, a historical fact in which a soul suffered after death and was conscious of that torment. Regardless of what conjectures are injected at this point, the conclusion is sure: there is conscious punishment after death; and whether it is accepted or not by Jehovah's Witnesses it still remains a Scriptural doctrine substantiated by God's Word.

Satan—The Devil

In Ezekiel 28:16–19 quoted in *Let God Be True*, page 65, Jehovah's Witnesses maintain Satan's annihilation, but in the light of the Scriptures before discussed, the area of meanings of the Hebrew words must be considered. The word for "destroy" (*'abad*) does not convey the meaning of annihilation or extinction. The term here used may be rendered validly "to reckon as lost, given up as lost, or cast away" (cf. Ecclesiastes 3:6b, and also Gesenius' *Hebrew-English Lexicon*). If Ezekiel, chapter 28, verse 19, is as translated in *Let God Be True*, page 65 "never shalt thou be anymore," the Hebrew word *'ayin* may properly be rendered "to fail" or "to be gone," *not* to cease to exist (cf. Isaiah 44:12; 1 Kings 20:40). The use of *'ayin* in Hebrew sentence structure is the standard means employed when negating noun clauses. In 1 Kings 20:40, for example, where the man is spoken of as "gone," the term *'ayin* is utilized to show the man's absence or escape, *not* his extinction. If Jehovah's Witnesses persist in their annihilation doctrine where Satan is concerned, they must also believe that the man was annihilated, and the context rules out that interpretation as absurd. The picture then is clear in the light of language interpretation. Satan *must* and *will* endure everlasting torment with his followers, and to this truth God's Word bears irrefutable testimony.

Man the Soul, His Nature and Destiny

Any critical thinker in examining this problem cannot escape the confusion of terms utilized by Jehovah's Witnesses to substantiate their argument that the soul is not an eternal entity. To carry this argument to any great length is foolish, for the Hebrew word (*nephesh*) and the Greek (*psuche*) possess great areas of meaning impossible to fathom without exhaustive exegesis of the original sources. The root of the problem lies in Jehovah's Witnesses misconception of the soul as merely a principle of life, not an entity. The Bible clearly teaches in numerous places (Genesis 35:18; 1 Kings 17:21, 22; Revelation 6:9–11 to state a few) that the soul departs at the death of the body, that it is not destroyed by physical death, and that it can be restored by God at His discretion.

In an exegetical study it is impossible to emphasize too much the importance of defining terms, and in the problem at hand it is of the utmost importance. Therefore, before we can decide who or what has immortality, we must know what the term immortality itself means. Due to the evolution of any language, we must realize that the area of meanings of words changes as time goes on. The English word "immortal" has, among others, a peculiar meaning of "not mortal." However, in most circles and also in theology, the word generally carries the meaning of "exemption from death." The question that will arise then is "When the Scriptures use the term 'immortal,' is this definition all that is meant?" Contrary to the belief of some, there is *no reference* in Scripture that can be given to show that man or his soul is immortal.

To go even one step farther, there is nothing in Scripture that states anything or anyone is immortal but God Himself. Let us analyze this problem. There are two words in the Greek text that are translated "immortality." The first is *athanasia*, and it appears three times and is translated "immortality" each time. The other term is *aphthartos*, and is translated "immortality" twice and "incorruption" four times. Now let us examine the use of these words. The former word *athanasian* is used in 1 Timothy 6:16 and is speaking of God "Who *alone* has immortality (*athanasian*) dwelling in the light which *no man* can approach unto." In 1 Corinthians 15:53, 54, we again have *athanasia* used twice, but in the same verse we have *aphthartos* used twice also. Paul here is speaking of the second coming of Christ, and declares (verse 53) "For this corruption must put on incorruption (*aphtharsian*) and this mortal must put on immortality (*athanasian*)." "So when this corruption *shall have put on* (aorist middle subjunctive of the verb *enduo*) incorruption (*aphtharian*) and this mortal *have put on* immortality (*athanasian*) *then* shall be brought to pass the saying that is written, *Death* is swallowed up in victory" (verse 54). We see here that in the two places where *athanasian* is used in reference to man, it is clear that it is an immortality to be given in the future, not one possessed at the present time.

Similarly, when an *aphtharsian* is used here and in Romans 2:7, "Something sought for," and 1 Peter 1:4, "reserved in heaven for you," it is speaking of the incorruption of man to be given at some future date, not possessed at the present time. Only when immortality or incorruption is used with God, is it in the present tense (1 Timothy 6:16, 1:17; Romans 1:23). Therefore, to say that the saints are immortal (if by immortality we mean *athanasian* or *aphtharsian*), we are not Scriptural. We must say the saints *will* be immortal. It is also plain to see in 1 Corinthians 15:53, 54, this immortality (*athanasian*) and this incorruption (*aphtharsian*) *will be put on* (*endusetai*) as one puts on a garment. Just as Paul exhorts us to put on (*endusasthe*) Christ (Romans 13:14; Galatians 3:27), the armor of light (Romans 13:12), the new man (Ephesians 4:24), and the armor or panoply of God (Ephesians 6:11), we must conclude then that *athanasian* or *aphtharsian* have a larger and broader meaning than to be "everlasting." It must be seen that immortality and incorruption, *when given*, will mean a change, not simply the giving and receiving of the attribute—"exemption from death." Jehovah's Witnesses have badly misconstrued the usage of immortality, and that error, coupled with their famous practice of term-switching has resulted in confusion and poor exegesis.

Now as to the eternity of the human soul, we must consult the existing language sources. When we use the term "eternal" in association with the soul of man, we mean that the human soul *after* its creating by God will (future) exist somewhere into the eternal, into the everlasting. Since there is only one place where the honest seeker can find pure information on the eternal existence of the soul, and that place is in the revelation which God, who created the soul, has given to man, namely His Word, let us turn to it and consider therein His revealed will.

Revelation does show first that God can be known, and secondly that man's soul is eternal. In Hebrews 1:1, we read, "God, who at sundry times and in divers manners spake in time past unto the fathers by the prophets, hath in these last days spoken unto us by his Son, whom he hath appointed heir of all things, by whom also he made the worlds." All through history God has manifested Himself to man in different ways, and at no time in history has man been left without a witness of God. In the Old Testament, God manifested Himself and His Will to man by the prophets, visions, and direct oral contact. However, when the fullness of time was come, God sent forth His Son in the likeness of sinful flesh and completed His progressive revelation. Man, since the time of his creation upon the earth, has always been able to know God and His will, if he so desired, and consequently since the day of Adam, men who know not God are without excuse.

God's revelation is not only a manifestation of God to man, but it also is the answer to the question, "Where did man come from? Is he a spiritual as well as natural being? What is his worth? and Where is he going?"

God's revelation shows that man is a creation of God, created in God's spiritual image, Genesis 1:26; Genesis 5:1; 1 Corinthians 11:7. He was created to have preeminence over other creatures, Genesis 1:28; Psalm 8:6; Psalm 82:6; Matthew 6:26; and Matthew 12:12. He is definitely a spiritual being, Job 32:8; Psalm 51:10; Ecclesiastes 12:7; Acts 7:59; and 2 Corinthians 4:13. He is an object of God's love, John 3:16; Revelation 1:5. He sinned and lost God's favor, Genesis 3:1–19. The consequences of Adam's sin passed upon all mankind, Romans 5:12. God sent His Son to redeem man, John 3:16. This redemption is by the vicarious death of Christ, Matthew 26:28; Acts 20:28; Romans 5:9; Hebrews 9:14; 1 Peter 1:18, 19; 1 John1:7; Revelation 1:5; Revelation 7:14; Colossians 1:20. This salvation is obtained by a new birth through faith in Jesus Christ, John 3:3–16.

We must then conclude that since "God is Spirit" (John 4:24) and as such is incorporeal, He must have imparted to man a spiritual nature created in His own image, or else Genesis 1:26 is not meaningful.

Now the question arises, "If Jesus redeemed those who accept His salvation, what is the difference between those who are redeemed and those who are not?" It is clear that redemption is not simply favor with God here upon earth. This brings us to the Scriptural teaching of the eternal existence of the soul. First of all, there is much evidence that the soul does exist as a conscious entity after it departs from the body, and there is no Scriptural evidence to the contrary. In Luke 20:37, 38, the Lord Jesus there speaking of the revelation God gave to Moses, makes it clear that when God said, "I am the God of Abraham, Isaac, and Jacob," that God was not the God of the dead, but of the living, though Abraham, Isaac, and Jacob had long since been physically dead. The only reasonable conclusion, then, is that these great Old Testament saints of God possessed spiritual natures that transcended physical death.

In the seventeenth chapter of Matthew we see Moses and Elijah on the Mount of Transfiguration with Christ, and communing with Him, yet we know that Moses had been physically dead for centuries, and no record of his resurrection exists in Scripture. Jehovah's Witnesses claim that this was a vision, not a "real" evidence of the soul's existence beyond the grave, and they point to Matthew 17:9, where the English rendition of the Greek (*orama*) is *vision*. However, this Greek term is translated literally in this context as "that which is seen—a spectacle" (see Thayer, op. cit., p. 451), not a mere *vision*.

In Luke 16:19–31, Jesus here (and this is not a parable) shows the difference between the state of the soul of the redeemed and the state of the soul of the wicked after death. In Revelation 6:9, we see the souls of those who had been martyred for Christ crying out for vengeance. In 2 Corinthians 5:1–9, Paul makes it clear that to be absent from the body is to be consciously "present" or "at home" with the Lord. But the Scriptures go even further, for they speak of a resurrection of the body, Job 19:25; 1 Thessalonians 4:16, 17; 1 Corinthians 15:35–57. In this last reference, 1 Corinthians 15, in verses 35–49, is found the answer to this question which the Jehovah Witnesses are laboring under, that is (verse 35), "How are the dead raised up? and with what body do they come?" We notice that in verse 36 Paul addresses one who labors under this question as "(thou) fool."

Now that we have considered the problem of the soul's existence after death, and the resurrection of the body, we find Scripture is clear in its teaching that those who reject God's salvation will suffer throughout eternity in outer darkness, Matthew 8:11, 12; 13:42–50; 22:13; 2 Peter 2:17; Jude 13; Revelation 14:9–11; 19:20, and those who accept God's salvation will dwell with Christ throughout eternity in joy and peace, John 14:1–3; 17:24;

Luke 20:36; 1 Thessalonians 4:17; Revelation 22:5. Here is revealed what we believe is the true meaning of the Scriptural terms "immortality and incorruption" (*athanasian, aphtharsian*). We must also realize that these words do not apply to God the Father in the same sense that they apply to God the Son. When we come "with" Him from heaven (1 Thessalonians 4:14), we shall be made like Him in the sense that we shall have a soul and body *incapable* of sin, not earthly but heavenly. We shall put on *aphtharsian* and *athanasian* and abide with Christ into the eternal.

As I stated at the beginning of this point, it would be futile to refute all the errors of thought in Jehovah's Witnesses theology. Therefore, I have presented what I feel is sufficient evidence to show that man has an eternal soul and will abide somewhere either in conscious joy or sorrow eternally, and that those who believe and trust in Christ as their personal Savior will "put on" that immortality when Jesus returns.

Regarding the Jehovah's Witnesses, we can only say as Paul said to the Corinthians in 2 Corinthians 4:3, 4, "But if our gospel be hid, it is hid to them that are lost: in whom the God of this world hath blinded the minds of them which believe not, lest the light of the glorious gospel of Christ, who is the image of God should shine unto them," and as he again states in 2 Thessalonians 2:10b, 11, "because they received not the love of the truth, that they might be saved. And for this cause God shall send them strong delusion, that they should believe a lie."

Honest study of this problem will reveal to any interested Bible student that man does possess an eternal immaterial nature which was fashioned to occupy an everlasting habitation whether in conscious bliss or torment. This then is the nature and certain destiny of man.

Author's Note

The following partial list of references to the soul and spirit of man as drawn from the Old and New Testaments will, we believe, furnish the interested reader with ample evidence that man is not just a combination of body and breath forming a living soul, as the Jehovah's Witnesses teach, but rather a soul, or spirit, possessing a corporeal form.

The Hebrew equivalent for soul as used in the Old Testament is *nephesh*, and for spirit *ruach*. The Greek equivalent for soul is *psuche* and for spirit *pneuma*.

1. It is an entity possessing the attributes of life (Isaiah 55:3). It is also separate from the body (Matthew 10:28; Luke 8:55; 1 Thessalonians 5:23; Hebrews 4:12; Revelation 16:3), *ie.*, it exists independent of material form.
2. A soul departs at the death of the form (Genesis 35:18).
3. The soul is conscious after death (Matthew 17:3; Revelation 6:9–11).
4. The soul of Samuel was conscious after death (1 Samuel 28:18, 19).
5. Stephen had a spirit which he committed to Christ at his death (Acts 7:59).
6. There is definitely a spirit and soul of man (Isaiah 57:16).
7. The spirit is independent of the body (Zechariah 12:1).
8. The spirit, the soul of man, does that which only a personality can do;

it "wills" (*prothumon*) (Matthew 26:41).

9. We are instructed to worship in the spirit (John 4:23; Philippians 3:3) since God is a spirit.
10. The spirit of man has the attribute of personality, the ability to testify (Romans 8:16, 26); also the faculty of "knowing" (1 Corinthians 2:11).
11. The spirit can be either saved or lost (1 Corinthians 5:5); it belongs to God, and we are instructed to glorify Him in it (1 Corinthians 6:20).
12. The spirit or soul goes into eternity and is a conscious entity (Galatians 6:8).
13. Christ is with our spirit (2 Timothy 4:22), for the spirit is the life of the body (James 2:26).
14. We are born of God's Spirit, and as such are spirits ourselves (John 3:5, 6).

These references will suffice to show that the immaterial nature of man is far from the combination of breath and flesh as Jehovah's Witnesses maintain.

The Kingdom of Heaven

The human soul, marred and stained as it is by the burden of personal sin, seeks constant escape from the reality of that sin and the sure penalty due because of it. Once the reality of eternal punishment is clouded by idealistic concepts of everlasting bliss without the fear of personal reckoning, the soul can relax, so to speak, and the sinner, unconscious of the impending doom, God's Justice, rests secure in the persuasion that "God is Love." Laboring under this delusion it is no wonder that Jehovah's Witnesses can so calmly construct "The Kingdom of Heaven," for to them God's infinite justice does not exist and eternal retribution is only an invention of "hell fire screechers."

The Biblical kingdom of heaven has many aspects, none of which includes the invented hierarchal construction so vividly outlined in *Let God Be True*. In Luke 17:20, 21 the Lord reveals the kingdom of heaven as within the believer in one aspect, but clearly states that the heavenly aspect will be visible and observable at His return (verses 23–26). In Matthew 13, the Lord Jesus portrays the kingdom of heaven symbolically in parables yet always it is pictured as reality, not as an invisible phantom government. Jehovah's Witnesses arrive at the year A.D. 1914 as the end of the Gentile times and the beginning of the reign of the invisible heavenly King Christ Jesus. How they arrived at this arbitrary date no one can reasonably or chronologically ascertain, but valuable evidence to the effect that "Pastor" Russell formulated the whole hoax is obtainable from the July 15, 1950, copy of *The Watchtower Announcing Jehovah's Kingdom*, where, on page 216, the following statements are found.

> Away back in 1880 the columns of *The Watchtower* had called notice to Bible chronology marking A.D. 1914 as the year for the 2,520 year period to end and referred to by Jesus as "the times of the Gentiles" in his prophecy on the world's end (Luke 21:24). In harmony with this it was expected that in 1914 the kingdom of God by Christ Jesus in the heavens would be fully established, while this world would be involved in an unprecedented "time

of trouble." The religious leaders and the systems of Christendom were all set to laugh at Brother Russell and his fellow witnesses of Jehovah over failure of his announced predictions concerning A.D. 1914. But it was no laughing matter when, at the end of July, World War I broke out and by October it had become global in its scope. Christendom's religious mouths were silenced at this frightening turn of events, but not Brother Russell's. October 1, 1914, on taking his place at the breakfast table in the Brooklyn Bethel dining room, he in a strong voice denoting conviction announced:

"The Gentile Times have ended!"

Knowing that the world had now reached the time for its dissolution he refused to heed the plea of U. S. President Wilson for all clergymen and preachers to join in nation-wide prayer for peace, . . .

Thus it was, that at the words of one colossally egotistical and unschooled haberdasher, the Times of the Gentiles ended.

To follow through Jehovah's Witnesses' interpretation of the Kingdom it is necessary to understand that only 144,000 faithful servants will rule with King Jesus in the heavenly sphere. They quote Revelation 7:4 and 14:1, 3, but neglect to notice that the 144,000 are of the tribes of Israel (Jews), 12,000 of each tribe, and are in no sense to be construed as anything else. This is not figurative; this is actual, since the tribes are listed by name. To follow out their own argument Jehovah's Witnesses must believe that only 144,000 Jewish members of their organization will be privileged to reign with Christ Jesus. The argument that they are spiritual Jews is invalid since even if they were, which they aren't, they would be "Children of Abraham" not Israel, and there is a vast difference in interpretation at this point (Galatians 3:29). Ishmael, the father of the Arab race, the ancestor of Mohammed, the founder of Islam, was a son of Abraham (Genesis 16) after the flesh even as Isaac the father of Jacob, so it can be seen that Abraham's seed differs from the selection of Israel's stock, as it is written ". . . for in Isaac shall thy seed be called" (Genesis 21:12). The texts are then clear that Israel after the flesh is mentioned and not spiritual symbolism; therefore, the 144,000 conjecture pertaining to kingdom rule as advanced by Jehovah's Witnesses crumbles under the light of Scriptural truth.

In concluding this point it is imperative to remember that there can be no kingdom without the King and the Scripture is clear when it states that the true kingdom will be instituted at Christ's visible return.

The Old and New Testaments corroborate each other in establishing the certainty of the visible return and reign of Christ. (Cf. Zechariah 14:4, Amos 9:8–15, Isaiah 11 and 12, Ezekiel 37:20–28, Luke 17:22ff. and Matthew 24:26–31 to mention just a few.) Jehovah's Witnesses unknowingly fulfill the prophecy of Christ in Matthew 24:23ff., where the Lord warns of false Christs and prophets who shall say Christ is here, Christ is there (in the desert, in the secret places, etc.), and shall deceive many with their deceit. Jehovah's Witnesses say He is here now but the Lord said He would be visible at His return, and every eye should see Him (Revelation 1:7; cf. Matthew 24:27–30). How then can we doubt His testimony when He Himself has said:

And the sign of the Son of Man will then appear in heaven and all the tribes of the earth will wail—*and they will see* [visible] the Son of Man coming on the clouds of heaven, with great majesty and power (Matthew 24:30).

To this we can only say with John:

"Even so come, Lord Jesus."

In drawing this portion of our study of Jehovah's Witnesses to a close it is expedient and vitally necessary that a clear picture of what this cult means to all Christians be presented. This organization has mushroomed from a meager beginning in 1881 until now it extends to every part of the globe. Because the cult does away with the doctrine of eternal retribution for sin it appeals greatly to those who believe they see in it an escape from the penalty of personal transgression. Jehovah's Witnesses offer an illusionary "Kingdom" to the personalities who desire importance, and most of all an outlet to vent their wrath upon religious leaders and organizations whose doctrines they assail as "of the Devil." We do not believe for one moment that the greater body of these people know the true implications of Russell's doctrines; however, let no Jehovah's Witnesses ever disclaim Russellistic origin. Charles Taze Russell founded, operated, propagated and gave his life to furthering this cult, and his teachings permeate every major phase of its doctrines despite the intense aloofness its leaders manifest when his past is mentioned. But now the question arises—"How can so many people be deceived by so obviously fraudulent a type of religion?" To understand this, the teachings and methods of propagation of the cult must be analyzed.

To begin with, no member of the Society is ever allowed to think independently for himself.

All religious leaders and organizations are pictured as false and anything they say is to be discounted as the "vain philosophies of men." The Scriptures are always made to conform to Jehovah's Witnesses' beliefs, never Jehovah's Witnesses' beliefs to the Scriptures. Rutherford's legal mind made most of this conjecture and linguistic chicanery reasonable to the minds of the people to whom he addressed it, and his books are masterpieces of illogical and invalid premises and conclusions.

To trace the logic and reasoning processes of Rutherford is the task of a logician, since for Russell or Rutherford a contradictory statement can be a premise which, regardless of the steps, always has a valid conclusion in their system of thinking. Jehovah's Witnesses' doctrine is a mass of half-truths and pseudo-scholastic material which to the untutored mind appears as "wonderful revelation."

Recently, when I was speaking to an ardent Jehovah's Witness, the following statement fell unashamedly from his lips: "I have never met anyone who knows more about Greek than the Society." In all probability he was right, for had he met someone who did know Greek he would never have become a member of the cult. The Society, to our knowledge, does not have any Greek scholars of any repute in their ranks, and if they do I would welcome any opportunity for them to come out from behind their lexicons and explain their rendition of John 1:1, 8:58 and Colossians 2:9, to mention just a few. Hebrew scholars are also included in this invitation.

Another trait of the Society is its aversion to attributing individual authorship to its publications since the death of Rutherford. All publications now appear anonymously, copyrighted and published by the Society. By not committing persons to their signatures the Society escapes the unpleasant task of having to answer for their numerous blunders. Their standard answer is, "Many persons worked on the books, not just one particular person," etc. In their predicament, having no recognized scholarship behind them, they have chosen the wisest possible course—silence. The plain truth of the matter is that the "new" books are just rephrases of Russell's and Rutherford's works and contain no originality other than up-to-date information on world conditions and new approaches to old material.

One of the distinguishing characteristics of an ardent Jehovah's Witness is his (or her) ability to handle the Scriptures. *The Emphatic Diaglott* and *The Kingdom Interlinear Translation of the Greek Scriptures* with their interlinear readings of the Greek facilitates their progress in this project. Any good Jehovah's Witness, sad to say, can cause the average Christian untold trouble in the Scriptures, though the trouble in most cases has an elementary solution. The Christian is bewildered by the glib manner in which they repeat Scripture verses (usually entirely out of context) and sprinkle their discourses with Greek or Hebrew grammatical terms of which they have no knowledge beyond their *Diaglott* and *Kingdom Interlinear*. The boldness with which they collar the unwary pedestrian, intrude on the quiet of a restful evening, attend their conventions, and propagate their literature, is a danger signal that evangelical Christianity would do well to heed and take definite steps to combat. As has been observed, the answer to Jehovah's Witnesses, or "Russellism" if you will, is the Deity of Jesus Christ, and in teaching that one cardinal doctrine of the Christian faith, all energy ought to be expended to the uttermost. All ministers, Sunday school supervisors, Bible and Tract Societies and teachers should drill their charges in Biblical memorization and doctrinal truths, that a united Christian front may be thrown up against this ever-growing menace to sound reasoning in Biblical exposition and study. The plan is not difficult, and only procrastination hinders its adoption. This problem is also the task of Christian colleges, seminaries and Bible schools, who too long have neglected the institution of strong cult courses in their curricula. The fruit of their neglect is before us today. Must we stand by in silence while the Word of God is defamed, the Lordship of Christ blasphemed, and the faith of generations still unborn is threatened by a group of people who will not listen to honest Biblical truths, and dare not contest them in scholastic discussion? It is frustrating and exasperating to carry on a discussion with a person or persons who argue in circles and dodge artfully from one refutation to another. These tactics characterize the preaching and argumentation of Jehovah's Witnesses, which must be met by calm dispositions and truthful Scriptural exegesis on the part of well-grounded Christians. Information in the form of documentary evidence and cold facts has met and can meet their perversions and emerge triumphant over them. We as Christians must perform this task without delay; we can ill afford to wait any longer.

The end product of this whole cult is the denial of the Lord Jesus Christ as "very God" and despite their protests that they honor Christ, they do indeed dishonor and "crucify Him afresh" since they deny His Deity and Lordship. Regardless of their Biblical names and proficiency in the Scriptures, they constantly reveal their true character in their actions, which are the diametric opposite of Scriptural teachings. The following old adage is most appropriate in describing the doctrines of Jehovah's Witnesses: "No matter how you label it or what color bottle you put it in, poison is still poison." "He that has ears, let him hear." On the cover of *The Watchtower Announcing Jehovah's Kingdom*, Isaiah 35:15 and 43:12 were quoted, and throughout all of their publications they boast themselves as "Jehovah's Witnesses."

There can be no kingdom without the King, however, and His return is visible, with power and glory (Matthew 24:30). Their kingdom has come (1914–1918 A.D.), but with no visible king, power or glory. Jehovah of the Watchtower is a conjectural myth, a creation of the reactionary theology of Charles Taze Russell, and is conformed to the pattern of Russell's mind and education, which continued through Rutherford and Knorr and now continues through Franz to the ever-increasing blindness of those misguided souls foolish enough to trust in the Russellite delusion. In comparison to the Scriptures this picture is infinite darkness, for its author is the "Prince of Darkness," and the Word of God clearly and incontestably reveals that "Jehovah of the Watchtower" is not the Jehovah of the Bible, for Jehovah of the Bible is Lord of all—"The great God and our Savior Jesus Christ" (Titus 2:13).

Selected Terms and Texts Misapplied by Jehovah's Witnesses

To review all the terms and texts which Jehovah's Witnesses have misinterpreted and misapplied to bolster up their fractured system of theology would be impossible in the space here available. Therefore, I have chosen to survey six of their worst perversions of common Biblical terms, and various texts which the Watchtower has mauled and mangled almost beyond recognition with little or no regard for hermeneutical principles, contexts, or the laws of sound exegesis.

These examples of Watchtower deceptions are found all neatly cataloged in their handbook of doctrinal subjects, entitled, *Make Sure of All Things* (Brooklyn: Watchtower Bible and Tract Society, 1953) upon which this study is principally based, should any care to check further their authenticity, etc.

Misapplied Terms

1. "Only begotten" (Greek: *monogenes*)—Jehovah's Witnesses in their zeal to establish the Christology of Arius of Alexandria have seized upon this Greek term, translated "only begotten" in the New Testament, and unfortunately they have been most successful in hoodwinking many uninformed persons into believing that "only begotten" really means "only generated." From this erroneous view they therefore suggest that since the term is applied to Jesus Christ five times in the New Testament Christ is but a creature, or as they love to quote Codex Alexandrinus, "The only begotten God" (John 1:18).

It should be noted in this connection, therefore, that the most authoritative lexicons and grammar books, not to mention numerous scholarly works, all render "monogenes" as "only or unique 'the only member of a kin or kind, hence generally only,' " (Liddell and Scott's *Greek-English Lexicon*, Vol. 2, page 1144). Moulton and Milligan in their *Vocabulary of the Greek New Testament*, pages 416 and 417, render "monogenes" as "one of a kind, only, unique," facts that establish beyond scholarly doubt the truth of the contention that in both classical and Koine Greek the term "monogenes" carries the meaning of "only," "unique," or "the only member of a particular kind." The Septuagint translation of the Old Testament also utilizes the term "monogenes" as the equivalent in translation of the Hebrew adjective "yachid" translated "solitary" (Psalm 68:6), etc. This interesting fact reveals that the translators understood "monogenes" to have the meaning of uniqueness attached to it, emphasis obviously being placed on "only" and decidedly not in "genus" or "kind."

In other places in the New Testament, such as Luke 7:11–18; 8:42; 9:38; Hebrews 11:17, etc., the rendering "only begotten" in the sense that Jehovah's Witnesses attempt to employ it in their translations and propaganda is an exegetical impossibility; especially in the instance of Hebrews 11:17, where Isaac is called the "only begotten" son of Abraham. Certainly he was not the eldest child, but rather he was the *sole or only* precious son in the sense that Abraham loved him in a unique way.

Dr. Thayer in his *Greek-English Lexicon of the New Testament*, page 417, referring to "monogenes," states, "single of its kind, only . . . used of Christ, denotes the only Son of God." Unfortunately in ancient literature "monogenes" became connected with the Latin term "unigenitus." However, such a translation is basically incorrect, as any lexicographical study will quickly reveal.

The early church fathers were in essential agreement that Jesus Christ preexisted from all eternity in a unique relationship to God the Father. In the year 325 at the Council of Nicaea it was officially proclaimed that Jesus Christ was of the same substance or nature as the Father, and those who differed from this pronouncement which the Church had always held were excommunicated. Among them was Arius of Alexandria, a learned Presbyter and the Christological father of Jehovah's Witnesses. Arius held that Jesus Christ was a created being, the first and greatest creation of God the Father, that He did not preexist from all eternity and that His only claim to Godhood was the fact that He had been created first and then elevated to the rank of a deity.

Arius derived many of his ideas from his teacher, Lucien of Antioch, who in turn borrowed them from Origen, who himself had introduced the term "eternal generation" or the concept that God from all eternity generates a second person like Himself, ergo the "eternal Son." Arius of course rejected this as illogical and unreasonable, which it is, and taking the other horn of the dilemma squarely between his teeth reduced the eternal Word of God to the rank of a creation! It is a significant fact, however, that in the earliest writings of the church fathers dating from the first century to the year 230 the term "eternal generation" was never used, but it has been this dogma later adopted by Roman Catholic theology which has fed the Arian heresy through the centuries and today continues to feed the Christology of Jehovah's Witnesses.

In the year A.D. 328, in his private creed, Arius interestingly enough applies the term "gegennemenon" in reference to Christ, not the terms "monogenes" or "ginomai." "Gegennemenon" is a derivative of the word "gennao" which is translated "begotten" and rightly so; further than this, Eusebius of Caesarea, a follower of Arius about 325 also utilized the term "gegennemenon" not "monogenes," a fact which throws a grammatical monkey wrench into the semantic machinations of the Watchtower.

We may see, therefore, that a study of this term "monogenes" reveals that in itself it is understood in both the classical and Koine vocabulary to be a term emphasizing uniqueness; i.e., the only one, the beloved, etc.; and there is no good grammatical ground for insisting as Jehovah's Witnesses do that it *must* mean "only generated," i.e., "only created."

Regarding the five times in the New Testament where the term "monogenes" is applied to Jesus Christ (John 1:14, 18; 3:16, 18; 1 John 4:9) it can be seen easily by the interested reader that the proper rendering "only" or "unique" in keeping with the historic usage of the term in no way disturbs the context but in fact makes it clearer Christologically, eliminating the concept fostered by the Arians and carried on by Jehovah's Witnesses that "only begotten" must infer creation which it most certainly does not!

As we mentioned before, the doctrine of eternal generation relative to the preexistence of the Lord Jesus Christ is one of the great stumbling blocks in any intelligent approach to the Christological problems of the New Testament. This fact being true, the authors feel it is wiser to return to the original language of Scripture in its description of the Lord Jesus and His preincarnate existence, where He is never referred to except prophetically in the Bible as the "eternal Son" but as the Word of God (John 1:1) who "was" from all eternity and who "became" flesh (John 1:14), taking upon Himself the nature of man, and as such was "begotten" of the Virgin Mary by the power of the Holy Spirit. The "unique," "only" Son of God, then, whose uniqueness stems from the fact that of all men He was the most precious in the Father's sight, beloved above all His brethren, so much that the Father could say of Him when He sent Him into the world, "Thou art my Son, this day have I begotten thee" (Hebrews 1:5), is not a creature or a demi-god but ". . . God over all, blessed forever. Amen" (Romans 9:5, RSV Footnote).

The Bible clearly teaches, then, that Jesus Christ before His incarnation was the eternal Word, Wisdom, or Logos, of God, preexistent from all eternity, co-equal, co-existent, co-eternal with the Father, whose intrinsic nature of deity He shared, and even though clothed in human form He never ceased to be deity, "God manifest in the flesh" (1 Timothy 3:16) or as Paul put it so directly, "in him dwells all the fulness of the Godhead bodily" (Colossians 2:9).

By insisting upon the correct title of the preexistent Christ, orthodox Christianity can successfully undercut the emphasis Jehovah's Witnesses place upon "monogenes," showing in contrast that "only begotten" is a term of time which can have no meaning outside of the sphere that man knows as recorded experience; and further, that Jesus Christ is not called by Scripture the "eternal Son," the error passed on from Origen under the title "eternal generation," but rather He is the Living Word of God (Hebrews 4:12), Creator of the Universe (2 Peter 3:5), Sustainer of all things (2 Peter 3:7), First Begotten from the dead (Acts 13:33), and our "Great High Priest, who has passed into the heavens, Jesus the Son of God . . . who can be touched with the feelings of our infirmities and who was in all points tempted like as we are, yet without sin." Let us fix these things in our minds, then: (a) the doctrine of "eternal generation" or the eternal Sonship of Christ, which springs from the Roman Catholic doctrine first conceived by Origen in A.D. 230, is a theory which opened the door theologically to the Arian and Sabellian heresies which today still plague the Christian Church in the realms of Christology.

(b) The Scripture nowhere calls Jesus Christ the eternal Son of God, and He is never called Son at all prior to the incarnation, except in prophetic passages in the Old Testament.

(c) The term "Son" itself is a functional term, as is the term "Father" and has no meaning apart from time. The term "Father" incidentally never carries the descriptive adjective "eternal" in Scripture; as a matter of fact, only the Spirit is called eternal[22] ("the eternal Spirit"—Hebrews 9:14), emphasizing the fact that the words Father and Son are purely functional as previously stated.

(d) Many heresies have seized upon the confusion created by the illogical "eternal Sonship" or "eternal generation" theory of Roman Catholic theology, unfortunately carried over to some aspects of Protestant theology.

(e) Finally; there cannot be any such thing as eternal Sonship, for there is a logical contradiction of terminology due to the fact that the word "Son" predicates time and the involvement of creativity. Christ, the Scripture tells us, as the Logos, is timeless, ". . . the Word *was* in the beginning" *not* the Son!

The Lord Jesus Christ, true God and true man, is now and for all eternity Son of God and Son of Man; therefore in this sense He is the eternal Son. But to be Biblical in the true sense of the term we must be willing to admit that He was known prior to His incarnation as the eternal Word, and knowledge of this fact cuts across the very basic groundwork and foundation of the Arian system of theology espoused by Jehovah's Witnesses. For if "only begotten" means "unique" or "only one of its kind," there cannot be any ground for rendering it "only generated" as Jehovah's Witnesses often attempt to do in a vain attempt to rob Christ of His Diety.

If then we relegate the terms "Father" and "Son" to the sphere of time as functional vehicles for the conveyance of the mysterious relationship which existed from all eternity between God and His Word, we will be probing deeper into the truth of the Scripture, which seems to teach us that God calls Christ His Eternal Word, lest we should ever forget that He is intrinsic Diety (for never was there a moment when God had a thought apart from His

---

[22]The Trinity as such is, however, spoken of as "the everlasting God" (Romans 16:26).

Logos or Reason). Further than this God calls Christ His "Son," lest we should think of the Word as being an impersonal force or attribute instead of a substantive entity existing in a subject-object relationship, the Eternal God "who is the Savior of all men, especially those who believe."

In summary, since the word "Son" definitely suggests inferiority and derivation it is absolutely essential then that Christ as the Eternal Word be pointed up as an antidote to the Arian heresy of Jehovah's Witnesses, and in this light we can understand quite plainly the usages of the term "monogenes" not in the Jehovah's Witnesses' sense of creatureliness but in the true Biblical sense of "uniqueness," i.e., "the unique or only Son of God," generated in the womb of a woman by the direct agency of the Holy Spirit, "God manifest in the flesh." "The great God and our Savior, Jesus Christ" (Titus 2:13).

2. "Greater"—(Greek: *meizon*). Another principal term utilized by Jehovah's Witnesses is the term "greater" translated from the Greek, *meizon* as it appears in the gospel of John, chapter 14, verse 28, "Ye have heard how I said unto you, I go away, and come again unto you. If ye loved me, ye would rejoice, because I said, I go unto the Father: for my Father is greater than I." From this particular text, lifted conveniently out of its context by the ever zealous Russellites, the Watchtower attempts to "prove" that since Jesus in His own words while He was on earth stated that His Father was "greater" than He was, therefore Christ could not be equal with God or one of the members of the Trinity which Jehovah's Witnesses deny so vehemently.

On the face of the matter this appears to be a good argument from Christ's usage of the word "greater," but a closer examination of the context and of the hermeneutical principles which govern any sound exegetical study of the New Testament quickly reveals that theirs is a shallow case indeed, and, one which rests rather unsteadily upon one Greek word in a most restricted context.

The refutation of this bit of Watchtower semantic double-talk is found in a comparison with Hebrews, the first chapter, verse 4, "Being made so much *better* than the angels, as he hath by inheritance obtained a more excellent name than they."

The careful student of Scripture will recognize immediately that in the first chapter of Hebrews, the verse previously cited, an entirely different word is utilized when comparing Christ and the angels. This word is *kreitton* and is translated "better" in the King James Version. Paralleling these two comparisons, then, that of Jesus with His Father in John 14:28, and Jesus with the angels in Hebrews 1:4, one startling fact immediately attracts attention. In the fourteenth chapter of John, as the Son of Man who had emptied Himself of His prerogatives of deity, Philippians 2:8–11, and taken upon Himself the form of a slave, the Lord Jesus Christ could truthfully say, "My Father is greater than I," greater being a *quantitative* term descriptive of *position*. Certainly in no sense of the context could it be construed as a comparison of nature or quality.

In the first chapter of Hebrews, however, the comparison made there between the Lord Jesus Christ and angels is clearly one of nature. The Greek *kreitton* being a term descriptive of quality, ergo, Christ was *qualitatively* better than the angels because He was their Creator (Colossians 1:16, 17) and as such He existed before all things and through Him all things hold together (Colossians 1:17–19). Since His intrinsic Nature is that of deity (John 8:58, compare Colossians 2:9), therefore *qualitatively* He was God manifest in the flesh, while *quantitatively* speaking He was limited as a man and could in all truthfulness state "My Father is greater than I." When this comparison of position in John 14:28 and the comparison of *nature* in Hebrews 1 are clearly understood, the argument Jehovah's Witnesses attempt to raise in order to rob Christ of His deity is reduced to rubble before one of the greatest of all truths revealed in Scripture, i.e., that "God who made the world and all things therein" so loved us as to appear in our form (John 1:1, 14) that the sons of men might through His measureless grace at length become the sons of God.

We should be quick to recognize, however, that had the Lord Jesus said in John 14:28 that His Father was *better* than He was and had used the proper Greek word denoting this type of comparison, another issue would be involved, but in actuality the comparison between Christ and His Father in that context and verse clearly indicates that Jesus was speaking as a man and not as the second person of the Trinity (John 1:1). Therefore it is perfectly understandable that He should humble Himself before His Father and declare that in the present form in which He found Himself, His Father most certainly was "greater," positionally, than He. One might be willing to admit that the President of the United States is a *greater* man by virtue of his present position, authority and recognition, etc., but it would be a far different matter to assent to the proposition that the President of the United States is a *better* man than his fellow Americans in the sense of *quality*, because such a comparison then involves a discussion of fundamental natures, attributes, etc. In like manner, then, Jesus, as the Incarnate Son of God who had by His own voluntary act of will divested Himself of His prerogatives of intrinsic deity, could speak of His Father as being *positionally* greater than He was without in any sense violating His true deity and humanity.

Hebrews 1:4 clearly teaches that Christ is better than the angels *qualitatively* from all eternity and that even while He walked the earth, though He was made lower than the angels *positionally* for the suffering of death in the form of a man, never for an instant did He ever cease to be the Lord of glory who could say with confident assurance "Before Abraham was I AM" (John 8:58).

Let us constantly be aware of these facts when discussing the nature of Christ with Jehovah's Witnesses, for once the distinction is made between "greater" and "better" their entire argument based upon John 14:28 melts into nothingness, and the deity of our Lord is completely vindicated by the whole testimony of Scripture.

3. "Born again"—Many times in their contacts with Christians, Jehovah's Witnesses utilize the evangelical terminology of the gospel of John, chapter 3, where Christ speaking to Nicodemus said, "Except a man be born again he cannot see the kingdom of God." The Witnesses utilize such ter-

minology because they realize that contemporary evangelical efforts, especially those of Dr. Billy Graham, have popularized this term, and the Watchtower is quick to capitalize on any popularization of a Biblical term, especially if it can be twisted to serve its own end! The definition which Jehovah's Witnesses give to the new birth or the act of being "born again" is found on page 48 of their textbook *Make Sure of All Things* and is as follows: "Born again means a birth-like realization of prospects and hopes for spirit life by resurrection to heaven. Such a realization is brought about through the water of God's truth in the Bible and God's holy spirit, his active force."

The interested student can see from this definition that the Witnesses reject flatly the concept of the new birth as taught in the New Testament. The Bible teaches us that when we are born again it is through repentance, the washing of water by the Word, and the direct agency of the third Person of the Trinity, God the Holy Spirit (John 3, Ephesians 5:26, 1 Peter 1:23, etc.). There is not one verse that may be cited in either the Old or New Testaments to prove that the new birth means "a birth-like realization of prospects and hopes for spirit life by resurrection to heaven," as Jehovah's Witnesses so brazenly misrepresent it. On the contrary, the new birth guarantees eternal life to *all* believers, entrance into the kingdom of Heaven, and a resurrection to immortality in a deathless, incorruptible form similar to that of the Lord Jesus Christ's form when He rose from among the dead.

The theology of Jehovah's Witnesses relevant to the new birth is that there will be only 144,000 "spiritual brothers" who will reign with Christ in heaven for a thousand years: and, further, that only these 144,000 will have a resurrection to heaven and a "spirit life" such as that now allegedly enjoyed by "Pastor" Charles Taze Russell and Judge J. F. Rutherford, who are carrying on the work of the Society "within the veil," according to Watchtower teaching.

In direct contrast to this the Lord Jesus Christ made a universal statement when He stated "Except a man be born again he cannot see the kingdom of God," and we find no record of either Christ, the disciples, or the apostles ever promulgating the 144,000 "spirit brothers" idea espoused so zealously by the Watchtower. A doctrine of such momentous importance, the author feels, would certainly have been carefully defined in the New Testament; yet it is not, and the only support Jehovah's Witnesses can garner for this weird Russellite interpretation is from the book of Revelation and the mystical number "144,000," which, incidentally, the Bible teaches, refers to the twelve tribes of Israel, twelve thousand out of each tribe, and therefore certainly *not* to members of the Watchtower's theocracy.

Christians therefore should be on guard continually against the Watchtower's perversion of common Biblical terms drawn from evangelical sources, for in 90% of the cases which the author has analyzed, the Witnesses *mean* just the opposite of what they *appear* to say. The new birth, Peter tells us, is a *past* event in the lives of those who have experienced the regenerating power of God's Spirit (Greek—"having been born again," 1 Peter 1:23); it is not something to be constantly experiencing or to be looking forward to in a type of ethereal spiritual resurrection as the Witnesses would have us believe. Rather it is a fact to be rejoiced in that we "have been born again" and are new creations in Christ Jesus (2 Corinthians 5:17), joint heirs in the glory of the Kingdom which is yet to be revealed.

The Watchtower Bible and Tract Society most decidedly has its "new birth" but it is not the new birth of Scripture, nor is their theory taught anywhere within the pages of the Bible. It is instead the theological brain child of Charles Taze Russell, to which the Witnesses cling so tenaciously, and which in the end will be found to have originated with "the god of this world" who has blinded their eyes "lest the glorious light of the Gospel of Christ, who is the image of God should shine unto them."

4. "Death"—In common with other deviant systems of theology Jehovah's Witnesses espouse a peculiar and definitely unbiblical concept of death, both in regard to the physical body and the soul and spirit of man.

According to the Watchtower publication, *Make Sure of All Things*, page 86, death is defined in the following manner: "Death—loss of life; termination of existence; utter cessation of conscious intellectual or physical activity, celestial, human, or otherwise."

Reverting to their basic trait of text-lifting and term-switching, Jehovah's Witnesses garner a handful of texts from the Old and New Testaments which speak of death as "sleep" or "unconsciousness," and from these out-of-context quotations attempt to prove that at the death of the physical form, man, like the beasts, ceases to exist until the resurrection.

Seizing upon such texts as Ecclesiastes 9:5, 6 and 10; Psalm 13:3; Daniel 12:2, etc., the Witnesses loudly contend that until the resurrection, the dead remain unconscious and inactive in the grave, thus doing away in one fell swoop with the doctrine of hell and the true Biblical teaching regarding the soul of man.

It is impossible in the time allotted here to place all the verses Jehovah's Witnesses lift out of their contexts back into their proper contextual-hermeneutical position, and by so doing to show that their theory is an exegetical nightmare, but the following observation can be made.

Despite the fact that in the Old Testament the term "sleep" is used to denote death, never once is such a term used to describe the immaterial nature of man, which the Scriptures teach was created in the image of God (Genesis 1:26, 27). This fact also holds true in the New Testament, as any cursory study of either Strong's or Young's concordances will reveal. The term "sleep" is always applied to the body, since in death the body takes on the appearance of one who is asleep, but the term "soul sleep" or "the sleep of the soul" is never found in Scripture and nowhere does it state that the soul ever sleeps or passes into a state of unconsciousness. The only way that Jehovah's Witnesses can infer such a doctrine is by assuming beforehand that death *means* sleep or unconsciousness; hence, every time they are confronted with the term "death" they assign the meaning of the temporary extinction of consciousness to it, and by so doing remove from Scripture the doctrine which they fear and hate the most—that of conscious punishment after death for unregenerate souls, continuing on into the everlasting ages of eternity (Jude 10–13; 2 Peter 2:17).

Since we have already covered the doctrine of hell in a previous section, the simplest refutation of Jehovah's Witnesses' perverted terms such as "death" can be found in the Scriptures themselves, where it easily can be shown that death does not mean "termination of existence"; "utter cessation of conscious intellectual . . . activity" as the Watchtower desperately attempts to establish.

The interested reader is referred to the following references: Ephesians 2:1–5; John 11:26; Philippians 1:21, 23; and Romans 8:10. The usage of death in these passages clearly indicates a state of existence solely in opposition to the definition which the Watchtower assigns to the word "death," and the reader need only substitute the Watchtower's definition in each one of these previously enumerated passages to see how utterly absurd it is to believe that the body has experienced "the loss of life" or "termination of existence" in such a context where Paul writes, "If Christ be in you, the body is dead because of sin" (Romans 8:10). The inspired apostle here obviously refers to a spiritual condition of separation—certainly not to "termination of existence," as the Watchtower's definition states.

We see, therefore, that death is a separation of the soul and spirit *from* the body, resulting in physical inactivity and a general *appearance* of sleep; however, in the spiritual sense death is the separation of soul and spirit from God as the result of sin, and in no sense of the term can it ever be honestly translated "unconsciousness" or "termination of existence" as Jehovah's Witnesses would like to have it.

In his first epistle to the Thessalonians, the fourth chapter, the Apostle Paul spoke of the return of the Lord Jesus Christ and most pointedly made use of the term "sleep" as a metaphor for death (1 Thessalonians 4:13–18), and it is interesting to note his concept: "But I would not have ye to be ignorant, brethren, concerning them which are asleep, that you sorrow not, even as others which have no hope. For if we believe that Jesus died and rose again, even so them also which sleep in Jesus will God bring *with* him. For this we say unto you by the word of the Lord, that we which are alive and remain unto the coming of the Lord shall not prevent them which are asleep. For the Lord himself shall descend from heaven with a shout, with the voice of the archangel, and with the trump of God: and the dead in Christ shall rise first: Then we which are alive and remain shall be caught up together with them in the clouds, to meet the Lord in the air: and so shall we ever be with the Lord. Wherefore comfort one another with these words."

Verse 14 of this previously quoted section indicates that Paul, while using the metaphor "sleep" to describe physical death, clearly understood that when Jesus comes again He will bring *with* (Greek: *sun*) Him those whose bodies are sleeping. To be more explicit, the souls and spirits of those who are with Christ now in glory (2 Corinthians 5:8; Philippians 1:22, 23) will be reunited with their resurrection bodies (1 Corinthians 15); that is, they will be clothed with immortality, incorruptibility, exemption from physical decay and they will be coming *with* Jesus. The Greek *sun* indicates in a "side by side" position, and the bodies that are sleeping will in that instant be quickened, raised to immortality and reunited with the perfected spirits of the returning saints.

This passage alone would be enough to convince any exegetical scholar that those "sleeping in Jesus" must refer to their *bodies*, since they are in the same verse spoken of as coming *with* Jesus, and by no possible stretch of the imagination could one honestly exegete the passage so as to teach anything to the contrary.

Jehovah's Witnesses are justly afraid of the "everlasting fire" prepared for the devil and his followers (Matthew 25:41), and their entire system of theology is dedicated to a contradiction of this important Biblical teaching of God's eternal wrath upon those who perpetrate the infinite transgression of denying His beloved Son. Rightly, then, does the Bible say that "The wrath of God continues to abide upon them" (John 3:36—literal translation) (Revelation 20:10; Mark 9:43, 48; Daniel 12:2).

For the Christian, then, physical death involves only the sleep of the body, pending the resurrection to immortality, when our resurrection bodies will be joined to our perfected souls and spirits; but in the intermediate state, should we die before the Lord comes, we have the assurance that we shall be *with Him* and that we shall return *with Him*, or as the Apostle Paul stated it, "To be absent from the body is to be at home (or present) with the Lord."

5. "Firstborn" (*prototokos*—Greek)—The author feels it necessary to include a brief resumé of Jehovah's Witnesses' misuse of the Greek term "prototokos" (Colossians 1:15), which the Watchtower lays much emphasis upon since it is used descriptively of the Lord Jesus Christ, and so in their Arian theology it is construed to teach that Christ is the first creature since the word "firstborn" implies that of the *first* child.

In Colossians 1 the Apostle Paul speaks of the Lord Jesus Christ as the firstborn of every creature or of all creation. And the Witnesses, always eager to reduce Christ to the rank of an angel, have seized upon these passages of Scripture as indicative of His creaturehood. The Watchtower teaches that since Christ is called the "firstborn of all creation," therefore He must be the *first one* created, and they cross-reference this with Revelation 3:14 which states that the faithful and true witness (Christ) is "the beginning of the creation of God."

On the surface the argument the Watchtower erects appears to be fairly sound, but underneath it is found to be both shallow and fraudulent. The term firstborn (*prototokos*) may also rightfully be rendered "first begetter" or "original bringer forth" (Erasmus), a term of preeminence, and in Colossians 1 it is a term of comparison between Christ and created *things*. In the first chapter of Colossians Paul points out that Christ is "before all things" and clearly establishes the fact that the eternal Word of God (John 1:1) existed before all creation (Hebrews 1), that He is preeminent over all creation, by virtue of the fact that He is Diety; and beyond this, that He is the Creator of all "things," which to any rational person indicates that if He is Creator of all things, He Himself is not one of the "things" created! In the eighth chapter of Romans, verse 29, the word "firstborn" is applied to Christ, clearly denoting His preeminence—not the concept that He is "the first creature made by Jehovah God," as the Witnesses would like us to believe—and in Colossians 1:18 we learn that Christ is "firstborn" from the dead, that is, the one with the preeminence, or right to rule, over death. Again the meaning is that of preeminence, not of creation.

Revelation 3:14, "The beginning of the creation of God" is easily harmonized with the rest of Scripture, which teaches the absolute Deity of the Lord Jesus Christ when we realize that the Greek word *arche*, which is translated "beginning," is translated by the Witnesses themselves as "originally" in John 1:1 of their own *New World Translation of the Christian Greek Scriptures*—and this is a good translation at this point—so applying it to Revelation 3:14 Christ becomes the "origin" or the "source" of the creation of God (Knox), and not the very beginning of it Himself in the sense that He is the *first* creation, a fact which Scripture most pointedly contradicts.

Christ is therefore "firstborn" or preeminent by virture of the fact that He is Deity, and by virtue of the fact that He is the first one to rise in a glorified body. He is therefore preeminent over all creation, and through His power all things consist or hold together. He is not one of the "things" (Colossians 1:16, 17) but He is the Creator of *all things*, the eternal Word who possesses the very nature of God (Hebrews 1:3).

6. "Soul and spirit" (Greek: *psuche, pneuma*)—Jehovah's Witnesses delight in the assertion that man does not possess an immaterial, deathless nature, and they never tire of proclaiming such teaching to be "a lie of the Devil" and a dogma derived from pagan religions (Egyptian, Babylonian, Greek, etc.). The literature of Jehovah's Witnesses is filled with condemnations of the doctrine of the immaterial nature of man. According to the Watchtower the soul is "a living, breathing, sentient creature, animal or human," and Jehovah's Witnesses also define a spirit as "a life force, or something wind-like" (page 357, *Make Sure of All Things*).

By so defining these two common Biblical terms, the Watchtower seeks to avoid the embarrassing Scriptural truth that since man is created in the image of God, and God is Spirit, man must possess a cognizant spiritual entity formed in the image of his Creator (Genesis 1:26, 27). To explode this Watchtower mythology is an elementary task when we realize that when the Lord Jesus Christ died upon the cross He said, "Father, into thy hands I commend my spirit," a fact Jehovah's Witnesses are hard put to explain, since if the spirit is nothing but breath or wind, and certainly not a conscious entity as the Bible teaches it is, then is would be fruitless for Christ to commit His breath to the Father, yet He did precisely that! The truth of the matter is that the Lord Jesus Christ committed to His Father His immaterial nature as a man, proving conclusively that the spirit and soul of man goes into eternity as a conscious entity (Galatians 6:8).

It will also be remembered that when Stephen was stoned, he fell asleep in death, but not before he said, "Lord Jesus, receive my spirit," and in that particular context it is rather obvious that he was not referring to the exhalation of carbon dioxide from his lungs! However, we may safely say that the meanings Jehovah's Witnesses give to soul and spirit will not stand the test of systematic exegesis in either the Old or New Testament, and no competent Hebrew or Greek scholar today has ever espoused their cause in open scholastic discussion.

Conclusion

Concluding this synopsis of the misapplications and misinterpretations of Jehovah's Witnesses where Biblical terms and texts are concerned, the author feels constrained to state that by no means has he thoroughly covered this vast subject.

Jehovah's Witnesses thrive on the confusion they are able to create, and in their door-to-door canvassing they accentuate this trait by demonstrating extreme reluctance to identify themselves as emissaries of the Watchtower until they have established a favorable contact with the prospective convert. To put it in the terms of the vernacular, until they have "made their pitch" they are careful to conceal their identity. To illustrate this particular point more fully, the *New Yorker Magazine,* June 16, 1956, carried a lengthy article by one of its feature writers, Richard Harris, in which Mr. Harris recounts his experiences with Jehovah's Witnesses. In this article, Mr. Harris relates that the Witnesses never identified themselves to prospective converts as Jehovah's Witnesses at first, when Mr. Harris accompanied a team of Witnesses on one of their daily canvassing routes in Brooklyn. Mr. Harris also pointed out in the article that the Witnesses openly admitted to him that it was necessary for them first to make a successful contact before they fully identified themselves. In short, Jehovah's Witnesses may be proud to be the only people standing for "Jehovah God," but they are not above neglecting to tell prospective converts their real affiliation if it will help their cause.

If evangelical Christianity continues to virtually ignore the activities of Jehovah's Witnesses, it does so at the peril of countless souls. Therefore let us awaken to their perversions of Scripture and stand fast in the defense of the faith "once delivered unto the saints."

Author's Note

Nowhere is this point more forcefully demonstrated than in a book written by a former member of the Watchtower Society, W. J. Schnell (*Thirty Years a Watchtower Slave,* Grand Rapids: Baker Book House, 1956). In this particular reference Schnell succinctly stated the Watchtower methodology in the following words:

"The Watchtower leadership sensed that within the midst of Christendom were millions of professing Christians who were not well grounded in 'the truths once delivered to the saints,' and who would rather easily be pried loose from the churches and led into a new and revitalized Watchtower organization. The Society calculated, and that rightly, that this lack of proper knowledge of God and the widespread acceptance of half-truths in Christendom would yield vast masses of men and women, if the whole matter were wisely attacked, the attack sustained and the results contained, and then re-used in an ever-widening circle" (page 19).

Chapter 5

CHRISTIAN SCIENCE

Historical Perspectives

For decades Christian Science was the matriarch of the Mind Science family. With a large and growing membership, secular and religious respect, and great wealth, the Mother Church predominated the Mind Science movement, more important in almost all respects than Unity School of Christianity, Mind Science, Religious Science, Divine Science, and their other siblings. However, during the 1960's a trend became apparent. Christian Science was losing members and income at a steady and significant rate. By the midseventies Christian Science members and even the public media were aware that the decline was long-term and steady. Scandal rocked the Mother Church in 1976 with charges of financial, moral, and spiritual corruption among the top leaders in the church. Today, in the early eighties, the Christian Science cult has regrouped its forces. Dissenting membership has been eliminated, financial waste reduced, and the cult presents a calm face to the world. The next couple of decades will tell whether Christian Science will be able to survive. Its forces are much diminished from what they once were. Only time will tell if the small core of faithful members will survive and spur growth in excess of attrition.

Yet, even now, the Christian Science cult is a powerful force with which evangelical Christians everywhere must deal. We shall examine its roots, founder, growth, and controversies, and contrast its teachings with the clear word of Scripture.

Of all the persons destined for religious prominence and success in the nineteenth century, none has eclipsed Mary Ann Morse Baker—better known among the band of faithful Christian Scientists as Mary Baker Eddy, "Mother" and Leader, the "Discoverer and Founder" of Christian Science.

Mary Baker was born in Bow, New Hampshire, in the year 1821 in the humble surroundings of a New Hampshire farm house, and was reared a strict Congregationalist by her parents, Mark and Abigail Baker. The life of young Mary Baker until her twenty-second year was marked with frequent illnesses of both emotional and physical nature,[1] and the then infant science of mesmerism was not infrequently applied to her case with some success.

In December of 1843, at the age of 22, the future Mrs. Eddy was married to George W. Glover, a neighboring business man, whose untimely death of

---

[1]Georgine Milmine, *The Life of Mary Baker G. Eddy and the History of Christian Science*, Grand Rapids, MI: Baker Book House, 1937, pp. 3–25.

yellow fever in Wilmington, South Carolina, some seven months later, reduced his pregnant wife to an emotional and highly unstable invalid, who, throughout the remaining years of her life, relied from time to time upon the drug morphine as a medication.[2]

To be sure, no informed person believes that Mrs. Eddy was a "dope addict," but much evidence from incontrovertible sources is available to show beyond doubt that throughout her life Mrs. Eddy made repeated use of this drug.[3]

A decade passed in the life of Mrs. Glover during which she had many trying experiences, and then on June 21, 1853, she married Dr. Daniel M. Patterson, a dentist, who, contrary to the advice of Mrs. Glover's own father, Mark Baker, took the emotionally unstable Mary Glover for his bride.

The advice of Mark Baker was indeed ominously accurate, for some years later Mrs. Eddy divorced Dr. Patterson, who, she claimed, had abandoned her, and thus her second attempt at matrimony met with crushing disaster.

The third and last marriage of Mary Baker Glover Patterson was to one Asa G. Eddy when Mrs. Eddy was fifty-six years of age. Asa Eddy's death of a coronary thrombosis prompted Mrs. Eddy to commit a nearly fatal mistake where Christian Science was concerned. She contested the autopsy report and the physician she chose confirmed her conviction that Asa died of "arsenic poisoning mentally administered."[4] Such a radical report prompted an inquiry into the credentials of Mrs. Eddy's physician, Dr. C. J. Eastman, Dean of the Bellvue Medical College, outside Boston. It was found that "Doctor" Eastman was running a virtual abortion mill, and had no medical credentials whatever to justify his title. He was sentenced to ten years in prison upon his conviction, and the Bellvue Medical College closed. Mrs. Eddy had contradicted her own advice concerning autopsies.[5] And she would have been far better off to have practiced in this instance what she preached and to have abandoned Asa's remains to the scrap heap of mental malpractice, but the error was virtually unavoidable since Mrs. Eddy was not to be outdone by any medical doctor. She was an expert healer by her own admissions; the autopsy was therefore inevitable.

Mrs. Eddy's letter to the *Boston Post* dated June 5, 1882, in which she accused some of her former students of mentally poisoning Asa Eddy with malicious mesmerism in the form of arsenic mentally administered is one of the most pathetic examples of Mrs. Eddy's mental state ever recorded and one which the Christian Science Church would like to forget she ever wrote.

The real history of Christian Science, however, cannot be told unless one P. P. Quimby of Portland, Maine, be considered, for history tells us that as Mrs. Eddy was the mother of Christian Science, so Phineas Parkhurst Quimby was undoubtedly its father. "Dr." Quimby in the late 1850's entitled

---

[2]*New York World*, October 30, 1906.
[3]Ernest Sutherland Bates and John V. Dittemore, *Mary Baker Eddy: The Truth and the Tradition*, New York: Knopf, 1932, pp. 41, 42, 151, 445.
[4]*The Boston Post*, June 5, 1882.
[5]See *Science and Health with Key to the Scriptures* by Mary Baker Eddy (Boston: Trustees under the Will of Mary Baker G. Eddy, 1934), p. 196 and the 1881 edition, vol. 1, p. 269.

his system of mental healing "The Science of Man," and had used the terms "The Science of Christ" and "Christian Science" for some time before Mrs. Eddy gratuitously appropriated the terminology as her own, something she dared not do while the old gentleman was alive and her relationship to him known to all.

Mrs. Eddy's relationship to Dr. Quimby began when she arrived in Portland, Maine, in 1862 and committed herself to his care for treatment of "spinal inflammation." In November of that same year Mrs. Eddy noised abroad to all men that P. P. Quimby had healed her of her infirmity. Said the then adoring disciple of Quimby, "I visited P. P. Quimby and in less than one week from that time I ascended by a stairway of 182 steps to the dome of the City Hall and am improving ad infinitum."[6]

In later years Mrs. Eddy's recollection of Quimby was somewhat different from her earlier echoes of praise, and she did not hesitate to describe him as a very "unlearned man," etc. Dr. Quimby termed his ideas "Science of Health." Mrs. Eddy entitled her book *Science and Health with Key to the Scriptures*, filled with numerous plagiarisms from the manuscripts of P. P. Quimby. Mrs. Eddy plagiarized a great part of her work from Quimby and other sources, and then had it all copiously edited by the Rev. J. H. Wiggin, a retired Unitarian minister. Wiggin revealed his part in her deceptive plan via the posthumus publication of an interview he gave to one Livingstone Wright, later published as a pamphlet entitled *How Reverend Wiggin Rewrote Mrs. Eddy's Book*.

Our authority for exposing this plagiarism on the part of "Mother" Eddy is none other than Mrs. Eddy herself, who wrote, "The best sermon ever preached is Truth practised. . . . We cannot build safely on false foundations. Truth makes a new creature, in whom old things pass away and 'all things are become new.' . . . The way to extract error from mortal mind is to pour in truth through flood-tides of Love. Christian perfection is won on no other basis" (*Science and Health*, p. 201). In addition, Mrs. Eddy made the following statement on the subject of plagiarism in her book *Retrospection and Introspection:* "There is no warrant in common law and no permission in the gospel for plagiarizing an author's ideas and their words" (p. 76). So it appears that out of her own mouth Mrs. Eddy has condemned plagiarism, a practice from which she seemed to have extreme difficulty abstaining.

Mrs. Eddy's plagiarism of Quimby's writings was well illustrated by *The New York Times* (July 10, 1904), which published parallel columns of Mrs. Eddy's and Dr. Quimby's writings, proving Quimby to have been at least a partial source of her "revelation" of "Science and Health."

From Quimby's *Science of Man*, expounded by Mrs. Eddy at Stoughton, 1868, 1869, 1870.	From Mrs. Eddy's *Science and Health*, the textbook of the "Christian Science" she now claims to have discovered in 1866.
If I understand how disease originates in the mind and fully believe it, why cannot I cure myself?	Disease being a belief, a latent delusion of mortal mind, the sensation would not appear if *this error was met and destroyed by Truth.*—page 61, edition of 1898.
Disease being made by our belief or	

---

[6]Portland *Evening Courier*, November 7, 1862.

by our parents' belief or by public opinion there is no formula of argument to be adopted, but every one must fit in their particular case. There it requires great shrewdness or wisdom to get the better of the error . . .

I know of no better counsel than Jesus gave to his disciples when he sent them forth to cast out devils and heal the sick, and thus in practice to preach the Truth, "Be ye wise as serpents and harmless as doves." Never get into a passion, but in patience possess ye your soul, and at length you weary out the discord and produce harmony by your Truth destroying error. Then you get the case. Now, if you are not afraid to face the error and argue it down, then you can heal the sick.

The patient's disease is in his belief. Error is sickness. Truth is health.

In this science the names are given; thus God is Wisdom. This Wisdom, not an Individuality but a principle every idea—form, of which the idea, man, is the highest— hence the image of God, or the Principle.

Understanding is God.

All sciences are part of God.

Truth is God.

There is no other Truth but God.

God is Wisdom.

God is Principle.

Wisdom, Love, Truth are the Principle.

Error is matter.

Matter has no intelligence.

To give intelligence to matter is an error which is sickness.

Matter has no intelligence of its own, and to believe intelligence is in matter is the error which produced pain and inharmony of all sorts; to hold ourselves we are a principle outside of matter, we would not be influenced by the opinions of man, but held to the workings only of a principle, Truth, in which there are not inharmonies of sickness, pain or sin.

For matter is an error, there being no substance, which is Truth, in a thing which changes and is only that which belief makes it.

Christ was the Wisdom that knew

Science not only reveals the origin of all disease as wholly mental, but it also declares that all disease is cured by mind.—page 62, edition of 1898.

When we come to have more faith in the Truth of Being than we have in error, more faith in spirit than in matter, then no material conditions can prevent us from healing the sick, *and destroying error through Truth.*—page 367, edition of 1898.

We classify disease as error which nothing but Truth or Mind can heal.— page 427, edition of 1898.

Discord is the nothingness of error. Harmony is the somethingness of Truth.—page 172, edition of 1898.

Sickness is part of the error which Truth casts out.—page 478, edition of 1898.

God is the principle of man; and the principle of man remaining perfect, its idea or reflection—man remains perfect.—page 466, edition of 1898.

Man was and is God's idea.—page 231, edition of 1898.

Man is the idea of Divine Principle. page 471, edition of 1898.

What is God? Jehovah is not a person. God is Principle.—page 169, edition of 1881.

Understanding is a quality of God.— page 449, edition of 1898.

All Science is of God.—page 513, edition of 1898.

Truth is God.—page 183, edition of 1898.

Truth, God, is not the Father of error.—page 469, edition of 1898.

How can I most rapidly advance in the understanding of Christian Science? Study thoroughly the letter and imbibe the spirit. Adhere to its divine Principle, and follow its behests, abiding steadily in Wisdom, Love and Truth.—page 491, edition of 1898.

Matter is mortal error.—page 169, edition of 1881.

The fundamental error of mortal man is the belief that matter is intelligent.—page 122, edition of 1881.

Laws of matter are nothing more or less than a belief of intelligence and life in matter, which is the procuring cause of

Truth dwelt not in opinion that could be formed into any shape which the belief gave to it and that the life which moved it came not from it but was outside of it.

all disease; whereas God, Truth, is its positive cure.—page 127, edition of 1881.

There is no life, truth, intelligence, or substance in matter.—page 464, edition of 1898.

Another instance of Mrs. Eddy's plagiarisms is worth documenting. There is no doubt that she copied almost an entire selection from a book by Lindley Murray entitled *The English Reader* (4th ed., Pittsburgh, 1823). This plagiarized material is to be found in Mrs. Eddy's *Miscellaneous Writings*, and is dated in that book September 30, 1895.

Murray's Reader, p. 98.	*Miscellaneous Writings, p. 147, 148.*
. . . the man of integrity . . . is one, who makes it his constant rule to follow the road of duty, according as the word of God, and the voice of his conscience, point it out to him. He is not guided merely by affections, which may sometimes give the colour of virtue to a loose and unstable character.	The man of integrity is one who makes it his constant rule to follow the road of duty, according as Truth and the voice of his conscience point it out to him. He is not guided merely by affections which may some time give the color of virtue to a loose and unstable character.
2. The upright man is guided by a fixed principle of mind, which determines him to esteem nothing but what is honourable; and to abhor whatever is base or unworthy, in moral conduct. Hence we find him ever the same; at all times, the trusty friend, the affectionate relation, the conscientious man of business, the pious worshipper, the public-spirited citizen.	The upright man is guided by a fixed Principle, which destines him to do nothing but what is honorable, and to abhor whatever is base or unworthy; hence we find him ever the same,—at all times the trusty friend, the affectionate relative, the conscientious man of business, the pious worker, the public-spirited citizen.
3. He assumes no borrowed appearance. He seeks no mask to cover him; for he acts no studied part; but he is indeed what he appears to be, full of truth, candour, and humanity. In all his pursuits, he knows no path but the fair and direct one; and would much rather fail of success, than attain it by reproachful means.	He assumes no borrowed appearance. He seeks no mask to cover him, for he acts no studied part; but he is indeed what he appears to be,—full of truth, candor, and humanity. In all his pursuits, he knows no path but the fair, open, and direct one, and would much rather fail of success than attain it by reproachable means. He never shows us a smiling countenance while he meditates evil against us in his heart. We shall never find one part of his character at variance with another.
4. He never shows us a smiling countenance, while he meditates evil against us in his heart. . . . We shall never find one part of his character at variance with another. . . . —*Blair*.	Lovingly yours, *Mary Baker Eddy*
	Sept. 30, 1895

Finally, the possibility that Mrs. Eddy plagiarized from a third source, a manuscript written by Francis Lieber, should be mentioned. Lieber was a distinguished German-American publisher and scholar. In 1936, a minister named Walter Haushalter published a book entitled *Mrs. Eddy Purloins from Hegel,* in which he made public the contents of a manuscript reportedly written by Lieber on "The Metaphysical Religion of Hegel." This twelve-page document appears to have been plagiarized extensively by Mrs. Eddy in *Science and Health*.

There is, however, some uncertainty as to the authenticity of the Lieber document. On the one hand, five top scholars examined the manuscript and in 1940 reported that, without a doubt, it was genuinely Lieber's, dated in 1866, and that it had been reproduced in portion without credit by Mrs. Eddy. These experts included John Calvin French, Ph.D., Johns Hopkins University Librarian; W. Stull Holt, Ph.D., also of Johns Hopkins; Johannes Mattern, Ph.D.; and a top handwriting and document authority, Arthur P. Myers. Another scholar, Arthur E. Overbury, examined the document personally and declared it authentic. No handwriting experts who have examined the original manuscript have ever declared it to be fraudulent (the study done by experts Osborn and Stein was based on a copy). These would appear to be strong reasons for accepting the Lieber document as genuine.

On the other hand, a great deal of evidence has also been brought to light that raises serious doubts as to its authenticity. A leading expert on Lieber, Frank Friedel, in his 1948 biography of Lieber gave several reasons why he did not accept the manuscript as genuine, and no recognized authority on Lieber has yet come out in support of the document. According to Friedel, the attitude toward Hegel in "The Metaphysical Religion of Hegel" is the exact opposite of that held by the historical Francis Lieber. Although Lieber was a German scholar, the manuscript contains a citation of the title of one of Immanuel Kant's books in German, containing the sort of errors in German which one might expect of an English-speaking person whose German was poor. Furthermore, the manuscript appears to have been plagiarized from a book written in the late 1880s by Otto Pfleiderer, which of course it could not have done if it was written in 1866.

In this light, the question of the authenticity of the Lieber document must be considered unsettled. There would appear to be strong reasons both for and against its genuineness. However, it is, at the very least, an example of the contemporary concensus of opinion in Mrs. Eddy's day that her writings were not original. On the counts of plagiarism from Murray's *Reader* and from Quimby, the impartial observer must find Mrs. Eddy guilty. Segments illustrating the parallels between Mrs. Eddy's work and the "Lieber" document are presented below.

The Metaphysical Religion of Hegel by Francis Lieber	*Science and Health with Key to the Scriptures* by Mary Baker Eddy
1. "For Hegel and his true disciples there is no truth, substance, life or intelligence in matter; all is Infinite Mind. Thus matter has no reality; it is only the manifestation of spirit . . . therefore science is spiritual, for God is Spirit" (page 85).	1. "There is no life, truth, intelligence nor substance in matter. All is Infinite Mind and its infinite manifestation, for God is all in all . . . Spirit is God, and man is His image and likeness. Therefore man is not material; he is spiritual" (p. 468, paragraphs 9–15).
2. "Hegel science brings to light truth	2. "Christian Science brings to light

and its supremacy, universal harmony, God's entirety, and matter's nothingness. For him there are but two realities, God and the ideas of God, in other words spirit and what it shadows forth. Properly, there is no physical science. The Principle of science is God, intelligence and not matter. Therefore science is spiritual, for God is Spirit and the Principle of the universe is (man). We learn from Hegel that Mind is universal the first and only cause of all that really is. Embryology affords no instance of one species producing another, the serpent germinating a bird, or a lion a lamb. The difference is not as great between the opposite species as between matter and spirit, so utterly unlike in substance and intelligence. That spirit propagates matter or matter spirit, is morally impossible. Hegel repudiates the thought" (pp. 85, 86).

3. "To conclude that Life, Love, and Truth are attributes of personal deity implies there is something in Person superior to Principle. What, then, is the Person of God? Hegel makes clear that He has no personality as we now know personality, for this would imply intelligence and matter.

The body of God is the Idea given of Him, harmonious order of the universe and in man (male and female) formed by Him" (p. 82).

4. "Beauty is also eternal. The beauty of matter passes away, fading at length into decay and ugliness. But beauty itself is a thing of Life, exempt from age or decay. To be this must be a thing of spirit" (p. 83).

5. "Hegel science brings to light Truth and its supremacy, universal harmony, God's entirety, and man's nothingness" (p. 85).

6. "As music is harmoniously controlled by its Principle, so man governed by his Principle and Being, by Soul and not senses, is harmonious, sinless, and immortal" (p. 91).

7. "The first step to understand Hegel is the Idea. He says the world would collapse without intelligence and Idea" (p. 74).

8. "These Ideas of God never amal-

Truth and its supremacy, universal mind, the entireness of God, good, and the nothingness of evil" (p. 293, paragraphs 28–31).

"There is no physical science, the principle of science is God, intelligence and not matter; therefore science is spiritual for God is Spirit and the Principle of the universe and man. We learn from science mind is universal, the first and only cause of all that really is."

"Embryology affords no instance of one specie producing another; of a serpent germinating a bird, or a lion a lamb. . . . The difference is not as great between opposite species as between matter and spirit, so utterly unlike in substance and intelligence. That spirit propagates matter, or matter spirit, is morally impossible; science repudiates the thought" (pp. 10, 264).

3. "To conclude, Life, Love, and Truth are attributes of a personal deity, implies there is something in Person superior to Principle."

"What is the Person of God? He has no personality, for this would imply Intelligence in matter; the body of God is the idea given of Him in the harmonious universe, and the male and female formed by Him" (p. 44, paragraphs 5–7; p. 221, paragraph 24; p. 222, paragraph 2).

4. "Beauty is eternal; but the beauty of matter passes away, fading at length into decay and ugliness."

"But beauty is a thing of Life, exempt from age or decay, and to be this it must be a thing of spirit" (p. 212, paragraph 7; p. 212, paragraph 10).

5. "Science brings to light Truth, and its supremacy, universal harmony, God's entirety, and matter's nothingness" (p. 28, paragraph 6).

6. "As music is harmoniously controlled by its Principle, so man governed by his Principle and Being, by Soul and not sense, is harmonious, sinless, and immortal" (p. 117, paragraph 29).

7. "This world would collapse without Intelligence and its Idea" (p. 185, paragraph 23).

8. "The ideas of God never amalgamate but retain their distinct identities,

gamate but retain their distinct identities, and are controlled only by the Principle that evokes them. The mineral, vegetable, and animal kingdoms have their distinct identities, wherein one does not create or control the other, but all are created and controlled by God, Spirit" (p. 76). and are controlled only by the Principle that evoked them. The mineral, vegetable, and animal kingdoms have their distinct identities, wherein one creates not nor controls the other, all are created and controlled by God" (p. 71, paragraphs 4–10).

Wrote Mrs. Eddy in *The First Church of Christ, Scientist, and Miscellany* (Boston: Trustees, 1941, p. 115), regarding her teachings:

"I should blush to write of *Science and Health with Key to the Scriptures* as I have, were it of human origin, and I, apart from God, were its author. But, as I was only a scribe echoing the harmonies of heaven in divine metaphysics, I cannot be super-modest in my estimate of the Christian Science textbook."

In a letter to a personal friend dated in 1877, Mrs. Eddy stated concerning Christian Science, "The idea given of God this time is higher, clearer and more permanent than before" (Milmine, p. 73).

Let it not be thought by anyone that Mrs. Eddy did not personally aspire to equality with Christ as some of her eager followers contend, for in the *Christian Science Journal* of April, 1889, Mrs. Eddy allowed the claim made in her behalf to the effect that she was the equal, as chosen successor, to Christ.

In a book entitled *Christ and Christmas* (published in 1884) appear pictures and captions of both Mrs. Eddy and Jesus Christ. That the two are considered at least on the same spiritual level, if Mrs. Eddy is not to be regarded higher, is plain to see.

The evidence of the Murray *Reader* and the Quimby manuscripts (and possibly the Lieber document as well) demonstrates Mrs. Eddy's total lack of ethics in borrowing what was not hers, and indicates that the Deity had no part in the authorship of *Science and Health*. One would be foolish indeed to accept her claim at face value in the face of such incontrovertible evidence.

The Figment of Divine Authorship

Let us return, however, to Mrs. Eddy's explanation of how she "discovered" Christian Science.

According to an authorized statement published by the Christian Science Publishing Society of Boston, Mrs. Eddy, after a fall on a slippery sidewalk February 1, 1866, was pronounced "incurable" and given three days to live by the attending physican (Dr. Alvin M. Cushing). The third day, allegedly her last on earth, Mrs. Eddy (the statement makes out) cried for a Bible, read Matthew 9:2 and rose completely healed. Thus the statement claims "she discovered" Christian Science.

Corroborating this new story, Mrs. Eddy in her book, *Retrospection and Introspection* (p. 38), declares that in February of 1886 (one month after Quimby's death), she was mortally injured in a sidewalk fall and was not expected to live. She, however, vanquished the angel of death in this skirmish, and on the third day emerged triumphant over her bodily infirmity. These two statements, the interested reader will note, substantiate each other in every detail; it is therefore most unfortunate that they should both be falsehoods. Mrs. Eddy never discovered Christian Science in the manner claimed, never was in danger of losing her life in the manner described, and never "rose the third day healed and free" as she maintained. Two incontrovertible facts establish these truths beyond doubt. They are as follows: (1) Dr. Alvin M. Cushing, the attending physican at this "illness" of Mrs. Eddy, denied under oath in a 1,000-word statement that he ever believed or said that she was in a precarious physical condition.[7] Moreover Dr. Cushing stated (contrary to the claims of Christian Scientists that Mrs. Eddy always enjoyed robust health) that he further attended her in August of the same year four separate times and administered medicine to her for bodily ailments. (2) Mr. Julius Dresser (pupil of the late "Dr." Quimby) received a letter from Mrs. Eddy dated February 15, 1866, two weeks *after* her alleged "recovery" from the fall on an icy sidewalk. In this letter Mrs. Eddy alludes to the fall and claims Dr. Cushing resigned her to the life of a cripple. Mrs. Eddy wrote:

> Two weeks ago I fell on the sidewalk and struck my back on the ice, and was taken for dead, came to consciousness amid a storm of vapors from cologne, chloroform, ether, camphor, etc., but to find myself the helpless cripple I was before I saw Dr. Quimby. The physician attending said I had taken the last step I ever should, but in two days I got out of my bed *alone* and *will* walk; but yet I confess I am frightened? . . . Now can't *you* help me? . . . I think I could help another in my condition . . . that yet I am slowly failing. . . .[8]

Barring the obvious medical error of a doctor administering chloroform and ether to an unconscious person, Mrs. Eddy's account once again demonstrates her ability to think in paradoxes and contradict all reason and logical expression. The accounts are therefore spurious and complete fabrications.

Mr. Horace T. Wentworth, with whose mother Mrs. Eddy lived in Stoughton while she was teaching from the *Quimby Manuscripts* (1867–1870), has made the following statement, and no Christian Scientist has ever refuted it:

> As I have seen the amazing spread of this delusion and the way in which men and women are offering up money and the lives of their children to it, I have felt that it is a duty I owe to the public to make it known.
> I have no hard feelings against Mrs. Eddy, no axe to grind, no interest to serve; I simply feel that it is due the thousands of good people who have made Christian Science the anchorage of their souls and its founder the infallible guide of their daily life, to keep this no longer to myself. I desire only that people who take themselves and their helpless children into Christian Science shall do so with the full knowledge that this is not divine revelation but simply the idea of an old-time Maine healer.

Further than this statement Mr. Wentworth has also recorded as incontestable evidence the *very* copy of P. P. Quimby's *Manuscripts* from which Mrs.

---

[7]The entire statement is reproduced in Milmine, pp. 84–86.
[8]F. W. Peabody, *The Religio-Medical Masquerade*, pp. 80–81.

Eddy taught during the years 1867–1870, which copy also contains corrections in Mrs. Eddy's *own* handwriting. Note, please, all this is undeniable fact—yet Mrs. Eddy maintains that she *alone* "discovered and founded" the Christian Science religion. What a historical perversion the prophetess of Christian Science has attempted to perpetrate. Let it also be remembered that Mrs. Eddy claimed for Quimby's theories, which she expanded, Divine import, owning that she only copied what God Almighty spoke.[9]

Let us return then to the personal history of the central figure of this analysis, Mary Baker Eddy—the still reigning Sovereign of Christian Science.

From the home of the Wentworths in Stoughton, Massachusetts, where she taught from the Quimby manuscripts, Mrs. Eddy went on to Lynn, Massachusetts, where she completed her "writing" of *Science and Health*, which she published in 1875. After leaving Lynn largely because of the revolt of most of her students, Mrs. Eddy came to Boston and opened what later became "The Massachusetts Metaphysical College" (571 Columbus Ave.) where she allegedly taught some 4,000 students at $300.00 per student for a period of eight years (1881–1889). One cannot help but wonder what would induce a reasonably intelligent person to spend that amount of money for a course which never lasted the length of a college half-semester and which was taught by a staff hardly qualified intellectually to instruct the ninth grade. Mrs. Eddy herself knew comparatively nothing of Biblical history, theology, philosophy or the ancient languages. Christian Science sources have attempted for years to prove that Mrs. Eddy was a scholar in these fields, but the Rev. J. H. Wiggin, her literary adviser for some years, and himself an excellent scholar, has gone on record as saying that she was grossly ignorant of the subjects in question.

When Mrs. Eddy left the thankless community of Lynn, Massachusetts, she was then 61 years old and possessed less than 50 persons she could call "followers." As the calendar neared 1896, however, the indomitable will and perseverance of Mary Baker Eddy had begun to pay sizable dividends. Her churches and societies numbered well over 400 and the membership in them eventually increased from 800 to 900 percent. Considering what she had to work with, Mrs. Eddy accomplished a financial miracle and a propaganda goal unrivaled for its efficiency and ruthlessness. From her ceaseless efforts for deification and wealth, there flowed continual revisions of *Science and Health*, which the "faithful" were commanded to purchase and sell, or stand in danger of excommunication from the Eddy Autocracy. Should the skeptical reader wish proof on this point of history, and on Mrs. Eddy's insatiable greed for the comforts of financial security and power, we quote her announcement to that effect in its entirety:

> Christian Scientists in the United States and Canada are hereby enjoined not to teach a student of Christian Science for one year, commencing on March 14, 1897.
>
> *Miscellaneous Writings* is calculated to prepare the minds of all true thinkers to understand the Christian Science textbook more correctly than a student can.

---

[9]*Christian Science Journal*, January, 1901.

The Bible, *Science and Health, With Key to the Scriptures* and my other published works are the only proper instructors for this hour. It shall be the *duty* of all Christian Scientists to *circulate* and to *sell* as many of these books as they can.

If a member of the First Church of Christ, Scientist shall fail to *obey* this *injunction* it will render him liable to *lose* his *membership* in this church.—Mary Baker G. Eddy.[10]

Please pay close heed to what Mrs. Eddy said. She did not ask, she commanded all Scientists as their duty to her church to "circulate" and "sell" her works and "obey" her "injunction" under penalty of loss of membership. If, perchance, a method of blackmail is ever rendered legal, it could not be stated in more compelling terminology than this encyclical from the Eddy throne.

But let it be observed that her religious pandering was not limited to just one edition of *Science and Health* alone—no, Mrs. Eddy even extended her tactics to other fields. For example, in February, 1908, she "requested" all Christian Scientists to read the "new" edition of *Science and Health* which contained on page 442, beginning at line 30, information she affirmed to be of "great importance." Said Mrs. Eddy:

TAKE NOTICE

I request Christian Scientists universally to read the paragraph beginning at line 30 on page 442 in the edition of *Science and Health* which will be issued February 29. I consider the information there given to be of *great importance* at this state of the workings of Animal Magnetism, and it will *greatly aid* the students in their individual experiences.—Mary Baker G. Eddy.[11]

One would assume from the tone of the language she used that here was a new revelation imperative to the defense against "Animal Magnetism" (the fiend all Christian Scientists continually war off mentally), but such was not the case; instead Mrs. Eddy merely wrote what she had written a hundred times previously in different language. Said the material of "great importance":

Christian Scientists, be a law to yourselves, that mental malpractice can harm you neither when asleep nor when awake.

Imagine $3.00 for these two sentences, the same old volume excepting this "new" sage advice, and countless loyal Scientists obliged her wish by dutifully pouring their money into the Eddy Treasury. It is no wonder that at her death Mrs. Eddy's personal fortune exceeded three million dollars. *None* of this, unfortunately, was left to charity.

Mrs. Eddy's reign had very little internal opposition and hence went unchallenged during her lifetime, but after her decease a definite scramble for control of her Empire ensued. All but the most exacting students of Christian Science history have overlooked this battle for the vacated throne

[10]*Christian Science Journal*, March, 1897.
[11]*Ibid.*, February, 1908.

of Christian Sciencedom, but it is an important historical conflict and one that deserves consideration. Upon the death of Mrs. Eddy the Christian Science Board of Directors, in good business fashion, assumed control of her thriving empire and consolidated this coup by obtaining from the Massachusetts Supreme Court authority for their self-perpetuating directorate. It was over this issue that a schism appeared in the ranks of Christian Science, and after assuming the title "The Christian Science Parent Church," under the leadership of Mrs. Annie C. Bill of London, the struggle commenced hot and heavy. John V. Dittemore, a member of the Christian Science Board of Directors, left the Boston camp and joined Mrs. Bill in editing the *Christian Science Watchman* and acclaimed her as Mrs. Eddy's successor. It was the contention of "The Parent Church" that Mrs. Eddy intended to have a successor within a half century of her demise and never intended a self-perpetuating Board of Directors. The directors, no doubt for good financial reasons, stoutly rejected this view and defended their new-found gold mine. On February 6, 1924, Mrs. Eddy's name was taken off *The Manual's* list of active officers and thus *The Watchman* claimed the Board had proven its original intentions by fully occupying the most powerful position in the Christian Science Church and forever eliminating the danger of a successor to Mrs. Eddy.[12] The claim by Mrs. Bill and Mr. Dittemore that the directors had usurped the authority of Mrs. Eddy and acted contrary to her expressed wishes went unchallenged for the most part by the Christian Science Board of Directors, for Mr. Dittemore had strong evidence from *The Memoirs of Adam Dickey*, which the Board suppressed, and excerpts from the unpublished writings of Mrs. Eddy's secretary, Calvin A. Frye, that she expected a personal successor within fifty years. Wrote Mrs. Eddy:

> In answer to oncoming questions will say: I calculate that about one-half century more will bring to the front the man that God has equipped to lift aloft His standard of Christian Science.[13]

But, Mrs. Eddy never picked her successor, and with the advancing years the Christian Science Parent Church and *The Watchman* faded into obscurity and the controversy has long since been forgotten.

Continuing further into the Eddy legend, we are once again confronted with the cold, impartial testimony of history where Mrs. Eddy's boundless "generosity" and "selflessness" are concerned. Shortly after the famous "Woodbury Suit" wherein Mrs. Eddy was accused of slandering a former disciple, the Christian Science treasury showed a marked decrease in volume, the result of large legal fees due in consideration of services rendered during the case. As a result of this, Mrs. Eddy perpetrated on the "faithful" the infamous "Teajacket swindle" calculated to draw from her gullible followers the revenue with which to further strengthen her treasury. In line with this scheme she drafted the following "request" to her Church universal which appeared in the *Christian Science Journal*, December 21, 1899:

> Beloved, I ask this favor of all Christian Scientists. Do not give me on, before, or after the forthcoming holiday aught material except three tea-

---

[12]*The Christian Science Watchman*, Vol. 4, No. 7, March, 1928, pp. 153–154.
[13]From *The Christian Science Watchman*, Vol. 4, No. 5, January, 1928.

jackets. *All may contribute to these.* One learns to value material things only as one needs them, and the costliest things are the ones that one needs most. Among my present needs material are these—three jackets, two of darkish, heavy silk, the shade appropriate to white hair; the third of heavy satin, lighter shade, but sufficiently sombre. Nos. 1 and 2 to be common-sense jackets for Mother to work in, and not overtrimmed by any means. No. 3 for best, such as she can afford for her dressing room.—Mary Baker Eddy

The key to this whole financial angle is tó be found in five short words, "*All may contribute to these.*" Notice Mrs. Eddy does not request two hundred thousand teajackets[14] merely "contributions" toward them. No one was to send them—only send the money to buy them. "Mother" Eddy must have enjoyed this neat trick of replenishing her gold reserve, and none can deny that it was carried off with a finesse that rivals any confidence game ever conceived. All this, mind you, in the name of Jesus Christ and under the banner of Christian Science, allegedly the true religion. Judge Rutherford of Jehovah's Witnesses could not have had Christian Science too far out of mind when he said, "Religion is a racket." Compared to Mrs. Eddy, "Pastor" Russell and Judge Rutherford of The Watchtower Society were rank amateurs at collecting money. She played for the highest stakes at all times, and with Mary Baker Eddy it was always "winner take all," and she did!

Theological Structure of Christian Science

In outlining this chapter on Christian Science, it is the conviction of the author that a series of primary quotations taken directly from official Christian Science books will prove far more useful to the average reader than any number of statements made by a non-Christian Scientist. Therefore to enable the reader to have this valuable source material at his fingertips, I have listed sixteen of the major doctrines of historic Christianity, and under each of their respective headings placed contradictory quotations derived from Mrs. Eddy's writings, which will, I believe, provide more than sufficient documentation should any dispute ever arise concerning the proper classification of Christian Science as an anti-Christian cult.

I. The Inspiration of the Bible

1. Referring to Genesis 2:7: "Is this addition to His creation real or unreal? Is it the truth, or is it a lie concerning man and God? It must be a lie . . . (*Science and Health*, p. 524).
2. ". . . the manifest mistakes in the ancient versions; the thirty thousand different readings in the Old Testament, and the three hundred thousand in the New,—these facts show how a mortal and material sense stole into the divine record, with its own hue darkening, to some extent, the inspired pages (*Ibid*, p. 139).

II. The Doctrine of the Trinity and the Deity of Christ

1. "The theory of three persons in one God (that is, a personal Trinity

---

[14]Estimated Christian Science Church membership in 1899.

or Triunity) suggests polytheism, rather than the one ever-present I AM" (*Ibid.*, p. 256).

2. "The Christian who believes in the First Commandment is a monotheist. Thus he virtually unites with the Jew's belief in one God, and recognizes that Jesus Christ is not God, as Jesus himself declared, but is the Son of God" (*Ibid.*, p. 361).

3. "The spiritual Christ was infallible; Jesus, as material manhood, was not Christ" (*Miscellaneous Writings*, p. 84).

III. The Doctrine of God and the Holy Spirit

1. "The Jewish tribal Jehovah was a man-projected God, liable to wrath, repentance, and human changeableness" (*Science and Health*, p. 140).

2. "God. The great I AM; the all-knowing, all-seeing, all-acting, all-wise, all-loving, and eternal; Principle; Mind; Soul; Spirit; Life; Truth; Love; all substance; intelligence" (*Ibid.*, p. 587).

3. "1. God is All-in-all. 2. God is good. Good is Mind. 3. God, Spirit, being all, nothing is matter . . . GOD: Divine Principle, Life, Truth, Love, Soul, Spirit, Mind" (*Ibid*, pp. 113, 115).

IV. The Virgin Birth of Christ

1. "A portion of God could not enter man; neither could God's fullness be reflected by a single man, else God would be manifestly finite, lose the deific character, and become less than God" (*Ibid.*, p. 336).

2. "Jesus, the Galilean Prophet, was born of the Virgin Mary's spiritual thoughts of Life and its manifestation" (*The First Church of Christ Scientist and Miscellany*, 1913, 1941, p. 261).

V. The Doctrine of Miracles

1. "The sick are not healed merely by declaring there is no sickness, but by knowing that there is none" (*Science and Health*, p. 447).

2. "Sickness is part of the error which Truth casts out. Error will not expel error. Christian Science is the law of Truth, which heals the sick on the basis of the one Mind or God. It can heal in no other way, since the human, mortal mind so-called is not a healer, but causes the belief in disease" (*Ibid.*, p. 482).

3. "The so-called miracles contained in Holy Writ are neither supernatural nor preternatural. . . . Jesus regarded good as the normal state of man, and evil as the abnormal. . . . the so-called pains and pleasures of matter were alike unreal to Jesus; for he regarded matter as only a vagary of mortal belief, and subdued it with this understanding" (*Miscellaneous Writings*, pp. 199, 200).

VI. The Atonement of Jesus Christ

1. "The material blood of Jesus was no more efficacious to cleanse from sin when it was shed upon 'the accursed tree,' than when it was flowing in His veins, as he went daily about his Father's business" (*Science and Health*, p. 25).

2. "The real atonement—so infinitely beyond the heathen conception that God requires human blood to propitiate His justice and bring His mercy—needs to be understood" (*No and Yes*, p. 34).

VII. The Death and Resurrection of Christ

1. "Jesus' students, not sufficiently advanced to understand fully their Master's triumph, did not perform many wonderful works until they saw him after his crucifixion and learned that he *had not died*" (*Science and Health*, pp. 45, 46).
2. "His disciples believed Jesus to be dead while he was hidden in the sepulchre, whereas he was alive, demonstrating within the narrow tomb the power of Spirit to overrule mortal, material sense" (*Ibid.*, p. 44).

VIII. The Ascension and Second Coming of Christ

1. ". . . until he himself ascended,—or, in other words, rose even higher in the understanding of Spirit, God. . . . Jesus' unchanged physical condition after what seemed to be death was followed by his exaltation above all material conditions; and this exaltation explained his ascension. . . . In his final demonstration, called the ascension, which closed the earthly record of Jesus, he rose above the physical knowledge of his disciples, and the material senses saw him no more" (*Ibid.*, p. 46).

IX. Satan and the Existence of Evil

1. ". . . Hence, evil is but an illusion, and it has no real basis. Evil is a false belief. God is not its author. The supposititious parent of evil is a lie" (*Ibid.*, p. 480).
2. "All these vagaries are at variance with my system of metaphysics, which rests on God as One and All, and denies the actual existence of both matter and evil. . . . There was never a moment in which evil was real" (*No and Yes*, p. 24).

X. The Nature and Existence of Hell

1. "The sinner makes his own hell by doing evil, and the saint his own heaven by doing right" (*Science and Health*, p. 266).
2. "The olden opinion that hell is fire and brimstone, has yielded somewhat to the metaphysical fact that suffering is a thing of mortal mind instead of body: so, in place of material flames and odor, mental anguish is generally accepted as the penalty for sin" (*Miscellaneous Writings*, p. 237).

XI. The Kingdom of Heaven—Its Reality and Significance

1. Definition: "HEAVEN. Harmony; the reign of Spirit; government by Principle; spirituality; bliss; the atmosphere of Soul" (*Science and Health*, p. 587).
2. "Heaven is harmony,—infinite, boundless bliss. . . . Heaven is the reign of Divine Science" (*First Church of Christ, Scientist and Miscellany*, p. 267).

XII. The Doctrine of Eternal Salvation

1. "Man as God's idea is already saved with an everlasting salvation" (*Miscellaneous Writings*, p. 261).
2. "One sacrifice, however great, is insufficient to pay the debt of sin" (*Science and Health*, p. 23).

XIII. The Doctrine of Prayer

1. "Prayer can neither change God, nor bring his designs into mortal modes—I have no objection to audible prayer of the right kind; but inaudible is more effectual" (*No and Yes*, pp. 39, 40).
2. "If prayer nourishes the belief that sin is cancelled, and that man is made better by merely praying, prayer is an evil. He grows worse who continues in sin because he fancies himself forgiven" (*Science and Health*, p. 4).

XIV. The Creation of Matter and Its Reality

1. "there is . . . no intelligent sin, evil mind or matter: and this is the only true philosophy and realism" (*No and Yes*, p. 38).
2. "There is no life, truth, intelligence nor substance in matter. All is infinite Mind and its infinite manifestation, for God is All-in-all" (*Science and Health*, p. 468).

XV. Man, the Soul, His True Nature and Destiny

1. "Man originated not from dust, materially, but from Spirit, spiritually" (*Miscellaneous Writings*, p. 57).
2. "Man is God's image and likeness; whatever is possible to God, is possible to man as God's reflection" (*Miscellaneous Writings*, p. 183).

XVI. The Existence of Sin, Sickness and Death

1. "DEVIL. Evil; a lie; error; neither corporeality nor mind; the opposite of Truth; a belief in sin, sickness, and death; animal magnetism or hypnotism; the lust of the flesh" (*Science and Health*, p. 584).
2. "DEATH. An illusion, the lie of life in matter; the unreal and untrue; the opposite of Life.
Matter has no life, hence it has no real existence. Mind is immortal. The flesh, warring against the Spirit; that which frets itself free from one belief only to be fettered by another, until every belief of life where Life is not yields to eternal Life. Any material evidence of death is false, for it contradicts the spiritual facts of being" (*Ibid.*, p. 584).

As the preceding quotations indicate, the teachings of Christian Science are vastly different than those generally understood to comprise the fundamental teaching of historic Christianity. And it would be a foolish student indeed who did not take cognizance of these severe deviations from Biblical theology, and mark them well as evidence of another gospel, the product of plagiarism, the amalgamation of sources suitably doctored by a professional literary adviser, and made palatable to the average mind by the semantic manipulations of Mary Baker Eddy.

The philosophy of Christian Science is basically syllogistic, embodying all the logical mazes that the confused and untrained mind of Mrs. Eddy wandered through. Theoretically Mrs. Eddy was an absolute idealist who denied outright the existence of matter from the tiniest insect to the most gigantic star in the celestial galaxies. But practically speaking Mrs. Eddy was a calculating materialist, an individual who thoroughly enjoyed all the material comforts derived from denying their existence. Hundreds of thousands of faithful Christian Scientists supplied their "leader" with all that money could buy, and every material benefit available, yet Mrs. Eddy continually affirmed the nonexistence of these material blessings by teaching in effect that they really did not exist to be enjoyed—they were "illusions of mortal mind," she said. In Mrs. Eddy's philosophy all that exists is "Mind" (God) and "It" is "Good"; matter has no "real" existence at all. It should be mentioned here that Mrs. Eddy never defined matter, to the satisfaction of any qualified logician, that is; so it must be assumed that she meant those elements which were recognizable to the five senses of man, etc.

However, Mrs. Eddy's vaunted metaphysical allegiance to this alleged rule crumbles weakly under the relentless hammering of sound logical principles. Let us see if the rule of inversion is always valid by applying it to similar constructions.

All rabbits are quadrupeds—(inverted) all quadrupeds are rabbits. Now of course any intelligent person can easily see that this inversion leads to a false conclusion since dogs, cats, horses and elephants are all quadrupeds and it is obvious they have no relation to the rabbit family. No rational person could therefore long entertain such logical absurdity, but it is exactly this kind of reasoning that forms the basis of Mrs. Eddy's philosophy and the entire foundation of Christian Science practice. Sin, sickness and death are equally relegated to these peculiar logical dungeons of Christian Science reasoning processes and then represented as "illusions of Mortal Mind." Regarding this phantom "Mortal Mind" Mrs. Eddy wrote:

> At best, matter is only a phenomenon of mortal mind, of which evil is the highest degree; but really there is no such thing as *mortal mind*,—though we are compelled to use the phrase in the endeavor to express the underlying thought (*Unity of Good*, p. 50).

These are strange words indeed, are they not—giving a name to an illusion that does not exist, representing it as evil which is equally nonexistent, and then blaming it for all physical woes which cannot exist, since there is no reality or existence apart from Mind, or God? This type of reasoning is considered sound thinking by Christian Scientists the world over; however, the reader is urged to form his own conclusions dictated by the obvious facts that matter is demonstrably "real" and its decay and death are an ever-present problem.

The syllogism—(1) God is all, God is Mind, therefore Mind is all, and (2) Mind is all, matter is not mind, therefore matter has no existence; these are only escape mechanisms from the objective world of material reality to the subjective world of idealism which can never answer the problems of evil, sin, sickness, or material death since they are negated by the assumption that only Mind exists and it is immaterial, therefore not included in material categories. By denying even that portion of the mind which recognizes these physical realities, and calling it "Mortal Mind," Mrs. Eddy has forever isolated herself and Christian Science from the realm of objective reality, since the mind that truly rejects the existence of matter must never allow the limitations of matter which constitute physical existence. But in practice no Christian Scientist holds these tenets as an Absolute—they all clothe, feed, and house the illusion of Mortal Mind called their bodies and many go to dentists and surgeons for the filling of imaginary cavities and the setting of nonexistent bones. If these facts are not proof positive that the entire philosophy of Christian Science in principle and practice is a huge philosophic hoax, then the author despairs of man's ability to analyze available evidence and arrive at logical conclusions. Even in its basic propositions the Eddy philosophy is a sorry foundation for faith by all standards and an almost unbelievable imposition upon the principles of sound logic.

Inspiration and Authority of the Bible

Christian Science, as a theology, and all Christian Scientists, for that matter, both affirm that the Bible is God's Word and quote Mrs. Eddy to "prove" that their whole religion is based upon the teachings of Scripture. Mrs. Eddy said:

> The Bible has been my only authority. I have had no other guide in 'the straight and narrow way' of Truth (*Science and Health*, p. 126).

However, Mrs. Eddy and Christian Science have repudiated and contradicted this affirmation numerous times (see *Miscellaneous Writings*, pp. 169–170, and *Science and Health*, pp. 517, 537, etc.), and in reality have perverted the clear teachings of the Bible to serve their own ends.

In Psalm 119 we read: "For ever, O Lord, thy *word* is settled in heaven . . . thy *word* is very pure . . . thy *word* is true from the beginning." The prophet Isaiah reminds us: "The *word* of our God shall stand for ever" (Isaiah 40:8), and Christ Himself confirmed these great truths when he said: "The scripture *cannot* be broken . . . Heaven and earth shall pass away but my words shall never pass away" (John 10:35; Matthew 24:35). It will be remembered also that St. Paul stamped with divine authority the testimony of the Scriptures when he wrote: "All scripture is given by inspiration of God, and is profitable for doctrine, for reproof, for correction, for instruction in righteousness" (2 Timothy 3:16).

Coupled with these unassailable voices of testimony as to the Bible's authority, it is evident from the words of Jesus Himself and the writings of His disciples and apostles that He believed in the authority of the Old Testament most emphatically, and even alluded to Old Testament characters and events, thus establishing the authenticity and trustworthiness of the Old Testament.

The Bible declares that *It*, not Mrs. Eddy and Christian Science, is the supreme authority on the activities of God and His relationship to man. Christian Science employs every art and method of paradoxical reasoning to escape the dilemma with which it is faced. It switches terminology about until the terms in question lose all logical meaning and spiritualizes texts until they are literally milked dry of any divine revelation whatsoever. To the average Christian Scientist the Bible is a compilation of ancient writings "full of hundreds of thousands of textual errors . . . its divinity is . . . uncertain, its inspiration . . . questionable . . . It is made up of metaphors, allegories, myths and fables . . . It cannot be read and interpreted literally . . ."[15] Consequently Christian Scientists believe, owing to the utter and hopeless confusion that the Bible allegedly engenders without a qualified interpreter, that it is necessary to have someone interpret the Bible for them. Mrs. Eddy is the divinely appointed person to fulfill this task. Through *Science and Health*, she, they affirm, "rediscovered the healing principle of Jesus and his disciples, lost since the early Christian era," and has *blessed the world* with Christian Science—the "Divine Comforter." To all Christian Scientists then, since they swear allegiance to Mrs. Eddy, "the material record of the Bible . . . is no more important to our well-being than the history of Europe and America" (*Miscellaneous Writings*, p. 170).

The reader is asked to compare this supposedly "Christian" view with the foregoing Scriptural references and the words of Christ and St. Paul, who said and wrote respectively:

> Sanctify them through thy truth: thy *word* is truth (John 17:17).
> But continue thou in the things which thou hast learned and hast been assured of, knowing of whom thou hast learned them; and that from a child thou hast known the *holy scriptures*, which are able to make thee wise unto salvation through faith which is in Christ Jesus (2 Timothy 3:14, 15).

We are told in the words of Peter:

> Knowing this first, that no prophecy of the scripture is of any private interpretation. For the prophecy came not in old time by the will of man: but holy men of God spake as they were moved by the Holy Ghost (2 Peter 1:20, 21).

By these things, of course, we do not mean that God dictated or mechanically reproduced the Bible, or even that He wrote tangibly, using the hands of men as an adult guides the hand of a child, but that God spoke and caused to be recorded truly and without error those things necessary for our salvation and an understanding of His sovereign purposes and love. The Bible is the inspired Word of God, and is wholly dependable in whatever fields it speaks. This, of course, holds true only for the original manuscripts of the Bible of which we have excellent reproductions. No scholar to our knowledge, however, holds to the infallibility of copies or translations which sometimes suggest textual difficulties. The Bible, therefore, stands paramount as God's revelation to man, the simple presentation of infinite values and truths clothed in the figures of time and space. Christian Science, by denying many of these truths and the veracity of the Bible itself in favor of

---

[15] I. M. Haldeman, *Christian Science in the Light of Holy Scripture*, p. 377.

Mrs. Eddy's "interpretations," disobeys directly the injunction of God to "study" and "believe" His Word which alone is able to make us "wise unto salvation through faith in Christ Jesus."

The Doctrine of the Trinity and the Deity of Christ

One prominent trait of all non-Christian religions and cults is their pointed denial of the Scriptural doctrine of the Trinity and the Deity of Jesus Christ. Christian Science ranges high in this category on the basis that it unequivocably denies the true Deity of our Lord and the triunity of the Godhead (Colossians 2:9). Mrs. Eddy said, and most decisively so, that "the theory of three persons in one God (that is, a personal Trinity or Tri-unity) suggests polytheism, rather than the one ever-present I AM" (*Science and Health*, p. 256). Going beyond this declaration Mrs. Eddy also wrote: "Jesus Christ is not God, as Jesus himself declared, but is the Son of God" (*Ibid.*, p. 361), and she then crowned this travesty with the astounding "revelation" that "Life, Truth, and Love constitute the triune Person called God" (*Ibid.*, p. 331). Thus it was that with one sweep of an unblushing pen, a vindictive, ignorant, untrained and egocentric old woman banished the God of the Bible from her religion forever. It is hardly necessary to examine at length the doctrine of the Trinity and the Deity of Christ to refute Mrs. Eddy's vague ramblings, but it is profitable, we believe, to review those passages of Scripture which so thoroughly unmask the pronounced shallowness of the Christian Science contentions.

In Genesis 1:26—"Let *us* make man in *our* image, after *our* likeness."

11:7—"let *us* go down, and there confound their language."

Isaiah 6:8—"who will go for *us*?"

Then we could mention Genesis 18 where Abraham addresses God personally as Lord (Jehovah) over ten times; the obvious plurality of the Godhead is strongly implied if not expressly declared. The fact that God intended to beget a Son after the flesh and of the line of David by virgin birth (Isaiah 7:14; 9:6; Micah 5:2; Matthew 1:23; Luke 1:35; cf. Psalm 2:7 and Hebrews 1:5; 5:5 and Acts 13:33), that this Son in the likeness of flesh was His eternal *Word* or *Wisdom* (John 1:1, 14, 18), and that He is true Deity (Colossians 2:9; Philippians 2:8–11; Revelation 1:8, 17, 18; Hebrews 1:1–4, etc.) and a separate Person from God the Father, is all indicative of the truth that Jesus Christ was truly the God-Man of prophecy and the *personal* Messiah of Israel. It is fruitful to note also that Mrs. Eddy recognizes the "true" God not as Jehovah but as "I Am" (*Science and Health*, p. 256), apparently oblivious of the fact that the word "Jehovah" is itself taken from the Hebrew verb form "to be" (Exodus 3:14), literally "I was, I am, I continue to be" or as the Jews render it "the Eternal"—(*Yhwh*—the tetragrammaton). Keeping with this vein of thought it will be easily recognized that Jesus identified Himself with the same "I Am" or Jehovah—and in fact claimed in no uncertain terms that He was that "I Am" John 8:58) for which the Jews were ready to stone Him to death on the grounds of blasphemy (John 8:59 and 10:30–33).

As to Mrs. Eddy's argument that Jesus was God's Son, *not* God, the answer is painfully simple when thoroughly analyzed. The solution is briefly this: Christ was God's Son by Nature, not creation, as we are; hence His intrinsic character was that of Deity—His attributes were divine—He possessed "all power," etc. (Matthew 28:18). He therefore could *not* be a true Son unless He were truly divine; therefore He could not be the Son of God at all without at once being "God the Son," i.e., of the very Nature of His Father. The Scriptures declare God's Son is Deity—"The mighty God . . . the Everlasting Father, or the Image of God . . . Impress of His Substance . . . Radiance of His glory" . . . etc. Innumerable testimonies as to His divinity are given, far too exhaustive to record here but evidence nonetheless, and beyond disputation. To reduce the Trinity so evident at Christ's baptism and the Great Commission ("In the name of the Father and of the Son and of the Holy Spirit," Matthew 28:19) to three of Mrs. Eddy's choice terms, "Life, Truth and Love," and declare all else "suggestive of heathen gods" (*Science and Health*, p. 256) is a prime demonstration of crass indifference to Biblical terminology and historical theology—an emphatic Christian Science attitude instituted by Mrs. Eddy.

John tells us that Christ was by His own admission *equal* in Deity to God the Father (John 5:18; cf. Philippians 2:8–11; Colossians 2:9; Hebrews 1:3), yet inferior in position and form during His earthly ministry (John 14:28) as a man. The Eternal Word voluntarily humbled Himself, became human and subject to our limitations even to the death of the cross, the Bible tells us, but *never* for a moment did He cease to be what by Nature and inheritance He always was and will be, God the Son, Second Person of the Trinity, Eternal Creator and Savior of the sons of men.

Therefore let us remember most clearly that Christian Science offers a dual Christ, a great man inspired by the "Christ idea" as Mrs. Eddy would have it, one who never really "died" at all for our sins.

The Scriptures hold forth as a ray of inextinguishable light the Deity of our Lord and the Trinity of God. We must therefore be ever vigilant in our defense of the *personal* Jesus who is our *personal* Savior, lest the *impersonal* Christ of Christian Science be allowed further opportunity to counterfeit the Christ of the Bible. This counterfeit so widely taught in Christian Science is merely another false theory that masquerades under the banner of the Christian religion and attempts to subvert the true Christian faith.

The Personality of God the Father and the Holy Spirit

In Christian Science theology, if it be properly understood, the term "God" is merely a relative one and bears no resemblance whatsoever to the Deity so clearly revealed in the Bible. As has been amply shown, Mrs. Eddy interchanges the terms "Life," "Truth," "Love," "Principle," "Mind," "Substance," "Intelligence," "Spirit," "Mother," etc. with that of God; thus Christian Science contends that God is *impersonal*, devoid of any personality at all. Biblically speaking, of course, this is a theological and historical absurdity since the core of Jehovah's uniqueness was His personal nature—I Am—indicative of a reflective and constructive Mind. Jesus repeatedly addressed His Father as a direct object, "I" and "Thou," postulating a logical subject-object relation in intercourse and at least twice the Father answered Him (see

Matthew 3:17 and Luke 17:5), establishing His independence of person. This would have been impossible if God were circumscribed by Mrs. Eddy's theology, for only a personality or cognizant ego can think reflectively, carry on conversation and use the personal pronouns "I" or "he," etc. The God of the Old Testament and the New is a personal transcendent Being, not an impersonal spirit or force, and man is created in His image, that of a personal, though finite, being. The higher animals, to whatever degree they "think," are incapable of rationality and, also unlike man, of the faculty of "knowing," as Descartes once put it "cogito ergo sum" ("I think, therefore I am").

But far surpassing this elementary distinction between the God of Christianity and that of Christian Science, is the inescapable fact that the God of the Bible does what only a personality can do, and these traits forever separate Him from the pantheistic god of Christian Science which is incapable by definition of performing these things. Briefly, God is described as capable of doing the following things:

1. *God remembers*—"I, even I, am he that blotteth out thy transgressions for mine own sake, and will not remember thy sins" (Isaiah 43:25; also compare Psalm 79:8; Jeremiah 31:20; Hosea 8:13).
2. *God speaks*—"I am the Lord: that is my name: and my glory will I not give to another, neither my praise to graven images" (Isaiah 42:8. See also Genesis 1:26; Isaiah 43:10–13; 44:6; Matthew 17:5; Hebrews 1:1).
3. *God hears, sees and creates*—
   A. "And God saw that the wickedness of man was great in the earth" (Genesis 6:5).
   B. "God heard their groaning" (Exodus 2:24), "and when the people complained . . . and . . . the Lord heard it . . ." (Numbers 11:1).
   C. "In the beginning God created the heaven and the earth" (Genesis 1:1).
4. *God "knows," i.e., He has a Mind*—
   A. "The Lord knoweth them that are his" (2 Timothy 2:19).
   B. "God is greater than our heart, and knoweth all things" (1 John 3:20).
   C. "For I know the thoughts that I think toward you, saith the Lord . . ." (Jeremiah 29:11).
5. *God will judge the world*—
   A. "Therefore I will judge you . . . saith the Lord God" (Ezekiel 18:30).
   B. "Therefore thus saith the Lord God unto them; Behold, I, even I, will judge . . ." (Ezekiel 34:20).
   C. "For we must all appear before the judgment seat of Christ" (2 Corinthians 5:10).
6. *God is a personal Spirit*—
   A. "God is a Spirit: and they that worship him must worship him in spirit and in truth" (John 4:24).
   B. "I am the Almighty God; walk before me, and be thou perfect" (Genesis 17:1).
   C. God's Son is declared to be the "express image of his person" (Hebrews 1:3), therefore God is a Person.
7. *God has a will*—
   A. "Thy will be done in earth, as it is in heaven" (Matthew 6:10).

B. ". . . prove what is that good, and acceptable, and perfect, will of God" (Romans 12:2).

C. ". . . he that doeth the will of God abideth for ever . . ." (1 John 2:17).

D. "Lo, I come to do thy will, O God" (Hebrews 10:7, 9).

From this brief resumé of some of God's attributes, the interested reader can doubtless see the vast difference between the God and Father of our Lord Jesus Christ and the "Divine Principle" of Mrs. Eddy's Christian Science. Psychologically speaking, a Principle cannot remember; "Life, Truth and Love" cannot speak audibly; nor can "Substance, Mind or Intelligence" hear, see, create, know, judge or will. The God of the Bible does these things; the god of Christian Science cannot. It is admitted, of course, that *a* mind or *an* intelligence can do those things, but then Mrs. Eddy does not recognize the existence of personality in the Deity and only *a* personality has *a* mind or *an* intelligence. Mrs. Eddy's god (Principle) cannot create nor can *it* exert a will because Principle or even *a* Principle, if you desire, does not possess a will, by any logical definition. The God of Christian Science is an *It*, a neuter gender—merely a name—incapable of metaphysical definition or understanding outside of the maze which is Christian Science theology. St. Paul triumphantly reminds us, "I know *whom* I have believed, and am persuaded that *he* is able to keep that which I have committed unto *him* against that day" (2 Timothy 1:12). The true Christian has a personal relationship with his Lord; he prays through Christ and the power of the Holy Spirit; he asks that it might be given; indeed, *personal* contact is the very source of the Christian's life and spiritual peace. Christian Scientists have no such contact, and consequently no real spiritual life or peace, only the riddles and incoherencies of Mrs. Eddy and a basic uncertainty about good health.

Concerning the doctrine of the Holy Spirit and the attitude of Christian Science toward it, little need be said since Mrs. Eddy's attitude was so obvious, but at the risk of repetition a short review may be profitable. As a matter of course, Mrs. Eddy denied both the personality and office of the Holy Spirit and for His exalted ministry substituted "Divine Science" (*Science and Health*, p. 55).

To refute such a decided perversion of Scripture and historical theology one need only recall who the writers of the Bible, and Christ Himself, considered the Holy Spirit to be in respect to personality and powers. In the sixteenth chapter of John's gospel Jesus instructed His disciples about their new ministry and duties and promised them a "Comforter" who would strengthen and guide them after His ascension. To quiet their fears Jesus told them that it was essential to the coming of the Comforter, who issued forth from the Father, that *He* go away. The Lord said:

". . . if I go not away, the Comforter will not come unto you; but if I depart, I will send him unto you. And when he is come, he will reprove the world of sin, and of righteousness, and of judgment" (verses 7 and 8).

It is useful to observe that the Greek text uses the masculine pronoun *"He"* and also *"Him"* for the Holy Spirit and ascribes to Him a *Will* (verse 7) and the power to "convince" the world of "sin, righteousness and judgment" (verse 8). "Divine Science" has not, will not, and cannot do any of these things since it denies the reality of sin, hence excluding the need for righteousness, and teaches in place of judgment the pernicious un-Biblical doctrine of man's *inherent* goodness. The Holy Spirit therefore is a Person with a Will and divine power to regenerate the soul of man (John 3) and glorify Jesus Christ. It should also be remembered that He does what only a person can do—He teaches us (Luke 12:12), He speaks to us (Acts 13:2), He thinks and makes decisions (Acts 15:28), and He moves us to do the will of God as He has moved holy men of God to serve in the past (2 Peter 1:21). Further than this the Holy Spirit can be lied to (Acts 5:3), He can be grieved (Ephesians 4:30), and He is often resisted (Acts 7:51). All these things denote dealings with a personality, not an impersonal force, and certainly not "Divine Science." Beyond these things the Holy Spirit sanctifies and separates us from sin and prays to the Father for us that we might be freed from great temptations (Romans 8:26).

Certainly these points of evidence disprove the meager attempts of Christian Science to reduce the Third Person of the Trinity to a metaphysical catchword ("Divine Science"), and reveal clearly for all to see the semantic deception Mrs. Eddy has utilized in attempting to undermine this great Scriptural truth.

The Miracles of Christ

The doctrine of the virgin birth of Jesus Christ is indissolubly joined with that of the validity of Old Testament prophecy concerning the Messiah of Israel. Isaiah the prophet tells us that "a virgin shall conceive, and bear a son, and shall call his name Immanuel" (7:14), and that this child was to be miraculous in every sense of the word. Indeed, so unique was this child to be that to Him alone of all the sons of men is the name God applied, the "mighty God" to be specific, the "everlasting Father," the "Prince of peace" (9:6). We are told that He shall reign forever (verse 7) and that the zeal of God Himself will bring this to pass. Unfolding further the panorama of Old Testament prophecy we are told that the child in question will be the Son of David (9:7), of royal lineage, that He will be born in Bethlehem of Judea (Micah 5:2). Even more remarkable than these rays of light from God, the Scriptures further tell us that He was to be crucified for the sins of Israel and the world (Isaiah 53, cf. Daniel 9:26), and that He would rise again to life and come in power to sift the sons of men with eternal judgment (Psalm 22, cf. Zechariah 12:10). But these facts are all a matter of history, which Jesus of Nazareth fulfilled to the letter and which only remain to be consummated at His triumphant return as Judge of the world. Both St. Matthew and St. Luke declare the human fulfillment of God's plan in Mary's conception of the Christchild (Matthew 1:18–25, cf. Luke 1:30–38). Thus the physical existence of Jesus Christ is a biologically established fact. Christian Science vehemently denies this fact and teaches instead that Mary conceived the spiritual idea of God and named *it* Jesus (*Science and Health*, pp. 29, 30). Denying as she did the reality of the physical universe, this was a strangely logical step for Mrs. Eddy as opposed to her usual contempt for all logical form whatsoever. But be that as it may, all the wanderings of Mrs. Eddy's mind, be they from Dan to Beersheba, can never change the testimony of

Old and New Testament Scripture that a demonstrably "real" child was born to Mary, not an "Idea," that this child existed as a concrete physical Being apart from His divine Nature and is now forever, for our sake, both God and Man in Jesus Christ. The virgin birth therefore is a well-supported Biblical doctrine which contradicts most forcibly the false concept Mrs. Eddy has incorporated into the Christian Science religion.

Respecting the miracles performed by Christ during His earthly ministry, Christian Scientists, whether they admit it or not, must logically deny that they were miracles in the first place and discount them as merely "illusions of mortal mind." Mrs. Eddy states that disease, sin, sickness and death are all illusions; they are not "real" since only Mind (God) is real and Mind is spiritual, not material. Therefore following Christian Science theology to its "logical" conclusions,—since the "illusion of disease" can exist only in "the illusion called matter," which is itself existent only in the illusion called "mortal mind" which Mrs. Eddy denies exists anyway—there were no miracles at all because there was no corporeal body to be diseased, hence no need to a cure. Mrs. Eddy wrote:

> The sick are not healed merely by declaring there is no sickness, but by knowing there is none (*Science and Health*, p. 447).

This reasoning on the part of Christian Science theology of course presupposes the assumption that there is no evil, since God-Good is *all* that really exists. Unfortunately it places them in the untenable position of having to account for the origin of the *idea* of evil, for even an illusion must have some basis in experience. Notwithstanding the circularity of this Christian Science argument, the Scriptures send a fresh breath of intellectual honesty into their account of Christ's true attitude toward disease, its reality and cure. The Lord Jesus never told the disintegrating leper as Mrs. Eddy's practitioner would, "You have no disease, it cannot exist, only God is good and He is all, etc." Rather, He recognized the physical decay and by an act of sovereign grace restored the damaged tissue with one short phrase, "I will, be thou clean." It will be recalled that the leper in question said, "Lord, if thou wilt, thou canst make me clean" (Matthew 8:2, 3). Christ's answer included none of Mrs. Eddy's "Divine Science" or treatments by paid "Quacktitioners" as they are sometimes called. He merely restored the form His power had originally created (Colossians 1:16) and destroyed the bacteria responsible for the disease. Jesus never healed by denying the reality of the disease He intended to cure. Rather, He affirmed its reality and glorified God for its cure. It will be recalled that at the raising of Lazarus (John 11) Christ waited until he was physically dead beyond question (four days) and then restored to the function of life every cell of his decaying body, and glorified God for the victory over man's second oldest enemy.[16] We should note in this connection that Jesus did not deny the reality of death, as do Christian Scientists. He did not consider it "an illusion"; rather He verbally confirmed it: "Lazarus *is dead*" (John 11:14).

Christian Science finds no support for its denial of the physical miracles

---

[16]Satan occupies the dubious honor of being the first.

of Christ; deny the physical though they may, the facts are established. Should further proof be desired, however, the reader is urged to consult the following Biblical references which prove, we believe, that the miracles of Christ were physical realities, the result of supernatural intervention on the part of God in behalf of His erring creatures:

1. Matthew 8:14, 15—the healing of Peter's mother-in-law.
2. Matthew 8:26, 27—Christ stills the tempest.
3. Matthew 9:2, 6, 7—Jesus heals the palsied man.
4. Matthew 9:27–30—Christ restores the sight of two blind men.
5. Mark 1:32–34—Jesus heals the sick and casts out devils.
6. John 2:1–11 and John 6:10–14—the miracles of changing water to wine and the feeding of 5,000 people.

Concluding this discussion, it should be noted in reference to John 2:1–11 and 6:10–14 that Christ would hardly have created wine from water or multiplied loaves and fishes to quench the thirst and satisfy the hunger of nonexistent bodies or "illusions of mortal mind," to quote Mrs. Eddy. The nature of all Christ's miracles was that of a divine-human encounter, comprising empirically verified physical events, to meet human needs whether hunger, thirst or suffering—not "illusions" as the theology of Christian Science attempts to make the gullible believe.

The Vicarious Atonement of Christ

There is no doctrine found within the pages of the Bible that is better supported or substantiated than that of the substitutionary death of Christ for the sins of the world. As far back in the Biblical record as Exodus, Moses wrote of God's symbolic use of blood for purification and sacrifice. It will be recalled that Jehovah delivered the Israelites from Egypt by causing all the firstborn of the nation, including Pharaoh's own son, to fall under the shadow of sudden death (Exodus 12). The Jews were instructed in this instance to sprinkle the blood of the young lamb on the doorposts and lintels of their homes, and God promised, "When I see the blood, I will pass over" (Exodus 12:13). The Lord also instituted the animal sacrifices of the Levitical era and expressly stated: ". . . It is the blood that maketh an atonement [covering] for the soul" (Leviticus 17:11). Following this typology through into the New Testament, we find that Jesus was called "the Lamb of God, which taketh away the sin of the world" (John 1:29), and further, that His blood shed upon the cross is our atonement or "covering" for sin, even for the sins of all mankind (Matthew 26:28; Romans 5:6–8; Ephesians 1:7; Colossians 1:20; etc.).

The believer in Christ, therefore, is saved by grace *alone*, through faith in His blood and its efficacy for the cleansing of all sin (Romans 3:25). John, the beloved disciple, reminds us in his powerful epistle, "The blood of Jesus Christ his Son cleanseth us from all sin" (1 John 1:7), and Peter no less resoundingly declares, ". . . ye were not redeemed with corruptible things, as silver and gold . . . But with the precious *blood* of Christ, as of a *lamb* without blemish and without spot" (1 Peter 1:18, 19). Indeed, like a crimson cord binding all the Bible into one compact testimony, the trail of blood courses from Genesis to Revelation, testifying from the mouths of unimpeachable witnesses the wondrous story of God's redemptive love. Listen for a moment to the record of Scripture and the picture comes clearly into focus—God loved us and sent His Son to be our Savior.

"Christ died for the ungodly," Paul triumphantly cries, and "Without shedding of blood there is no remission" (Romans 5:6; Hebrews 9:22); He purchased the church with His own blood (Acts 20:28) Luke informs us, and John adds to the witness by declaring that Christ "washed us from our sins in His own blood" (Revelation 1:5). This was not a pagan sacrifice to placate the wrath of a heathen god's justice as Mrs. Eddy wrote, but a sacrifice offered "through the eternal Spirit" to free the sons of men from the curse of sin, and open the path of salvation by which now we can have "boldness to enter into the holiest by the *blood* of Jesus—a new and living way" to the very throne room of God our Father (Hebrews 10:19, 20).

Contrasting this picture of concrete Biblical theology with the views of Christian Science, no better illustration of Mrs. Eddy's repudiation of this doctrine can be shown than that which comes from her own pen. Said Mrs. Eddy in speaking of the atonement:

> The material blood of Jesus was no more efficacious to cleanse from sin when it was shed upon "the accursed tree," than when it was flowing in his veins . . . (*Science and Health*, p. 25).

According to Mrs. Eddy, then, Jesus, the disciples and apostles, and the early Christian theologians did not understand the meaning of the vicarious atonement, but *she* did and so she wrote:

> He atoned for the terrible unreality of a supposed existence apart from God (*No and Yes*, p. 35).
> The efficacy of the crucifixion lies in the practical affection and goodness it demonstrated for mankind (*Science and Health*, p. 24).

This is, of course, the opposite of anything the Bible teaches, and when Jesus said, "This is my flesh which I shall give for the life of the world," and "This is my blood shed for many for the remission of sin," Mrs. Eddy would have us believe that He anticipated no sacrifice for man's sin at all but merely martyrdom for "the terrible unreality of a supposed existence apart from God." Further comment on this problem is not deemed necessary in the light of the obvious denial by Christian Science of this historically accepted Biblical doctrine, so strongly supported by the Scriptures of both Testaments.

The Death, Resurrection and Ascension of Christ

In our age of advanced medicine we read of many miracles ascribed to the labors of medical science; but all these advancements, marvelous though they may be, have only delayed the inevitable decay and death of the body and have yet to guarantee us physical immortality. The Scriptures clearly teach us that there is given to all men first death, and then the judgment (Hebrews 9:27) even as they tell us that our Lord Himself physically died at Calvary (Philippians 2:8). In fact the death of Jesus upon the cross is more thoroughly substantiated from Biblical and secular history than is His birth, which makes it even more difficult to believe that rational persons would deny it; however, Mrs. Eddy and Christian Science do deny it, hence the necessity of refuting their illogical contentions.

Joseph of Arimathaea, it will be remembered, requested the dead body of Jesus from Pontius Pilate (Matthew 27:58) and properly prepared it for burial (verses 59–60) as was the custom of the Jews. One thing that Joseph knew above anything else in the gathering shadows of the Sabbath that marked a solemn hour rent by bitterness, sorrow and fear, was that the body of the Galilean Prophet he buried was physically incapable of life; Jesus of Nazareth was dead. The absolute terror and doubt that gripped the immediate followers of Jesus could have come only from the personal knowledge that He had perished under the Judaeo-Roman conspiracy and that their cause was without a visible leader and apparently doomed to failure. The Apostle Paul tells us repeatedly "Christ died" (Romans 5:6); Peter recounts that He "bare our sins in his own body on the tree" (1 Peter 2:24), and John testifies that the soldiers "saw" . . . when they came to Jesus . . . "that he was dead already" (John 19:33). Certainly such intimate accounts cannot be lightly dismissed, yet Mrs. Eddy and Christian Science boldly assert "His disciples believed Jesus to be dead while he was hidden in the sepulchre, whereas he was alive . . ." (*Science and Health*, p. 44), and once again she states:

> Jesus' students . . . did not perform many wonderful works until they saw him after his crucifixion and learned that he had not died (*Science and Health*, pp. 45, 46).

The issue therefore is a clean-cut one. The Bible says Christ died upon the cross; Mrs. Eddy and Christian Science say He did not. For those who call themselves Christians the choice is not a difficult one to make, and for those who are not Christians we are certain they will accept the words of the Scripture in preference to Mrs. Eddy anyhow, if only on general principles and the testimony of history.

The Resurrection of Christ is treated on a similar basis by the Christian Science religion, which affirms that He never rose from the dead physically any more than He died physically, Mrs. Eddy deliberately perverting numerous texts of Scripture to glean support for her wobbly propositions.

So it is that we learn how Christian Science often attempts to change the obvious meaning of texts. In the twentieth chapter of John's gospel, the resurrected Jesus, to prove to the doubting Thomas that He was not a spirit but genuine "flesh and bones," presented His body bearing the imprint of nails and spear for the disciple's examination. To His disciples at another time Jesus also said, "Handle me, . . . for a spirit hath not flesh and bones, as ye see me have" (Luke 24:39). The Resurrection of Christ and its startling revelation—namely, that He was who He claimed to be, the Son of God—is the one factor which most probably accounts for the rapid rise of Christianity's power over the lives of men. Here was a genuine opportunity to believe in a Savior who proved His Divinity by vanquishing death, and who promised the same victory to those who believe and preach His Gospel. It is no wonder Satan has so strenuously opposed this doctrine of Scripture, for upon it hangs the verity of our Gospel. As St. Paul puts it, "If Christ be not raised, your faith is vain; ye are yet in your sins (1 Corinthians 15:17). Mrs. Eddy and Christian Science may oppose this truth vigorously, as indeed they do—but the Gospel of Christ will not be hindered by merely denials, and their unbelief does not in any sense nullify the truth of God as the Scriptures so powerfully declare it:

> But now is Christ risen from the dead, and become the firstfruits of them that slept. For since by man came death, by man came also the resurrection of the dead. For as in Adam all die, even so in Christ shall all be made alive[17] (1 Corinthians 15:20–22).

As to the doctrine of the Ascension of Christ into heaven, physically, another denial is vouchsafed from the pen of Mrs. Eddy. By the same method she uses to spiritualize the Resurrection of Christ, Mrs. Eddy also spiritualizes His Ascension. She describes it thusly:

> (the disciples) dear Master would rise again in the spiritual realm of reality, and ascend far above their apprehension. As the reward for his faithfulness, he would disappear to material sense in that change which has since been called the ascension (*Science and Health*, p. 34).

Now to any alert Bible student the Ascension of Christ was a physical one; the disciples *saw* Him carried into the heavenlies visibly; it was not merely an upward stroke on the "spiritual scale" of existence as Mrs. Eddy put it, but a change of position from one sphere to another visible in part to the human eye. In connection with this, one need only remember the testimony of the angels who escorted their Lord to His throne:

> Ye men of Galilee, why stand ye gazing up into heaven? this same Jesus, which is taken up from you into heaven, shall so come in like manner as ye have seen him go into heaven (Acts 1:11).

Beside these great declarations of Scripture the confused writing of Mrs. Eddy is conspicuously immature and inadequate, since, as always, the Bible, which is the supreme Christian authority, confirms the truth as it really happened, not as Christian Science has imagined it happened.

The Existence of Satan, Evil and Sin

Probably one of the most obvious doctrines of Biblical theology is that of the origin, existence and final disposition of evil. From Genesis to Revelation one can distinguish the powers set in array against God and His people, powers whose ultimate end is spiritual judgment of the most terrible order. We are told in the Scripture that Satan or Lucifer, the "god of this world," was once a mighty and perfect angelic son of God whose dazzling and wondrous countenance earned for him the titles, "Son of the Morning" and "Covering Cherub" (Isaiah 14:12 and Ezekiel 28:14). The Scriptures also tell us that this powerful angel secretly cherished the desire to usurp the throne of his Maker (Isaiah 14:13, 14) and upon gathering numerous supporters he rebelled against the sovereignty of Jehovah. The outcome of this wicked

---

[17]Or to more properly grasp the sense of the Greek, "As in Adam all die, so then through Christ shall all be resurrected."

rebellion was the driving from heaven of Satan and the fallen angels that followed him, and he was subsequently allowed dominion over the celestial universe for reasons best known to God and himself, hence his title "prince of the power of the air" (Ephesians 2:2).

With this rebellion commenced the beginning of all evil or sin, i.e., that which is opposed to the will of God. After his rout in the heavenly encounter, Satan extended his kingdom over the heavenlies and earth, determined to disrupt, if possible, the plans of God. In the Garden of Eden Satan's desires reached fruition and he succeeded in spiritually corrupting the future parents of the human race, Adam and Eve (Genesis 3). As punishment for this sin against the Lord, Satan was sentenced to a humiliating defeat by the "Seed" of the very creatures he had so willfully wronged (Genesis 3:15). This promised Seed who would bruise the head of Satan was to be the Messiah of Israel, who we have already seen is the Lord Jesus Christ. The final judgment of Satan will come after his complete and utter defeat at Armageddon, when he and all his followers from the ancient days of his heavenly citizenship will then be cast into the lake of fire, there to suffer eternally the righteous judgment of God (Revelation 20:10).

Despite this graphic Biblical portrayal of Satan available for all to see, Mrs. Eddy and Christian Science energetically deny his existence. Further establishing her contention that evil is nonexistent, Mrs. Eddy flatly states:

. . . Hence, evil is but an illusion, and it has no real basis. Evil is a false belief. God is not its author. The supposititious parent of evil is a lie (*Science and Health*, p. 48).

There never was a moment in which evil was real (*No and Yes*, p. 24).

Since Christian Science denies the origin of evil or Satan, it is only logical that it should deny evil, and sin as the result of evil. Concerning sin Mrs. Eddy wrote:

. . . the only reality of sin, sickness, or death is the awful fact that unrealities seem real to human, erring belief, until God strips off their disguise. They are not true, because they are not of God (*Science and Health*, p. 472).

. . .Sin, sickness, and death are to be classified as effects of error. Christ came to destroy the belief of sin (*Ibid.*, p. 473).

Placing this declaration on a level plane with the Biblical definition and development of the doctrine of sin, it is seen to be at complete odds with the Biblical record. John reminds us that sin, far from being an "illusion" or a nonexistent force, is in reality a very potent enemy of man. "Sin," writes John, "is the transgression of the law," and further, "All unrighteousness is sin" (1 John 3:4 and 1 John 5:17). Paul also admonishes "for the wages of sin is death" (Romans 6:23). One can hardly be expected to believe that the Christian Science teaching about sin is truthful when both John and Paul, inspired spokesmen of God, so clearly contradict it. The Bible innumerable times declares: "All have sinned, and come short of the glory of God" (Romans 3:23), and "if we say we have not sinned, we make him [God] a liar, and his word is not in us" (1 John 1:10). As to the personality and power of a personal force of evil (Satan), the Bible equally establishes his existence as opposed to Mrs. Eddy's denials. Jesus, it will be remembered, spoke with

Satan, who tempted Him (Luke 4:3–6). This could hardly have been an illusion even of the Christian Science variety, and the Lord also announced that He had come "to destroy the works of the devil" whom He described as a liar and a murderer from the beginning who abode not in the truth, a liar and the father of it (John 8:44). Mrs. Eddy's devil, as Mr. Wiggin so aptly put it, was Malicious Animal Magnetism, which she invented to explain away the rather obvious fact that evil and sin existed despite her affirmations to the contrary. This doctrine eventually became a mania with Mrs. Eddy and drove her to irrational behavior and fantastically absurd demonstrations of temper, illness and rapid excursions to different communities, "when she felt the fiend closing in."

The Scriptures, therefore, give more than convincing proof "that God will judge sin" and that it is not an illusion but an ever-present enemy which all men and even Christian Scientists must reap the wages of in the end. It is comforting to know from a Biblical standpoint that though "the wages of sin is death . . . the gift of God is eternal life through Jesus Christ our Lord" (Romans 6:23).

The Doctrines of Prayer and Eternal Salvation

The doctrines of prayer and salvation are inseparably joined in the Scripture with the decree and plan of God to redeem the fallen race of men. The Bible, in places too numerous to recount, encourages, instructs and even commands us to "pray without ceasing" (1 Thessalonians 5:17) that God may reward our faith in His righteous judgments. The Lord Jesus often prayed to His Father for strength to meet the physical and spiritual rigors of daily life and finally the cross itself (Matthew 26:36). We remember also at the raising of Lazarus, pictured so vividly in the eleventh chapter of John's gospel, Jesus prayed:

> Father, I thank thee that thou hast heard me. And I knew that thou hearest me always . . . (John 11:41, 42).

and that He further instructed us to "pray to thy Father which seeth in secret; and thy Father which seeth in secret shall reward thee openly" (Matthew 6:6). Above and beyond these elementary examples of Christ's attitude toward prayer, it is a well-established Biblical fact that prayer by definition is a direct personal request to God for His intervention, whether it be for the purpose of healing the sick, raising the dead or simply asking for grace and strength to live our separate lives (Philippians 4:6, 7). The entire context of John's seventeenth chapter, for example, is devoted to recording the prayer of Christ for *all* His disciples present and future, that they might be protected from Satan and the powers of darkness during their ministry of gospel truth. Jesus understood only too well the need for personal prayer to God in order to maintain close fellowship with our Father, and it is of this that He reminds us when He said:

> Men ought always to pray, and not to faint (Luke 18:1).

Prayer, to Christian Scientists, however, carries none of the meaning that the Bible so clearly portrays because, as Mrs. Eddy wrote:

> Prayer to a personal God hinders spiritual growth.[18]

We have seen, of course, that the God of the Bible is a Personal Being, not a mere "Principle" as Christian Science contends; therefore it is easy to see why the meaning of prayer to a Christian and to a Christian Scientist differs markedly. Mrs. Eddy also wrote concerning prayer:

> Audible prayer can never do the works of spiritual understanding, which regenerates . . . (*Science and Health*, p. 4).
> The danger from prayer is that it may lead us into temptation (*Ibid.*, p. 7).
> The mere habit of pleading with the divine Mind, as one pleads with a human being, perpetuates the belief in God as humanly circumscribed,— an error which impedes spiritual growth (*Ibid.*, p. 2).

It is singularly peculiar, in view of these contradictory claims of Mrs. Eddy, that Jesus addressed His Father as a *personal* Being and commanded us to pray a *personal* prayer, "Our Father which art in heaven, Hallowed be *thy* name, *Thy* kingdom come. *Thy* will be done in earth, as it is in heaven" (Matthew 6:9, 10).

If "Give us this day our daily bread, and forgive us our debts, as we forgive our debtors," etc., is not a plea to God, then, perhaps, Mrs. Eddy's followers can tell us what in the name of reason it is. Mrs. Eddy says, further:

> Prayer cannot change the Science of being, but it tends to bring us into harmony with it (*Science and Health*, p. 2).

What is more evident from this bold negation of Scripture than the fact that Christian Scientists cannot even logically claim that they pray in the Biblical sense at all, disbelieving as they do the clear definitions the Bible gives of what prayer and communication with God really mean. It was written of the Lord Jesus that prayer was His constant habit, His unceasing attitude and unwearied occupation; it is difficult, therefore, to believe that He would urge us to pray in the sure knowledge that it "might lead us into temptation" as Mrs. Eddy implied it did. Moreover, the Lord Jesus prayed audibly, and commanded His disciples to emulate Him "Lead us *not* into temptation." But Mrs. Eddy says audible prayer itself may lead us into temptation (*Science and Health*, p. 7). One need look no further for evidence of where she obtained her inspiration—it was obviously supplied by the great Counterfeiter (Genesis 3:4, 5). Paul, that noble apostle of personal prayer, instructs us to ". . . let your requests be made known unto God" and to pursue "everything by prayer and supplication with thanksgiving" (Philippians 4:6). Once again the inspired apostle flatly contradicts Mrs. Eddy's unscriptural teachings and those of Christian Science, a fact hardly necessitating further comment upon the subject here. Prayer is the lifeblood of the Christian's spiritual existence, and personal communion with *the* personal God our ever-present help in trouble, a relationship no Christian Scientist can ever enjoy since they have never known the God of the Bible, or Jesus Christ, both of whom Biblically speaking they and Mrs. Eddy, their "leader," unreservedly deny.

The doctrine of eternal salvation is so well documented in the Scripture

---

[18]Quoted in I. M. Haldeman, *Christian Science in the Light of Holy Scripture*, p. 268.

that I feel sure no major comment at this stage of study is necessary; however, to clarify the doctrine as opposed to Christian Science perversions of it, I shall briefly summarize it here.

Eternal life, the Bible reveals to us, is to be found only in the cross of Christ, that supreme symbol of God's immeasurable love toward a lost and dying world. This life, the Scripture tells us, resides in the Person of His Son, Jesus, "the true God and eternal life" (1 John 5:20, and John 17:3; 3:16; 5:24; 6:47; 10:28; 14:6, etc.). The Scriptures further testify that God sent His Son to be the "Savior of all men, specially of those that believe" (1 Timothy 4:10). The Lord Jesus Christ by His sacrifice on Calvary has purchased "eternal redemption" for us, promising that if we trust Him fully we shall at length be with Him where He is (John 17:24). God's Word assures us that our Savior is now at the "right hand of the Majesty on high" (Hebrews 1:3), and that some day by His matchless grace, we, too, shall leave this vale of tears, forever free of earthly shackles, to "dwell in the house of the Lord for ever" (Psalm 23:6).

> For by grace are ye saved through faith; and that not of yourselves: it is the gift of God: Not of works, lest any man should boast (Ephesians 2:8, 9).

This, then, is the true, the Christian meaning of salvation, not only freedom from fear, judgment and the uncertainties of this earthly life, but the knowledge of peace *with* God "through the blood of His cross," and justification *before* God by "the power of His resurrection." All these things, according to both John and Peter, are the result of the operation of God's Holy Spirit in the hearts of men, regenerating, renewing, recreating, until eventually, in His redeemed own, the perfect reflection of Christ, God's "express image" (Hebrews 1:3), shall shine forth triumphant over Satan, the flesh and death itself.

"Ye must be born again," said our Lord to Nicodemus (John 3:3); "having been born again of incorruptible seed," writes Peter; and Paul adds, "Therefore if any man be in Christ, he is a new creature: old things are passed away; behold, all things are become new" (2 Corinthians 5:17). Thus it is seen that God's salvation is not a reformation of man, but a regeneration, not just a reorganization of his social habits, but a literal saving of his spiritual life—a complete deliverance of the completely lost.

Christian Science, unfortunately, does not hold this view but teaches instead, as Mrs. Eddy put it, that salvation is *not* a personal deliverance from *real* sin and wickedness, but ". . . boundless freedom and sinless sense," or, as she further stated, "Man as God's idea is already saved with an everlasting salvation" (*Miscellaneous Writings*, p. 261).

Christian Science does away altogether with the necessity of Christ's death on the cross for sin:

> According to divine law, sin and suffering are not cancelled by repentance or pardon (*Ibid.*).

These are strange words in contrast to what Christ said, "I am not come to call the righteous, but sinners to repentance" (Matthew 9:13), and to Peter's immortal sentence, "Christ died for *our* sins, the just for the *unjust*, to reconcile *us* to God" (1 Peter 3:18). Christian Science offers no eternal life and no salvation for the soul, denying as it does, sin, and hence the necessity of redemption from it. But God's Word stands sure, in powerful opposition to the falsehoods of Mrs. Eddy and Christian Science: "All have sinned, and come short of the glory of God," and "There is none righteous, no, not one" (Romans 3:23 and 3:10); but, "Believe on the Lord Jesus Christ, and thou shalt be saved" (Acts 16:31). This is God's salvation; this is the central message of the Bible; this is eternal life.

Man, His Spiritual and Material Natures

Without fear of contradiction all rational persons will admit the reality of their physical existence. There are three principal reasons for this admission, which, briefly stated, are these:

1. Man is capable of perceiving his corporeal form.
2. The demands of the body, such as food, clothing, etc., prove that it has a material existence.
3. The human mind is capable of discerning the difference between concrete and abstract ideas, the body being easily discerned as a concrete proposition.

In view of these three facts, it is worthwhile to note that Christian Science denies without reservation all physical existence, as Mrs. Eddy wrote:

> Man is not matter; he is not made up of brain, blood, bones, and other material elements. . . . Man is spiritual and perfect; and because he is spiritual and perfect, he must be so understood in Christian Science. Man is idea, the image, of Love; he is not physique (*Science and Health*, p. 475).

Not only did Mrs. Eddy deny the materially verifiable fact that the body exists, but she even went so far as to correct God in His creative office by asserting that "Man is the offspring and idea of the Supreme Being whose law is perfect and infinite. In obedience to the law, man is forever unfolding the endless beatitudes of Being; for he is the image and likeness of infinite Life, Truth, and Love" (*Miscellaneous Writings*, p. 82). At this point in her incoherent ramblings and deplorable mental condition, Mrs. Eddy did the one thing which, by itself devoid of any theological speculation whatsoever, characterizes her system of reasoning as that of a gross philosophic perversion. To deny the reality of matter, philosophically speaking, is to predicate the worst type of absurdity, and Mrs. Eddy was not above such a perpetration. Genesis 2:7 plainly states that "God formed man of the dust of the ground, and breathed into his nostrils the breath of life; and man became a living soul." Moses further tells us that God created the material Eve, using a part of the material Adam, and David said, "It is he that hath made us, and not we ourselves" (Psalm 100:3). The Scriptures irrefutably declare that God created matter (Genesis 1:1), all forms of living organisms, and finally man himself in the spiritual image and likeness of his immaterial Father. There is therefore no conceivable ground, logically speaking, for denying that man exists physically as well as spiritually, and Mrs. Eddy's repeated attempts to do away with the human body, and for that matter the material universe itself, is only one more evidence of her unsound reasoning processes.

In regard to the spiritual nature of man, Christian Science takes a peculiar attitude, but for once an attitude that is logically consistent when followed through. Since man is totally spiritual ("the reflection of God" as Christian Science would have it), and God is perfect and incapable of sin, therefore man must also be perfect as His reflection and hence incapable of sin. This is exactly what Mrs. Eddy taught. Witness her own words:

> ... man is the ultimate of perfection and by no means the medium of imperfection. ... If God is upright and eternal, man as His likeness is erect in goodness and perpetual in Life, Truth, and Love. ... The spiritual man is that perfect and unfallen likeness, coexistent and coeternal with God (*Miscellaneous Writings*, p. 79).

The logical mind can only deduce from these statements that the Biblical account of man's fall from perfection (Genesis 3:6, 7) and his definition as a finite being (Psalm 89:48 and 1 Corinthians 15:47) are totally in error and that man *is* God, because if he coexists with an eternal being (*Miscellaneous Writings*, p. 79), he himself is eternal. The weakness of this position can easily be demonstrated by the fact that all material things, including the human body, eventually return to the basic elements of existence, and since God is said to have created all that exists, both material and spiritual (John 1:3), therefore man in both his physical and spiritual forms is a creature, a creation not of a coexistent or inherently eternal character.

In conclusion, it is obvious that the identification of man and God by Christian Science on the basis of a spiritual nature is completely erroneous, if the Judaeo-Christian viewpoint be accepted as to the identity of the true God. Christian Science, it should be noted, claims that it holds the Christian position, and Christian Scientists violently repudiate any attempts to show that their teachings are the opposite of what Jesus taught; yet in every possible sense of the Biblical record, all things having been considered, there is not the slightest possibility that the theology of Christian Science resembles even vaguely the revelation of the Bible concerning the teachings of Jesus Christ. The soul of man, it is true, is immaterial and was created in the image of God, but the body of man is purely physical in every sense of the word. To deny its reality as does Christian Science and attempt to prove that man is totally spiritual, and spiritually perfect at that, is, to say the least, a flagrant perversion of what Biblical theology plainly portrays. The soul of man wilfully sinned against God in the person of Adam (Isaiah 43:27; Romans 5); the souls of all men have forever been in rebellion against Almighty God from that day forward. It is only through the Gospel of Jesus Christ that this rebellion is brought into submission and that the sins of man's evil soul are cleansed, and the soul regenerated to eternal life. To deny these facts on a Biblical basis is dangerous: they are far too obvious. To explain them away as does Christian Science is fruitless; for the "word of the Lord endureth forever," and "it is this Word which through the gospel we preach unto you" (1 Peter 1:25).

Christian Science and Healing

The central claim of Mrs. Eddy and Christian Science is that she has "restored" to Christendom the power of healing "lost" since the days of the early church. It is continually reiterated in the literature of the cult that their "leader" healed as Jesus did and demonstrated, through Divine Science. Not only this, but Mrs. Eddy herself boldly asserted that she healed all types of diseases including cancer, tuberculosis and diphtheria. Mrs. Eddy wrote to the *New York Sun*, December 19, 1898:

> I challenge the world to disprove what I hereby declare. After my discovery of Christian Science I healed consumption in the last stages that the M.D.'s by verdict of a stethoscope and the schools declared incurable, the lungs being mostly consumed. I healed malignant tubercular diphtheria and carious bones that could be dented by the finger, saving them when the surgeon's instruments were lying on the table ready for their amputation. I have healed at one visit a cancer that had so eaten the flesh of the neck as to expose the jugular vein so that it stood out like a cord.

Notice here Mrs. Eddy gives no particulars, names of patients, localities, dates or witnesses. Indeed the only persons who ever witnessed her "miraculous" cures were either lackeys of Mrs. Eddy's without medical training to justify their diagnosis of disease, or Christian Scientists of another era who unfortunately believed as God-breathed truth any claim that either Mrs. Eddy or her contemporary worshipers have conjured up. Mrs. Eddy's claim of the power to heal presents us with a challenge. Since she denied all of the cardinal doctrines of the Christian faith, we know that her so-called power to heal did not come from God. We are left, then, with two alternatives. Either the so-called healings were not supernatural at all (being actually fraudulent, spontaneous, psychosomatic, etc.) and Mrs. Eddy stands condemned as a fraud; or they were accomplished by the power of Satan, in the pattern of the magicians of Pharaoh's court in Moses' day (Exodus 7:11, 22). Briefly then, let us consider this phase of "Mother" Eddy's long career.

To begin with, it should be realized in the process of investigating Mrs. Eddy's healing claims that she refused outright to treat identical cases of diseases she claimed to have cured. Even when a prominent Cincinnati physician offered her every such opportunity, Mrs. Eddy remained strangely silent; indeed she never mentioned the issue again.[19] This is hardly the attitude one would expect from the alleged "successor to Jesus Christ." The foregoing is only one fact of a large number which proved beyond doubt that Mrs. Eddy did not heal as she claimed. During her long life Mrs. Eddy allowed her own little granddaughter, her beloved brother Samuel's wife, and her close friend, Joseph Armstrong, all to die painful deaths of cancer, pneumonia and pleurisy, and never, to any known evidence of the contrary, did she ever lift her "healing" hand to save them.[20] Instead she recommended "absent treatment" in all three cases, which consisted of reading her book, *Science and Health*, and concentrating upon mentally repulsing the organic deterioration. Mrs. Eddy could have at least paid a call on them, and if her claims were true, healed them "at one visit," but she did not because she

---

[19]*New York Sun*, January 1, 1899, by Dr. Charles A. L. Reed.
[20]She did, however, send her personal check to defray the cost of her sister-in-law's operation, but by the time the surgeon operated, the time taken in useless Christian Science treatments had taken a fatal toll and she died.

could not, and no one knew it better than Mary Baker Eddy. There is an overwhelming mass of evidence from sources unchallengeable that this fact is absolute truth, and no better authority can be quoted than the sworn testimony of Mr. Alfred Farlow, then chairman of the Publications Committee of the Christian Science Church and President of the Mother Church in Boston. Mr. Farlow's testimony, that of a Christian Scientist in excellent standing with his church and certainly in a position to know the facts about Mrs. Eddy, clearly stated that he did not know of *any* healing *ever* having been made by Mrs. Eddy of *any* organic disease in her entire life but that of stiff leg—hardly a major illness by any reasonable diagnosis (*The Religio-Medical Masquerade*, F. W. Peabody, p. 113). Much more material could be introduced to further verify this contention of history against the Eddy healing legend, but it is sufficient to say that the issue needs no further support. She who professed to "succeed Jesus Christ" as the great healer of our age could not heal even her closest emotional contacts; and to conceal this great threat to her system which was based squarely on her alleged failure to heal, Mrs. Eddy and her contemporaries have masqueraded to the world and to her gullible followers the legend of her miraculous curative power. This power, so widely trumpeted by Christian Science propaganda, history tells us she never exercised or demonstrated openly, for the obvious reason that it was a complete illusion, a phantom of Christian Science publicity and the delusions of Mary Baker Eddy.

Mrs. Eddy however was not above attaching a price tag to the miraculous healings she claimed for her religion, and so she wrote:

> When teaching imparts the ability to gain and maintain health, to heal and elevate man in every line of life,—as this teaching certainly does,—is it unreasonable to expect in return something to support one's self and a Cause? If so, our whole system of education, secular and religious, is at fault, and the instructors and philanthropists in our land should expect no compensation. "If we have sown unto you spiritual things, is it a great thing if we shall reap your carnal things?" (*Miscellaneous Writings*, p. 38).

But that was Mrs. Eddy, clever to the last and beyond the comprehension and understanding of even her most intimate friends.

It must never be forgotten that Mrs. Eddy once wrote:

> A patient hears the doctor's verdict as the criminal hears the death-sentence (*Science and Health*, p. 198).

Yet she made very rare, but real use of doctors for her spasmodic attacks of hysteria, and toward the end of her life even allowed Christian Scientists the right to use anesthetics, surgery, and the services of orthopedists for breaks and fractures, etc. This although she stoutly opposed such practices at the outset of her career!

However, no one can ever accuse Mrs. Eddy of being foolish, since she seemingly made allowance for some situations, but while she provided in a measure for the bodies of her followers she left their souls poverty stricken, barren and destitute, robbed of the true Christ and His Gospel of life.

The chief attraction of Christian Science then lies in its seeming power over disease and mental conflict, but to quote Psychologist David S. Davis:

"What has been induced by suggestion can be cured by suggestion."[21]

Most illnesses "cured" by Christian Scientists are imagined illnesses which lack medical documentation and are seldom thoroughly verified by anyone other than the Scientists or their sympathizers. The physical world to most Christian Scientists is an "illusion of mortal mind," but they are quick to seize every opportunity to avail themselves of all the comforts this same "mortal mind" conjures up.[22]

With this philosophy it is easy to see how even sin, with all its hideousness, is reduced to a state of mind, and death to a flighty "illusion."

Since the central doctrine of almost all cults is the denial of both the Deity and Saviorhood of the Lord Jesus, we must exert renewed effort in preaching and teaching these major doctrines of our Christian heritage. We must be quick to expose error and even still quicker to extend to all cultists the love of God and the assurance of forgiveness through His Eternal Son, if they will but come to the Christ of Calvary.

Let us not forget, however, that Christian Science can temporarily induce peace of mind, and this cannot be doubted; but, that it is able to cure "diagnosed diseases," give peace of soul, or most of all, peace with God, is a question to which the Bible emphatically says—No! The Bible clearly teaches that salvation is effected solely through the Grace of God as revealed in Jesus Christ and His substitutionary atonement on the cross. The Christ of Christianity is a Personality—God Incarnate (John 1:1–14)—not the "Divine Idea" of a pantheistic nonentity, as Mrs. Eddy has portrayed Him to be.

It is therefore important to remember that Mrs. Eddy never believed in a Personal God nor does any true Christian Scientist today. Mrs. Eddy's last words, which she scrawled with a trembling hand on a scrap of paper shortly before her death, "God is my life," might just as well have read, "Principle, Love, Spirit or Intelligence is my life." To her utterly confused mind the God of the Bible did not exist; for her, God was not personal in any sense, since her limited theology only permitted an "It" which was "all in all." Aside from adoring this pantheistic, impersonal deity, Mrs. Eddy, and consequently all Christian Scientist practitioners today, expound this principle as the Master Key to all human misery. Paradoxically, however, they deny misery exists in the first place but never tire of trying to convince anyone who will listen, for a handsome fee, that Christian Science can remove this "error of mortal mind" through "prayer." The great byword of Christian Science, incidentally, is "prayer," and they never cease reminding their audience that they always pray to "God" for healing. But is it really prayer? The Scriptures teach that prayer is one's petition to a personal God who sees our needs and answers them (Philippians 4:6, 7). Not so in Christian Science. Mrs. Eddy many times reaffirmed her conviction that prayer to a personal God is a hindrance, not a help. To her and Christian Science the only true prayer is the affirmation of Principle Allness and the identification of one's self with this pantheistic

---

[21]Prof. David S. Davis, "A Psychologist Views the Cults," from *The Examiner*, Vol. I, January–February No. 1, p. 11.

[22]Scripture, however, does cite evidence that Satan can counterfeit the miracles of God (Exodus 7:22ff.) and whatever "cures" Christian Science can present are not the work of our Christ.

Principle. From this basic misconception stems the illusion of man's inherent goodness and the denial of the "erroneous" ideas that evil, or for that matter, sin, suffering, disease, or even death, is real. With this view of life it is easy to see how Christian Scientists can appear so apparently happy and so oblivious to everyday worries. Whenever they encounter evil they deny its reality; whenever they behold misery, they affirm its nonexistence; and even when death comes to a loved one, they simply assert that it is an "illusion" since Principle (God) is All, and "It" is *good*.

It would be possible to go on indefinitely with the many strange interpretations which Mrs. Eddy gave to the Scriptures. Suffice it to say, that she never believed in them as God's Word, nor worshiped the Savior within its pages. The Christian's most holy and sacred doctrine of love, which is Christ crucified for us and His sacrificial blood our atonement with God, Mrs. Eddy abruptly dismissed as unnecessary. She equally ignored the existence of hell, Satan, or, for that matter, a literal heaven. (For her it was a "state of mind.") Nowhere in the annals of cultism is there to be found a person who camouflaged so expertly the "broad way of destruction" under a canopy of apparent serenity as did Mary Baker Eddy. Nevertheless, beneath this "serenity" lies a denial of almost all orthodox Christianity.

In concluding this survey of Mrs. Eddy's religion, it is extremely important that the implications of Christian Science be thoroughly understood by Christians and non-Christians alike. It is important for Christians because ignorance of Christian Science has been one of the main contributing factors to the success of its rapid development. For non-Christians it is important because it is an imitation of the true Gospel which bears no resemblance whatsoever to the historic Christian faith.

Christian Science must be understood and its teachings refuted from the Scriptures which it perverts and wrests to the destruction of many misled souls. But Christian Scientists must be loved and evangelized for the cause of the Gospel and because this is God's command to His Church. Here lies the greater challenge by far.

Biblical Texts Helpful in Refuting Christian Science Theology

1. *The Authority of the Bible*: Psalm 119:140; Isaiah 40:8; Matthew 24:35; John 10:35; 17:17; 2 Timothy 3:16.
2. *The Trinity and Deity of Christ*: Genesis 1:26; 11:7; 18:1–33; Exodus 3:14; Isaiah 6:8; 9:6; John 1:1, 14; 8:58; Colossians 1:15; 2:9; Hebrews 1:3; Revelation 1:7, 8, 16.
3. *The Personality of the Holy Spirit*: Luke 12:12; John 16:7, 8; Acts 13:2.
4. *The Virgin Birth and Miracles of Jesus*: Isaiah 7:14; 9:6; Micah 5:2; Matthew 1:18–25; Luke 1:30–38. *Miracles*: Matthew 8:14, 15, 26, 27; 9:2, 6, 7, 27–30; Mark 1:32–34; John 2:1–11; 6:10–14.
5. *The Atonement, Death and Resurrection of Christ*: Exodus 12:13; Leviticus 17:11; Psalm 22; Isaiah 53; Daniel 9:26; Matthew 26:28; 28:5–7; Luke

24:39; John 1:29; 19:33; Romans 5:6–8; Ephesians 1:7; Colossians 1:20.
6. *The Doctrine of Eternal Retribution*: Matthew 13:42, 50; 22:13; Mark 9:44, 46, 48; Luke 3:17; Revelation 20:10.
7. *The Doctrine of Christian Prayer*: Matthew 6:5–15; 7:7–11; Luke 18:1; Philippians 4:6; 1 Thessalonians 5:17; James 5:16.
8. *The Doctrine of Sin*: Romans 3:23; 6:23; 1 John 1:10; 3:4; 5:17.

Chapter 6

MORMONISM—THE LATTER-DAY SAINTS

Historical Perspective

The Church of Jesus Christ of Latter-Day Saints is distinctive among all the religious cults and sects active in the United States in that it has by far the most fascinating history, and one worthy of consideration by all students of religions originating on the American continent.

The Mormons, as they are most commonly called, are divided into two major groups, The Church of Jesus Christ of Latter-Day Saints, with headquarters in Salt Lake City, Utah, and The Reorganized Church of Jesus Christ of Latter Day Saints with headquarters in Independence, Missouri. Today, over 150 years after the movement's founding, the Mormons number more than 5.3 million adherents, own considerable stock in the agricultural and industrial wealth of America, and circle the earth in missionary activities, energetically rivaling evangelical Christianity. The former group, which is the main concern of this chapter, claimed a membership in excess of 5.1 million in April of 1983. The Reorganized Church has just over 200,000 members worldwide, and has won acceptance in some quarters as a "sect of fundamentalism." The Reorganized [Missouri] Church, which rejects the name "Mormon," is briefly reviewed in this chapter, but there can be little doubt that it has gained much ground in recent decades and is composed of a zealous group of dedicated people. They irritate the Utah Church consistently by pointing out that court decisions have established their claim that they are the true church and Utah the schismatic. From its founding the Mormon Church has been characterized by thriftiness, zeal and an admirable missionary spirit, and even before the advent of World War Two, it had more than 2,000 missionaries active on all the mission fields of the world. Since the close of World War Two, however, and in keeping with the acceleration of cult propaganda everywhere, the Mormons have more than 26,000 "missionaries" active today.

One interesting fact, however, accounts for this large missionary force and that is the practice of the Mormon Church to encourage its most promising young people, boys aged 19 and girls aged 21, to dedicate two years of their lives to missionary work on a self-supporting basis. In some cases the parents support the young people during this tour of duty, but it is significant to note that approximately every two weeks some seventy to ninety young men and women begin such missionary activities.

Membership in the Mormon Church now increases each year at an average rate of 200,000 conversions, and the Mormons have a birthrate of 28.1 per thousand, in contrast to the average 15.9 birthrate of the United States.[1] According to the teaching of the Mormon Church, Mormons are to preserve their bodies always in the best of health and are cautioned against the use of tabacco and alcohol, and even the drinking of tea, coffee, and other caffeine-bearing drinks, such as Coca-Cola. Strongly insistent upon the Old Testament principle of tithing, the Mormon Church requires all members to meet the Biblical one-tenth, with the result that in 1982 the church had accumulated assets estimated to exceed $2 billion,[2] a tremendous figure for a comparatively small organization. The reader should bear in mind that the Mormons put this money to good use in the expansion of their church, a truth borne out by the fact that the church is rapidly expanding its real estate holdings, both for commercial and ecclesiastical purposes. The "Saints" now have more than 20 temples in operation, with an additional 20 or so in design or under construction on every continent on the globe. The Mormon university in Utah, Brigham Young University, boasts more than 27,000 students on two campuses.

Promulgated as it is by determined, zealous, missionary-minded people who have a practical religion of "good works" and clean living, the Mormons each year spend millions of dollars in the circulation of the teachings of their chief prophets, Joseph Smith and Brigham Young, while proselyting any and all listeners regardless of church affiliation.[3] In addition to their regular tithing fund, the Mormon Church also encourages what it terms "fast offerings." This unusual practice involves the giving up of two meals on the first Sunday of each month, the price of which is turned over to the church as a voluntary contribution to support and feed the poor.

Since education ranks high in Mormon circles, the existence of their "seminary" and "institute" programs for high school and college students with an enrollment of over 320,000, is what could be expected of such systematic growth. The church also has more than 50 schools outside of the United States, most of which are in Mexico and the South Pacific.

Mormonism, then, is not one of the cults tending to appeal merely to the uneducated, as for the most part Jehovah's Witnesses do, but instead it exalts education, which results in huge amounts of printed propaganda flowing from its presses in the millions of copies annually. The Mormons are also great chapel and temple builders, temples being reserved for the solemnization of "celestial" marriages, sealings, plus proxy baptisms and other ordinances for the dead (nearly 4.5 million sacred endowment rituals performed in 1982 alone). Such temples are forbidden to "Gentiles" (a Mormon term for all non-Mormons) and are truly beautiful buildings, usually ex-

---

[1]The growth of the Mormons since 1900 is an outstanding story. 1900—268,331; 1910—393,437; 1920—526,032; 1930—672,488; 1940—862,664; 1950—1,111,314; 1960—1,693,180; 1970—2,930,810; and 1980—4,633,000.

[2]In 1975 the Associated Press estimated the church's daily income to be at least $3 million per day—with 60% of it tax-free.

[3]As an example, in April of 1978 the *Reader's Digest* published an eight-page removable advertisement about church programs, the first of a $12 million series aimed at nearly 50 million *Digest* readers.

tremely costly both in construction and furnishings. Along with their strong emphasis on education, the Mormons believe in sports, hobbies, dramatics, music, homemaking courses for prospective brides, dances and dramatic festivals. The Mormon organization which sponsors a good deal of this is known as the Mutual Improvement Association and has sponsored literally thousands and thousands of dances and other programs designed to attract and entertain young people. Each Mormon dance is begun with prayer and closed with the singing of a hymn. Mormonism does all that is humanly possible to make its church organization a home away from home for Mormon children and young people, and the absence of juvenile delinquency is in a marked proportion among Mormons, testifying to the success of the church-centered program.[4]

Emphasizing as they do the importance of missions, the Mormon Tabernacle Choir has become famous and is well known to all radio listeners. The choir contains 350 singers and has a repertoire of 810 anthems. It recently completed its fiftieth year of network broadcasting. Those who would tend to write off the Mormons as an influential force in the United States would do well to remember that Mormons have more adherents listed in Who's Who in America than any other one religion, and this also holds true for the scientific honor societies of our nation. Mormon leaders have become powerful in almost all branches of American government, headed by former Secretary of Agricultrue, Ezra Taft Benson, one of the Twelve Apostles who govern the Mormon Church; Treasury Secretary David M. Kennedy (now using his cabinet credentials effectively as an ambassador-at-large for the church); Treasurers Angela (Bay) Buchanan and the late Ivy Baker Priest; Education Secretary Terrel H. Bell; former Michigan governor George Romney; Marriner S. Eccles; three U.S. ambassadors to Scandinavia; and a dozen U.S. senators, to name but a few. Far from being an organization of minor influence, the Mormons are indeed a potent political and social force to be reckoned with, a fact that few informed persons would doubt.

Church Organization

The organization and general administration of the Mormon Church is directed by its "General Authorities." At the top is the First Presidency (presently composed of 88-year-old "prophet" Spencer W. Kimball and two "counselors"), assisted by a "Council of Twelve" apostles, the "First Quorum of the Seventy" and its Presidency, a "Presiding Bishopric," and the Patriarch of the Church. All authority resides in the Mormon "priesthood," established under the titles "Aaronic" (lesser) or "Melchizedek" (higher), to either one of which nearly every active male Mormon twelve years of age or over, belongs. The Mormon Church administration is divided into territories made up of "wards" and "stakes," the former consisting of from five hundred to a thousand people. Each ward is presided over by a bishop and his two counselors. The wards are all consolidated into stakes, each of which is supervised

---

[4]However, a review of social statistics in the state of Utah, which is at least 70% Mormon, shows that rates of divorce, child abuse, and teenage pregnancy and suicide are above the national average and climbing.

by a stake president and two counselors, aided in turn by twelve high priests known as the "stake high council." Today there are approximately 8,900 wards, 1,400 stakes, 2,000 branches, and 180 missions functioning in the Mormon Church. These various auxiliary groups form a powerful coalition for mutual assistance among Mormons, and it is noteworthy that during the depression in 1929, the Mormon "storehouse" saw to it faithfully that few worthy members were in want of the necessities of life.

In their missionary program the Mormons continue to manifest great zeal. Missionaries are well trained in their dogmas and quote the Bible profusely. Thus it is that many true Christians have often unfortunately been literally quoted into silence by the clever disciples of Joseph Smith and Brigham Young, who flourish a pseudo-mastery of Scripture before the uninformed Christian's dazzled eyes and confuse him, sometimes beyond description.

In common with most cults, Mormonism has had its siege of persecutions and slander, but unlike many of the other cults who prefer to "let sleeping dogs lie" the Mormons have attempted at times to defend their "prophets." This has led them into more than one precarious historical dilemma.[5]

The average active Mormon is usually marked by many sound moral traits. He is generally amiable, almost always hospitable, and extremely devoted to his family and to the teachings of his church. Sad to say, however, the great majority of Mormons are in almost total ignorance of the shady historical and theological sources of their religion. They are openly shocked at times when the unglamorous and definitely un-Christian background of the Mormon Church is revealed to them. This little known facet of Mormonism is "a side of the coin" which innumerable Mormon historians have for years either hidden from their people or glossed over in an attempt to suppress certain verifiable and damaging historical evidences. Such evidence the author has elected to review in the interest of obtaining a full picture of Joseph Smith's religion.

Early Mormon History

The seeds of what was later to become the Mormon religion were incubated in the mind of one Joseph Smith, Jr., "The Prophet," better known to residents of Palmyra, New York, in 1816, as just plain "Joe Smith."

Born in Sharon, Vermont, December 23, 1805, fourth child of Lucy and Joseph Smith, the future Mormon prophet entered the world with the proverbial "two strikes" against him in the person of his father and his environment.

Joseph Smith, Sr., was a mystic, a man who spent most of his time digging for imaginary buried treasure (he was particularly addicted to Captain Kidd's legendary hoard!). Besides this failing he sometimes attempted to mint his own money, which at least once brought him into decided conflict with the local constabulary. This fact is, of course, well-known to any informed student of Mormonism, and is bolstered by the testimony of the late Hon. Judge

---

[5]See Hugh Nibley, *The Myth Makers*, Salt Lake City, UT: Bookcraft, Inc., 1958.

Daniel Woodard of the County Court of Windsor, Vermont, a former neighbor of the Smith family. Judge Woodard went on record in the *Historical Magazine* in 1870 with a statement to the effect that the elder Smith definitely was a treasure hunter and that "he also became implicated with one Jack Downing, in counterfeiting money, but turned State's evidence and escaped the penalty."[6]

The mother of the future prophet was as much as her husband the product of the era and her environment, given as she was to extreme religious views and belief in the most trivial of superstitions. Lucy Smith later in her life "authored" a book entitled *Biographical Sketches of Joseph Smith and His Progenitors for Many Generations*. When published by the Mormon Church in Liverpool, England, however, it incurred the enduring wrath of Brigham Young, the first successor to Smith, who brought about the suppression of the book on the grounds that it contained "many mistakes" and that "should it ever be deemed best to publish these sketches, it will not be done until after they are carefully corrected" (*Millennial Star*, Vol. 17, pp. 297, 298, personal letter dated January 31, 1885).[7]

Mrs. Smith, of course, was totally incapable of writing such a work, the "ghost writing" being done by a Mrs. Coray, who faithfully recorded what came to be known as "Mother Smith's History." This work will be discussed as we progress, as also will the personal history of Joseph Smith, Jr. It is merely mentioned now to indicate the contradictory views held by the Mormon Church and by Smith's mother concerning the prophet's home life, background and religious habits.

I return now to the central character of our survey, Joseph Smith, Jr. The year 1820 proved to be the real beginning of the prophet's call, for in that year he was allegedly the recipient of a marvelous vision in which God the Father and God the Son materialized and spoke to young Smith as he piously prayed in a neighboring wood. The prophet records the incident in great detail in his book, *The Pearl of Great Price* (Joseph Smith—History 1:1–25), wherein he reveals that the two "personages" took a rather dim view of the Christian church, and for that matter of the world at large, and announced that a restoration of true Christianity was needed, and that he, Joseph Smith, Jr., had been chosen to launch the new dispensation.

It is interesting to observe that Smith could not have been too much moved by the heavenly vision, for he shortly took up once again the habit of digging for treasure along with his father and brother, who were determined to unearth Captain Kidd's plunder by means of "peep stones," "divining rods," or just plain digging.[8]

History informs us that the Smith clan never succeeded at these multitudinous attempts at treasure hunting, but innumerable craters in the Vermont and New York countryside testify to their apparent zeal without knowledge.

---

[6]*Historical Magazine*, News Series, Vol. 8, No. 5, November, 1870, pp. 315–316.
[7]*Millennial Star*, Vol. 27, No. 42, October 21, 1885.
[8]Peep Stones, or Peek Stones: supposedly magical rocks which when placed in a hat and partially darkened allegedly reveal lost items and buried treasure. Divining rods were sticks supposed to lead to treasure or water, etc.

In later years, the "prophet" greatly regretted these superstitious expeditions of his youth and even went on record as denying that he had ever been a money-digger. Said Prophet Smith on one such occasion: "In the month of October, 1825, I hired with an old gentleman, by the name of Josiah Stoal, who lived in Chenango County, State of New York. He had heard something of a silver mine having been opened by the Spaniards in Harmony, Susquehannah County, State of Pennsylvania; and had, previous to my hiring with him, been digging, in order if possible, to discover the mine. After I went to live with him, he took me, among the rest of his hands, to dig for the silver mine, at which I continued to work for nearly a month, without success in our undertaking, and finally I prevailed with the old gentleman to cease digging after it. Hence arose the very prevalent story of my having been a money digger."[9]

This explanation may suffice to explain the prophet's treasure hunting fiascos to the faithful and to the historically inept; but to those who have access to the facts, it is at once evident that Smith played recklessly, if not fast and loose, with the truth. In fact, it often appeared to be a perfect stranger to him. The main source for promoting skepticism where the veracity of the Prophet's explanation is concerned, however, is from no less an authority than Lucy Smith, his own mother, who, in her account of the very same incident, wrote that Stoal "came for Joseph on account of having heard that he possessed certain keys by which he could discern things invisible to the natural eye" (Linn, *The Story of the Mormons*, p. 16).

Further evidence, in addition to Mrs. Smith's statement (and prima facie evidence, at that), proves beyond a reasonable doubt that the prophet was a confirmed "Peek Stone" addict, that he took part in and personally supervised numerous treasure-digging expeditions, and further that he claimed supernatural powers which allegedly aided him in these searches. To remove all doubt the reader may have as to Smith's early treasure hunting and "Peek Stone" practices, we shall quote three of the best authenticated sources which we feel will sustain our contention that Smith was regarded as a fraud by those who knew him best. It should also be remembered that Joseph Smith, Sr., in an interview, later published in the *Historical Magazine* of May, 1870, clearly stated that the prophet had been a "Peek Stone" enthusiast and treasure-digger in his youth, and, further, that he had also told fortunes and located lost objects by means of a "Peek Stone" and alleged supernatural powers therein. Substantiating Joseph's father's account of his rather odd activities is the testimony of the Reverend Dr. John A. Clark after "exhaustive research" in the Smith family's own neighborhood.

"Long before the idea of a Golden Bible entered their minds, in their excursions for money digging . . . Joe used to be usually their guide, putting into a hat a peculiar stone he had through which he looked to decide where they should begin to dig" (*Gleanings by the Way*, p. 225, 1842).

The proceedings of a court trial dated March 20, 1826—*New York* v. *Joseph Smith*—revealed that Joseph Smith "had a certain stone which he had occasionally looked at to determine where hidden treasures in bowels of the

---

[9]*Millennial Star*, Vol. 14, Supplement, p. 6.

earth were . . . and had looked for Mr. Stoal several times."[10] Therefore the court found the defendant guilty of money digging.

Joseph Smith, Jr., in 1820, claimed a heavenly vision which, he said, singled him out as the Lord's anointed prophet for this dispensation, though it was not until 1823, with the appearance of the angel Moroni at the quaking Smith's bedside, that Joe began his relationship to the fabulous "golden plates," or what was to become the *Book of Mormon*.

According to Smith's account of this extraordinary revelation, which is recorded in the *Pearl of Great Price* (Joseph Smith—History 1:29–54), the angel Moroni, the glorified son of one Mormon, the man for whom the famous book of the same name is entitled, appeared beside Joseph's bedside and thrice repeated his commission to the allegedly awe-struck treasure hunter. Smith did not write this account down until some years later, but even that fails to excuse the blunder he made in transmitting the angelic proclamation. This confusion appears chiefly in the earlier edition of the *Pearl of Great Price* wherein the former Moroni is named as messenger; yet in the latter, Joseph, with equal prophetic authority, identifies the messenger as Nephi, an entirely different character found in the *Book of Mormon*! This unfortunate crossing up of the divine communication system was later remedied by thoughtful Mormon scribes who have exercised great care to ferret out all the historical and factual blunders not readily explainable in the writings of Smith, Young and other early Mormon writers. In current editions, therefore, both the "revelations" agree by identifying Moroni as the midnight visitor. However, whether Nephi or Moroni carried the message to Smith apparently makes little difference to the faithful.

In 1827 Smith claimed to receive the golden plates upon which the *Book of Mormon* is alleged to have been written. Shortly after this historic find, unearthed in the hill Cumorah near Palmyra, New York, Smith began to "translate" the "reformed Egyptian"[11] hieroglyphics inscribed thereupon by means of the "Urim and Thummim," a type of miraculous spectacles which the always thoughtful angel Moroni had the foresight to provide for the budding seer. The account of how Smith went about "translating" the plates and of the attendant difficulties with one Martin Harris, his wife, and Professor Charles Anthon, a noted scholar, will be dealt with more fully later in this chapter. However, the plot is obvious to anyone who is even basically informed concerning the real character of Joseph Smith; so we will continue with the prophet's history.

During the period when Joseph was translating the plates (1827-29) one Oliver Cowdery, an itinerant school teacher, visited Smith at the home of his father-in-law (who after some months, for the sake of his daughter, had received Joseph into his home) where he was duly "converted" to the prophet's religion and soon after became one of several "scribes" who wrote down what Joseph said the plates read, in spite of the fact that he never actually saw them. In the course of time, Smith and Cowdery became fast friends;

---

[10]*Frazers Magazine* (New Series), Vol. 7, February, 1873, p. 229.
[11]Reformed Egyptian is a nonexistent language according to every leading Egyptologist and philologist ever consulted on the problem. However, the Mormons still maintain their claim with the full knowledge that these are the facts.

and the progression of the "translation" and spiritual zeal allegedly attained such heights that, on May 15, 1829, heaven could no longer restrain its joy; and so John the Baptist in person was speedily dispatched by Peter, James and John to the humble state of Pennsylvania with orders to confer the "Aaronic Priesthood" on Joe and Oliver.

This amazing event is recorded in the *Pearl of Great Price* (Joseph Smith—History 1:68–73), following which Oliver baptized Joe and vice versa; and they apparently had a real time blessing one another and prophesying future events "which should shortly come to pass." Smith was careful not to be too specific in recording these prophecies, because of the fact that more often than not, Mormon prophecies did not come in on schedule, which no doubt accounted for Smith's hesitancy in alluding to details.

From the now hallowed state of Pennsylvania, immortalized by Smith's initiation into the priesthood of Aaron by John the Baptist, Joe returned shortly to the home of Peter Whitmer in Fayette, New York, where he remained until the "translation" from the plates was completed and the *Book of Mormon* published and copyrighted in the year 1830. On April 6th of this same year, the prophet, in company with his brothers, Hyrum and Samuel, Oliver Cowdery and David and Peter Whitmer, Jr., officially founded a "new religious society" entitled "The Church of Christ" (later to be named the Church of the Latter-day Saints, and finally as the Church of Jesus Christ of Latter-day Saints). Thus it was that one of the more virulent strains of American cults came into existence—Mormonism had begun in earnest.

Following this "momentous" occasion, a conference consisting of thirty men was called by the "prophet" on June 1, 1830, at which time missionary efforts were decided upon and some of the newly ordained elders were set aside to become missionaries to the Indians. In August of 1830 a zealous preacher, one Parley P. Pratt, was "converted" to Mormonism, and allegedly in September Sidney Rigdon, a powerful Campbellite preacher from Ohio, "saw the light" and "converted" his congregation to Smith's religion, which had begun to take root outside of New York State and Pennsylvania, for reasons which we shall view a little later on.

Sidney Rigdon and Parley Pratt, it should be noted, were almost from the day of their "conversions" slated for greatness in the Mormon hierarchy, as was Orson Pratt; and it is their writings, along with those of Young, Orson Pratt, Charles Penrose and James Talmage, which best argue in favor of the Mormon cause, even to this very day. The role Sidney Rigdon played in the Mormon saga will be discussed in a later chapter, but it must be remembered that Rigdon was later accused of apostasy and excommunicated from the Mormon Church, largely because of his famous "Salt Sermon," which was delivered in 1833 in Jackson County, Missouri. In the course of its presentation, Rigdon soared to the heights of inflamatory rhetoric against the citizens of Jackson County, virtually challenging the whole state to do pitched battle with the "saints," who were subsequently terribly persecuted and expelled in November of 1833.

This volatile bit of rabble-rousing did Sidney no good with his fellow Mormons; and it became known rather bitterly as "Sidney's Salt Sermon," due to the fact that his text was drawn from Matthew and dealt with salt having lost its savor. Rigdon's devastating evaluation of "Prophet" Smith from the "inside" is a masterful piece of factual dissection and should be read by anyone tempted to deify the questionable character of the first Mormon prophet.

Shortly after the Fayette meeting, the nucleus of the Mormon Church moved to Kirtland, Ohio, where in a period of six years they increased to over 16,000 souls. It was from Kirtland that Smith and Rigdon made their initial thrust into Jackson County, Missouri. Joseph and Sidney were no strangers to persecution and suffered the indignity of an old fashioned "tar-and-feathering" accompanied by a trip out of town on the proverbial rail. While in Missouri, Smith purchased sixty-three acres which he deemed "holy ground" and there marked the exact spot on which he declared that the temple of Zion, the earthly headquarters of the kingdom of Jesus Christ, was eventually to be built. It is an interesting fact of history that one small branch of Mormonism (the Church of Christ, Temple Lot) today owns that temple site and claims that it once refused five million dollars from the Utah church for the "hallowed ground."

In Kirtland also the First Stake of Zion was established and a quorum of twelve apostles was chosen, presided over by a First Presidency of three, supervised by the president, Joseph Smith, the Seer. Chief reason for the Mormons moving to Kirtland, Ohio, however, was the extreme unpopularity of Smith and his revelations among the people who knew him best and who regarded his new religion as a sham and a hoax, thus hardly recommending them as prospective converts. Smith, of course, conjured up a revelation from God as authorization for the move. In fact, between the years 1831 to 1844, the "prophet" allegedly received well over 135 direct revelations from God, revelations which helped build Kirtland and, later, the Mormon metropolis of Nauvoo, Illinois. Smith's infamous practice of polygamy was instituted at Kirtland and later confirmed by "divine revelation." Some misinformed persons have declared that Smith was not a polygamist, but one needs only to search the famous Berrian collection in the New York Public Library for volumes of primary information to the contrary, written by Mormon men and women who lived through many of these experiences and testified to the outright immorality of Smith and the leaders of the Mormon Church. Gradually, of course, polygamy filtered down through the entire Mormon Church so that it was necessary for the United States government to threaten to confiscate all Mormon property and to threaten them with complete dissolution in order to stamp out the then widely accepted practice.

In 1890, President Wilford Woodruff officially abolished polygamy as a practice of the Mormon Church, one concrete instance at least of the fact that the religious convictions of the Mormons were sacrificed for their political and economic survival, something more often discussed in Mormon circles today. The facts still remain that in Kirtland, Nauvoo, Jackson County, etc., the Mormons had a chance to win converts to Smith's religion because they were strangers and the character of the prophet was unknown in those areas. But in New York, Smith was known by the most uncomplimentary terms, some of which have a direct bearing upon a proper understanding of his character. Pomeroy Tucker, in his classic work, *The Origin, Rise and Prog-*

ress of Mormonism (New York, 1867), collected a number of duly sworn statements by neighbors of the Smith family and by acquaintances of Joseph
Smith, Jr., particularly. According to the unanimous consensus of those who
testified at the time, Joseph Smith, Jr., was known for "his habits of exaggeration and untruthfulness . . . by reason of his extravagancies of statement,
his word was received with the least confidence by those who knew him best.
He could utter the most palpable exaggeration or marvelous absurdity with
the utmost apparent gravity" (p. 16).

One of the most interesting statements concerning the early life of the
Smith family and of Joseph, Jr., was obtained by E.D. Howe, a contemporary
of Smith's, who did tremendous research during the lifetime of Joseph which
has never been successfully impugned by any Mormon historians. Smith
himself never dared to answer Howe's charges, though they were well known
to him, so great was the weight of contemporary evidence.

Mr. Howe obtained a statement signed by sixty-two residents of Palmyra,
New York, one that cannot be ignored by any serious student of Mormonism:

> "We, the undersigned, have been acquainted with the Smith family, for
> a number of years, while they resided near this place, and we have no
> hesitation in saying, that we consider them destitute of that moral character,
> which ought to entitle them to the confidence of any community. They were
> particularly famous for visionary projects, spent much of their time in dig-
> gings for money which they pretended was hid in the earth; and to this day,
> large excavations may be seen in the earth, not far from their residence,
> where they used to spend their time in digging for hidden treasures. Joseph
> Smith, Senior, and his son Joseph, were in particular, considered entirely
> destitute of *moral character*, and *addicted to vicious habits"* (*Mormonism Unveiled*,
> Zanesville, Ohio, 1834, p. 261).

Some persons reading this may feel that it is unfair to quote only one
side of the story; what about those who are favorable to the Mormons, they
will ask. In answer to this, the amazing fact is that *there exists no contemporary
pro-Mormon statements from reliable and informed sources who knew the Smith family
and Joseph intimately*. It has only been the over-wise Mormon historians, utilizing hindsight over a hundred-year period, who have been able to even
seriously challenge the evidence of the neighbors, Joseph's father-in-law, and
many ex-Mormons who knew what was going on and went on record with
the evidence not even Mormon historians have bothered seriously to dispute.

As the Mormons grew and prospered in Nauvoo, Illinois, and as the
practice of polygamy began to be known by the wider Mormon community
and outsiders as well, increasing distrust of Prophet Smith multiplied, especially after one of his former assistants, John C. Bennett, boldly exposed
the practice of polygamy in Nauvoo. When the prophet (or "general," as he
liked to be known in this phase of his career) could tolerate this mounting
criticism no more and ordered the destruction of its most threatening mouthpiece, an anti-Mormon publication entitled *The Nauvoo Expositor*, the State of
Illinois intervened. The "prophet" and his brother, Hyrum, were placed in
a jail in Carthage, Illinois, to await trial for their part in the wrecking of the
Expositor. However, on June 27, 1844, a mob comprised of some two hundred
persons stormed the Carthage jail and brutally murdered Smith and his

brother, Hyrum, thus forcing upon the vigorously unwilling prophet's head the unwanted crown of early martyrdom, thus insuring his perpetual enshrinement in Mormon history as a "true seer."

With the assassination of Joseph Smith, the large majority of Mormons accepted the leadership of Brigham Young, then forty-three years of age and the man who had previously led the Mormons to safety from the wrath of the Missouri citizenry.

In 1846, Young announced that the "saints" would abandon Nauvoo. In 1847, after a brutal trek through the wilderness of the Southwest, Young brought the first band of Mormons to the valley of the great Salt Lake and with the exclamation, "This is the place!" sealed the destiny of the "saints"— they were in what was to become the state of Utah.

For more than thirty years, Brigham Young ruled the Mormon church, and as is still the case, he inherited the divinely appointed prophetic mantle of the first prophet. So it is that each succeeding president of the Mormon church claims the same authority as Joseph Smith and Brigham Young—an infallible prophetic succession.

The "spiritual deed" which the Mormons felt entitled them to possession of the valley of the great Salt Lake was "granted" in June of 1848 when the first Mormon crops were largely saved from a plague of locusts by a vast armada of sea gulls; thus, according to Mormon teaching, God gave visible evidence of His blessing upon the Latter-Day Saint Church.

We cannot, of course, discuss the history of the Mormons under Brigham Young in great detail because that would easily necessitate a full volume by itself, but suffice it to say that Smith gave the movement its initial thrust and Brigham Young supplied the needed momentum necessary to establish it as a bona fide religion. Young himself was a character of many facets, and one cannot understand the theology of Mormonism without understanding the tremendous influence exercised upon it by the person of "Prophet" Young and his teachings. Smith and Young, in company with the pronouncements of the succeeding presidents, have made Mormon theology what it is, and apart from Brigham Young, Mormonism cannot be thoroughly understood.

Young was a man of indomitable courage, possessed of a canny nature, but given to fits of ruthlessness now conveniently forgotten by Mormon historians. One such evidence of his determination to control Utah was the order which he gave to massacre over 100 non-Mormon immigrants in what has now become known as the infamous Mountain Meadows massacre. In this particular instance, for reasons known only to himself, Young entrusted to Bishop John D. Lee in 1857 the task of annihilating a wagon train of virtually helpless immigrants. This, Bishop Lee did faithfully, and 20 years later he was imprisoned, tried, convicted and executed by the government of the United States for this vicious, totalitarian action.

In his memorable book, *The Confessions of John D. Lee,* a consistent sore spot in the Mormon scheme of historical "reconstruction," Lee confessed to his part in the infamous doings, but he swore that he acted upon the orders of Brigham Young. However, the testimony of Lee and of some of his lieutenants and others connected with the massacre indicates beyond question that Young ordered and sanctioned the action. As we further study Mormon theology, it will become apparent that this was not at all beyond the limits of Young's character; he was the law in Utah; and as it has been so wisely observed, "Power corrupts and absolute power corrupts absolutely."

Mormonism today, then, is a far cry from quite a number of the principles and practices of its early founders. To be sure, it remains faithful to their basic tenets, but, as in the case of polygamy, when those tenets come in conflict with government statutes or political influence, the Latter-day Saints have wisely chosen to ignore (the word commonly used is "re-interpret") the counsels of their two chief prophets. The history of the Mormons is a vast and complex subject; it is a veritable labyrinth of books, testimonies, affidavits, photographs, hearsay and opinions, and it is only after the most careful analysis of the contemporary evidence that a picture emerges consistent with verifiable facts. For the average faithful Mormon, one can but have sympathy and regard. He is, by and large, honest, industrious, thrifty and zealous in both the proclamation and promulgation of his beliefs. One only regrets that he has accepted at face value a carefully edited "history" of the origin and doctrinal development of his religion instead of examining the excellent sources which not only contradict but irrefutably prove the falsity of what is most certainly a magnificent reconstructed history. It is to be hoped that as we further study the unfolding drama of Mormon doctrine, and the basis of such doctrine, the reader will come to appreciate the evolution of Mormonism and the pitfalls which most certainly exist in taking at face value the gospel according to Joseph Smith and Brigham Young. The verdict of history, then, is overwhelmingly against the Mormon version, particularly where Smith and Young are concerned; and there is a vast amount of documentation all but a few Mormons seem content to ignore, but the facts themselves remain too well verified to be ignored.

A New Revelation—the "Mormon Bible"

Aside from the King James Version of the Bible, which the Mormons accept as part of the Word of God "insofar as it is correctly translated," they have added the *Doctrine and Covenants,* the *Pearl of Great Price,* and the initial volume, the *Book of Mormon,* to the canon of what they would call authorized scripture—the "Four Standard Works." The last mentioned is a subject of this chapter since it occupies a pivotal place in Mormon theology and history and therefore must be carefully examined. A great deal of research on the part of a number of able scholars and organizations has already been published concerning the *Book of Mormon*, and I have drawn heavily upon whatever documented and verifiable information was available. The task of validating the material was enormous, and so I have selected that information which has been verified beyond refutation and is available today in some of our leading institutions of learning (Stanford University, Union Theological Seminary, the Research Departments of the Library of Congress, the New York Public Library, and others).

It is a difficult task to evaluate the complex structure of the *Book of Mormon,* and the reader is urged to consider the bibliography at the end of this volume if he should desire further and more exhaustive studies.

The Story of the Ancient People

The *Book of Mormon* purports to be a history of two ancient civilizations which were located on the American continent. According to the Mormon version, the first of these great civilizations left the tower of Babel (about 2,250 B.C. by Mormon reckoning), crossed over into Europe and emigrated to the eastern coast of what we know as Central America.

The second group allegedly left Jerusalem somewhere in the neighborhood of 600 B.C., before the destruction of the city and the Babylonian captivity of Israel. According to traditional Mormon thinking, that group crossed the Pacific Ocean, landing on the west coast of South America. The *Book of Mormon* is supposedly a condensation of the high points of these civilizations. The author of the book was a prophet named Mormon. The book is "the translation of the abridgment of the record of these civilizations" and "includes a brief outline of the history of the earlier Jaredite people, an abridgment made by Moroni, son of Mormon, taken from the Jaredite record found during the period of the second civilization."

The Jaredites were destroyed as the result of "corruption" and were punished for their apostasy, their civilization undergoing total destruction.

The second group, who came to America about 600 B.C., were righteous Jews, the leader of which group was named Nephi. This group eventually met a fate similar to the Jaredites' and were divided into two warring camps, the Nephites and the Lamanites (Indians). The Lamanites received a curse because of their evil deeds, and the curse took the form of dark skins.

The Mormon's record claims that Christ visited the American continent, revealed Himself to the Nephites, preached to them the Gospel, and instituted both baptism and the communion service.

The Nephites, unfortunately, proved to be no match for the Lamanites; and they were defeated by them and annihilated in a great battle near the hill Cumorah in Palmyra, New York, approximately A.D. 385.

Some fourteen hundred years later, the Mormons claim, Joseph Smith, Jr., unearthed Mormon's abridgment which was written in reformed Egyptian hieroglyphics upon plates of gold, and with the aid of Urim and Thummin (supernatural spectacles) translated the reformed Egyptian into English. It thus became the *Book of Mormon* which was published in 1830, bearing the name of Joseph Smith, Jr., as "Author and Proprietor."

Lest there be any confusion, there are four classes of record plates which were allegedly revealed to Smith: (1) the plates of Nephi, (2) the plates of Mormon, (3) the plates of Ether, and (4) a set of plates mentioned throughout the *Book of Mormon* known as the "plates of brass" or brass plates of Laban.

The plates of Nephi recorded mostly the secular history, although the smaller plates of Nephi allegedly recorded sacred events. The second group is an abridgment from the plates of Nephi which was made by Mormon and which included his commentaries and additional historical notes by his son, Moroni. The third set of plates recorded the history of the Jaredites, also abridged by Moroni, who added his own comments. It is now known as the *Book of Ether*.

The fourth set of plates are alleged to have come from Jerusalem and appear in the form of extracts in Nephite records. They are given over to quotations from the Hebrew Scriptures and genealogies.

Joseph Smith is alleged to have received the plates from the hand of Moroni, "a resurrected personage," in the year 1827.

Purpose of the Book of Mormon

The purpose of the *Book of Mormon* and its mission generally eludes Christian theologians, archeologists, and students of Anthropology because of the many difficulties which the book introduces in the light of already established facts. But a Mormon explanation of the purpose of the book ought to be considered:

It is a principle of divine and civil law that, "In the mouth of two or three witnesses every word shall be established" (II Corinthians 13:1). The Bible, its history of the dealings and providences of God with man upon the eastern continent, is one witness for the truth. The *Book of Mormon* is another witness to the same effect. It recites that providences of God in the basic and vastly important matter of redemption, as also in general in the laws of nature, and indicates that such provisions were not limited, not confined to the Eastern world, "God so loved the *world*" (John 3:16), not a mere portion of it, that he likewise ministered in behalf of the race in the great western continent. Being the seat of mighty civilizations, it was entitled to and partook of the ministrations of the Father of the race.

The stated purpose of the *Book of Mormon* (in its introduction) is universal: to witness to the world the truth and divinity of Jesus Christ, and his mission of salvation through the gospel He taught. Its witness is for Jew and Gentile. The house of Israel rejected its Messiah, and in consequence was rejected, scattered, and the government overthrown. The gospel refused by them was then preached to the Gentiles. Israel has ever since remained in unbelief in Christ and without the ministration of inspired men. Bible prophecy frequently declares their restoration in the latter days to divine favor, the gathering of Israel and their permanent establishment in their ancient homeland of Palestine. The sealed book, the *Book of Mormon*, is predicted by Bible prophecy and by its own declarations to be a confirming, additional revelation from God of the Messiahship of Jesus Christ, and of the covenants made with their fathers. It repeatedly predicts regathering, restoration, and other manifold blessings to Israel. The God of Israel is to make a "new covenant" with that people—not the old Mosaic covenant, but another and later one, by which they are to be reinstated as a nation in their holy land. (See also Jeremiah 31:34; Ezekiel 20:33–38, etc., Bible predictions to the same effect.) The *Book of Mormon* interprets Old Testament prophecy to that effect, as it recites predictions of its inspired men. It claims to be part of the new covenant to Israel.

It claims to be the sealed book of Isaiah, chapter 29, which it quotes and interprets. It recites that as a result of its revealment, Israel would come to understanding of the Christ message of salvation; that they would no longer fear but be secured and greatly blessed by divine favor; that the coming forth of its record would be followed by physical blessing upon Palestine to its redemption from sterility to fertility, and thus made capable of maintaining that nation as in ancient times. It is a fact that since the appearance of the book that land has been favored. It produces abundantly.

The Jews are now permitted to return and establish cities and industrial and agricultural units. Many Jews, according to predictions of the book, are beginning to believe in Christ. Proponents of the book state that with such predictions fulfilled it is now too late for any similar fulfillment by another record.

The book declares also that the remnants of the former inhabitants of Ancient America, scattered throughout North, Central, and South America—the Indian populations—will by means of the coming to light of the record of their fathers, be converted to the faith and share in the covenants made with their progenitors. It indicates their emergence from primitive conditions to enlightenment. It declares that the Gentile nations occupying their lands would favor their emancipation from degenerate conditions. This is part of the purpose of the book.

The Gospel of Saint John 10:16 contains a statement of Jesus Christ quoted by believers in the divinity of the *Book of Mormon*. It reads: "And *other sheep I have, which are not of this fold*: them also I must bring, and *they shall hear my voice*; and there shall be one fold, and one shepherd." Citing also that Christ declared these words: "I am not sent but unto the lost sheep of the house of Israel" (Matthew 15:24), they believe that since Jesus Christ, according to the record, never appeared to the Gentiles, and "salvation is of the Jews," or Israel (John 4:22), the promise concerning "other sheep" was realized by the appearance of Christ to the Nephites.[12]

For the Mormons, then, the Bible predicts the *Book of Mormon*; the *Book of Mormon* interprets Old Testament prophecy and it claims to be part of the new covenant to Israel. It is also supposed to be "another witness" to the truth of the Christian Gospel. It is unfortunate for the Mormons that this witness is so often found in conflict with the Biblical revelation, as we shall see. It is at the very least a gross assumption unjustified by any of the internal evidence of the book or the testimony of science and history, that the *Book of Mormon* should be considered "part of the new covenant" in any sense.

Scientific Evidence Against the Book of Mormon

In an attempt to validate and justify the claims of the *Book of Mormon*, the highest authority in Mormonism, Joseph Smith, Jr., the Mormon prophet, related an event which, if true, would add significant weight to some of the Mormon claims for their Bible. Fortunately, it is a fact on which a good deal of evidence can be brought to bear.

Smith put forth his claim in the book, the *Pearl of Great Price*, (Joseph Smith—History 1:62–64, 1982 edition), and it is worthwhile to examine it:

> . . . I commenced copying the characters off the plates. I copied a considerable number of them, and by means of the Urim and Thummim I translated some of them . . . Mr. Martin Harris came to our place, got the characters which I had drawn off the plates, and started with them to the city of New York. For what took place relative to him and the characters, I refer to his own account of the circumstances, as he related them to me after his return, which was as follows: "I went to the city of New York, and

---

[12]*The Book of Mormon* by R. K. Salyards, Sr., Herald House, Independence, MO: n.d., pp.13–16.

presented the characters which had been translated, with the translation thereof, to Professor Charles Anthon, a gentleman celebrated for his literary attainments. Professor Anthon stated that the translation was correct, more so than any he had before seen translated from the Egyptian. I then showed him those which were not yet translated, and he said that they were Egyptian, Chaldaic, Assyriac, and Arabic; and he said they were true characters" (Section 2, verses 62, 63, 64).

According to Joseph Smith then, Martin Harris, his colleague, obtained from the learned Professor Charles Anthon of Columbia University a validation of Smith's translation of the reformed Egyptian hieroglyphic characters found on the plates which Moroni made available to him. The difficulty with Smith's statement is that Professor Anthon never said any such thing, and fortunately he went on record in a lengthy letter to Mr. E. D. Howe, a contemporary of Joseph Smith who did one of the most thorough jobs of research on the Mormon prophet and the origins of Mormonism extant. Howe has never been refuted, and because of this he is feared and hated by Mormon historians and not a few contemporary Mormons.

Upon learning of Smith's claim concerning Professor Anthon, Mr. Howe wrote him at Columbia. Professor Anthon's letter reproduced here from Howe's own collection is a classic piece of evidence the Mormons would like very much to see forgotten.

> New York, N.Y., Feb. 17, 1834
> Mr. E.D. Howe
> Painesville, Ohio

Dear Sir:

I received this morning your favor of the 9th instant, and lose no time in making a reply. The whole story about my having pronounced the Mormonite inscription to be "reformed Egyptian hieroglyphics" *is perfectly false.*[13] Some years ago, a plain, and apparently simplehearted farmer, called upon me with a note from Dr. Mitchell of our city, now deceased, requesting me to decipher, if possible, a paper, which the farmer would hand me, and which Dr. Mitchell confessed he had been unable to understand. Upon examining the paper in question, I soon came to the conclusion that *it was all a trick, perhaps a hoax.* When I asked the person, who brought it, how he obtained the writing, he gave me, as far as I can now recollect, the following account: A "gold book," consisting of a number of plates of gold, fastened together in the shape of a book by wires of the same metal, had been dug up in the northern part of the state of New York, and along with the book an enormous pair of "gold spectacles"! These spectacles were so large, that, if a person attempted to look through them, his two eyes would have to be turned towards one of the glasses merely, the spectacles in question being altogether too large for the breadth of the human face. Whoever examined the plates through the spectacles, was enabled not only to read them, but fully to understand their meaning. All this knowledge, however, was confined at the time to a young man, who had the trunk containing the book and spectacles in his sole possession. This young man was placed behind a curtain, in the garret of a farm house, and, being thus concealed from view, put on the spectacles occasionally, or rather, looked through one of the glasses, deciphered the characters in the book, and, having committed some of them to paper, handed copies from behind the curtain, to those who stood on the outside. Not a word, however, was said about the plates having

---

[13]Italics are the author's for emphasis.

been deciphered "by the gift of God." Everything, in this way, was effected by the large pair of spectacles. The farmer added, that he had been requested to contribute a sum of money towards the publication of the "golden book," the contents of which would, as he had been assured, produce an entire change in the world and save it from ruin. So urgent had been these solicitations, that he intended selling his farm and handing over the amount received to those who wished to publish the plates. As a last precautionary step, however, he had resolved to come to New York, and obtain the opinion of the learned about the meaning of the paper which he brought with him, and which had been given him as a part of the contents of the book, although no translation had been furnished at the time by the young man with the spectacles. *On hearing this odd story, I changed my opinion about the paper, and, instead of viewing it any longer as a hoax upon the learned, I began to regard it as a part of a scheme to cheat the farmer of his money, and I communicated my suspicions to him, warning him to beware of rogues.* He requested an opinion from me in writing, which of course I declined giving, and he then took his leave carrying the paper with him. *This paper was in fact a singular scrawl. It consisted of all kinds of crooked characters disposed in columns, and had evidently been prepared by some person who had before him at the time a book containing various alphabets. Greek and Hebrew letters, crosses and flourishes, Roman letters inverted or placed sideways, were arranged in perpendicular columns, and the whole ended in a rude delineation of a circle, divided into various compartments, decked with various strange marks, and evidently copied after the Mexican Calendar given by Humboldt, but copied in such a way as not to betray the source whence it was derived.* I am thus particular as to the contents of the paper, inasmuch as I have frequently conversed with my friends on the subject, since the Mormonite excitement began, and well remember that *the paper contained anything else but "Egyptian Hieroglyphics."* Some time after, the same farmer paid me a second visit. He brought with him the golden book in print, and offered it to me for sale. I declined purchasing. He then asked permission to leave the book with me for examination. I declined receiving it, although his manner was strangely urgent. I adverted once more to the roguery which had been in my opinion practiced upon him, and asked him what had become of the gold plates. He informed me that they were in a trunk with the large pair of spectacles. I advised him to go to a magistrate and have the trunk examined. He said the "curse of God" would come upon him should he do this. On my pressing him, however, to pursue the course which I had recommended, he told me that he would open the trunk, if I would take the "curse of God" upon myself. I replied that I would do so with the greatest willingness, and would incur every risk of that nature, provided I could only extricate him from the grasp of the rogues. He then left me.

I have thus given you a full statement of all that I know respecting the origin of Mormonism, and must beg you, as a personal favor, to publish this letter immediately, should you find my name mentioned again by these wretched fanatics.

Your respectfully,
Charles Anthon, LL.D.
Columbia University.

Professor Anthon's letter is both revealing and devastating where Smith's and Harris' veracity are concerned. We might also raise the question as to how Professor Anthon could say that the characters shown to him by Martin Harris and authorized by Joseph Smith as part of the material copied from the revelation of the *Book of Mormon* were "Egyptian, Chaldaic, Assyriac, and Arabic" when the *Book of Mormon* itself declares that the characters were "reformed Egyptian," the language of the Nephites. Since the language of the *Book of Mormon* was known to "none other people," how would it be conceivably possible for Professor Anthon to have testified as to the accuracy of Smith's translation? To this date, no one has ever been able to find even the slightest trace of the language known as "reformed Egyptian"; and all reputable linguists who have examined the evidence put forth by the Mormons have rejected them as mythical.

Archeological Evidence

The *Book of Mormon* purports to portray the rise and development of two great civilizations. As to just how great these civilizations were, some excerpts from the book itself adequately illustrate:

"The whole face of the land had become covered with buildings, and the people were as numerous almost, as it were the sand of the sea" (Mormon 1:7).

". . . fine workmanship of wood, in buildings, and in machinery, and also in iron and copper, and brass and steel, makings [*sic.*] all manners of tools. . ." (Jarom 1:8 and 2 Nephi 5:15).

". . . grain . . . silks . . . cattle . . . oxen . . . cows . . . sheep . . . swine . . . goats . . . horses . . . asses . . . elephants. . ." (See Ether 9:17-19).

". . . did multiply and spread . . . began to cover the face of the whole earth, from the sea south to the sea north, from the sea west to the sea east" (Helaman 3:8).

". . . had been slain . . . two millions" [Jaredites] (See Ether 15:2).

". . . their shipping and their building of ships, and their building of temples, and of synagogues and their sanctuaries. . ." (Helaman 3:14. See also 2 Nephi 5:15, 16 and Alma 16:13).

". . . there were ten more who did fall . . . with their ten thousand each. . ." (See Mormon 6:10–15).

". . . swords . . . cimeters . . . breastplates . . . arm-shields . . . shields . . . head-plates . . . armor" (See Alma 43:18, 19; 3:5 and Ether 15:15).

". . . multiplied exceedingly, and spread upon the face of the land, and became exceeding rich. . ." (Jarom 1:8).

See 3 Nephi 8:9, 10, 14 and 9:4, 5, 6, 8: where cities and inhabitants were sunk in the depths of the sea and earth.

In addition to the foregoing statements from the *Book of Mormon* which indicate the tremendous spread of the culture of these races, there are some thirty-eight cities catalogued in the *Book of Mormon*, evidence that these were indeed mighty civilizations which should, by all the laws of archeological research into the culture of antiquity, have left vast amounts of "finds" to be evaluated. But such is not the case as we shall show. The Mormons have yet to explain the fact that leading archeological researchers not only have repudiated the claims of the *Book of Mormon* as to the existence of these civilizations, but have adduced considerable evidence to show the impossibility of the accounts given in the Mormon Bible.

The following letter was addressed to the Rev. R. Odell Brown, pastor of the Hillcrest Methodist Church, Fredericksburg, Virginia, an ardent student of Mormonism and its claims. Dr. Brown, in the course of his research, wrote to the Department of Anthropology at Columbia University in New

York City. The answer he received is of great importance in establishing the fact that the *Book of Mormon* is neither accurate nor truthful where the sciences of archeology and anthropology are concerned.

> Dear Sir:
>   Pardon my delay in answering your letter of January 14, 1957. The question which you ask concerning the *Book of Mormon* is one that comes up quite frequently. . . . However, . . . I may say that I do not believe that there is a single thing of value concerning the prehistory of the American Indian in the *Book of Mormon* and I believe that the great majority of American archeologists would agree with me. The book is untrue Biblically, historically and scientifically,
>   Concerning Dr. Charles Anthon of Columbia University, I do not know who he is and would certainly differ with his viewpoint, as the Latter Day Saints (Mormons) tell it. What possible bearing Egyptian hieroglyphics would have on either the *Book of Mormon* or the prehistory of the American Indian I do not know . . . I am,
>   Very sincerely yours,
>   Wm. Duncan Strong (Signed).

The Smithsonian Institution in Washington has also added its voice against the archeological claims of the *Book of Mormon*. Such a highly regarded scientific source the Mormons can ill afford to ignore.

> 1. The Smithsonian Institution has never used the Book of Mormon in any way as a scientific guide. Smithsonian archeologists see no direct connection between the archeology of the New World and the subject matter of the book.
>   2. The physical type of the American Indian is basically Mongoloid, being most closely related to that of the peoples of eastern, central, and northeastern Asia. Archeological evidence indicates that the ancestors of the present Indians came into the New World—probably over a land bridge known to have existed in the Bering Strait region during the last Ice Age—in a continuing series of small migrations beginning from about 25,000 to 30,000 years ago.
>   3. Present evidence indicates that the first people to reach this continent from the East were the Norsemen who arrived in the northeastern part of North America around A.D. 1000. There is nothing to show that they reached Mexico or Central America.
>   4. One of the main lines of evidence supporting the scientific finding that contacts with Old World civilizations, if indeed they occurred at all, were of very little significance for the development of American Indian civilizations, is the fact that none of the principal Old World domesticated food plants or animals (except the dog) occurred in the New World in pre-Columbian times. American Indians had no wheat, barley, oats, millet, rice, cattle, pigs, chickens, horses, donkeys, camels, etc., before 1492. The domesticated dogs of the Indians accompanied their ancestors from northwestern Asia. Domesticated sweet potatoes occurred in both hemispheres, but probably originated in the New World and spread from there into the Pacific.
>   5. Iron, steel, glass, and silk were not used in the New World before 1492 (except for occasional use of unsmelted meteoric iron). Nuggets of native copper were used in various locations in pre-Columbian times, but true metallurgy was limited to southern Mexico and the Andean region,

where its occurrence in late pre-historic times involved gold, silver, copper, and their alloys, but not iron.

6. There is a possibility that the spread of cultural traits across the Pacific to Mesoamerica and the northwestern coast of South America began several hundred years before the Christian era. However, any such inter-hemispheric contacts appear to have been the results of accidental voyages originating in eastern and southern Asia. It is by no means certain that even such contacts occurred; certainly there were no contacts with the ancient Egyptians, Hebrew, or other peoples of Western Asia and the Near East.

7. No reputable Egyptologist or other specialist on Old World archeology, and no expert on New World prehistory, has discovered or confirmed any relationship between archeological remains in Mexico and archeological remains in Egypt.

8. Reports of findings of ancient Egyptian, Hebrew, and other Old World writings in the New World in pre-Columbian contexts have frequently appeared in newspapers, magazines, and sensational books. None of these claims has stood up to examination by reputable scholars. No inscriptions using Old World forms of writing have been shown to have occurred in any part of the Americas before 1492.

Summer 1979

From this evidence, it is clear that the cities mentioned in the *Book of Mormon* are imaginary, that elephants never existed on this continent, and that the metals described in the *Book of Mormon* have never been found in any of the areas of contemporary civilizations of the New World. Here is not a theologian attempting to discredit the Mormons on the basis of their theology, but recognized archeological experts challenging the *Book of Mormon* on the basis of the fact that its accounts are not in keeping with the findings of science. Mormon missionaries are generally reluctant to discuss these areas when the evidence is well known, but evidence it is and from most authoritative sources.

The Mongoloid Factor

It is one of the main contentions of Mormon theology that the American Indians are the descendants of the Lamanites and that they were of the Semitic race, in fact of Jewish origin. As we have seen, this claim is extensive in Mormon literature; and if evidence could be adduced to show that the American Indian could not possibly be of Semitic extraction, the entire story of Nephi and his trip to America in 600 B.C. would be proven false.

It is, therefore, of considerable value to learn that in the findings compiled by anthropologists and those who specialize in genetics, the various physical factors of the Mediterranean races from which the Jewish or Semitic race spring bear little or no resemblance of those of the American Indian! Genotypically, there is therefore little if any correlation, and phenotypically speaking the American Indians are considered to be *Mongoloid* in extraction, not Mediterranean Caucasoids.

Now, if the Lamanites, as the *Book of Mormon* tells it, were the descendants of Nephi, who was a Jew of the Mediterranean Caucasoid type, then their descendants, the American Indians, would by necessity have the same blood factor genotypically; and phenotypic, or apparent characteristics, would be the same. But this is not at all the case. Instead, the American Indian, so say anthropologists, is not of Semitic extraction and has the definite phenotypical characteristic of a Mongoloid. A thorough study of anthropology and such writers as W. C. Boyd (The Contributions of Genetics to Anthropology) and Bentley Glass, the gifted geneticist of Johns Hopkins University, reveals that the Mormon claims based upon the *Book of Mormon* are out of harmony with the findings of geneticists and anthropologists. There simply is no foundation for the claims that the American Indian (Lamanites according to the Mormons) is in any way related to the race to which Nephi (a Semite) allegedly belonged.

Corrections, Contradictions and Errors

There is a great wealth of information concerning the material contained in the *Book of Mormon* and the various plagiarisms, anachronisms, false prophecies and other unfortunate practices connected with it. At best then we can give but a condensation of that which has been most thoroughly documented.

Since the publication of the *Book of Mormon* in 1830, the first edition has undergone extensive "correction" in order to present it in its present form. Some of these "corrections" should be noted.

1. In the book of Mosiah, chapter 21, verse 28, it is declared that "King Mosiah had a gift from God"; but in the original edition of the book, the name of the king was Benjamin—an oversight which thoughtful Mormon scribes corrected. This is, of course, no typographical error as there is little resemblance between the names Benjamin and Mosiah; so it appears that either God made a mistake when He inspired the record or Joseph made a mistake when he translated it. But the Mormons will admit to neither, so they are stuck, so to speak, with the contradiction.

2. 1 Nephi 19:16–20:1, when compared with the edition of 1830, reveals more than fifty changes in the "inspired *Book of Mormon*," words having been dropped, spelling corrected, and words and phraseology added and turned about. This is a strange way to treat an inspired revelation from God!

3. In the book of Alma 28:14–29:1–11, more than thirty changes may be counted from the original edition, and on page 303 of the original edition the statement, "Yea, decree unto them that decrees which are unalterable," has been expurged. (See Alma 29:4.)

4. On page 25 of the edition of 1830, the *Book of Mormon* declares:

"And the angel said unto me, Behold the Lamb of God, yea, even the eternal Father."

Yet in 1 Nephi 11:21, the later editions of the book read:

"And the angel said unto me: Behold the Lamb of God, yea even the son of the eternal Father!"

5. The Roman Catholic Church should be delighted with page 25 of the original edition of the *Book of Mormon* which confirms one of their dogmas, namely, that Mary is the mother of God.

"Behold, the virgin which thou seest, is the mother of God."

Noting this unfortunate lapse into Romanistic theology, considerate Mormon editors have changed 1 Nephi 11:18 so that it now reads:

"Behold, the virgin whom thou seest, is the mother of the son of God."

From the foregoing which are only a handful of examples of the nearly 4,000 word changes to be found in the *Book of Mormon*, some made as recently as 1981, the reader can see that it is in no sense to be accepted as the Word of God. The Scripture says: "The word of the Lord endureth for ever" (1 Peter 1:25); and our Savior declared:

"Sanctify them through thy truth: thy word is truth" (John 17:17).

The record of the Scripture rings true. The *Book of Mormon,* on the other hand, is patently false in far too many places to be considered coincidence.

Added to the evidence of various revisions, the *Book of Mormon* also contains plagiarisms from the King James Bible, anachronisms, false prophecies and errors of fact which cannot be dismissed. Some of these bear repetition, though they are well known to students of Mormonism.

The testimony of the three witnesses which appear at the front of the *Book of Mormon* (Oliver Cowdery, David Whitmer, and Martin Harris) declares that ". . . an angel of God came down from heaven, and he brought and laid before our eyes, that we beheld and saw the plates, and the engraving thereon. . . ."

It is quite noteworthy that Martin Harris, in his conversation with Professor Anthon relative to the material "translated" from these miraculous plates, denied that he had actually seen them. In fact, when pressed, he stated that he only saw them "with the eye of faith," which is vastly different from a revelation by an angelic messenger.

The Mormons are loath to admit that all three of these witnesses later apostatized from the Mormon faith and were described in most unflattering terms ("thieves and counterfeiters") by their Mormon contemporaries.

A careful check of early Mormon literature also reveals that Joseph Smith and his brother Hyrum wrote three articles against the character of the witnesses of the *Book of Mormon*, which in itself, renders their testimony suspect.

Plagiarisms—The King James Version

According to a careful survey of the *Book of Mormon*, it contains at least 25,000 words from the King James Bible. In fact, verbatim quotations, some of considerable length, have caused the Mormons no end of embarrassment for many years.

The comparison of Moroni chapter 10 with 1 Corinthians 12:1–11, 2 Nephi 14 with Isaiah 4, and 2 Nephi 12 with Isaiah 2 reveals that Joseph Smith made free use of his Bible to supplement the alleged revelation of the golden plates. The book of Mosiah, chapter 14 in the *Book of Mormon,* is a reproduction of the fifty-third chapter of Isaiah the prophet; and 3 Nephi 13:1–18 copies Matthew 6:1–23.

The Mormons naively suggest that when Christ allegedly appeared on the American continent after His resurrection and preached to the Nephites he quite naturally used the same language as recorded in the Bible. They also maintain that when Nephi came to America he brought copies of the Hebrew Scriptures, which account for quotations from the Old Testament. The only difficulty with these excuses is that the miraculous plates upon which they were all inscribed, somehow or another, under translation, came out in King James English without variation approximately a thousand years before this 1611 version was written. Such reasoning on the part of the Mormons strains at the limits of credulity and only they are willing to believe it.

There are other instances of plagiarisms from the King James Bible including paraphrases of certain verses. One of these verses (1 John 5:7) is reproduced in 3 Nephi 11:27, 36. The only difficulty with the paraphrase here is that the text is considered by scholars to be an interpolation missing from all the major manuscripts of the New Testament but present in the King James Bible from which Smith paraphrased it not knowing the difference.

Another example of this type of error is found in 3 Nephi 11:33–34, and is almost a direct quotation from Mark 16:16, a passage regarded by many New Testament Greek scholars as an addition to that gospel by an overzealous scribe. But Joseph Smith was not aware of this either, so he even copied in translational errors, another proof that neither he nor the alleged golden plates were inspired of God.

Two further instances of plagiarisms from the King James Bible which have backfired on the Mormons are worth noting.

In the third chapter of the book of Acts, Peter's classic sermon at Pentecost paraphrases Deuteronomy 18:15–19. While in the process of writing 3 Nephi, Joseph Smith puts Peter's paraphrase in the mouth of Christ when the Savior was allegedly preaching to the Nephites. The prophet overlooked the fact that at the time that Christ was allegedly preaching His sermon, the sermon itself had not yet been preached by Peter.

In addition to this, 3 Nephi makes Christ out to be a liar, when in verse 23 of chapter 20 Christ attributes Peter's words to Moses as a direct quotation when, as we have pointed out, Peter paraphrased the quotation from Moses; and the wording is quite different. But Joseph did not check far enough, hence this glaring error.

Secondly, the *Book of Mormon* follows the error of the King James translation which renders Isaiah 4:5: "For upon all the glory shall be a defense" (See 2 Nephi 14:5).

Modern translations of Isaiah point out that it should read "For over all the glory there will be a canopy," not a defense. The Hebrew word, "chuppah," does not mean defense but a protective curtain or canopy. Smith, of course, did not know this nor did the King James translators from whose work he copied.

There are quite a number of other places where such errors appear, including Smith's insistence in Abraham 1:20 that "Pharaoh signifies king by royal blood," when in reality the dictionary defines the meaning of the term Pharaoh as "a great house or palace."

The Revised Standard Version of the Bible renders Isaiah 5:25: "And their corpses were as refuse in the midst of the streets," correctly rendering the Hebrew *suchah* as refuse, not as "torn." The King James Bible renders the passage: "And their carcases were torn in the midst of the streets." The *Book of Mormon* (2 Nephi 15:25) repeats the King James' text word for word, including the error of mistranslating *suchah,* removing any claim that the *Book of Mormon* is to be taken seriously as reliable material.

Anachronisms and Contradictions

Not only does the *Book of Mormon* plagiarize heavily from the King James Bible, but it betrays a great lack of information and background on the subject of world history and the history of the Jewish people. The Jaredites apparently enjoyed glass windows in the miraculous barges in which they crossed the ocean; and "steel" and a "compass" were known to Nephi despite the fact that neither had been invented, demonstrating once again that Joseph Smith was a poor student of history and of Hebrew customs.

Laban, one of the characters of the *Book of Mormon* (1 Nephi 4:9), makes use of a steel sword; and Nephi himself claims to have had a steel bow (the Mormons justify this by quoting Psalm 18:34 as a footnote in the *Book of Mormon*), but modern translations of the Scripture indicate that the word translated steel in the Old Testament (since steel was nonexistent) is more properly rendered bronze.

Mormons sometimes attempt to defend Nephi's possession of a compass (not in existence in his time) by the fact that Acts 28:13 states: "And from thence we fetched a compass." Modern translations of the Scripture, however, refute this subterfuge by correctly rendering the passage: "And from there we made a circle."

Added to the preceding anachronisms is the fact that the *Book of Mormon* not only contradicts the Bible, but contradicts other revelations purporting to come from the same God who inspired the *Book of Mormon*. The Bible declares that the Messiah of Israel was to be born in Bethlehem (Micah 5:2), and the gospel of Matthew (chapter 2, verse 1) records the fulfillment of this prophecy. But the *Book of Mormon* (Alma 7:9, 10) states:

". . . the son of God cometh upon the face of the earth. And behold, he shall be born of Mary, at Jerusalem, which is the land of our forefathers . . ."

The *Book of Mormon* describes Jerusalem as a city (1 Nephi 1:4) as was Bethlehem, so the contradiction is irreconcilable.

There are also a number of instances where God did not agree with Himself, if indeed it is supposed that He had anything to do with the inspiration of the *Book of Mormon*, the *Pearl of Great Price*, the *Doctrine and Covenants*, or the other recorded utterances of Joseph Smith.

In the *Book of Mormon*, for instance, (3 Nephi 12:2 and Moroni 8:11) the remission of sins is the result of baptism:

"Yea, blessed are they who shall. . .be baptized, for they shall. . .receive the remission of their sin. . .Behold baptism is unto repentance to the fulfilling of the commandments unto the remission of sin."

But in the *Doctrine and Covenants* (Section 20, verse 37), the direct opposite is stated:

"All who humble themsleves. . .and truly manifest by their works that they have received of the spirit of Christ unto the remission of their sins, shall be received by baptism into his church."

This particular message from the heavenlies almost provoked a riot in the Mormon Church, and Mormon theologians conspicuously omit any serious discussion of the contradiction.

Joseph Smith did not limit his contradictions to baptism; indeed polygamy is a classic example of some of his maneuvers.

"God commanded Abraham, and Sarah gave Hagar to Abraham to wife. And why did she do it? Because this was the law; and from Hagar sprang many people. . .Go ye, therefore, and do the works of Abraham; enter ye into my law and ye shall be saved" (*Doctrine and Covenants*, 132:34, 32).

The *Book of Mormon,* on the other hand, categorically states:

"Wherefore, I the Lord God will not suffer that this people shall do like unto them of old. . .for there shall not any man among you have save it be one wife; and concubines he shall have none; for I, the Lord God, delight in the chastity of woman" (Jacob 2:26–28).

It appears that Joseph could manufacture revelations at will, depending upon his desires. In the last instance, his reputation and subsequent actions indicate that sex was the motivating factor.

A final example of the confusion generated between the *Book of Mormon* and other "inspired" revelations is found in this conflict between two works in the *Pearl of Great Price*: the *Book of Moses* and the *Book of Abraham.*

"I am the Beginning and the End, the Almighty God; by mine Only Begotten I created these things; yea, in the beginning I created the heaven, and the earth upon which thou standest" (Moses 2:1).

The *Book of Abraham,* on the other hand, repudiates this monotheistic view and states:

"And then the Lord said: Let us go down. And they went down at the beginning, and they, that is the Gods, organized and formed the heavens and the earth" (Abraham 4:1).

Just how it is possible to reconcile these two allegedly equal pronouncements from Mormon revelation escapes this author, and the Mormons themselves appear reluctant to furnish any concrete explanation.

The question of false prophecies in Mormonism has been handled adequately in a number of excellent volumes, but it should be pointed out that Joseph Smith drew heavily upon published articles both in newspapers and magazines. In fact, one of his famous prophecies concerning the Civil War is drawn chiefly from material published in New York State at the time.

Smith declared in *Doctrine and Covenants*, Section 87:

". . .At the rebellion of South Carolina. . .the Southern States will call on other nations, even the nation of Great Britain. . .and then war shall be poured out upon all nations. . .And. . .slaves shall rise up against their masters. . .and that the remnants. . .shall vex the Gentiles with a sore vexation."

Though the Civil War did break out some years after Smith's death (1844), England did not become involved in war against the United States. "All nations" were not involved in war as prophesied. The slaves did not rise up against "their masters," and the "remnants" who were Indians were themselves vexed by the Gentiles, being defeated in war and confined to reservations.

Prophet Smith was an extremely ineffective prophet here, as he was when in *Doctrine and Covenants* 124:22, 23, 59, he also prophesied that he would possess the house he built at Nauvoo "for ever and ever."

The fact of the matter is that neither Joseph nor his seed "after him" lived from "generation to generation" in Nauvoo house, which was destroyed after Smith's death, and the Mormons moved to Utah.

These, and other instances, indicate that Smith was not only a poor scribe but a false prophet, and his prophecy concerning the restoration of Israel to Palestine clearly reveals that he anticipated the millennium in his own lifetime, whereas in reality the prophecy of Ezekiel 37 began to be fulfilled in 1948, more than a hundred years after Smith's death.

The question quite naturally arises in summing up the background of the *Book of Mormon* —Where did the book come from, since it obviously did not come from God? The answer to this had been propounded at great length by numerous students of Mormonism, particularly E. D. Howe, Pomeroy Tucker and William A. Linn.

All concur that the *Book of Mormon* is probably an expansion upon the writings of Solomon Spaulding, a retired minister who was known to have written a number of "romances" with Biblical backgrounds similar to those of the *Book of Mormon*. The Mormons delight to point out that one of Spaulding's manuscripts, entitled "Manuscript Story," was discovered in Hawaii more than 100 years ago, and it differed in many respects from the *Book of Mormon*.

But in his excellent volume (*The Book of Mormon?*), Dr. James D. Bales makes the following observation, which is of great importance and agrees in every detail with my research over the last decade:

> It has long been contended that there is a connection between the *Book of Mormon* and one of Solomon Spaulding's historical romances. The Latter-day Saints, of course, deny such a connection.
>
> What if the Latter Day Saints are right and there is no relationship between the *Book of Mormon* and Spaulding's writings? It simply means that those who so contend are wrong, but it proves nothing with reference to the question as to whether or not the *Book of Mormon* is of divine origin. One could be wrong as to what man, or men, wrote the *Book of Mormon*, and still know that it was not written by men inspired of God. One can easily prove that the *Book of Mormon* is of human origin. And, after all, this is the main issue. The fundamental issue is not *what* man or men wrote it, but whether it was written by men who were guided by God. We know that men wrote it, and that these men, whoever they were, did not have God's guidance.
>
> This may be illustrated by *Science and Health With Key to the Scriptures*— the textbook of Christian Science churches. Mrs. Eddy claims to have been its author, under God's direction. There are others who claim she reworked and enlarged a manuscript of Mr. Quimby and the evidence seems to prove that such is the case. But what if those who so maintained failed to prove their case? Would that prove that it was inspired of God? Not at all, it would prove only that Quimby's manuscript had nothing to do with it. But it would not prove that some other uninspired being did not write it. Regardless of what human being or beings wrote *Science and Health*, it is of human, not

divine origin. Just so the *Book of Mormon* is of human origin and uninspired, even though it were impossible to prove what particular man wrote it.

It has not been maintained that all the *Book of Mormon* was written by Spaulding. Thus, it has not been claimed that the theological portions were put in by him. Those portions bear the imprint of Smith, Cowdery and Sidney Rigdon (see the proof offered in Shook's *The True Origin of the Book of Mormon*, pp. 126–). It is maintained, however, that some things, including a great deal of Scripture, were added to one of Spaulding's manuscripts and that his work was thus transferred into the *Book of Mormon* (see the testimony of John Spaulding, Solomon's brother; Martha Spaulding, John's wife): They maintained that the historical portion was Spaulding's. (E. D. Howe, *Mormonism Unveiled*, 1834, pp. 278–; Shook, *The True Origin of the Book of Mormon*, pp. 94–).

The Mormons contend that the discovery of one of Spaulding's manuscripts demonstrates that it was not the basis of the Book of Mormon.

"I will here state that the Spaulding manuscript was discovered in 1884, and is at present in the library of Oberlin College, Ohio. On examination it was found to bear no resemblance whatever to the *Book of Mormon*. The theory that Solomon Spaulding was the author of the *Book of Mormon* should never be mentioned again—outside a museum." (William A. Morton, *op. cit.*, p. 6.)

There are three errors in the above paragraph: viz, that Spaulding wrote but one manuscript; that the manuscript discovered in 1884 is the one which non-Mormons have claimed constituted the basis of the *Book of Mormon*; that the manuscript in Oberlin bears no resemblance whatever to the *Book of Mormon*.

(a) *Spaulding wrote more than one manuscript.* This was maintained by D. P. Harlburt and Clark Braden before the Honolulu manuscript was found (Charles A. Shook, *op. cit.*, p. 77). Spaulding's daughter also testified that her father had written "other romances." (Elder George Reynolds, *The Myth of the "Manuscript Found,"* Utah, 1833, p. 104). The present manuscript story looks like a rough, unfinished, first draft.

(b) *The manuscript found in Honolulu was called a "Manuscript Story" and not the "Manuscript Found."* This Honolulu manuscript, *The Manuscript Story*, was in the hands of anti-Mormons in 1834. However, they did not claim that it was the manuscript which was the basis of the *Book of Mormon*. It was claimed that another manuscript of Spaulding was the basis of the *Book of Mormon*, (Charles A. Shook, *op. cit.*, pp. 77, 15, 185. The *"Manuscript Found or Manuscript Story"* of the late Rev. Solomon Spaulding, Lamoni, Iowa: Printed and Published by the Reorganized Church of Jesus Christ of Latter-day Saints, 1885, p. 10).

(c) Although the *Manuscript Story* has not been regarded as the *Manuscript Found*, which constituted the basis of the *Book of Mormon*, there is a great deal of resemblance between the *Manuscript* and the *Book of Mormon*. These points of similarity can be accounted for upon the basis that the *Manuscript Story* was the first, and rough draft of one of Spaulding's works which he reworked into the *Manuscript Found*.

"Howe, in 1834, published a fair synopsis of the Oberlin manuscript now at Oberlin (Howe's *Mormonism Unveiled*, p. 288) and submitted the original to the witnesses who testified to the many points of identity between Spaulding's *Manuscript Found* and the *Book of Mormon*. These witnesses then (in 1834) recognized the manuscript secured by Harlburt and now at Oberlin, as being one of Spaulding's, but not the one which they asserted was similar to the *Book of Mormon*. They further said that Spaulding had told them that he had altered his original plan of writing by going farther back with his dates and writing in the old scripture style, in order that his story might appear more ancient" (Howe's *Mormonism Unveiled*, p. 288; Theodore Schroeder, *The Origin of the Book of Mormon, Re-Examined in Its Relation to Spaulding's "Manuscript Found,"* p. 5).

This testimony is borne out by the fact that there are many points of similarity between the manuscript in Oberlin College and the Book of Mormon.[14]

It is then fairly well established, historically, that the Mormons have attempted to use a manuscript admittedly *not* the one from which Smith later copied and amplified the text of what is now known as the *Book of Mormon* as the basis for denying what eye witnesses have affirmed, namely that it was another Spaulding Manuscript (*Manuscript Found*) which Smith drew upon to fabricate the Mormon Bible.

Dr. Bales is right when he states:

There are too many points of similarity for them to be without significance. Thus, the internal evidence, combined with the testimony of witnesses, as presented in Howe's book and reproduced in Shook's, show that Spaulding revised the Manuscript Story. The revision was known as the *Manuscript Found*, and it became the basis of the *Book of Mormon* in at least its historical parts. Also its religious references furnished in part the germs of the religious portions of the *Book of Mormon*.

However, in ordinary conversation, and in public debate on the *Book of Mormon*, it is unnecessary to go into the question of who wrote the *Book of Mormon*. The really important issue is whether or not the *Book of Mormon* is of divine origin. There are some Mormons who seem to think that if they can prove that Spaulding's manuscript had nothing to do with the *Book of Mormon*, they have made great progress toward proving its divine origin. Such, however, is not the case. And one should show, from an appeal to the Bible, and to the *Book of Mormon* itself, that the *Book of Mormon* is not of divine origin.[15]

Let us not forget that the *Manuscript Story* itself contains at least 75 similarities to what is now the *Book of Mormon* and this is not to be easily explained away.

Finally, students of Mormonism must, in the last analysis, measure its content by that of Scripture, and when this is done it will be found that it does not "speak according to the law and the testimony" (Isaiah 8:20) and it is to be rejected as a counterfeit revelation doubly condemned by God Himself (Galatians 1:8, 9).

Joseph Smith, the author of this "revelation," was perfectly described (as was his reward) in the Word of God almost thirty-three hundred years before he appeared. It would pay the Mormons to remember this message:

If there arise among you a prophet, or a dreamer of dreams, and giveth thee a sign or a wonder,

And the sign or the wonder come to pass, whereof he spake unto thee,

[14]*The Book of Mormon?* by James D. Bales, Ph.D., The Manney Company, Fort Worth 14, Texas, pp. 138–142.
[15]*Ibid.*, pp. 146, 147.

saying, Let us go after other gods, which thou hast not known, and let us serve them;

Thou shalt not hearken unto the words of that prophet, or that dreamer of dreams: for the Lord your God proveth you, to know whether ye love the Lord your God with all your heart and with all your soul.

Ye shall walk after the Lord your God, and fear him, and keep his commandments, and obey his voice, and ye shall serve him, and cleave unto him.

And that prophet, or that dreamer of dreams, shall be put to death; because he hath spoken to turn you away from the Lord your God, which brought you out of the land of Egypt, and redeemed you out of the house of bondage, to thrust thee out of the way which the Lord thy God commanded thee to walk in. So shalt thou put the evil away from the midst of thee.

If thy brother, the son of thy mother, or thy son, or thy daughter, or the wife of thy bosom, or thy friend, which is as thine own soul, entice thee secretly, saying, Let us go and serve other gods, which thou has not known, thou, nor thy fathers;

Namely, of the gods of the people which are round about you, nigh unto thee, or far off from thee, from the one end of the earth even unto the other end of the earth:

Thou shalt not consent unto him, nor hearken unto him; neither shall thine eye pity him, neither shalt thou spare, neither shalt thou conceal him:

But thou shalt surely kill him; thine hand shall be first upon him to put him to death, and afterwards the hand of all the people.

And thou shalt stone him with stones, that he die; because he hath sought to thrust thee away from the Lord thy God, which brought thee out of the land of Egypt, from the house of bondage (Deuteronomy 13:1–10).

The *Book of Mormon,* then, stands as a challenge to the Bible because it adds to the Word of God and to His one revelation, and the penalty for such action is as sobering as it is awesome:

For I testify unto every man that heareth the words of the prophecy of this book, If any man shall add unto these things, God shall add unto him the plagues that are written in this book:

And if any man shall take away from the words of the book of this prophecy, God shall take away his part out of the book of life, and out of the holy city, and from the things which are written in this book.

He which testifieth these things saith, Surely I come quickly. Amen. Even so, come, Lord Jesus (Revelation 22:18–20).

We need not make this a personal issue with the Mormons but a historical and theological issue which, for all the politeness and tact demonstrably possible, cannot conceal the depth of our disagreement. Even the famous "witnesses" to the veracity of the *Book of Mormon* are impugned by history, since Prophet Smith wrote two articles against them and Hyrum, his brother, wrote one. This does not speak well for the characters of those concerned, nor for their reliability as witnesses.

It was Joseph Smith who declared theological war on Christianity when he ascribed to God the statement that branded all Christian sects as "all wrong," their creeds as "abominations," and all Christians as "corrupt. . .having a form of godliness, but they deny the power thereof" (Joseph Smith—History 1:19).

The onus of hostility rests upon the Mormons, and their history of persecution (largely the result of their mouthing of Smith's abusive accusations and their practice of polygamy) may be properly laid at their own doorstep. They were the initial antagonists, *not* the Christian Church. We do not excuse those who persecuted the early Mormons, but they were in a great many instances provoked to action by Mormon excesses. (Note: An example of this would be the Mormon expulsion from Jackson County, Missouri.)

We may, then, safely leave the Mormon Bible to the judgment of history and Mormon theology to the pronouncements of God's immutable Word. But we must speak the truth about these things and keep foremost in our minds the fact that the sincerity of the Mormons in their faith is no justification for withholding just criticism of that faith or of its refuted source, the *Book of Mormon* and the "revelations" of Joseph Smith. The truth must be spoken in love, but it must be spoken.

The Theology of Mormonism

The Mormon church almost from its inception has claimed what no other church today claims to possess, namely, the priesthoods of Aaron and Melchizedek.

The Mormons maintain that Joseph Smith and Oliver Cowdery received the Aaronic priesthood from the hand of John the Baptist on May 15, 1829, and that "the Melchizedek priesthood was conferred upon Joseph Smith and Oliver Cowdery through the ministration of Peter, James, and John, shortly after the conferring of the Aaronic order."[16]

In the theology of Mormonism, both the Melchizedek and Aaronic orders are considered to be but one priesthood "without beginning of days or end of years" (*Doctrine and Covenants* 84:17), and through the authority of this priesthood alone, they maintain, men speak and act in the name of the Lord for the salvation of humanity. In order that this may be clearly understood, the following quotation from the leading Mormon volume on the subject of the priesthood must be considered:

> This authoritative Priesthood is designed to assist men in all of life's endeavors, both temporal and spiritual. Consequently, there are divisions or offices of the Priesthood, each charged with a definite duty, fitting a special human need.
>
> The Prophet Joseph Smith once said that all Priesthood is Melchizedek. That is to say that the Melchizedek Priesthood embraces all offices and authorities in the Priesthood. This is clearly stated in the *Doctrine and Covenants*, Section 107, Verse 5: "All other authorities or offices in the church are appendages to this Priesthood."
>
> There are two Priesthoods spoken of in the Scriptures, the Melchizedek and the Aaronic or Levitical. Although there are two Priesthoods, yet the Melchizedek Priesthood comprehends the Aaronic or Levitical Priesthood;

---

[16]John A. Widtsoe, *The Priesthood and Church Government*, Salt Lake City, UT: Deseret Book Company, 1939, p. 107.

and is the grand head, and holds the highest authority which pertains to the Priesthood, and the keys of the Kingdom of God in all ages of the world to the latest prosperity on the earth; and is the channel through which all knowledge, doctrine, the plan of salvation and every important matter is revealed from heaven.[17]

The Mormon concept of the priesthood, then, holds that God has placed in that church presidents, apostles, high priests, seventies, elders; and that the various offices all share specific authorities.

The president of the church, they maintain, "may hold and dispense the powers of the administrative responsibilities of that office, the power of the Priesthood is decentralized; first according to offices and the jurisdictions of those respective offices; second according to individual Priesthood-bearers. This means that while the Church as a whole is delicately responsive to central authority for church-wide purposes, the central-local relationships in the organization do not restrict the full initiative and free development of either territorial divisions of the Church individual quorums, groups of quorums, or the member as an individual. . .The Priesthood provides a "functional" instrumentality for Church Government which is at once efficient and responsible in centralization, but flexible and decentralized in actual administration."[18] It is apparent, then, that in Mormon theology the priesthood occupies a position of great importance and comprehends nearly every male member of the church above the age of twelve in one capacity or another; and therefore by necessity the refutation of the Mormon claims to its possession undercuts the very foundations of Mormonism.[19]

With the foregoing in mind, let us examine the Scriptures which most thoroughly refute the Mormon contentions, and the Scripture indeed provides a wealth of information.

In the seventh chapter of the epistle to the Hebrews, Melchizedek, who was the king of Salem and priest of the Most High God is mentioned briefly in connection with Abraham. The author of Hebrews points out that the priesthood of Melchizedek is superior to the Aaronic priesthood and the administrations of the Levites because Abraham, who was the father of the sons of Levi paid tithe to Melchizedek. This establishes the fact that Melchizedek was superior to Abraham. The writer of Hebrews puts it this way: "And without all contradiction the less is blessed of the better. And here men that die receive tithes; but there he receiveth them, of whom it is witnessed that he liveth. And as I may so say, Levi also, who receiveth tithes, paid tithes in Abraham. For he was yet in the loins of his father, when Melchizedek met him" (verses 7–10).

The establishment of the fact that the Melchizedek priesthood is superior to the Aaronic would be virtually meaningless unless the writer of Hebrews had gone on to say:

"If therefore perfection were by the Levitical priesthood (for under it

[17]*Ibid.*, pp. 102, 103.
[18]*Ibid.*, p. 103.
[19]Until June of 1978, men of African descent were denied the priesthood because of a teaching that they were under a curse for their lack of valiance in their pre-mortal existence. Under this ban they were unable to attain the status of "exaltation" (godhood).

the people received the law) what further need was there that another priest should rise after the order of Melchizedek, and not be called after the order of Aaron? For the priesthood being *changed*, there is made of necessity a change also of the law."

The whole point of the seventh chapter of Hebrews, as any careful exegesis will reveal, is the fact that Jesus Christ who is "a priest forever after the order of Melchizedek" (verse 17) has, by virtue of His sacrifice upon the cross, changed the priesthood of Aaron (verse 12), instituting in its place His own priesthood of the Melchizedek order.

Christ was not of the tribe of Levi and not of the priesthood of Aaron; He was of the tribe of Judah, yet His priesthood is infinitely superior to that of Aaron. It is quite evident that the Levitical priesthood could not evolve into the Melchizedek priesthood, but that it passed away as symbolized by the tearing of the veil leading to the Holy of Holies at the crucifixion (Matthew 27:51).

The writer of Hebrews further states that Christ is our great High Priest and that He has "passed through the heavenlies" to "appear in the presence of God for us." In addition to this, it is declared that "Christ is not entered into the holy places made with hands, which are the figures of the true; but into heaven itself. . .Nor yet that he should offer himself often, as the high priest entereth into the holy place every year with blood of others; for then must he often have suffered since the foundation of the world: but now once in the end of the world hath he appeared to put away sin by the sacrifice of himself" (Hebrews 9:24–26).

The previous reference is clearly to the truth that the old priesthood, which enabled the priests to enter into the temple apartment once every year on the day of atonement, had come to a close because Christ has once offered an eternal atonement for the sins of all the world (1 John 2:2).

How significant indeed are these facts when placed beside the Mormon claim to possession of the Aaronic priesthood which God's Word says has been "changed" and completely consummated in the Priest whose order is after Melchizedek, Jesus Christ Himself.

Our Lord's priesthood is not dependent upon its continuation from father to son, as the Aaronic was through the Levitical order, something which was necessitated by virtue of the fact that all men die; hence its transference. But the writer of Hebrews tells us that the Lord Jesus Christ "arose after the similitude of Melchizedek." He is "another priest" who is made "not after the law of carnal commandment," (which is temporary by nature) but after the power of imperishable life. The Greek word, *akatalutou*, is rightly translated "imperishable, indestructible and indissoluble"; and in this context it refers to His life. He was not consecrated a priest as were the Levites from father to son, but His priesthood is after the order of endless Being. His is an infinite priesthood because He is eternal.

All this background is of vital importance in refuting the Mormon claims to the perpetuity of the Aaronic priesthood, but even more so in refuting their concept of the Melchizedek priesthood which they also claim to have received.

In the same seventh chapter of Hebrews, this second Mormon claim is tersely dispensed with by the Holy Spirit in an emphatic and irrevocable manner.

> By so much was Jesus made a surety of a better testament. And they truly were many priests, because they were not suffered to continue by reason of death: But this man, because he continueth ever, hath an unchangeable priesthood. Wherefore he is able to save them to the uttermost that come unto God by him, seeing he ever liveth to make intercession for them. For such an high priest became us, who is holy, harmless, undefiled, separate from sinners, and made higher than the heavens; who needeth not daily, as those high priests, to offer up sacrifice, first for his own sins, and then for the people's: for this he did once, when he offered up himself. For the law maketh men high priests which have infirmity; but the word of the oath, which was since the law, maketh the Son, who is consecrated for evermore" (verses 22–28).

Particular attention should be paid to verse 24, which, in the Greek, is devastating to the Mormon claim. Verse 24, in Greek, literally reads:

"But he continues forever, so his priesthood is untransferable"[20] (Goodspeed).

The Greek word, *aparabatos*, literally rendered as *untransferable*, carries the note of finality. Thayer's *Greek-English Lexicon* puts it this way:

"Priesthood unchangeable and therefore not liable to pass to a successor, Hebrew 7:24" (p. 54).

Since the word appears but once in New Testament Greek, there is not even the appeal to possible contextual renderings. Here is one instance where no amount of semantic juggling can escape the force of the context and grammar.

The writer of Hebrews, under the the inspiration of the Holy Spirit, declares that the priesthood of Melchizedek is the peculiar possession of Jesus Christ, not only by virtue of the fact that He is God, and possessed of imperishable life, but because it cannot be transferred to another. It consummated the Aaronic priesthood; it terminated the Levitical order; it resides in the Son of God, and by the will of His Father, it cannot be transferred. There is no escape from the force of these revelations of Scripture, and no exegetical theologian or commentator has ever held otherwise. It is all well and good for the Mormons to claim the priesthoods of Aaron and Melchizedek, but it should be pointed out that they do so by contradicting the expressed teaching of the Word of God which they claim to respect. And this discrepancy no Mormon theologian has ever attempted to explain.

In his interesting and informative booklet, *Gods, Sex, and the Saints*, Dr. George Arbaugh makes the following observation. "The Mormons are advised that the harvest is ripe and that the sickle should be thrust into the Christian churches. The bold proselyting usually includes certain stereotyped challenges, questions and arguments" (p. 39).

---

[20]The Mormon claim that Melchizedek conferred his priesthood on Abraham when the latter paid tithe to him (Genesis 18) finds no support in Scripture. (*Priesthood and Church Government*, John A. Widtsoe, p. 109). Mormons should be pressed at this juncture for the Biblical evidence, the absence of which affords further opportunity to undercut their already weakened position.

Dr. Arbaugh then goes on to point out that the priesthood is one of the areas the Mormons emphasize. They never tire of stating to any and all who will listen, particularly to those who are likely proselytes, "You do not have the priesthood!"

To answer this, the alert Christian should point out that the Mormons themselves do not have any priesthood but that the Church of Jesus Christ has always had a priesthood, a priesthood very clearly taught in the New Testament. This priesthood was emphasized by the great Reformation theologian, Martin Luther, who described it as "the priesthood of all believers."

Dr. Arbaugh rightly observes:

"There are many millions more priests in the Lutheran Church than in the Latter-day Saint organization, for this reason that every believer is a priest. There is a universal priesthood of believers. This means that each believer can come to God in prayer, in his own right, and that he can speak about his Lord to his fellow men. He need not wait for some priest to do the essential Christian things for him. For that matter how could any priest do the essential Christian thing for you, namely, to love God and your fellow man also?

"In the original Mormon Church the only officers were elders, but subsequently many additional offices were established. For this reason *Doctrine and Covenants*, Section 20, verses 65 through 67, was 'corrected' from the original form in the *Book of Commandments*. Mormonism even stoops to falsifying its scriptures in order to pretend that there have been the same priestly offices in all ages" (p. 44).

The True Priesthood

In the opening sentences of the book of the Revelation, John the Apostle makes an astounding statement when he declares:

"Blessing and peace to you from him who is, and was, and is coming, and from the seven spirits before his throne and from Jesus Christ, the trustworthy witness, the first born of the dead, the sovereign of the kings of the earth. To him who loves us and has released us from our sins by his own blood—he has made us a kingdom of priests for his God and Father—to him be glory and power forever" (Goodspeed, verses 4–6).

How incisive is this plain declaration by apostolic authority. Jesus Christ who is the sovereign of the kings of the earth, the one who continues to love us and who has released us from our sins through His own blood, has also made us "a kingdom of priests for His God and Father." Here is the true priesthood indeed.

The Christian does not need any temples, secret services, rituals, and mysteries. His priesthood knows no special offices and power to communicate with the dead, something which the Mormon priesthood most definitely claims (See *Leaves from the Tree*, a catechism for young people by Mormon leader Charles Penrose, p. 38). The Christian priesthood embraces all those who have been loosed from their sins by the blood of Jesus Christ, and who enjoy the perpetual love of the Lamb of God who takes away the sins of the world.

This concept is further developed in the writings of Peter, who affirms that:

"You are the chosen race, the *royal priesthood,* the consecrated nation, his own people, so that you may declare the virtues of him who has called you out of darkness into his wonderful light; you who were once no people, but are now God's people; once unpitied, but now pitied indeed. . ." (1 Peter 2:9 and 10, Goodspeed).

In this context, the words of the apostle establish that long before there were any mythological Mormon priesthoods, there was a priesthood embracing all the redeemed, a "royal priesthood," neither Aaronic nor Melchizedek. This priesthood is composed of all consecrated "ambassadors for Christ," to quote the Apostle Paul, whose task it is to exhort men to "be reconciled to God," "knowing the terror of the Lord" (2 Corinthians 5:20 and 11).

As has been observed, Mormonism places great stress upon the priesthood. But as we have also seen, it is not the priesthood described in the Scriptures. Instead they have substituted the revelation of "Prophet" Smith concerning a priesthood which has been changed (Hebrews 7:12) and a priesthood which by its nature is "untransferable" (7:24). The resulting dilemma is that they have no priesthood at all since their denial of the true Deity of Jesus Christ and the nature of God rules out the possibility that they could share in the priesthood of all believers. In order for one to be one of the "kingdom of priests to God His Father" (Revelation 1:4–6) and a member of the "royal priesthood" (1 Peter 2:9, 10), one must first have undergone personal regeneration in a saving encounter or experience with the God-Man of Scripture—Jesus Christ. Mormon theology with its pantheon of gods, its perverted view of the Virgin Birth, and its outright condemnation of all churches as an "abomination" (Joseph Smith—History 1:19), removes itself from serious consideration as a form of Christianity. There is more to Christianity than the application of the Christian ethic. There is a great deal more to the Gospel than the similarity of terms, albeit redefined. Christianity is not just a system of doctrinal pronouncements (though they are of vast importance). It is a living vital experience with the God of the Bible as He was incarnate in the man from Nazareth. Mormonism, with its many doctrinal vagaries and outright denials of historic Christian teachings, disqualifies itself. And its priesthood, on which it places so much emphasis, is shown to be the antithesis of the divine revelation.

It is to be earnestly hoped that more Christians will acquaint themselves with the Biblical evidence concerning the true priesthood in which we all participate. It is only when a thorough understanding of the fundamentals of Christian theology is obtained that it is possible to successfully encounter and refute the Mormon doctrine of the priesthood.

The Mormon Doctrine of God

It will be conceded by most informed students of Christianity that one cannot deny the existence of the one true God of Scripture and at the same time lay claim to being a Christian. The New Testament writers, as well as our Lord Himself, taught that there was but one God, and all church theologians from the earliest days of church history have affirmed that Christianity is monotheistic in the strictest sense of the term. Indeed it was this fact that so radically differentiated it and the parental Judaism from the pagan, polytheistic societies of Rome and Greece. The Bible is particularly adamant in its declaration that God recognizes the existence of no other "deities." In fact, on a number of occasions the Lord summed up His uniqueness in the following revelation:

> Ye are my witnesses, saith the Lord, and my servant whom I have chosen: that ye may know and believe me, and understand that I am he: before me there was no God formed, neither shall there be after me. I, even I, am the Lord; and beside me there is no savior. . .Thus saith the Lord the King of Israel, and his redeemer the Lord of hosts; I am the first, and I am the last; and *beside me there is no God.* . .Ye are even my witnesses. Is there a God beside me? *yea, there is no God; I know not any.* . .I am the Lord, and there is none else, *there is no God beside me:* I girded thee, though thou hast not known me: . . . *There is no God else beside me;* a just God and a Saviour; *there is none beside me.* Look unto me, and be ye saved, all the ends of the earth: *for I am God, and there is none else* (Isaiah 43:10, 11; 44:6, 8; 45:5, 21, 22).

Throughout the Old Testament, God is known by many titles. He is Elohim, Jehovah, Adonai, El Gebor, and He is also spoken of by combinations of names, such as Jehovah-Elohim, Jehovah-Sabaoth, etc. If the Hebrew Old Testament tells us anything, it is the fact that there is but one God: "Hear, O hear, Israel: The Lord our God is one Lord" (Deuteronomy 6:4). And Jewish monotheism, as all know, at length gave birth to Christian monotheism, the one developing from the other by progressive revelation from God the Holy Spirit. It is not necessary to belabor the point; it is common knowledge that the facts as they have been stated are true. But as we approach our study of the Mormon concept of God, a subtle yet radical change takes place in the usage of the vocabulary of Scripture as we shall shortly see.

It must also be admitted at the outset that the Bible does designate certain individuals as "gods," such as Satan who is described by Christ as "the prince of this world" and elsewhere in Scripture as "the god of this world." It must be clearly understood, however, that whenever this term is assigned to individuals, to spirit personalities, and the like, metaphorical and contextual usage must be carefully analyzed so that a clear picture emerges. For instance, the Lord declared to Moses: "See, I have made thee a god to Pharaoh: and Aaron thy brother shall be thy prophet" (Exodus 7:1). The Hebrew indicates here, when cross-referenced with Exodus 4:16 ("And he shall be even to thee in place of a mouth, and thou shalt be to him in place of God") that a definite relationship was involved. The context also reveals that Moses, by virtue of the power invested in him by God, became in the eyes of Pharoah "a god." Aaron in turn became a prophet of the "god" (Moses) that Pharaoh beheld, since he was the spokesman for Moses. So metaphorical usage is obviously intended, from the very usage of the language and its contextual analysis. On this point all Old Testament scholars are agreed. But this should never cloud the issue, that there is only one true and living God as the previous quotations readily attest.

Another instance of similar usage is the application of the term "Elohim," the plural usage of the term often translated God in the Old Testament. In some contexts the judges of Israel are referred to as "gods," not that they themselves possessed the intrinsic Nature of Deity but that they became in the eyes of the people as gods, or more literally "mighty ones" (Psalm 82 cf. John 10) representing, as they did, the Lord of Hosts. In the New Testament usage, the Apostle Paul is quite explicit when he declares that in the world, i.e., as far as the world is concerned, "there are lords many and gods many, but to us there is one God the Father and one Lord Jesus Christ" (1 Corinthians 8:5), a statement emphasized by our Lord when He stated: "I am the first and I am the last, I am He that liveth and became dead, and behold I am alive for evermore" (Revelation 1:17, 18). We conclude, then, that polytheism is totally foreign to the Judeo-Christian tradition of theology. In fact, it is the antithesis of the extreme monotheism portrayed in Judaism and Christianity. The God of the Old Testament and the God and Father of our Lord Jesus Christ are one and the same Person; this the Christian Church has always held. In addition to this, God's Nature has always been declared to be that of pure spirit. Our Lord declared that "God is spirit, and they that worship Him must worship Him in spirit and in truth" (John 4:24—Greek). In numerous other places within the pages of the inspired Word of God, the Holy Spirit has been pleased to reveal God's spiritual nature and "oneness." The Apostle Paul reminds us that "a mediator is not a mediator of one, but God is one" (Galatians 3:20), the Psalmist reminds us of His unchangeable Nature, "From everlasting to everlasting thou art God" (Psalm 90:2), and Moses records in the initial act of creation that "the Spirit of God brooded over the face of the waters" (Genesis 1:2). The "gods" mentioned in Scripture, then, are never gods by either identity or nature, they are "gods" by human creation or acclamation as we have seen. This, then, is a far cry from comparison with the one true and living God described by the writer of the epistle to the Hebrews as "the Father of spirits" (Hebrews 12:9; Galations 4:8, 9).

The Truth About the god of the Mormons

In sharp contrast to the revelations of Scripture are the "revelations" of Joseph Smith, Brigham Young, and the succeeding Mormon "prophets." So that the reader will have no difficulty in understanding what the true Mormon position is concerning the Nature of God, the following set of quotations in the context, derived from recognized Mormon sources fully portray what the Mormons mean when they speak of "God."

1. "In the beginning, the head of the Gods called a council of the Gods; and they came together and concocted a plan to create the world and people it" (*Teachings of the Prophet Joseph Smith,* p. 349).

2. *"God himself was once as we are now, and is an exalted man, . . ."*(*Teachings of the Prophet Joseph Smith,* p. 345).

3. "The Father has a body of flesh and bones as tangible as man's: the Son also; but the Holy Ghost has not a body of flesh and bones, but is a personage of Spirit. . . " (*Doctrine and Covenants* 130:22).

4. "Gods exist, and we had better strive to be prepared to be one with them" (Brigham Young, *Journal of Discourses*, Vol. 7, p. 238).

5. "As man is, God once was: as God is, man may become" (Prophet Lorenzo Snow, quoted in Milton R. Hunter, *The Gospel Through the Ages*, pp. 105, 106).

6. "Each of these Gods, including Jesus Christ and His Father, being in possession of not merely an organized spirit, but a glorious immortal body of flesh and bones. . ." (Parley P. Pratt, *Key to the Science of Theology*, ed. 1965, p. 44).

7. "And then the Lord said: Let us go down. And they went down at the beginning, and they, that is the Gods, organized and formed the heavens and the earth" (Abraham 4:1).

8. "Remember that God, our heavenly Father, was perhaps once a child, and mortal like we ourselves, and rose step by step in the scale of progress, in the school of advancement; has moved forward and overcome, until He has arrived at the point where He now is" (Apostle Orson Hyde, *Journal of Discourses*, Vol. 1, p. 123).

9. "Mormon prophets have continuously taught the sublime truth that God the Eternal Father was once a mortal man who passed through a school of earth life similar to that through which we are now passing. He became God—an exalted being—through obedience to the same eternal Gospel truths that we are given opportunity to obey" (Hunter, *op. cit.*, p. 104).

10. " Christ was the God, the Father of all things. . .Behold, I am Jesus Christ. I am the Father and the Son" (Mosiah 7:27 and Ether 3:14, *Book of Mormon*).

11. "When our father Adam came in the garden of Eden, he came into it with a celestial body, and brought Eve, one of his wives, with him. He helped to make and organized this world. He is MICHAEL, the Archangel, the ANCIENT OF DAYS! about whom holy men have written and spoken— HE is our FATHER and our GOD, and the only God with whom we have to do"[21] (Brigham Young, in the *Journal of Discourses*, Vol. 1, p. 50).

12. Historically this doctrine of Adam-God was hard for even faithful Mormons to believe. As a result, on June 8, 1873, Brigham Young stated:

"How much unbelief exists in the minds of the Latter-day Saints in regard to one particular doctrine which I revealed to them, and which God revealed unto me—namely that Adam is our father and our God. . . .

" 'Well,' says one, 'Why was Adam called Adam?' He was the first man on the earth, and its framer and maker. He with the help of his brethren, brought it into existence. Then he said, 'I want my children who are in the spirit world to come and live here. I once dwelt upon an earth something like this, in a mortal state. I was faithful, I received my crown and exaltation' " (*Deseret News*, June 18, 1873, p. 308).

It would be quite possible to continue quoting sources from many volumes and other official Mormon publications, but the fact is well established.

The Reorganized Church of Jesus Christ of Latter Day Saints which

---

[21]It is important to note that Brigham Young taught that he had "never yet preached a sermon and sent it out to the children of men, that they may not call *Scripture*" (*Journal of Discourses*, Vol. 13, p. 95). That includes the Adam-God Doctrine.

disagrees with the Utah church on the subject of polytheism, steadfastly maintains that Joseph Smith, Jr. never taught or practiced either polygamy or polytheism, but the following direct quotation from Smith relative to the plurality of gods and the doctrine that Mormon males may attain to godhood vexes the Reorganized Church to no end. But, it is fact, nonetheless.

The following quotations are excerpted from a sermon published in the Mormon newspaper *Times and Seasons* (August 15, 1844, pp. 613–614) published four months after Smith delivered it at the funeral of Elder King Follet and only two months after Smith's assassination in Carthage, Illinois.

This discourse was heard by more than 18,000 people and recorded by four Mormon scribes. It is significant that the split in Mormonism did not take place for more than three and one-half years. So apparently their ancestors did not disagree with Smith's theology, as they themselves do today. Nor did they deny that Smith preached the sermon and taught polytheism, as does the Reorganized Church today. But the facts must speak for themselves:

"I want you all to know God, to be familiar with him,. . .What sort of a being was God in the beginning?

"First, God himself, who sits enthroned in yonder heavens, is a man like unto one of yourselves,. . .if you were to see him today, you would see him in all the person, image and very form as a man. . .

"I am going to tell you how God came to be God. We have imagined that God was God from all eternity. These are incomprehensible ideas to some, but they are the simple and first principles of the gospel, to know for a certainty the character of God, that we may converse with him as one man with another, and that God himself; the Father of us all dwelt on an earth the same as Jesus Christ himself did . . . what did Jesus say? (mark it elder Rigdon;) Jesus said, as the Father hath power in himself, even so hath the Son power; to do what? Why what the Father did, that answer is obvious. . .Here then is eternal life, to know the only wise and true God. You have got to learn how to be Gods yourselves; to be kings and priests to God, the same as all Gods have done; by going from a small degree to another, from grace to grace, from exaltation to exaltation, until you are able to sit in glory as do those who sit enthroned in everlasting power. . . ."

Mormon theology then is polytheistic, teaching in effect that the universe is inhabited by different gods who procreate spirit children which are in turn clothed with bodies on different planets, "Elohim" being the god of this planet (Brigham's teaching that Adam is our heavenly Father is now officially denied by Mormon authorities, but they hold firm to the belief that our God is a resurrected, glorified man). In addition to this, the "inspired" utterances of Joseph Smith reveal that he began as a Unitarian, progressed to tritheism and graduated into full fledged polytheism, in direct contradiction to the revelations of the Old and New Testaments as we have observed. The Mormon doctrine of the Trinity is a gross misrepresentation of the Biblical position, though they attempt to veil their evil doctrine in semi-orthodox terminology. We have already dealt with this problem, but it bears constant repetition lest the Mormon terminology go unchallenged.

On the surface, they appear to be orthodox; but in the light of unimpeachable Mormon sources, Mormons are clearly evading the issue. The truth of the matter is that Mormonism has never historically accepted the Christian doctrine of the Trinity; in fact, they deny it by completely perverting the meaning of the term. This is one of the chief reasons why they have never been accepted by any Christian council of churches (National Association of Evangelicals, National Council of Christian Churches, World Council of Churches, American & International Council of Churches, etc.). The Mormon doctrine that God the Father is a mere man is the root of their polytheism, and forces Mormons to deny not only the Trinity of God as revealed in Scripture but the immaterial nature of God as pure spirit. The Mormons, in *Look* magazine, stated that they accepted the Trinity but as we have seen, it is *not* the Christian Trinity. God the Father does not have a body of flesh and bones, a fact clearly taught by our Lord (John 4:24, cf. Luke 24:39). Mormon apostle James Talmage describes the church's teaching as follows in his book *The Articles of Faith:*

> The Church of Jesus Christ of Latter-day Saints proclaims against the incomprehensible God, devoid of "body, parts, or passions," as a thing impossible of existence, and asserts its belief in and allegiance to the true and living God of scripture and revelation. . .Jesus Christ is the Son of Elohim both as spiritual and bodily offspring; that is to say, Elohim is literally the Father of the spirit of Jesus Christ and also of the body in which Jesus Christ performed His mission in the flesh. . .Jehovah who is Jesus Christ the Son of Elohim, is called "the Father". . .That Jesus Christ, whom we also know as Jehovah, was the executive of the Father, Elohim, in the work of creation is set forth in the book *Jesus the Christ,* chapter IV (pp. 48, 466, 467).

In these revealing statements, Talmage lapses into the error of making Elohim and Jehovah two separate gods, apparently in complete ignorance of the fact that Elohim "the greater god" and Jehovah—Jesus the lesser god, begotten by Elohim, are compounded in the Hebrew as "Jehovah the Mighty One," or simply "Jehovah God" as any concordance of Hebrew usage in the Old Testament readily reveals (Lord—Yahweh; God—Elohim). This error is akin to that of Mary Baker Eddy, who, in her glossary to *Science and Health With Key to the Scriptures* made exactly the same error, she too being in complete ignorance of the Hebrew language. In this grammatical error, Christian Science and the Mormons are in unique agreement, though it is virtually certain that they are unaware of it.

Talmage's argument that "to deny the materiality of God's person is to deny God; for a thing without parts has no whole and an immaterial body cannot exist" is both logically and theologically an absurdity. To illustrate this, one need only to point to the angels whom the Scriptures describe as "ministering spirits" (Hebrews 1:7), beings who have immaterial "bodies" of spiritual substances and yet exist. The Mormons involve themselves further in a hopeless contradiction when, in their doctrine of the preexistence of the soul, they are forced to redefine the meaning of soul as used in both the Old and the New Testaments to teach that the soul is not immaterial, while the Bible clearly teaches that it is. Our Lord upon the cross spoke the words, "Father, into thy hands I commend my spirit." Certainly this was immaterial. And Paul, preparing to depart from this world for the celestial realms, indicated that his real spiritual self (certainly immaterial, since his body died) was yearning to depart and to be with Christ, which is far better (Philippians 1:21–23). The martyr Stephen also committed his spirit (or immaterial nature) into the hands of the Father, crying, "Lord Jesus, receive my spirit" (Acts 7:59). And there are numerous passages in both the Old and New Testaments which indicate that an "immaterial body" can exist, provided that form is of a spiritual substance as is God the Father and the Holy Spirit, and as was Jesus Christ as the pre-incarnate Logos (John 1:1, cf., John 1:14). Far from asserting their "belief and allegiance to the true and living God of Scripture and revelation," as Talmage represents Mormonism, Mormons indeed have sworn allegiance to a polytheistic pantheon of gods which they are striving to join, there to enjoy a polygamous eternity of progression toward godhood. One can search the corridors of pagan mythology and never equal the complex structure which the Mormons have erected and masked under the terminology and misnomer of orthodox Christianity, as previously demonstrated. That the Mormons reject the historic Christian doctrine of the Trinity no student of the movement can deny, for after quoting the Nicene creed and early church theology on the Trinity, Talmage, in *The Articles of Faith,* declares: "It would be difficult to conceive of a greater number of inconsistencies and contradictions expressed in words as here. . .The immateriality of God as asserted in these declarations of sectarian faith is entirely at variance with the Scriptures, and absolutely contradicted by the revelations of God's person and attributes. . ."(p. 48).

After carefully perusing hundreds of volumes on Mormon theology and scores of pamphlets dealing with this subject, the author can quite candidly state that never in over a decade of research in the field of cults has he ever seen such misappropriation of terminology, disregard of context, and utter abandon of scholastic principles demonstrated on the part of non-Christian cultists than is evidenced in the attempts of Mormon theologians to appear orthodox and at the same time undermine the foundations of historic Christianity.The intricacies of their complex system of polytheism causes the careful researcher to ponder again and again the ethical standard which these Mormon writers practice and the blatant attempts to rewrite history, Biblical theology, and the laws of scriptural interpretation that they might support the theologies of Joseph Smith and Brigham Young. Without fear of contradiction, I am certain that Mormonism cannot stand investigation and wants no part of it unless the results can be controlled under the guise of "broadmindedness" and "tolerance."

On one occasion when the Mormon doctrine of God was under discussion with a young woman leaning in the direction of Mormon conversion, I offered in the presence of witnesses to retract this chapter and one previous effort (*Mormonism,* Zondervan Publishing House, 1958), if the Mormon elders advising this young lady would put in writing that they and their church rejected polytheism for monotheism in the tradition of the Judaeo-Christian religion. It was a bona fide offer; the same offer has been made from hundreds of platforms to tens of thousands of people over a twenty-year period. The Church of Jesus Christ of Latter-day Saints is well aware of the offer. To the unwary, however, they imply that they are monotheists, to the informed they defend their polytheism, and like the veritable chameleon they change color to accommodate the surface upon which they find themselves.

G. B. Arbaugh, in his classic volume, *Revelation in Mormonism* (1932), has documented in exhaustive detail the progress of Mormon theology from Unitarianism to Polytheism. His research has been invaluable and available to interested scholars for fifty years, with the full knowledge of the Mormon Church. To this date they have never refuted Arbaugh's evidence or conclusions: in fact, they are significantly on the defensive where the peculiar origins of the "sacred writings" are involved or when verifiable evidence exists which reveals their polytheistic perversions of the Gospel of Jesus Christ. It is extremely difficult to write kindly of Mormon theology when they are so obviously deceptive in their presentation of data, so adamant in their condemnation of all religions in favor of the "restored gospel" allegedly vouchsafed to the prophet Joseph Smith. We must not, however, confuse the theology with the person as is too often the case, for while hostility toward the former is scriptural, it is never so with the latter.

Continuing with our study, apostle Orson Pratt, writing in *The Seer*, declared: "In the Heaven where our spirits were born, there are many Gods, each one of whom has his own wife or wives which were given to him previous to his redemption, while yet in his mortal state" (p. 37). In this terse sentence, Pratt summed up the whole hierarchy of Mormon polytheism, and quotations previously adduced from a reputable Mormon source support Pratt's summation beyond reasonable doubt. The Mormon teaching that God was seen "face to face" in the Old Testament (Exodus 33:9, 11, 23; Exodus 24:9–11; Isaiah 6:1, 5; Genesis 5:24; Genesis 6:5–9, etc.) is refuted on two counts, that of language and the science of comparative textual analysis (hermeneutics).

From the standpoint of linguistics, all the references cited by the Mormons to prove "that God has a physical body that could be observed" melt away in the light of God's expressed declaration, "Thou canst not see my face: for there shall no man see me and live" (Exodus 33:20).

Exodus 33:11 (face to face) in the Hebrew is rendered "intimate" and in no sense is it opposed to verse 20. Similar expressions are utilized in Deuteronomy 5:4, while in Genesis 32:30 it is the angel of the Lord who speaks, *not* Jehovah Himself. The Old Testament is filled with theophanies (literally, Godforms), instances where God spoke or revealed Himself in angelic manifestations, and it is accepted by all Old Testament scholars almost without qualification that anthropomorphisms (ascribing human characteristics to God) are the logical explanation of many of the encounters of God with man. To argue, as the Mormons do, that such occurrences indicate that God has a body of flesh and bone, as Prophet Smith taught, is on the face of the matter untenable and another strenuous attempt to force polytheism on a rigidly monotheistic religion. Progressing beyond this, another cardinal Mormon point of argument is the fact that because expressions such as "the arm of the Lord," "the eye of the Lord," "the hand of the Lord," "nostrils," "mouth," etc., are used, all tend to show that God possesses a physical form. However, they have overlooked one important factor. This factor is that of literary metaphor, extremely common in Old Testament usage. If the Mormons are to be consistent in their interpretation, they should find great difficulty in the Psalm where God is spoken of as "covering with his feathers," and man "trusting under his wings." If God has eyes, ears, arms, hands, nostrils, mouth, etc., why then does He not have feathers and wings? The Mormons have never given a satisfactory answer to this, because it is obvious that the anthropomorphic and metaphorical usage of terms relative to God are literary devices to convey His concern and association with man. In like manner, metaphors such as feathers and wings indicate His tender concern for the protection of those who "dwell in the secret place of the Most High and abide under the shadow of the Almighty." The Mormons would do well to comb the Old Testament and the New Testament for the numerous metaphorical usages readily available for observation, and they must admit, if they are at all logically consistent, that Jesus was not a door (John 10:9), a shepherd (John 10:11), a vine (John 15:1), a roadway (John 14:6), a loaf of bread (John 6:51), and other metaphorical expressions any more than "our God is a consuming fire" means that Jehovah should be construed as a blast furnace or a volcanic cone.

The Mormons themselves are apparently unsure of the intricacies of their own polytheistic structure, as revealed in the previously cited references from Joseph Smith, who made Christ both the Father and the Son in one instance, and further on indicated that there was a mystery connected with it and that only the Son could reveal how He was both the Father and the Son. Then to compound the difficulty, Smith later separated them completely into "separate personages," eventually populating the entire universe with his polytheistic and polygamous deities. If one peruses carefully the books of Abraham and Moses as contained in the *Pearl of Great Price* (allegedly "translated" by Smith), as well as sections of Ether in the *Book of Mormon*, *Doctrine and Covenants*, and *Discourses of Brigham Young*, the entire Mormon dogma of the preexistence of the soul, the polygamous nature of the gods, the brotherhood of Jesus and Lucifer, and the hierarchy of heaven (telestial, terrestrial, and celestial—corresponding to the basement, 50th floor, and observation tower of the Empire State Building respectively), and the doctrines of universal salvation, millennium, resurrection, judgment and final punishment, will unfold in a panorama climaxing in a polygamous paradise of eternal duration. Such is the Mormon doctrine of God, or, more properly, of the gods, which rivals anything pagan mythology ever produced.

The Holy Spirit in Mormonism

Having discussed the nature and attributes of God in contrast to Mormon mythology and its pantheon of polygamus deities, it remains for us to understand what the Mormon teaching concerning the third person of the Christian Trinity is, since they do deign to describe Him as "a personage of spirit."

It is interesting to observe that in their desire to emulate orthodoxy where possible, the Mormons describe the Holy Ghost in the following terms:

"The term Holy Ghost and its common synonyms, Spirit of God, Spirit of the Lord, or simply Spirit, Comforter, and Spirit of Truth occur in the Scriptures with plainly different meanings, referring in some cases to the person of God the Holy Ghost, and in other instances to the power and authority of this great personage, or to the agency through which He ministers. . .The Holy Ghost undoubtedly possesses personal powers and affections; these attributes exist in Him in perfection. Thus He teaches and guides, testifies of the Father and the Son, reproves, rebukes, speaks, commands, commissions. . .These are not figurative expressions but plain statements of the attributes and characteristics of the Holy Ghost" (*The Articles of Faith*, p. 115).

It is interesting to recall that, according to Talmage, who wrote *The Articles of Faith* (as we previously mentioned): "It has been said, therefore, that God is everywhere present; but this does not mean that the actual person of any one member of the Godhead can be *physically* present in more than one place at one time. . .Admitting the personality of God, we are compelled to accept the fact of His materiality; indeed, an 'immaterial being,' under which meaningless name some have sought to designate the condition of God, cannot exist, for the very expression is a contradiction in terms. If God possesses a form, that form is of necessity of definite proportions and therefore of limited extension in space. It is impossible for Him to occupy at one time more than one space of such limits. . ." (pp. 42, 43).

Here exists a contradiction in Mormon theology if ever there was one. Talmage declares that the Holy Spirit is a personage of spirit, obviously "an immaterial being" and obviously God (cf. *Doctrine and Covenants* 20:28), and yet not possessing a form of material nature; hence, not limited to extension and space, and therefore rendering it possible for Him to occupy at one time more than one space of such limits, in direct contradiction to Talmage's earlier statements in the same volume. For the Mormon then, "a thing without parts has no whole and an immaterial body cannot exist" (*Articles of Faith*, p. 48), and yet the Holy Spirit is a "personage of Spirit," one of the Mormon gods, according to *Doctrine and Covenants*. To cap it all, "He is an immaterial being possessed of a spiritual form and definite proportions!" Mormon theology here appears to have really become confused at the roots, so to speak; but Talmage does not agree with Talmage, nor does *Doctrine and Covenants*; they are forced into the logical position of affirming the materiality of God in one instance, and denying that materiality in the next instance where the Holy Spirit is concerned. It would be enlightening to see how Mormon theologians reconcile this logical and theological contradiction.

Parley P. Pratt, the eminent Mormon theologian, further complicated the doctrine of the Holy Spirit in Mormon theology when he wrote: "This leads to the investigation of that substance called the Holy Spirit or Light of Christ. . .There is a divine substance, fluid or essence, called Spirit, widely diffused among these eternal elements. . .This divine element, or Spirit, is immediate, active or controlling agent in all holy miraculous powers. . .The purest, most refined and subtle of all these substances, and the one least understood, or even recognized, by the less informed among mankind, is that substance called the Holy Spirit" (*Key to the Science of Theology*, pp. 45, 105, 46).[22]

---

[22]Some Mormons quoting early Mormon writers have attempted to differentiate between the Holy Spirit and the Holy Ghost! This is linguistically impossible in New Testament Greek as any lexicon reveals.

In the thinking of Pratt, then, certainly an official source of Mormon theology and a man whose writings are still circulated today by his church as authoritative and representative, the Holy Spirit is both a substance, a fluid, and a person, but this is not the teaching of Scripture, which consistently portrays God the Holy Spirit, Third Person of the Trinity, as an eternal, omnipotent, omnipresent, and omniscient Being, sharing all the attributes of Deity and one with the Father and the Son, in unity of substance. Mormons are, to say the least, divided in their theology on the issue, although Talmage bravely attempts to synthesize the mass of conflicting information and "revelations" found within the writings of Smith and Young and the early Mormon writers. Try as he will, however, Talmage cannot explain the Mormon confusion on the subject, as evidenced by the following facts.

In *Doctrine and Covenants* 20:37 the following statement appears:

"All those who humble themselves. . .and truly manifest by their works that they have received of the Spirit of Christ unto the remission of their sins, shall be received by baptism into His church."

Joseph Smith the prophet was the recipient of this alleged revelation from the throne room of the "gods," and he is to be believed at all costs; yet the same Joseph Smith translated the *Book of Mormon,* which unreservedly declared:

"Yea, blessed are they who shall. . .be baptized, for they shall. . .receive a remission of their sins. . .Behold, baptism is unto repentance to the fulfilling of the commandments unto the remission of sins" (3 Nephi 12:2; Moroni 8:11).

In one instance, Smith taught that baptism follows the initial act—remission of sins—and in the second instance, the initial act—remission of sins—reverses its position and follows baptism. According to Talmage, "God grants the gift of the Holy Ghost unto the obedient; and the bestowal of this gift follows faith, repentance, and baptism by water. . .The apostles of old promised the ministration of the Holy Ghost unto those only who had received baptism by water for the remission of sins" (*The Articles of Faith,* p. 163).

The question naturally arises—When, then, is the Holy Spirit bestowed? Or indeed, can He be bestowed in Mormon theology when it is not determined whether the remission of sins precedes baptism or follows it? Here again, confusion on the doctrine of the Holy Spirit is evidenced in Mormon thinking.

It would be possible to explore further the Mormon doctrine of the Holy Spirit, especially the interesting chapter in President Charles Penrose's book, *Mormon Doctrine* (Salt Lake City, 1888), in which over twenty times he refers to the Holy Spirit as an "it" devoid of personality, although, in the usual polytheistic Mormon scheme, endowed with Deity. Penrose closes his comment by stating, "As baptism is the birth of water, so confirmation is the birth or baptism of the Spirit. Both are necessary to entrance into the Kingdom of God. . .The possessor of the Holy Ghost is infinitely rich; those who receive it can lose it, and are of all men the poorest, but there are various degrees of its possession. Many who obtain it walk, but measurably, in its light. But there are few who live by its whisperings and approach by its mediumship into close communion with heavenly beings of the highest order. To them, its light grows brighter every day" (pp. 18, 19).

Mormonism then, for all its complexities and want of conformity to the revelation of God's Word, indeed contradicts the Word of God repeatedly, teaching in place of the God of pure spiritual substance (John 4:24), a flesh-and-bone deity and a pantheon of gods in infinite stages of progression. For Mormons, God is restricted to a narrow, rationalistic and materialistic mold. He cannot be incomprehensible, though Scripture indicates that in many ways He most certainly is. "My thoughts are not your thoughts, neither are your ways my ways, saith the Lord. For as the heavens are higher than the earth, so are my ways higher than your ways, and my thoughts than your thoughts" (Isaiah 55:8, 9). Mormon theology complicates and confounds the simple declarations of Scripture in order to support the polytheistic pantheon of Joseph Smith and Brigham Young. It is obvious, therefore, that the God of the Bible and the "god" of the Mormons, the "Adam-god" of Brigham Young and the flesh-and-bone deity of Joseph Smith, are not one and the same; by their nature all monotheistic and theistic religions stand in opposition to Mormon polytheism. Christianity in particular repudiates as false and deceptive the multiplicity of Mormon efforts to masquerade as "ministers of righteousness" (2 Corinthians 11:15).

The Virgin Birth of Christ

One of the great doctrines of the Bible, which is uniquely related to the supreme earthly manifestation of the Eternal God, is the doctrine of the Virgin Birth of Jesus Christ. In one very real sense, this doctrine is indissolubly linked with that of the Incarnation, being, so to speak, the agency or instrument whereby God chose to manifest Himself. Time and again the Bible reminds us that Deity was clothed with humanity in the manger of Bethlehem, and Christians of all generations have revered the mystery prefigured by the cryptic words of Isaiah the prophet:

> Behold, a virgin shall conceive, and bear a son, and shall call his name Immanuel. For unto us a child is born, unto us a son is given: and the government shall be upon his shoulder: and his name shall be called Wonderful, Counselor, The mighty God, The everlasting Father, The Prince of Peace (Isaiah 7:14 and 9:6).

The Apostle Paul numerous times refers to the Deity of our Lord, declaring that "In Him dwells all the fullness of the Deity in the flesh" (Colossians 2:9).

Attempts to minimize the virgin birth of Christ, or to do away with it altogether, as some liberal theologians have energetically tried to do, have consistently met with disaster. This was true because the simple narratives of this momentous event recorded in Matthew and Luke refuse to surrender to the hindsight reconstruction theories of second-guessing critics.

Some persons have, on the other hand, decided upon a middle course where this doctrine is concerned. They affirm its biological necessity. In a word, Matthew and Luke, who had access to eyewitness testimonies (Mary, Joseph, Elizabeth, etc.), never really believed the teaching as recorded; rather it was a pious attempt to endow Christ with a supernatural conception in order to add glory to His Personality. Regardless of how distasteful the un-biblical concepts of liberal and so-called Neo-orthodox theologians may be concerning the virgin birth of our Savior, no group has framed a concept of the virgin birth doctrine in the terms employed by the Mormon prophet Brigham Young. Mormon doctrine concerning the virgin birth of Christ is derived directly from the pronouncements of Brigham Young and as we have previously pointed out, no higher authorities can be quoted in Mor-monism than Joseph Smith and Brigham Young.

Relative to the doctrine of the virgin birth of Christ, Brigham Young has unequivocally stated: "When the Virgin Mary conceived the child Jesus, the Father had begotten him in his own likeness. He was *not* begotten by the Holy Ghost. And who was the Father? He is the first of the human family; and when he took a tabernacle [body], it was begotten by his Father in heaven, after the same manner as the tabernacles of Cain, Abel, and the rest of the sons and daughters of Adam and Eve; from the fruits of the earth, the first earthly tabernacles were originated by the Father, and so on in succession . . . Jesus, our elder brother, was begotten in the flesh by the same character that was in the garden of Eden, and who is our Father in Heaven" (*Journal of Discourses*, Vol. I, pp. 50 and 51).

Now, in order to understand what "Prophet" Young was saying, another of his pronouncements found in the same context should be considered:

> "When our father Adam came into the garden of Eden, he came into
> it with a celestial body, and brought Eve, *one of his wives*, with him . . . He *is*
> our FATHER *and our* GOD, *and the only God with whom* WE *have to do.*"

As we have seen in the Mormon doctrine of God, Mormon theology teaches that polytheism is the divine order. Belief in many gods is the cor-nerstone of their theology, and polygamous gods they are. Parley Pratt, a leading Mormon writer whose books are recommended by Mormon pub-lishing houses as representing their theological views, also writes concerning this doctrine:

> "Each of these Gods, including Jesus Christ and his Father, being in
> possession of not merely an organized spirit, but a glorious immortal body
> of flesh and bones. . ." (*Key to the Science of Theology*, Ed. 1966, p. 44).

Added to this polytheistic picture are other official Mormon sources, many of whom confirm the sexual conception of Jesus enunciated by Young and many others. Wrote apostle James Talmage in *The Articles of Faith*:

> ". . . His [Christ's] unique status in the flesh as the offspring of a mortal
> mother [Mary] and of an immortal, or resurrected and glorified, Father
> [Elohim]" (p. 473, ed. 1974).

Brigham Young, therefore, taught this anti-Biblical doctrine of which he spoke openly more than once as recorded in *Journal of Discourses*, Vol. 8, p. 67; Vol. 4, p. 218; Vol. 4, p. 216; Vol. 10, p. 192; Vol. 13, p. 145; Vol. 9, p. 291; Vol. 3, p. 365; Vol. 4, p. 27:

> "When the time came that His first-born, the Saviour, should come into
> the world and take a tabernacle, (body) the Father came Himself and fa-

voured that spirit with a tabernacle instead of letting any *other* man do it" (*Journal of Discourses*, Vol. 4, p. 218).

The crass polytheism of Mormonism was never more clearly dissembled than in the foregoing statements, and Young's classification of the Father as a glorified, resurrected "man" cannot be misunderstood. The phrase "any *other* man" rules out the efforts of Mormon apologists to defend Young and unmasks the entire anti-Christian teaching.

We see, then, the Mormon teaching concerning our Lord's birth is a revolting distortion of the Biblical revelation and one which is in keeping with the Mormon dogma of a flesh-and-bone god. In Mormon thinking, as reflected in the authoritative declarations of one of their prophets, our Savior was produced, not by a direct act of the Holy Spirit but by actual sexual relations between "an immortal or resurrected and glorified Father," and Mary—a blasphemous view which takes its place beside the infamous mythology of Greece, wherein the gods fathered human sons through physical union with certain chosen women.

Brigham Young further declared: "He (Christ) was *not* begotten by the Holy Ghost. . . Jesus, our elder brother, was begotten in the flesh by the same character that was in the garden of Eden, and who is our Father in Heaven" (*Journal of Discourses*, Vol. 1, pp. 50, 51). There can be no mistaking the fact that the Adam-god doctrine is meant here, no matter how vehemently the Mormon apologists of today may deny that it was ever taught. The language is too clear, the cross-reference easily demonstrable, and the denial of His conception by the Holy Spirit evident for all to see.

Mormon leaders, however, while accepting the doctrine as Young declared it, are extremely careful not to allow "the Gentiles" (all non-Mormons) to understand the full impact of the teaching until they have come under extremely favorable Mormon influences. This is understood by the fact that in *Look* magazine,[23] later reproduced in Leo Rosten's *A Guide to the Religions of America* (1963, pp. 131–141), the Mormons employed the subterfuge of semantics to escape declaring this position to the general public.

In the *Guide* book, the question was asked, "Do Mormons believe in the Virgin Birth?" (p. 134). To which the Mormon spokesman, a high-ranking member of the Mormon hierarchy, replied, "Yes. The Latter-day Saint accepts the miraculous conception of Jesus the Christ."

Now, it is obvious that if apostle Richard L. Evans, the Mormon spokesman, had set forth the doctrine of Brigham Young, a doctrine which has been taught by his church and which appears in authoritative publications, even nominal Christians would have been shocked and goaded to some comments, and the one thing the Mormon Church does not desire is adverse publicity. Indeed they maintain a public relations staff in order to avoid such embarrassments, so Mr. Evans resorted to semantic vagaries in an attempt to make his religion appear "orthodox," which it is not!

According to the revelation of the virgin birth as recorded within the Scripture, our Lord was conceived by a direct act of God the Holy Spirit, wholly apart from human agency. The Scripture is explicit in declaring that

---

[23]October 5, 1954.

this conception took place while Mary was "espoused to Joseph, *before* they came together." Matthew, therefore, flatly contradicts Brigham Young in no uncertain terms, declaring: "She was found with child by the Holy Spirit" (Matthew 1:18). And the angel Gabriel, who appeared to Joseph to reassure him concerning the divine origin of Christ's conception, reiterated this fact by declaring, "That which is conceived in her is *by* the Holy Spirit" (verse 20).

Luke, the beloved physician, in his narrative of the virgin birth, describes the revelation of our Lord's conception in unmistakable terms: "The Holy Ghost shall come upon thee, and the power of the Highest shall overshadow thee: therefore also that holy thing which shall be born of thee shall be called the Son of God" (Luke 1:35).

Some Mormon apologists have attempted to prove from this verse, however, that the phrase "the power of the Highest shall overshadow thee" in fact refers to the Mormon god's impregnation of Mary, thus proving "the truthfulness" of Brigham Young's assertion. But as we shall see from Matthew's account, this is an impossible contention and is unworthy of further refutation.

It is true that many debates have been instigated over the nature of the virgin birth of Christ, but the Christian position has always been based upon a literal acceptance of the event as recorded in the first chapters of Matthew and Luke. It might be noted that even liberal and Neo-orthodox scholars have repudiated the grossly polytheistic and pagan concept enunciated by Brigham Young and handed down through Mormon theology.

We would do well to remember "Prophet" Young's denials: "He (Jesus) was not begotten by the Holy Ghost . . . Jesus, our elder brother, was begotten in the flesh by the same character that was in the garden of Eden, and who is our Father in Heaven," and contrast it with the reliable testimony of the Word of God:

> "When as his mother Mary was espoused to Joseph, before they came together, she was found with child of the Holy Ghost . . . The angel of the Lord appeared unto him in a dream, saying, Joseph, thou son of David, fear not to take unto thee Mary thy wife: for that which is conceived in her is of the Holy Ghost" (Matthew 1:18-20).

The Mormon Church today finds itself, no doubt, in a very difficult position where this heinous teaching concerning our Lord's conception is concerned. Some Mormons with whom the author has spoken repudiate violently Brigham Young's doctrine of the virgin birth, maintaining that he never really taught such a thing; but upon being faced with statements from Young's *Journal of Discourses* and quotations from Mormon periodicals and magazines between the years 1854 and 1878, particularly, they are forced to admit that such was the teaching of their church under Brigham Young. Then, not wanting to appear before a Mormon "court" for failure to uphold the prophetic office of Young, they lapse into silence or reluctantly affirm it.

One Mormon writer and historian, B. H. Roberts, writing in the *Deseret News* (July 23, 1921, Section 4, p. 7) went so far as to deny that the Mormon church taught the Adam-god doctrine or the doctrine of the virgin birth as pronounced by Young. Wrote Mr. Roberts in answer to the charge of the Presbyterian Church that "the Mormon church teaches that Adam is God . . . and that Jesus is his son by natural generation":

> "As a matter of fact, the 'Mormon' church does not teach that doctrine. A few men in the 'Mormon' church have held such views: and several of them quite prominent in the councils of the church . . . Brigham Young and others *may* have taught that doctrine but *it has never been accepted by the church as her doctrine.*"

The unfortunate thing about Mr. Roberts' statement is that (1) he was not empowered to speak for the church and (2) he is in direct conflict with the teachings of his church on the subject of prophetic authority, not to mention Talmage's *Articles of Faith* previously cited. He also used a carefully qualified term when he said that "Brigham Young and others *may* have taught that doctrine." As we have seen, Brigham Young *did* teach that doctrine; and according to the Mormon faith, Brigham Young was a prophet of God as was Joseph Smith, in the same category as Jeremiah, Ezekiel or Daniel. So, if Brigham taught it—especially at the church's Semiannual General Conference—then it *is* the doctrine of the Mormon Church, by definition, a fact challenged only by uninformed students of Mormonism. That the Mormon Church accepts as her doctrine whatever Joseph Smith and Brigham Young taught must, we feel, be documented beyond reasonable doubt so that the reader will become familiar with the unfortunate Mormon habit of redefining terms and qualifying statements to elude detection of their true teachings. The following quotation is taken from *The Latter Day Saints Biographical Encyclopedia* (January 5, 1901, No. 1, Vol. 1), an official publication of the Mormon Church, and clearly reveals the authority of Brigham Young and his high position in the church. In the light of this statement and numerous others, it is hard to see how his doctrines can be denied by the Mormons, which in fact *they have never been.*

> In a revelation given through the Prophet Joseph Smith, Jan. 19, 1841, the Lord says: "I give unto you my servant, Brigham Young, to be a president over the Twelve traveling council, which Twelve hold the keys to open up the authority of my kingdom upon the four corners of the earth, and after that to send my word to every creature."
>
> The Quorum of the Twelve stands next in authority to the Presidency of the Church, and in the case of the decease of the Prophet the Twelve preside over the Church with their president at the head, and thus was brought to the front Brigham Young, the man whom God designed should succeed the Prophet Joseph Smith . . . When the Twelve were sustained as the presiding authority of the Church; Brigham Young arose to speak, and in the presence of the multitude was transfigured by the spirit and power of God, so that his form, size, countenance and voice appeared as those of the martyred Prophet. Even non-members were struck with amazement and expected to see and hear the departed Seer. From that moment doubt and uncertainty were banished from the hearts of the faithful and they were fully assured that the mantle of Joseph Smith had fallen upon Brigham Young. After the martyrdom of Joseph and Hyrum, persecution did not cease; the Prophets were slain but truth did not die. The man who stood at

the earthly head was taken away, but the authority he held had been conferred upon others . . . During his administration of thirty years as President of the Church, he made frequent tours, accompanied by his associates in the Priesthood . . . Though he did not utter so many distinct prophecies, he builded faithfully upon the foundation laid through the Prophet Joseph Smith, and all his movements and counsels were prophetic, as fully demonstrated by subsequent events. He was a Prophet, statesman, pioneer and colonizer (pp. 11, 13, 14).

Supplementing this detailed account of Brigham Young's authority and position as a source of doctrinal reliability, the reader will find innumerable statements concerning the government of the Mormon Church in their circulated literature, all of which indicate that every succeeding first president of the church wears the "prophetic mantle" of Joseph Smith and Brigham Young; they, too, are considered prophets of God as were Joseph and Brigham.

When all the facts are considered, two things emerge from the mass of evidence available, which no Mormon writer has yet attempted to explain away—that is, the fact that the Mormon Church teaches the absolute authority of its prophetic office and that Brigham Young is regarded as *second* greatest in lineage. When one reads, therefore, Young's statements concerning the nature of God and the virgin birth of our Lord in particular, and duly notes the circuitous tactics of the Mormons and their pointed lack of official denial where the teachings of Young and other prominent Mormons are involved, there is very little left to the imagination as to their true teachings. The Christian, who reverences the revelation God has given concerning the nature of His Son's birth, cannot find fellowship with the Mormons, who subscribe to the teachings of their prophet. Henceforth, when Mormons speak of "the miraculous conception of Jesus the Christ," let it be well remembered what they mean by these terms, for in no way can they be equated with the teaching of the New Testament wherein God has so effectively spoken: "That which is conceived in her is *of* the Holy Spirit" (Matthew 1:20).

Salvation and Judgment in Mormonism

Personal salvation in Mormonism is one of the doctrines most heavily emphasized, and since Christianity is the Gospel or "Good News" of God's redemption in Christ, it is inevitable that the two should come into conflict.

The Mormon doctrine of salvation involves not only faith in Christ, but baptism by immersion, obedience to the teaching of the Mormon Church, good works, and "keeping the commandments of God (which) will cleanse away the stain of sin" (*Journal of Discourses,* Vol. 2, p. 4). Apparently Brigham was ignorant of the Biblical pronouncement that "without the shedding of blood there is no remission [of sin]" (Hebrews 9:22).

The Mormon teaching concerning salvation is, therefore, quite the opposite of the New Testament revelation of justification by faith and redemption solely by grace through faith in Christ (Ephesians 2:8–10).

Brigham Young, an authoritative Mormon source by any standards, was quite opposed to the Christian doctrine of salvation which teaches that a person may at any time sincerely repent of his sins, even at the eleventh hour, and receive forgiveness and eternal life. Wrote Brigham:

"Some of our old traditions teach us that a man guilty of atrocious and murderous acts may savingly repent on the scaffold; and upon his execution will hear the expression—'Bless God! he has gone to heaven, to be crowned in glory, through the all-redeeming merits of Christ the Lord!' This is all nonsense. Such a character will never see heaven" (*Journal of Discourses*, Vol. 8, p. 61).

Prophet Young never did explain the words of the Lord Jesus Christ addressed to the thief on the cross who had repented of his sins at the last moment, so to speak, crying: "Jesus, Lord, remember me when thou comest into thy kingdom" (Luke 23:42). The answer of our Savior was unequivocal: "Today shalt thou be with me in paradise" (Luke 23:43).

The parable of the laborer (Matthew 20:1–16) which presents Christ's teaching that God agrees to give to all who will serve Him the same inheritance, i.e., eternal life, was also ignored by Brigham Young, who would most likely have been numbered among the voices which "murmured against the good man of the house, saying: these last have worked but one hour and you have made them equal with us, who have borne the burden and the heat of the day" (verses 11 and 12).

The answer of the Lord is, however, crystal clear: "Friend, I do thee no wrong: did you not agree with me for a penny? Take what is thine, and go thy way: I will give unto the last workers, even as unto thee. Is it not lawful for me to do what I will with mine own? Is thine eye evil, because I am good?" (verses 13–15).

Our Lord was obviously teaching, to use a modern illustration, that the "base pay" given to all laborers in the Kingdom is the same; namely, eternal redemption. But the rewards are different for length and content of the services rendered, so whoever comes to Christ for salvation receives it, whether at the first hour or the eleventh hour. The "gift of God," the Scripture tells us, is "eternal life," and although rewards for services may be earned as the believer surrenders himself to the power of the Holy Spirit and bears fruit for the Lord, God is no respecter of persons. His salvation is equally dispensed without favor to all who will come.

According to the Mormon scheme of salvation the gods who created this earth actually planned that Adam, who was to become ruler of this domain, and his wife, Eve, were predestined to sin so that the race of man who now inhabit this earth might come into being and eventually reach godhood. The fall in the Garden of Eden was actually the means "by which act Adam and Eve became mortal, and could beget mortal children" (J. Widtsoe, *A Rational Theology*, Deseret Publishing Company, p. 47).

Since Mormons believe in the preexistence of the human soul, it is part of their theology that these preexistent souls must take human forms since it is necessary, in order to enjoy both power and joy, that bodies be provided. This was the early Mormon justification for polygamy which accelerated the creation of bodies for these preexistent offsprings of Joseph Smith's galaxy of gods. A careful reading of the *Book of Abraham* will reveal that life on this earth was designed by the gods to discipline their spirit children and at the same time provide them with the opportunities to reproduce and eventually inherit godhood and individual kingdoms of their personal possessions.

According to Mormon revelation, the great star Kolob was the site for the conception of these plans, and it will come as no surprise to students of Mormonism to learn that Lucifer, who was a spirit brother of Jesus prior to His incarnation, fell from heaven because of his jealousy of Christ. Christ was appointed by the gods to become the redeemer of the race that would fall as a result of Adam's sin, and it was this office to which Lucifer aspired, hence his antipathy.

Lucifer is even quoted as saying: "Behold, here am I, send me, I will be thy son, and I will redeem all mankind, that one soul shall not be lost, and surely I will do it; wherefore give me thine honor" (Chapter 4 of the *Book of Moses*, found in the *Pearl of Great Price*, catalogs all of these events, including the fall of Satan and the establishment of the Garden of Eden, Chapter 6, which Joseph Smith elsewhere "revealed" was really located in Missouri and not the Mesopotamian area!).

The *Book of Moses* also records the fact that Cain, the first murderer, was the progenitor of the Negro race, his black skin being the result of a curse by God. On this basis the Mormons for years avoided and ignored blacks in their missionary work, believing that preexistent souls which were considered less than valiant in the "war in heaven" between Christ and Satan were punished by being assigned to black bodies during their mortality. Until 1978 they were denied all of the "blessings" and "privileges" of the priesthood, but a revelation of convenience gave them full access to these glories and neatly removed the last major obstacle to the Mormon "evangelization" of Africa and the rest of the free world.

The Indians, who are supposedly the descendants of the *Book of Mormon*'s wicked Lamanites, have allegedly been cursed by the Mormon deity with dark skins as a punishment for the misdeeds of their forefathers. Mormonism, then, is clearly a religion with a shameful history of white supremacist doctrines and practices.

These and many other interesting factors comprise the background of the Mormon doctrine of salvation, but it is also important to understand the Mormons' teaching concerning their redeemer, one of the main areas of their controversy with historic Christianity.

The Mormon Savior

The record of the Bible concerning the Savior of the world, the Lord Jesus Christ, is well known to students of the Scriptures. In Christian theology, there is but one God (Deuteronomy 6:4, 1 Corinthians 8:4–6) and Jesus Christ is His eternal Word made flesh (John 1:1 and 1:14). It was the function of the Second Person of the Trinity, upon His reception by the sons of men, to empower them to be the sons of God (John 1:12); and this the Scripture teaches came about as a result of God's unmerited favor and His great love toward a lost race.

The Lord Jesus offered one eternal sacrifice for all sins and His salvation comes not by the works of the law or any human works whatever (Galatians

2:16 and Ephesians 2:9), but solely by grace through faith (Ephesians 2:8). The Savior of the New Testament revelation existed eternally as God; lived a holy, harmless and undefiled life, separate from sinners, and "knew no sin." He was "a man of sorrows and acquainted with grief," "the Lamb of God that takes away the sin of the world" (John 1:29).

The Savior of Mormonism, however, is an entirely different person, as their official publications clearly reveal. The Mormon Savior is not the second person of the Christian Trinity since, as we have seen previously, Mormons reject the Christian doctrine of the Trinity, and he is not even a careful replica of the New Testament Redeemer. In Mormon theology, Christ as a pre-existent spirit was not only the spirit brother of the devil (as alluded to in the *Pearl of Great Price*, Moses 4:1–4, and later reaffirmed by Brigham Young in the *Journal of Discourses*, Vol. 13, p. 282), but celebrated his own marriage to both "the Marys and Martha, whereby he could see his seed before he was crucified" (apostle Orson Hyde, *Journal of Discourses*, Vol. 4, pp. 259–260). As we have seen previously, the Mormon concept of the virgin birth, alone, distinguishes their "Christ" from the Christ of the Bible.

In addition to this revolting concept, Brigham Young categorically stated that the sacrifice made upon the cross by Jesus Christ in the form of His own blood was ineffective for the cleansing of *some* sins. Brigham went on to teach the now suppressed but never officially repudiated doctrine of "blood atone-ment."

To better understand Young's limitation of the cleansing power of Christ's blood, we shall refer to his own words:

"Suppose you found your brother in bed with your wife, and put a javelin through both of them, you would be justified, and they would atone for their sins, and be received into the kingdom of God. I would at once do so in such a case; and under such circumstances, I have no wife whom I love so well that I would not put a javelin through her heart, and I would do it with clean hands . . .

"There is not a man or woman, who violates the covenants made with their God, that will not be required to pay the debt. The blood of Christ will never wipe that out, your own blood must atone for it; and the judgements [*sic.*] of the Almighty will come, sooner or later, and every man and woman will have to atone for their covenants . . . All mankind love themselves, and let these principles be known by an individual, and he would be glad to have his blood shed . . . I could refer you to plenty of instances where men have been righteously slain, in order to atone for their sins . . . This is loving our neighbor as ourselves; if he needs help, help him; and if he wants salvation and it is necessary to spill his blood on the earth in order that he may be saved, spill it" (*Journal of Discourses*. Vol. III, p. 247, and Vol. IV, pp. 219–220). So clear-cut was Brigham's denial of the all sufficiency and efficiency of the atoning sacrifice of Christ in the foregoing quotation that Mormons have had to develop an argument "to explain" what the prophet really meant. It is their contention that a criminal is "executed to atone for his crimes and this is all Brigham Young meant."

However, they completely omit any discussion of the fact that Young's statement is not dealing with this subject at all. Young's statement declared that what Christ's blood could *not* cleanse, a man's own blood atonement could. This teaches that in some instances human sacrifice, which Brigham states took place and which he sanctioned, were efficacious where Christ's blood was not!

The Mormons want no part of the Biblical doctrine of the all-sufficiency of Christ's atonement, in the words of John, "The blood of Jesus Christ, His Son, cleanses us from *all* sin" (1 John 1:7), for this both contradicts Young and reveals the true Biblical teaching.

There can be no doubt from the Biblical record that it is in Jesus Christ that we have redemption and that His blood is the means of the cleansing of the conscience (Hebrews 9:14) and of the loosening from sin (Revelation 1:5). It is the very basis of our justification (Romans 5:9).

The Christ of the Mormons cannot save, for he is as the Apostle Paul describes him, "another Jesus," the subject of "another gospel," and the originator of a "different spirit," whose forerunner (the angelic messenger, Moroni) was anticipated by the Apostle (Galatians 1:8 and 9) and who along with the entire revelation is to be considered "anathema" or more literally from the Greek, "cursed" by God.

It may be difficult for some to grasp what is in fact an incredible concept, but Mormonism fits perfectly into the descriptions given by the Word of God. The greatest of the apostles, in his second letter to the Corinthian church, after mentioning a counterfeit Jesus, gospel and spirit, goes on to state that such occurrences should not come as a surprise to the Christian church:

"For such are false apostles, deceitful workmen, transforming themselves into apostles of Christ, and it is not surprising, for Satan himself transforms himself into an angel of light. It is therefore no great marvel if his servants also transform themselves as servants of righteousness whose end will be according to their works" (2 Corinthians 11:13–15, Greek).

This is harsh language indeed, but it is the language of God's choosing and it cannot be ignored by anyone who takes seriously the revelations of Scripture and apostolic authority.

Mormonism, with the apostles, priesthood, temples, secret signs, symbols, hand shakes and mysteries, quite literally masquerades as "the church of the restoration"; but at its heart, in its doctrine of the Messiah, it is found to be contrary to every major Biblical pronouncement.

Salvation by Grace?

It is common to find in Mormon literature the statement that "all men are saved by grace alone without any act on their part." Although this appears to be perfectly orthodox, it is necessary to study *all* the Mormon statements relative to this doctrine in order to know precisely what they mean by what they appear to say.

In one such official Mormon publication (*What the Mormons Think of Christ* by B.R. McConkie), the Mormons give their own interpretation:

> Grace is simply the mercy, the love and the condescension God has for
> his children, as a result of which he has ordained the plan of salvation so

that they may have power to progress and become like him ... All men are saved by grace alone without any act on their part, meaning that they are resurrected and become immortal because of the atoning sacrifice of Christ ... In addition to this redemption from death, all men, by the grace of God, have the power to gain eternal life. This is called salvation by grace coupled with obedience to the laws and ordinances of the gospel. Hence Nephi was led to write: "We labor diligently to write, to persuade our children, and also our brethren, to believe in Christ, and to be reconciled to God; for we know that it is by grace that we are saved *after all we can do.*"

Christians speak often of the blood of Christ and its cleansing power. Much that is believed and taught on this subject, however, is such utter nonsense and so palpably false that to believe it is to lose one's salvation. Many go so far, for instance, as to pretend and at least, to believe that if we confess Christ with our lips and avow that we accept Him as our personal Saviour, we are thereby saved. His blood, without other act than mere belief, they say, makes us clean ... Finally in our day, he has said plainly: "My blood shall not cleanse them if they hear me not" ... Salvation in the kingdom of God is available because of the atoning blood of Christ. But it is received only on condition of faith, repentance, baptism, and *enduring to the end in keeping the commandments of God* (pp. 27–33).

The foregoing is a typical example of what might be termed theological double talk which in one breath affirms grace as a saving principle and in the next declares that it is "coupled with obedience to the law and ordinances of the gospel" and ends by declaring that confession of Christ and acceptance of Him as "personal Saviour" is "utter nonsense" and "palpably false." McConkie decries the fact that Christ's blood "without other act than mere belief ... makes us clean" (p. 31).

The Biblical position is, however, quite clear in this area; we are saved by grace alone, as previously mentioned, but it in no way enables us to "have power to progress and become like Him." As we have seen, in the Mormon sense such a progression refers to becoming a god, not to the Christian doctrine of sanctification, or of the life of the believer being brought into conformity to the Holy Spirit as clearly enunciated in the epistle to the Romans (chapters 8 and 12).

Mr. McConkie's assertion, that "salvation by grace" must be "coupled with obedience with the laws and ordinances of the gospel" in order for a person to be saved, introduces immediately the whole Mormon collection of legalistic observances and requirements. In the end, salvation is not by grace at all, but it is in reality connected with human efforts: "baptism, and enduring to the end in keeping the commandments of God" (p. 33).

This is not the Christian doctrine of redemption which the Apostle Peter described graphically when he wrote:

"Forasmuch as ye know that ye were not redeemed with corruptible things, as silver and gold, from your vain conversation received by tradition from your fathers; but with the precious blood of Christ, as of a lamb without blemish and without spot ... Being born again, not of corruptible seed, but of incorruptible, by the word of God, which liveth and abideth for ever" (1 Peter 1:18, 19, 23).

In diametric opposition to the Mormon concept, the confession of Christ with the lips and the acceptance of Him as "our personal Savior" is indeed the very means of personal salvation. It is the Biblical record which states that "with the heart man believeth unto righteousness and with the mouth confession is made unto salvation" (Romans 10:10). The Gospel's command is "believe on the Lord Jesus Christ and thou shalt be saved" (Acts 16:31). This is, of course, totally foreign to what the Mormon would have us believe. Jesus Christ did not die merely to insure our resurrection, as Mr. McConkie declares (p. 27), but He died to reconcile us to God, to save us by grace, to redeem us by blood, and to sanctify us by His Spirit. But such Biblical doctrines the Mormons most decidedly reject. It appears that they cannot conceive of a God who could save apart from human effort, and Nephi's statement betrays this: "For we know it is by grace that we are saved *after all we can do*" (p. 28).

In Mormonism it is they who must strive for perfection, sanctification, and godhood. Grace is merely incidental.

It was no less an authority than Brigham Young who taught concerning salvation:

"But as many as received Him, to them gave he power to *continue* to be the sons of God" (*Journal of Discourses*, Vol. 4, p. 7).

In Brigham's theology, "instead of receiving the gospel to become the sons of God, my language would be—to receive the gospel that we may *continue* to be the sons of God. Are we not all sons of God when we were born into this world? Old Pharaoh, king of Egypt, was just as much a son of God as Moses and Aaron were His sons, with this difference—he rejected the word of the Lord, the true light, and they received it."

In agreement with their doctrine of the preexistence of souls, the Mormons believe that they are already the sons of God and that the acceptance of God merely enables them to "continue to be the sons of God," a direct contradiction of the Biblical record which states:

"But as many as received him, to them gave he power to become the sons of God, even to them that believe on his name" (John 1:12).

The Apostle Paul points out, with devastating force, the fact that: "They which are the children of the flesh, these are *not* the children of God: but the children of the promise are counted for the seed" (Romans 9:8).

The Apostle, with equal certainty, affirms that only those who are led by God's Spirit can be called the sons of God (Romans 8:14). It is difficult to see how in any sense of the term, "Old Pharaoh, king of Egypt, was just as much a son of God as Moses and Aaron were His sons," as Brigham Young declared.

The Biblical teaching is that "Ye are all the children of God *by faith* in Christ Jesus" (Galatians 3:26), a fact Brigham obviously overlooked.

It is one of the great and true statements of the Word of God that salvation is not "of him that wills or of him that strives, but of God who shows the mercy" (Romans 9) and that Jesus Christ has redeemed us from the curse of the law, having become a curse for us (Galatians 3:13).

It was the teaching of our Lord that: "All that the Father giveth me shall come to me; and him that cometh to me I will in no wise cast out" (John 6:37), and the salvation which He still offers to lost men is "not by any works of righteousness which we have done, but according to his mercy he saved us" (Titus 3:5).

In the Mormon religion, they boldly teach universal salvation, for as Mr. Evans, the Mormon apostle and spokesman, put it: "Mormons believe in universal salvation that all men will be saved, but each one in his own order" (*Look* magazine, Oct. 5, 1954).

It is the teaching of the Scripture, however, that not all men will be saved and that at the end of the ages some shall "go away into everlasting punishment, but the righteous unto life eternal" (Matthew 25:41, 46).

The somber warnings of the Apostle John stand arrayed against the Mormon doctrine of universal salvation:

> And I saw the beast, and the kings of the earth, and their armies, gathered together to make war against him that sat on the horse, and against his army. And the beast was taken, and with him the false prophet that wrought miracles before him, with which he deceived them that had received the mark of the beast, and them that worshipped his image. These both were cast alive into a lake of fire burning with brimstone. And the devil that deceived them was cast into the lake of fire and brimstone, where the beast and the false prophet are, and shall be tormented day and night for ever and ever. And whosoever was not found written in the book of life was cast into the lake of fire. But the fearful, and unbelieving, and the abominable, and murderers, and whoremongers, and sorcerers, and idolators, and all liars, shall have their part in the lake which burneth with fire and brimstone: which is the second death. The same shall drink of the wine of the wrath of God, which is poured out without mixture into the cup of his indignation; and he shall be tormented with fire and brimstone in the presence of the holy angels, and in the presence of the Lamb: And the smoke of their torment ascendeth up for ever and ever: and they have no rest day nor night, who worship the beast and his image, and whosoever receiveth the mark of his name (Revelation 19:19, 20; 20:10, 15; 21:8; 14:10, 11).

By no conceivable stretch of the imagination is universal salvation to be found in these passages where the Greek words in their strongest form indicate torment, judgment, and eternal fire that defies human chemical analysis.

The Mormon doctrine of "celestial marriage" derived from their original concept of polygamy and substituted for it in 1890, when they were forced to abandon this immoral conduct under penalty of losing the state of Utah, is tied to their doctrine of salvation. The Mormons believe that the family unit will endure unto the eternal ages, hence their insistence upon the sealing of Mormon men to many women and sealing of their families. It was for this reason that there are many special rites and ceremonies instituted in behalf of the dead (particularly relatives); hence, their practice of baptism for the dead and laying on of hands (for the bestowing of the gift of the Holy Ghost), all by proxy.

Mormon Eschatology

Believing as they do in the literal second advent of Christ, the Mormons teach that at His return the Jews will have been gathered to Palestine, the

Mormons will be miraculously gathered together in Missouri and the judgment of the Lord will be poured out upon the earth everywhere except on old and new Jerusalem. (See *Doctrine and Covenants* 29:9–11.)

The Mormons also have something in common with the cult of Anglo-Israel, believing as they do in the restoration of the ten lost tribes. The difference is that the Anglo-Israelites believe that the ten lost tribes are the English people, whereas the Mormons believe the ten lost tribes are somewhere in the polar region and will be released and transported to Zion (Missouri) where all the riches they have accumulated will be shared with the rest of the "saints." "Men have lost millions of dollars, and hundreds of lives to find a country beyond the northpole; and they will yet find that country—a warm, fruitful country, inhabited by the ten tribes of Israel, a country divided by a river, on one side of which lives half the tribe at Mannasseh, which is more numerous than all the others. So said the Prophet (Joseph Smith)" (*The Young Woman's Journal*, Vol. 3, pp. 263–264. See also *Mormonism and the Mormons*, D. P. Kidder, p. 91).

Mormons also believe in the bodily resurrection of all men and in salvation in a three-fold heaven. In Mormon theology, there are three heavens: the telestial, the terrestrial and the celestial. The lowest heaven is designed for the heathen people who rejected the Gospel and those who are at that time suffering in hell, pending the last resurrection. The second heaven will be inhabited by Christians who did not accept the Mormon message, Mormons who did not live up to their church's requirements, and men of good will of other religions who rejected the revelations of the saints. The final or celestial heaven is itself divided into three levels, the highest of which is godhood or the possession of a kingdom for one's self and one's family. This particular estate has as its prerequisite the candidate's having been sealed by celestial marriage in a Mormon temple while upon the earth. Even in the celestial kingdom godhood is by slow progression, and in the end each who becomes a god will, with his family, rule and populate a separate planet of his own.

It is almost superfluous to comment that this entire scheme of the consummation of Mormon salvation is the antithesis of the Biblical revelation, which knows nothing of godhood, either constituted or progressive, and which teaches instead that in heaven the destiny of the redeemed will be the special providence of God Himself, which "eye hath not seen, ear hath not heard" and which has "never entered into the mind of men" for these are "the things which God hath prepared for them that love Him." God has revealed many of these things to us by His Spirit; but as Paul so eloquently puts it, we "see through a glass darkly, but *then* face to face" (1 Corinthians 13:12).

Let us understand clearly, then, that salvation in the Biblical sense comes as the free gift of God by grace alone through faith in the vicarious sacrifice of Christ upon the cross. The Lord Jesus Christ said: "He that hears my word and believes Him that sent me *has* eternal life, and shall never come into judgment; but has passed out of death into life" (John 5:24, Greek).

The command of the Gospel is to all men everywhere "Repent! for God has appointed a day in which he will judge the world in righteousness by that man whom he has ordained; whereof he has given assurance unto all men, in that he has raised him from among the dead" (Acts 17:31).

The Scriptures disagree with the Mormons in their insistence upon good works as a *means* of salvation. The book of James clearly teaches (chapter 2) that good works are the *outgrowth* of salvation and justify us before men, proving that we have the faith which justifies us before God (Romans 4 and 5).

No Mormon can today claim that he *has* eternal life in Christ. This is the very power of the Gospel which is entrusted to Christ's church (Romans 1:16, 17). Let us therefore use it in an attempt to bring them to redemptive knowledge of the true Christ of Scripture and the costly salvation He purchased for us with His own blood.

John, the beloved apostle, has summed it up thus:

> If we receive the witness of men, the witness of God is greater: for this is the witness of God which he hath testified of his Son. He that believeth on the Son of God hath the witness in himself: he that believeth not God hath made him a liar; because he believeth not the record that God gave of his Son. And this is the record, that God hath given to us eternal life, and this life is in his Son. He that hath the Son hath life; and he that hath not the Son of God hath not life. These things have I written unto you that believe on the name of the Son of God; that ye may know that ye have eternal life, and that ye may believe on the name of the Son of God. And this is the confidence that we have in him, that, if we ask any thing according to his will, he heareth us: And if we know that he hear us, whatsoever we ask, we know that we have the petitions that we desired of him. And we know that we are of God, and the whole world lieth in wickedness. And we know that the Son of God is come, and hath given us an understanding, that we may know him that is true, and we are in him that is true, even in his Son, Jesus Christ. This is the true God, and eternal life (1 John 5:9–15, 19, 20).

Let us follow in his train "for the hour is coming in which no one can work" and the Mormons too are souls for whom Christ died.

We have seen in the preceding pages how the Mormon religion utilizes Biblical terms and phrases and even adopts Christian doctrines in order to claim allegiance to the Christian faith. Mormons have also come to lay much stress upon public relations and take pains to make certain that they do not use language which might reveal the true nature of their theological deviations. We have also seen that the Mormon Church considers itself alone the true church of Christ in our age, and further that they consider all other groups to be Gentiles and apostates from the true Christian religion.

We further read into the words of Joseph Smith himself, whom all Mormons are bound to recognize as the prophet of God, equal if not superior, to any of the Old Testament prophets.

Wrote prophet Smith concerning an alleged interview with the deity:

"My object in going to inquire of the Lord which of all the sects was right, that I might know which to join. No sooner therefore, did I get possession of myself so as to be able to speak, then I asked the Personages who stood above me in the light, which of all the sects was right and which I should join.

"I was answered that I must join none of them, for they were all wrong, and the personage who addressed me said that all their creeds were an abomination in His sight; those professors were all corrupt; they draw near to Me with their lips but their hearts are far from Me; they teach the doctrines and commandments of men having a form of godliness but they deny the power thereof.

"He again forbade me to join any of them; and many other things did he say unto me which I cannot write at this time."[24]

In addition to this statement of Smith's, Samuel W. Taylor, noted Mormon author, wrote in answer to the question, "Are Mormons Christians?" the following reply:

"Yes, indeed, but neither Protestant nor Catholic. Mormons believe that there was a breaking away of the other churches from true Christianity and that their religion is the restored gospel."[25]

From these facts it is evident for all to see that Mormonism strives with great effort to masquerade as the Christian church complete with an exclusive message, infallible prophets, higher revelations for a new dispensation which the Mormons would have us believe began with Joseph Smith, Jr.

But it is the verdict of both history and Biblical theology that Joseph Smith's religion is a polytheistic nightmare of garbled doctrines draped with the garment of Christian terminology. This fact, if nothing else, brands it as a non-Christian cult system.

Those who would consider Mormonism would be greatly profited by a thoughtful consideration of the facts and evidence previously discussed, lest they be misled into the spiritual maze that is Mormonism.

---

[24]Joseph Smith—History 1:1–25.
[25]The American Weekly, April 3, 1955.

Chapter 7

SPIRITISM—THE CULT OF ANTIQUITY

By far the oldest form of religious cult extant today, and certainly one of the deadliest where the certainty of divine judgment is concerned, is that of Spiritism, often erroneously referred to as "Spiritualism." However, in speaking of this cult, it is sometimes necessary to use that term in order to communicate in the vernacular of our day.

In 1949, Dr. Charles Braden wrote that in America, Spiritist leaders "estimate [there are] from 500,000 to 700,000 spiritualists in the United States; and . . . 1,500,000 to 2,000,000 in the world" (*These Also Believe*, New York: Macmillan Company, 1960, p. 356).

This estimate, as far as the United States is concerned, is very outdated. The International General Assembly of Spiritualists, the Nationalist Spiritualist Alliance of the United States of America, and the National Spiritualist Association of Churches reported (latest figures 1976) more than 200 churches, with a total membership of over 10,000, and more than 200 clergy. This does not include statistics for other countries of the world, notably in Europe and South America, where the movement is much stronger than in the States. In South America alone there are more than 4,000,000 Spiritists. Spiritism is finding new life, even in what is referred to as the scientific age of physics and quantum mechanics!

Dr. Marcus Bach, the noted liberal scholar, who has examined a great deal of spiritistic phenomena, states that, in his opinion, "The *raison d'etre* of Spiritualism is . . . demonstration and proof of the continuity of life, coupled with the comforting assurance that the life is good."

Dr. Bach went on in the same context to explain that in a séance, he saw the apparent reunion of a family, "a son telling his mother that life over there was just a continuation of life on earth. There were not two worlds at all; there was but one interblended, interrelated world, closely interwoven by memory and the love of life. Consciousness could not die. Personality could not be destroyed. The spirit of man was indeed eternal."

Dr. Bach concluded his observation with the statement:

> I left the room overpowered by a strange onrush of comfort about life and death. If this is all true, I thought, it will be difficult to speak of it without emotion. I have always believed in life after death. The traditional church has believed it too. Spiritism went a step further. It asked us to believe that the spirits were interested and active in human affairs; that they could be reached, seen and communicated with. The sense of assurance and comfort lingered. The feeling of genuineness persisted. I walked past the Chesterfield grotto. Someone was praying within the shrine. For those who believe, Spiritualism leads to God.[1]

---

[1]Marcus Bach, *They Have Found a Faith*, New York: Bobbs-Merrill, 1946, pp. 116, 121.

We cannot agree with Dr. Bach that "for those that believe, Spiritualism leads to God," for it is the direct testimony of Holy Scripture that Spiritualism is the masquerade of demonic forces, who pretend to be departed spirits with the intent of deceiving through the power of Satan those foolish enough to believe the testimony of demons in preference to the authority of the Word of God Himself. One need only to read 1 Samuel 28 to learn that King Saul's encounter with the medium of Endor brought divine condemnation and Saul's death; for God interrupted the séance, shocked the medium (verse 12) who was expecting the usual counterfeiting of personalities by her own familiar spirit, and allowed Samuel to speak to Saul of God's displeasure and coming wrath.

Spiritists repeatedly attempt to prove that the Bible endorses Spiritism, in fact, they cite any number of references in an attempt to prove that many Biblical characters, not excepting the apostles and our Lord Himself, were indeed mediums, and encouraged such practices.

Spiritism does indeed have a tremendous appeal to the minds of many persons, because, as Dr. Bach points out, it confirms for them life after death and reunion with their loved ones, something which the Scriptures also teach, and further declares that it is not necessary to confirm such truth through Satanic channels, unless one wishes to court the judgment of God.

Spiritism—Yesterday and Today

Since the first World War the religious horizons of the globe have seen the rapid rise of various forms of Spiritism, a religion unique in that it offers contact with and information from, beings beyond the grave. Much of contemporary Spiritism has been exposed by competent professionals as fraudulent. The classic exposé was by Houdini and Dunninger (*Magic and Mystery*, New York: Weathervane Books, 1967). Other exposés include that by former "psychic" M. Lamar Keene (*The Psychic Mafia*, New York: St. Martin's Press, 1976) and a joint investigation by a Christian physician, Paul Meier, and a Christian magician, Danny Korem (*The Fakers*, Grand Rapids: Baker Book House, 1980).

However, not all psychic or spiritistic phenomena can be exposed as fraudulent. There is a spiritual dimension which cannot be ignored. Authentic spiritists draw their power from the one the Bible calls "a roaring lion" who seeks "whom he may devour" (1 Peter 5:8), who is Satan. Spiritism, as we shall see, directly contradicts the Bible, God's Word. As well as constituting something akin to consumer fraud, spiritism also constitutes Biblical heresy.

In contemporary American life, so acute and complete is the recognition of supernatural sensitivity of communication and spirit manifestations, that Duke University set up a special division for the study of extrasensory perception (ESP, as it commonly is referred to in discussion). There are other such centers for psychic research and the studies of perception which transcends the normal senses, but all are calibrated to achieve the same end—confirmation of what God has forbidden—the exploration of the psychic dimension.

The greatest of all source books on the subject of Spiritism is, of course, the Bible, which gives a historical outline of Spiritism in a most concise and dependable form.

Beginning graphically in Exodus, Scripture reveals that the ancient Egyptians were practitioners of cultism of magic sorcery and necromancy, which were utilized by the priests of the demon gods of Egypt to duplicate the miracles of Moses when he appeared before Pharaoh with the divine command (Exodus 7:11, 22; 8:18).

The attitude of God toward those who practice the forbidden sin is also clearly outlined in Scripture. The Lord ordered the death penalty for all sorcerers as recorded in Exodus 22:18; Leviticus 20:27, to cite two specific instances. The Old Testament also named as those cursed by God, persons consorting with "familiar spirits" and "wizards" (Leviticus 19:31 and 20:6), in our language demons and mediums.

In company with these violators of divine command, Daniel the prophet often speaks of the magicians, sorcerers, soothsayers and astrologers (Daniel 1:20; 2:2, 27; 4:7 and 5:7), who specialized along with the Chaldeans, in the art of interpreting dreams and visions. The prophet Isaiah also speaks of ancient spiritists as casting sorceries upon Israel (Isaiah 8:19; 19:3; 47:9), and King Saul, before his apostasy, under God's command drove such practitioners from Israel (1 Samuel 28:3, 9) as did the righteous King Josiah after him (2 Kings 23:24, 25).

The Scriptures likewise bear record that Manassah's downfall came about as the result of his delving into Spiritism (2 Kings 21:6; 2 Chronicles 33:6) and his ensuing practice of idolatry in defiance of the command of God. The Bible then presents a devastating resumé of man's forbidden desire to uncover the hidden spiritual mysteries of the universe, even if witchcraft, divination, or enchantments must be employed to further his unholy quest. Egyptians, Babylonians, Chaldeans and the Canaanites, the Scriptures tell us, all practiced Spiritism, which practice, in one form or another, continued through the ages. In 1848 Spiritism received its modern rebirth at Hydesville, New York, in the persons of Kate and Margaret Fox, two of the best-known of the nineteenth century promulgators of Spiritism. (For further Biblical references to the practices of Spiritism, see such verses as Exodus 8:18; Leviticus 19:31; 1 Samuel 15:23; 2 Kings 9:22; 2 Chronicles 33:6; Daniel 2:2; Micah 5:12; and Nahum 3:4.)

The Revival of Modern Spiritism

Modern Spiritism had its birth, as far as most church historians are concerned, on March 31, 1848. On that date Mrs. John Fox, of Hydesville, New York, heard peculiar noises in the upstairs rooms and cellar of her home. Margaret and Kate Fox seemed to be peculiarly sensitive to these noises, and through this sensitivity they developed into mediums, and their communications became known as "The Rochester Rappings."

Some time afterward, the Fox sisters allegedly stated that the noises originated from their cracking the joints of their toes, but modern-day spiritists scorn this explanation, and today in Lilydale, New York, the Fox sisters' cottage has become a spiritualistic shrine, with a large marker, "There Is No Death," reaffirming the ancient practices of those whom God condemned as practitioners of abominations (Deuteronomy 18:9–12).

The roster of those interested in Spiritism is not inconsiderable. Dr. Bach lists a number of "great names" interested in psychic phenomena and research, names such as James Fenimore Cooper; William Cullen Bryant; Robert Dale Owen; Daniel Webster; Harriet Beecher Stowe; Elizabeth Barrett Browning; Horace Greeley; Elisha Cane; Sir Oliver Lodge, English physicist and author; E. Lee Howard, former pastor of the historic Congregational Church at Painesville, Ohio; Sherwood Eddy, world traveler and writer; Arthur Conan Doyle and Sir William Crooks, the last of whom was honored with degrees from at least five English universities and was inventor of the Crooks tube and discoverer of thallium. According to Bach, "Crooks reported 'that he had seen manifestations of levitation, and heard accordions play without being touched by human hands; had seen a luminous hand write upon the wall, and a medium handle live coals with bare hands.' All of this he had subjected to scientific tests to prove there were forces at work which could not be explained by any known physical law."

While some of these names might be readily challenged, we are concerned only with the judgments of the Bible, in which we are admonished to "prove [test] all things; hold fast that which is good" (1 Thessalonians 5:21).

It is interesting to note that Spiritism has made its strongest appeal to those who have suffered great loss, and after each great war, Spiritism always seems to be on the upgrade following the death of loved ones.

One of the great early prophets of modern-day Spiritualism was Andrew Jackson Davis, a poorly educated but extremely earnest disciple of spirit communication.

In 1847 Davis published his *Principles of Nature, her Divine Revelations and a Voice to Mankind*, which is reputed to have gone through over fifty editions in the United States. To this day Davis is revered by modern spiritualists as one of the great prophets of the movement. In 1852 Spiritualism was introduced into England, and in Germany in 1856 there were exhibitions or so-called "Spiritistic or Automatic Writings."

Other famous mediums were Daniel Douglas Home, William Stainton Moses and Leonora Piper. Chiefly through the works of these people, the famous British scientist Sir William Crooks accepted Spiritualism as genuine, and his testimony in no small way influenced Dr. William James, the noted philosopher and psychologist at Harvard.

The American Mercury carried in detail one of James' exhaustive verifications of spiritistic phenomena which stands today as a scientific confirmation of supernatural activity and empirical evidence of an existence that transcends the death of the body. Extensive quoting from that article follows.

From *The Housewife Who Confounded Two Countries*

In the city of Boston in 1885, Mrs. Leonora E. Piper, wife of a Boston merchant, and possessed of but limited education, began what was to be a

forty-year career as a spiritistic medium, a career which was to confound
the best minds in psychical research in both the United States and Europe
with scientifically validated evidence which has never been refuted. Mrs.
Piper became interested in Spiritism after visiting a clairvoyant for the relief
of severe pain after the birth of her first child. It was during sessions with
him that she lapsed into trances during which period she could answer with
amazing accuracy questions concerning persons who had died.

For some 26 years she continued under the various "spirit controls"
that possessed her during her trances as a medium and stopped only in
1911 when "the spirits" suggested that her health would not bear the strain
of their manifestation.

In 1924 Mrs. Piper conducted a special series of séances and the records
of these séances run more than 3,000 pages in length with a fantastic score
for accuracy.

Mrs. Piper gave some 88 sittings, for example, carefully observed at all
times by members of the British Society for Psychical Research. Professor
Oliver Lodge, later Sir Oliver Lodge, one of England's most brilliant scientists
and a careful psychic investigator, compiled a checklist of some 41 specific
incidents wherein Mrs. Piper stated facts and general information concerning those who attended her séances, facts which were unknown to those
persons at the very time the séances were in session! This was carefully
verified and is beyond refutation.

Mrs. Piper also had the amazing capacity to find lost objects and to
relate incidents which were taking place many hundreds of miles away from
where she was in a trance. Professor William James testified to this when
Mrs. Piper informed him that his aunt living over two hundred miles away
in New York had died early that very morning. According to James:

"On reaching home an hour later I found a telegram reading as follows:
'Aunt Kate passed away a few minutes after midnight.'"

Dr. James, undaunted by Mrs. Piper's capabilities, went so far as to
bring visiting professors from foreign universities with whom Mrs. Piper
was not acquainted only to have her give the correct names of the professors,
some of their parents, and the illnesses from which they died. James once
wrote of her:

"I now believe her to be in possession of a power as yet unexplained."

The British Society for Psychical Research enlisted the aid of detectives
and investigators who observed Mrs. Piper under all conditions while she
was in England, and Dr. Richard Hodgson, who had dedicated his life to
exposing "psychic wonders," threw up his hands in complete capitulation
when without any previous encounter with him, she informed him of his
real name, members of his family which were still living and two who had
died.

Hodgson brought her to England only to have her go under the control
of a spirit named Dr. Phinuit who communicated through her to Dr. Hodgson during the course of three months of exhaustive investigation. During
the course of that investigation she told him the exact movements of persons
in distant cities, and at another time under the control of a spirit who identified himself as "George Pellew," Mrs. Piper informed Dr. Hodgson of
events and facts which were subsequently verified by more than thirty of
Pellew's friends. Pellew correctly rejected more than a hundred persons

claiming to have known him in life and showed only those whom he had known!

Under the control of Pellew, Mrs. Piper translated perfectly a Greek phrase composed on the spur of the moment by a classical Greek scholar. Mrs. Piper knew no Greek whatever, but George Pellew did. She also reported under Pellew's control with complete accuracy what Pellew's father, who lived in another city, was doing at that moment.

Professor James Hyslop, of Columbia University, was totally bewildered by Mrs. Piper when with the cooperation of Dr. Hodgson, he interviewed Mrs. Piper in Sion seventeen times, only to be told by her his correct name and perfect answers to the questions which he addressed to her though she could not possibly have an access to the answers. Dr. Hyslop ended up believing that through Mrs. Piper he had actually communicated with the spirit of his departed father!

Mrs. Piper herself believed that the powers which she possessed were not supernatural. In fact, she stated:

"I never heard of anything being said by myself during the trance which might not have been latent in my own mind or in the mind of the sitters or in the mind of some absent person alive somewhere else in the world. The theory of telepathy strongly appeals to me as the most plausible solution of the problem."

Despite this modest statement, Mrs. Piper convinced Sir Oliver Lodge, Sir William Crooks, Dr. William James, Dr. Hodgson and Dr. Hyslop (after more than $150,000 was spent on "the most prolonged investigation in the history of psychical research"), that she was indeed possessed of supernatural capacities.

Evidence such as this cannot be dismissed but must indeed be studied carefully and will, I believe, demonstrate beyond a question of a doubt not only the existence of a spiritual dimension of reality but of the capacity of some to penetrate this dimension. In the terms of Scripture such a penetration can only culminate in a liaison with the forces of darkness of whom, in the light of Scripture, Mrs. Piper was the vehicle of communication.

It would be negligent to give the reader the impression that all so-called psychic phenomena is genuine, albeit demonic. By far the majority of such activity is fraudulent. There is abundant testimony (see Bibliography) to the consistently fraudulent world of spiritism. Christian authors Danny Korem and Paul Meier reflect some of the balance that a Christian should have in his assessment of psychic phenomena: "The reader, because of my perspective may assume that I have ruled out the possiblility of the intervening of supernatural agents in the flow of day-to-day existence. I *do* believe such intervention can and does take place. . . . The goal of this treatise is not only to debunk much of what is considered supernatural phenomena, but *also* to come full circle and identify those supernatural powers that do exist and their origins" (Korem and Meier, p. 32).

It is important to reiterate that much psychic activity is in reality fraud, deception, or even just misplaced sincerity. This pseudo-spiritism is, in one way, as dangerous and non-Christian as actual demonic communication. As Houdini and Dunninger stated in their classic exposé of fraudulent mediums: "The fact remains that a great number of self-styled mediums have played upon the credulity and sufferings of a public anxious to believe any-thing—anything which seems to assure continued life to those who have been loved, and who have passed the barrier of this life" (Houdini and Dunninger, p. 17).

The history of Spiritism literally spans the ages, but throughout it all, two things remain constant. The first is that Spiritism is to be found every-where posing as a universal, common denominator for all religious groups, not excepting Judaism and Christianity. It teaches the continuity of life and the eternal progression of man toward perfection in the spirit realm. Second, the Eternal God has condemned its practice in the sternest possible terms, maintaining that the interpretation of the supernatural realms belongs solely to Him (Genesis 40:8), and that those who practice intrusion into these realms are worthy of death (Exodus 22:18).

We are repeatedly warned in the strongest terms not to seek after me-diums and not to dabble in the realms of divine dominion (Leviticus 19:31). Only the deluded prefer the doctrines of demons to faith in the Word of God, and, as we shall see, the doctrines of Spiritism are precisely of such a nature.

Verified Instances of Spiritistic Phenomena

Below are two instances of spiritistic phenomena which I accept as in-dicative of true occultic/demonic involvement as described by the Bible. Both I feel have sound evidence attesting to their validity. There are many Chris-tians, unfortunately, who suffer from the illusion that all Spiritism, or spir-itistic evidence, is fraudulent, and prefer to rest in the falsely secure belief that Spiritism can never be demonically empowered.

I do believe that much spiritistic evidence is manufactured and comes from over-active imaginations or outright deception on the part of the "per-former." Spiritism, legitimate or fraudulent, is big business. The lure of easy money is more than enough to draw many unsuspecting would-be mediums into occultic and/or deceptive spiritistic practices. Ex-psychic M. Lamar Keene said of the largest Spiritist camp, Chesterfield, that it was "spiritualism's an-swer to Disneyland. That first season of mine, more than 65,000 pilgrims crowded onto the grounds from here, there, and everywhere. They spent more than a million dollars to commune with their beloved dead."[2]

Case I

The first of these instances was reported by Dr. Marcus Bach, a well-known religious observer and writer whose unbiased approach to Spiritism led him to visit the largest Spiritist camp, Chesterfield, and to attend séances that his investigation convinced him were authentic.

On August 26 I drove into Chesterfield, Indiana, and proceeded im-mediately to the spiritualist camp adjoining the town. It is called a city of

---

[2]*The Psychic Mafia*, New York: St. Martin's Press, 1976, p. 43.

peace, a New Jerusalem, a Great Mecca. Expecting a morbid cloister for communication with the dead, I found to my surprise a bucolic vacationland. Two large hotels and twenty cottages look out upon a grass-carpeted amphitheater and a grotto in a "garden of prayer."

Symbolizing the unbroken tradition of spiritualism, there is a "Trail of Religions." Spiritualists say there is nothing like it in the world. Life-sized busts of Abraham, Buddha, Zoroaster, Mohammed, Lao-tse, Confucius, Vardhamana, Zeus, Osiris, and Jesus suggest that spiritualism is universal in appeal and application. Overlooking the scene, an Indian stands with face uplifted to the invisible heavens of the spirit world.[3]

After arriving at this Mecca of modern American Spiritism, Dr. Bach visited two séances. He records this for us as a skeptic who became a believer in the phenomena of Spiritism:

The moments passed. My eyes became accustomed to the dark and I could make out the vague outline of Pressing next to me. He leaned over and whispered somberly, "Well, when's something going to happen?"

Before I could answer—

"How do you do, Dr. Bach! How do you do, Mr. Pressing!" came to us out of the darkness. It was a tantalizing, childish voice with a slightly roguish touch. It might have been a winsome little prodigy stepping out in the debut. It might have been a tiny actress in a puppet show.

"Good afternoon," responded Mr. Pressing.

"Who are you?" I asked.

With a friendly lilt the answer came, "I'm Sylvia. . . . We are glad you are here, Dr. Bach," she said with a neat curtsy in her voice. "This is going to be a good séance. There are good vibrations. Look!"

The small trumpet was slowly rising from the floor. It stopped slightly above the larger one and hovered uncertainly. . . .

"But who are you?" I insisted.

"Sylvia!" said the voice emphatically. "Didn't I tell you I am Sylvia? . . . I can get other spirits for you, if you want me to."

"How?" I demanded. "With millions of spirits in the spirit world, how do you get them? Call Bob Whitehand for me."

"Bob Whitehand?" The voice seemed to drift from us for a moment. "Bob Whitehand?" it returned reflectively. "I'll try. It is done by vibrations. . . . I'll try to get Bob Whitehand afterwhile. But look at the trumpet now, Dr. Bach!"

It had risen to five or six feet above the floor and was slowly floating in space. . . .

"Where would you like the trumpet to go?" asked Sylvia.

"Bring it close to me," I told her.

Outlined by the luminous bands, the trumpet floated toward me. It stopped close to my right ear.

"Put it in my hands, Sylvia," I said.

"Hold them out!"

I extended my hands and the trumpet came to rest in them. Now, I thought, here's my chance to find those strings. Balancing the feather-light tube in my left hand, I passed my right hand completely around it. No strings.

[3]*They Have Found a Faith*, Marcus Bach, p. 99.

"Put your hands on each end of the trumpet," Sylvia directed.
I did, holding the trumpet about elbow's length from my body.
"Now I'll talk to you from inside the trumpet."
A whispered voice—Sylvia's—came from within the trumpet. I put it
to my right ear—the voice was there; to my left ear—Sylvia speaking.
"Well," I admitted, "that's interesting." Then I withdrew both hands
quickly. Unaided, the trumpet remained fixed in space.
A conversation between Sylvia and Pressing was lost in the amazement
upon seeing the other trumpet begin a slow take-off. Without stopping, it
ascended to a point near the ceiling. It hung there, then started a slow
swinging motion, round and round, like the retarded movement of a heli-
copter.[4]

Dr. Bach continued the discussion of the séance to point out that Dr.
William James then addressed him for perhaps fifteen or twenty minutes.
The trumpet continued its levitating motion and, after Dr. James stopped
speaking, Sylvia, the capricious spirit creature, took the trumpet which seemed
suspended from the air, and caused it to crash with a bang against the wall
behind Dr. Bach. Dr. Bach records Mr. Pressing asking, "What the devil was
that?"

Sylvia's impish laugh was the answer. "I wanted to show you how pol-
tergeists work! Well, that's the way!" The room was quiet for a few moments.
Nothing could be seen save the luminous bands of the small trumpet. Then
Sylvia's voice said, "I think I have Bob Whitehand for you."
"Good!" I said, in a tone of co-operation. "Bob? Bob? Can you hear
me?"
A luminous head appeared levitated about four feet from the floor. It
was not materialized in the way that materialization is usually described. It
simply appeared out of nothingness. It was like a blurred flashlight reflected
on a human face. I made out the unmistakable features of my friend who
had been killed in France. This apparition hovered in the room for only a
few seconds and then blacked out. How should I explain it? If it were
actually a human face illuminated by a flashlight, it must have been shrouded
in a curtain in the center of the room. But I knew there had been no curtain.
Besides, why would the flashlight diffuse over no other single part of the
room, curtain or apparatus—if apparatus were used? And if it were someone impersonating Bob Whitehand, how could he make up such a marked
resemblance of Bob, inasmuch as no one knew that I would request Bob's
appearance? It was an inexplicable happening and remained the most vivid
of the afternoon's demonstration.
Sylvia was now bidding us good-by. The little trumpet returned to its
original position.[5]

Dr. Back records one more confrontation in the séance which certainly
bears close study and analysis because it was of a closely personal nature. He
described it this way:

I was making minute mental notations of all that was happening—the
hovering, swaying motion of the "spirits," the rhythm of life, like the rise
and fall of a tide, as many as four speaking simultaneously in whispered

---

[4]*Ibid.*, pp. 104–106.
[5]*Ibid.*, pp. 108, 109.

voices, excited, hurried persuasive. Suddenly the galaxy of spirits melted away. For a long still moment nothing happened. Then the swirling ectoplasmic effluvia glowed from the floor and quickly took on the form of a girl. Before the figure was complete, it spoke.

"Marc, dear—Marc, dear—Marc, dear."

Those who know me well call me Marc; those who know me better call me Marc, dear, so I knew this must be a "familiar spirit!" I got up and walked over until there was a space of less than four feet between us. "Yes?" I said. "Who are you?"

The answer was fraught with disappointment. "Don't you know me?"

I did not. I had no idea who this might be. I had really been too absorbed to think very much about personal contact with the spirits. . . . Nor did I propose to offer any hint of whom I thought she *might represent*. No leads, I determined.

"I do not know you. Who are you?"

"Paula," came the answer.

The name and soft manner in which it was uttered brought the sudden unfolding of a forgotten drama. Twenty years ago my sister Paula had died at the age of twenty-three. Her child Janette had died shortly before. These deaths had been among the deep sorrows of our family, but time and travel reduce the past into forgetfulness. No medium or spirit had plucked this name out of my mind because I wasn't thinking of Paula. I had not thought of her even once during the séance.

I looked at the presence before me closely.

"How do I look?" she asked.

"You look fine," I replied.

"The right height?" she whispered. "Do you think I should be taller?"

"No. You are about the height I remember."

"I wanted to do a good job," she told me earnestly. "Do I look all right?"

"Yes," I assured her, recalling that one theory of materialization is that the spirit "takes" the ectoplasm and fashions according to its memory the human form which clothed it on earth.

. . . Did this form and these features resemble Paula? I must admit they did. Very much. The outline of the figure was recognizable and convincing. It was like a "false front," a flat, two-dimensional body with the semblance of arms clothed in a shadowy gray-white film. The face, though typically masklike, was strikingly reminiscent. There was an illusion of long blond hair. I cannot say whether the voice was Paula's or not. After twenty years I would not remember. Just now, however, it was Paula returned.

But why shouldn't it be? I asked myself as I stood there. The spiritualists at Chesterfield knew I was coming. If, as some people say, they have a well-laid system of espionage they could easily have traced my family and got Paula's description. If this was someone "dressed up," play-acting, if this was a marionette using the voice of a ventriloquist, naturally it would be constructed as to represent Paula. This thought haunted me more than the presence. I wished I could convince myself some way. The impulse to reach out and touch the figure became stronger. I moved closer. I moved slightly to one side so that the red light would strike the spirit's face more directly. We were about three feet apart now. Paula was talking about life in the spirit world. I was asking hasty questions: Have you seen Jesus? What is heaven like? What about the element of time? Can you be everywhere at once? Are terms like Methodist, Reformed, Presbyterian, Catholic ever used where you are?

Her voice seemed to laugh. She answered, "No, no," to all questions save the one about heaven. It was like speaking to a living person secretly, clandestinely, knowing that time was running out. Her features seemed to become clearer. Perhaps it was my mind playing tricks.

And then a thought came to me. "Paula," I said, "do you remember the catechism we learned at home?"

"Of course!"

"Paula, do you remember the first question in that catechism?"

"I remember."

"What was it?" I asked almost fearfully.

The answer came at once. " 'What is your chief comfort in life and in death?' "

"Go on," I urged.

" 'That I, with body and soul, both in life and in death am not my own—' " She interrupted herself. "Here where we are the words have a greater meaning!"

Then quickly, breathlessly, she told me that serving God means personal development. Life on the spirit plane is an evolvement. Like the breaking of a chrysalis. Like the ascent in a spiral. Like the growth of moral affection to higher and higher "heavens." Several times she interrupted herself with "Do you understand? Is that clear?" as if she felt her message was vital, all-absorbing. Death, she insisted, was not a violent result of sin. It had no sting. It was neither friend nor enemy. It was part of the divine purpose, a purpose without beginning or end.

The whispering grew fainter. "I can stay no longer. I must go now."

"Paula, one more thing. Can you put your arms around me?"

"I'll give you a kiss," she said. "Come closer."

"You come close to me." I wanted her to come nearer the red light. She did. There was now scarcely a foot between us. Her face was luminous, seemingly transparent, and without depth.

I leaned forward and lowered my head. The weblike texture of ectoplasmic arms encircled my neck. Something soft and flaxen brushed my forehead. Then Paula vanished—into the floor, it seemed.

I walked back to my chair and sat down. . . . The séance was ended.[6]

Camp Chesterfield has not always enjoyed such favorable inspection as it received from Dr. Bach. In 1960 a Spiritist advertising project blew up in the Spiritists' faces, exposing some of the fraudulent activities occurring there. M. Lamar Keene, ex-psychic and ex-Chesterfield staff member recounts:

Two sympathetic researchers, Tom O'Neill and Dr. Andrija Puharich, had tried to get the first motion pictures ever of the materialization of a spirit. O'Neill was a believing spiritualist, editor of the monthly newspaper *Psychic Observer*, an ordained minister of the Indiana Association of Spiritualists . . . and a close friend of . . . other stalwarts at the camp. Puharich was a physician and psychical researcher whom O'Neill had recruited to give the project scientific credibility. . . .

The experiment was a disaster for the spiritualists. Peering through the snooperscope in the dark, Puharich saw that what were supposed to be spirit forms of shimmering ectoplasm materializing out of thin air, were actually figures wrapped in chiffon entering the séance room through a

[6]*Ibid.*, pp. 117–121.

hidden door from an adjacent apartment.

The infrared motion picture confirmed Puharich's observations. There, etched unmistakably on the film, were the familiar faces of camp mediums, dressed up in gauze, impersonating departed spirits (Keene, *op. cit.*, pp. 41, 42).

Case II

An example of spiritistic demonstration is recorded by J. Arthur Hill in his book, *Spiritualism: Its History, Phenomena, and Doctrine* (New York: George Doran, 1919, pp. 74, 75), wherein Mr. Hill cites the case of Daniel Douglas Home, medium extraordinary, who practiced communication and levitation:

In 1885, Daniel D. Home, a young man of Scottish-American descent, arrived in the British Isles, and it is in the case of Home and his claims of spiritistic mediumship, that the objective observer finds evidence of supernatural manifestations that has been challenged by no one who has thoroughly investigated the life of Mr. Home.

There are many instances recorded of Home's ability to communicate with forces beyond this earth, but the physical phenomena or manifestations of spirit influence which reveal themselves in Home's fantastic ability, are the best testimonies to his possession by supernatural powers.

Sir Wm. Crooks, famed British scientist and acknowledged authority on the phenomena of spiritualism, testified that beyond a shadow of a doubt in the case of Mr. Home, there was "definitely the operation of some agency unknown to science."

In the presence of Sir William and Home, "an accordion placed under the table and untouched by the medium, played tunes, and could manage a few notes, though no tune, when it was held by Mr. Crooks himself. A lath of wood on a table, three feet from Home, rose 10 inches and floated about in the air for more than a minute, moving gently up and down as if it were on rippling water, the medium's hands, meanwhile, being held by Mrs. Walter Crooks and Mrs. William Crooks. A pencil on the table stood up on its point and tried to write, but fell down: the lath then slid across to it and buttressed the pencil, while it tried again. Tables slid about, untouched. Luminous clouds were seen and materialized hands, which carried flowers about. And Home himself was lifted into the air, thus paralleling the levitations of many saints. All this in a fair light, usually one gas burner.

The most famous of the levitations, however, occurred in 1868, at 5, Buckingham Gate, London, in the presence of Lords Lindsay and Adare, and Captain Wynne. Home floated or appeared to float out of one window and in at another. The windows were 76 inches apart, 85 feet above the ground, and there was no ledge or foothold between them. . . . It is difficult to believe that the whole of Home's phenomena were due to fraud or hallucination. As we so often have to say, certainty concerning matters of history, which are vouched for only by a few people, most or all of whom are now dead, is not attainable, and when the alleged events are of a kind to which our own experience supplies no parallel, it is easiest to suppose that the things were done fraudulently somehow. But we must admit that this conclusion is due to prejudice, for in any other matter we should unhesitatingly accept as final the word of so distinguished a man of science as Sir William Crooks, especially when supported by such massive testimony.

It must be noted that not every investigator of psychic phenomena accepts the validity of this particular event. Houdini and Dunninger remained unconvinced as have some others.[7]

There are many other instances which we could cite to demonstrate the claims of spiritists, that they do indeed make contact with powers beyond this earth, and such claims are doubtless quite valid. The question is, are such contacts approved of in the Word of God, and if not, then is not the practice of such contacts disobedience to the expressed will of God, and harmful to the soul of man?

As we have noted, the Bible speaks emphatically on this very point, and as we move on to discuss doctrinal content and contrasts of spiritistic teachings with those of Christianity, we shall be better able to understand the divine viewpoint where Spiritism and the practices of spiritists are concerned.

In this connection, let us note at least two specific things in the account given us by Dr. Bach and Mr. Hill. In the case of Dr. Bach, it will be remembered that the apparition which purported to be his departed sister, Paula, completely contradicted the New Testament, particularly the fifteenth chapter of 1 Corinthians, where death is described as an enemy (verse 26). Death does indeed have a sting for mankind that can only be removed by faith in the resurrection of Jesus Christ, which makes possible the resurrection of those who believe in Him (verses 55–57).

It might also be profitably recalled that in his epistle to the Romans, the Apostle Paul spoke quite markedly of the reality of sin, evil, and spiritual death or separation from fellowship with God. Chapters five and six particularly point out that Christ alone restores man to fellowship, and this He did by ruining Satan's power. (See Hebrews 2:14.) In the revelation of the New Testament, death is indeed the result of sin. (See also Genesis chapter three.) It is a part of the divine purpose which God has permitted to take place and has provided a solution for: i.e., its eventual destruction by resurrection, in Christ. Although it is a part of the divine purpose, it is not neutral; it is indeed the "last enemy" to be destroyed (1 Corinthians 15:26).

Though we may also find ourselves in agreement with the statement of Mr. Hill concerning Daniel Home and his supernatural powers, we ought not to forget that Home was a true spiritist-medium who denied the Deity of Jesus Christ, the atonement and the bodily resurrection of our Lord. The powers which controlled him (spiritists are wrong when they claim to control the spirits) were not powers from God. On the contrary, they were the demonic spirits spoken of and condemned in the Bible. The Father of Spirits, God Almighty, will be the eventual judge of him who is known as "the prince of the powers of the air," Satan.

The Theology of Spiritism

Its "Seven Principles" have been set forth as follows.

    I. The Fatherhood of God
   II. The Brotherhood of Man
  III. Continuous Existence

---

[7]*Magic and Mystery*, New York: Weathervane Books, 1967, p. 97.

IV. Communion of Spirits and Ministry of Angels
V. Personal Responsibility
VI. Compensation and Retribution Hereafter for Good and Evil Done on Earth
VII. A Path of Endless Progression

Secretary of the Spiritualists' National Union,
The Seven Principles of Spiritualism (pp. 2, 3).

1. Spiritualism is the Science, Philosophy and Religion of continuous life, based upon the demonstrated fact of communication, by means of mediumship, with those who live in the Spirit world.

2. A Spiritualist is one who believes, as the basis of his or her religion, in the communication between this and the spirit world by means of mediumship, and who endeavors to mold his or her character and conduct in accordance with the highest teachings derived from such communion.

National Spiritualist Association,
Definitions, 1914, 1919.

Infinite Intelligence pervades and controls the universe, is without shape or form and is impersonal, omnipresent and omnipotent.

It teaches that the spark of divinity dwells in all.

That every soul will progress through the ages to heights, sublime and glorious, where God is Love and Love is God.

"What Spiritualism Is and Does,"
Spiritualist Manual, 1940.

Man is a spiritual being, evolved from the lower forms of life, up through the period of consciousness, to the state of the higher moral and spiritual faculties, which survive, unaffected, the decomposition of the physical body.

Good deeds, springing from a good heart, have a creative force in building pleasant abodes in spirit life, and conversely the sinful create their own unhappy habitations. The wicked must compensate for their evil deeds, here or hereafter, and attain a state of justice before they are prepared to enter upon the path which leads to spiritual happiness and progression.

"Philosophy of Spiritualism," *Ibid*.

Spiritualism is an outpouring of the spirit upon humanity, a divine revelation from the spheres of light. It is the highest message of truth which we have, as yet, grown to grasp; and one whose depth, beauty and mighty significance we still imperfectly realize.

Spiritualism is the broad educator, the great redeemer, the emancipator which releases human souls from the bondage of superstition and ignorance, lifts the clouds or error that have so long enshrouded the world, and illumines the darkness of the world's materiality.

"What is Spiritualism?," *Ibid*.

The Spiritualistic Hymnal indicates changes made on well-known hymns and we have listed one to demonstrate their theological position in so doing.

Just As I Am

Just as I am, without one plea,
But that, O God, Thou madest me,

And that my life is found in Thee
O God of Love, I come, I come.

Just as I am, nor poor, nor blind,
Nor bound by chains in soul or mind;
For all of Thee within I find
O God of Love, I come, I come.

Just as I am, Thou wilt receive,
Tho' dogmas I may ne'er believe,
Nor heights of holiness achieve
O God of Love, I come, I come.

It is an absurd idea that Jesus was any more divine than any other man.—*Weisse*

Tom Paine is the seventh sphere, one above our Lord, though he was so many centuries behind him in entering into the spirit life.—*Weisse*

The miraculous conception of Christ is merely a fabulous tale.—*Haweis*

Advanced spirits do not teach the atonement of Christ—nothing of the kind.—*Nocholas*

Your doctrine of the atonement is the very climax of a deranged imagination, and one that is of the unrighteous and immoral tendency.—*Hall*

We regret and condemn the practice of Spiritualists sending their children to be instructed in the teaching of a vicarious atonement, or salvation by faith and not of works.—A resolution passed at the Spiritualistic Convention in Bradford, England.

All advanced Spiritualists—though few have the courage to confess it—repudiate marriage in its legal sense, and believe in the doctrine of affinities.—The Founder of the Free Love Society, a Spiritualist, in a letter to the *New York World* in 1856.

> Quotations from the writings of noted Spiritualists
> as recorded in William Edward Biederwolf's *Spiritualism*,
> Grand Rapids, MI: Eerdmans, 1952, p. 32.

I am here tonight as one of the founders of Spiritualism to denounce it as an absolute falsehood from beginning to end, as the flimsiest of superstitions, the most wicked blasphemy known to the world.—R. B. Davenport, *The Deathblow to Spiritualism*, 1888, p. 76; cf. *The New York Daily Tribune*, for Oct. 22. See also *New York World*, Oct. 21, 1888.

> LeRoy Edwin Froom, *Spiritualism Today*,
> Washington D. C.: Review and Herald, 1963, p. 6.

Lord Dowding, a strong advocate of Spiritualism, says in his book, *Many Mansions* (p. 107): "The first thing which the orthodox Christian has to face is that the doctrine of the Trinity seems to have no adherents in advanced circles of the spirit world. The Divinity of Christ as a co-equal partner with the Father is universally denied. Jesus Christ was indeed the Son of God, as also are we sons of God. . . . We (i.e., orthodox Christians) are taught to believe in the remission of sins to the penitent, through the virtue of Christ's sacrifice and atonement. This doctrine Imperator (the pseudonym of one of these advanced spirits) vigorously combats in a score of passages."

Quoted in J. Stafford Wright's *Spiritualism*,
London, England: The Church Book Room Press, 1959, p. 11.

Sir Arthur Conan Doyle: "Spiritualism is the greatest revelation the world has ever known."

I have seen spirits walk around the room and join in the talk of the company.

We are continually conscious of protection around us.

General experience shows that a facile acceptance of these claims of spirit is very rare among earnest thinkers and that there is hardly any prominent Spiritualist whose course of study and reflection has not involved a novitiate of many years.

"The History of Spiritualism,"
Spiritualist Manual, op. cit., p. 131.

Every Human Soul born into life is a child of GOD and the opportunity for development will at some time be realized and taken advantage of by each one. Spiritualism proclaims "THE DOORWAY TO REFORMATION IS NEVER CLOSED AGAINST ANY SOUL HERE OR HEREAFTER."

Ibid., p. 181.

We do not believe in "fairies," "demons," "elementals," "astral shells," nor any such imaginary beings, whose existence cannot be proven. We know no reason why such creatures should exist. Such beliefs are neither scientific, nor do they follow the Laws of Nature, as these are disclosed by our science and philosophy or by the other natural sciences. We impress upon you once more that our belief contains nothing but what is in accord with Natural Law and which can be concretely proven.

Ibid., p.181.

We believe in intelligent and ignorant spirits. No being is naturally "bad"— evil always originates in ignorance. Merely leaving the physical body does not change the condition of the spirit, which is the actual personality. It must learn to desire, and to progress to higher and better conditions, just as we do on earth.

"Miracle" means something done in defiance of Natural Law, therefore there are no Miracles. The demonstrations you speak of can be manifested today by our Sensitives (often called mediums) by the application of perfectly natural forces, when necessary conditions for such manifestations are provided.

Ibid., p. 182.

We do not believe in such places as Purgatory and Hell. Communicating spirits have merely graduated from this form of life into another. That life can be heaven or hell-like, just as each spirit chooses to make it; the same applies to our life here.

Ibid., p. 183.

Even the most degraded personality can in time attain to the greatest heights. It is easier, however, to begin progression in earth life.

Each must work out his own salvation; each has an equal opportunity to do this when he shall have atoned for the wrongs and overcome the temptations and allurements to the sense gratifications of earth life.

Ibid., p. 184.

The Verdict of the Holy Spirit

The previously cited quotations show most clearly some of the basic teachings of Spiritism. Such quotations from their representative literature, when contrasted with familiar Christian truths, reveal that Spiritism cannot in any sense qualify as Christianity. In fact, it is a particularly virile form of cultism, opposed in almost every specific to the historic doctrines of the Christian faith. It is hardly necessary therefore to refute Spiritism since its own statements are of such an anti-Christian nature as to be self-convicting.

Perhaps the most striking example in the New Testament of the immutable attitude of God toward Spiritism and mediums is recorded in the thirteenth chapter of the Book of Acts and merits careful scrutiny:

> Now there were in the church that was at Antioch certain prophets and teachers; as Barnabas, and Simeon that was called Niger, and Lucius of Cyrene, and Manaen, which had been brought up with Herod the tetrarch, and Saul. As they ministered to the Lord, and fasted, the Holy Ghost said, Separate me Barnabas and Saul for the work whereunto I have called them. And when they had fasted and prayed, and laid their hands on them, they sent them away. So they, being sent forth by the Holy Ghost, departed unto Seleucia; and from thence they sailed to Cyprus. . . . And when they had gone through the isle unto Paphos, they found a certain sorcerer, a false prophet, a Jew, whose name was Bar-jesus; which was with the deputy of the country, Sergius Paulus, a prudent man; who called for Barnabas and Saul, and desired to hear the word of God.
>
> But Elymas the sorcerer (for so is his name by interpretation) withstood them, seeking to turn away the deputy from the faith. Then Saul, (who also is called Paul,) filled with the Holy Ghost, set his eyes on him, And said, O full of all subtilty and all mischief, thou child of the devil, thou enemy of all righteousness, wilt thou not cease to pervert the right ways of the Lord? And now, behold, the hand of the Lord is upon thee, and thou shalt be blind, not seeing the sun for a season. And immediately there fell on him a mist and a darkness; and he went about seeking some to lead him by the hand (Acts 13:1–4, 6–11).

The context of this chapter indicates that Paul and Barnabas were set apart specifically by the Holy Spirit (verses 2, 4) to preach the Word of God as the Spirit directed.

In the course of discharging the duties assigned to them by the Holy Spirit, they found a certain magician or medium, a false prophet, a Jew, whose name was Bar-jesus (verse 6).

We learn from the account that this man deliberately obstructed the preaching of the Gospel to the deputy of the country, Sergius Paulus, a man of integrity who desired to hear the Word of God (verse 7). The judgment of God fell upon this man (verse 11). But it is not significant until it is noted that in verses 9 and 10 the judgment was preceded by the announcement that Paul, was "filled with the Holy Spirit," when he set his eyes upon him. Paul's scathing denunciation of the medium identifies him as a destructive, mischievous son of Satan, the enemy of all divine righteousness, and the perverter or twister or the right pathway of the Lord.

The Scripture reminds us that we are the temple of the Holy Spirit (1 Corinthians 6:19). The Spirit of God dwells within each Christian, and Scripture assures us that "greater is he that is in you, than he that is in the world" (1 John 4:4). The Christian, then, can never be possessed by demonic forces; he is constantly shielded and protected by the power of the indwelling Spirit. There is no demonic force that can withstand the presence and power of the Holy Spirit. This is why in the thirteenth chapter of Acts, the Scripture reminds us that Paul dealt with forces of darkness in his capacity as a believer filled with the Holy Spirit, and with complete assurance and confidence that God's power, grace and all-pervading presence would give him the victory over any medium, false prophet or "son of Satan" (as the Holy Spirit, through Paul, so graphically describes Bar-jesus).

As we close our study of Spiritism, three important factors can be gleaned from the comparison of Spiritism historically and theologically with the Gospel of Jesus Christ.

First, Spiritism as a cult has been from its beginning in opposition to the Judaeo-Christian religions. In order for one to embrace its teachings, every major doctrine of the Christian faith must be rejected, including the inspiration and final authority of the Bible, the doctrines of the Trinity, the Deity of Christ, the Virgin Birth, Vicarious Atonement, and Bodily Resurrection of our Lord from the grave. The Biblical doctrine of salvation by grace alone, through faith in Christ, apart from the works of the Law, is anathema to spiritist theology which relies on progressive evolution or growth in the "spirit world," to attain final perfection.

No informed student of Spiritism for a moment denies these things, and the previously noted quotations taken from bonafide spiritist publications more than substantiate the validity of this contention.

Second, it cannot be forgotten that amidst the vast majority of spiritistic phenomena which are fraudulent, there are truly supernatural manifestations. Authorities have given credence to a number of those which do not readily admit to natural or trick explanations. True Spiritism, then, can produce supernatural manifestations, which the Bible describes as originating in demonic forces, and thus under the judgment of God (Deuteronomy 18:9–11; Leviticus 19:31; 20:6; 1 Samuel 28:3–9; 2 Kings 21:6; 2 Chronicles 33:6; and Isaiah 47:9).

Third, Christians must realize that Spiritism is practiced by persons who willfully ignore the God of the Bible and His declared means of making men holy, i.e., the sending of His Son into the world that the world through Him might be saved (John 3:16, 36).

In the spirit of Christian love, we are committed to bear witness to Spiritists, refute their teachings, and confront them with the Christ of Calvary, who alone can "take away the sins of the world" (John 1:29). Spiritism properly understood, is indeed a cult of antiquity, but its motivating force comes from Satan who said long ago, in pristine Eden, "You shall not surely die," and of whom Jesus Christ said, "He is a liar" and "a murderer from the beginning and obeyed not the truth" (John 8:44).

Chapter 8

THE THEOSOPHICAL SOCIETY

Theosophy as a cult system derives its name from the Greek term *theosophia*, literally, divine wisdom. And, in the words of J. H. Fussell, its teachings are,

at the same time religious, philosophic and scientific, . . . (postulating) one eternal, immutable, all-pervading principle, the root of all manifestation. From that one existence comes forth periodically the whole universe, manifesting the two aspects of spirit and matter, life and form, positive and negative, "the two poles of nature between which the universe is woven." Those two aspects are inseparably united; therefore all matter is ensouled by life while all life seeks expression through forms. All life being fundamentally one with the life of the Supreme Existence, it contains in germ all the characteristics of its source, and evolution is only the unfolding of those divine potentialities brought about by the conditions afforded in the various kingdoms of nature. The visible universe is only a small part of this field of evolution.[1]

Theosophy then, may be recognized at the outset as a pantheistic form of ancient Gnosticism, which attempts to embrace religious, philosophic and scientific truth as it is found in all religio-philosophic sources.

According to the views of Theosophists, their Society "is a growing system of thought, the result of careful study and research" and further "it is nothing less than the bedrock upon which all phases of the world's thought and activity are founded."[2]

This enobling ideal dreams of a brotherhood of all faiths, or, if we may use the term, a type of homogenized religion, in which all men will agree to the cardinal tenets of Theosophy, in one degree or another. In this respect, it is related to Spiritism, Rosicrucianism, Baha'ism and the Great I Am cults.

In theory of course, and quite apart from the Christian Scriptures, this idea is most appealing. But even a cursory perusal of man's demonstrably depraved nature, as revealed in history and in the Bible, renders this Utopian concept an absurd theological farce.

Theosophy as a religion is opposed to virtually every cardinal doctrine of the Christian faith, and finds no support from Judaism, little from Islam, and certainly none from the majority of world religions, with the exception of Buddhism and Hinduism. Christianity, Judaism and Islam all confess a personal God; all believe in a resurrection of the body, and in the authority

[1]J. H. Russell, in "Theosophy," *The New Shaff-Herzog Encyclopedia of Religious Knowledge*, Grand Rapids, MI: Baker Book House, 1977 (repr.), vol. 11, p. 407.
[2]Irving S. Cooper, *Theosophy Simplified*, Wheaton, IL: The Theosophical Press, 1964 (7th ed.), pp. 22, 23.

of the Old Testament. Theosophy, on the other hand, rejects *all* these doctrines. Yet it continues to qualify for the role as a "unifier and peace-maker in religion."

It is an interesting fact that Theosophy speaks in glowing terms of the ancient cult of Gnosticism, which thrived in the first three centuries of the Christian era, and which almost succeeded in doing irreparable damage to historic Christian faith. Paul's epistle to the Colossians, and the epistle of 1 John are recognized by all Biblical scholars to be direct apologetic thrusts against this cult which spiritualized the Old Testament, redefined contemporary Christian terminology, substituted an impersonal God for the God of revelation, and reduced Jesus Christ to a demi-god, or a pantheistic emanation from the unknowable divine essence. The well-known Theosophical writer L. W. Rogers, however, disdains the counsel of the Holy Spirit, not to mention the warnings of the apostles Paul and John when he states:

> The antagonism between scientific and religious thought was the cause of great controversy that occurred in the intellectual world in the late nineteenth century. If the early teaching of the Christian Church had not been lost, the conflict could not have arisen. The gnostic philosophers who were the intellect and heart of the Church had a knowledge of nature so true that it could not possibly come into collision with any fact of science; but unfortunately, they were enormously outnumbered by the ignorant, and the authority passed wholly into the hands of the latter. It was inevitable that misunderstanding followed.[3]

Theosophists then are great admirers of the Gnostics, and this is not at all surprising, since they have adopted much of the terminology and vocabulary of ancient Gnosticism, which looked with disdain upon the material properties of both the world and man, depersonalized God and created various planes of spiritual progression culminating in universal salvation and reconciliation through reincarnation and the wheel concept of progression borrowed unblushingly from Buddhism.

Theosophy does not hesitate to declare that:

> God and man are the two phases of the one eternal life and consciousness that constitutes our universe! The idea of the immanence of God is that He is the universe; although he is also more than it is; that the solar system is an emanation of the Supreme Being as clouds are an emanation of the sea. This conception makes man a part of God, having potentially within him all the attributes and powers of the Supreme Being. It is the idea that nothing exists except God, and that humanity is one portion of him—one phase of his Being.[4]

In the theology of Theosophy there are seven distinct planes in the universe. The Physical is the most dense of these planes; that which is next in the order is called the Astral Plane, and above it, the Mental. There are four higher spiritual planes, but to all except initiates and adepts they are as yet "mere names." Man of course has a physical body, a mental body and an astral body. But at this particular stage of cosmic evolution, with but few

---

[3]L. W. Rogers, *Elementary Theosophy*, Wheaton, IL: The Theosophicals Press, 1956, p. 22.
[4]*Ibid.*, p. 23.

exceptions, the so-called higher spiritual bodies are still awaiting organization.[5]

A little further on in the chapter, we shall see what relationship this has to the basic doctrines of Christianity. But there can be little doubt that such hypothetical fancies, saturated with gnostic terminology and concepts, cannot help but generate conflict where Biblical theology is concerned.

Historical Sources

It is one of the strange historical peculiarities of the saga of cultism that some cults were either started by women or were influenced in a major way by the allegedly weaker sex: Christian Science, Mary Baker Eddy; Unity, Myrtle Fillmore; Spiritism, the Fox sisters; Jehovah's Witnesses, Marie Russell; Theosophy, Helena Blavatsky and Annie Besant; The Peace Mission Movement (Father Divine), Sister Penny and Faithful Mary (Viola Wilson).

A woman founded this modern form of Hindu and Buddhistic philosophy, popularized in our age as The Theosophical Society.

The term "theosophy" was introduced, to the best knowledge of reputable scholars, in the third century by a noted philosopher, Ammonius Saccas, the teacher of Plotinus, the great Roman philosopher. Theosophy, however, has a long history traceable directly to the Orient, particularly India, where the Upanishads and Vedas or Hindu Scriptures form the basis for no small part of the doctrines. The writings of Gautama Buddha and the early Christian Gnostics also heavily influenced the formulation of Theosophical doctrines.

Theosophy claims to be a universal world religion of a distinct nature all its own. But any careful study of its eclectic background readily reveals that much of its "original theology" is borrowed from easily recognizable sources. The modern American history of Theosophy began with the activities of the young and mystically inclined Russian lady, Madam Helena Blavatsky, in the year 1875 in New York City. Helena Petrovna was born in Ekaterinoslav, Russia, in 1831, the daughter of Peter Hahn, the son of the noble Von Hahn family of Germany. At the age of seventeen, Helena married the Czarist general Blavatsky, a cultured gentleman many years her senior, whom she promptly left after only three months of marriage. It is a known fact that Madam was notoriously short of the virtue of patience and had a violent temper. It is asserted by at least one of her biographers that she married General Blavatsky merely to spite her acid-tongued governess, who, in a moment of sarcasm, declared that even the noble old gentleman would not marry a shrew like Helena. To her credit, Madam Blavatsky repented quite hastily of her revenge upon the governess, but she had already beguiled the General and was forced into a position of compliance with matrimony.[6]

Shortly after her separation from General Blavatsky, Helena embarked upon a long career of travel which eventually led her into the field of mystical religion, which she studied from Tibet, India, Egypt to Texas, Louisiana,

---

[5]H. P. Blavatsky, *Theosophical Glossary*, Los Angeles, CA: The Theosophy Company, 1892, 1973.
[6]Baseden G. Butt, *Madam Blavatsky*, London: Marchand Bros., 1926, p. 13.

Cuba and Canada, landing eventually in New York long enough to found, in the year 1875, The Theosophical Society, in conjunction with Colonel H. S. Olcott and W. Q. Judge, two ardent devotees.

In 1879, Madam Blavatsky left the United States for India, and later died in London, England, in 1891. W. Q. Judge split the Society in 1895 and then saw his organization also divided into the "Universal Brotherhood and Theosophical Society" and "The Theosophical Society in America."

Mrs. Blavatsky held Judge in the highest esteem, and Judge wore her mantle of leadership to all intents and purposes as head of the Aryan Theosophical Society of which he was president until 1896 when he died. Madam Blavatsky also founded the Esoteric School of Theosophy in London in 1888, and during her travels in India and England, influenced profoundly one Annie Wood Besant, who took over the reins of leadership after the deaths of Madam Blavatsky, Judge, and his successor, Catherine Tingley.

Helena Blavatsky was a woman of tremendous physical proportions with piercing, almost hypnotic eyes, and she ruled the Theosophists during her life and in many areas, even after her death, through her literary works—principally, *The Secret Doctrine*—which is still regarded as divinely inspired interpretations or oracular instructions by most loyal Theosophists.

Annie Besant (1847–1933) was the most prominent of all the British Theosophical luminaries, and one destined to become a bright star in the political fortunes of India. Among her many accomplishments, Mrs. Besant founded the Central Hindu College at Benares, India, in 1898, and also the Indian Home Rule League in 1916. In the year 1917 she was elected president of the Indian National Congress, and was almost always regarded as a powerful figure in Indian politics.

In 1889, Mrs. Besant, a native of London, became enthralled by the personality and teachings of Madam Blavatsky and forthwith became a devout pupil and disciple. Mrs. Besant believed firmly in the teachings of Madam Blavatsky, and her writings best represent the true doctrines of the cult and are always laudatory of the departed Russian seer.

Mrs. Besant herself had not a few idiosyncrasies, and was highly mystical in her approach to both life and religion, as evidenced in 1925, when she claimed for her adopted son Krishnamurti, an Indian mystic, the title of "Messianic Leader and Reincarnation of the World Teacher."

Such grandeur, however, was renounced by the new Messiah on November 20, 1931, at Krotana, California, then headquarters of the American branch of Theosophy. Mrs. Besant died in 1933, after which time George Arundale and C. Jinara Jodosa succeeded to the presidency of the Society.[7]

It should be remembered that the Apostle Paul strictly enjoined the Christian Church to forbid women to usurp the authority of her male head, and leadership roles should more properly be filled by men where available to meet this need:

---

[7]See Horton Davies, *The Challenge of the Sects*, Philadelphia, PA: Westminster Press, 1961; Charles Ferguson, *New Books of Revelation*, Garden City, NY: Doubleday, 1929; and J. K. Van Baalen, *The Chaos of the Cults*, Grand Rapids, MI: William B. Eerdmans Publishing Company, 1962.

> Let the woman learn in silence with all subjection. But I suffer not a woman to teach, nor to usurp authority over the man, but to be in silence. For Adam was first formed, then Eve. And Adam was not deceived, but the woman being deceived was in the transgression (1 Timothy 2:11–14).

It can be clearly seen from the study of non-Christian cults, ancient and modern, that the female teaching ministry has graphically fulfilled what Paul anticipated in his day by divine revelation, and brought in its wake, as history tells us, confusion, division and strife. This is true from Johanna Southcutt to Mary Baker Eddy to Helena Blavatsky and the Fox sisters, all of whom were living proof of the validity of our Lord's declaration that "if the blind lead the blind, both shall fall into the ditch" (Matthew 15:14b).

Theosophy and Christian Theology

According to the literature of the Theosophical cult as represented chiefly by Madam Blavatsky, Mrs. Besant, I. C. Cooper, A. P. Sinnett, L. W. Rogers and C. W. Leadbeater, there is a great fraternity of "Mahatmas" or "Masters," who are highly evolved examples of advanced reincarnations whose dwelling place is somewhere in the far reaches of remote Tibet.[8] These divine beings possessed Madam Blavatsky, and utilized her services to reach the generations now living upon the earth with the restored truths of the great religions of the world, which have been perverted by mankind. In this highly imaginative picture the Theosophists add seven planes of progression previously noted, through which the souls of men must progress, on their way to the Theosophist's "heaven" or Devachan.

In keeping with the Theosophists' concept of heaven in the final analysis, is the Nirvana of Buddhism, where the absorption of the personality or the soul into a type of world soul eventually extinguishes personal cognizance— the Theosophists also have their "hell," which, oddly enough, resembles the Roman Catholic purgatory, with indescribable tortures and degrees of degradation. The name for this intermediate state of existence where the departed souls suffer for their past sins while awaiting reincarnation, or the chance to start living in a new body, is Kamaloka, where the atmosphere is ". . . gloomy, heavy, dreary, depressing to an inconceivable extent. . . . the man who is full of evil passions *looks* the whole of them; bestial appetites shape the astral body into bestial forms, and repulsively human animal shapes are the appropriate clothing of brutalized human souls. No man can be a hypocrite in the astral world, and cloak foul thoughts with a veil of virtuous seeming; whatever a man is that he appears to be in outward form and semblance, radiant in beauty if his mind be noble, repulsive in hideousness if his nature be foul."[9]

Contrary to the Christian doctrines of redemption and punishment, Theosophy offers no forgiveness for sin except through myriads of reincarnations ever progressing toward Devachan, and no eternal retribution for man's rebellion or sin, only the evolutionary terrors of Kamaloka. The Theo-

---

[8]See Blavatsky's *The Theosophical Glossary*, op. cit.
[9]Annie Besant, The Ancient Wisdom: *An Outline of Theosophical Teachings*, London: Theosophical Publishing Society, 1897, pp. 92, 93.

sophical Society maintains that it has three primary objectives which are: "(1) to form a nucleus of the brotherhood of humanity, without distinction of race, creed, sex, caste or color; (2) to encourage the study of comparative religion, philosophy, and science; (3) to investigate the unexplained laws of nature and the powers latent in man. Assent to the first of these objects is required for membership, the remaining two being optional. 'The Society has no dogmas or creed, is entirely non-sectarian and includes in its membership adherents of all faiths and of none, exacting only from each member their tolerance for the beliefs of others that he would wish them to exhibit toward his own.' "[10]

Theosophy, then, makes no demands of absolute allegiance to any religion or religious leader, and is resolutely opposed to any form of dogmatism, particularly that type manifested by the Son of God, who said: "I am the way, the truth and the life: no man cometh unto the Father, but by me" (John 14:6).

God and Man in Theosophy

In common with Christian Science, Unity and other pantheistic theologies, Theosophy conceives of God in strictly impersonal terms, while asserting that man is in a spiritual sense, part of God. L. W. Rogers put it this way, when he wrote:

In divine essence, latent power and potential spirituality, man is an image of God, because he is part of Him. The same idea is more directly put in the Psalms, with the assertion "ye are gods." If the idea of the immanence of God is sound, then man is a literal fragment of the consciousness of the Supreme Being, is an embryo-god, being destined to ultimately evolve his latent powers into perfect expression. The oneness of life was explicitly asserted by Jesus. . . . It is an unqualified assertion that humanity is a part of God as leaves are part of the tree, not something a tree has created, in the sense that a man creates a machine, but something that is an emanation of the tree and is a living part of it. Thus only has God made man. Humanity is a growth, a development, an emanation, an evolutionary expression of the Supreme Being. . . . It is simplicity itself when we think of the solar system as just an emanation of the Supreme Being, as something generated from a central life, an expression of that life which gives rise to the poles within it that we know as consciousness and matter. The human soul is an individualized fragment of that divine life . . . is literally a spark of the divine fire, and latent within it are the characteristics of that central light from which it originated. The theosophical conception of the soul is that it is literally an emanation from God, and since it is therefore of its own essence, it becomes clear why Theosophists assert that man is a god in the making.[11]

In keeping with this position, Mrs. Besant once declared, "man is spiritual intelligence, a fragment of divinity clothed in matter."[12] Mrs. Besant's adopted son Krishnamurti once declared that all of us are a part of God and

[10]J. H. Russell, op. cit., pp. 408, 409.
[11]Rogers, op. cit., pp. 22–25, 19, 20.
[12]Annie Besant, Man's Life in Three Worlds, London: Theosophical Publishing Society, 1899, p. 3.

must dig down within ourselves to find the God within us.

These pantheistic views of the Deity are drawn from the deadly trinity of Hinduism, Buddhism and Gnosticism. And one wonders why Theosophy even attempts to use Christian terms at all, except when it is realized that it is easier to reach the Western mind in terms of the Christian religion, than in the language of Hinduism, Buddhism and Gnosticism! So this is the obvious reason for the utilization of redefined Christian terminology by Theosophists.

Concerning the Deity of Jesus Christ and His unique place as *the* Savior of the world, Theosophy declares that all men are innately divine, "so that in time all men become Christs."[13]

The clearest position on this subject, however, is declared by Rogers, who summed up the position of Theosophy where our Lord and His mission are concerned, when he wrote:

> Most readers will probably agree that a world teacher known as the Christ did come, and that he founded a religion nearly 2,000 years ago. Why do they think so? They reply that God so loved the world that he sent his son the Christ to bring it light and life. If that is true, how can we avoid the conclusion that he or his predecessors, must have come many times before. The belief that he came but once is consistent only with the erroneous notion that Genesis is history, instead of allegory . . . when a new era in human evolution begins, a world teacher comes in a voluntary incarnation and founds a religion that is suited to the requirements of the new age. Humanity is never left to grope along alone. All that it can comprehend and utilize is taught in the various religions. World teachers, the christs and saviours of the age, have been appearing at propitious times since humanity began existence. . . . In the face of such facts, what becomes of the assertion that God so loved the world that he sent his son to help ignorant humanity about 2,000 years ago—but never before? What about the hundreds of millions of human beings who lived and died before that time? Did he care nothing for them? Did he give his attention to humanity for a period of only 2,000 years and neglect it for millions of years? Has anybody believed that God in his great compassion sent just *one* world teacher for that brief period. . . . If God so loved the world that he sent his son 2,000 years ago, he sent him, or some predecessor very many times before.
>
> Supermen are not myths, or figments of the imagination. They are as natural and comprehensive as human beings. In the regular order of evolution, we shall ourselves reach their level, and join their ranks, while younger humanity shall attain our present state. As they rose, we too shall rise. Our past has been evolution's night. Our present is its dawn. Our future shall be its perfect day. . . . That is the magnificent future the Theosophist sees for the human race.[14]

The refutation of these non-Christian concepts concerning God and the Lord Jesus Christ are clearly found in various places in the Bible. The personality of God and the Deity of Christ are forcefully set forth along with many of the other things that Theosophists deny. The God of the Bible

---

[13]Annie Besant, *Is Theosophy Anti-Christian?*, London: Theosophical Publishing Society, 1901, p. 16.
[14]*Ibid.*, pp. 260–263.

created man, and is separate and distinct from him (Genesis 1:27). He is a cognizant ego or personality (Exodus 3:14; Isaiah 48:12; John 8:58), and He is triune, three separate persons, Father, Son and Holy Spirit, yet one in essence or nature (Deuteronomy 6:4; Galatians 3:20). The God of the Bible cannot be equated with the God of Theosophy, nor can Jesus Christ be redefined so that Christ becomes innately divine, "so that in time all men become Christs."[15] Neither the laws of language, logic, nor Biblical theology can permit such extravagances as the Theosophists must insist upon to arrive at such inconceivable equations.

The Theosophist, in his depersonalization of God, however, fails to recognize that man is a cognizant, reflective ego, and that he is a creation of God, in the divine spiritual image, debased though he may be by sin. How is it possible to claim for the creation what is not possessed by the Creator, namely, personality? Are we to assume that the creation, even though part of the divine, is greater in that part, i.e., the possession of ego and personality, than the divine itself? To use the analogy of Mr. Rogers, is the spark greater than the flame, the ray greater than the source from which it emanated? Of course not! So then, neither is man greater than God. If man possesses personality and ego, and the Theosophists grant this, then God, by definition, must be personality and ego—a disconcerting fact, but a fact, nonetheless!

The Bible gives much evidence to this effect by underscoring the personality of God in terms of attributes which only a personality can manifest. These traits forever separate Him from the pantheistic God of Theosophy, which is incapable, by definition, of performing these things.

1. *God remembers*—"I, even I, am he that blotteth out thy transgressions for mine own sake, and will not remember thy sins" (Isaiah 43:25). 2. *God creates*—"In the beginning God created the heavens and the earth" (Genesis 1:1). 3. *God knows*—i.e., He has a mind—"The Lord knoweth them that are his" (2 Timothy 2:19). "For I know the thoughts that I think toward you, saith the Lord" (Jeremiah 29:11). 4. *God is a Personal Spirit*—"I am the Almighty God; walk before me, and be thou perfect" (Genesis 17:1). 5. *God has will*—"Lo, I come to do thy will, O God" (Hebrews 10:9).

From this brief resumé of some of God's attributes, the interested reader can doubtless see the vast difference between the God and Father of our Lord Jesus Christ and the impersonal God of Theosophy. Theosophy's God is not a personal being. He cannot remember, He cannot create, He cannot will, He cannot know, because He is not a personality, but an impersonal "it," an abstract, pantheistic principle, not the God of divine revelation.

Theosophy makes the grave error of all gnostic cults; it divides Jesus and Christ, making Jesus only the outer man and Christ a divine consciousness immanent within Him and within all men, to a greater or lesser degree. For Theosophists, Jesus is not *the* Christ of divine revelation, as distinct from the Christ who is immanent within all men. They do not understand that the word *Christ* (*Christos* in the Greek) is a title corresponding to the Hebrew *Messiah*. It is not a force, essence, or divine spark, as any careful reading of a good Greek lexicon will speedily reveal. In the sixteenth chapter of Mat-

---

[15]Besant, *Anti-Christian, op. cit.*

thew's gospel, the Apostle Peter affirmed this truth by pointing out in his confession of faith, "Thou art the Christ, the Son of the living God" (Matthew 16:16). And John reminds us that, "Who is a liar but he that denieth that Jesus is the Christ? He is antichrist, that denieth the Father and the Son" (1 John 2:22).

It is unnecessary to pursue this point any further since Christian theology has always maintained that Jesus of Nazareth was the Christ, the Anointed Redeemer of God, very God Himself (Isaiah 9:6; Micah 5:2; John 1:1, 14, 18; Colossians 2:9; Revelation 1:16, 17; Isaiah 44:6; etc.). He is the second person of the Trinity, not the theosophical emanation from the impersonal essence they acknowledge as God. And this is why Theosophy is not Christian, and is indeed the very antithesis of historic Christian theology.

In regard to the lengthy statement previously quoted from Rogers, the argument that God must have sent other "world teachers" to meet the requirements for humanity's redemption prior to Christ is the purest speculation and directly contradicts the statement of our Lord who affirmed:

> Verily, verily, I say unto you, He that entereth not by the door into the sheepfold, but climbeth up some other way, the same is a thief and a robber. But he that entereth in by the door is the shepherd of the sheep. To him the porter openeth; and the sheep hear his voice: and he calleth his own sheep by name, and leadeth them out. All that ever came before me are thieves and robbers: but the sheep did not hear them. The thief cometh not, but for to steal, and to kill, and to destroy: I am come that they might have life, and that they might have it more abundantly" (John 10:1-3, 8, 10).

The epistle to the Romans points out that God has revealed Himself to the hundreds of millions of human beings about whom Rogers is so concerned, and that in the face of His revelation, "professing themselves to be wise, they became fools, and changed the glory of the uncorruptible God into an image made like to corruptible man, and to birds, and four-footed beasts, and creeping things. Wherefore God also gave them up to uncleanness through the lusts of their own hearts, to dishonor their own bodies between themselves: who changed the truth of God into a lie, and worshipped and served the creature more than the Creator, who is blessed for ever" (Romans 1:22–25). And as a direct result of this, the Apostle Paul informs us, God abandoned them to themselves so that ". . . when they knew God, they glorified him not as God . . . but became vain in their imaginations, and their foolish heart was darkened" (Romans 1:21).

So it is apparent that mankind has never been without a witness of God's grace and love, but that every time it has been manifested, in His law, His prophets, and finally, in His Son, men have responded with violence, evil and sin of every proportionate degree, so that they are without excuse, and deserving of eternal condemnation.

Quite to the contrary, the idea is not preposterous, as Rogers suggests, but quite consistent with the character of God and His judgment upon depraved human nature (Romans 3:23). It is a fact that Theosophists refuse to face despite the atrocities frequent in even modern society, the horrible Nazi concentration camps, the selective incarceration, torture, and even murder by modern communistic regimes, and the other testimonies to the fallen nature of mankind. They apparently think that when Adam sinned (an allegory) the race fell spiritually upward, a condition controverted by all the facts of history!

It is true that God so loved the world that He gave His only begotten Son, but it is not true that He has many sons, that they came many times, and that Christ was only one among them. This He Himself denied, and on far better authority than any Rogers or Theosophy can muster (John 12:44–50).

The Vicarious Atonement

Theosophy is opposed to not only the true Biblical teaching of God's personality and nature, as well as the Deity of His Son, but it also vigorously denies Christ's substitutionary sacrifice for all sin (1 John 2:2).

One of the most concise statements concerning the views of Theosophy in this area comes from the pen of L. W. Rogers, who wrote:

> Back of the ancient doctrine of the vicarious atonement is a profound and beautiful truth, but it has been degraded into a teaching that is as selfish as it is false. That natural truth is the sacrifice of the Solar Logos, the Deity of our system. Sacrifice consists of limiting himself in the manner of manifested worlds, and it is reflected in the sacrifice of the Christ and other great teachers. Not the sacrifice of life, but a voluntary returning to live in the confinement of material body. Nobody more than the Theosophist pays to the Christ the tribute of the most reverent gratitude; we also hold with St. Paul that each must work out his own salvation. Were it not for such sacrifice, the race would be very, very far below its present evolutionary level. The help that such great spiritual beings have given mankind is incalculable, and is undoubtedly altogether beyond what we were able to comprehend. But to assume that such sacrifice has relieved man from the necessity of developing his spiritual nature, or in any degree nullify his personal responsibility for any evil he has done, is false and dangerous doctrine. . . . And true too, we know that any belief that is not in harmony with the facts of life is a wrong belief . . . the vital point against this plan of salvation is that it ignores the soul's personal responsibility, and teaches that whatever the offenses against God and man have been, they may be cancelled by the simple process of believing that another suffered and died in order that those sins might be forgiven. It is the pernicious doctrine that wrongdoing by one can be set right by the sacrifice of another. It is simply astounding that such a belief could have survived the middle ages and should continue to find millions who accept it in these days of clearer thinking.
>
> The man who is willing to purchase bliss by the agony of another is unfit for heaven, and could not recognize it if he were there.
>
> A heaven that is populated with those who see in the vicarious atonement the happy arrangement letting them in pleasantly and easily, would not be worth having. It would be a realm of selfishness, and that would be no heaven at all. . . . The hypothesis of reincarnation shows our inherent divinity, and the method by which the latent becomes the actual. Instead of the ignoble belief that we can fling our sins upon another, it makes personal

responsibility the keynote of life. It is the ethics of self-help. It is the moral code of self-reliance. It is the religion of self-respect![16]

The inconsistency of Theosophists is eclipsed only by their apparent lack of concern for the validity of established terms in both philosophy and theology. Here is a classic example of what we mean. Rogers wants Christians to believe that "nobody more than the Theosophist pays to the Christ the tribute of the most reverent gratitude." But he denies categorically the expressions of that very Christ and the prophecies concerning Him, which state that He came for the express purpose of paying the penalty for all sin.

The Theosophist wants no part of the vicarious sacrifice of Jesus; in fact, it is personally repugnant to him. By his own admission, he considers it "an ignoble belief" that we can fling our sins upon another. But this is exactly what we are called upon to do in the New Testament!

The Scriptures bear incontrovertible witness to the truth that, "Christ died for the ungodly" (Romans 5:6), and that "The blood of Jesus Christ . . . cleanses us from all sin" (1 John 1:7). There is no doctrine found within the pages of the Bible that is better supported or substantiated than that of the substitutionary death of Christ for the sins of the world. As far back in the Biblical record as Exodus, Moses wrote of God's symbolic use of blood for purification and sacrifice. It will be recalled that Jehovah delivered the Israelites from Egypt by causing all the firstborn of the nation, including Pharaoh's own son, to fall under the shadow of sudden death (Exodus 12). The Jews were instructed in this instance to sprinkle the blood of the young lamb on the doorpost and lintels of their homes, and God promised "When I see the blood, I will pass over" (Exodus 12:13). The Lord also instituted the animal sacrifices of the Levitical era and expressly stated, "It is the blood that maketh an atonement for the soul" (Leviticus 17:11).

Following this typology through into the New Testament, we find that Jesus was called the Lamb of God, who takes away the sin of the world (John 1:29), and further, that His blood, shed upon the cross, is our atonement or covering for sin, even for the sins of all mankind (Matthew 26:28; Romans 5:6-8; Ephesians 1:7; Colossians 1:20).

The believer in Christ therefore is saved by grace alone through faith in His blood, and its efficacy for the cleansing of all sin (Romans 3:25). John, the beloved disciple, reminds us in his powerful epistle of this fact (1 John 1:7), and Peter declares, ". . . we were not redeemed with corruptible things, such as silver and gold . . . but with the precious blood of Christ, as a lamb without blemish and without spot" (1 Peter 1:18, 19).

The pages of the New Testament bear incontrovertible testimony that Jesus Christ on Calvary "purchased the church with his own blood" (Acts 20:28), and in the great message of Christ to John recorded in the Book of Revelation, we are told that He "washed us from our sins in his own blood" (Revelation 1:5). This was not a pagan sacrifice to placate the wrath of a heathen god's justice. The sacrifice was offered through the Eternal Spirit, to free the sons of men from the curse of sin and to open the path to salvation, through which we now can have boldness to enter into the holiest by the

---

[16]*Ibid.*, pp. 201–206.

blood of Jesus—a new and living way to the very throne of God our Father (Hebrews 10:19, 20).

Contrasting this picture of concrete Biblical theology with the views of Theosophy, the facts speak for themselves, and they cannot honestly be ignored.

Theosophy, on the other hand, refuses to accept the vicarious atonement of Jesus Christ for the forgiveness of all sin. Instead, Theosophy teaches the inexorable law of Karma (the accumulated weight of one's bad actions which can only be "atoned for" through personal and individual good actions during a succession of lives [reincarnation] and which is sometimes called "the Law of Cause and Effect"). Annie Besant described it as the "law of causation . . . bidding man . . . surrender all the fallacious ideas of forgiveness, vicarious atonement, divine mercy and the rest of the opiates which superstition offers to the sinner."[17]

Through the application of the law of Karma then, the Biblical doctrine of the atonement is neatly supplanted and the authority of Scripture circumvented or negated. Mrs. Besant once wrote that "The atonement wrought by Christ lies not in the substitution of one individual for another. . . ."[18]

As the daughter of an Anglican clergyman, and the former wife of another, Mrs. Besant must have known better. But despite this, she never does satisfactorily explain what the Biblical doctrine of the Atonement *does* mean, if it does not mean what the Christian Church has always maintained.

For Theosophists then, the redemptive love of a personal God as revealed in the substitutionary sacrifice of His most precious possession, His Son, Jesus Christ, is totally unnecessary, and is not the way of salvation. This fact alone would remove Theosophy from any serious consideration of compatibility with Christianity, and we can be grateful that the cult today is so insignificant in number that it does not even appear in the Yearbook of *American and Canadian Churches 1975* (Constant H. Jacquet, Jr., ed., New York: Abingdon Press, 1975), although its "chapters" or centers can be found in many major cities of the United States and throughout the world. Its rate of growth seems considerably slower than it was in the 1920's, and we can hope that the very fact of its complexity and the involved vocabulary utilized to describe its mazelike theology may yet render it more ineffective in an age in which precision of definition is at last coming into its own.

In order to be Christian, one must conform to the Scriptures. Theosophy fails to meet this requirement and must be considered as anti-Christian.

Sin, Salvation and Prayer

The Christian concepts of sin, salvation and prayer need but passing mention relative to the reinterpretation they receive at the hands of Theosophical writers. The teaching of Theosophy on these principal Christian doctrines is very definite and important and should be understood.

The Bible plainly states that all men have come under the divine in-

---

[17]Annie Besant, *Karma*, London: The Theosophical Publishing Society, 1904, p. 23.
[18]Besant, *Anti-Christian?, op. cit.*, p. 11.

dictment of sin (Romans 3:23). The divine remedy for sin, as we have seen, is the redemptive work of Jesus Christ who "died, the just for the unjust, to bring us to God" (1 Peter 3:18). So hideous and degrading was human sin in the eyes of the Holy God, that it required the God-man's death to satisfy the righteous judgment of His Father. Salvation from sin, then, is full and complete by faith in Jesus Christ "once for all" (Hebrews 10:10); "for the wages of sin is death" (Romans 6:23). Since the Theosophist wants no part of the redeeming sacrifice of the cross, and since he denies that personal sin must be atoned for by a power outside himself, like Petra of old, he is deceived by the pride of his heart (Obadiah 3). There can be little doubt that Theosophists, like Unitarians, make salvation by character and progression. Theirs must be a God of love, who allows the penalty of sin to be worked out on the wheel of reincarnation and by infinite progression. He does not judge; He cannot, for the spectacle of an impersonal principle judging the actions of a personal being is too much for any serious student of the philosophy of religion, not excepting Theosophists!

The Biblical doctrine of prayer also suffers at the hand of Theosophy. In the Biblical vocabulary, prayer is personal communion with a personal God, not an abstract force or a cosmic consciousness. Jesus Christ Himself encouraged us to pray many times. (See Matthew 5:44; 6:6, 7, 9; 9:38.) He repeatedly emphasized its virtues and benefits. For the Christian, then, prayer is the link with the Eternal by which man can come to "the throne of grace" in the power of the Holy Spirit and find "grace to help in time of need" (Hebrews 4:16).

Salvation for the Christian is by grace and true faith in God's only method for making men holy and through the only "name under heaven given among men, whereby we must be saved" (Acts 4:12). Human sin makes it necessary for this grand redemption, and since Theosophy denies it, it follows of a necessity that redemption would also be negated. Since Theosophy rejects the God of the Bible or any concept of a personal God, prayer in the Biblical sense becomes impossible and the sinner's most desperate need, which is to "call upon the name of the Lord" that he might be saved, not from a wheel of incarnations, but from eternal, spiritual and conscious separation from the life and fellowship of God Himself, is ignored or denied.

Contrasted to this Biblical picture of sin, salvation and prayer, Theosophy equates God the Father with the pagan gods, Buddha and Vishnu, [19] and defines prayer, not as personal supplication for divine mercy and grace (Philippians 4:6, 7), but as "concentrated thought."[20] Theosophists also believe that personal sin is removed only by suffering in Kamaloka, "the semi-material plane, to us subjective and invisible, where the disembodied 'personalities,' the astral forms . . . remain. . . . It is the Hades of the ancient Greeks and the Amenti of the Egyptians, the land of Silent Shadows. . . ."[21] Personal salvation is obtained through various reincarnations, ending in ab-

[19]Annie Besant, The Seven Principles of Man, London: The Theosophical Publishing Society, 1902, p. 58.

[20]Annie Besant, The Changing World, London: The Theosophical Publishing Society, 1901, p. 68.

[21]H. P. Blavatsky, op. cit., pp. 171, 172.

sorption of the individual ego. These cannot be viewed as pleasant alternatives to Biblical revelation, but they are all that Theosophy offers.

Resurrection versus Reincarnation

In bringing to a conclusion this chapter on Theosophy, it is necessary for the Christian to understand the one great doctrine which forever removes any possibility of realizing fellowship with Theosophists.

The Apostle Paul, in his great and grand chapter on the resurrection of the body (1 Corinthians 15), cites the Resurrection of Christ and its subsequent effect upon the bodies of all mankind as *the* proof that God exists, that Christ is His Son and that the redemption of all believers is assured by His personal triumph over the grave.

Paul goes to great lengths in this chapter to show that "if Christ be not raised, your faith is vain; ye are yet in your sins" (verse 17). For the great apostle, our hope for physical immortality lies alone in the triumphant physical Resurrection of Christ (verse 14), who visibly and tangibly presented Himself alive "with many infallible proofs" (Acts 1:3) to over 500 persons who knew that it was indeed Jesus who had conquered the grave in their behalf.

Our risen Lord also promised that one day we should be physically and morally as He is, and that God the Father, through Him, would raise the believing dead and clothe them with immortality at His second advent (1 Thessalonians 4).

The condition of the Christian in death, however, is not one of suffering, or repeated reincarnations while atoning for sin, as Theosophy would have it, but one of cognizant personal joy, literally the state of being "at home with the Lord" (2 Corinthians 5:8).

The Resurrection of Jesus Christ then, and for that matter, the resurrection of all mankind, leaves no room for the Theosophical dogma of concurrent reincarnations. We indeed concur with the Apostle Paul that, "If in this life only we have hope in Christ, we are of all men most miserable" (1 Corinthians 15:19). The souls of the dead do not pass through various reincarnations as Theosophy contends; rather, these souls are either experiencing happiness in Christ's presence (Philippians 1:21), in which case, to die is gain; or they are suffering conscious separation from His presence (Luke 16:19–31). In any case, Scripture clearly shows that reincarnation is not man's destiny, nor is it God's revealed plan for perfecting the souls of men. The Bible tells us that Christ died to fully redeem (Romans 5:6; Hebrews 9:26; 10:12).

Out of the Labyrinth, Into the Light

To wend our way completely out of the mazelike labyrinth of Theosophy and its anti-Christian doctrines into the light of Biblical reality, would probably take many volumes of exacting systematic analysis of this cult. But suffice it to note that Theosophy offers to the sinner no hope of full redemption from sin, only seemingly endless reincarnations; it guarantees no personal relationship with a loving, personal heavenly Father, and it ignores completely the true nature, person and work of the Lord Jesus Christ.

The entire system is Eastern in its origin; it is Hinduistic and Buddhistic in its theology, Gnostic in its vocabulary and Christian only in its key terminology, which is specifically designed to imitate the true content of the Gospel.

The Theosophist proudly rejects the atonement on the cross, preferring to trust in his own righteousness (and the working out of the law of Karma), and is willing to brave the terrors of Kamaloka itself, rather than to bow the knee to Jesus Christ (Philippians 2:10, 11).

Let us not then be deceived by the veneer of the intellectual and metaphysical jargon the Theosophist has mastered, nor retreat before his attempt to belittle the preaching of the Cross as "foolishness." We need not defer to his alleged "deeper revelation," to his claims that Theosophy is a higher form of revelation for our age. We are informed in Scripture repeatedly that, "The preaching of the cross is to them that perish foolishness; but unto us which are saved, it is the power of God" (1 Corinthians 1:18). Theosophy is just one more attempt to supplant the authority of Christ and Scripture with "the philosophy and empty deceit" of the world (Colossians 2:8).

Theosophy, in common with the other non-Christian religions of the world, offers no living Redeemer, no freedom from the power of sin, and in the end, no hope for the world to come. Jesus Christ, on the other hand, offers promises by the mouths of prophets and the God who cannot lie, that those who trust in and serve Him shall "receive [for their faith] an hundredfold, and shall inherit everlasting life" (Matthew 19:29).

We must seek to win Theosophists to a saving knowledge of the Gospel, but we must not forget that its theology has many labyrinths, for "there is a way which seemeth right unto a man," in the words of Solomon, "but the end thereof are the ways of death" (Proverbs 14:12).

Chapter 9

ZEN BUDDHISM

The second oldest of all the cult systems considered in this book is a form of Buddhism, one of the major world religions with a following of many millions.

"Zen," as it is known in America, is derived from the Japanese branch of the "meditation" school of Buddhist philosophy introduced into Japan from China in the seventh century A.D.

The two great pioneers of Zen in Japan were Eisai, who originated the Rinzai sect in A.D. 1191, and Dogen, who founded the Soto sect in A.D. 1227. The Rinzai emphasized the protection of the Japanese nation and the Dogen emphasized the centralization of power in the Emperor, thus fusing Zen with the very life of the Japanese people and their government.

Today, Zen claims more than three million followers in Japan, and in America there are around 300,000 Buddhists, many of whom practice Zen. Many prominent Americans practice Zen, including former California governor Jerry Brown.

Zealous followers of Zen trace their origin to Buddha, who, they claim, imparted to one of his disciples, Mahakasyapa (or Kasyapa), what has become known as "the doctrine of the Buddha mind." Buddha, as the legend goes, merely picked the flower in silence, and thus communicated the mystical fragment of his mind, hence the emphasis upon the "Buddha mind" in Zen.

This school of Buddhism, the forerunner of Zen, was formally established in China by the famous Bodhi-Dharma (A.D. 480–528) around A.D. 528, although it supposedly had been passed down through twenty-eight patriarchs, starting with the great Buddha himself.

In the United States Zen has grown by leaps and bounds in the last few years. This is largely because of American's disillusionment with a valueless system of society and their turning to the counterfeit values of Eastern religion and philosophy.

Zen cannot be taken lightly, especially when it receives favorable attention from magazines of the standing of *Time, Newsweek, Life, U.S. News and World Report*, and *Reader's Digest*, to name a few. Zen itself is far more complex than the garbled jargon of pseudo-intellectuals who desperately want "a place in the sun," not by virtue of their capacity to earn it, but on the singularly selfish principle that they are entitled to it because of their own imagined intellectual and philosophical superiority to their fellow man. This is no exaggeration, and anyone acquainted with pseudo adherents to Zen will readily testify to it. They literally believe that the world owes them a living. So, ceaselessly mouthing fragmented sentences, liberally sprinkled with symbolic language, Zen terminology and fractured logic, they urge the general populace to embrace what they claim has emancipated them.

The Theological Implications of Zen

Gautama Buddha, who founded the Buddhist religion, was the son of Suddhodana, a chieften reigning over a district near the Himalayas in what is known today as the country of Nepal. At an early age, Siddhartha Gautama, his true name, observed the many contradictions and problems of life; he abandoned his wife and son when he felt he could no longer endure the life of a rich nobleman, and became a wandering ascetic in search of the truth about life. Buddhist historians tell us that after almost seven years of wandering, inquiring, meditating and searching, he found "the true path," and "great enlightenment," under the legendary bo tree (tree of wisdom), and thus attained Nirvana, that most desirable of all states which Zen Buddhism says can be the experience of any member of the meditation school. In this they differ with classical Buddhist thought which maintains that cycles of reincarnations are necessary in order to attain Nirvana. Zen maintains that it is a here and now possibility.

The teachings of Buddha are concerned with the ramifications of the "Four Noble Truths": (1) Suffering; (2) Its cause; (3) Its cessation; and (4) The Way which leads to this cessation. According to Buddhism:

> . . .Three elements common to all post-Vedic Hindu thought are at once discernible in this teaching; viz., transmigration, karma, and the dissolution of individuality. In its shortest form Buddha's teaching may be summarized as follows: Birth is sorrow, age is sorrow, sickness is sorrow, death is sorrow, clinging to earthly things is sorrow. Birth and rebirth, the chain of reincarnation, result from the thirst of life together with passion and desire. The only escape from this thirst is to follow the Eightfold Path: Right belief, right resolve, right word, right act, right life, right effort, right thinking, right meditation.
>
> The goal of Buddhism is Nirvana. A definition of this term is almost impossible for the simple reason that Buddha himself gave no clear idea, and in all probability possessed none, of this state. He was indeed asked by more than one of his disciples whether Nirvana was postmundane or postcelestial existence, or whether it was annihilation. To all these questions, however, he refused an answer, for it was characteristic of his teachings that they were practically confined to the present life, and concerned themselves but little either with problems of merely academic philosophy or with the unknowable. . . . the *summum bonum* is release from karma and reincarnation, a goal which is to be attained by knowledge, and which consists in absorption into or reunion with the Over-Soul. This involves the annihilation of individuality, and in this sense Nirvana is nihilism, so that with the tacit ignoring of any real conception of the divine in the teachings of Buddha, Nirvana seems to imply the annihilation of the soul rather than its absorption.[1]

When we come to the Zen variety of Buddhism, we find a strong emphasis on the present and on practical meditation. The late Alan Watts, American proponent of Zen, described it this way:

---

[1]Samuel Macauley Jackson, ed., *The New Schaff-Herzog Encyclopedia of Religious Knowledge*, Grand Rapids, MI: Baker Book House, 1977 reprint, volume 2, p. 293.

Perhaps the special flavor of Zen is best described as a certain directness. In other schools of Buddhism, awakening or *bodhi* seems remote and almost superhuman, something to be reached only after many lives of patient effort. But in Zen there is always the feeling that awakening is something quite natural, something startlingly obvious, which may occur at any moment. If it involves a difficulty, it is just that it is much too simple. Zen is also direct in its way of teaching, for it points directly and openly to the truth, and does not trifle with symbolism.[2]

Zen is hence revolutionary, holding that enlightenment comes with clarification and simplification through acting out of old values of time and experience, and depending upon only the supreme experience, "now." One state of consciousness and the next cannot be measured by hours or miles, as the Master tries to say, in a *koan* . . . the standard advice of Zen, using one of the 1700 traditional questions to highlight it. The snap of a finger can be a lesson . . . indicating that this very moment is the immediate experience of reality, past time and embracing all dimensions.

Zen is brusque in its teachings, aimed at the roots of inconsistency. It demands action of a curious sort. This can only be achieved when it is simple, natural and totally correct. It finds truth through shrinking away from error, not discovering a way to truth.

Such a mystic philosophy, oddly enough, bears a kinship to primitive Christianity. Like the ardent fundamentalist awaiting the second coming which will bring heaven to earth, the Zen ideal is to achieve a Nirvanic state and a saintly condition on this earth. . . . The *koan*, which goes back to the twelfth century, when it was devised to test the students' understanding of the Zen spirit and shake his mind from conventional thinking, leaves most professed Zen followers in Japan uninterested today. And, of course, one can never achieve *satori*—the nonrational, clear and intuitive understanding of reality—until he understands the exercises of *koan*. . . .

Zen is a paradox within a paradox, a mystical doctrine which laughs at all doctrines and dogma, and becomes a doctrine and dogma in the doing (Richard Mathison, *God Is a Millionnaire*, New York: The Bobbs-Merrill Company, Inc., 1960, pp. 365, 367–368).

With a philosophy such as this, it is easy to understand how Zenists can sit cross-legged (*zazen*—Japanese), meditating upon a flower petal or a rock thrown haphazard over a floor or on a garden path. For them, reality is not objective correlative truth, but subjective, egocentric reflection, which becomes reality if they deign to participate in its manifestation. The following quotations deal with the theology of Zen Buddhism in a general way, for if ever a system was devoid of a theology, except by implication and interpretation, it is Zen.

Zen Teachings

1. *Revelation*

Zen is at once the knower and the known. It is also the factor which unites the two in one. It is a way to Truth and not facts about Truth. As

---

[2] Alan W. Watts, *The Way of Zen*, New York: The New American Library, 1957, p. 83.

Dr. Suzuki puts it, "When we think we know something, there is something we do not know." For there is still an antithesis, the known and the knower, and Zen seeks that which lies beyond antitheses, however subtle (Christmas Humphreys, *Zen Buddhism*, London: George Allen and Unwin Ltd., 1957, p. 2).

Strictly speaking, however, Zen is incommunicable. Even as "The Tao that can be expressed is not the Eternal Tao," so Zen translated into the terms and apparatus of the intellect is not true Zen. There is therefore an inevitable distinction between Zen and the forms of Zen, between expressions *of* Zen, and facts *about* Zen. . . (*Ibid.*).

[In Zen] the Scriptures are useful on the foothills of our understanding, but as soon as they are seen as so much paper they are better put to useful purposes (Christmas Humphreys, *Buddhism*, Baltimore, MD: Penguin Books, 1951, p. 179).

2. *Authority*

Zen, however, is *ex hypothesi* beyond the intellect, and the coins of intellectual usage, such as words and diagrams, have no validity (Humphreys, *Zen, op. cit.*, p. 3).

Zen has nothing to teach us in the way of intellectual analysis; nor has it any set doctrines which are imposed on its followers for acceptance. In this respect Zen is quite chaotic if you choose to say so. Probably Zen followers may have sets of doctrines, but they have them on their own account, and for their own benefit; they do not owe the fact to Zen. Therefore, there are in Zen no sacred books or dogmatic tenets, nor are there any symbolic formula through which an access might be gained into the signification of Zen. If I am asked, then, what Zen teaches, I would answer, Zen teaches nothing. Whatever teachings there are in Zen, they come out of one's own mind. We teach ourselves; Zen merely points the way. Unless this pointing is teaching, there is certainly nothing in Zen purposely set up as its cardinal doctrines or as its fundamental philosophy (Daisetz Teitaro Suzuki, *An Introduction to Zen Buddhism*, London: Rider and Company/The Buddhist Society, n.d., p. 38).

3. *The Nature of God (Pantheism) and Morality*

Meister Eckhart, a German mystic in the fourteenth century, is still read by many Western people, and I see much common ground in Zen and his mysticism. He wrote:

The eye by which I see God is the same as the eye by which God sees me. My eye and God's eye are one and the same—one in seeing, one in knowing, and one in loving. . . .
When I have shut the doors of my five senses, earnestly desiring God, I find him in my soul as clearly and as joyful as he is in eternity. . . .

Such statements have found a welcomed home in Zen literature (Sohaku Ogata, *Zen for the West*, Westport, CN: Greenwood Press, Publishers, 1959, pp. 17, 18).

Zen consciousness is a mind made one with life, and even at its lowest produces a sense of one-ness with all humanity. Who, having this, needs rules of morality? (Humphreys, *Zen, op. cit.*, p. 178).

Is Zen a religion? It is not a religion in the sense that the term is popularly understood; for Zen has no God to worship, no ceremonial rites to observe, no future abode to which the dead are destined, and last of all, Zen has no soul whose welfare is to be looked after by somebody else and whose immortality is a matter of intense concern with some people. Zen is free from all these dogmatic and "religious" encumbrances.

When I say there is no God in Zen, the pious reader may be shocked, but this does not mean that Zen denies the existence of God; neither denial nor affirmation concerns Zen. When a thing is denied, the very denial involves something not denied. The same can be said of affirmation. This is inevitable in logic. Zen wants to rise above logic, Zen wants to find a higher affirmation where there are no antitheses. Therefore, in Zen, God is neither denied nor insisted upon; only there is in Zen no such God as has been conceived by Jewish and Christian minds. For the same reason Zen is not a philosophy, Zen is not a religion (Suzuki, *op. cit.*, p. 39).

4. *Self-Salvation*

. . . for it is not the life of the soul that lives in perfect freedom and in perfect unity? There is no freedom or unity in exclusion or in limitation. Zen is well aware of this. In accordance with the demands of our inner life, therefore, Zen takes us to an absolute realm wherein there are no antitheses of any sort (*Ibid.*, pp. 67, 68).

Therefore, Zen does not mean a mere escape from intellectual imprisonment, which sometimes ends in sheer wantonness. There is something in Zen that frees us from conditions and at the same time gives us a certain firm foothold, which, however, is not a foothold in a relative sense. The Zen master endeavours to take away all footholds from the disciple which he has ever had since his first appearance on earth, and then to supply him with one that is really no foothold (*Ibid.*).

In Zen there are no miracles, supernatural interventions, ways nor refuges. We bear the whole responsibility for our actions and no Sage whomsoever he be has the right to encroach on our free will.

We are at the same time responsible for our slavery and our freedom; the chains of our enslavement have been forged by ourselves, and only we can break them. . . .

Nor have we anything to acquire, say the Zen Masters. We have nothing either to receive from the outside, nor anything to build up or "make" in the usual sense of the word. Rather have we to "undo" the complex accumulations of our false values.

Everything is present. We are the Real but we do not know it, as Zen tells us repeatedly. From the depths of our spirit to the material structures of our physiology, *nothing is lacking*. It suffices merely to establish a coordination, a functional harmony between the different components of which we are made up. The lack of harmony between the different levels of our beings, and the very sense of division into different compartments which our spirit loves to create, come from an essential error of our mental vision. The mirages engendered by it, however, disappear as soon as it is adjusted by "correct attention" (Robert Linssen, *Living Zen*, London: George Allen and Unwin Ltd., 1958, p. 74).

5. *Sin and Evil*

The opposites (*dvandva*) of light and darkness, good and evil, pleasure and pain, are the essential elements of the game, for although the Godhead is identified with Truth (*sat*), Consciousness (*chit*), and Bliss (*ananda*), the dark side of life has its integral part in the game just as every drama must have its villain, to disrupt the *status quo*, and as the cards must be shuffled, thrown into chaos, in order that there may be a significant development of the play. For Hindu thought there is no Problem of Evil. The conventional, relative world is necessarily a world of opposites. Light is inconceivable apart from darkness; order is meaningless without disorder; and likewise, up without down, sound without silence, pleasure without pain (Watts, *op. cit.*, pp. 45, 46).

For this reason the masters talk about Zen as little as possible, and throw its concrete reality straight at us. This reality is the "suchness" (*tathata*) of our natural, nonverbal world. If we see this just as it is, there is nothing good, nothing bad, nothing inherently long or short, nothing subjective and nothing objective. There is no symbolic self to be forgotten, and no need for any idea of a concrete reality to be remembered (*Ibid.*, p. 127).

From the foregoing, the deep-seated philosophical mysticism of the Zen school of meditation of Buddhism is accurately reflected, revealing Zen to be a philosophy that negates a personal God. Secondly, it denies the reality of sin due to the absence of an absolute standard of revealed law and holiness. Thirdly, it rejects the necessity of personal redemption from the penalty of sin revealed in the Person of Jesus Christ, who is *the* Way.

It was the Apostle John who declared, "If we say that we have no sin, we deceive ourselves, and the truth is not in us" (1 John 1:8), and this is the curse of Zen, with which its adherents are forced to live and from which they can never fully escape, psychologically or spiritually. The transgression of the law of God does produce guilt in the soul and mind of men which no amount of meditation, cross-legged or head-standing, can obliterate. Adherents of the Zen cult dislike intensely the Christian doctrine of personal responsibility for sin. They quite naturally revolt against any form of authority, particularly if it be a revealed authority, outside of their own subjective criterions of morality, reality and truth. In dealing with the Zenist, it is wise to concentrate upon the fact of human depravity, and the truth of their famous eternal *now* that, "the heart [of man] is deceitful above all things, and desperately wicked" (Jeremiah 17:9).

Zenists have no antidote for the piercing analytical pronouncements of Scripture: "All have sinned, and come short of the glory of God. There is none righteous, no not one" (Romans 3:23; 3:10). And the reality of divine judgment can be brought to bear upon them through proper use of the Scriptures and logic. As we have mentioned previously, one trip through the gas ovens of Dauchau, Belsen, Auschwitz and Buchenwald is worth a thousand theological propositions, and Zenists ought to be reminded of this fact— the fact that those crimes were crimes against an absolute standard which is not subjective, but objective and universal, i.e., "Thou shalt not kill" (Exodus 20:13).

The true nature of Zen is, in reality, that of ego-absorption, to the extent that one becomes obsessed with himself, not with his sins and the desperate need for their erasure. The Zenist is a stranger to social responsibility also, which leaves little to justify his existence.

The finest work from a Christian standpoint on the subject of Zen Buddhism was written by Lit-Sen-Chang, a Christian convert from Zen, the former President of Kiang-nan University, and Special Lecturer in Missions at Gordon Divinity School in Massachusetts. Mr. Chang has performed a real service for evangelical Christianity by analyzing Zen from the inside, so to speak, in his illuminating book *Zen-Existentialism: The Spiritual Decline of the West*.

Excerpts below illustrate some of the foundational defects and inadequacies of Zen:

> Thus, while Zen is seemingly commendable in some features, with its plausible teachings, it is nevertheless objectionable by reason of its serious inadequacy and sheer futility.... Even though there is some truth in Zen, it is from general revelation which does not convey to man any absolutely reliable knowledge of God, nor acquaint man with the only way of salvation. In this regard, we need further discussion....
>
> 1. It supersedes the doctrine of a real Creator. In the first place, Zen is a very peculiar and subtle form of Atheism. It denies the infinity and transcendence of a living personal God by identifying Him with nature. All visible objects thus become subjective modifications of self-existence, unconscious and impersonal essence, which may be called God, Nature, the Absolute, Oneness, Suchness, or Tathata, etc. It robs God of His sovereignty by denuding Him of His power of self-determination in relation to the world. God is reduced to the hidden ground. Since Zen does not affirm the existence of God, it is not only absolutely destitute of the special revelation of God in His Word, but it is also alien to the God of revelation....
>
> 2. It engenders a spirit of mysticism. Secondly, it has a strong tendency to engender (although they deny it) a spirit of mysticism by taking refuge in its doctrines of radical intuition, i.e., "No dependence upon words and letters"; "Special transmission of the Mind"; ... Satori is almost entirely lacking in intellectual content and yet filled with intense emotion of conviction and the mystic returns from it with a sense of great illumination. "The source phenomenon is common among Christian mystics who frequently after ecstasy assert that they have had tremendous revelation, yet are unable to state explicitly any of them."
>
> Furthermore, mysticism without divine revelation is dangerous and will lead men to destruction....
>
> 3. It disregards the holiness of God. Thirdly, Zen is a very radical form of iconoclasm. According to Prajnaparamita-hrdaya Sutra, "The void nature of all dharmas is not arising or extinction, not pure or impure, not increasing nor decreasing.... If one understands that reality is neither pure nor impure, he finds the Buddha in the dung as well as in Heaven. "... In the conception of Zenists, sin against God does not exist. As they boldly declare that the "immaculate Yogins do not enter Nirvana and the precept violating monks do not go to hell; to avoid sin and evil by obedience to any moral law is only an idle attempt...."

4. It denies the need of a Savior. Fourthly, Zen is a most radical form of auto-soterism. The principle of heathenism, as Herman Bavinck remarks, is negatively the denial of the true God and the gift of His grace; and positively, the notion that salvation can be secured by man's own power and wisdom. In the sayings of Linchi, we read, "Smash whatever you come across. Smash Buddha, smash your parents, and relations. You will be in real emancipation!" In Zen, "there is no supernatural intervention, ways or refuges. We bear the whole responsibility for our actions and no Sage whosoever he be has the right to encroach on our free will. . . ." Although they contend that this is not a proof of their pride, this teaching will surely result in self-deification which is the blasphemous characteristic and idolatrous fallacy of heathenism.

III. The Utter Failure of Zen

1. In "seeing into one's own nature." Certain of the philosophers have called man a microcosm, as being a rare specimen of divine power, wisdom and goodness and containing within himself wonders sufficient to occupy our minds. This is not altogether improper. For Paul, after reminding the Athenians that they "might feel after God and find him," immediately adds that "He is not far from everyone of us"; every man having within himself undoubted evidence of the heavenly grace by which "he lives and moves and has his being!" . . .

Since there was life in Christ from the beginning that the whole world had lost, it is necessary to return to that foundation of life, and by believing in His name, become again the sons of God. Therefore, it is rather necessary to destroy our former nature, instead of "seeing into one's own nature"; and to form in us anew the image of God which was sullied by the transgression of Adam.

2. In the attainment of Enlightenment. In 1 Corinthians 2:5, Paul well said that: "Your faith should not stand in the wisdom of man, but in the power of God." . . .

Zen asserts that without "Satori" (Enlightenment), "Zen is a sealed book." But the problem is that without special revelation, "Satori" can never be real. This is not our prejudice against Zen, even a psychologist as sympathetic to Zen as Dr. Carl G. Jung shares the same opinion. He says, "We can never decide definitely whether a person is really enlightened, or whether he merely imagines it, we have no criterion of this." . . .

. . . Zen masters . . . are often known in China as "mo-wang" (demon-king). For, while they claim to have attained Satori (Enlightenment) or to have seen their own nature; and while they talk and write with the charms of seductive eloquence, they do not realize that they are shut up in the shadow of death and that they remain in their miserable condition of perdition. . . .

3. In the way of salvation. Can Zen offer the way of salvation? . . . Satori always requires a certain amount of subconscious incubation. It is said that a merely chance occurrence—a sight, a sound—may bring it about. Often it is accompanied by intense emotional phenomena such as a trembling, a rash of tears or a cold sweat. . . .

IV. Conclusion

From the foregoing discussions, it is evident that Zen attracts people by its specious arguments, but offers no truth. It is the delusion of "blind guides," but is not the true way. It casts some dim light, but does not give the true light, nor the life, "the life (that) was the light of man." The whole creation groans and travails in pain, searches and probes in darkness. Yet man comprehended not the light which is come into the world and shines in darkness; they loved the darkness rather than the light and thus became easy preys of the false prophets.

Zen is objectionable not only because it is inadequate in its teachings but also futile in its effects. Zen is inadequate, because (1) it denies the infinity and transcendence of a living and personal God by identifying Him with nature. It is in fact a very subtle form of Atheism, disguised by the language of theism, and embellished with seductive eloquence. (2) It engenders a spirit of mysticism by taking refuge in its doctrine of radical intuition by looking into one's own nature. But to look "within" for an authoritative guide without divine revelation will surely fall into the delusion of Satan. . . . (3) It denies the need of external rules of morality. This will inevitably plunge mankind into pure anarchic relativism. (4) It rejects the grace of God and the need of a Savior by exalting and deifying man. This will surely lead the world to eternal perdition because "the whole godless world lies in the power of the evil one." Indeed, it is "a way which seems right unto a man, but the end thereof are the ways of death!" . . .

In a word, Zen is not only Biblically and theologically untenable, but also psychologically and socially detrimental. As we pointed out in another chapter, Zen is a technique by which to achieve "a mental breakdown." . . . Now many Westerners, weary of their conventional religion and philosophy, find some charm in Zen and have become prey to its plausible teachings. If unchecked, the consequences will be surely disastrous to our culture.[3]

The Core of Zen

Zen Buddhism is one of the more philosophic and orientally flavored imports of cultism, peculiarly adapted to the Western mind in that it decidedly shuns outright supernaturalism, but encourages a "Satori" (enlightenment) experience, "an awakening of our original inseparability with the universe." The ultimate goal of Zen Buddhism is "the freeing of the will," so that "all things bubble along in one interrelated continual." Those who would be disciples of Zen must allow their ego to be detached until "one's real self calmly floats over the world's confusion" like a ping-pong ball skimming over the turbulent rapids of life. In a world faced with deprivation, hunger, disease, death and the ever-present shadow of nuclear warfare, the denial of such reality borders on the criminal. Zen Buddhism, in our opinion, is the most self-centered, selfish system of philosophy that the depraved soul of man can embrace, for it negates the two basic principles upon which all spiritual reality exists, "Thou shalt love the Lord thy God with all thy heart, with all thy soul and with all thy mind . . . and thy neighbor as thyself" (Matthew 22:37, 39).

For Zenists, it is love of self first, last and always. This is the core of Zen, which releases one from spiritual responsibility and substitutes intellectual

[3]Lit-sen Chang, *Zen-Existentialism: The Spiritual Decline of the West*, Nutley, NJ: Presbyterian and Reformed Publishing Company, 1969, pp. 128–147.

enlightenment for conversion, and the absence of concern for one's fellow man for peace with God. Historically, Buddhism has produced nothing but indescribable conditions under which its subjects live. For in almost every area of the world where Buddhism of any form holds sway, there stalks the spectre of disease, hunger, and moral and spiritual decay. The peoples of the Orient are the slaves of their religions, and Buddhism, with its egocentricity, inherently selfish concept of life and of responsibility to society, is by all odds one of the greatest offenders. Let those who consider Zen as a superior form of religious philosophy look well at its history and its fruit, for "by their fruits ye shall know them" (Matthew 7:20).

Chapter 10

THE BAHA'I FAITH

The Baha'i World Faith is a non-Christian cult of distinctly foreign origin that began in Iran in the nineteenth century with a young religious Iranian businessman known as Mírzá' Ali Muhammad, who came to believe himself to be a divine manifestation projected into the world of time and space as a "Bab" (Gate) leading to a new era for mankind.

As Christianity almost since its inception has had heretics and heresies within its fold, so Islam was destined to experience the same fragmenting forces. Mírzá' Ali Muhammad, alias the "Bab," thus became one of the sorest thorns in the flesh of Islamic orthodoxy; so much so, that he was murdered by Islamic fanatics in 1850 at the age of 31. He had derived much of his early encouragement and support from a small Islamic sect in Iran, and was a prominent teacher among them for six years prior to his death. Though Christians have not been known historically for putting to death those who disagreed with them (notable exceptions are the Reformation and Counter-Reformation, the Inquisition and certain phases of the Crusades), violence may generally be said to follow in the wake of "new" revelations in most other religions, and unfortunately, in the case of Mírzá' the pattern held true.

The history of the Baha'i World Faith, then, began with the stupendous claims of a young Iranian to the effect that "the religious leaders of the world had forgotten their common origin. . . . Moses, Jesus and Mohammad were equal prophets, mirroring God's glory, messengers bearing the imprint of the Great Creator."[1]

Today this still remains the basic tenet of the Baha'i faith, albeit with the addition of Zoroaster, Buddha, Confucius, Krishna, Lao and Bahá'u'lláh, the last great manifestation of the Divine Being, whose name literally means, "the glory of God."

As Baha'i history records it, the Bab was sentenced to death and was executed July 8, 1850, at Tabriz. In the view of thousands, as the Baha'is tell it, 750 Armenian soldiers raised their rifles and fired at the figure of the prophet. When the smoke cleared, the Bab had not only emerged unscathed from the fusilade of bullets, but the bullets had burned through the ropes which held him, and he stood unfettered.

The story goes on to relate that he then disappeared from their vision, but upon returning to his cell, the guards found him lecturing his disciples. After he had finished his speaking with them, he is reported to have said, "I have finished my conversation. Now you may fulfill your intention."

He was then led out before the same firing squad and this time they did not miss.

---

[1]Richard Mathison, *Faith, Cults and Sects in America*, New York: Scribners, 1952, p. 105.

All of these events were accompanied by the cries of "Miracle! Miracle!" from the assembled populace, who, though they outnumbered the luckless Armenian soldiers, failed to rescue the Bab from his appointment with the Dark Angel.

The Baha'i history of the event also records that a fierce black whirlwind swept the city immediately after the execution of the Bab, somewhat reminiscent of the earthquake and darkness which fell over the earth upon the death of Jesus Christ on Golgotha, eighteen centuries before.

The death of the Bab, however, did not dim the rising star of the new faith. Instead, he had, according to his followers, prophesied that "The oneness of all mankind" was an inevitability, and that in time there would come, "a Promised One" who would unify all the followers and would himself be a manifestation of the only true and living God.

Modern Baha'ism considers that the Bab's great prophecy has been fulfilled by Mirza Husayn' Ali, better known to the initiated as "Bahá'u'lláh," who succeeded the Messianic throne of Baha'ism upon the death of his unfortunate predecessor, the Bab.

In the year 1863, this same Bahá'u'lláh declared himself as that one prophesied by the Bab thirteen years previously, the One who was "chosen of God, and the promised one of all the prophets."[2]

Apparently Bahá'u'lláh's conviction that he was to play Christ to the Bab's John the Baptist, convinced the majority of "Babis," as they were then known. However, his brother, Mirza Yahya, apparently did not receive the message clearly, for he forthwith renounced Bahá'u'lláh and allied himself with the enemies of the new-found religion, the Ski-ihs.

His nefarious plot, however, miserably failed, and the Baha'i movement gradually evolved into what is known today as the Baha'i World Faith, a worldwide religious organization which continues to teach in the tradition of Bahá'u'lláh, who, despite his claims to immortality, was rather unceremoniously deprived of his earthly existence by the Angel of Death who overtook him in 1892 in Bahji in Palestine. He was seventy-five at the time.

The Baha'is have had their share of persecution, and more than nine thousand were killed between 1850 and 1860. But in their emigration to America in the person of 'Abdu'l Bahá, son of Bahá'u'lláh, who arrived in the United States in 1912, Baha'ism truly received "a new birth of freedom," and today carries on its work in more than 100 countries, claiming a world membership around six million. While actual membership statistics are not given, it would appear that in 1975 they had approximately 5,500 communities in the United States. Since the Baha'is are not overly strong in publication of statistics and the information must literally be ferreted out, it is hard to estimate their rate of growth. However, they have gained some notable converts in the past, and no less a figure than Count Leo Tolstoy spoke warmly of their "spirit of brotherhood," and Woodrow Wilson's daughter became one of the first converts to Baha'ism through the work of Bahá'u'lláh in the United States. Some members of the rock music group, Crosby, Stills,

---

[2]J. E. Esslemont, *Bahá'u'lláh and the New Era*, Wilmette, IL: Baha'i Publishing Committee, 1951, p. 38.

Nash, and Young, shared their new faith in Baha'ism during public concerts and network television talk shows.

The world headquarters of the Baha'i World Faith is in Haifa, Israel, from whence are circulated the writings of Bahá'u'lláh and 'Abdu'l Bahá. Bahá'u'lláh reputedly left behind him 200 books and tablets, which, along with the writings of his son, constitute the final authority for religious faith and conduct where members of the cult are concerned.

The writer had the opportunity to visit the famous nonagon structure or Temple, as it is known, in Wilmette, Illinois; a building which utilizes the symbolic number nine, sacred to Baha'is. Its architecture is a combination of synagogue, mosque and cathedral, in which there are nine concrete piers, nine pillars representing the nine living world religions, and nine arches. The building is beautifully centered in a park having nine sides, nine avenues and nine gateways, and containing nine fountains. The worship service consists of readings from Bahá'u'lláh, 'Abdu'l Bahá, and whatever sources from the major religions are thought to be meaningful for the worshipers that day. Around the central dome of the building are various quotations both inside and out, all of which emphasize the unity of all the great religions of the world.

The Baha'i World Faith utilizes the calendar for observances designed by the Bab, which consists of nineteen months, each having nineteen days. New Year's Day falls on March 21. There are no ministers, and no ecclesiastical machinery or organization. The Baha'is employ only teachers who conduct discussion groups in homes or Baha'i Centers, and who are willing to discuss with anyone the unity of all religion under Bahá'u'lláh.

The Baha'i cult also maintains schools for study in Colorado Springs, Colorado; Geyserville, California; Eliot, Maine and Davison, Michigan.

Baha'ism, then, is an Iranian transplant to the United States, a syncretistic religion which aims at the unity of all faiths into a common world brotherhood, in effect, giving men a right to agree to disagree on what the Baha'is consider peripheral issues, but unifying all on the great central truths of the world religions, with Bahá'u'lláh as the messiah for our age. 'Abdu'l Bahá did his work well, and when he died at the age of seventy-seven in Palestine (1921), he bequeathed a budding missionary arm of his father's faith to Shoghi Effendi (Guardian of the Faith), whose influence continues in and through the teaching hierarchy of the contemporary Baha'i movement in America.

An Interview with a Baha'i Teacher

In the course of researching the history and theology of Baha'ism, I conducted numerous interviews with authoritative spokespersons for the Baha'i movement. The following is a transcription of relevant portions of an interview I conducted with one well-prepared and candid Baha'i teacher.

QUESTION: Do you in Baha'ism believe in the Holy Trinity?

ANSWER: If by the Trinity you mean the Christian concept that the three persons, Father, Son and Holy Spirit, are all the one God, the answer is No. We believe that God is one person in agreement with Judaism and Islam.

We cannot accept the idea that God is both three and one and find this foreign to the Bible which Christianity claims as its source. Not a few Jewish scholars are in complete agreement with us on this point, as is the Koran.

QUESTION: Is Jesus Christ the only manifestation of Deity, that is, is He to be believed when He said, "I am the Way, the Truth and the Life, no one comes to the Father but by me" (John 14:6)?

ANSWER: No, we believe that Jesus was only one of nine manifestations of the divine being and appeared in His era of time to illumine those who lived at that time. Today Bahá'u'lláh is the source of revelation.

Jesus was the way, the truth and the life for His time but certainly not for all time.

'Abdu'l Bahá points out that we are to honor all the major prophetic voices, not just one of them. He said:

"Christ was the prophet of the Christians, Moses of the Jews—why should not the followers of each prophet recognize and honor the other prophets?"[3]

'Abdu'l Bahá also occupied an exalted place in the thinking of Baha'is. It was he who said:

"The revelation of Jesus was for His own dispensation, that of the Son, and now it is no longer the point of guidance to the world. Baha'is must be severed from all and everything that is past—things both good and bad—everything. . . . Now all is changed. All the teachings of the past are past" (from the official Baha'i brochure, *Star of the West*, December 31, 1913).

QUESTION: Since you believe that Jesus spoke to His own dispensation, how do you account for the fact that in numerous places in the New Testament both He and His apostles and disciples asserted that He was the same "yesterday, today and forever" (Hebrews 13:8), and that His words were binding and "would never pass away"?

ANSWER: You must realize that many of the things written in the New Testament were written long after Jesus died, hence it is impossible to have absolute accuracy in everything. It would be natural for His followers to assert such things, but the revelation of Bahá'u'lláh supersedes such claims.

QUESTION: The resurrection of Jesus Christ from the dead is the true foundation of Christian experience. Does Baha'ism accept His bodily resurrection and ascension into heaven, and do you believe that He is indeed a high priest after Melchizedic's order as intercessor before the throne of God for all men?

ANSWER: The alleged resurrection of Jesus and His ascension into heaven may or may not be true depending upon your point of view. As I said before, we are concerned with Bahá'u'lláh and the new era or age, and while we reverence Jesus as we do the great prophets of other religions, we do not believe that it is necessarily important that the Baha'i faith recognize every tenet of a specific religion. We believe that Jesus conquered death, that He triumphed over the grave, but these are things which are in the realm of the spirit and must receive spiritual interpretation.

QUESTION: Then you do not actually believe in the bodily resurrection of Christ?

---

[3]*The Wisdom of Bahá'u'lláh*, Willmette, IL: Baha'i Publishing Committee, n.d., p. 43.

ANSWER: Personally, No. But we do believe that resurrection is the destiny of all flesh.

QUESTION: In Jewish theology and Christian theology much stress is laid upon sacrificial atonement for sin. The theology of Christianity in particular emphasizes that Jesus Christ is the Lamb of God who takes away the sin of the world. It was John the Baptist who so identified Him, and the New Testament gives ample testimony to His substitutionary atonement for the sins of the world. If, as Christianity maintains, "He is the satisfaction for all our sins, not for ours only, but for the sins of the whole world" (1 John 2:2), why, then, is 'Abdu'l Bahá, or for that matter, Bahá'u'lláh important? If God has revealed Himself finally and fully as the New Testament teaches in Jesus Christ (Colossians 2:9), why should further manifestation be necessary?

ANSWER: But you see that is precisely our position. God has not finally and fully revealed Himself in any of the great manifestations but through all of them, culminating in Bahá'u'lláh. A Christian may find spiritual peace in believing in a substitutionary atonement. In Baha'ism this is unnecessary. That age is past. The new age of spiritual maturity has dawned through Bahá'u'lláh, and we are to listen to his words.

QUESTION: If, as you say, Moses, Buddha, Zoroaster, Confucius, Christ, Mohammed, Krishna, Lowe and Bahá'u'lláh are all equal manifestations of the divine mind, how do you account for the fact that they contradict each other, for we know that God is not the author of confusion, or is He?

ANSWER: While it is true that there are discrepancies between the teachings of the great prophets, all held to basic moral and spiritual values. So we would expect unity here, and in the light of man's perverse nature, variety of expression in the writings and teachings of their disciples.

QUESTION: Do you accept all of the sacred books of the world religions, that is, do you consider them all to be of equal authority with the writings of Bahá'u'lláh?

ANSWER: The writings of Bahá'u'lláh, since they are the last manifestation, are to be considered the final authority in matters of religion so far as the Baha'i faith is concerned.

QUESTION: Jesus Christ taught that salvation from sin could be effected only by acceptance of Him as the sin-bearer mentioned so prominently in the fifty-third chapter of the Prophet Isaiah. Just how in Baha'ism do you deal with the problem of your own personal sin?

ANSWER: We accept the fact that no one is perfect, but by the practice of principles laid down by Bahá'u'lláh and by making every effort through prayer and personal sacrifice to live in accord with the character of the divine being revealed in him, we can arrive at eventual salvation as you like to term it.

QUESTION: What you mean then is that you, yourself, are cooperating with God in working for your salvation?

ANSWER: Yes, in a sense I suppose you could say this is true, though God in the end must be merciful to us or no one would be fit to escape the divine judgment.

QUESTION: Then you do believe in final judgment and the existence of paradise and hell?

ANSWER: Yes, the Baha'i faith recognizes divine judgment though not in the graphic terms which Christians portray it. We know nothing of eternal flames where sinners will be confined forever without respite. We do believe in the paradise of God which will be the abode of the righteous and in the resurrection and the final writing of all things.

QUESTION: Putting this on a personal basis without meaning to be offensive, might I ask you if you personally this moment believe that you are a good practicing disciple of Bahá'u'lláh; and, this being true, do you at this moment know with certainty that your sins have all been forgiven you, and that if you were to be called to accounting tonight before the throne of God, you would be adjudged fit and worthy to enter His kingdom?

ANSWER: I don't believe any person can make that statement, for no one is perfect or holy enough to merit the paradise of God, and those who so claim to have attained this exalted position are in the eyes of the Baha'i faith presumptuous, to say the very least. I could not at the moment say this for myself, but I hope that this will be the case when I die.

QUESTION: Does the Baha'i faith recognize the personality and deity of the Holy Spirit of God as revealed in the New Testament?

ANSWER: I believe it is in your Gospel of John that Jesus promised another Comforter who would abide always. We understand this to be the coming of Bahá'u'lláh, a direct fulfillment of the words of Jesus.

QUESTION: Is it not true that a great deal of your theology is borrowed from Islam and that Muslims have made the same claim for Mohammad where Christ's prophecy in John 14 is recorded as you have for Bahá'u'lláh?

ANSWER: There is no doubt that we reverence the Koran as one of the divine manifestations of illumination and Mohammed as one of the nine revelators, but Islam historically has persecuted us; in fact, it was followers of Islam who killed the Bab and persecuted Bahá'u'lláh.

With reference to the Islamic claim in John 14, I believe it is true they also make this claim.

The above excerpt has much more impact than my analysis alone would have. From an authoritative Baha'i spokesperson, it most clearly expresses what separates Baha'ism from historic Christianity. No true follower of Bahá'u'lláh, by his own admission, can claim this moment peace with God and the joy of sins forgiven, an experience which belongs only to those who have put their faith and trust in the grace and sacrifice of the Son of God (John 5:26; 6:47; Ephesians 2:8–10).

The fact that the major prophets of Baha'ism contradict each other is paradoxically overlooked by Baha'ism, which in its quest for an ecumenical syncretism prefers to avoid rather than explain the great contradictions between the major faiths.

As do most cults, the Baha'i faith will pick and choose out of the Bible that which will best benefit the advancement of their own theology, irrespective of context or theological authority. The author was impressed during this interview with the fact that the Baha'i teacher who granted it had been a disciple for more than fifty years and was certainly in a position to understand the historic views of Baha'ism. Throughout the course of the interview which was held at a Baha'i meeting in her home, we had the opportunity time and time again to present the claims of Jesus Christ, and it became apparent that her "god" was Bahá'u'lláh. The Baha'i plan of salvation is faith in him plus their own good works. Their concept of hell is largely remedial, not punitive. Their eschatology, a combination of Islam, Judaism and Christianity; and their authority, the writings of Bahá'u'lláh and 'Abdu'l Bahá.

All of the some thirty persons present took extreme pride in the fact that they had arrived at a faith which was progressively superior to all other religions and which magnanimously was willing to embrace the truth that was in every one of them to bring about the new era of which their leader had prophesied.

There was no virgin-born Son, there was only an Iranian student; there was no miraculous ministry, there was only the loneliness of exile; there was no power over demons, there were only demons of Islam; there was no redeeming Savior, there was only a dying old man; there was no risen Savior, there was only 'Abdu'l Bahá; there was no Holy Spirit, there was only the memory of the prophet; there was no ascended High Priest, there were only the works of the flesh; and there was no coming King, there was only the promise of a new era. In that room the words of the Lord of hosts were fulfilled with frightening accuracy:

"This people honor me with their lips but their heart is far from me; in vain do they worship me, teaching for doctrines the commandments of men" (Matthew 15:8, 9).

All the Baha'i temples in the world and all the quotations from sacred books cannot alter the fact that the heart of man is deceitful above everything and desperately wicked. Who can understand it? Bahá'u'lláh could not, but could his disciples today? Penned in the words of our Lord:

> If ye were blind, ye should have no sin: but now ye say, We see; therefore, your sin remaineth. Ye are from beneath; I am from above: ye are of this world; I am not of this world. I said therefore unto you, that ye shall die in your sins: for if ye believe not that I am he, ye will die in your sins. When ye have lifted up the Son of man, then shall ye know that I am he, and that I do nothing of myself; but as my Father hath taught me, I speak these things. He that believeth on me, believeth not on me, but on him that sent me. And if any man hear my words, and believe not, I judge him not: for I came not to judge the world, but to save the world. He that rejecteth me, and receiveth not my words, hath one that judgeth him: the word that I have spoken, the same shall judge him in the last day. For I have not spoken of myself; but the Father which sent me, he gave me a commandment, what I should say, and what I should speak. And I know that his commandment is life everlasting: whatsoever I speak therefore, even as the Father said unto me, so I speak (John 9:41; 8:23, 24, 28; 12:44, 47–50).

Conclusion

Looking back over our survey of Baha'ism, we can learn a number of things about this strange cult. First, we can discern that, although it is Islamic in its origin, Baha'ism has carefully cloaked itself in Western terminology and has imitated Christianity in forms and ceremonies wherever possible in order to become appealing to the Western mind.

Second, Baha'ism is eager *not* to come into conflict with the basic principles of the Gospel, and so, Baha'is are perfectly willing that the Christians should maintain their faith in a nominal sense, just so long as they acknowledge Bahá'u'lláh and the general principles of the Baha'i World Faith.

Third, Baha'ism deliberately undercuts the foundational doctrines of the Christian faith by either denying them outright or by carefully manipulating terminology so as to "tone down" the doctrinal dogmatism which characterizes orthodox Christianity.

Baha'ism has few of the credentials necessary to authenticate its claims to religious supremacy. An honest Baha'i will freely admit that in not a few respects, their system was patterned after many of the practices of Islam and Christianity.

Baha'is will quickly draw upon the scriptures of any religion of their sacred nine to defend the teachings of Bahá'u'lláh and 'Abdu'l Bahá. In this they have a distinct advantage because not a few of them are well informed concerning the Scriptures of the religions of the world, particularly, the Old and New Testaments and the Koran.

Thus, it is possible for a well-trained Baha'i cultist literally to run the gamut of the theological quotations in an eclectic mosaic design to establish their basic thesis, i.e., that all men are part of a great brotherhood revealed in this new era by the manifestation of Bahá'u'lláh.

The cardinal doctrines of the Christian faith, including the absolute authority of the Bible, the doctrines of the Trinity, the Deity of Jesus Christ, His Virgin Birth, Vicarious Atonement, Bodily Resurrection and Second Advent are all categorically rejected by Baha'ism. They maintain that Christ was *a* manifestation of God, but not the "*only* manifestation" of the Divine Being.

There is very little indeed that a true Christian can have in common with the faith of Baha'i. There is simply no common ground on which to meet or to talk once the affirmations have been made on both sides of Jesus Christ, as opposed to Bahá'u'lláh. Of course, there is the common ground of Scripture upon which we can meet all men to proclaim to them the indescribable gift of God in the Person of Christ, but there can be no ground for fellowship with the Baha'i World Faith, which is, at its very core, anti-Christian theology.

Finally, as is always the case with non-Christian cults, the refutation of Baha'ism must come from a sound knowledge of doctrinal theology as it appears in the Scriptures. No Christian can refute the perversions of the Baha'i World Faith unless he is first aware of their existence and of their conflict with the doctrines of the Bible. We must therefore be prepared to understand the scope of the teachings of the Baha'is, their basic conflict with the Gospel and the means by which we may refute them as we witness for Christ.

Chapter 11

THE UNITY SCHOOL OF CHRISTIANITY

The Unity School of Christianity, with a reputed world membership of approximately 1.5 million, is the largest gnostic cult in Christendom. It is also by far the best advertised, through the printed page, correspondence courses, and multiple publications, which have made it the largest mail-order religious concern in the world. After a careful study of its history and present-day methods of doing business with the United States mails, this writer is convinced that Unity supplies salvation as Sears Roebuck supplies overalls, cut to size and delivered parcel post. The direct-mail approach of Unity has catapulted it to a phenomenal rate of growth, especially when one realizes that it has grown from two people in a rented hall in Kansas City in 1889, to an entire city (Unity Village) in Lees Summit, Missouri. The United States government has had to supply this city with its own post office in order to process the correspondence of America's largest mail-order religion. From the presses of Unity each year flow literally tons of printed matter, dutifully shipped to the faithful in Uncle Sam's mail sacks. For a nominal fee the prospective convert may purchase magazines, newspapers, pamphlets and numerous books, all telling of the marvelous benefits to be derived from accepting the philosophy of Unity, and filling the mind with "happy thoughts," and "kind ideas," thereby banishing forever the awful concept that man is essentially an unregenerate rebel against the laws of the Holy God and desperately in need of personal redemption through Jesus Christ.

Unity, as it is known to millions of persons, is probably the most inoffensive of all the cults, since its adherents usually retain their membership in the church of their choice, while at the same time subscribing to the Unity publications, thus giving them a direct access to many churches and many congregations where the Unity cult teachings are subtly disseminated under the guise of a higher plane of Christian experience. As we shall see in the pages to follow, Unity has not been judged as a non-Christian cult solely on this basis. But it is non-Christian on the basis that it violates virtually every cardinal doctrine of the Christian faith necessary to salvation as outlined within the pages of Scripture. It is for this reason that it comes under our scrutiny as we obey the command of the Holy Spirit to "prove all things; hold fast that which is good" (1 Thessalonians 5:21).

As we have seen in our study of Christian Science, Mary Baker Eddy was definitely not its originator. And in studying the Unity cult, careful historical examination will readily reveal that Charles and Myrtle Fillmore, who began the operation of the Unity School of Christianity, were no more *its* theological parents than was Mrs. Eddy of Christian Science. Both of these cult systems, Christian Science and Unity, are the twin sisters of American

Gnosticism, and were fathered by the writings of Phineas Parkhurst Quimby, an old time Maine mental healer whom Mrs. Eddy credited with restoring her to perfect health when she was on the verge of despair.[1]

Both Mrs. Eddy and the Fillmores merely played Trilby to Quimby's theological Svengali, and the result was the birth of two variations of Quimby's pantheistic, metaphysical system, neither of which is willing to own Quimby as its legitimate parent. But a careful perusal of the *Metaphysical Bible Dictionary* published by the Unity School will quickly show that Christian Science, Unity and New Thought (which *does* recognize Quimby) have an almost interchangeable vocabulary, a fact denied by only the uninformed and those who are unwilling to study the facts of history and semantics.

Literature of the Unity School is published in the best taste. The paper is good and the bindings are excellent. Style of writing is also very appealing since it makes much of Biblical references and illustrations. Unfortunately, the average person either listening to a Unity broadcast or reading from its numerous publications doubtless believes Unity to be a form of Christian theology. It is not, however, in any sane use of the word, as we shall see. For, like other non-Christian cults, the Unity School adopts Biblical language to portray its essentially anti-Christian theological propositions. But when its true theological teachings are projected against the backdrop of Biblical revelation and stripped of their protective terminology camouflage, the entire system is revealed to be a Gnostic masquerade and a clever counterfeit of the genuine Gospel of Jesus Christ.

Openly rivaling the propaganda activities of Jehovah's Witnesses, Mormonism and Herbert W. Armstrong, Unity continues to grow in power and prestige throughout America, especially in the Midwest and the Eastern seaboard. The activities of Unity are not restricted however to "air mail or special delivery" salvation, since over its own and numerous other radio stations across the United States and Canada, the movement broadcasts its metaphysical remedies for everything from sin, sickness and death to domestic troubles and the incessant demands of the local finance companies. Unity teaches that there is no problem insoluble if one practices its tenets faithfully, and offers not only health and happiness, but financial security as well. Couple if you will these material benefits with an extremely palatable theology (palatable, that is, to those uninstructed in the Word of God), and one can easily see why Unity is a certain prospect for popularity and expansion in the Kingdom of the Cults.

Unity Village, which is the central headquarters of the cult, is located in Lees Summit, Missouri, and houses a huge printing operation, including a Sunday school quarterly, *Wee Wisdom*, for children; *Good Business*, for the working man; and *Weekly Unity*, a devotional magazine. Since one of the major tenets of the theology of Unity is reincarnation, which frowns upon the consumption of flesh foods, Unity maintains a large vegetarian cafeteria that has no equal, either for variety or quality, anywhere.

With the advent of such non-Christian cults as Theosophy, Rosicrucianism, Spiritism, etc., all emanating from Oriental sources in greater or lesser

---

[1]*Portland Evening Courier*, November 7, 1862.

degrees, reincarnation has taken on a new look, especially in Europe and America, and, from all appearances, an eminently successful one.

This new look has been specifically designed for consumption by the occidental mind and frowns upon the thought of passing from a human form to that of a snail or a chimpanzee. It is, however, receptive to the thought of reincarnation or rebirth in another human form. It comes as no surprise, then, that the most vocal proponent of this modern school of trans-migrational thought should be the Unity School of Christianity, which is in agreement in many areas with the before-mentioned cults, primarily where reincarnation is involved.

We deal more thoroughly with this when we come to Unity's concept of reincarnation, but it is one of the most effective doctrines of the cult from an evangelical standpoint, since it becomes a substitute for hell and eternal punishment—unpleasant subjects which the human mind, experience teaches us, seeks to avoid contact with at all costs.

The Beginnings of Unity

Though Phineas P. Quimby was the father of Christian Science, New Thought and Unity, Myrtle Fillmore was the theological mother of Unity. She formed Unity into a system which today resembles all three, but which clings to the special designation, "School."

Myrtle Fillmore was raised a Methodist and earned her living as a school teacher. Her early New England background was reflected in the naming of her sons, Lowell and Waldo after James Russell Lowell and Ralph Waldo Emerson. There is no doubt that she became interested in transcendental philosophy at an early age.

Mrs. Fillmore moved to Kansas City, Missouri, in 1884, and became a convert to Christian Science in 1887.

Her conversion to Mrs. Eddy's version of Quimby's theology came about when she realized that "I am a child of God and therefore I do not inherit sickness."

Mrs. Fillmore credits her own appropriation of this principle with her healing from a variety of physical problems. She then converted her husband, Charles, a former real estate salesman who had built a considerable fortune, only to lose both it and his health.

Charles Fillmore dabbled in spiritism and later became interested in Hinduism, from which the Fillmores derived a concept of reincarnation, properly modified, of course, so as to appeal to the Western mind.

Burning with zeal for their new religious discovery, Myrtle and Charles Fillmore rented a small hall in Kansas City. Thus began the great religious cult which today girdles the globe.

In April of 1889, the Fillmores published their first magazine, *Modern Thought*, which they changed in 1890 to *Christian Science Thought*. Mary Baker Eddy, however, strongly objected to the Fillmores apparently capitalizing upon the terminology she popularized. Therefore, in 1891, the title of the publication was changed to *Thought*.

The name Unity was adopted in 1891, "devoted" as Charles Fillmore stated, "to the spiritualization of humanity from an independent standpoint. . . ." a religion which ". . . took the best from all religions" (quoted in James Dillet Freeman's *The Story of Unity*, Lees Summit, MO: Unity School of Christianity, 1954, pp. 55, 61).

Unity was a member for many years of the International New Thought Alliance, from which they withdrew in 1922, having far outstripped in membership both New Thought and Christian Science.

During this period, notably, at the Columbian exposition in Chicago in 1893, the Fillmores became intensely interested in the philosophy of Hinduism and Yogaism as later popularized by Swami Vivekananda of India. Charles Fillmore, who was no stranger to the writings of Spiritualists and Theosophists, drew heavily upon this encounter, and became an admirer of Vivekananda, incorporating many of the concepts of Yogaism, reincarnation, diet (vegetarianism), etc., into the theology of the emerging Unity School.

Unity differs primarily from Christian Science in that it admits that God is expressed in matter as well as in mind or spirit, whereas Christian Science maintains that matter is illusory and has no real existence.

Myrtle Fillmore, as a result of her experience with Christian Science and Swami Vivekananda, went on to found, with her husband, such publications as *Unity* magazine, *Good Business, Wee Wisdom, Progress, Weekly Unity* and *Daily Word*. Unity also set about establishing centers throughout the South and Middle West, and constructing a publishing house from which poured multiple millions of copies of tracts, pamphlets, books and magazines, all propagating the theology of the Fillmores.

In 1903, Unity established its own ordination machinery. In 1918, Unity Field Department was established, and, in 1921, the Unity Statement of Faith was adopted.

Three years after the adoption of the Statement, the Fillmores established the Unity Church Universal, which became the Unity annual conference that ordains ministers, approves their standings on a yearly basis and supervises the operation of Unity centers, radio and television broadcasts, literature and lecturers.

Charles Fillmore ran Unity alone after Myrtle's death in 1931, until he married his longtime secretary, Cora Dedrick. Following their deaths, Charles' sons assumed control. The family still leads the organization today.

Charles Fillmore had little or no contact with orthodox Christianity, for, as Freeman put it:

> Charles Fillmore had always been interested in religion, though his approach to it was an unorthodox one. He had occasionally gone to church with his mother, who had been reared as an Episcopalian and knew the litanies by heart. But it was not from the standpoint of one who has been reared in a doctrine from childhood and simply accepts it as part of his life, that Charles approached religion. His approach was from a philosophic standpoint (*Ibid.*, p. 40).

From this unusual union then, a Methodist turned Christian Scientist and a religious agnostic turned reincarnationist, came the Unity School of Christianity, in which many well-meaning persons are today imprisoned, totally unaware of the great debt that Unity owes to Phineas Quimby, Warren

Evans and Mary Baker Eddy. In fact, they are unlikely to uncover this, since those who at the helm of the Unity barque are most careful never to discuss in detail the various origins of the cult, doubtless because they wish to continue representing it as an original "higher form" of Christianity.

Through Myrtle Fillmore's conviction and drive came the Unity School of Christianity, with its Society of Silent Help, now known as "Silent Unity." Of Mrs. Fillmore's abilities and accomplishments, Dr. James Teener, whose outstanding research of the history and theology of this cult must be considered by any serious student of Fillmore's religion, has declared:

> This silent and absent healing agency became most important in Unity, and also the most productive financially. Through it wealth has come. As need arose, other organizations were set up, the Unity Tract Society, the Unity Correspondence School, the Silent Seventy and the Unity Pure Food Company. All were consolidated into corporation as the Unity School of Christianity in 1914. The founders and their two living sons became the trustees with power to operate the business and determine their own compensation and to appoint their successors. The Fillmores did not start out to develop a sect or denomination. They have insisted that they merely had "an independent educational institution, teaching the use of the Jesus Christ doctrine in every day life."
>
> Nevertheless, their activity has been an increasing annunciation of this avowed purpose. Very early they developed their own Sunday school and worship services, putting them at the same time as the established denominational meetings. How then could their students be faithful to their individual churches? . . . Unity's strength does not lie in its theology. It is more effective than most of the mental cure agencies, because it has added religious motivation and warmth to mental and emotional guidance. Added to this is the personal interest of authors to those who approach it. People are assured that Silent Unity operates twenty-four hours a day. There is always someone in the prayer room. Letters, telegrams asking for help, are promptly answered. . . . God is always successful. "God is your highest self, and is constantly waiting upon you." This is also a weakness of Unity, for in experience, we discover that our "highest self" is still far short of the glory of God the Father of our Lord Jesus Christ.[2]

The history of Unity, then, is one of unbounded success from humble beginnings, springing from a relatively small gathering of persons under the tutelage of Myrtle Fillmore, who held twice-weekly meetings, setting forth a redefinition of the theology of Phineas P. Quimby and the "love principle, as taught by Christ."

Leaving the historical picture of Unity, we shall now allow the doctrinal teachings to speak for themselves and then examine them in the light of the Word of God.

Some of the Doctrines of Unity

1. *The Authority of the Bible.*

". . . spiritual principle is embodied in the sacred books of the world's living religions. Christians hold to the Bible as the supreme exponent of

---

[2]James W. Teener, "The Challenge of Unity," *Crossroads Magazine*, July 6, 1952, pp. 9–11.

spiritual principle. They believe that the Bible is the greatest and most deeply spiritual of all the Scriptures, though they realize that other Scriptures, such as the Zend-Avesta, and the Upanishads, as well as the teachings of Buddha, the Koran, and the Tao of Lao-tse and the writings of Confucious, contain expressions of eminent spiritual truths. . ." (*What Unity Teaches*, Lees Summit, MO: Unity School of Christianity, 1952, p. 4).

". . . Scripture may be a satisfactory authority for those who are not themselves in direct communion with the Lord" (*Unity*, October 1896, vol. 7, p. 400).

2. *The Triune God (the Trinity).*

"The Father is Principle, the Son is that Principle revealed in the creative plan, the Holy Spirit is the executive power of both Father and Son carrying out the plan" (*Metaphysical Bible Dictionary*, Unity School of Christianity, p. 629).

"God is not loving. God is love, the great heart of the universe and of man, from which is drawn forth all feeling, sympathy, emotion, and all that goes to make the joys of existence.

"Yet God does not love anybody or anything. God is the love in everybody and everything. God is love; man becomes loving by permitting that which God is to find expression in word and act" (Charles Fillmore, *Jesus Christ Heals*, Lees Summit, MO: Unity School of Christianity, 1947, p. 27).

"Drop from your mind the idea that God is a being of majesty and power in the sense that you now interpret majesty and power.

"Drop from your mind the belief that God is in any way separated from you, that He occupies form or space outside of you, or that he can be manifested to your consciousness in any way except through your own soul" (*Ibid.*, pp. 27, 28).

"God is not a . . . person, having life, intelligence, love, power. God is that invisible, intangible, but very real, something we call life. God is perfect love and infinite power. God is the total of these, the total of all good, whether manifested or unexpressed" (H. Emily Cady, *Lessons in Truth*, Lees Summit, MO: Unity School of Christianity, 1944, p. 6).

"To the individual consciousness God takes on personality, but as the creative underlying cause of all things, He is principle, impersonal; as expressed in each individual, He becomes personal to that one—a personal, loving, all-forgiving Father-Mother. All that any human soul can ever need or desire is the infinite Father-Principle, the great reservoir of unexpressed good. There is no limit to the Source of our being, nor to His willingness to manifest more of Himself through us, when we are willing to do His will" (*Ibid.*, p. 11).

3. *The Deity of Jesus Christ.*

"Christ, meaning 'messiah' or 'anointed,' designates one who had received a spiritual quickening from God, while Jesus is the name of the personality. To the metaphysical Christian—that is, to him who studies the spiritual man—Christ is the name of the supermind and Jesus is the name of the personal consciousness. The spiritual man is God's Son; the personal man is man's son" (*Jesus Christ Heals, op. cit.*, p. 10).

"Jesus Christ Himself was a parable, and his life an allegory of the experiences that man passes through in development from natural to spiritual consciousness" (Charles Fillmore, *Christian Healing*, Lees Summit, MO: Unity School of Christianity, 1942, p. 68).

"Christ is the only begotten Son of God, the one complete idea of perfect man and divine Mind. This Christ or perfect-man idea existing eternally in divine Mind is the true, spiritual, higher-self of every individual" (*Metaphysical Bible Dictionary, op. cit.*, p. 150).

"The difference between Jesus and us is not one of inherent spiritual capacity, but in difference of demonstration of it. Jesus was potentially perfect, and He expressed that perfection; we are potentially perfect, and we have not yet expressed it" (*What Unity Teaches, op. cit.*, p. 3).

4. *The Atonement of Jesus Christ.*

"The atonement is the union of man with God the Father in Christ. Stating it in terms of mind, we should say that the atonement is the At-one-ment or agreement or reconciliation of man's mind with divine Mind, through the superconsciousness of Christ-mind" (*What Unity Teaches, op. cit.*, p. 5).

"We have thought that we are to be saved by Jesus' making personal petitions and sacrifices for us, but now we see that we are to be saved by using the creative principles that he developed in Himself and that He is ever ready to co-operate with us in developing in ourselves by observing the law as He observed it. 'I in them, and thou in me, that they may be perfected into one' " (*Jesus Christ Heals, op. cit.*, p. 162).

"These theories of the sin offering of Jesus are conceived with the personal God idea. They carry out the pagan concept of a big god who becomes very angry with his disobedient children and can be mollified only with a human sacrifice. A correct understanding by man of God as the supreme creative Mind creating under laws that must be observed by both Creator and creation, reveals how broken law may be mended by one who is willing to make certain sacrifices" (Charles and Cora Fillmore, *Teach Us to Pray*, Lees Summit, MO: Unity School of Christianity, 1946, p. 150).

5. *Salvation.*

"The Christ in man never changes; it always has been and always will be the perfection that God created" (*What Unity Teaches, op. cit.*, p. 8).

"Being 'born-again' or 'born from above' is not a miraculous change that takes place in man; it is the establishment of that which has always existed as the perfect man idea of divine Mind" (*Christian Healing, op. cit.*, p. 24).

"No one can do this for you. You do not really want another to do it although you sometimes think how nice it would be if some master of spiritual ideas would suddenly help you right into his understanding. But this is a childish dream of the moment. You want to be yourself, and you can be yourself only by living out your own life and finding its issues at the Fountainhead. If it were possible for one person to reveal the Truth to another, we should have heaven cornered by cunning manipulators of mind and its glories stored up in warehouses awaiting a higher market. Let us be thankful that God is no respecter of persons; that Truth cannot be revealed by one mortal to another. God is a special, personal Father to every one of His children, and from no other source can they get Truth" (*Jesus Christ Heals, op. cit.*, p. 98).

6. *The Holy Spirit.*
"The Spirit *of wholeness quickens and heals me.* The Spirit of wholeness is called the Holy Spirit in the New Testament. In classical mythology it is called Hygeia. Modern medical men refer to it as the restorative power of nature. It has been recognized by savage and civilized in every land and age. It has many names, and they all identify it as a universal urge toward perfection in man and the universe and toward keeping things going regardless of any retarding or interfering force" (*Ibid.*, p. 182).

"Do not be misled by the personality of the Holy Spirit and the reference to it as 'he.' This was the bias of the Oriental mind, making God and all forms of the Deity masculine" (*Ibid.*, p. 183).

7. *The Resurrection.*
"Jesus spent whole nights in prayer, according to the Gospels, and it is quite evident that He was resurrecting His body by realizing, as we do in our prayers, that God was His indwelling life" (*Ibid.*, p. 13).

"Eventually all souls reincarnate on the earth as babes and in due time take up their problems where they left off at death" (*Teach Us to Pray, op. cit.*, p. 50).

". . . Jesus demands of the Pharisees, 'What think ye of Christ? whose son is he?' They answered, not as one might ordinarily expect, 'The son of Joseph,' but '*The son* of David.' In other words He was the reincarnation of David" (Ernest C. Wilson, *Have We Lived Before?*, p. 41).

8. *Sin.*
"Pain, sickness, poverty, old age and death are not real, and they have no power over me. There is nothing in all the universe for me to fear" (*Lessons in Truth, op. cit.*, p. 35).

"1. I deny that I have inherited disease, sickness, ignorance or any mental limitation whatsoever. 2. I deny that I am a child of the flesh. I deny all belief in evil, for God made all that really is and pronounced it good. 3. Therefore no such deception as a belief in evil can darken my clear understanding of Truth. 4. I deny that the sins and omissions of my ancestors can reflect upon me in any way. Selfishness, envy, malice, jealousy, pride, arrogance, cruelty, hypocrisy, obstinancy and revenge are not part of my present understanding and I deny all such beliefs" (*Christian Healing, op. cit.*, pp. 250, 251).

9. *The Reality of Matter.*
"God, then, is the substance (from *sub*, under and *state*, to stand), or the real thing standing under every visible form of life, love, intelligence, or power. Each rock, tree, animal, everything visible, is a manifestation of the one Spirit—God—differing only in degree of manifestation; and each of the

numberless modes of manifestation, or individualities, however insignificant, contains the whole" (*Lessons in Truth, op. cit.*, p. 8).

Refuting the Teachings of Unity

The theology of the Unity cult, as revealed in the previously quoted extracts from some of its standard publications, is far removed indeed from the Gospel of Jesus Christ as preached by the early apostles and as transmitted through the centuries by faithful witnesses of God in each age.

We cannot, of course, in the space allotted for a publication of this type cover in any extensive detail the various perversions so apparent in the teachings of Unity, but we shall for the remainder of this chapter concern ourselves with the dogmas of Unity as they affect some well-known Biblical doctrines, which are, in order: (1) The Bible; (2) The Trinity; (3) The Deity of Christ; (4) The Atonement of Christ; (5) The Doctrine of Salvation; (6) The Resurrection of Christ; (7) The Second Coming of Christ.

It is hoped, by contrasting the clear, historical teachings of Christianity which the Bible forthrightly states, with the teachings of Unity, that the reader may be able to discern the vast difference which exists between the doctrines of the Unity cult and those of orthodox Christianity.

1. *The Bible.*
We have seen in our study of the Unity cult that the use of the Scriptures is an integral part of their entire system of teachings. By this we do not mean that teachings of Unity conform to the Scriptures, but rather that the Unity adherents use the Scriptures in a vain attempt to bolster up the unscriptural doctrines of the Fillmores.

Dr. James Teener, in his thorough analysis of Unity, has stated that for Unity ". . . the Bible is one of many sacred books, all of which are to be treated with reverence as 'records of men as to what their experiences have been communing with the omnipresent God.' The general tendency of Unity, however, is not to criticize statements of the Bible but to reinterpret them by the process of allegorization. The Fillmores belong in the lineage of Origen, Swedenborg and Mrs. Eddy in this respect. Thus they are able to unite the metaphysical-mystical East and the practical-ethical West, but the East is always regent" (James Teener, *Unity School of Christianity*, Chicago, IL: University of Chicago Library, 1942, p. 13).

With Dr. Teener's analysis this writer is in wholehearted agreement, having studied numerous publications of the Unity School of Christianity. In his *Twelve Powers of Man* (Lees Summit, MO: Unity School of Christianity, 1930, p. 114), Charles Fillmore stated, "Scripture may be a satisfactory authority for those who are not themselves in direct communion with the Lord." From this it is at once obvious that Scripture is for those dwelling on a lower plane of spiritual development, whereas personal experience with God transcends the authority of Scripture!

Proof that the Unity School continues to spiritualize and allegorize all passages of the Bible which are in direct contradiction to their jumbled theological structure, can be found in any edition of *Unity* magazine, where the

International Sunday School Lessons (a Biblical presentation) are reinterpreted in the framework of Unity theology. This writer challenges anyone to read the parallel columns therein contained and by any conceivable stretch of the imagination or rational exercise of the mind in the light of the plain declarations of Scripture, to reconcile them as Unity claims it has done.

In company with Mrs. Eddy and most other gnostic religious thinkers, Unity refuses the historic exegetical positions of the Bible, and deliberately shuns any controversy with informed Bible scholars, lest their shallow pretentions and fraudulent scholarship be exposed to the glaring light of Biblical truth. The Christian faith is founded upon belief in the Bible as the Word of God, or, as Paul put it, "All Scripture is given by inspiration of God [God-breathed], and is profitable for doctrine, for reproof, for correction, for instruction in righteousness that the man of God may be perfect, thoroughly furnished unto all good works" (2 Timothy 3:16, 17).

The Lord Jesus Christ, in referring to the Word of His Father said, "Sanctify them through thy truth,. thy word is truth" (John 17:17); and it was the Psalmist who stated, "For ever, O Lord, thy word is settled in heaven" and "Thy word is very pure" (Psalm 119:89, 140).

It is a well-known fact that Christ, during His lifetime, recognized the three-fold division of the Old Testament—the law, the prophets and the writings—and referred to them in their proper order at various times during the course of His ministry. Therefore, it is inconceivable that the early church should not have held in great esteem the record of the Old Testament, as well as the then-forming record of the new covenant, for which many of them eventually were to pay with their very life's blood.

Christians of all denominations who confess the cardinal doctrines of the Scripture (The Trinity, The Deity of Christ, The Virgin Birth, The Sinless Nature of Christ, The Vicarious Atonement, The Physical Resurrection, The Second Coming of Christ, etc.), recognize the importance of accepting the Bible in its historic and linguistic framework. Only those with no concern for the testimony of history and the facts of sound exegesis, allegorize and spiritualize texts which they know reinforce the foundational doctrines of historic Christianity.

The adherents of the Unity cult are guilty of allegorization and spiritualization of all the cardinal doctrines of the Christian faith, and rather than to criticize outright the statements of Scripture, they subtly undercut the great pronouncements of the Word of God by reinterpreting them, allegorizing them and spiritualizing them, until they have sapped all of the revealed power of the Word of God, twisted it into the mold of the Fillmore religion and, in effect, "wrested the Scriptures to their own destruction" (2 Peter 3:16).

Let us keep in mind, then, that the members of the Unity cult speak devotedly of the Bible, but they utilize the Bible *only* insofar as it can be wielded as a successful tool to lure the unwary soul into the meshes of the Fillmore cult. But for the true Christian, the Bible in its proper context and framework of history, must ever remain the Word of God, inviolate, the final authority for the Church of Jesus Christ and the individual Christian life.

2. *The Trinity.*

It is the clear teaching of the Word of God that the nature of God is spirit (John 4:24), and further, that He has manifested Himself in the Old Testament in different ways (the Angel of Jehovah—Exodus 23:20; Judges 6:12 and 13; Judges 13, etc.; the Son of God—Daniel 3:25; as Emmanuel, *God with us*—Isaiah 7:14, etc.). In the eighteenth chapter of Genesis, for instance, it is recorded that Abraham entertained three visitors on the plains of Mamre, two of whom were angels (Genesis 19:1), the other whom Abraham addressed fourteen times as Jehovah God! To further clarify the picture where an understanding of the true nature of God is concerned, the Bible in the creation account (Genesis 1:26, 27) quotes the Lord as saying, "Let *us* make man in *our* image after *our* likeness . . . so God created man in his own image, in the image of God created he him, male and female created he them," utilizing the Hebrew plural "us" and "our" while at the same time returning to the singular "his" in verse 27, clearly a Trinitarian indication.

As we approach the New Testament revelation of God we also find something far beyond the Jewish interpretation of solitary unity (Deuteronomy 6:4), for both at the baptism of the Lord Jesus Christ and His last resurrection appearance (Matthew 3:16, 17; cf. Matthew 28:19), three distinct Persons are viewed as the one God, and nothing could be clearer than Christ's command to baptize in this threefold name of the Deity, Jehovah!

The God of the Bible and Father of our Lord Jesus Christ is a personal Being, a personal Spirit. This Almighty Person performs acts that only a personality is capable of: God hears (Exodus 2:24); God sees (Genesis 1:4); God creates (Genesis 1:1); God knows (2 Timothy 2:19, Jeremiah 29:11); God has a will (1 John 2:17); God is a cognizant reflectable ego, i.e., a personal being "I AM that I AM" (Exodus 3:14; Genesis 17:11). This is the God of Christianity, an omnipotent, omniscient, and omnipresent Personality, who manifests every attribute of a personality. He is therefore definitely not the God of Unity theology for Unity teaches that "belief" in a personal God has retarded the progress of the race![3]

According to the theology of Unity, "The Father is principle, the Son is that principle revealed in the creative plan, the Holy Spirit is the executive power of both Father and Son, carrying out the plan" (*Metaphysical Bible Dictionary, op. cit.,* p. 629). However, this description does not coincide with the Biblical revelation of the character of God, for Unity is at its very core a pantheistic form of religion, maintaining that man is in effect, part of God; whereas the Scriptures clearly teach that man is the result of God's creative power and separate from Him, as every creation is by its very nature, separate from its creator.

Bear in mind that whenever the adherents of Unity speak of "God," they do not speak of the God of Christianity or of the Judaeo–Christian heritage. They speak, instead, of an abstract Principle, a divine Mind, which in no sense has a personality, neither can "it" be addressed as a personal being.

Unity perverts the doctrine of the Trinity, spiritualizing the very terms used to describe the relationship between the members of the godhead (Fa-

[3]Sarah B. Scott, *The True Character of God*, Lees Summit, MO: Unity School of Christianity, n.d., p. 3.

ther, Son, Holy Spirit), and this dishonest practice should be unmasked at every opportunity by those interested enough in the truth concerning the character of God as we find it within the pages of Scripture.

3. *The Deity of Christ.*

One needs only to peruse superficially the literature of the Unity cult to realize quickly that in the theology of Unity, Jesus Christ is not the God-man of the New Testament doctrine.

The New Testament, which is in reality the continuation or the unfolding of the expression of God's will under the old covenant, categorically teaches that Jesus Christ is the Eternal Word of God (John 1:1), that He took upon Himself the form of a man (John 1:14; Philippians 2:6, 7), and further, that He is the Redeemer of Israel and the Savior of the world (Matthew 1:21–24; Acts 4:12).

Unity, in company with Christian Science, New Thought, Religious Science, etc., divides Jesus and Christ, reducing the God-man of Scripture to a perfect man indwelt by the Christ-consciousness, a consciousness present in *every* human being and which only needs to be cultivated and developed. Or, as the *Metaphysical Bible Dictionary* states it on page 150, "Christ is the only begotten son of God with one complete idea of perfect man and divine Mind. This Christ, or perfect-man idea, existing eternally in divine Mind is the true spirit and higher self of every individual." We see, then, that all men are miniature "christs" so to speak, and in no sense whatsoever does Unity teach the intrinsic Deity and uniqueness of the incarnate Word of God.

By subtly making a differentiation between the man Jesus and "the Christ, the spiritual identity of Jesus," Unity attempts to divest the Lord Jesus Christ of His true identity, which the Scriptures reveal to be that of incarnate Deity (see Isaiah 9:6; John 5:18; Colossians 1:15–18; 2:9; Revelation 1:7, 8, 17, 18).

Charles Fillmore, in *Christian Healing* (*op. cit.*, pp. 106, 107), counsels the adherents of Unity when in doubt to "claim your Christ understanding at all times. . . ." which in one short phrase sums up the position of Unity regarding the Lord Jesus Christ. For Mr. Fillmore taught that "Christ" is in reality "the superconscious mind, Christ-conscious, or spiritual-consciousness. . . ." (*Metaphysical Bible Dictionary, op. cit.*, p. 155), a position which is directly opposed to the teaching of Scripture; for there has been but one Christ, of whom Peter spoke when he said, "Neither is there salvation in any other, for there is none other name under heaven given among men, whereby we must be saved," and "this same Jesus, God hath made Lord and Christ" (Acts 4:12; 2:36).

Jesus Christ then, was not Jesus and Christ as the Unity cultists would have us believe; rather, He was the God-man—two natures in one being, "Jesus Christ the same, yesterday, today and for ever" (Hebrews 13:8). In the eighth chapter of John's gospel, verse 58, the Lord Jesus Christ unmistakably identified Himself with Jehovah when He stated that "Before Abraham was, I AM" (cf. Exodus 3:14). And it is this one fact that establishes the unity of Christ with the Eternal Trinity, Father, Son and Holy Spirit, and establishes beyond question in the mind of any intelligent exegetical student of Scripture the identity and Deity of Jesus Christ. "This is the true God, and eternal life" (1 John 5:20).

4. The Atonement of Christ.

The verdict of the Scriptures on the state of unregenerate mankind is most explicit: "All have sinned and come short of the glory of God" (Romans 3:23). Punishment for this is declared to be "everlasting" (Matthew 25:46), unless one accepts the death of Jesus Christ upon Calvary's cross in his stead, for then, and then alone, the Scriptures teach, can a man find peace with God (Romans 5). The Bible declares in unmistakable terms that the atonement (reconciliation) of Christ was the fulfillment of the Old Testament sacrifice of the lamb for the sins of the people (Exodus 12:5–14) and further, that Jesus Christ as the Lamb of God (John 1:29) made atonement for all sin forever upon the cross of Calvary "once," then seated Himself on the right hand of the "Majesty on High" (Hebrews 1:3 and 9:26). Through His substitutionary sacrifice we "have peace with God" (Colossians 1:20) and "the blood of Jesus Christ his Son, cleanseth us from all sin" (1 John 1:7). In his book, *What Practical Christianity Stands For* (Lees Summit, MO: Unity School of Christianity, 1947, p. 5), Charles Fillmore made the following statement: "The atonement is the unity of man with God the Father, in Christ. Stating it in terms of mind, we should say that the atonement is the At-one-ment or agreement or reconciliation of man's mind with divine Mind through the superconsciousness of Christ Mind."

It is hardly necessary to expand upon the direct contradiction which exists between these two positions. The atonement of the cross is a great deal more than the "reconciliation of man's mind with divine Mind through the superconsciousness of Christ Mind," as Mr. Fillmore would have us believe.

According to the testimony of Scripture, Christ "bore in his own body our sins upon the tree" (1 Peter 2:24), and the Scriptures irrevocably state that, "Without the shedding of blood there is no remission" (Hebrews 9:22), a vastly different position from that of Mr. Fillmore and the Unity cult.

Peter, in his first epistle, states the doctrine of the atonement in a nutshell, when he writes:

> Forasmuch as ye know that ye were not redeemed with corruptible things, as silver and gold, from your vain conversation received by tradition from your fathers; But with the precious blood of Christ, as of a lamb without blemish and without spot. . . . Being born again, not of corruptible seed, but of incorruptible, by the word of God, which liveth and abideth forever. . . . But the word of the Lord endureth for ever. And this is the word which by the gospel is preached unto you (1 Peter 1:18, 19, 23, 25).

Christ, therefore, upon Calvary's cross, ransomed the souls of all who will believe, from the power of eternal death, and as John so beautifully puts it in the Apocalypse, "From Jesus Christ, who is the faithful witness and the first begotten of the dead, and the prince of the kings of the earth. Unto him that loved us and washed [loosed] us from our sins in his own blood" (Revelation 1:5).

The theology of the Unity School, then, is directly opposed to the clear revelation of Scripture which teaches that it is through the blood of the Lord

Jesus Christ shed in a vicarious effort that man has peace with God (Colossians 1:20; cf. Romans 5), and with Moses of old we can rest in the sure Word of God which states, ". . . for the blood through the life in it serves for expiation" (Leviticus 17:11, Berkeley Version).

5. The Doctrine of Salvation.

There are many who will ask, "Since Unity denies practically every cardinal doctrine of the Christian faith, how then can they claim any kind of salvation; and if so, what type of salvation is it?"

To answer these questions, we must understand that Unity denies the existence of a literal heaven or hell (Luke 16). Indeed, all the heaven or hell a man is likely to get, according to the Fillmores, he will get here upon this earth, either in this incarnation or in future incarnations, dependent upon his behavior during each incarnation. In *Jesus Christ Heals* (*op. cit.*, p. 162), Charles Fillmore summed up the Unity teaching on salvation when he wrote, "We have thought that we were to be saved by Jesus' making personal petitions and sacrifices for us, but now we see that we are to be saved by suing the creative principles that He developed in Himself and that He is ever ready to cooperate with us in developing in ourselves by observing the law as He observed it. 'I in them, and thou in me, that they may be perfected into one.' "

The Unity cult today continues to hold this teaching and knows nothing of the "eternal life" offered to mankind by the Lord Jesus when He said, "Come unto me all ye that labor and are heavy laden and I will give you rest" (Matthew 11:28) and "Ye must be born again" (John 3:5). Let us then beware of Unity's perversions of Scripture and cling to the Gospel of the Son of God, "who loved us and gave Himself for us" (Ephesians 5:2), for He alone is the "author of eternal salvation to all them that obey Him" (Hebrews 5:9).

6. The Resurrection of Christ.

Unity, through its various publications and especially its *Statement of Faith*, Article 22, has gone on record as stating the following things relative to the Resurrection.

"We believe the dissolution of spirit, soul and body, caused by death, is annulled by rebirth of the same spirit and soul in another body here on earth. We believe the repeated reincarnations of man are the merciful provision of our loving Father to the end that all may come to obtain immortality through regeneration, as did Jesus."

In lieu of the great doctrine of the bodily resurrection as taught in both the Old and the New Testaments, the Unity cult teaches cycles of reincarnation until eventual perfection is reached. The true Christian position concerning death, however, is taught in numerous places in Scripture as, for example in 2 Corinthians 5:8, where Paul emphatically states that "to be absent from the body is to be present with the Lord [or at home with the Lord]." And again, in Philippians 1:21–23, the great apostle anticipates his departure from this life to be with Christ, and certainly not to go through repeated incarnations until he was found worthy to share the glory of the Lord.

To refute the Unity position, reincarnation vs. resurrection, the reader is referred to the fifteenth chapter of 1 Corinthians where the doctrine of the physical resurrection of the body to immortality is clearly stated. After reading this, the writer feels, the observant reader will immediately note the difference between the theology of Paul under the inspiration of the Holy Spirit, and the theology of the Fillmores and Unity, via the medium of the "great deceiver!"

In *Jesus Christ Heals* (*op. cit.*, p. 165), Charles Fillmore wrote: "Salvation through Jesus Christ is not accomplished by looking forward to freedom but by realizing that we are now free through His freeing power, which we are using to cut the bonds with which our thoughts have bound us. Then we have only to establish ourselves in real life and strength by understanding that these attributes of Being are omnipresent and that our affirmations of that presence, will cause us to become conscious that we do now and here live, move, and have our being in eternal life and strength." The Unity cult has not departed from this teaching of Fillmore, which directly contradicts the testimony of the Lord Jesus Christ in the fourteenth chapter of John, when He said, "Let not your heart be troubled, ye believe in God, believe also in me. In my Father's house are many mansions: if it were not so I would have told you. I go to prepare a place for you. And if I go and prepare a place for you, I will come again and receive you unto myself; that where I am, there ye may be also" (verses 1–3). Contrary to the teachings of Unity, then, "it is appointed unto men once to die, but after this the judgment" (Hebrews 9:27); and "It is a fearful thing to fall into the hands of the living God" (Hebrews 10:31), pronouncements which, while they held no terror for the Fillmores during their long lives, doubtless are most meaningful today, since both the first Mrs. Fillmore and her patriarchal husband, Charles, have departed this life to face the judgment of the God of the Bible and not the god that they fashioned with deceptive words and metaphysical speculations. The God who is not a respecter of persons (2 Samuel 14:14), and who is the Judge of all the earth, has commanded that all men honor His Son, even as they honor Him (John 5:23). And He has especially stated His intention of eventually raising the dead (1 Corinthians 15), not subjecting them to repeated reincarnations in the traditions of the Fillmores and the Unity cult.

7. *The Second Coming of Christ.*

It is quite unnecessary to go into detail relative to the teaching of Unity on the Second Coming of the Lord Jesus Christ, except to note that Unity recognizes no personal return of Jesus Christ to judge the world (see 1 Thessalonians 4:13–18).

In direct contradiction to this unscriptural teaching, the Bible clearly prophesies the return of the Messiah of Israel and the Savior of mankind to execute righteous judgment upon the earth (Zechariah 12:10; cf. Revelation 1:7; also Matthew 25:31–46; and 2 Thessalonians 1:7–10).

The great expectation of the Church of Christ has been the imminent return of her blessed Lord, which Paul describes in his letter to Titus as "looking for that blessed hope and the glorious appearing of the great God and our Savior Jesus Christ, who gave himself for us, that he might redeem us from all iniquity, and purify unto himself a peculiar people, zealous of good works" (2:13–15).

When we consider these objective facts of Scripture and carefully compare them with the mangled jargon of the Unity School, it becomes increasingly apparent that our faith must rest as always, upon the sure revelations of Scripture. We must be prepared for the "scoffers" who the Holy Spirit through Peter said, would come toward the end of the age (2 Peter 3:3), and whom we are to "reprove, rebuke and exhort with all longsuffering and doctrine" (2 Timothy 4:2), that we may be faithful to Christ, "who is over all, God blessed for ever. Amen" (Romans 9:5).

Before closing our study of the Unity School, we believe it is necessary to examine one of the major tenets of Unity, which makes it so attractive to so many persons in our day. We make reference to the doctrine of reincarnation which the Unity School propagates, in company with other reincarnationists, and which should be analyzed and answered from the Bible.

The Reincarnation Theory of Unity

The theory of reincarnation, transmigration or rebirth, is best described briefly as a process whereby at the death of the body, the soul passes into the bodies of lower animals or other human beings in an ever-rotating cycle (from body to body) until purification from sin is accomplished. When this sinless state has been attained, the soul passes thence to Nirvana (Buddhism) or the dwelling place of Brahma (Hinduism). These places consist of nothing more than "the eternal peace," reached by absorption of the soul and all vestiges of individual personality into the world soul or whatever philosophical abstraction it may constitute.

In the case of the Unity School, as we have previously observed, reincarnation has been given a new facade, and a good deal of "evidence" has been introduced to show that the Unity concept of reincarnation is not only logical and rational, but that it is the only "reasonable" solution to many so-called insoluble problems that orthodox Christianity cannot solve.

We shall consider at this time only those evidences most frequently submitted, the remainder being largely peripheral in character.

The Evidence

(1) There are persons, places and experiences with which we do not have to become acquainted. Somehow we feel we already know them. Have you ever felt that you have been to a place or known a person before you experienced the meeting? This is evidence of reincarnation.

(2) All men are not born equal in regard to either station in life, opportunity or condition of health. Some babies are born blind, deaf or diseased, many persons are cut down in the flower of youth. If God is just, He cannot allow such things to happen to the apparently innocent. Therefore, He must be punishing them for their previous sins while in another form, and this will continue on until all are purified of past mistakes. Reincarnation, then,

is the only fair evidence of God's being perfectly just to all men.

(3) Unfinished thoughts and unfinished work abound in everyone's experience, and God could not justly waste these undeveloped talents. Rather, He gives us countless opportunities to utilize them by supplying concurrent rebirths in which to bring our thoughts and works to fruition.

(4) Many documented and verified cases of persons who have been able to recount their previous lives in detail are recorded in the files of reputable professional hypnotists, psychologists and research organizations; these establish the fact of reincarnation beyond reasonable doubt, and are available for evaluation.

These four points in one form or another make up the basic premises upon which the theory of reincarnation is based; abundant "evidence" is also submitted from the "inspired" writings of numerous Eastern religions and Western cults, but the pattern is always uniformly the same. The Unity School, however, differs slightly from the more "orthodox" systems of transmigration in that Unity claims that reincarnation is a "Christian doctrine" (Ernest Wilson, *op. cit.,* p. 28) and that the Bible fully teaches and supports it as such. Some of the common texts cited are: Matthew 16:17; 17:11; 22:42; John 9:2; Revelation 5:5 and 22:16). We shall discuss these and their contextual meanings contrasted with the interpretation of reincarnationists a little later on, but the fact remains that not a few have dared to claim support from the Scriptures for this pagan dogma.

The Biblical Position

Reincarnation can easily be refuted from the Bible by at least ten Old and New Testament doctrines, but for the sake of brevity, we have elected to list only four, all of which those believing in reincarnation, including the Unity School, deny automatically, by accepting their transmigration hypothesis. These Biblical doctrines are: (1) The Personality of God; (2) The Atonement of Christ; (3) The Physical Resurrection and (4) Divine Retribution.

1. For some unknown reason, all reincarnationists reject the Personality of God, that He is a personal cognizant Spirit, a divine Ego (Exodus 3:14) capable of a subject-object relationship with man and within the Godhead.

All reincarnationists, then, are committed to a pantheistic concept of Deity, that is, God is conceived of as being the fountain of all existence from the tiniest atom to the most gigantic forms of matter, and further, these things are all part of His Substance, which permeates every particle of existence.

This position that God is all and all is God or a manifestation of Him, is thoroughly refuted by the following verses of Scripture, which teach incontrovertibly that God is a Personal Spirit possessed of attributes which only a personality has, immanent in creation, but apart from it as Creator. Transcendent in that He does not share His spiritual substance (John 4:24; Hebrews 1:3) with the products of His creative will.

A. God remembers. Isaiah 43:25; Jeremiah 31:20; Hosea 8:13.
B. God speaks (Subject-object relationship). Exodus 3:12; Matthew 3:17; Luke 17:6.

C. God sees, hears and creates. Genesis 6:5; Exodus 2:24; Genesis 1:1.
D. God knows (has a mind). Jeremiah 29:11; 2 Timothy 2:19; 1 John 3:20.
E. God is a personal spirit. John 4:24; Hebrews 1:3.
F. God has a will. Matthew 6:10; Hebrews 10:7, 9; 1 John 2:17.
G. God will judge. Ezekiel 18:30; 34:20; 2 Corinthians 5:10.

2. Reincarnation is refuted most decisively by the atonement of Jesus Christ, since the doctrine of the atonement teaches that God, through Christ's sacrifice on the cross, has "purged" believers from all their sins (Hebrews 1:3) and counted them righteous for the sake of His Son (2 Corinthians 5:21). Reincarnationists, on the other hand, claim that successive "rebirths" are the instrument of cleansing for the soul and thereby do away with not only the efficacy of the atonement, but the very necessity itself of Christ's dying at all for the sins of the world.

The Bible, however, clearly teaches that "without the shedding of blood is no remission" (Hebrews 9:22) of sin, and Christ purchased the church with His own blood which is not corruptible as silver or gold are (1 Peter 1:18, 19), but which is precious and the price of the soul's redemption.

For the Unity adherent of the reincarnation theory, then, almost endless cycles of rebirth are necessary to cleanse the soul from sin, but for the Christian the blood of Jesus Christ, God's Son, cleanses us from all sin (1 John 1:9). This is the message of the Bible from Genesis to Revelation, redemption by blood through the sacrifice of "him that loved us and washed us from our sins in his own blood" (Revelation 1:5). (For further Scriptures see Matthew 26:28; Romans 5:6–8; Ephesians 1:7; Colossians 1:20, etc.)

3. The doctrine of the physical resurrection of Jesus Christ (and all men, for that matter!) is the foundation stone upon which the validity of Christianity stands, for in the words of the Apostle Paul—"If Christ be not raised, your faith is vain; ye are yet in your sins" (1 Corinthians 15:17). The Bible plainly states that Jesus arose from the grave in a physical form (John 20:27), that He was not raised a spirit (Luke 24:39–44) and that Christ Himself after He had risen, rebuked His disciples for their unbelief in His physical Resurrection (Mark 16:14*). It is evident, therefore, that though Jesus Christ was raised physically, He had what the Bible terms a "spiritual body" (1 Corinthians 15:44–49), not a spirit form, but an immortal, incorruptible physical body possessed of spiritual characteristics forever exempt from death (Romans 6:9), a body the like of which all believers shall one day possess at His glorious return and our resurrection (1 John 3:2; 1 Corinthians 15:52–54).

The Unity School, however, does away altogether with physical resurrection, and even claims that Christ rose spiritually, not physically, pointing to the facts that Mary Magdalene (John 20:14, 15) and the Emmaus disciples did not recognize their risen Lord until He revealed Himself (Luke 24:16, 31). Whereas, it is claimed, they would have known Him immediately, if His body had been a physical resurrection. Further than this, such persons often

---

*Though obviously a disputable source, a valuable historical witness to the bodily resurrection.

refer to 1 Peter 3:18, where it states that Christ was "made alive in the spirit," the inference being that His was a spiritual resurrection. These objections, though apparently valid, crumble under the relentless pressure of sound exegesis, for in no way does Christ's veiling His identity from some persons after His Resurrection prove that He was not physically raised, as any cursory study of the Greek at the respective texts clearly indicates. The key to understanding these veiled appearances is found in Luke 24:16 and 31, two texts reincarnationists religiously avoid commenting upon for the obvious reason that a correct exegesis of them destroys their spiritual resurrection claims.

Luke 24:16 in the Greek states simply that the eyes of the disciples "were kept from recognizing Him" (Greek—*ekratounto*), which proves conclusively that Christ willed that they should behold His features yet be incapable of knowing that it was He, not because His form had changed but because His will had dictated otherwise!

The other text, Luke 24:31, fully substantiates the Greek of 24:16 by showing that, although the disciples had been conversing with Christ, *the eyes of their understanding were closed* by His will, so that they could not comprehend until He chose to reveal it, that the risen Christ was their companion (Greek—*dienoichthesan*—opened).

In regard to 1 Peter 3:18, a word study of the Greek completely corroborates the testimony of Scripture that Christ was raised in a physical form by God the Father but *through* the agency of the Holy Spirit (Romans 8:11). Thus, when Peter says "put to death in the flesh," he quickly announces the triumph of God the Father, who raised His Son Jesus from the dead (Acts 17:31) "by the spirit" (1 Peter 3:18). Going beyond this, we further see that Jesus Christ was not raised *a* Spirit (John 20:28) and that in the Bible a spiritual resurrection is never taught at all, for His body did not know corruption (Acts 2:31; 13:37) and on the third day His Spirit and soul returned to that *same* body and brought it to life (Matthew 28:9). Henceforth, it was a glorified body (Philippians 3:21), a model of all the bodies of the saints (1 John 3:2). It could pass through walls (John 20:19), but it could be handled and felt (Luke 24:36–39). It could ascend into heaven (Acts 1:9), but before it did so, it could eat fish and honey (Luke 24:41–43). What is unmistakably asserted, then, is that while Christ died on Calvary, He was "made alive" in a spiritual body; thus we see that the eternal Word made flesh for the suffering of death ceased living a mortal, fleshly existence, and began to live a resurrection life in a spiritual body. As Luther so succinctly stated it:

> . . . Christ by His suffering was taken from the life which is flesh and blood . . . and is now placed in another life and made alive according to the Spirit . . . He has now passed into a spiritual and supernatural life.

The great doctrine of the physical resurrection of all men, saved and unsaved (John 5:28, 29), therefore eliminates the necessity of concurrent reincarnations and proves once more the fallacy of the entire system.

4. Reincarnation is further refuted by the Biblical doctrine of divine retribution for sin, a doctrine inseparably connected with the nature of man and the state of the dead.

The Bible unmistakably teaches that at the death of the physical form, the soul leaves the body (Genesis 35:18) and if saved, is instantly transported to the Presence of God (2 Corinthians 5:8; Philippians 1:21–23). Those who have rejected Jesus Christ, on the other hand, go instantaneously to hell, a place of conscious separation from God and spiritual torment of a terrible nature (Luke 16:19–31). In addition to this, the Bible further warns that at the last judgment (Matthew 25:31–46) the unsaved dead will be cast into "outer darkness," there to be forever in conscious separation and the indescribable retribution of eternal fire for the endless ages of eternity (Matthew 8:12; 25:41, 46; 2 Peter 2:17; Jude 13; Revelation 20:15).

Such is the divine Will, Scripture tells us, for those who have committed the infinite transgression of rejecting God's love as expressed in Jesus Christ (John 3:16, 36). To this eternal pronouncement, reincarnationists can offer no refutation, only a denial, and the pretended mysticism which dictates cycles of reincarnations in a clever attempt to accomplish what the Lord in His Word has already ordained, perfect justice at the hands of God's Son, the perfect righteous Judge (John 5:22).

Explanation of the Texts Misapplied to Prove Reincarnation[4]

1. Matthew 16:17; 22:42. "Jesus calls Simon Peter, 'Bar-Jonah,' or literally, 'son of Jonah.' The use of 'son' here is figurative, implying that the present incarnation is the 'son' or offspring of the previous life. This explains the passage (Matthew 22:42) in which Jesus demands of the Pharisees, 'What think ye of Christ?, whose son is he?' They answered, not as one might ordinarily expect, 'The son of Joseph,' but 'The *son* of David.' In other words He was the reincarnation of David" (p. 39).

Comment—These texts hardly need to be explained, since the context in which they appear explains them perfectly and rules out any such attempts as Mr. Wilson makes to read into them reincarnation.

In both cases the usage of common Hebrew expressions is indicated in the Greek. Jesus called Simon "Son of Jonah" as a means of contrasting Peter's background with the character of the revelation Peter had declared (Matthew 16:16–18), thus revealing that the source of Peter's knowledge of His true identity—"the Christ, the Son of the Living God"—was God the Father, Himself. Neither the Greek grammar nor the context allows such a fanciful interpretation as reincarnationists read into the text at Matthew 16:17.

Regarding Matthew 22:42 and the illogical and unorthodox interpretation read into the text by Mr. Wilson, the context is decidedly one of Judaistic theology and history. The Pharisees and Sadducees, it can be seen from the preceding narrative, had tried to trap Christ with trick questions, but having failed in this, they were in turn asked a searching question by Christ Himself (verse 21), regarding David's relationship to his coming son, the Messiah. The answer of the Pharisees, "the son of David" (verse 42) merely expressed their common acceptance of the fact that Messiah was to

---

[4]Ernest C. Wilson, *op. cit.*, pp. 37–60.

be of David's lineage, no more, no less. Certainly, they never meant that Messiah was to be the reincarnation of David, as Mr. Wilson states, since the idea of reincarnation was as totally foreign to Old Testament theology as it is to that of the New; therefore, that argument cannot stand.

2. Matthew 11:14. "Jesus . . . when speaking of John the Baptist (Matthew 11:14) . . . said, 'And if ye are willing to receive *it*, this is Elijah, that is to come' " (*Ibid.*, p. 42).

Comment—Jesus was here commenting on Malachi 4:5 and applying to John the Baptist the mantle of prophecy in the tradition of Elijah. So Christ, in answering the Jews, merely gave the prophecy its true meaning. Neither the context nor the prophecy refers in any way to John being a reincarnation of Elijah, as Mr. Wilson so vainly strives to establish, and no exegetical Bible scholar has ever supported reincarnationists on this point.

3. Revelation 5:5; 22:16. "In Revelation 5:5 Jesus is called 'the Lion that is of the tribe of Judah, the Root of David'. . . . In Revelation 22:16 Jesus says, 'I, Jesus . . . am the root (as Joshua) and the offspring (as Jesus) of David' " (*Ibid.*, p. 41).

Comment—These texts have been so sorely tortured out of their historical and contextual meanings that it seems almost unbelievable that supposedly honest people would stoop to such depths. The argument that since the Hebrew form of Jesus is Joshua, and since Jesus was of David's line, therefore Joshua and David were previous incarnations of the man later called Jesus of Nazareth, is completely without Biblical foundation!

4. John 9:12ff. These particular texts are favorites of reincarnationists, because it is claimed that the man born blind was suffering for sins he committed in a previous incarnation (*Ibid.*, pp. 45–48).

As is the case with most text-lifting cultists, the Unity School never looks beyond the passages it contextually abuses, and where, in many cases, the explanation usually lies.

In verse 3 of John 9, Christ explained that the man was born blind, not as a result of the sins of his parents or his own sins for that matter, but "that in him works of God should be displayed" (Berkeley Version). Following this thought out, in verses 6 and 7 of the same chapter, Jesus restored the man's sight to the glory of His Father, and once again testified to His intrinsic Deity.

The thought of reincarnation, then, never once enters the context of John 9 in any form, as even Mr. Wilson could learn by *reading* it thoroughly, instead of trying to *read into it* his preconceived theory of reincarnation.

The Son of God warns in the closing verses of the Revelation (22:18, 19) that the plagues there recorded will be the certain destiny of those who tamper with His Word, and that their very names will be *subtracted* from the Book of Life if they *subtract* from His Word.

Evaluation of the Evidences for Reincarnation

1. The familiarity with persons, places and things never consciously traceable to experienced events is one of the strongest pillars on which the faith of the Unity cultist rests. It must, therefore, be duly examined. The question is: Do such occurrences prove that one has lived before in similar

circumstances? The opinions of leading scientists, psychologists, psychiatrists and hypnotists are almost all to the contrary. It is quite possible, they tell us, to connect subconscious memories of "forgotten" stories and facts with religious beliefs. Through hypnotic regression, it is possible to weave strange tales, many of which dwarf "Bridey Murphy," and are also recorded in the files of reputable, competent evaluators (see *Life*, March 19, 1956). Such feelings, then, are largely the result of pure subjectivism, and as empirical evidence are therefore valueless.

2. The argument from equality. This particular argument attempts to show that the evils and inequalities that beset mankind are the result of sins committed in previous incarnations. This argument is weak, however, in that it does not recognize the prerogative of God to discipline His creatures or His children for His own purposes (Romans 8:28) that He might refine us in the fires of testing (1 Peter 4:12). While it is true, however, that there are inequalities in the world, the Scriptures never indicate that sins committed in a previous life are their logical antecedents, and no reincarnationist, living or dead, has ever been able to prove that any connection exists at all between divine judgment and alleged pre-birth existences. On the contrary, the Bible formally and flatly states that sin is in this world as the result of the sin of Adam (Romans 5:12). We must never forget that God is Sovereign and that He orders all things after the good pleasure of His will. It is man who is accountable to God, and *never* is God accountable to man. Let us not forget, though, as do the pantheists, that the God of the Bible is not just a set of cold, abstract attributes. He is a Personality, for there is a Person behind the decrees of God and His attributes, who is definitely perfect, loving, just and good—a Person whose fullness has been seen for all time in the face of Jesus Christ, as it is written, "He that hath seen me hath seen the Father" (John 14:9).

3. Unfinished thought and unfinished work. This "evidence" for the necessity of reincarnation is totally worthless, since God, in order to be just, does not "have" to allow man to finish all his thoughts or works, or, for that matter, any of them! In fact, it was Solomon, the wisest man who ever lived, who stated that the wisdom of man and his works perish in the grave, a hard pill indeed for reincarnationists to swallow (Ecclesiastes 9:10; see also Psalm 146:4).

4. The final "evidence" for reincarnation is that of various cases (Bridey Murphy, etc.), which are adduced as incontestable proof of the theory. With reference to many of such occurrences, *Life* magazine has presented logical, scientific explanations which largely answer the questions raised. In many cases, however, for purposes of deception, Satan has in the past and most certainly still does, exercise demonic forces to lead the unwary soul from God's truth into the dark passages of occultism (Exodus 7:11, 12).

Were not the New Testament doctrine of the new birth or regeneration tied to the "Bridey Murphy" and similar so-called reincarnationist cases, then Christians might well write the whole affair off as a hoax or as the pranks which our human mental processes sometimes play on us. The attempt, however, to reinterpret the new birth as reincarnation, by both Unity and the "Bridey Murphy" believers, stamps the entire subject as demonic in origin and purpose, to be avoided by the Christian.

The Christian doctrine of the new birth plainly teaches that when one receives Jesus Christ as Lord and Savior, the Holy Spirit of God regenerates his soul (John 3:3; 1 Peter 1:23), restores his relationship to God, lost because of sin, and creates a sinless nature within (2 Corinthians 5:17). This nature will eventually through progressive sanctification, enable us to reach perfection, either at the death of the body and the reunion of the soul with Christ (2 Corinthians 5:8); or, if we survive to the Second Coming of Christ, at our translation or resurrection to immortality (1 Thessalonians 4:14–17 and 1 Corinthians 15:51–54).

This great Biblical truth, then, can never be logically, rationally, or exegetically connected to or compared with the rebirth or new birth of reincarnation, and it is best that the Christian public be alerted to the "new" menace which Unity advocates, which "tickles the ears" and the vanity of many deluded souls today, and leads them away from the Prince of life (Acts 3:15) and into the chasm of spiritual death.

In order to join the Unity School of Christianity, it must be understood that one would have to renounce every basic doctrine of the Christian faith—denying the Deity of, physical resurrection and personal Second Coming of our Lord, and believing in the reincarnation of the soul as opposed to the doctrine of the physical resurrection of the body,

Let us not forget, then, that under the apparent sugar-coated shell of tolerance and pseudo-love which characterizes the Unity School of Christianity, there lies a subtle, but firm denial of the basic principles of the Gospel of Jesus Christ.

To those who would drink at this well of supposed spiritual refreshment, our warning must be clear and definite:

> Try the spirits whether they are of God: because many false prophets are gone out into the world (1 John 4:1).

Even in this brief study of the Unity cult, no objective student of Scripture can deny that Unity is distinctly within the boundaries of this warning, and we would be bereft of wisdom not to listen to this counsel from the Word of God.

Charles W. Ferguson, the great liberal critic of cultism, writing in his revealing book, *The New Books of Revelation*, has summed up the Unity School in a masterful way, and we close our study with his succinct appraisal (with which, the facts of both history and theology force us to agree):

> Thus it is that, with much wind and high sales pressure, the Unity School of Christianity serves the multitudes. It gets results. It offers a philosophy that sounds good and works better. It has demonstrated its success for the millions of adherents who have been swept into the paper fold. Underpinning its vast machinery are of course, the cases in which it has cured diseases of every sort and its glib promise of physical immortality to its followers. The machinery is not to be despised.
>
> We have in Unity an enormous mail order concern dispensing health and happiness on the large scale of modern business enterprise. It is mass production in religion, and its work is carried on shrewdly and systematically with infinite pains to capitalize upon the old demand and extend the

market. It is the work of a retired realtor, and his inspired wife, and with its tedious array of tabulated facts and its insufferable efficiency, it suggests pretty well what Americans want in the realm of the spirit.[5]

---

[5]Charles W. Ferguson, *The New Books of Revelation*, Garden City, NJ: Doubleday and Sons, 1929, p. 250.

Chapter 12

HERBERT W. ARMSTRONG AND THE WORLD-WIDE CHURCH OF GOD—ANGLO-ISRAELISM

The Worldwide Church of God, founded and lead by octogenarian Herbert W. Armstrong, could more properly be designated "The New Galatianism" because of its emphasis on legalism. Since this group has media visibility throughout the entire world, it is essential that its theological system be analyzed in the light of the Word of God, to see whether or not it is, as advertised, "The Plain Truth."

To facilitate a clearer understanding of this twentieth century cult system, some historical background is necessary.

The Rise of Herbert W. Armstrong

Herbert Armstrong began his cult in this century and is its founder and present dynamic leader. The details of his early life and of the beginnings of his system are sketchy at best. Two publications by the Worldwide Church's Ambassador Press, *The Inside Story of the World Tomorrow Broadcast,* and *The Autobiography of Herbert W. Armstrong,* list some significant historical highlights of the life of Armstrong and the growth of his cult, but even these two volumes present incomplete histories. Armstrong's life before his "calling" is summarized in both publications approximately as follows. Armstrong began his professional career as an advertising and promotional man who wrote copy for the *Merchants Trade Journal* in Des Moines, Iowa (1912-1915). His whole advertising business was destroyed, however, in 1920 in what the books term "a flash depression."[1] In 1924 Armstrong moved to the Pacific Northwest where twice his business ventures failed, due to "forces beyond Mr. Armstrong's control."[2]

Mr. Armstrong's spiritual odyssey was launched primarily through his wife's discovery that "obedience to God's spiritual laws summed up in the Ten Commandments is necessary for salvation. Not that our works of keeping the commandments save us, but rather that sin is the transgression of God's spiritual law. Christ does not save us in our sins but from our sins. We must repent of sin, repent of transgressing God's law which means turning from disobedience as a prior condition to receiving God's free gift."[3]

Mr. Armstrong's Sunday school days had taught him that there are no works to salvation . . . God's law was done away with. To him religion had

[1]Herbert W. Armstrong, *The Autobiography of Herbert W. Armstrong*, Pasadena, CA: Ambassador Press, 1967, vol. 1, p. 234.
[2]*Ibid.*, p. 284.
[3]*Ibid.*, pp. 281-284, 286ff.

not been a way of life but a mere belief, an acceptance of the fact of God's existence, Christ's virgin birth, the efficacy of Christ's shed blood. Controversy arose between Mr. and Mrs. Armstrong. She refused to give up the truths she had found. He was angered into his first real study of the Bible, undertaken for the avowed purpose of proving to his wife that "all these churches can't be wrong."[4]

Armstrong's long solitary study of the Scriptures led him to the same conclusions he had fought so bitterly against with his wife. Ambassador Press publications indicate that Armstrong's struggle to change from "traditional" Christian belief to this new-found "legalism" caused within him "a furious inner struggle."[5]

After the study of his Bible and much prayer, we are informed, Mr. Armstrong began writing and doing evangelical work. It was in June of 1931 that Armstrong conducted an evangelistic campaign in Eugene, Oregon, and at that time was "ordained as a minister of Jesus Christ."

His tremendous zeal, tireless energy, writing, speaking and promotional ability stood Armstrong in good stead through the years and culminated in the founding of the Ambassador College, located in Pasadena, California; *Plain Truth Magazine,* which was started in February 1934; and *The World Tomorrow Program,* which originated in Eugene, Oregon, January 1934.

Of all the cultic structures, the Worldwide Church of God sponsors more radio broadcasts and television programs on more stations than any other cultic group in the world, and in fact more than its five top competitors combined! Herbert Armstrong has made it a career to become a senior statesman of diplomacy for his church, and visits the various leaders of established and emerging nations, attracting their attention by his expensive gifts and direct aid programs in areas where the individual country may be in need.

An example of Armstrong's diplomacy is his high standing with the Israeli government, for whom he has sponsored archeological digs, not the least of which are his much-publicized excavations around and underneath the site of the second temple in Jerusalem.

The Armstrong religion is strong in England, throughout the United Kingdom, and on the European continent, as well as in the United States. It should be noted that Radio Luxembourg and other stations beam Armstrong's material all over Europe and behind the Iron Curtain, so the work of the Worldwide Church of God is not strange to them.

The Eclecticism of Herbert W. Armstrong

Armstrong's biographer, Roderick Meredith, goes to great pains to point out that "there was never any association in any way with Jehovah's Witnesses, Seventh-day Adventists, Mormons, or any such sects as some accusers have falsely claimed."[6]

---

[4]Roderick Meredith, *The Inside Story of the World Tomorrow Broadcast,* Pasadena, CA: Ambassador Press, n.d., p. 47.
[5]*Ibid.,* p. 48.
[6]*Ibid.,* pp. 48ff.; cf. *Autobiography, op. cit.,* p. 302, where Armstrong denies having attended any Seventh-day Adventist church services, although he admits becoming familiar with their literature. He also denies being a member of that denomination (*Ibid.,* p. 338).

1. *Seventh-day Adventism and Herbert Armstrong.*

Unfortunately for Mr. Meredith, the Seventh-day Adventist denomination has done a complete historical résumé of Herbert Armstrong and his association with them. Writing for the Ministerial Association of the Seventh-day Adventists, George Burnside states concerning Mr. Armstrong:

". . . Mr. Armstrong is an off-shoot of an off-shoot of an off-shoot of the Seventh-day Adventist church." The information from Burnside is summarized as follows.

In 1886 Elders B. F. Snook and W. H. Brinkerhoff, two ministers of the small and newly organized Iowa Conference of Seventh-day Adventist, apostatized, and with a few members formed a group of their own. They directed their work from Marion, Iowa. In 1889 they centered their work in Stanbury, Missouri, calling their company "the Church of God (Adventist)."

Mr. Armstrong joined this church and after a stormy experience with them, he reported that Mr. Duggar, in a dispute over leadership, led off a sizable part of the membership and called their group "the Church of God (Seventh-day)." Mr. Armstrong joined this off-shoot movement. Sometime later, because of Mr. Armstrong's acceptance of the British-Israelism theory and other subjects, he went out on his own and formed his own church, calling it "The World Church of God," known today as the Worldwide Church of God.[7]

Having checked the Adventists' documentation on this thoroughly, and finding it to be accurate, what Mr. Meredith glosses over lightly now takes on significance. The neighbor lady who revealed the great discovery to Mrs. Armstrong about the law of God was a former member of the Seventh-day Adventist Church and also a member of the splinter group. Mr. Armstrong's theology in many areas paralleled Seventh-day Adventism. His theology insists upon observance of the Seventh-day Sabbath, abstinence from certain articles of food as unclean, a general Adventist system of prophetic interpretation (albeit with his own peculiar modifications), his extreme legalism and the observance of feasts and new moons, and his denunciation of the doctrines of hell and eternal punishment for which he has substituted the Adventist doctrine of the annihilation of the wicked. Mr. Armstrong owes a considerable debt to Seventh-day Adventism, as he does to Jehovah's Witnesses (with whom he agrees in his denial of the doctrine of the Trinity and the bodily resurrection of Christ) and the Mormon Church (whose teaching that man may become as God was appropriated by Armstrong without even the slightest acknowledgment to Joseph Smith and Brigham Young).

Mr. Meredith seems overly eager to pass by these facts, but facts they are. His blanket dismissal "there was never any association in any way with Jehovah's Witnesses, Seventh-day Adventism and Mormons" is a clear misrepresentation of historical fact.

2. *Anglo-Israelism.*

Anglo-Israelism (sometimes called British-Israelism) is, properly speaking, neither a sect nor a cult since it transcends denominational and sectarian

---

[7]The above material is summarized from George Burnside's series on Herbert W. Armstrong as published in the *Bulletin of the Ministerial Association of Seventh-day Adventist Ministers.*

lines and because it does not set up an ecclesiastical organization. It has existed for more than a century in the United States, having come to this hemisphere from England. Apparently it originated there shortly after the close of the Elizabethan era, its "first apostle" being Richard Brothers (1757-1824).

The most vocal proponents of the Anglo-Israelic system of Biblical interpretation in North America were James Lovell of Fort Worth, Texas, and Howard Rand of Destiny Publishers.

The teachings of these men and their followers are comparatively innocuous and free from serious doctrinal error. The chief harm results from the appeal to nationalism with its accompanying vanity and the two-fold way of salvation which some advocates have implied (see below).

a. Herbert Armstrong and Anglo-Israelism.

In addition to the two groups headed by James Lovell and Howard Rand, there were several other groups which also teach some of the doctrines of Anglo-Israelism. The largest of all these groups is headed by Herbert Armstrong, founder of the Worldwide Church of God and the World Tomorrow radio and television broadcasts.

Armstrong is also the founder of Ambassador College in Pasadena, and is by far the most well-known and widely heard and read of all Anglo-Israelite cultists. Mr. Armstrong is editor of *The Plain Truth*, a monthly magazine with a circulation of around 1,000,000 and is a strong influence in the publishing world of the cults.

The Worldwide Church of God is outside the historic Christian Church because it denies foundational Christian truth. All other forms of Anglo-Israelism (or at least the vast majority of them) maintain a guarded orthodoxy at least in the areas of the Nature of God, personal redemption, and the Person and Work of Jesus Christ.[8] However, it is very clear that the Worldwide Church of God and Mr. Armstrong do not share essential Bible doctrine with these other Anglo-Israelism groups. The essential doctrines of the Worldwide Church of God are absolutely heretical and without any Biblical foundation, as we shall see in the body of this chapter.

To sum up the theories of the Anglo-Israel cult in a concise manner is not difficult, and to refute them from the Scriptures as noted scholars and Biblical expositors have done many times, is essentially an elementary task. But with the advent of Herbert Armstrong's version of the old error and his utilizaton of it as a cloak for his own confusion on Biblical theology, the problem is no longer elementary, in fact, it is quite complex and deserves the careful consideration of responsible Christian ministers and laymen. For it is certain that they will be affected, sooner or later, by the plausible propaganda which flows from the Armstrong presses and out over the airwaves.

---

[8]A few of them have taught, by implication at least, a form of salvation by physical birth into the nation Israel (i.e., Great Britain or the United States, for example) along with the usual Christian teachings of individual personal salvation. Some also have suggested some rather naive ideas, such as the belief that the city of Jerusalem in the Bible is really what we know today as Edinburg, Scotland. (See, for example, Comyns Beaumont, *Britain—The Key to World History*, London: Rider & Co., 1948.)

We shall deal with Anglo-Israelism, then, only as a prelude to dealing with the theology of Herbert Armstrong, with which it has now become identified in the minds of most people—in England, Canada and the United States.

The basic premise of the Anglo-Israelite theory is that ten tribes were lost (Israelites) when the Jews were captured by the Assyrians under King Sargon and that these so-called "lost" tribes[9] are, in reality, the Saxae, or Scythians, who surged westward through Northern Europe and eventually became the ancestors of the Saxons, who later invaded England. The theory maintains that the Anglo-Saxons are the "lost" ten tribes of Israel and are substituted, in Anglo-Israel interpretation and exegesis, for the Israel of the Bible.[10]

In the heyday of the British Empire, when their colonies spanned the globe under Victoria, Anglo-Israelites were in their glory, maintaining that, since the British were the lost tribes and, therefore, inheritors of the covenants and blessings of God, it was obvious that God was honoring His promises and exalting His children in the latter days.

In light of recent history, however, and the loss by Britain of virtually all her colonial possessions, Anglo-Israelites are content to transfer the blessings of the Covenant to the United States, maintaining as they do that Ephraim is Great Britain and Manasseh, the United States. The fact that Ephraim is called "the exalted one" in Scripture and that Manasseh is designated as the inferior of the two, creates both historical and exegetical problems for the Anglo-Israelites. This is particularly true because the United States, the inferior (Manasseh), has now far surpassed the allegedly superior Ephraim, a minor problem that will not long forestall the cogitations and prophetic conjectures of the Anglo-Israelites' school of Biblical interpretation.

Relative to the relationship of Israel to Judah in Scripture, Anglo-Israelism maintains that Judah represents the Jews who are still under the divine curse and are not to be identified with Israel at all. In this line of reasoning, all the promises recorded in the Scripture are applied, not to a nation (Israel), which, as we have seen, is, in their system of thought, to be identified with Great Britain and the United States!

Herbert Armstrong, in dealing with this subject, enunciates the basic idea of Anglo-Israelism that Israel is to be distinguished from the Jews[11] (Judah) in these words:

> We want to impress here that Israel and Judah are not two names for

---

[9]J. H. Allen, *Judah's Sceptre and Joseph's Birthright*. 6th ed., Boston: A. A. Beauchamp, Pub., 1918, pp. 124-145.

[10]Rev. Commander L.G.A. Roberts, *Commentary on the Book of the Prophet Isaiah*. London: The Covenant Publishing Co., Ltd., 1931, p. 159.

[11]"There is not a particle of evidence to support that the Jews of today are other than the house of Judah, or that they represent the lost Twelve Tribes. The evidence is clear that Israel did not rejoin the Jews" (J. Llewellyn Thomas, *God and My Birthright*, London: The Covenant Publishing Company, Ltd., n.d., p. 21). It should be noted that the Covenant Publishing Company is in no way associated with Herbert Armstrong or his teaching, does not subscribe to his beliefs, does not believe he has the correct interpretation of prophecy, and does not think he has rightly drawn conclusions concerning modern Israel in the latter days.

the same nation.[12] They were and still are, and shall be until the Second Coming of Christ, two separated nations. The House of Judah always means Jew.

This distinction is vital if we are to understand prophecy. Because most so-called Bible students are ignorant of this basic distinction; they are unable rightly to understand prophecy!

The next place where the term "Jew" is mentioned in the Bible, the House of Israel had been driven out in captivity, lost from view, and the term only applies to those of the House of Judah. There are no exceptions in the Bible.[13]

It is further maintained by Anglo-Israelites that in their migration of the Mediterranean area across Europe to the British Isles, the "lost" tribes left behind them landmarks, bearing names of the tribes. Thus, the Danube River and Danzig are clear indications to them of the Tribe of Dan.[14] The term Saxon is obviously derived from the Hebrew and means Isaac-son, or "the son of Isaac!"[15]

Another Anglo-Israel exercise in semantics is their insistence that the Hebrew term for covenant (*berith*), and for man (*ish*), is to be interpreted as meaning "the man of the covenant,"[16] a fact that would be amusing, if it were not for the unpleasant truth that the Hebrew and Anglo-Saxon tongues have as much in common as do Chinese and Pig-Latin!

Herbert Armstrong, however, who can read neither Hebrew, Aramaic nor Greek, states with dogmatic authority:

> The House of Israel is the covenant people. The Hebrew word for covenant is *beriyth*, or *berith*. . . . The Hebrew word for man is *iysh*, or *ish*. In the original Hebrew language, vowels were never given in the spellings, so omitting the vowel *e* form *berith*, but retaining the *i* in its Anglicized form to perserve the *y* sound, and you have the Anglicized Hebrew word for covenant, *brith*. The Hebrews, however, never pronounced their h's. The Jew, even today, in pronouncing the name Shem will call it Sem. Incidentally, this ancient Hebrew trait is also a modern British trait, so the Hebrew word for covenant would be pronounced, in its Anglicized form as Brit.
>
> And the word for covenant man or covenant people would therefore be British. So the true covenant people today are called the British. And they reside in the British Isles. . . .
>
> To Abraham God said, "In Isaac shall thy seed be called," and this name is repeated in Romans 9:7, and Hebrews 11:18. In Amos 7:16 they are called the "house of Isaac."
>
> They are descended from Isaac, and therefore are Isaac's sons. Drop the "i" from Isaac (vowels are not used in Hebrew spelling) and we have

---

[12]Thomas (*Ibid.*, p. 5) states: "All Jews and Levites were Israelites, but all Israelites were not Jews or Levites."

[13]Herbert W. Armstrong, *Where Are the Ten Lost Tribes?*, Pasadena, CA: Ambassador Press, n.d., p. 8.

[14]Adam Rutherford, *Israel-Britain or Anglo-Saxon Israel*. London: publ. by author, 1936, 3rd ed. p. 36.

[15]Anon., *The Roadbuilder: God's Commonwealths, British and American*, Toronto, Canada: Commonwealth Publishers, Ltd., 1930, pp. 161ff. (See also Rutherford, p. 9.)

[16]Cf. Rutherford, *op. cit.*, p. 30.

the modern name, Saac's sons, or, as we have spelled it in shorter manner, Saxons.[17]

It is sufficient to point out at this stage that the Hebrew words *berith* and *ish* literally mean "covenant and man," not, "men of the covenant," as Armstrong and Anglo-Israelites maintain. When to this is added the unbiased and impeccably researched conclusions of the venerable *Oxford English Dictionary* and every other major English work on etymology, there is absolutely no evidence or support for the Anglo-Israelite contention that there is a connection between the Anglo-Saxon tongue and the Hebrew language, the paucity of their claims becomes all too apparent.

Moreover, it should be noted that the Anglo-Israelite theory and the Worldwide Church of God both maintain that the throne of England is the throne of David. In the June 1953 issue of *The Plain Truth* appears the statement:

> Herman L. Hoeh now reveals the astonishing fact that Elizabeth II actually sits on the throne of King David of ISRAEL—that she is a direct descendant, continuing David's dynasty[18]—the VERY THRONE on the which Christ shall sit after his return . . . Elizabeth II was crowned "Queen of thy people Israel."[19] Turning to the article by Hoeh, it clearly states that: the throne upon which she was crowned (i.e., the "Stone of Scone," lodged in Westminster Abbey) is really the stone which Jacob used for a pillow, which he took with him when he departed from Bethel, and which later came under the care of Jeremiah the Prophet, who took it with him to England, where it became the Coronation Stone for the British (Davidic) dynasty.[20]

The disturbing scientific fact that the Stone of Scone has been examined and analyzed, and found to be . . . "calcareous, a sandstone of a reddish or purplish color, with heterogeneous pebbles and of Scottish origin"[21] does not deaden the enthusiasm of Anglo-Israelites, who must make Jacob a native of Scotland, and Bethel, a suburb of London, if they are to maintain the fiction that the Stone of Scone is of Middle Eastern origin.[22]

---

[17]Anon., *The United States and British Commonwealth in Prophecy*, London: The Covenant Publishing Co., Ltd., n.d., pp. 17, 18.

[18]Dr. Henry Hedyt of the American Board of Mission to the Jews has a letter from the Office of the Lord Chamberlain which states that no known reason exists why any assertion should be made that Her Majesty Queen Elizabeth was crowned Queen of Israel. It goes on to say that she is demonstrably not the Queen of Israel and cites a portion of the Coronation Service in which the Queen took the oath. He also has a letter from Brigadier Wieler, the Resident Governor of the Tower of London, which states clearly that in the Tower of London and in the Public Records Office no ancestral chart is known which substantiates the claim, "Yes, on the throne of England reigns a daughter of David, . . . a dynasty that has ruled Ireland, Scotland and England for over 2500 years!" Hoeh, "The Coronation Stone," *Plain Truth*, June 1953, p. 640.

[19]Richard D. Armstrong (son of Herbert W. Armstrong), "Why Was Elizabeth II crowned Queen of Israel?" in *The Plain Truth*, June 1953, p. 8.

[20]Herman L. Hoeh, "The Coronation Stone" in *The Plain Truth*, June 1953, p. 64.

[21]W. H. Smith, *The Ten Tribes of Israel Never Lost*, n.p., p. 91. Enthusiasts like Beaumont (pp. 128ff.), have no difficulty since they identify Bethel with Glastonburg and Jerusalem with Edinburgh, Scotland (*Ibid.*, pp. 259ff.).

[22]Beaumont, *et. al.*, maintain the fiction that the British Isles contain the Biblical Holy Land cities.

The Anglo-Israelites school of interpretation claims more than 3,000,000 adherents in England, Canada, the British Commonwealth and throughout the world, including the United States. They are found in many already-established denominations in Christian Churches and so do not constitute a separate denomination, preferring to work through all groups, instilling its propaganda and its fierce emphasis upon racial pride as a type of nationalistic leaven grounded in what is known to be a totally discredited method of scholarship and linguistic analysis.

Were it not for the fact that Herbert Armstrong has capitalized so successfully upon it as a means of inculcating his own peculiar interpretation of the Bible for almost a half-million readers and millions of listeners, we might well ignore Anglo-Israelism. But Armstrong has, in a very real sense, resuscitated what was a gradually dying theological body, and its death throes have now given way to militant life with which the Church of Jesus Christ must come to grips.

b. The Biblical Answer to Anglo-Israelism.

There are two principal areas in which the Anglo-Israel theory must either stand or fall. They are, first, the question whether any tribes *were* lost, and therefore later reappeared as the British and American nations; second, there is the question of whether or not it is possible, in either the Old or New Testaments, to teach that

> Israel and Judah are not two names for the same nation. They were and still are, and shall be until the Second Coming of Christ, two separate nations. The House of Judah always means Jew. . . . the term applies only to those of the House of Judah. There are no exceptions in the Bible![23]

Rather than become bogged down in an attempt to interpret Anglo-Israel chronology and methodology in the Old Testament, we have elected to let one of the greatest Hebrew scholars of the Christian Church, Dr. David Baron, an Englishman, answer the first question. It should be remembered that Dr. Baron's answer is substantiated in every detail by scholars of the Old Testament, whether or not they are Christian.

> The Anglo-Israelite theory . . . I cannot help regarding as one of the saddest symptoms of the mental and spiritual shallowness of the present day. . . . I believe that you . . . like many other simple-minded Christians are perplexed and imposed upon by the plausibilities of the supposed identifications (of British Israelism), and are not able to detect the fallacies and perversions of Scripture and history upon which the whole theory is based.
>
> Let us glance at the question of the so-called "lost" ten tribes in the light of Scripture history and prophecy. Anglo-Israelism first of all loses the ten tribes, claiming for them a different destiny from the Jews, whom it supposes to be descendants of the two tribes only. And then it identifies this "lost" Israel with the British race. But there is as little historical reason for the supposition that the ten tribes are lost, in the sense in which Anglo-Israelism uses the term, as there is scriptural basis for a separate destiny for "Israel" apart from "Judah."
>
> The most superficial reader of the Old Testament knows the origin

---

[23]*Where Are the Ten Lost Tribes?*, *op. cit.*, p. 8.

and cause of the unfortunate schism which took place in the history of the elect nation after the death of Solomon. But this evil was to last only for . . . a limited time; for the very commencement of this it was announced by God that He would in this way afflict the seed of David, but *not for ever* (1 Kings 11:39).

The final overthrow of the northern kingdom took place, as we have seen, in the year 721 B.C., but when we read that the "king of Assyria took Samaria and carried Israel away into Assyria," we are not to understand that he cleared the whole land of all the people, but that he took the strength of the nation with him.

Jerusalem was finally taken in 588 B.C., by Nebuchadnezzar—just 133 years after the capture of Samaria by the Assyrians. Meanwhile the Babylonian Empire succeeded the Assyrian; but although dynasties had changed, and Babylon, which had sometimes, even under the Assyrian *régime*, been one of the capitals of the Empire, now took the place of Nineveh; the region over which Nebuchadnezzar now bore rule was the very same over which Shalmaneser and Sargon reigned before him, only somewhat extended.

With the captivity (Assyrian and Babylonian) the divisions and rivalry between "Judah" and "Israel" were ended, and the members of all tribes who looked forward to a national future were conscious not only of one destiny but that such a destiny was bound up with the promises to the house of David, and with Zion or Jerusalem as its center, in accordance with the prophecies of Joel, Amos, and Hosea, and of the other inspired messengers who ministered and testified more especially among them until the fall of Samaria. This conviction of a common and united future, no doubt, facilitated the merging process, which cannot be said to have begun with the captivity. It commenced almost immediately after the rebellion under Jeroboam, but which was certainly strengthened by it.

Glimpses into the feeling of the members of the two kingdoms for one another, and their hopes and aspirations for unity, we get in the writings of Jeremiah, Ezekiel, and Daniel, who prophesied during the period of exile. The most striking prophecy in relation to this subject is Ezekiel 37:15-17: "The word of the Lord came again unto me, saying, Moreover, thou son of man, take thee one stick, and write upon it, For Judah, and for the children of Israel his companions (that is, those of Israel who before the captivity fell away from the ten tribes and joined the southern kingdom): then take another stick, and write upon it, For Joseph, the stick of Ephraim, and for all the house of Israel his companions: and join them one to another into one stick; and they shall become one in thine hand."

Then follows the divine interpretation of this symbol: "Behold, I will take the stick of Joseph, which is in the hand of Ephraim, and the tribes of Israel his fellows, and will put them with him (or literally, I will add them upon, or to him), even with the stick of Judah, and make them one stick, and they shall be one in mine hand. And the sticks whereon thou writest shall be in thine hand before their eyes. And say unto them. Thus saith the Lord God; Behold, I will take the children of Israel from among the heathen, whither they be gone, and will gather them on every side, and bring them into their own land; and I will make them one nation in the land upon the mountains of Israel; and one king shall be king to them all: and they shall be no more two nations, neither shall they be divided into two kingdoms any more at all: neither shall they defile themselves any more with their idols, nor with their detestable things, nor with any of their transgressions: but I will save them out of all their dwelling-places, wherein they have sinned, and will cleanse them; so shall they be my people, and I will be their God. And David my servant shall be king over them; and they all shall have one shepherd; they shall also walk in my judgments, and observe my statutes, and do them. And they shall dwell in the land that I have given unto Jacob my servant, wherein your fathers dwelt; and they shall dwell therein, even they, and their children, and their children's children for ever: and my servant David shall be their prince for ever" (Ezekiel 37:19-25).

In 458 B.C. Ezra, "the scribe of the law of the God of heaven," in accordance with the decree of Artaxerxes organized another large caravan of those whose hearts were made willing to return to the land of their fathers. Part of this most favorable royal proclamation, was as follows: "I make a decree that all they of the people of Israel, and of his priests and Levites in my realm, which are minded of their own free will to go up to Jerusalem, go with thee"; and in response to it "this Ezra went up from Babylon . . . and there went up (with him) of the children of Israel, and of the priests, and the Levites, and the singers and the porters, and the Nethinims, unto Jerusalem in the seventh year of Artaxerxes the king" (Ezra 7:13, 6, 7).

This party consisted of about one thousand eight hundred families, and apart from the priests, Levites, and Nethinims, was made up of "the children of Israel," irrespective of tribal distinctions, from all parts of the realm of "Babylon," or Assyria, now under the sway of the Medo-Persians.

The narratives contained in the books of Ezra and Nehemiah, under whose administration the position of the restored remnant became consolidated, covers a period of about 115 years, and brings us down to about 420 B.C.

Anyhow it is a fact that the remnant in the land grew and grew until, about a century and a half later, in the time of the Maccabees, and again about a century and a half later still, in the time of our Lord, we find "the Jews" in Palestine a comparatively large nation, numbering millions, while from the time of the downfall of the Persian Empire, we hear but very little more of the Israelite exiles in ancient Assyria or Babylon. By the conquest of Alexander, who to this day is a great favorite among the scattered nation, the regions of ancient Babylonia and Media were brought comparatively near and a highway opened between East and West. From about this time settlements of "Jews" began to multiply in Asia Minor, Cyprus, Crete, on the coasts of the Aegean, in Macedonia and other parts of Southern Europe, in Egypt and the whole northern coast of Africa, whilst some made their way further and further eastward as far as India and China. There is not the least possibility of doubt that many of the settlements of the Diaspora in the time of our Lord, north, south, and west, as well as east of Palestine, were made up of those who had never returned to the land of their fathers since the time of the Assyrian and Babylonian exiles, and who were not only descendants of Judah, as Anglo-Israelism ignorantly presupposes, but of all the *twelve tribes scattered abroad* (James 1:1).

As a matter of fact, long before the destruction of the second Temple by Titus, we read of currents and countercurrents in the dispersion of the "Jewish" people.

To summarize the state of things in connection with the Hebrew race at the time of Christ, it was briefly this:

I. For some six centuries before, ever since the partial restoration in the days of Cyrus and his successors, the descendants of Abraham were no longer known as divided into tribes but as one people, although up to the time of the destruction of the second temple tribal and family genealogies were for the most part preserved, especially among those who were settled in the land.

II. Part of the nation was in Palestine, but by far the larger number were scattered far and wide, and formed innumerable communities in many different lands, north and south, east and west. But wherever dispersed and to whatever tribe they may have belonged, they all looked to Palestine and Jerusalem as their center. They felt they were of the same stock, stood on the same ground, cherished the same memories, grew up under the same institutions, and anticipated the same future. They had one common center of worship in Jerusalem, which they upheld by their offerings; and they made pilgrimages thither annually in great numbers at high festivals.

The name of "Jew" and "Israelite" became synonymous terms from about the time of the Captivity. It is one of the absurd fallacies of Anglo-Israelism to presuppose that the term "Jew" stands for a bodily descendant of "Judah." It stands for all those from among the sons of Jacob who acknowledged themselves, or were considered, subjects of the theocratic kingdom of Judah, which they expected to be established by the promised "Son of David"—the Lion of the tribe of Judah—whose reign is to extend not only over *all the tribes of the land,*" but also "from sea to sea, and from the river unto the ends of the earth."

"That the name 'Jews,' " writes a Continental Bible scholar, "became general for all Israelites who were anxious to preserve their theocratic nationality, was the more natural, since the political independence of the ten tribes was destroyed." Yes, and without any hope of a restoration to a separate national existence! What hopes and promises they had were, as we have seen, linked with the Kingdom of Judah and the House of David.

Anglo-Israelism teaches that members of the ten tribes are never called "Jews," and that "Jews" are not "Israelites," but both assertions are false. Who were they that came back to the land after the Babylonian exile? Anglo-Israelites say they were only the exiles from the southern kingdom of Judah, and call them "Jews."

It is clear from the prophecies of Amos and Hosea, which were primarily addressed to the ten tribes, that if they were in the first instance "cast out" by force from their own land (as the word in the Hebrew means), it was with a view that they should be "tossed about" and "wander" among "all nations."

Now note, Anglo-Israelism tells you to identify the ten tribes with one nation, but if you are on the line of scripture and true history, you will seek for them "among all nations." He that scattered Israel will gather him, and by His own Divine power and omniscience separate them again into their tribes and families.

My last words on this subject must be those of warning and entreaty. Do not think, as so many do, that Anglo-Israelism, even if not true, is only a harmless speculation. I consider it nothing short of one of the latter-day delusions by which the Evil One seeks to divert the attention of men from things spiritual and eternal.

Summing up his judgments on the Anglo-Israel question relative to their methods of interpretation, Dr. Baron stated:

One of its foundation fallacies is that it anticipates the millennium and interprets promises which will only be fulfilled in that blessed future period, after Israel as a nation is supernaturally converted. There is no way the Scriptures can be stretched to identify that Israel with the British nation at the present time. By such a faulty identification, such "interpreters" make all prophetic Scripture meaningless. It fosters national pride, and nationalizes God's blessings in this dispensation which is individual and elective in its character. It diverts man's attention from the one thing needful, and from the only means by which he can find acceptance with God. . . . After all, in this dispensation, it is a question only as to whether men are in Christ, or not. If they are Christians, whether Jew or Gentile, their destiny is not linked either with Palestine or with England, but with that inheritance which is incorruptible and undefiled, and which fades not away; and if they are not Christians, then instead of occupying their thoughts with vain speculations as to a supposed identity of the British race with the lost ten tribes, it is their duty to seek the One and only Savior, whom we must learn to know, not after the flesh, but after the Spirit, without whom a man, either an Israelite or not, is undone.

And finally, it not only robs the Jewish nation, the true Israel, of many promises in relation to their future by applying to the British race in the present time, but it diverts attention from them as the people in whom is bound up the purpose of God in relation to the nations, and whose receiving again to the heart of God after the long centuries of unbelief, will be as life from the dead to the whole world.[24]

Dr. Baron's brilliant and thorough refutation cannot be improved upon. And excerpts from this personal letter which he addressed to a Christian, perplexed by Anglo-Israelite perversions of history and Biblical interpretation, remain a classic, and the letter has never been refuted by Anglo-Israelites.

The second barrier is that of the identification of Israel and Judah as separate nations, as seen by Mr. Armstrong's previously quoted statement. This matter can be summarily dismissed by careful consideration of the following facts.

First, after the Babylonian captivity, from which the Jews returned, Ezra records that the remnant were called by the name Jews (eight times), and by the name Israel, forty times. Nehemiah records eleven times that they were Jews, and proceeds to describe them as Israel, twenty-two times. The Book of Esther records their partial restoration, calling them Jews forty-five times, but never Israel. Are we to conclude that only Judah (the Jews), and not Israel, were restored under Zerubbabel and Joshua? History, archaeology and a study of Hebrew, refute this possibility completely.

The sixth chapter of Ezra describes the sin offering, mentioning specifically that ". . . twelve he goats, according to the number of the tribes of Israel" were offered for all Israel (v. 17), a fact attested to by Ezra 8:35.

While it is true that in the post-exilic period, we no longer have two kingdoms, but one nation, the prophet Zechariah describes them in comprehensive terms as "Judah, Israel and Jerusalem" (Zechariah 1:19), literally, "the House of Judah, and the House of Joseph" (Zechariah 10:6). Zechariah 8:13 identifes Judah and the House of Israel as one nation, and Malachi called the Jews Israel or Jacob, in contrast to Esau.

The coup de grace to Anglo-Israelism's fragmented exegesis is given by

---

[24]David Baron, *A Letter to an Inquirer*, London: privately published, n.d., pp. 36-38.

the prophet Amos of Judah, a man specifically set apart by God to prophesy to the ten-tribed kingdom of the North. Dr. Baron points out that he "abode in Bethel, which was a center of the idolatrous worship set up by Jeroboam ... there his duty was to announce the coming judgment of God on the Israel of the ten tribes on account of their apostasy" (*Ibid.*, p. 34).

In the last chapter of his book, Amos in approximately 728 B.C. declares:

> Behold, the eyes of the Lord God are upon the sinful kingdom, and I will destroy it from off the face of the earth; saving that I will not utterly destroy the house of Jacob, saith the Lord. For, lo, I will command, and I will sift the house of Israel among all nations, like as a corn is sifted in a sieve, yet shall not the least grain fall upon the earth. All the sinners of my people shall die by the sword, which say, The evil shall not overtake nor prevent us (9:8-10).

We learn from this prophecy that as a kingdom, the ten tribes were to suffer destruction and their restoration would never be realized. How then is it possible for them to be "lost" for almost three millenniums, and then reappear as the British Kingdom when the kingdom was never to be restored?

The Prophet Jeremiah informs us that Israel and Judah are both declared to be "an outcast" (chapter 30), which, in combination with Isaiah 11, proves that they are considered to be one nation in both the eyes of the prophets and in the eyes of God.

Anglo-Israelism would do well to consider these facts, as would Mr. Armstrong in particular, who speaks perpetually with breath-taking dogmatism on subjects about which he apparently knows very little historically, theologically or linguistically. He therefore pours forth interpretations which can only be construed to have progressed out of the abundance of his ignorance.

Second and finally, the New Testament speaks on the subject of the equation of Israel and Judah as one nation, described alternately and interchangeably as "the Jews" and "Israel."

Peter at Pentecost, proclaims the message of redemption to "all the house of Israel." Paul in Acts 26:6 and 7 apparently took Zechariah's statement:

> And it shall come to pass, that as ye were a curse among the heathen, O house of Judah, and house of Israel; so will I save you, that ye shall be a blessing ... (Zechariah 8:13).

In this context, Israel shall indeed be scattered among the nations, and so will Judah, and they shall be redeemed again together to bring forth a blessing in the Person of the Messiah, whose Gospel is to the Jew first, (not just to the house of Israel but as a separate nation), and also to the Gentiles (Romans 1:16b).

A cursory reading of the tenth chapter of Matthew indicates that Jesus Christ Himself considered "the lost sheep of the house of Israel," to include "the Jews," since the missionary journeys of the twelve were limited to the environs of Palestine.

It should be recalled also that Pauline theology, especially in the Book of Romans (chapters 9-11), deals specifically with Israel, not as a nation in the sense of geography, but in the sense of spiritual transgression. He refers to them as God's people who have not been cast away.

If Israel and Judah are separate nations, why then does the Apostle describe the Jews as "his brethren" and as "kinsmen according to the flesh," and then identify them as "Israelites, heirs to the promises of God," as those promises are provided for in the coming Messiah?

The Apostle Paul made this clear by declaring "I am a man which am a Jew . . . for I am also an Israelite . . . are they Israelites? So am I." (Acts 21:39; 22:3; Romans 11:1; 2 Corinthians 11:22; Philippians 3:5).

Jesus Christ sprang from Judah "a Jew," in Anglo-Israelite reckoning, and the Apostle Paul declares in Romans that it was in Israel that "Christ came, who is God over all, blessed for ever" (9:5, Greek).

Let it not be forgotten that Anna the Prophetess was "of the tribe of Aser" (Israel), but she is called "a Jewess" of Jerusalem, facts which forever decimate the concept of Armstrong and the British Israelites that England is the throne of David and is Ephraim, while America is Manasseh.

The words of Jeremiah the Prophet conclude our observations, where he states:

> In those days, and in that time, saith the Lord, the children of Israel shall come, they and the children of Judah together. . . (50:40).

This is proof positive that both the house of Israel and the house of Judah would return from the captivity, and that as the New Testament amply demonstrates, it would be considered as one nation, no longer a kingdom in the historic meaning of that term.

Anglo-Israelism stands refuted by the facts of Scripture and history, and it would be unworthy of attention, if it were not being utilized as a tool by the Armstrong cult, which opens a Pandora's box of multiple and destructive heresies, some of which we shall consider.

c. Other Eclectic Sources and Traits of Herbert Armstrong.
Like so many other non-Christian cultists, Herbert Armstrong claims for himself a divine mandate and nowhere is this more clearly exemplified than in his own writing:

> Yet, is there *anything* so shocking—so hard to believe—as this flat Biblical statement that the whole world is religiously deceived?
> Thirty-seven years ago *I* simply couldn't believe it—until I found it *proved*! And even then, my head was swimming: I found myself all mixed up. To see with my own eyes in the Bible the *opposite* of what I had been taught from boyhood in Sunday school, well this was pretty hard to take, yet there it was in plain type before my eyes!
> If this were the year A.D. 30 and you took a trip to Jerusalem and there speaking to a throng around him you should see an ordinary looking young man about the age of 33 teaching the same things you hear me and Garner Ted Armstrong say over the raido today, it would have been just as astonishing to you then as it is today—and it was to those who heard Him then. . . . You would have been truly astonished! His doctrine was so different! And He spoke dogmatically with assurance, with power and authority. . . . Yet He had foretold a prophecy. He had foretold wolves coming in sheep's clothing to deceive the world. He had said they would enter in profession

to come in His name claiming to be Christian, yet deceiving the whole world. That happened!

For two 19-year time cycles the original apostles did proclaim this Gospel, the Gospel of the Kingdom of God, but in A.D. 69 they fled. In A.D. 70 came the military siege against Jerusalem. The ministers of Satan had wormed their way in, had gained such power that by persecution of political influence they were able to brand the true people of God as heretics and prevent further organized proclaiming to the same Gospel Christ brought from God. For eighteen and one-half centuries that Gospel was not preached. The world was deceived into accepting a false gospel. Today Christ has raised up His work and once again allotted two 19-year time cycles for proclaiming His same Gospel, preparatory to His Second Coming. . . . *The World Tomorrow* and *The Plain Truth* are Christ's instruments which He is powerfully using. Yes, His message is shocking today. Once again it is the voice in the wilderness of regilious confusion![25]

Mr. Armstrong's son, Garner Ted, once heir-apparent to his father's throne, carries the same theme through:

"No man ever spoke like this man," reported their officers to the Pharisees regarding Jesus. The multitudes "were astonished at His doctrine."

Today that same *living Christ*, through *The World Tomorrow* broadcast, *The Plain Truth* magazine, and *this Work*, proclaims in mighty power *around the world* His *same Gospel*—the *same* Gospel preached by Peter, Paul, and the original Apostles.[26]

As did Joseph Smith, "Pastor" Russell, and Mary Baker Eddy before him, so does Mr. Armstrong pose his efforts as the only work which is accurately representing Christianity today. But a tree is known by its fruit, and fruits are not only manifested in a life which is lived, but also in doctrines which are believed and taught. And so it is to the doctrines and teachings of The Worldwide Church of God that we shall now turn for a closer look at what Mr. Armstrong calls The Plain Truth.

The Theology of the Worldwide Church of God

I. *The Divine Origin Of The Worldwide Church Of God*

I'm going to give you the frank and straight answer. You have a right to know all about this great work of God, and about me. First, let me say—this may sound incredible, but it's true—*Jesus Christ foretold this very work—it is, itself the fulfillment of his prophecy* (Matthew 24:14 and Mark 13:10).

Astounding as it may seem, there is no other work on earth proclaiming to the whole world *this very same gospel* that Jesus taught and proclaimed!

And *listen again*! Read this twice! Realize this, incredible though it may seem—no other work on earth is proclaiming this true Gospel of Christ to the world as Jesus foretold in Matthew 24:14 and Mark 13:10! This is the most important activity on earth today![27]

The prophecies bring this Church into concrete focus in the 12th chapter of Revelation. There she is shown spiritually, in the glory and splendor

[25]*The Inside Story. . . , op. cit.,* pp. 7-11.
[26]*Ibid.,* p. 2.
[27]Personal letter to Robert Sumner, November 27, 1958.

of the Spirit of God, but visibly in the world as a persecuted, Command-ment-keeping Church *driven into the wilderness*, for 1,260 years, through the middle ages!

In New Testament prophecy *two churches* are described.

One, the great and powerful and universal church, a *part* of the world, actually ruling in its politics over many nations, and united with the "Holy Roman Empire," brought to a concrete focus in Revelation 17.

. . . She is a *mother* Church! Her daughters are also *churches* who have come out of her, even in protest, calling themselves Protestant—but they are fundamentally of her family in pagan doctrines and practices! They, too, make themselves a *part of* this world, taking active part in its poli-tics—the very act which made a "whore" out of their *Mother*!

The entire apostate family—Mother, and more than 500 daughter de-nominations, all divided against each other and in *confusion* of doctrines and festivals—has a family *name*! They call themselves "Christian," but God calls them something else—"*Mystery, Babylon the Great*!"

But the true Church of God is pictured in prophecy as the "*Little* Flock!" . . . It has kept God's festivals . . .

That Church always has existed, and it exists today!"[28]

II. *The Trinity of God and the Divinity of Man*

The *purpose* of life is that in us God is really re-creating his *own kind* —*reproducing himself* after His own kind—for we are, upon real conversion, actually *begotten* as sons (yet unborn) of [God]; then, through study of God's revelation in His Word, living by His every Word, constant prayer, daily experience with trials and testings, we grow spiritually more and more like God, until, at the time of the resurrection we shall be instantaneously *changed* from mortal into *immortal*—we shall then be *born of* [God]—*We shall then be God!*[29]

. . . Yes, and as a *born* [son of god], Christ *is* God! God Almighty His Father is god. They are two separate and individual Persons (see Revelation 5:1, 6, 7).[30]

. . . I suppose most people think of God as one single individual Person. Or, as a "*trinity*." *This is not true*.

. . . But the theologians and "Higher Critics" have blindly accepted the heretical and false doctrine introduced by *pagan* false prophets who crept in, that the *Holy Spirit* is a *third person* — the heresy of the "*trinity*." This *limits* God to "Three Persons."[31]

Do you really grasp it? The *purpose* of your being alive is that finally you be *born* into the Kingdom of God, when you will actually *be God*, even as Jesus was and is God, and His Father, a different Person, also is God!

You are setting out on a training to become *creator*—to become *God!*[32]

III. *The Nature of Christ*

Jesus, *alone*, of all humans, has so far been *saved*! By the resurrective

---

[28]Herbert W. Armstrong, *Easter Is Pagan*, Pasadena, CA: Ambassador Press, n.d., pp. 8, 9.
[29]Herbert W. Armstrong, *Why Were You Born?*, Pasadena, CA: Ambassador Press, n.d., pp. 21, 22.
[30]Herbert W. Armstrong, *Just What Do You Mean—Born Again?*, Pasadena, CA: Ambassador Press, n.d., p. 16.
[31]*Ibid.*, pp. 17, 19.
[32]*Why Were You Born?*, *op. cit.*, pp. 21, 22.

power of *God*! When Jesus comes, at the time of the resurrection of those in *Christ*, He then brings His reward with *Him*![33]

Christ, one of the beings in the Godhead, had now been *changed* into flesh—still having the *personality* and *will* to do right which distinguished Him as an entity—yet now had become human, having *human nature* with all of its *desires*, *weaknesses* and *lusts*—and subject to *death* just like any other human.

This is a truth about which *millions are deceived*.

The Satan-inspired doctrine that Jesus was *not* human, that He did *not* inherit the human nature of Adam, that He did *not* have all the normal human nature of Adam, that He did *not* have all the normal human passions and weaknesses against which all of us have to struggle—in a word, that Jesus did *not* really come "in the flesh" as a normal human being—*This is the doctrine of the anti-Christ*. Notice Romans 8:3: "God sending His own Son in the likeness of sinful flesh."

The idea Satan is trying to put across is that it is *impossible* for man to keep the spiritual law of God, and so Jesus came as our Savior—not "in the flesh" with normal human nature—but through "special process" so that He could keep the law of God *in our stead* to *die* for us! But His *obedience* was our example!

. . . that Jesus taught, *"If* thou wilt enter into life, *keep the commandments"* (Matthew 19:17).

. . .We are not only to keep the letter of the law, but to follow it as it is magnified throughout the Bible in "every word of God" (2 Corinthians 3:6).

Satan the Devil, through His *false ministers* who appear as "ministers of righteousness" (2 Corinthians 11:13-15), is trying to deceive the world into believing in a *false Christ* — a Christ who *did away* with the Father's spiritual *law* and made it possible for us to inherit eternal life without having to build, with the help of God's Spirit, the kind of holy, righteous *character* which would enable us to obey God's eternal, spiritual *law* both now and forever.[34]

How plain! How abundantly clear! Not having *human nature* with its *passions and lusts*, God *cannot* be tempted with evil. And on the contrary, *every* man is tempted by his own *lust* — because every man does have *human nature*.

So it is not only *possible* — but *obligatory* — that we obey God's spiritual law, the Ten Commandments, as they are, magnified throughout the Bible. Keeping them in the spirit does *not* mean "spiritualizing" them away, but really obeying them as Jesus set us the example, through the power of God's Holy Spirit, which He gives to them that obey Him (Acts 5:32).

The *only difference* between Jesus and any other human is that He was conceived of the Holy Spirit. Therefore He obeyed God's laws *from birth* — and never had to go through the process of repenting of going the wrong way, of *unlearning* wrong ideas and habits, and of gradually learning to exercise His will to do right continually.

. . . And, praying for the strength He needed through the Holy Spirit, *He always* did *right*.

Yes, Jesus had *sinful* flesh — human nature. But by exercising the *will* to always obey God, and by receiving the extra help He needed to *master* His fleshly desires, Jesus *repudiated* the sway of sin in the human flesh and showed that the law of God *could be kept*.

---

[33]*Ibid*., p. 12.
[34]*The Plain Truth*, November 1963, pp. 1, 4, 7, 8.

. . . They were not worshiping Jesus as just another *Man*.

. . . Christ came *in the flesh* to set us a *perfect example*, then *to die* in payment for our sins and make it possible for us to be reconciled to a holy, righteous God and receive of His Spirit—His very *life and character* implanted within us.[35]

That is, He who had existed from eternity — He by whom God created the worlds and all things therein — He who was and is *Life* — He who was God — He *was made flesh* — converted *into flesh*, until He *became flesh* and then He *was* flesh!

Yes, Jesus was a fleshly *man*. He was God, come in human flesh. And, when converted into human flesh the *life* that kept Him alive resided *in the blood*, as in all who are *flesh* (Leviticus 17:11).

. . . But He was not God inside of, yet separate from the body of flesh — He, God, was *made flesh*, until He, still *God*—God, with us — God *in* (not inside of) the human flesh — God manifest *in the flesh* (1 Timothy 3:16).

If there was no other Person in the Godhead, then the Giver of all Life was dead and all hope was at an end!

If there was no *Father* in heaven while Jesus Christ lay dead — His blood in which resided His *life* shed from *His* veins, given for you and for me — then all life everywhere had come to an end.

. . . That's where His life resided — in His *blood*, not in spirit! He did not shed *a spirit* to save us from our sins — He shed His *blood, and* in so doing *gave His life*.

But, "as the Father hath life *in Himself*; so hath He given to the Son to have life in Himself" (John 5:26). God the Father raised Jesus from the dead. Cf. John 2.

Not Resurrected in Same Body

Now notice carefully, God the Father did not cause Jesus Christ to get back into the body which had died.

Some seem to believe that it was only the *body* which died — that Jesus Christ never died.

. . . What they believe is that a *body* Christ lived in died, but Christ *Himself* never died, Christ was God, and they argue, God could not die!

If they are right, they are lost and doomed to eternal punishment! If Christ did not die for their sins — if it was only a mortal *body which* died — then we have no Savior, and we are *lost*.

What happened is that the Logos — the *Word* — the Eternal — was *made flesh*. He was converted into — changed into flesh. Now He was flesh and blood, exactly as you and I.

His *life* was in His blood, and He gave His *life* by the fact His blood poured out while He was on the cross! He had taken on a *human* nature. He was God — but now God changed *into* flesh and blood — God with us — Emmanuel!

Yes, the Word was *made flesh*, and He was flesh and blood, not just an immortal Spirit *in* a body of flesh and blood.

It was *Christ Himself* who was *dead*. He was *revived*. Nowhere does the Scripture say He was alive and active, or that God had Him get back into the human *body*, that had died and was now resurrected.

Jesus Christ was *dead*. He was as much "out" as a boxer knocked sense-

---

[35]*Ibid*., pp. 11, 12.

less — much *more*, for the boxer usually is not dead but only unconscious. Jesus was *dead* — but was *revived!*

And the resurrected body was no longer human — it was the Christ resurrected, *immortal*, once again *changed!* As He had been changed, converted *into* mortal human flesh and blood, subject to death, and for the *purpose* of *dying for our sins, now,* by a *resurrection from the dead, He was again changed, converted, into immortality* — and He is alive forevermore! Now a *living* Savior, not a *dead* Savior, He *was* dead — but only for three days and three nights.[36]

IV. *The Personality of the Holy Spirit*

God's Holy Spirit is His *life. It* imparts His *life* to you! *It* imparts more as we shall see!

One thing more, the Holy Spirit is *divine, spiritual love* — the love of God flowing into you from God Almighty — through the living Christ! (Romans 5:5).[37]

But the theologians and "Higher Critics" have blindly accepted the heretical and false doctrine introduced by *pagan* false prophets who crept in, *that the Holy Spirit is a Third Person* — the *heresy of the "trinity."* This limits God to "Three Persons." This *denies* that Christ, through His Holy Spirit actually comes now *into* the converted Christian and does His saving work on the *inside* — "Christ in you, the hope of glory" (Colossians 1:27).

Jesus Christ is *come* in the flesh, as inspired in its original Greek language means, literally, *present tense* — that *Christ is now coming.* . . .

. . .If the Holy Spirit were a third *person* that would be impossible!

. . .That heresy *denies* the *true born-again* experience![38]

V. *Salvation by Grace and Law*

Salvation, then, is a *process!*

But how the god of this world would blind your eyes to that! He tries to deceive you into thinking all there is to it is just "accepting Christ" with *"no works"*—and presto-chango, you are pronounced "Saved."

But the *Bible* reveals that *none* is yet "saved."[39]

The *blood* of Christ does not finally save any man. The death of Christ merely paid the penalty of sin in our stead — it wipes the slate clean of past sins — it saves us merely from the *death penalty* — it removes that which separated us from God and reconciles us to God.

But we are *saved* — that is, given immortal life — by Christ's *life*, not by His death (Romans 5:10).

It is *only those* who, during this Christian, Spirit-begotten life, have grown in knowledge and grace, have overcome, have developed spiritually, done the works of Christ, and endured unto the end, who shall finally be given *immortality*—finally changed from mortal to *immortal* at the time of the Second Coming of Christ (1 Corinthians 15:53, 54).[40]

People have been taught, falsely, that "Christ *completed* the plan of sal-

---

[36]*The Plain Truth*, April 1963, p. 10.

[37]Herbert W. Armstrong, *What Do You Mean—Salvation?*, Pasadena, CA: Ambassador Press, n.d., p. 19.

[38]*Just What Do You Mean Born Again?*, *op. cit.*, p. 13.

[39]*Why Were You Born?*, *op. cit.*, p. 11.

[40]Herbert W. Armstrong, *All About Water Baptism*, Pasadena, CA: Ambassador Press, n.d., pp. 1-3.

vation on the Cross"—when actually it was only *begun* there. The popular denominations have taught, "Just *believe*—that's all there is to it; believe on the Lord Jesus Christ, and you are that instant *saved!*"

That teaching is false! And because of deception—because the *true Gospel* of Jesus Christ has been all but blotted out, lo these 1900 years by the preaching of a false gospel *about [the] person* of Christ—and often a false Christ at that—millions today *worship Christ—and all in vain!*

The blood of Christ does not finally save any man. The death of Christ did pay the penalty of sin in our stead—it wipes the slate clean of past sins—it saves us merely from the *death penalty*—it removes that which separated us from God and reconciles us to God.[41]

. . . So it is not only *possible* but obligatory—that we obey God's spiritual law, the *ten commandments*, as they are magnified throughout the Bible. Keeping them in the spirit does *not mean* "spiritualizing" them away.

. . . But by exercising the *will* to always obey God, and by receiving the extra help He needed to master His fleshly desires, Jesus *repudiated* the sway of sin of the human flesh and showed that the law of God *could be kept.*[42]

VI. *The New Birth and the Resurrection*

But, He was then *born [of God], how?* By a resurrection from the dead (Romans 1:4). *When? At the time* of His resurrection!

And *that is* the way *you* and I shall look, if and when we are finally *born [of God]!* These deceived people who talk about having had a "born again experience" certainly don't look like *that!*

That tremendous, glorious event of being *born of God* is to take place *at the resurrection of the just*— at the time of Christ's Second Coming to earth![43]

It is *only* those who, during this Christian, Spirit-begotten life, have grown in knowledge and grace, have overcome, have developed spiritually, done the works of Christ, and endured unto the end, who shall finally be given *immortality*—finally changed from mortal to *immortal* at the time of the Second Coming of Christ (1 Corinthians 15:53-54).[44]

The real *source of this whole stupendous error* is this. In the English language, we have *two different* words to express the *two phases* that occur in the reproductive process of all mammals.

The one, which is the very Start of the new life, we call *conception*, or a *begettal*.

But *no one ever calls this beginning of the process a* birth!

The phase of the process which in the English language we call being *born* is that process by which the foetus is *delivered* from the mother's womb, and out into the world comes a little baby to gasp its own first breath. It has then *been born!*

But if you would try to tell a doctor, or a nurse, that the yet unborn foetus has already been *born*, as soon as you knew it had been *conceived*, or *begotten*, the doctor or nurse would surely think you ignorant, and probably try to explain.

The New Testament of the Holy Bible was originally written in the *Greek* language. And, in this case, the Greeks had *only one word* for the *two* vitally *different* phases of the process!

---

[41]*All About Water Baptism, op. cit.*, p. 6.
[42]*The Plain Truth*, November 1963, pp. 11, 12.
[43]*Just What Do You Mean Born Again?, op. cit.*, p. 13.
[44]*All About Water Baptism*, pp. 1, 3.

That Greek word is "gennao"(pronounced ghen-ah-o). The Greek-English dictionary (lexicon) gives this definition of the Greek word; *to procreate* (properly of the father, but by extension of the mother): beget, be born, bring forth, conceive, be delivered of, gender.

Four of those definitions mean to beget or to conceive—but *not* to be *born*. To *procreate means to beget*. To *conceive* has the same meaning. Webster's dictionary defines "gender" as to beget, breed, generate. It does *not refer* to the birth. But three of the Lexicon definitions of "gennao" mean the actual *birth*: "be born," "bring forth" and "be delivered of."

. . . and since the "scholars" of our comparatively recent years who translated the Bible into English did not, themselves, *understand* God's Plan—they often translate the Greek word "gennao" into the English word "*born*" where it actually meant "begotten."

". . . for in Christ Jesus I have *begotten* you through the gospel." There it is correctly translated, showing that Paul's converts at Corinth, as his "spiritual children," had been *begotten* of God, *but not yet born.*

The experience of conversion, in this life, is a *begettal*—a "conception—an impregnation" — but *not yet a birth.* This we shall make *plain.*

All who *now* are *begotten* sons of God shall then be *born* — elevated from mortal to *immortal*, from decaying *flesh* to *spirit*, from *human to divine!* And that *true born-again experience* will be as incomparably more *glorious* than the fake, vague, meaningless, so-called "born-again experience" that deceived *thousands think* they have had, now, as the present transcending *glory of Christ* is superior to the status of sickly, diseased, sinning, suffering *humanity today!*[45]

. . . After people are actually *born of God*, they, too, shall *be spirit, just as* God is Spirit. They will be invisible to material human sight, just as angels are.

He is now *begotten* of God. The very *life* and *nature* of God has *entered into* him, impregnating him with immortal spirit—life, exactly as the physical sperm cell from the human father enters into the ovum or physical egg-cell when a new *human life* is first *conceived, impregnated, or begotten.* But, just as that tiny ovum, as small as a pin-point, is merely *begotten* of its human father — *not yet born* — so the converted human is, at what we properly call, conversion, merely *begotten* of God the heavenly Father — *not yet born.*

He is *still* material *flesh*, even though God's Spirit has now *entered into* his *mind.* He is *still visible.*

A newly converted human is actually *begotten of* God. Such a person is, already, an actual begotten *son of God.* He can call God "Father." *But He is Not Yet Born of God.*[46]

All true Christians who shall have died before Christ's coming shall rise first — in a resurrection — and then all Christians *still alive*, in mortal flesh, shall be instantaneously — in the twinkling of an eye — *changed from mortal to immortal* — from material flesh to immaterial spirit — from *human* to *divine*, at last *born of God!*

We are now *flesh* — vile, corruptible flesh subject to rotting and decay. But at Christ's coming, when we shall be *born of God*, this vile body shall be *changed*, and made exactly like Jesus in His *glorified body.*[47]

[45]*Just What Do You Mean Born Again?* pages 6, 18, 19, 20.
[46]*Ibid.*, p. 11.
[47]*Ibid.*, pp. 13-15.

VII. *The Guilt of God and the Nature of Man*

God has *made* man's natural mind so that it wants to do things that are contrary to His laws; "The carnal mind (with which we are all born) is enmity against God" (Romans 8:7). Compare this with Romans 3:9–18. "The flesh (man's natural heart and mind) *lusteth* against the Spirit and the Spirit against the flesh: and these are *contrary* the one to the other" (Galatians 5:17). *All*, as originally born, have a desire-lust—to go contrary to God's Laws! (James 1:4 and Psalm 81:11, 12).

It *is by man's own carnal mind that God blinds him* . . .

God, in love and wisdom, blinds human beings who by nature reject the truth so they will unwittingly *sin all the more often* and thereby *learn their lesson all the more deeply.*[48]

VIII. *The Sabbath, Unclean Foods and Legalism*—1 Timothy 4:4

Passover, the days of unleavened bread, Pentecost, and the holy days God had ordained *forever* were all observed by Jesus . . .

The New Testament reveals that Jesus, the apostles, and the New Testament Church, both Jewish and Gentile-born, observed God's Sabbath, and God's festivals—weekly and annually.[49]

The Theology of Biblical Christianity

In the tradition of Jehovah's Witnesses whom he follows concerning the doctrine of eternal retribution and the Resurrection of Jesus Christ, Herbert Armstrong's theology has no room for the deity or personality of the Holy Spirit.

For Armstrong, God's Holy Spirit is an impersonal "it," and though he makes a pathetic effort to rescue the divinity of the Spirit, he only succeeds in reducing Him to "the love of God" on abstract principle at best.

In our analysis of the theology of Jehovah's Witnesses we observed how the depersonalization of the Holy Spirit strikes at the very heart of the Christian Gospel, for it is through the agency of the third person of the Trinity that God regenerates men to eternal life (John 3:5). By denying the personality of the Spirit, i.e., that the Spirit is a personal ego and one of the persons of the Holy Trinity, Armstrong invalidates the only means whereby a man can be saved. All too few listeners to his program are aware of this particular serious deviation from historic Christianity. It is always wise to keep in mind that the more vigorously they enunciate what small fragments of truth that somehow manage to escape the multiple strands of error woven into the very fabric of the The Worldwide Church of God, the more carefully one ought to listen for the inevitable overtones of Armstrong's interpretations which nullify the small percentage of truth he does retain.

It is unnecessary to repeat what we have stated before, but even a careful consideration of the thirteenth chapter of Acts reveals that the Holy Spirit uses the personal pronoun "I," denoting ego or personality. He also commands the Church to set apart Paul and Barnabas, then He sends them forth (verses 2 through 4).

---

[48]C. P. Meredith, *Is This the Only Day of Salvation?*, Pasadena, CA: Ambassador Press, n.d., p. 2.
[49]Herbert W. Armstrong, *Easter Is Pagan*, Pasadena, CA: Ambassador Press, n.d., pp. 4, 12.

The twenty-first chapter of the Book of Acts pictures the Spirit instructing the prophet, Agabus, to speak: "Thus says the Holy Spirit, So shall the Jews at Jerusalem bind the man that owns this belt, and shall deliver him into the hands of the Gentiles" (verse 11).

Thus Luke reveals that the third person of the Trinity has the capacity to think, command and prophesy. This certainly does not correspond to Mr. Armstrong's caricature of the Spirit as an "it." For even an elementary knowledge of psychology reveals that an "it" is devoid of personality and cannot speak, command or prophesy!

Further analysis of the fifth chapter of Acts underscores that the Holy Spirit is deity and is so designated by the Apostle Paul (verses 3 and 4). That the Holy Spirit is considered a member of the heavenly Trinity is evident by His presence at the incarnation (Luke 1:35), the baptism of Christ (Matthew 3:16), the Resurrection of Christ (Romans 8:11 and 1 Peter 3:18), and in the Great Commission (Matthew 28:19).

One cannot read Mr. Armstrong's writings without becoming increasingly aware of the fact that he is radically anti-Trinitarian. A perusal of the quotation from his writings found in the earlier part of this chapter indicates forcefully that he wants no part of Christian theology in this and far too many other areas for the spiritual good of himself or his listeners.

In the theology of Herbert Armstrong:

> Genesis 1:1 gives God's name as in the Hebrew Elohim. This is a uni-plural name. It means more than one person, but combined into the family, which family is God. . . . For the word "God" comes to us from the Hebrew word "Elohim" which means "living, eternal, creating, all-powerful, governing kingdom." Elohim means one God, not many gods. But that one God is a kingdom. There is but one true church—one church but many members! (1 Corinthians 12:20). So it is with God.
>
> Do you really grasp it? The purpose of your being alive is that finally you will be born into the kingdom of God when *you will actually be God* even as Jesus was and is God and His Father a different person also is God! . . . You are setting out on a training to become Creator, to become God![50]

The similarity to Mormonism in Armstrong's theology at this point is quite striking, for as previously observed in our chapter on the Mormons, they, too, believe and teach that men may become members of the God-family and become gods. Armstrong, on the other hand, exceeds even the Mormon fantasy, boldly teaching what appears to be a pantheistic unity of God in which all the members of the "family" participate. This is certainly a view which is not shared by any of the inspired writers of the Scripture, and his recourse to the Hebrew plural (Elohim) in which he stretches it beyond all proportion and contextual meaning to the forced interpretation of a "family" or "kingdom," is indirectly a pathetic admission of the extremely limited knowledge he possesses of the language.

Armstrong's usage of Elohim is not consistent with any scholarly presentation; in fact, as he uses it, it is simply a perversion tailored to impress those who can be impressed with the ludicrous.

---

[50] *Just What Do You Mean Born Again?*, *op. cit.*, pp. 16-20.

The followers of Armstrong's cult should consult the third chapter of Genesis where they will find that Satan first taught the "God family" doctrine to Adam and Eve. Both Armstrong and the Mormons have received and believed the same perversion which ushered in the reign of sin and death upon the human race, for if Satan lied when he said "you shall be as gods" (verse 5), so does Mr. Armstrong "wrest the Scripture to his own destruction" and sadly to the destruction, spiritually speaking, of those who follow in his training.

The plain truth of this whole matter is that we do indeed grasp what Mr. Armstrong is teaching. His Worldwide Church of God serves only as a camouflage for his doctrinal deviations which are mixed with orthodox terminology and evangelical clichés and infused with numerous half-truths. This concoction is enunciated with a dogmatism and arrogance akin to that of the late Judge Rutherford of Jehovah's Witnesses. And were it not for Armstrong's dynamic presentation and wide media coverage coupled with the spiritual vacuum which today pervades many quarters of Christendom, his entire system of interpretation would be the object of humor instead of the serious consideration it now demands.

The Armstrong cult appeals to the Hebrew and Greek languages and is conspicuously devoid of the scholastic background or knowledge of the languages which Armstrong so glibly quotes. The Hebrew plural Elohim, as we have stated, does not refer to any family or kingdom of God; it is one of the divine names utilized in Scripture and is distorted by the Mormons, Jehovah's Witnesses and Mr. Armstrong in a vain attempt to alter the nature of God which, as revealed in the Bible, controverts their respective theologies.

In our study of Jehovah's Witnesses the doctrine of the Trinity has been given full consideration, so it will not be necessary to go into further detail on this subject. But it should not be forgotten that every major non-Christian cult system either perverts subtly or denies outright the Christian doctrine of the Trinity; and Mr. Armstrong's cult is no exception to the rule, even though he mixes the theologies of Jehovah's Witnesses and Mormonism with his own peculiar interpretations. The denial is uniquely his own and should be recognized for what it is.

The New Birth — A New Twist

The doctrine of the New Birth or Spiritual Regeneration as it is taught in the New Testament apparently has an effect upon Mr. Armstrong when he either hears or reads it which is little short of hysterical. In his pamphlet, *Just What Do You Mean Born Again* he vigorously criticizes the Christian doctrine of regeneration, and in its place substitutes by all odds, one of the strangest doctrines in the area of cultism. Through it he has quite literally given the new birth a new twist!

According to the theology of The Worldwide Church of God, the doctrine of the new birth is divided into two segments or areas. In the first or initial area which takes place upon the acceptance of Jesus Christ as the Son of God, the believer is impregnated with the life of God through the Holy Spirit which Armstrong terms "begetting." The second phase is the new birth itself which he informs us takes place not at the moment of faith but at the resurrection of the body!

Mr. Armstrong strenuously maintains that it is "a universal error" to believe that when a person is converted and has fully repented and accepted Christ in faith that that person is born again in the Biblical sense. For Herbert Armstrong the original Greek word *Gennao* is the pivot point of the controversy. Armstrong holds that since the word can also be translated "beget" or "conceive," the translators of the Bible erred in not rendering the word consistently as "begotten" instead of "born," and this they did because "they did not themselves understand God's plan . . . the experience of conversion in this life in a begettal, a conception, an impregnation, but not yet a birth."

It is worthwhile to note in studying this particular phase of Mr. Armstrong's theology that his appeal to the Greek, which was meant by him to carry the convincing weight of scholastic authority, in reality becomes the proverbial albatross around his neck. Mr. Armstrong's contention that "the original Greek in which the New Testament was written has only the one word for both meanings" is a most damaging remark, for any good lexicon reveals immediately that the Greek has at least four other terms to describe the idea of conception and birth (*sullabousa, tiktei, apotelestheisa,* and *apokuei*) which are translated variously as "conceive," "bring forth," "delivered," "born," "when finished," and "begat." One need only study Luke 1:24, 37; 2:21, 36; James 1:15, 18 and not a few others, and he will come to the immediate conclusion that Mr. Armstrong has no concept whatever of New Testament Greek. In fact, the Greek language even has a term which describes pregnancy from conception to delivery!

Mr. Armstrong's blatant statement to the effect that "the Greek had only one word for two vitally different phases of the process . . . since the original Greek in which the New Testament was written had only the one word for both meanings (*gennao*)," is either a product of his own ignorance or a deliberate falsehood. Since he seems to be aware of the existence of lexicons and concordances, this writer is convinced that it is the latter.

It is only necessary to look for a moment at Mr. Armstrong's manufactured distinction between the uses of *gennao* in the New Testament to see that his attempt to stretch the term beyond all limits of its usage in New Testament Greek, is only done in order to teach that no one is *now* born again of the Holy Spirit, but that instead this can only take place at the resurrection.

The followers of Mr. Armstrong must settle for an impregnation by the Spirit and a gestation period (their entire life!) before they can be born again. This new birth is dependent upon keeping the commandments of God and enduring to the end in Mr. Armstrong's theology, a fact overlooked by some of his more zealous disciples.

The fact that the new birth has nothing to do with the resurrection is demonstrated by the usage of the term by the Apostle Peter who reminds us that through faith in the Lord Jesus Christ we have been "born again (past tense) not of corruptible seed, but of incorruptible, by the Word of God which liveth and abideth forever" (1 Peter 1:23).

The new birth in the New Testament is synonymous with spiritual regeneration to eternal life, and the very fact that Jesus Christ and the apostles described the possessors of the new birth as "saved" decimates Mr. Armstrong's contention that one must wait until the resurrection in order to be born again.

In his epistle to the Ephesians the Apostle Paul is adamant in his declaration that "by grace you have been saved through faith; and this is not your own doing, it is the gift of God — not because of works, lest any one should boast" (Ephesians 2:8, Greek). Here is the usage of the past tense in reference to Christians, an instance which is amply supplemented throughout the New Testament by such passages as John 5:24; 3:36; 6:47; Romans 8:1; 1 Peter 1:18 and 1 John 5:1, 11-13 and 20.

It is wholly unnecessary to pursue this thought further since Mr. Armstrong has no scholarly precedent for subdividing the new birth and attempting to attach it to the resurrection of the body, something which the Scripture nowhere does. His is a lame attempt to distort the basic meaning of *gennao* which he, himself, admits is listed in the lexicon as "to be born, to bring forth, to be delivered of." It is only one more indication of the limitations of his resources.

When Jesus Christ addressed Nicodemus (John 3) and spoke of the new birth, He connected this birth to the person of the Holy Spirit whom the disciples received in the Upper Room (John 20) and whose power and presence were manifested at Pentecost (Acts 2). This has always been accepted in Christian theology for just what the Bible says it is, an instantaneous experience of spiritual cleansing and re-creation synonymous with the exercise of saving faith in the person of Jesus Christ and through the agency of the grace of God (Acts 16:31; 2:8–10; Colossians 1:13, 14; Galatians 2:20; 1 Corinthians 6:11, 19; 2 Corinthians 5:17).

The Apostle Paul instructs us that our salvation has been accomplished not by any efforts on our part, but by "the kindness and love of God our Savior" (Titus 3:4-7). It is not something we must wait for until the resurrection; it is our present possession in Christ totally separate from the immortality of the body which is to be bestowed at the return of Christ and the resurrection of the body (1 Corinthians 15:49–54; 1 John 3:2; Romans 6:5).

It is all well and good if Mr. Armstrong's followers wish to make the new birth a process, as indeed they do with the doctrine of salvation, but we must be quick to point out that this is not the Christian doctrine of the new birth and as such is not consistent with the revelation of the Bible. Mr. Armstrong's new twist to the new birth is just that, and the Christian Church can ill afford to sit by in silence while The Worldwide Church of God propagates it as Biblical theology.

The Resurrection of Christ

The Resurrection of Jesus Christ along with the Christian doctrine of the Trinity is assailed most vigorously by the majority of non-Christian religious cultists. Such persons steadfastly maintain that they believe in the Resurrection of Christ, but then proceed to redefine the term "resurrection" until it generally comes to mean merely the conquest of death by the spiritual nature of Jesus. Herbert Armstrong is no exception in this category, teaching as he does that Jesus Christ was raised from the dead as a spirit and that the saints will be resurrected as spirits.

Wrote Mr. Armstrong:

> The saints of God now born of the spirit and become spirit at the resurrection will be able to be invisible or visible at will.[51]

The Worldwide Church of God does not hesitate to state that "the resurrected body was no longer human. . . ." and that Jesus Christ Himself was spirit in His Resurrection:

> Now notice carefully God the Father did not cause Jesus Christ to get back into the body which had died. Nowhere does the Scripture say He was alive and active or that God had Him get back into the human body that had died and was now resurrected . . . and the resurrected body was no longer human . . . He was again changed and converted into immortality . . .[52]

What has been said about Jehovah's Witnesses' doctrine of the Resurrection of Christ can also be said about Armstrong's position.

The reader can consult the second chapter of John's gospel (verses 19–21) to ascertain from the lips of the Lord Jesus that He promised to raise His own body from the grave. The Greek word as has been observed (soma) refers to a physical form not to an immortal spirit!

Luke goes to great pains to point out that Christ identified the body in which He conquered death as physical in nature (flesh and bone), and further that this body had the marks of the cross in the hands and feet (Luke 24:37–39).

The Apostle Thomas could not doubt that Christ had risen in the physical form after our Lord's appearance in the Upper Room (see John 20), for it was there that the risen Christ invited him to place his fingers into the wounds in His hand and his hand into the spear wound in His side. One thing is certain from all this, Jesus Christ conquered death *as a man not* as a spirit, and at this juncture Mr. Armstrong's theology is in complete opposition to the revelation of the Scripture. At the Second Coming of Christ (1 Thessalonians 4) when the dead in Christ rise, they will rise immortal according to the Apostle Paul (1 Corinthians 15) and will possess a form like Christ's own form (1 John 3:2). This form will be composed of flesh and bone in the structural composition of Christ's resurrected body (Luke 24), for nowhere does the Bible say that either Christ or the resurrected bodies of Christians are composed of spirit.

In the 26th chapter of Matthew's gospel, Jesus Christ promised His disciples that they would drink wine with Him in the kingdom of His Father (verse 29), and He reiterated this same promise in Luke's gospel, "you may eat and drink at my table in my kingdom" (Luke 22:30).

It is the hope of Christians that at His glorious appearing Jesus Christ will "change our vile body that it may be fashioned like unto His own glorious

---

[51]*The Plain Truth*, October 1959, p. 30.
[52]*The Plain Truth*, April 1963, pp. 10, 40.

body" (Philippians 3:21). And if He is indeed the firstfruits of them that slept (1 Corinthians 15:20), then we shall indeed be like Him (1 John 3:2); and He is an immortal man, not a spirit as Mr. Armstrong's theology so erroneously declares.

Salvation and Atonement

As the theology to The Worldwide Church of God does violence to the true nature of the new birth, so also does it categorically deny the Biblical doctrine of the Atonement.

According to Mr. Armstrong:

> Salvation then is a process but how the god of this world would blind your eyes to that! He tries to deceive you into thinking all there is to it is just accepting Christ with no works, and presto changeover, you are pronounced saved! . . . But the Bible reveals that none is as yet saved . . . people have been taught falsely that Christ completed the plan of salvation on the cross when actually it was only begun there. The popular denominations have taught just believe that's all there is to it, believe on the Lord Jesus Christ and you are that instant saved. That teaching is false . . . the blood of Christ does not finally save any man, the death of Christ merely paid the penalty of sin in our stead and wipes the slate clean of *past* sins . . . it is only those who during this Christian spirit-begotten life have grown in knowledge and grace, have overcome, have developed spiritually, done the works of Christ and endured to the end who shall finally be given immortality, finally changed from mortal to immortal, at the time of the Second Coming of Christ. So being, as we say, converted, receiving the Holy Spirit of God is merely the beginning! Then begins a life long of living under the government of God by God's laws which expresses His will instead of by self-will and desire.[53]

After reading Mr. Armstrong's statements, any serious student of the Bible wonders how anyone could take seriously his theological interpretations, for if there is one thing that the Bible does emphatically teach, it is the fact that salvation is *not* a process but an accomplished fact based upon the completed sacrifice of Jesus Christ (Hebrews 1:3; 9:26, 28).

Regarding Mr. Armstrong's shocking statement to the effect that the blood of Christ does not finally save anyone, it is in direct contradiction to the words of the Apostle Peter who taught that persons have not been redeemed by anything corruptible but "by the precious blood of Christ" (1 Peter 1:19). It should be noted that this is the *past tense* as an accomplished fact, a teaching amplified in the Book of Hebrews repeatedly. The writer of Hebrews tells us that "by one offering He has perfected forever them that are sanctified" and that by the will of God "we are sanctified through the offering of the body of Jesus Christ once for all" (Hebrews 10:14, 20).

The Lord Jesus has entered

> not into a sanctuary made with hands, a copy of the true one, but into heaven itself, now to appear in the presence of God on our behalf. . . . But as it is, he has appeared once for all of the end of the age to put away sin by the

---
[53]*Why Were You Born?*, p. 11.

sacrifice of himself. And just as it is appointed for men to die once, and after that comes judgment, so Christ, having been offered once to bear the sins of many, will appear a second time, not to deal with sin but to save those who are eagerly waiting for him (Hebrews 9:24–28, RSV).

Mr. Armstrong and his Worldwide Church of God consistently ignore the fact that

Christ had offered for all time a single sacrifice for sins. Therefore, brethren since we . . . have confidence to enter the sanctuary by the blood of Jesus, by the new and living way which he opened for us through the curtain, that is, through his flesh, and since we have a greater priest over the house of God, let us draw near with a true heart in full assurance of faith, with our hearts sprinkled clean from an evil conscience and our bodies washed with pure water. Let us hold fast the confession of our hope without wavering, for he who promised is faithful (Hebrews 10:12–23, RSV).

The Apostle Paul reiterates the completed nature of the atonement upon the cross when he deals with the subject in such passages as Ephesians 1:7, Colossians 1:20 and Romans 5:9. The Apostle John's reminder that God has provided for continual cleansing from sin (1 John 1:7, 9) should only serve to strengthen Christians in the knowledge that Jesus Christ has indeed by the sacrifice of the cross "loosed us from our sins in His own blood" (Revelation 1:5, Greek). This is a completed act, the benefits of which are shed abroad in the hearts of all true believers by the Holy Spirit. Nowhere does the Bible teach that the atonement of Christ is *yet* to be completed! This particular doctrine is drawn from the early writings of Seventh-day Adventists with whom, as we mentioned, Mr. Armstrong was associated at one time. It is to the credit of the Adventists that their denomination has officially repudiated this position, maintaining that the atonement has already been completed.

Pauline theology makes clear the fact that in Jesus Christ God has determined to redeem men by sovereign grace, and the record still stands:

For what saith the scripture? Abraham believed God, and it was counted unto him for righteousness. Now to him that worketh is the reward not reckoned of grace, but of debt. But to him that worketh not, but believeth on him that justifieth the ungodly, his faith is counted for righteousness. Even as David also describeth the blessedness of the man, unto whom God imputeth righteousness without works, Saying, blessed are they whose iniquities are forgiven, and whose sins are covered. Blessed is the man to whom the Lord will not impute sin (Romans 4:3–8).

The theology of The Worldwide Church of God in regard to the doctrine of salvation is refuted thoroughly by the Apostle Paul in his epistle to the Galatians. When describing the purpose of the law of God, Paul points out that its primary function was to "lead us to Christ" that we might be justified by faith. The law was a pedagogue, a teacher, but it was finally and completely fulfilled in the person of the incarnate Jesus Christ. Love is the universal, all fulfilling principle which is implemented through grace, first toward God and then toward one's neighbor. (See Romans 13:8–11.)

Mr. Armstrong attaches to salvation the requirement of "keeping the law and commandments of God." This can only be described as adding to the gospel of grace the condition of law-keeping, a first century heresy scathingly denounced in the Galatian epistle as "another gospel" by no less an authority on the law than St. Paul (Galatians 2:16, 21; 1:8, 9).

If all law is fulfilled in love as Christ and the apostles taught, then the insistence upon observance of the Ten Commandments (or, for that matter, the over six hundred laws of Moses) on the part of Mr. Armstrong and his followers as a condition of salvation injects into the Christian Church what the apostles so successfully expelled (Matthew 22:36-40; Acts 15:24).

It is certainly true that no informed Christian believes in the destruction or setting aside of the laws of God, but, as we shall see, when dealing with the Seventh-day Adventists' concept of this subject, there is a vast difference between the abolition of law and the fulfillment of law, which fulfillment Christ accomplished once for all on the cross (Romans 3:31; 10:4).

The theology of Herbert Armstrong includes what can only be termed a type of universalism where the redemption of man is concerned:

> As Lord of lords Christ will begin to convert and save the entire world during His reign . . . all peoples will then come to know God. Their blindness and religious confusion will be removed and they will finally be converted. The resurrected saints will teach the people God's way.[54]

The New Testament repeatedly urges men to assume the forgiveness God has provided now, not during some future millennial reign. "Now is the accepted time; behold, now is the day of salvation" (2 Corinthians 6:2), is the watchword of the New Testament theology. Along with "Pastor" Russell, the founder of Jehovah's Witnesses, Armstrong teaches what amounts to a second chance for unregenerate men.

Jesus Christ urged men to accept Him "for the Son of man is come to seek and to save that which was lost" (Luke 19:9, 10) and the writer of Hebrews emphasizes "how shall we escape if we neglect so great salvation" (Hebrews 2:3).

The writer of Hebrews also exploded another of Mr. Armstrong's theological fantasies when he wrote that during the millennial kingdom "they shall not teach every man his neighbor, and every man his brother, saying, Know the Lord: for all shall know me, from the least to the greatest" (Hebrews 8:11). The followers of The Worldwide Church of God would do well to put Mr. Armstrong's theology to the test (1 Thessalonians 5:21), for then it would be apparent that what he says is anything but "the plain truth."

Inherent within the theological structure of The Worldwide Church of God and stemming from Mr. Armstrong's perversion of the Biblical doctrine of salvation, is his insistence (also borrowed from the Seventh-day Adventist) that Christians abstain from specific types of food which he claims are "unclean."

No devoted follower of The Worldwide Church will therefore eat pork, lobster, clams, shrimp or oysters or any of the prohibitions of the Mosaic system. They are in effect Orthodox Jews in this particular area of theology! In his first epistle to Timothy the Apostle Paul recognized among the

---

[54]*The Plain Truth*, October 1959, p. 30.

Gentiles the problem of so-called unclean foods and dealt with it in the following manner:

> Now the Spirit expressly says that in later times some will depart from the faith by giving heed to deceitful spirits and doctrines of demons, through the pretensions of liars whose consciences are seared, who forbid marriage and enjoin abstinence from foods which God created to be received with thanksgiving by those who believe and know the truth. For everything created by God is good, and nothing is to be rejected if it is received with thanksgiving; for then it is consecrated by the word of God and prayer (1 Timothy 4:1–5, RSV).

Further comment on this particular subject is unnecessary in the light of the Apostle's clear statement, but a reading of the fourteenth chapter of Romans reveals instantly that Christians are not to sit in judgment upon one another relative to days of worship or foods to be consumed. We are not to judge spirituality on the basis of diet or the observance of days. But in The Worldwide Church of God this is not true, for Mr. Armstrong does indeed sit in judgment upon all those who do not subscribe to his particular interpretation of dietary laws allegedly enforced in this era of history.

Relative to the problem of Sabbath-keeping, Mr. Armstrong also derived this from the Seventh-day Adventist denomination, but he has gone further than the Adventist have ever even intimated.

The literature of The Worldwide Church of God is literally filled with insistence upon the observance of the Jewish feast days, new moons, festivals and sabbaths, all of which were dealt with fully and finally by the Apostle Paul in his Colossian epistle.

> And you who were dead in trespasses and the uncircumcision of your flesh, God made alive together with him, having forgiven all our trespasses, having canceled the bond which stood against us with its legal demands; this he set aside, nailing it to the cross. He disarmed the principalities and powers and made a public example of them, triumphing over them in him. Therefore, let no one pass judgment on you in question of food and drink or with regard to a festival, a new moon or a sabbath. These are only a shadow of what is to come; but the substance belongs to Christ (2:13–17, RSV).

When the preceding quotation from Paul is placed beside his counsel in Romans 14, the picture is transparently clear:

> Let not him who eats despise him who abstains, and let not him who abstains pass judgment on him who eats; for God has welcomed him. Who are you to pass judgment on the servant of another? It is before his own master that he stands or falls. And he will be upheld for the Master is able to make him stand. One man esteems one day as better than another, while another man esteems all days alike. Let everyone be fully convinced in his own mind. He who observes the day, observes it in honor of the Lord. He also who eats, eats in honor of the Lord, since he gives thanks to God; while he who abstains, abstains in honor of the Lord and gives thanks to God. . . . Why do you pass judgment on your brother? Or you, why do you despise your brother? . . . Then let us no more pass judgment on one another, but rather decide never to put a stumbling-block or hindrance in the way of a

brother. I know and am persuaded in the Lord Jesus that nothing is unclean in itself; but it is unclean for anyone who thinks it unclean. . . . Do not, for the sake of food, destroy the work of God. Everything is indeed clean, but it is wrong for anyone to make others fall by what he eats; it is right not to eat meat or drink wine or do anything that makes your brother stumble (14:3–21, RSV).

There is a memorable passage in the Book of Acts where the Council of Jerusalem was in session concerning the problem of Jewish prohibitions on diet and practice as it affected the Gentile converts. Apostle James once for all time dealt with the issue, a fact Mr. Armstrong seems content to ignore:

> Therefore my sentence is, that we trouble not them, which from among the Gentiles are turned to God; But that we write unto them, that they abstain from pollutions of idols, and from fornication, and from things strangled, and from blood . . . Forasmuch as we have heard, that certain which went out from us have troubled you with words, subverting your souls, saying, Ye must be circumcised and keep the law: to whom we gave no such commandment. . . . For it seemed good to the Holy Ghost, and to us, to lay upon you no greater burden than these necessary things; that you abstain from meats offered to idols, and from blood, and from things strangled, and from fornication: from which if ye keep yourselves, ye shall do well (Acts 15:19, 20, 24–29).

It is evident that law keeping, dietary prohibitions, the Mosaic ordinances which were binding upon Israel, and the Jewish customs of observances of feasts, etc., were abrogated by the Holy Spirit (verse 28), and it is certainly not amiss to comment that what the Spirit of God saw fit to lift as restrictions upon the Church of Jesus Christ, the so-called Worldwide Church of God has no right to reimpose! Mr. Armstrong, however, has done precisely this and his action stands condemned not only by the Council at Jerusalem and the Apostle James but by the clear words of the Apostle Paul and the pronouncement of the Holy Spirit Himself.

The Indictment of God

We close our observations on the theology of the Armstrong cult by pointing out that he has not hesitated to indict God for the guilt of man.

> God has made man's natural mind so that it wants to do things that are contrary to His laws . . . it is by man's own carnal mind that God blinds him . . . God in love and wisdom blinds human beings who by nature reject the truth so they will unwittingly sin all the more often and thereby learn their lesson all the more deeply . . .[55]

While it is certainly true that the carnal mind "is enmity against God" (Romans 8:7) and that "the natural man does not receive the things of the Spirit" and by nature rebels against the decrees of the Creator, nowhere in Scripture does it state that God "made man's natural mind so that it wants to do things contrary to His laws," as Mr. Armstrong's theology teaches. Rather, it is the clear testimony of Scripture that each member of the human

---

[55]*Is This the Only Day of Salvation?*, p. 2.

race has chosen to voluntarily and freely rebel against the Lord, thereby, coming into possession of carnal or fleshly natures which are at enmity with God.

The fifth chapter of Romans informs us that the spiritual attributes of rebellion are in all men because of Adam's disobedience and that only in Christ can these be changed by the creation of a new nature, thus restoring man to fellowship with God.

In the theology of Mr. Armstrong's cult, then, God is ultimately responsible for the evil nature of man, and he has not even hesitated to state concerning the human nature and character of the Lord Jesus Christ:

> Christ now had become human having human nature with all of its desires, weaknesses and lusts . . . and subject to death just like any other human. This is a truth about which millions are deceived.[56]

When dealing with the sinless nature and character of Christ, Mr. Armstrong states:

> . . .He was the first human ever to achieve it — to be perfected, finished as a perfect character.[57]

In the fifteenth chapter of 1 Corinthians the Apostle Paul contradicts Mr. Armstrong in the strongest possible terms by referring to Jesus Christ as "the last Adam," (verse 45) thereby teaching incontrovertibly that Jesus Christ had a perfect human nature and character and was never under obligation to achieve it or "to be perfected, finished as a perfect character." He was perfect as the last Adam and as the eternal Word made flesh (John 1:1, 14).

It is perfectly true that the Scriptures speak of Christ as "learning obedience as a faithful son." It is also true that He was made "complete" (Hebrews 2:10; 5:9; 7:28). The Greek word translated "perfect" in the passages from Hebrews basically means "completion," a fact demonstrated by Jesus Christ Himself when in speaking of Herod, He said:

"And He said unto them, go ye and tell that fox, Behold, I cast out devils, and I do cures today and tomorrow, and the third day I shall be perfected" (Luke 13:32).

The Revised Standard Version correctly renders the word "finish," carrying with it the meaning of the completion of a plan, literally "I finish my course." Far from being imperfect and in need of suffering and death to perfect His character and human nature as Armstrong maintains, these terms only describe the completion of the divine plan of the ages whereby God brought to completion or fulfillment the foreordained consummation of His majestic design for human redemption. The attempt by Mr. Armstrong to imbue Jesus Christ with a tainted human nature and to seize upon the word "perfect" as the means to accomplish this, cannot alter the plain declarations of Scripture which describe our Lord in His human nature and character in far different terms than does Mr. Armstrong. When applied to our Lord, the term "perfect" or "perfected" refers only to Christ's completion of His

---

[56]*The Plain Truth*, November 1963, pp. 11, 12.
[57]*Why Were You Born?* p. 14.

human life and sacrifice for our sins. He became complete only in the sense of perfect obedience and submission to the Father's will. He was always "holy" and without sin in His human nature and character.

In the gospel of Luke which describes the annunciation to the virgin Mary by the angel Gabriel, the child to be born is designated as "the son of the Highest" by the angelic messenger who does not hesitate to emphasize "that holy thing which shall be born of thee shall be called the Son of God" (1:32, 35).

The Apostle Peter in the course of one of his great sermons in the Book of Acts quotes David in his description of the Messiah as God's "Holy One" (2:27) and reiterates this title in the third chapter as "the Holy One and the Just" (verse 14).

The Apostle John, preaching with Peter further on in the Book of Acts, states in a stirring prayer to God: "For of a truth against thy holy child Jesus, whom thou hast anointed, both Herod, and Pontius Pilate, with the Gentiles, and the people of Israel, were gathered together" (4:27).

The word translated "child" can also be rendered "servant" in Greek, but regardless of which way one takes it, it is qualified by the word "holy" which any lexicon or dictionary defines as "without sin — pure." Our Lord made this claim for Himself when, in conflict with the Jews, He challenged them to dare to accuse Him of sin (John 8:46), and the writer of the epistle to the Hebrews declares Him to be "holy, harmless and undefiled, separate from sinners" (7:26). None of these pronouncements of the Scripture are in agreement with Mr. Armstrong's contention that Jesus Christ had a sinful nature and a character that needed to be perfected due to defects which he implies existed, thereby necessitating a "perfecting" process.

The Worldwide Church of God does indeed honor Christ with its lips, but in the cold analytical dawn of Biblical examination and analysis, there can be little doubt that its heart is far from Him.

There are many other errors in the theology of Mr. Armstrong which could easily fill a small volume, but space does not allow us to deal with it in the confines of a chapter. Let it be said, however, that the theology of Herbert Armstrong and his Worldwide Church of God contains just enough truth to make it attractive to the listener who is unaware of the multiple sources of heretical doctrine he has drawn upon for the balance of his theological system, enough of which permeates both his radio programs and his publications to insure the uninformed listener a gospel of confusion unparalleled in the history of American cultism. The Worldwide Church of God is all the more dangerous as it makes profuse use of the Bible and professes to swear allegiance to only "the plain truth of the Scripture," while, in reality, its allegiance is to the interpretations of the Scripture propagated by Herbert W. Armstrong whom one magazine has aptly described as "Mr. Confusion." Since "God is not the author of confusion," and this "plain truth" no student of the Scripture will deny, there is one sure remedy to the problem of the spread of Mr. Armstrong's religion. Turn off the set and open your Bible, for within its pages God is always broadcasting the eternal message of the Gospel of Grace impregnated by the Spirit of God in every essential necessary to the redemption of the soul and re-creation and living of the Christian life.

When this is supplemented by attendance in a truly Christian Church where that Gospel is preached, there is no need to listen to the Herbert Armstrongs of our day, for as the Psalmist so beautifully described it, "the entrance of thy Word giveth light."

Chapter 13

UNIFICATION CHURCH

The Unification Church, founded and led by Korean-born Rev. Sun Myung Moon, represents a new kind of cultic influence popular in America today. The distinctive features of this kind of cult include (1) its special appeal to educated young people from the middle class; (2) its habit of conducting business, especially recruiting, under multiple pseudonyms or anonymously; (3) its Westernization of Eastern religious ideas; and (4) its misinterpretations of scripture to persuade outsiders that its Eastern religious orientation is compatible with and, indeed, is the fulfillment of, biblical Christianity. Such groups as the Unification Church are further characterized by what appears to be obvious, widespread, and forceful psychological pressure on members to conform and remain loyal to the group at all costs. This psychological pressure is present in all the cults, as we noted in the opening chapters of this book. It is perhaps more obvious with groups newly arrived in America and whose converts are mainly young people whose families have had little or no previous exposure to the group.

The Hare Krishnas, Transcendental Meditation, the followers of the Oregon-based guru Rajneesh, the Church Universal and Triumphant, and other such groups share the same features, although in their own unique expressions. In this short review of Unification theology and practice, we will touch on some of the teachings which cause the Unification Church to be classified as a non-Christian cult both by theology and practice.

History

On January 6, 1920, Yong Myung Moon (Shining Dragon Moon) was born of Christian parents in the Pyungan Buk-do province of what is now North Korea. There is evidence that young Moon dabbled in spiritist practices, and he recounts that at age 16 he was visited by Jesus Christ himself in a vision. In this vision Jesus Christ declared that the world would be changed through Moon.[1] However, Moon's unique position of leadership and spiritual authority, as well as his unique doctrinal teachings and practices do not appear to have been formulated until the 1940s.

The young Moon continued independent Bible study and attended school in Japan, formulating his religious system through 1945. This system is most fully presented in the Unification textbook *Divine Principle*. After World War

---

[1]The exact content of Jesus' speech seems to vary. Some say Jesus told him he was to accomplish a "great mission." Others say he was told he would establish God's kingdom on earth. Others that he would complete man's salvation as the Second Coming of Jesus Christ. He later claimed that both Buddha and Mohammed also endorsed his mission.

II, in North Korea, Moon joined a group of underground Pentecostals with some strange beliefs:

> After World War II, while living in North Korea, he became involved with a group that was deeply entrenched in mystical revelations, awaiting the impending appearance of a new Messiah. They also believed that Korea was the New Jerusalem of the Bible and that the Messiah would be born in Korea. These elements are all found in Rev. Moon's theology and in the *Divine Principle*).[2]

In 1945 Moon received the revelation that began the Unification Church. At this visionary ceremony, Moon was declared to be the one through whom the world would be saved:

> After nine years of search and struggle, the truth of God was sealed into his [Moon's] hands. At that moment, he became the absolute victor of heaven and earth. The whole spirit world bowed down to him on that day of victory, for not only had he freed himself completely from the accusation of Satan, but he was now able to accuse Satan before God. Satan totally surrendered to him on that day, for he had elevated himself to the position of God's true son. The weapon to subjugate Satan then became available to all mankind.[3]

Symbolic of his spiritual mastery, he changed his name to Sun Myung Moon ("Shining Sun and Moon") in 1946.

Moon was imprisoned by Communist forces twice in the next three years, and his followers claim that this was persecution for his faith. Critics cite allegedly official records which indicate that his problems with the communist leaders stemmed instead from his capitalist pursuits and/or bigamy.

Moon was freed from communist imprisonment and moved to Pusan in South Korea. He continued his unique preaching ministry, combining his own spiritist revelations with more familiar Christian terminology, and founded his church in 1954 in Seoul. The new church was called the Holy Spirit Association for the Unification of World Christianity and it has caused controversy almost from its beginning. In 1955 he was arrested by South Korean officials and charged with draft evasion and sexual promiscuity. Although the charges were later dropped, testimonies of ex-members who had been in the church at that time lend credence to the charge that an early practice of the new church may have been for female members to be "purified" through sexual intercourse with Rev. Moon. Christian author James Bjornstad reported one ex-follower's comments:

> One long-time follower of Rev. Moon added an interesting sidelight to this. He said, "It is entirely possible that those sexual rituals were a part of the early church in Korea. Since original sin came through the woman's [Eve's] intercourse with Lucifer through which she received his evil characteristics, it is perfectly logical that the reversal of this, woman's intercourse with the perfect man through which she could receive his perfect charac-

---

[2]James Bjornstad, *Sun Myung Moon and the Unification Church*, Minneapolis, MN: Bethany House, 1984, p. 10.

[3]Sun Myung Moon, *Message to the World Unification Family*, Washington, D.C.: The Holy Spirit Association for the Unification of World Christianity, 1964, p. 4.

teristics, would liquidate original sin. Then, as Adam received Satan's evil characteristics from Eve through intercourse, so man would receive perfect characteristics through intercourse with the woman."[4]

The Unification Church "Bible," *Divine Principle*, was published in 1957. It was actually written by a church member, but contains all of Moon's teachings to his followers. Through *Divine Principle* in its latest version, Moonies understand and interpret the Bible. As is true with all cults, the Unification Church members cannot understand the Bible as it is. It must be explained by the organization and God's "prophet" for today: Rev. Sun Myung Moon.

Moon's power (and his church) grew in South Korea, greatly aided by Moon's secular business activities. His strong anti-communist activities won him the support of the South Korean government.

In 1972 Moon announced that the United States was to become the beneficiary of his missionary activities. God had called him to bring Unification theology to America. As part of his missionary preparation, he accumulated an enormous missionary fund, largely from Japanese followers' contributions. This money was deposited in a Chase Manhattan Bank in New York in Rev. Moon's name rather than in the unincorporated name of the Unification Church. (The Unification Church was not incorporated in the United States until 1976.) It was the U.S. government's questioning of the use and tax status of this money which resulted in Moon's trial and conviction of tax fraud in 1983. Rev. Moon began his eighteen month prison term July 20, 1984.[5] Despite criticism of Moon and his church by most major religious bodies in the United States, many religious spokespersons have testified in Moon's behalf in this instance, citing First Amendment freedoms. John McClaughry, former Reagan Senior Policy Advisor, summarized this opinion of Moon's conviction:

> One may concede that the government was clever in its choice of victims. Reverend Moon is not a popular figure in the American religious world. He is a non-white, a foreigner who speaks only halting English. His theology is highly unorthodox. In addition, he is outspokenly anti-Communist and sees himself as a rallying force for a great American struggle to roll back the Communist tide in the world. Then there are the allegations concerning the Moonies' fundraising and recruitment practices. If the government wanted to establish a new doctrine of government supervision of churches, it could hardly have chosen a better target to make its case.
>
> But the case of Reverend Moon is not just his own problem. It should be a matter of grave concern for all those who defend freedom of religion against unwarranted government intrusion. For if Reverend Moon goes to jail—this time not in Communist North Korea, but in the United States of America, the great bastion of religious liberty—something of vital importance to all American religions goes with him.[6]

We must never forget, as Mr. McClaughry rightly observes, that religious

[4]James Bjornstad, *The Moon Is Not the Sun*, Minneapolis, MN: Bethany House, 1976, pp. 31.
[5]Contrary to his followers' claims that Moon is now a martyr, he is a common convicted criminal.
[6]John McClaughry, "The Uneasy Case Against Reverend Moon" in *National Review*, December 23, 1983, p. 1162.

liberty is to be guarded jealously, but it must not be used as an excuse to avoid prosecution for unlawful acts.

The story of the Unification Church in America since 1972 has been a startling combination of good and devastating publicity. The Unification Church has been praised for pouring millions of dollars into struggling local economies. Moon lives on a twenty-five acre estate in Irvington, New York. The $850,000 Belvedere Estate in Tarrytown, New York, is campus for the Unification seminary. Moon's net worth is somewhere over $15 million. The church frequently buys struggling industries in depressed areas (fishing co-ops in Louisiana, for example) and turns them into good profit-making companies with member help, much of which is volunteer. However, critics claim that the money raised comes largely from donations which are coerced from the unsuspecting public by members who are said to be dupes of Moon, soliciting donations while not telling their "marks" that the Unification Church is the recipient of their donations. Those who live and work around the Moonie businesses often complain that the cheap member labor increases local unemployment.

The Unification Church has also hosted a number of professional symposia for scientists, philosophers, and theologians. While those sympathetic to the Unification Church see this as a philanthropic, ecumenical gesture, critics point out that the Unification Church seems to hide its involvement in such meetings in order to increase attendance, and then after the meetings exploit their involvement for publicity. Evangelical Christians who have attended the Moonie religious conventions or seminars sometimes feel that the purpose of the meeting is more for the Moonies to learn Christian vocabulary and apply it to their unorthodox theology than for open dialogue. NEW ERA is the Moonie front organization which sponsors these meetings, and its purposes were described by *Washington Post* writer Martha Barnette, summarizing the thought of NEW ERA consultant and religious writer Richard Quebedeaux:[7]

> Quebedeaux said the conferences, which he estimated cost the Unification Church "several millions of dollars a year," are designed to provide an ecumenical forum for theological discussions and to counter what he called "so much negative publicity" and "the uniform nastiness" of press coverage of the controversial church.[8]

Barnette also noted that "critics of the church, however, said they viewed the conference as part of the church's increasing public relations efforts to gain legitimacy by associating itself with members of the religious and intellectual establishment."[9]

---

[7]The curious role of Mr. Quebedeaux, a proclaimed Christian, has puzzled and confused not a few of his colleagues. Using his Christian credentials, he encourages Christian leaders to "dialogue" with what he admitted to me is a non-Christian cult. While the Unification Church claims to be open, none of these meetings has had any effect in changing the essentially non-Christian Unification theology. It is sad that some evangelicals, by their participation at such conferences, encourage the goals of a cult whose basic theology is decidedly unbiblical.

[8]Martha Barnette, " 'Moonies' Offer Expense-Paid Lure" reprinted from the *Washington Post* in the *Los Angeles Times*, August 29, 1981.

[9]*Ibid.*

In 1982 the ill-fated, anti-communist World War II movie, *Inchon*, was released to bad reviews and bad attendance. The movie was one of the most expensive ever produced, costing $48 million dollars, almost all of which was paid for by the Unification Church. Even this publicity-seeking, anti-communist propaganda vehicle backfired on the Moonies. There was little critical or box office acclaim and much public controversy over its funding and distribution publicity (all by Unification organizations and money).

The Unification Church was in the news again in 1982 with a mass wedding at Madison Square Garden, where Rev. Moon united 2,075 couples, all his followers. Caroli Agus of *Newsday* reported,

> . . .Wearing identical wedding uniforms, an army of brides married an army of grooms at Madison Square Garden in a wedding that began with "Here Comes the Bride" and ended in a shower of balloons.
>
> Strangers married strangers. Before the wedding the Moonies, celibates all, lived separately from the opposite sex. They related to each other as brother and sister and called each other by those names. The wedding was preceded by a "matching" June 25 and 26, held at the New Yorker Hotel, which is Unification Church property. It took a few seconds or a few minutes to match a couple.[10]

Rather than improving Moonie public relations, the ceremony served to highlight the Moonies' non-traditional social and cultural habits and their unorthodox theology. Some critics declared that this was just another example of the drastic mind control and brainwashing executed upon Moonie converts.

As we survey the history of Rev. Moon and his Unification Church, we find that his practices depart from what is commonly accepted in American culture and contrast sharply to traditional Christian values. Below is a short presentation of Unification theology, which will show it is as far removed from biblical Christianity as is Unification culture.

Unification Theology vs. the Bible

God. "God's essential positivity and essential negativity are the attributes of His essential character and essential form. . . . Here we call the positivity and negativity of God 'masculinity' and 'femininity', respectively."[11]

"God either projected the full value of Himself in His object, or He created nothing at all. . . . So man is the visible form of God, and God is the invisible form of man. Subject and object are one in essence. God and man are one. Man is incarnate God."[12]

In the theology of the Unification Church relative to God, there are traces of Mormonism and spiritism flavored with Moon's ever present psycho-sexual emphasis.

The Bible categorically teaches that man, far from being "incarnate God,"

[10]Caroli Agus, "Strangers Commit Selves Spiritually in Moonie Marriages" reprinted from *Newsday* in the *Los Angeles Times*, December 10, 1982.
[11]*Divine Principle*, p. 24.
[12]Sun Myung Moon, *New Hope*, Washington, D.C.: HSA-UWC, 1974, p. 5.

is a creation "lower than the angels" (Heb. 2:6–8) and a transgressor of the laws ordained by God.

The only time that God "projected the full value of himself" was in the person of Jesus Christ (John 1:1, 14, 18). Moon's theology is also anti-trinitarian[13] and inevitably ends in the error of blurring the distinction between man and God.

Such passages as 2 Peter 1:17 when compared with Titus 2:13 and Acts 5:3–4 are clearly indicative of trinitarian theology and Matthew 28:19 indicates trinitarian thinking on the part of our Lord when He gave the great commission. As early as the second century of the Christian Church the word trinity was invoked as a means of expressing the mysterious relationship extant between the Father, Christ, and the Spirit.

All cultic structures as we have seen deny biblical trinitarianism which is totally monotheistic and usually introduce some variation which distorts the revelation God has given concerning himself.

Jesus Christ. "The Principle does not deny the attitude of faith held by many Christians that Jesus is God, since it is true that a (any) perfected man is one body with God."[14]

"We must understand that this (John 8:58) also does not signify that Jesus was God Himself. Jesus, on earth, was a man no different from us except for the fact that he was without original sin."[15]

If there were no other quotation from the teaching of Sun Myung Moon, this would be quite sufficient to reveal the essential anti-biblical nature of his Christology.

The Lord Jesus, while on earth, was both God and man and indicated this on numerous occasions by forgiving sins (Mark 2:5), raising the dead (John 11), casting out demons (Mark 5:7–13), and affirming to the Jews who challenged his identity that He was indeed the eternal Being who spoke with Moses at the burning bush (Exodus 3:14, 15; cr. John 8:58).

The Unification Church's theology also denies the bodily resurrection of Jesus Christ from the dead and teaches that He was raised as a spirit.[16] In the light of our Lord's discourse with Thomas as recorded in the twentieth chapter of John and His appearance to His disciples where He offered His body as tangible proof of the resurrection (Luke 24:36–39), the theology of the Unification Church collapses. The utilization of such passages as John 2:19–22 and John 20:28 can be most effective in showing "Moonies" the gross nature of Mr. Moon's error at this crucial point of Christian doctrine.

Salvation. "We must realize that through the crucifixion on the cross, God and Jesus lost everything. . . . At that moment of crucifixion, nothing was there—nothing—no nation of Israel, no Jewish faith, no disciples, no family, not at all, no Christianity. There was no redemption; there was no salvation; and there was no beginning of Christianity. So there on the cross, salvation was not given."[17]

---

[13]*Divine Principle*, p. 68.
[14]*Ibid.*, p. 209.
[15]*Ibid.*, p. 212.
[16]*Ibid.*, p. 36; *Master Speaks 4*, p. 9.
[17]Sun Myung Moon, *The Way of the World*, Washington, D.C.: HSA-UWC, 1973, p. 13.

It is hardly necessary to make any extended comment upon the Moon doctrine of salvation since it is totally eclipsed by the cross. Multiple passages of Scripture teach us that at Calvary redemption was fully accomplished, that the old covenant was fulfilled and that Christ "by himself purged us of our sins" and became "the satisfaction for all our sins, and not for ours only but for the sins of the whole world" (1 John 2:2 and Hebrews 1:3).

In Unification theology salvation is not by grace through the all sufficient sacrifice of the Lord Jesus but must be augmented by human works and by the teachings, revelations, and requirements of Mr. Moon.

The warning of the Lord Jesus against false Christs and false prophets is most apropos where Moon is concerned, for he can make no genuine claim to messianic office being Korean, for as Christ said, ". . . salvation is *from* the Jews" (John 4:22).

Chapter 14

L. RON HUBBARD AND SCIENTOLOGY

Scientology is a cult which thrives on glowing promises that are heady stuff for the lonely, the weak, the confused, the ineffectual, and the mentally or emotionally ill. For a healthy fee, Scientology claims it can "help people do something about the upsets and travails of life. Hope and happiness can return again through Scientology."[1]

Why is this movement called Scientology? It claims to be a "church" and an "applied religious philosophy." How do its teachings compare to the teachings of the Bible? What background and qualifications does founder L. Ron Hubbard have for developing a system which claims to be "the most vital movement on Earth today"?[2] In this brief analysis of a complex religious and philosophical system, we will explore some answers to these questions. We will provide a survey of Scientology and, by contrast, show the major points at which statements in Scientology materials contradict biblical teaching.

L. Ron Hubbard

The founder of Scientology, L. (Lafayette) Ron Hubbard, was born in Nebraska, March 13, 1911. Scientology publications long claimed that Hubbard graduated in civil engineering from George Washington University as a nuclear physicist, although the university records show that he attended for two short years, during the second of which he was on academic probation, and failed physics. Hubbard's Ph.D. was said to be from a Sequoia University in California, although there is no proof of the existence of any accredited institution in California by that name that grants doctorates.

However, Hubbard did become an accomplished (if not entirely successful) science fiction and novel writer in the 1930s. Some of the ideas common to Scientology first appeared in his 1938 manuscript titled *Excalibur*. In May of 1950, Hubbard collected and published many of these ideas in an article in *Astounding Science Fiction*. During the same year, the systematic presentation of his quasi-psychotherapeutic and religious ideas were published as the non-fiction *Dianetics: The Modern Science of Mental Health*. The book has now sold millions of copies, and Hubbard has written prolifically about his revolutionary new way to promote mental, emotional, and spiritual perfection in literally dozens of Scientology books.

Hubbard's movement was known as Dianetics until, in 1952, Hubbard

---

[1]Ralph Lee Smith, "Scientology—Menace to Mental Health" in *Today's Health*, December 1968, p. 34.
[2]L. Ron Hubbard, "The Aims of Scientology," Hollywood, CA: The Church of Scientology Celebrity Centre, 1974, 1977, one page flyer.

reorganized it, renamed it Scientology, and declared it a religious system and its centers of instruction, churches. Counselors are now called ministers and have even adopted clerical clothing. While the sales of *Dianetics* and the growth of the Scientology centers were extremely impressive, the claims of Scientology often sounded more like science fiction than religion. Ralph Smith recounts,

> One preclear [student of Scientology] said that this thetan [somewhat similar to "soul" or "spirit"] had inhabited the body of a doll on the planet Mars, 469,476,600 years ago. Martians seized the doll and took it to a temple, where it was zapped by a bishop's gun while the congregation chanted "God is Love." The thetan was then put into an ice cube, placed aboard a flying saucer, and dropped off at Planet ZX 432, where it was given a robot body, then put to work unloading flying saucers. Being a bit unruly, it zapped another robot to death and was shipped off in a flying saucer to be punished. But the flying saucer exploded, and the thetan fell into space.[3]

For many years, Scientology's international headquarters was located at Saint Hill in England. From 1966 through 1975, Hubbard lived aboard the group's floating headquarters, the 300-foot boat *Apollo*. He ruled the organization from behind an almost impenetrable wall of trusted associates and aids, spending most of the time from 1975 through 1979 in seclusion in the desert (probably in California). No one, including his wife or any Scientologists, will admit to having seen Hubbard personally since March of 1980.

Hubbard's estranged son, Ron DeWolf, tried unsuccessfully in 1983 to have his father declared legally dead and his estate turned over to him. The courts finally ruled that a written statement purporting to be from Hubbard and attested to by handwriting experts constituted legal proof that Hubbard was still alive and still mentally competent to manage his own affairs. However, even some upper echelon of Scientology have expressed doubts that Hubbard is still alive. Whether dead or alive, the enigmatic Hubbard was well described by *Time* magazine:

> A reclusive multimillionaire who preferred to work all night. A man terrified of germs who fought his growing array of ailments with a variety of drugs and massive vitamin injections. A brilliant and dominating figure who built an empire and who was both revered and feared. And now, to make the comparison [to the late Howard Hughes] more compelling still, the question of his fate. Even longtime intimates have not seen him in more than two years. They do not know whether he is living in seclusion by his own choice, or whether he is mentally incompetent and a captive of former underlings. Some of his old aides think he may even be dead.[4]

A stinging indictment of Hubbard and Scientology and their tactics in silencing critics was delivered by Los Angeles Superior Court Judge Paul G. Breckenridge J. in his legal opinion on a case involving a Scientology critic and ex-Scientologist, Gerald Armstrong, who was at one time commissioned by Scientology to write Hubbard's authorized biography. The judge's opinion reads, in part:

---

[3]Ralph Lee Smith, *op. cit.,* p. 38.
[4]*Time*, January 31, 1983, p. 64.

In addition to violating and abusing its own members' civil rights, the organization over the years with its "Fair Game" doctrine has harassed and abused those persons not in the church whom it perceives as enemies. The organization clearly is schizophrenic and paranoid, and this bizarre combination seems to be a reflection of its founder. . . . The evidence portrays a man who has been virtually a pathological liar when it comes to his history, background and achievements. The writings and documents in evidence additionally reflect his egoism, greed, avarice, lust for power and vindictiveness and aggressiveness against persons perceived by him to be disloyal or hostile.[5]

The Church of Scientology

As recounted above, the basic ideas of the Church of Scientology can be traced back to the science fiction of founder L. Ron Hubbard, and to its early propagation as Dianetics. Throughout its evolution into an "applied religious philosophy," Scientology's history has been as stormy and paradoxical as the life of its founder.

National governments of a number of countries (including the United States, Australia, Great Britain, and France) have investigated the Scientology organization and have issued warnings about the veracity of its claims. Scientology's troubles with the United States government have included a raid by the Food and Drug Administration in 1963; Internal Revenue Service audits, rulings, and judgments concerning the collection and taxation of the millions of dollars of annual church income; an FBI raid of church offices in Washington, D.C., and Los Angeles in 1977; and indictments and/or convictions in federal court of leading Scientologists (including Hubbard's wife, Mary Sue) for "burglary, obstruction of justice, wiretapping, harboring a fugitive, and conspiracy."[6] The alleged extent of Scientology's operations against the government were described by *Time* magazine:

> . . . . bugging and burglarizing the Washington offices of the IRS, the Federal Trade Commission, the Drug Enforcement Administration and the Justice, Treasury and Labor departments. These break-ins were part of a vast spying operation, created by Hubbard and directed by his wife, to gather information on "enemies" of the church. One Scientology document so identifies 136 governmental agencies at home and abroad. At its height, the espionage system, called "Operation Snow White" by Hubbard, included up to 5,000 covert agents who were placed in government offices, foreign embassies and consulates, as well as in private organizations critical of Scientology. Hubbard even assembled a dossier on President Richard Nixon and individuals ranging from U.S. Senators to members of the Rockefeller family.[7]

Numerous mental health organizations, professionals, and periodicals (including *Today's Health* and *Psychology Today*) have decried Scientology for

---

[5]Paul G. Breckenridge, Jr., quoted by Myrna Oliver, "Ex-Scientology Aide Absolved by Ruling" in the *Los Angeles Times*, June 22, 1984, part one, p. 20.
[6]Cheryl McCall, "Federal Prosecutors Unveil the Astonishing Intrigues of the Scientology Church" in *People* magazine, August 14, 1978, p. 20.
[7]*Time*, op. cit., p. 64.

its unorthodox methods which some see as psychologically dangerous. Other more general periodicals (including the *Saturday Evening Post, Life, Time*, and *People*) have chronicled the many problems with Scientology over the years.

Scientology has long supported a large legal and public relations department staffed by Scientologists dedicated to protecting the interests of Scientology from any critics or detractors. Books critical of Scientology have been swiftly removed from the market by publishers unwilling to fight the intense pressure against them.

Although some estimates put Scientology's all-time high membership at more than three million, *Time* magazine estimates the number at two million in the mid-1970s. Membership in 1983 was estimated at 200,000. Well-known Scientologists include actress Karen Black, singer Lou Rawls, actor John Travolta, and jazz musician Stanley Clarke.[8]

Some of the Teachings of Scientology

God

Scientology says: "There are gods above all other gods, and gods beyond the gods of the universes."[9]

The Bible says: "Ye are my witnesses, saith the Lord, and my servant whom I have chosen: that ye may know and believe me, and understand that I am he: before me there was no God formed, neither shall there be after me. I, even I, am the Lord; and beside me there is no saviour" (Isaiah 43:10, 11). "Thus saith the Lord the King of Israel, and his redeemer the Lord of hosts; I am the first, and I am the last; and besides me there is no God" (Isaiah 44:6; see also Isaiah 45:18, 22; Mark 12:28–29, 32).

Jesus Christ

Scientology says: "You will find the cross as a symbol all over the universe, and the CHRIST LEGEND as an implant in preclears a million years ago."[10]

The Bible says: "For we have not followed cunningly devised fables, when we made known unto you the power and coming of our Lord Jesus Christ, but were eyewitnesses of his majesty" (2 Peter 1:16; see also John 20:19–20, 24–28).

Scientology says: "Neither Lord Buddha nor Jesus Christ were OTs [Operating Thetans, the highest Scientology level] according to evidence. They were just a shade above clear."[11]

The Bible says: "[Christ] who is the image of the invisible God, the first-born of every creature: for by him were all things created, that are in heaven, and that are in earth, visible and invisible, whether they be thrones, or dominions, or principalities, or powers: all things were created by him, and for

[8]*People*, op. cit., pp. 22, 23.

[9]L. Ron Hubbard, *Scientology 8–8008*, Los Angeles, CA: Publications Organization, 1953, 1967, p. 73.

[10]L. Ron Hubbard, *Professional Auditor's Bulletin #31*, one page flyer.

[11]L. Ron Hubbard, *Certainty Magazine*, Los Angeles, CA: Publications Organization, vol. 5, no. 10. n.d.

him: and he is before all things, and by him all things consist" (Colossians 1:15–17; see also Hebrews 1:13).

Sin and Salvation

Scientology says: "It is despicable and utterly beneath contempt to tell a man he must repent, that he is evil."[12]

The Bible says: "When Jesus heard it, he saith unto them, They that are whole have no need of the physician, but they that are sick: I came not to call the righteous, but sinners to repentance" (Mark 2:17; see also Luke 19:10).

Scientology says: ". . . personal salvation in one lifetime [is] freedom from the cycle of birth and death [reincarnation]. . . . Religious practice of all Faiths is the universal way to Wisdom, Understanding and/or salvation."[13]

The Bible says: "Jesus saith unto him, I am the way, the truth, and the life: no man cometh unto the Father, but by me" (John 14:6; see also Acts 4:12 and Hebrews 2:3).

Eternal Punishment (Hell)

Scientology says: ". . . hell is a total myth, an invention just to make people very unhappy and is a vicious lie."[14]

The Bible says: "Then shall he say also unto them on the left hand, Depart from me, ye cursed, into everlasting fire, prepared for the devil and his angels" (Matthew 25:41). "And these shall go away into everlasting punishment: but the righteous into life eternal" (Matthew 25:46).

"You Shall Know Them by Their Fruits"

"Beware of false prophets, which come to you in sheep's clothing, but inwardly they are ravening wolves. Ye shall know them by their fruits. Do men gather grapes of thorns, or figs of thistles?" (Matthew 7:15–16).

Professor of Philosophy and Bible at Westminster College, Joseph Hopkins, writing in *Christianity Today*, presented a succinct summary of one of the most valid criticisms of Scientology's failure to demonstrate altruistic social concern:

> Another liability of Scientology is its utter lack of social concern. It could hardly be criticized for this omission were it to abandon the pretense of being a religion. But to pose as a church, while neglecting the responsibilities of a church in the community, nation, and world, is reprehensible. Scientology offers society nothing except an expensive and highly dubious method of psycho-therapy, the goal of which is *self*-improvement, *self*-mastery, *personal* happiness. The door to salvation is shut to those who cannot afford to pay the price of processing. Nothing is said about the plight of the poor, the sick, the homeless, the oppressed. . . .

---

[12]*Prof. Aud.*, op. cit.
[13]*Scientology: A World Religion*, op. cit., pp. 16, 35.
[14]*Prof. Aud.*, op. cit.

As Paul deplored the legalism that diverted the Galatian Christians from the doctrine of salvation by faith alone, so evangelicals must deplore those false premises that divert Scientologists from God's grace in Christ: the naive assumption that our human nature is untainted with evil, that man's computer-brain is capable of errorless understanding and judgment, that perfect knowledge automatically produces perfect behavior, that human repentance and divine grace are unnecessary, and above all that God (most Scientologists will grant his existence) is really irrelevant to the human situation.[15]

---

[15]*"Scientology: Religion or Racket?"* in *Christianity Today*, December 21, 1969, p. 12.

Chapter 15

EASTERN RELIGIONS

Rajneeshism, ISKCON and Transcendental Meditation

This book has undertaken to survey some of the major cults that exist and are active in the United States today. During my ministry of more than thirty years in this field of apologetics, I have seen hundreds of smaller cults come and go. During this time, I have observed trends in cultic structures. Often, the fads of society are reflected in the fads of cults or cultic belief. Nowhere is this more evident than in the general American culture's strange preoccupation with anything Eastern or Oriental. This "fad" traces its roots to the appearance of a Hindu guru at the Chicago World's Fair at the turn of the century, although popular interest in Eastern things did not explode in American society until the 1960s and 1970s. From Nehru jackets in the 1960s to tao and the new physics in the 1980s, Eastern influence has pervaded Western society.

The last fifteen years have seen the explosive growth of new-age (or occultic) religious cults with their roots in classic Hindu thought. Today, there are literally hundreds of large and small cults in America with Eastern ideas and practices. In this short summary, we will survey the Hindu roots of these cults and then present a quick look at three of the most well-known imports, Rajneeshism, the International Society for Krishna Consciousness (ISKCON, or Hare Krishnas), and Transcendental Meditation (TM). What follows is a brief history and description of Hinduism and a brief introduction to and doctrinal summary of Rajneeshism, ISKCON and TM.

Hinduism

Hinduism, today, is not the same as Hinduism five thousand years ago. The Hindu religion has evolved over the past five thousand years of Indian religious history. Hinduism seeks to be a synthesis of the various religious ideas and influences from throughout the Indian subcontinent, representing hundreds of separate cultural, social, and tribal groups. The term "Hindu" itself is not indigenous to India. It comes from the Persian designation of the Indus River. Yogi Ramacharaka notes,

> The different Hindu sects, while practically appearing as different re-
> ligions, in reality regard themselves as but different sects and divisions of
> the One Eternal Religion of India, of which each, of course, considers itself
> the best and most favored channel of expression and interpretation.[1]

---

[1]Yogi Ramacharaka, *The Philosophies and Religions of India*, Chicago, IL: The Yogi Publication Society, 1930, pp. 271, 272.

Scripture

The Hindu scriptures were collected over hundreds of years, beginning with the writing of the oral traditions around the last half of the second millenium B.C. These scriptures are known as the *Vedas* ("wisdom" or "knowledge"). The concluding portion of the *Vedas* are called the *Upanishads*, which are a synthesis of Vedic teachings. The general assumptions of the *Upanishads* include a belief in pantheism, karmic retribution, and reincarnation. Perhaps the most well-known section of the *Vedas* is the Hindu epic called the Bhagavad-Gita, which tells the story of the warrior-prince, Arjuna, and his charioteer, Krishna, who is actually the disguised incarnation of the Hindu god Vishnu. The Gita was written down and subsequently modified between 200 B.C. and A.D. 200.

An illustration of the pluralism or contradictory nature of Hinduism is found by comparing the God of the Gita with the God of earlier Vedic literature. God, as described by the Gita, is personal and often sounds even monotheistic (only one God who is personal and not a part of creation exists). However, when one reads earlier Vedic scripture, God is presented as being definitely pantheistic (all of existence is, in some way, divine) and perhaps even monistic (all of existence is one, whether any divinity exists at all). The monotheistic characteristics of the Gita were appropriated by the founder of ISKCON, and consequently ISKCON teaches a more monotheistic rather than pantheistic idea of God today.

Contemporary Hinduism

There are three basic classifications into which the hundreds of Hindu sects can be divided: (1) the abstract monists, who stress the philosophical oneness of the universe instead of religious or theistic ideas; (2) the Vishnuites, who are devoted to the worship (in many different manners) of the god Vishnu (in many different manifestations) as the supreme form of divinity; and (3) the Shivaites, who are devoted to the worship of the god Shiva as the highest manifestation of divinity. TM, with its philosophical concentration, relates to the monistic classification, while ISKCON believes that Krishna, the supreme God, is also known as Vishnu and so they are identified with the Vishnuites. Rajneesh differs from them both in that he is philosophically agnostic and pragmatically Hindu. He has no inhibitions about subjecting Hinduism to any interpretation that fits his presuppositions, particularly in the realm of morality.

World religion expert Professor Ninan Smart notes the problems of the varieties of contemporary Hindu systems:

> It might be asked, by way of conclusion, What is the essence of Hinduism? A hard question. There are orthodox Hindus who deny the existence of God. There are others who while not denying God, relegate him to a second place, as a secondary or illusory phase of the Absolute. Amid such a variety of theological views, what remains as necessary to Hindu belief? Certainly the doctrines of rebirth and that of an eternal soul. The picture of the world as a place where the immortal spirit within man is virtually endlessly implicated in the round of reincarnation has dominated the Indian imagination for about three millenia. In addition, a complex social system has given shape to the actual religion of the subcontinent over a long period.[2]

---

[2]Ninan H. Smart, *The Religious Experience of Mankind*, New York: Charles Scribner's Sons, 1976, pp. 155, 156.

Hindu Beliefs

God. There is no single Hindu idea of God. Hindu concepts of deity can include any of the following: monism (all existence is one substance); pantheism (all existence is divine); panentheism (God is in creation as a soul is in a body); animism (God or gods live in nonhuman objects such as trees, rocks, animals, etc.); polytheism (there are many gods); henotheism (there is one god we worship among the many that exist); and monotheism (there is only one God).

Karma and Samsara. Fundamental to Hindu thought is the idea that all souls are eternal and accountable for their own actions throughout time. Karma refers to the debt of one's bad actions which must be atoned for (through various Hindu systems) in order for one to escape the wheel of *samsara*, or reincarnation (the soul inhabits successive human bodies) or transmigration (the soul inhabits successive bodies—human, animal, or even plants or inanimate objects).

Salvation. The three major paths to Hindu "salvation" include *karma marga* (method), the way of disinterested action; *bhakti marga*, the way of devotion; and *jnana marga*, the path of knowledge or mystical insight. *Jnana marga* achieves self-realization through intuitive awareness and mystical insight. *Bhakti marga* achieves self-realization through ritualistic sacrifice and discipline.

Bhagwan Shree Rajneesh (Rajneeshism)

In terms of media attention and exposure, *Bhagwan Shree* (Sir God) *Rajneesh* (born 1931) has gradually achieved greater notoriety than any living cult leader—with the possible exception of Sun Myung Moon. He is indisputably the preeminent Eastern guru of the 1980s.

In an interview in *Forward* magazine, Eckart Flother, a former follower of Rajneesh, gave an excellent thumbnail sketch of the cult leader's background:

> Rajneesh Chandra Mohan was born on the 11th of December, 1931, in a village in central India, the eldest in a family of five sisters and seven brothers. His childhood was overshadowed by the fact that his father, an unsuccessful businessman, was often on the road. The "father figure" in Rajneesh's life was instead occupied by his grandfather, to whom he became very attached. His grandfather died when he was seven years old. This was a very traumatic experience for young Rajneesh. From then on he felt strangely attracted to the subject of death. In his 1979 diary (which is made public), it is reported that he followed after funerals as other children would follow circuses.
>
> Rajneesh pursued his education and in 1957 obtained a Master of Arts in Philosophy. He proceeded to teach philosophy in two universities between 1957 and 1966. In 1966, Rajneesh resigned from his service as a teacher in order to, as he puts it, concentrate on the wish of God. He felt called to work for the spiritual regeneration of humanity, which he feels is necessary in order to survive the holocaust which he is predicting and fearing.
>
> Rajneesh then became a "master" and called himself "Acharya"[3]

---

[3]"Acharya" means *teacher*.

Rajneesh, and he walked and rode a donkey around India in various states in order to teach people that they have to change their lives and turn around in order to survive.

His mission wasn't very successful, and in 1970 he was a tired and poor man who nevertheless recognized that he possessed charisma and power. In Bombay he decided to gather people around him to whom he could teach his message. As more and more disciples flocked around him, the apartment where he lived was unable to accommodate them. Thus, in 1974 he moved to Poona, 120 miles south of Bombay, rented several houses, and founded his ashram.[4] There he changed his name from Acharya to Bhagwan (which means God), designed orange robes and a wooden bead necklace for his disciples, and started the movement we are dealing with today.

Rajneesh, bald, bearded and photogenic, first attained major media exposure in the U.S. in early 1978 when *Time* magazine featured an article on the guru entitled " 'God Sir' at Esalen East." *Time* magazine reported that the charismatic guru had come into vogue among certain celebrities and prominent apostles of the Human Potential Movement who were joining thousands of other spiritual seekers in making the pilgrimage to Rajneesh's ashram in Poona, India. Rajneesh's appeal stemmed partly from his use of "tantric yoga" (involving nudity and free sex) and partly from his incorporation of a wide variety of popular "psychospiritual" therapies and techniques.

In the late '70s and early '80s, Rajneesh's acclaim continued to spread within the New Age Movement in America, Great Britain, Germany, and nearly every free-world, industrialized nation. With as many as 6,000 Westerners in Poona at a time, the ashram population rose to 10,000 while 500 Rajneesh centers were established in 22 nations by orange and red garbed *Sannyasins*[5] (now more commonly called *Rajneeshees*) returning from Poona to their homelands. As of 1984, Rajneesh had gathered some 350,000 followers, whose average age was 34.

Rajneesh's discourses, which are delivered daily, have been transcribed into over 350 books and diaries which average between $15 and $22 in cost. Video tapes of each discourse range in price between $50 and $170, while audio tapes cost almost $10 each. These are all disseminated by Rajneesh Foundation International, a multimillion dollar corporation. As a follower stated in the film *Ashram*, a documentary on the Rajneesh cult, "The organization understood long ago what powerful energy money is." Rajneesh, whose ever-growing fleet of Rolls Royces numbered more than 70 at the time of this writing, believes that "spirituality is the luxury and privilege of the rich."[6]

Rajneesh is a self-proclaimed spiritual rebel who thrives on the controversy that he has created, first in India, and now in America. Tal Brooke, a former devotee of the popular Indian guru Sathya Sai Baba, after visiting Poona effectively summed up the scene there:

An object of media fascination and horror, Rajneesh is known for his

---

[4]Religious community/monastery.
[5]Initiated disciples. Males take on the title "Swami," and females go by the appellation "Ma."
[6]Russell Chandler and Tyler Marshall, "Guru Brings His Ashram to Oregon," *Los Angeles Times*, August 13, 1981, part 1, p. 14.

bizarre revelations on sex. He has constructed a vision of the New Man that repudiates all prior norms and traditions. Man, by Rajneesh's thinking, is the hedonist-god, fully autonomous (barring the inner voice of Rajneesh), and free to carve out the cosmos in his own image. He is the sovereign pleasure seeker, self-transcender, who owes nobody anything. The family is anathema, children extra trash. And so long as the Neo-sannyasin has the money the fun ride continues. Afterward, however, he or she is usually a nonfunctional casualty. Homicides, rapes, mysterious disappearances, threats, fires, explosions, abandoned ashram children now begging in Poona's streets, drug busts—all done by those amazing hybrids in red who believe they are pioneering new and daring redefinitions of the word "love." Christians working in a Poona asylum confirm such accounts, adding the breakdown rate is so high the ashram has wielded political power to suppress reports.[7]

Rajneesh has often openly expressed hostility toward established religions: "This is a revolution . . . I am burning scriptures here, uprooting traditions . . . unless I am shot I'll not be proved right."[8]

By early 1981, threats on Rajneesh's life were reported. The ashram was heavily guarded, and no one was allowed to enter without first being searched for weapons. Then an ashram warehouse was set on fire, and an explosion was set off near the cult's health center. According to the cult's own account, when an actual attempt on the guru's life was made in February, ashram officials hastened a process (which had already been initiated) of looking for a new headquarters.

According to the reputable magazine *India Today*, however, ". . . both police and . . . officials in [Poona] are unanimous in their charge that the incidents were rigged by Rajneesh followers."[9] Why? The Indian periodical explains that "Disclosures in [Poona] last fortnight revealed that the Rajneesh Foundation was up to its neck in income tax arrears, defalcation with the charities commissioner, a major insurance fraud, and a string of cases for criminal offenses which were still being investigated when they left."[10]

The U.S. Consulate in Bombay issued Rajneesh a visa, and on June 1, 1981, he secretly flew to New York with 17 of his closest disciples.

Since Rajneesh left Poona, his followers spread throughout the West. "In Europe the present strategy is to establish 'Sacred Cities.' The European Newsletter, issue 8, 1981 says: 'A Sannyasin city is to be set up in each major European country. Bhagwan has suggested that the cities should be self-supporting, alternative societies, which will be models of sannyas.' "[11]

In America, efforts were undertaken to create the ultimate "sacred city," one fit for the "master" himself. On July 10, 1981, the Chidvilas Rajneesh Meditation Center of Montclair, New Jersey, purchased the Big Muddy Ranch (where the John Wayne movie *Big Muddy* was filmed) for $6 million ($1.5 million of it in cash) from an investment company in Amarillo, Texas. The land, near Madras, Oregon, covers more than 100 square miles. The Center

[7]"Pied Piper of Poona," *Eternity*, September 1981, p. 14.
[8]*This Is a Revolution*, Bhagwan Shree Rajneesh, Videocassette 18C236, December 28, 1980.
[9]Chander Uday Singh, "Sins of Bhagwan," *India Today*, June 15, 1982.
[10]*Ibid*.
[11]Jens Johansen, "The Master Will Not Speak Again," *New Religious Movements Update*, Vol. 5, No. 3/4, Dec. 1981, p. 81.

also managed to lease 14,889 acres in the same area from the U.S. Bureau of Land Management.

Two hundred Rajneeshees from sixteen Western countries soon flocked to the Big Muddy, and in September they jubilantly welcomed their master to his new home.

Not long after the ranch was purchased, plans were announced to build "America's first enlightened city," which was to be called *Rajneeshpuram* (expression or city of Rajneesh). On November 4, 1981, the Wasco County Commission voted two-to-one to allow an election to be held the following May to determine if the Big Muddy property should be incorporated as a city.

Since the only ones allowed to vote in such an election are those who *live* on the site (in this case, the Rajneeshees), the outcome was predictable: 154 votes in favor of the incorporation of Rajneeshpuram, none opposed. Rajneesh, his followers, and their "enlightened city" have been making headlines ever since.

Working twelve hours a day, seven days a week for no wages (their basic necessities are provided for), the 2,000 members of the Rajneesh Neo-Sannyas International Commune have been appropriately tagged the "red ants" because of their impressive industry and accomplishments. "The Rajneeshees have taken 81,000 acres of rocky, steep, dry and useless land . . . and are building a self-sufficient city complete with dam, substation, parks, housing developments, roads, fields, greenhouses and airport."[12]

From the beginning, the cult's efforts to carve a paradise out of the Oregon desert have been heatedly opposed. The legal status of the city has been challenged on two grounds: (1) that it violates the constitutional separation of church and state, and (2) that the Wasco County Commission's decision to allow an incorporation election violated state land-use zoning laws. At the time of this writing, neither issue had been resolved. A final ruling against the city on either count could result in the dismantling of most of its buildings.

As a security measure in case Rajneeshpuram is disincorporated (to make sure the cult has access to municipal powers and services), the Rajneeshees have politically taken over a nearby town, changing its name from Antelope to Rajneesh. Most of Antelope's original forty residents (mostly elderly), after being subjected to constant observation by the Sannyasin-manned police force, having their taxes tripled to support cult interests, and watching the Rajneesh-dominated city council designate an area within a local park for nude sunbathing, have quit fighting and moved away.

The town has been growing, nonetheless, as Rajneeshees buy existing homes and build new ones.

In the meantime, the Immigration and Naturalization Service (INS) has been "conducting an ongoing investigation into suspected violations of immigration laws and related criminal statutes by the Rajneesh Foundation International and related organizations and/or their members," said Carl Houseman, Portland's INS District Director.[13] Twenty-five to thirty Rajnee-

---

[12]Bill Dietrich, "Conflict Over Rajneeshpuram," Seattle *Times*, Sept. 9, 1984, p. A2.
[13]Win McCormack and Bill Driver, "Rajneeshpuram: Valley of Death?" *Oregon Magazine*, Sept. 1984, p. 26.

shees (including top leaders) are suspected of engaging in "marriages of convenience" between U.S. citizens and foreign nationals. The permanent resident status of Rajneesh himself is also in jeopardy if the INS can prove that his original travel visa was granted on the basis of an exaggerated illness.

It was the takeover of Antelope, in particular, that fed the surrounding communities' worst fears about the cult's political ambitions. The Rajneesh Humanity Trust's "share a home" experiment in the fall of 1984, which imported 3,500 street people to the ranch, was interpreted by most observers as a bold (though abortive) attempt to establish a large enough voting bloc to gain political mastery over Wasco County.

The Rajneeshees eclipsed even the national elections in the Oregon media that November, and "rumor controls" had to be started to quiet runaway fears, such as a concern that the cult was threatening to take over the entire state.

Visions of a Jonestown-like confrontation between the Rajneeshees and governmental authorities, entertained ever since the cult purchased the Big Muddy, have been fueled by Sheela Silverman, Rajneesh's personal secretary and president of Rajneesh Foundation International. The pugnacious Indian disciple, whose word is final in earthly matters, has persistently taken an inflammatory stance.

> In an interview on KGW-TV aired June 29 [1984] . . . Sheela . . . told how she would deal with any attempt to dismantle buildings at Rajneeshpuram. "I will be dead," she said. "I will paint the bulldozers with my blood." Then, in a July 5 article in the *San Francisco Chronicle*, quotations from Sheela implied that she would block any attempt to arrest people at Rajneeshpuram for immigration or other legal violations. "I mean business," Silverman said through (according to the *Chronicle* account) lips trembling with anger. "You will find out what will happen to you if you come here to harm me or Bhagwan or any of my people . . . I'll take things as they come. We are willing to die for human freedom. I have 100 percent support from my people."[14]

While it is uncertain at this time how seriously Sheela's threats are to be taken, there is no doubt that Rajneesh has been inculcating a catastrophic mind-set in his followers. In 1983, the guru published his vision of a worldwide crisis:

> The period of this crisis will be between 1984 and 1999. During this period there will be every kind of destruction on earth including natural catastrophes and man manufactured auto-suicidal efforts. In other words there will be floods which have never been known since the time of Noah, along with earthquakes, volcanic eruptions and everything else that is possible through nature. . . . There will be wars which are bound to end in nuclear explosions, hence no ordinary Noah's arks are going to save humanity. Rajneeshism is creating a Noah's ark of consciousness, remaining centered exactly in the middle of the cyclone.
>
> I say to you that except this [i.e., Rajneeshism] there is no other way.
> Tokyo, New York, San Francisco, Los Angeles, Bombay, etc.—all these cities are going to disappear and the holocaust is not going to be confined

---

[14]*Ibid.*, pp. 30–31.

to certain places. It is going to be global so no escape will be possible. You can only escape within and that's what I teach.[15]

In early 1984, Rajneesh further expounded his vision of impending disaster by specifying that, in supposed fulfillment of a prediction made by Nostradamus, Acquired Immune Deficiency Syndrome (AIDS) will kill two-thirds of the world's population.

As the quote above indicates, Rajneesh perceives himself as a Savior, comparable (indeed, even superior) to Jesus. The key to understanding his sense of mission is discovered in these anticipated global catastrophes. He is hurriedly attempting to build his "Noah's ark of consciousness" in his followers, before mankind destroys itself. He teaches that "A revolution in human consciousness is no more a luxury, it has become an absolute need as there are only two alternatives—suicide or a quantum leap in consciousness which Nietzsche called Superman."[16]

When asked if Rajneeshees would survive the predicted nuclear holocaust, Rajneesh replied:

> . . . monkeys took a jump and became human beings, but not all monkeys did. The remaining ones are still monkeys. . . .
> I will not say that Rajneeshees will survive the holocaust, but I can say with an absolute guarantee that those who will survive will be the Rajneeshees and the remaining will be monkeys [i.e., humans who did not evolve into "Superman"] or commit suicide. In fact, *the remaining don't matter*[17] (emphasis ours).

Since Rajneesh believes he is the only "Awakened One" on the face of the earth, he also believes he is the only one capable of orchestrating this "quantum leap in consciousness" to save the race. Therefore, all of "Bhagwan's work is directed toward creating the circumstances for this change of consciousness to take place."[18]

Rajneeshpuram, then, can be viewed as a colossal human experiment: the "enlightened Master" trying to create the conditions and spiritual energy (*Buddhafield*, as Rajneesh calls it) necessary to give birth to a super race. Those who cannot or will not fit in with this group "don't matter." All that really matters is that the spiritual aspirations of Bhagwan Shree Rajneesh for mankind be fulfilled.

And what is the spirituality upon which these aspirations are based? Even the briefest exposure to Rajneesh's teachings makes it explicitly clear that "Rajneeshism" is in every respect hostile to the Christian faith. Consider the following samplings from his discourses.

> You can be a Christ: Why be a Christian?[19]
> Let *me* be your death and resurrection.[20]

---

[15]Bhagwan Shree Rajneesh, *Rajneeshism*, An Introduction to Bhagwan Shree Rajneesh and his Religion (Rajneeshpuram, Oregon: Rajneesh Foundation International, 1983), pp. 56–57.

[16]Rajneesh, *Rajneeshism*, op. cit., p. 60.

[17]*Ibid.*, p. 61.

[18]*Ibid.*, p. 15.

[19]The quote cited is the title of Videotape 18C144, September 2, 1980.

[20]*Discourses on the Sufi Way*, quoted in the *Victor Valley Daily Press*, September 18, 1981, p. B3.

Nobody is a sinner. Even while you are in the darkest hole of your life, you are still divine; you cannot lose your divinity. I tell you, there is no need for salvation, it is within you.[21]

... disobedience is not a sin, but a part of growth.[22]

God is neither a he nor a she ... if you say he is a she, I will say he is a he and if you say he is a he, I will say he is a she ... *whatsoever your belief is, I'm going to destroy it.* ..[23] (emphasis ours).

If [Jesus] had a little intelligence and rationality he would not have gone [to Jerusalem and the cross]. But then, there was no need [for Him] to declare [that He was] the Messiah and Son of God. . . . Those messiahs are basically insane. He believed totally that crucifixion is going to prove him right, that's why I believe there was a hidden current of suicidal intent. . . . If anyone is responsible for the crucifixion, he himself is responsible. He asked for it. And no Jewish source or contemporary source says there was resurrection. Only the New Testament. It is fictitious. There was no resurrection.[24]

The argument the devil gave Eve was that God wants you to remain ignorant. . . . He is jealous. And it makes sense, because the Jewish God is very jealous. He doesn't want them to become equal. This is not a loving father. . . . Knowledge is not a sin ... I counsel you to eat of the tree of knowledge. . . .[25]

To anyone who takes biblical teaching seriously, the above quotes unmask once and for all the true spirit underlying and driving Rajneesh and his "religion" (1 Tim. 4:1–6; Matt. 24:2, 4, 5, 23–24; 7:15).

... every spirit that does not confess Jesus is not from God; and this is the spirit of antichrist, of which you have heard that it is coming, and now it is already in the world (1 John 4:3).

It would seem evident that the same spiritual power that spoke through the serpent in the Garden of Eden speaks through Rajneesh freely. He appears to be unreservedly given over to it. The danger that this fact portends for the thousands of sincere seekers of truth who now adoringly sing to Rajneesh "I place my heart, my heart, in your hand"[26] is a matter demanding serious prayer from the concerned Christian.

The ultimate significance which Rajneesh and his followers attach to their experiment at Rajneeshpuram could lead to violent confrontation if the government determines to step in and dismantle their dream. And, far from being "centered exactly in the middle of the cyclone," Rajneesh's "ark of consciousness" is fated to capsize in the storm of God's judgment against man's idolatry (e.g., Rev. 16:17–21). Those who have naively fled to him for refuge will, instead, find themselves swept up in the consequences of his own extreme rebellion and blasphemy.

Sannyasins, and especially those more reachable seekers who are con-

---

[21]*Sannyas*, April, 1978, p. 18.
[22]*Jesus, Buddha: Their Days Are Finished*, Videocassette 18C321 and 18C322, March 7, 1981.
[23]*He or She? On Beliefs—The Book of the Books VI*, Videocassette 18S133, April 22, 1980.
[24]Bhagwan Shree Rajneesh in a discourse given to 30 disciples at Rajneeshpuram, Nov. 12, 1984.
[25]*Ibid.*
[26]Dietrich, "Conflict over Rajneeshpuram," *op. cit.*, p. B3.

sidering, but have not yet made a commitment to Rajneesh, need to be alerted to the true antihuman, antichrist nature of his teachings, and pointed instead to the *biblical* Jesus, who is as different from Rajneesh as light is from darkness.

Eckart Flother is the only person, known to date, who, after his conversion to Christ, confronted Rajneesh. His own words are, to say the least, compelling:

> In July, right as I was getting more deeply involved with the ashram, I had a very extraordinary experience. On one of those hot, humid Indian nights filled with mosquitos, I was sitting in my hotel room and reading Rabi Maharaj's book, *Death of a Guru*. Suddenly I saw a brilliantly shining being standing in the hotel room, and He said to me with a mighty voice, "I want you to become my disciple." I immediately understood that Jesus had called me, yet I really didn't know what to do with it.
>
> I went to Rajneesh and told him what had happened to me. As I was talking to him about this experience, I could feel a kind of very warm energy or light radiating from me and I saw that Rajneesh was very irritated, and even startled as he looked at me. He was unable to speak. At that moment I could see that he was not a master like Jesus Christ, as he claims. It was at this time I decided to become a disciple of Jesus.

Flother left Rajneeshism and today devotes considerable time to helping people escape from the system which imprisoned him both spiritually and mentally.

How to Reach the Sannyasins for Christ[27]

In seeking to communicate with sannyasins from the Christian standpoint, there is the obvious difficulty of their not wanting to use their minds, not wanting to think objectively about what they are experiencing. The more they have progressed within the movement, the more difficult this becomes. Are there any means of approaching them in which one can get them to think critically about what they are experiencing, and to look objectively at what Rajneesh is doing to them and to others?

E.F.: I found by working with people who wanted to get out that any logical or rational argument does not help at first.

The approach that I have found useful is to create an emotional situation, such as helping them to recall a childhood situation in the family, or a situation where they felt they needed privacy (which they don't have in the ashram), or a situation where they helped others. I have advised parents and friends to recreate a situation where they showed charity to others. Reliving this normally creates an emotional outburst, a flashback of a previous experience, which is called "snapping back."

After this I have found that I can talk to them on a rational level again, and most of them shake their heads as if to say, "I must have been in a long, long dream."

So one has to first create a situation where they can feel something very deeply that they felt before joining the movement, in order to help them to

---

[27]Vol. 5, No. 1, Spring 1982, *Forward* magazine. Eckart Flother's responses are indicated by his initials EF.

go back and become whole again. Then let them ask questions, because normally they say, "Where am I? What was happening?" and they have many questions. Then one can come with a message.

The best approach is not to criticize at first what Rajneesh was doing, but to go through the differences between his teaching and that of Jesus Christ point-by-point and show the ways in which the teachings of both cope with reality. In this way one can help people make up their minds by themselves, and not impose a certain belief system on them.

So you find criticizing Rajneesh or coming against his philosophy in a direct manner is not effective?

E.F.: Not in the first attempt, because one has to realize that Rajneesh was, in effect, the foundation of their lives, and his belief system was their structure of reference. So if one starts stripping his foundation out from under them, it could be considered dangerous, and no sannyasin would be likely to go for it.

To criticize Rajneesh and his system can be left to the man or woman who comes out, because he or she will find out sooner or later what has happened. If this critical attitude is not appearing two or three weeks after the person has left the movement, it will be important to initiate criticism, but not at first.

What are the needs of an individual coming out of involvement with this cult?

E.F.: It is very important that the family and friends create a very strong and loving support system. It is important that somebody who has been with Rajneesh not only feels supported, loved, and wanted by family and friends, but *needed* as well. They need to feel that they have not only been missing something, but that they've been *missed*.

A second important point I've found is that one of the reasons why people leave their families and join Rajneesh is because their parents and friends very often pretended that everything was all right, and nobody had a problem. So parents, family members, and friends must share their problems in dealing with life, and their struggles in coping with reality, to show that they are human too. It is important that somebody who comes out realizes that to be human means to be imperfect. It means to have problems and not always know how to resolve them.

Above all, not only the sannyasins but also their families and friends must realize that our problems can only be *ultimately* resolved through a personal relationship with Jesus Christ. *He* has the answers that we so often lack.

ISKCON (Hare Krishnas)

The second major Hindu sect is ISKCON, a modern school of Vishnu Hinduism which developed from the fifteenth century teachings of a man named Chaitanya, who instituted worship of Vishnu as God against the prevailing local worship of Shiva. Chaitanya taught that Krishna was the supreme personality of the Godhead.

ISKCON itself began in the 1960s in New York City, founded by the Vishnu yogi His Divine Grace Abhay Charan De Bhaktivedanta Swami Prabhupada, born in Calcutta, India, in 1896. Hare Krishnas, the followers of

ISKCON, are well-known today in America for their fund-raising activities through public solicitation and their public *sankirtanas*, or spiritual chanting.

ISKCON Beliefs

God. Although the bulk of Hindu scripture is pantheistic (everything is a part of God), portions of the Hindu scripture, notably the Bhagavad-Gita, are basically monotheistic presentations of Hinduism. Hinduism, in seeking to be a synthesis of a variety of Indian thought and belief, contains within its vast scripture tradition a variety of beliefs about God, even though those beliefs may contradict one another. Since the Bhagavad-Gita, which implies a form of monotheism, is the most sacred scripture to ISKCON, we find that the ISKCON belief in God is essentially monotheistic, and Krishna is said to be the supreme personality of the Godhead. Any incarnation of the one God is an incarnation of Krishna: "ALL the lists of the incarnations of Godhead are either plenary expansions or parts of the plenary expansions of the Lord, but Lord Sri Krsna is the original Personality of Godhead Himself."[28]

Christ. To ISKCON, Jesus Christ is Krishna's Son, but in a position no more unique to God than any other man could strive to attain. To the Hare Krishna, then, Jesus Christ is not the unique Son of God, God manifest in the flesh. He is not an incarnation of Krishna.

Salvation. Salvation in ISKCON is obtained by removing one's karmic debt through devotion to Krishna and right actions through multiple incarnations: "All these performers who know the meaning of sacrifice become cleansed of sinful reactions, and, having tasted the nectar of the remnants of such sacrifices, they go to the supreme eternal atmosphere."[29] ISKCON also says, "From the body of any person who claps and dances before the Deity, showing manifestations of ecstacy, all the birds of sinful activities fly away upwards."[30]

TM (Transcendental Meditation)

TM is a spiritual practice or yoga which was first introduced to the Western world by its founder, Maharishi Mahesh Yogi, as a religious exercise or philosophy. Encountering skepticism from nonreligious Westerners, Maharishi revamped his TM program. In the 1970s, he promoted the movement as a scientifically sound, nonreligious psychological exercise designed to relieve stress, to bring peace to the inner man, thereby having a positive effect on society, and to enable the advanced practitioner to participate in astral projection (his soul leaving his body) and levitation.

TM still wears its secular label in its own promotions today, and most Westerners are unaware of its religious presuppositions and nature.

---

[28]Siddha Swarup Ananda Goswami, *Jesus Loves KRSNA*, Vedic Christian Committee and Life Force, Krsan Yoga Viewpoint, 1975, p. 14.
[29]A. C. Bhaktivedanta Swami Prabhupada, *Bhagavad-Gita As It Is*, New York: The Bhaktivedanta Book Trust, 1968, p. 81.
[30]Prabhupada, *The Nectar of Devotion*, New York: The Bhaktivedanta Book Trust, 1970, p. 75.

TM Beliefs

God. TM concentrates on those Hindu scriptures which present a pantheistic view of God. Therefore, God in TM is pantheistic, and one's goal is to lose his own personality in the oneness of God. This also, of course, takes away from the unique and separate personality of God: "Being is the living presence of God, the reality of life. It is eternal truth. It is the absolute in eternal freedom."[31]

Jesus Christ. TM ignores Jesus Christ almost totally, although Maharishi teaches that anyone can become as enlightened as Jesus Christ through the application of TM techniques. It is clear from his neglect of Jesus Christ and from his world view that he does not consider Jesus Christ to be the unique Son of God, God manifest in the flesh (see, for example, Maharishi Mahesh Yogi, *Meditation of Maharishi Mahesh Yogi*, pp. 123, 124).

Salvation. Salvation in TM is accomplished by realizing that one is in union with the Creative Intelligence: "The answer to every problem is that there is no problem. Let a man perceive this truth and then he is without problems."[32] This realization comes through practicing the meditations of TM: ". . . a huge mountain of sins extending for miles is destroyed by Union brought about through transcendental meditation, without which there is no way out."[33] Salvation is almost a misnomer, since one is not truly a sinner, but just forgetful of his oneness with the divine.

Conclusion

There are hundreds of other Eastern groups. Rajneeshism, ISKCON, and TM have served as just three examples of Eastern thought. For further information on Eastern groups and Hinduism in general, the reader is directed to the bibliography.

In conclusion, Hinduism, for all of its diversity and contradictions, is not compatible with Christianity. In all its forms, Hinduism denies the biblical Trinity, the Deity of Christ, the doctrines of the atonement, sin, and salvation by grace through the sacrifice of Jesus Christ. It replaces resurrection with reincarnation, and both grace and faith with human works. One cannot, then, achieve peace with God through Hinduism or any of its sects. C. S. Lewis wisely observed that at the end of all religious quests one must choose between Hinduism and Christianity; the former absorbs all others and the latter excludes them. Peace with God is not achieved by looking inside oneself but by looking up to Him of whom Moses and the prophets did write—Jesus of Nazareth, the Son and Christ of God.

---

[31]Maharishi Mahesh Yogi, *The Science of Being and the Art of Living*, New York: The New American Library, 1968, p. 22.
[32]Maharishi Mahesh Yogi, *Maharishi Mahesh Yogi on the Bhagavad-Gita*, New York: Penguin Books, 1967, p. 257.
[33]*Ibid.*, p. 299.

Chapter 16

ISLAM: THE MESSAGE OF MUHAMMED

Islam is not a cult, but a major world religion distinctly different from Christianity. Only cults were included in this book's original edition. Since then, the West has experienced an unanticipated invasion—Islam. Mosques are springing up in many "Christian" areas, and if you live in a city, you probably live near several Muslims. Unfortunately, most Christians understand very little about Islamic teaching and are afraid to witness to them. This chapter will help you prepare to talk with the Muslims you meet.

"There is no god but Allah, and Muhammed is the prophet of Allah" is the great *Shahada,* or "confession," which faithful Muslims around the world declare daily. This declaration of faith effectively distinguishes Muslims from every other world religion, including Christianity and Judaism. Between 400 and 700 million people worldwide claim Allah as their God and Muhammed as their prophet. Islam is one of the four largest religions in the world, along with Christianity, Judaism, and Hinduism. In this short survey of Islam, we will define the most important terms of this religion, mention its most prominent sects and summarize its basic teaching contrasted to biblical Christianity. We will also give some practical advice for sharing the gospel with a Muslim.

Millions of people embrace the Islamic faith. Entire countries are ruled and dominated by Islamic teachings, practices, and laws. Much of the Western world is dependent on Islamic nations for a major portion of its petroleum needs. Western towns, universities, and businesses are seeing a larger influx of Muslims than has ever been seen before. Islam is a religious, social, and political force which every American should be aware of.

Western Christians, especially, need to equip themselves to give an active defense of the biblical faith against the claims of Islam, and to share the gospel of Jesus Christ in love with followers of Muhammed. Aware of this challenge, let us begin our survey of Islam.

Definitions

Islam, like many religions, has its own vocabulary to describe its beliefs. A quick look at some of the most important religious terms in Islam will provide a basis for further discussion of Islamic history and belief.

Islam[1] is the name of the religion which came out of the revelations and teachings of Muhammed. Islam is the Arabic term for "submission."

Muslim[2] is the name given to one who adheres to the religion of Islam.

---

[1]Since there is no standardized method of transliterating Arabic script into Roman script, one often finds Islamic terms spelled in a variety of ways (e.g., Muhammed, Mohammed; Moslem, Muslim, etc.). We have chosen to use the spelling most popular with Muslims who write in English.

[2]It is incorrect to refer to a Muslim as a "Mohammedan." Muslims have a strong aversion to anything resembling idol worship. If a Muslim would accept the appelation "Mohammedan," he would think that he could be accused of worshiping Mohammed.

Muslim is an Arabic cognate of Islam, and means "one who submits." The Muslim submits to the will of Allah as revealed by Muhammed. *Allah* is the Islamic name for God and cannot be translated easily into English. One Muslim writer defined it thusly: "The word means the unique God Who possesses all the attributes of perfection and beauty in their infinitude. Muslims feel strongly that the English word 'God' does not convey the real meaning of the word 'Allah.' "[3] *Muhammed* was the common name of an Arabic man born in the city of Mecca in A.D. 570 (d. A.D. 632). He claimed that he was the prophet to restore true religion and the praise of Allah throughout the world, just as Jesus Christ was a prophet in his time for his people. Muhammed means "the one who is praised."

Quran (also spelled *Koran*) is Arabic for "the recitation," and refers to the collection of revelations supposedly given by Allah through his archangel to Muhammed and preserved as the Islamic scripture. Muslims believe in the Law of Moses, the Psalms of David, and the *Injil,* or gospel of Jesus Christ. However, they believe that those scriptures were superseded by the scripture given through Muhammed, and that the Bible used by Christians and Jews is a distorted version of those other scriptures. Wherever the Bible contradicts Islam, the Muslim says the Bible is incorrect. *Surah* refers to the divisions within the Quran, and roughly corresponds to our "chapter." The Quran contains 114 revelations, each composing one surah or chapter. The shortest revelations appear first, the longest ones last. There is no chronological arrangement in the Quran. Also important in Islamic literature is the *Hadith,* Arabic for the "collected traditions." These customs provide source material for the intricate political and social structure of Islam. *Caliph* is Arabic for leader and refers to the main leaders of Islam, especially the immediate successors of Muhammed. *Ayatollah* refers to a spiritual master or leader in Islam.

Sects of Islam

Out of the 400 to 700 million Muslims worldwide, by far the greatest number are members of the Sunnite sect. They accept the four caliphs in direct succession from Muhammed and no others. The Sunnis practice a moderate form of Islamic interpretation. Ninety percent of the Muslims in the Mideast are Sunnis (e.g., 90% of the Egyptian Muslims, 90% of the Jordanian Muslims, 90% of the Saudi Arabian Muslims, 98% of the Libyan Muslims).

The second largest sect of Islam is the Shia'ite sect. Although much smaller than the Sunnite sect, the Shia'ite sect is much more literal in its interpretation and application of the Quran and is much more militant and fanatical than the Sunnis. Ninety-three percent of Iran's Muslims are Shia'ites, led by the most powerful Shia'ite Ayatollah, Khoumeni (var. sp.).

Another Muslim sect of note is the Ahmdiyan sect, which was founded in the 1800s. This small sect has produced the bulk of Islamic apologetics against Christianity and Judaism over the last forty years. The Ahmdiyans are highly visible on American campuses and practice strong proselytizing techniques on American students.

---

[3]Badru D. Kateregga, with David W. Shenk, *Islam and Christianity*, Grand Rapids, MI: William B. Eerdmans Publishing Company, 1980, p. 1.

The Sufi sect is the mystical sect of Islam. Sufis are rejected by many conservative Muslims. Some Sufi writings seem to reject the strict unitarian monotheism of traditional Islam for a form of "immanent pantheism."

Islamic Beliefs

At first glance, Islamic belief appears to be almost compatible with Christianity and/or Judaism. Often people claim that the Muslims believe in the same God as Christians: "They just don't accept Jesus Christ." However, as we shall see, the Muslim God is not like the Christian God. Islam rejects the biblical doctrines of the Trinity and the Deity of Christ.

God

For the Muslim, Allah is the only true God. There is no such blasphemous thing as the "Trinity." Jesus Christ is a prophet of Allah; he is not the Son of God or God himself (Surah 4:171). The Muslim God is unapproachable by sinful man. He is so perfect and holy He can only communicate with mankind through a progression of angels and prophets. The Muslim God is a god of judgment, not grace; a god of wrath rather than love. The Muslim's desire is to submit to the point where he can hold back the judging arm of Allah and, perhaps, through the capricious whim of Allah, inherit eternal life in an earthly paradise of gluttony and sexual gratification. Muslims have no concept of God as a loving and compassionate Father.

Jesus Christ

As we mentioned above, Jesus Christ to the Muslim is just one of many prophets of Allah. Jesus Christ was the prophet for His people in His day. The prophet Muhammed supercedes Jesus Christ. Jesus Christ is not the Son of God or a part of any Trinity. Jesus Christ did not atone for anyone's sins, although He was himself sinless. Jesus Christ did not die on the cross. Various Muslim traditions say that He either miraculously substituted Judas Iscariot for himself on the cross, or that God miraculously delivered Him from the hands of the Romans and Jews before He could be crucified. Most Muslims believe that Jesus Christ was taken bodily into heaven without having died (Surah 4:157).

Sin and Salvation

Sin and salvation in Islam is associated with two concepts: works and fate (*kismet*). Every Muslim who hopes to escape the judgment of Allah must fulfill the works of the Five Pillars of the Faith (Surah 10:109). These include: (1) Recitation of the Shahadah ("There is no god but Allah and Muhammed is the prophet of Allah"); (2) Five daily prescribed prayers (*Salat* or *Namaz*) in Arabic. These prayers include genuflection and prostration in the direction of the holy city, Mecca; (3) Almsgiving (*Zakat*), which is unlike tithing since Muslims are only required to give one-fortieth of their income as charitable contributions; (4) Fasting (*Saum* or *Ruzeh*) during the entire month of Romadan, when Muslims are supposed to fast from all food and drink from sunrise to sunset in atonement for their own sins over the previous year (However, after sunset many Muslims enjoy a feast and some get up before sunrise to eat some more before the sun rises and the fast begins again); and (5) A pilgrimage (*Hajj*) to Mecca, the holy city at least once in a Muslim's lifetime.

Holy War (*Jihad*) used to be a condition of faith, and early Muslims believed it was their sacred duty to murder anyone who would not embrace the one true faith. Contemporary Islam is much more moderate, although some Shia'ites talk of restoring *Jihad* as one of the essentials of Islamic faith.

Sharing the Gospel with a Muslim

The three key topics of discussion between a Christian and a Muslim should be the nature of God, the identity and Deity of Jesus Christ, and salvation by grace alone apart from works. Christians can share with Muslims that the Christian God transcends man's finitude and sinfulness because He cares about people individually, and He loves individuals. Divine love is a concept missing from Islam and yet essential to human peace and happiness with God. A powerful witness of Scripture to God's love is John 3:16: "For God so loved the world, that he gave his only begotten Son, that whosoever believeth in him should not perish, but have everlasting life." When told about Jesus, many Muslims will refuse to listen, claiming that our scriptures are distorted and untrustworthy. The Christian can refer the interested Muslim to the many fine Christian volumes available showing the inerrancy and inspiration of the Bible, both Old and New Testaments. (See Authority of the Scriptures Bibliography.) This can provide a foundation for the Christian to present the New Testament teaching that Jesus Christ is truly God and is the only way to salvation (see the chapter on Jehovah's Witnesses for a thorough discussion of the Deity of Christ).

Next, tell the Muslim the good news that salvation and peace with God does not depend on his own insufficient efforts, but on the grace of God displayed through the atonement of Jesus Christ on the cross. No one can work his way to heaven (or Muslim paradise). The Muslim will agree that Allah could justly choose to bar all men from paradise since no man is perfect as Allah is perfect. However, *biblical* salvation does not depend on man's imperfections. Biblical salvation depends on the work and love of God. "For by grace are ye saved through faith; and that not of yourselves; it is the gift of God: not of works, lest any man should boast" (Eph. 2:8–10).

Finally, the Christian should love the Muslim. Muslims have a definite zeal for God. They desire to follow God and express their worship of God through their lives. The Christian should respect Muslims' sincere intentions and share with them the life-changing gospel of Jesus Christ. When a Christian can demonstrate the power of the Word of God through the Holy Spirit, and use his own life as an example of the joy and peace possible to those who love Jesus Christ, he becomes an effective example to the Muslim of the opportunity to know and worship the true God rather than Muhammed's distorted concepts about God.

Chapter 17

THE CULTS ON THE WORLD MISSION FIELDS

We have observed in our study of the various cults that the cults are particularly effective among those in whom the early seeds of Christianity have previously been planted. It is much easier for them, therefore, to promulgate their doctrines among young Christians, nominal Christians, and those who have only a passing acquaintance with the Scriptures. Throughout the United States, the various non-Christian cults are in evidence everywhere; they boldly advertise themselves and eagerly covet the one great prize that all of them desperately seek—prestige and recognition as "Christians." This, however, is not always the case, especially on the foreign mission field, and it is with this area that we shall now briefly concern ourselves.

In the summer of 1958 it was the privilege of the author to be a part of the Pastor's Conference Team of World Vision Incorporated, then headed by Dr. Bob Pierce. These conferences were specifically designed to meet the needs of pastors, missionaries, and Christian workers on the various foreign mission fields of Asia and Africa. In the course of this tour of some 25,000 miles, I had opportunity to meet and speak to over 5,000 dedicated Christian workers and students on the problem of non-Christian cults on those mission fields. Beginning in Japan with the largest pastors' conference in Japanese church history (1560 persons), we journeyed through Formosa, Hong Kong, Singapore, Thailand, Burma, India and Ghana, Africa. At the conclusion of the African meetings I had the opportunity to travel throughout Europe, meeting and interviewing Christian workers there, so it was possible for me to get a fairly well-rounded picture of what the various cults were doing in these specific locales. I returned to Europe in 1961 to lecture on the cults, and then interviewed missionaries whose work ranged from Scandanavia through Germany, Switzerland, Italy, Belgium, Holland and France. I traveled in most of these countries and gathered first-hand impressions which gave me the theological pulse of cultism in Europe.

A few things emerged very clearly from this unprecedented opportunity, which Dr. Pierce made possible, as well as from my subsequent European trip. I say unprecedented, because never before in the history of Christian missions has any researcher in the field of cults been able to visit so many mission fields in so short a time (two and one-half months), delivering lectures and gathering information on a subject about which very little is known. In the course of my travels I learned much about cult methodology on the mission fields, and in contrast to our previous statements concerning their activities in the United States, the cults generally are happy to remain virtually anonymous, until they have established a bridgehead. This is important in an area where a work has already begun or has been functioning for many years. One missionary explained to me that young converts in particular, were the prey of such cults as Jehovah's Witnesses and Mormonism, two of the most virulent strains of non-Christian cults, and a duo which are found on practically every major mission area throughout all of the continents of the world. In addition to their evangelical endeavors, the cults specialize in reaching people in their own language and it is here that the printing establishments of Jehovah's Witnesses, the Mormons and the Unity School of Christianity are revealed at their effective best. The average missionary who encounters a Jehovah's Witness in Japan, for instance, can expect to find copies of *The Watchtower* and *Awake* magazines translated into the language of the people and dutifully mailed from cult headquarters in Brooklyn, New York. There is also the very real problem of literature to combat these movements; literature which itself must, by the very nature of cult propaganda, also be in the language of the country in question and such literature today is virtually unobtainable. At the Japanese conference many hours were consumed, both in the lecture period and in private counseling sessions with missionaries and native pastors, explaining the vulnerable areas of cult theology and in turn, gleaning much valuable information on the tactics of cults abroad.

We learned that Jehovah's Witnesses were making an attempt to convince people that their own translation of the Bible (*The New World Translation*) is "the latest American translation," and should be accepted in questionable areas of theology as "the best and most recent rendering of the original languages."

The informed person, of course, knows that the Watchtower's translation is accepted as sound *only* by the Watchtower and those who have not carefully checked its many perverted renderings. But when one is 15,000 miles from home, laboring among people of a foreign tongue, and generally beset by the pressing problems of hostile indigenous religions (Buddhism, Islam, Shintoism, Taoism, Confucianism, Hinduism, etc.), it is difficult to check these things. And the Watchtower eagerly supplies *their* Bible to all interested persons, converts and pagans alike—something the Christian Church has found it difficult to accomplish, even in the twentieth century.

The startling growth of Jehovah's Witnesses, and the astronomical figures in publishing and distribution that the Watchtower yearly accomplishes, can only be appreciated when one sees a mission field, literally inundated by tracts, pamphlets, Bibles, books and magazines, all stamped Brooklyn, New York, U.S.A.! The world today is hungry to read, and the underdeveloped countries of Asia and Africa will read anything, even Watchtower propaganda, which appears as a torrent in comparison with the trickle of Christian literature currently in circulation.

It also became apparent while questioning missionaries, that many of them are disturbed by the fact that Watchtower people always seemingly have enough literature to proselytize Christian converts, but the missionary has little, if any, literature which will answer such cultists, much less evangelize them or their converts.

A chart of growth for Jehovah's Witnesses over four recent years illustrates the growing danger of the major cults today.

This information has been compiled from the Watchtower's own publications and one cannot but be astounded at their steady growth and the dedication of their members, of whom those who contributed extraordinary amounts of volunteer door-to-door "missionary" time are called "Kingdom Publishers."

GROWTH COMPARISONS FOR JEHOVAH'S WITNESS PUBLISHERS AND BAPTISMS

Year	Average # of publishers	% change from previous year	Total baptisms	% change from previous year
1978	513,673	− 3.15	20,469	− 26.9
1979	521,370	+ 1.50	26,958	+ 31.7
1980	543,457	+ 4.24	27,811	+ 3.16
1981	563,453	+ 3.68	28,496	+ 2.46

From the above chart, Christian Missions can draw little comfort, and Christian Bible colleges, institutes and seminaries would do well to consider the ramifications of such rapid growth, since very little, if anything, is being done to prepare missionaries and ministers to meet these problems, either at home or on the field of world missions.

When we remember that approximately 33 per cent of the membership of Jehovah's Witnesses reside in the United States, and almost 67 per cent on the mission field, the gravity of the problem which confronts the Christian Church is apparent to all but the most adamantly obtuse.

The Witnesses in 1975, at their worldwide communion service known as their Memorial, numbered 4,550,459 persons, as over against 1,553,909 persons in 1961, a total increase of almost 3,000,000 persons!

It is no wonder that many missionaries are discouraged and that in the United States an increasing number of pastors are beginning to share that discouragement. This stems from the fact that a cult so obviously non-Christian as Jehovah's Witnesses, is becoming increasingly successful in its missionary outreach, particularly in the field of literature, when both clergy and missionary representing the historic Gospel of Jesus Christ find little or no support in this vital area of literary mass evangelism.

The Watchtower Society has not restricted itself, however, to just the publication of literature on the mission field. Their two-by-two doorstep evangelism has become the plague of the British Commonwealth, most of the countries of Europe, Asia and Africa.

The Worldwide Growth of the Watchtower Bible & Tract Society

Total amount of fieldwork for 1975:

28,410,783　Books and Bibles placed in homes
12,163,807　Booklets placed in homes

293,705,005 *Watchtowers* and *Awakes* placed in homes
155,336,481 Calls back to interested families
  1,411,256 Home Bible Studies conducted
382,296,208 Hours in America spent in proslytizing efforts

Watchtower missionaries also have made it extremely difficult for Christian missions throughout the various trouble spots of the world, such as East Germany, Africa, Japan, Indonesia, Viet Nam and Cuba, by emphasizing their rigid anti-government stand, based upon their theological presupposition that all governments are under the direct supervision of Satan and are opposed to the theocracy rule of Jehovah. It is unnecessary to observe that since they identify themselves as Christian, utilize the Bible and vocabulary of Christianity, those who are by nature hostile to the Christian message, and who are seeking only the opportunity to persecute it and restrict its activities, seize upon the Watchtower organization's many statements that to them, at least, seem to incite disloyalty to governmental authority, as well as a militant pacifism and allegiance to a theocracy, in place of the individual nation.

The Watchtower Society seems totally oblivious to the thirteenth chapter of Romans and its demand that "every soul be subject unto the higher powers, for the powers that be are ordained of God." And for the average Jehovah's Witness, all governments and all forms of supposed Christianity, except his own, are enemies to be harassed, vilified and condemned as tools of Satan. This hardly makes for good public relations, and in the fervent spirit of emerging nationalism, particularly in the so-called underdeveloped countries of the world, those in authority have taken a rather dim view of the Watchtower's activities, resulting in their persecution of true disciples of the cross, who suffer because of the Watchtower's identification, albeit mistaken, with Biblical Christianity.

All in all, Jehovah's Witnesses are a growing concern everywhere and a challenge to evangelical Christianity, which desires to win them to a redemptive knowledge of Jesus Christ and in the process, to give every man an answer, "a reason for the hope that is in us—Christ in you, the hope of glory" (1 Peter 3:15; Colossians 1:27).

Mormon Missionary Efforts

Even surpassing the Jehovah's Witnesses is the rapidly burgeoning missionary effort of the Church of Jesus Christ of Latter-day Saints (Mormon).

Boasting a missionary force approaching 23,000 full-time workers, and bolstered by a church whose gross income last year was well over 1 billion dollars, the Mormon cult is moving at a rapid pace, particularly in its new mission fields of South America and Africa.

The following chart demonstrates the growth of Mormon missions over the last few years and should suffice to remind us that Jehovah's Witnesses are not the only cult which competes with Christianity on a large scale on most of the large mission fields.

The Growth of the Mormon Church

1900	268,331
1910	393,437
1920	526,032
1930	672,488
1940	862,664
1950	1,111,314
1960	1,693,180
1962	1,965,786
1975	3,700,000
1982	5,000,000+

Mormon missionary work far surpasses that of the Jehovah's Witnesses, and together the missionary efforts of the two cults present a real and present danger to the spread of the true gospel throughout the world today.

The methodology of Mormon missionaries is similar in many respects to that of Jehovah's Witnesses. They, too, are door-to-door canvassers and tireless, round-the-clock "back-callers," on contacts previously made either by themselves or by those missionaries who preceded them. Mormon missionaries, unlike those of the Jehovah's Witnesses, come fully equipped with slick multi-media presentations and free copies of the *Book of Mormon, Doctrine and Covenants* and *Pearl of Great Price*, the sacred books which they believe "properly interpret" the Bible. Whereas the Jehovah's Witnesses will emphasize the absolute authority of the Scriptures as a supreme criterion for truth, the Mormons will hedge at this juncture, maintaining that the Bible is the Word of God insofar as it is "correctly translated." They will insist gently, but firmly, that the *Book of Mormon* and the other two sacred books "throw light upon the Bible, and explain the Bible in the light of restored Christianity and the ministry of the prophet, Joseph Smith." In England, where the Latter-day Saints once doubled their membership, they are particularly proud to point out that Brigham Young came from English background and did missionary work in England himself, prior to the assassination of Joseph Smith in 1844. Young returned from England to assume the leadership of the Mormon Church, and some of his wives were English girls whom Brigham Young recruited on his missionary journey. It is not unusual to find second generation Mormons returning to the same country where their parents did missionary work, to carry on the family tradition.

Another aspect of Mormon missionary activity is their preoccupation with the anthropological background of the *Book of Mormon*, which leads them to declare that the American Indian and the Central and South American Indian races have similar origins and are mentioned in the *Book of Mormon*. They do not hesitate to suggest the linkage of the Inca civilization, the Aztec civilization and other such archaeologically verified Indian groups as giving credence to the teachings of the *Book of Mormon*. The fact that no reputable archaeologist has ever verified their hypothetical and unsupported propositions (in fact, others have gone on record as repudiating them outright [see chapter on Mormonism]), apparently does not hinder the zeal of Mormon missionaries one whit.

Such archaeological and anthropological razzle-dazzle, however, does have quite an effect on the untutored and uninformed mind outside the United States, where verifications or contradictions of the Mormon claims would be difficult, if not impossible, to obtain. Thus we see that in Mexico and South America particularly, Mormon missionaries appealing to the nationalistic pride of both Indians and Latins, are telling them that they are the heirs of great civilizations which the *Book of Mormon* reveals are connected with the origins of Christianity and its nineteenth century "restoration," through the establishment of the Mormon Church. By utilizing the *Book of Mormon* as a prophetic volume and "new light on the Bible," the Mormons have succeeded to an amazing degree in Mexico and in South America, to the great dismay of many mission agencies and a large company of missionaries. As we previously observed, however, the Mormons are careful not to point out their previous discrimination against the black race, for it simply would not do for the "Restored Church of Jesus Christ" to be on the one hand, busily engaged in promoting the archaeological myth of the *Book of Mormon* and the races of the Americas, while virtually ignoring the black race, purely on the ground of their skin color and imagined curse! Wherever possible, it is good for missionaries to point out this glaring inconsistency, which is well-known in Africa where the Mormons in force have been, until recently, conspicuously absent. For almost all of its controversial history, Mormon missionary efforts were confined to those races which qualified in the theology of Joseph Smith and Brigham Young, but one could hardly seriously consider, on the basis of such racial discrimination, the claims of the Mormons to being the restored church of Christ.

The Mormon missionary approach also differs from that of other cults, particularly Jehovah's Witnesses, in that it emphasizes the need for education, preferring to reach a higher strata of intellect, generally speaking, than the Jehovah's Witnesses have been able to attain. From a standpoint of educational background, social graces and personal habits which include a quiet, tolerant regard for evangelical Christianity (something lacking most pointedly in the methods of Jehovah's Witnesses), the Mormons make a good impression on prospective converts and many ex-members of Christian denominations are now the disciples of Joseph Smith and Brigham Young because of this distinctive Mormon emphasis.

A typical Mormon missionary approach is oriented around three prime factors:

1. The Mormon Church alone has the marks of true Christianity. It is called the Church of Jesus Christ; it has apostles and prophets; it has a priesthood (Melchizedek and Aaronic) as well as elders and other New Testament practices.

The Mormons claim the unique ability to baptize for the dead (1 Corinthians 15:29) and sacred extra-Biblical literature which interprets the Bible.

2. The Mormons maintain that Christianity is an open apostasy, as evidenced by the rise of Roman Catholicism during the dark ages and the various and multiple divisions in Christendom since the Reformation.

3. The outward success of the Mormon Church, its enormous prosperity and growth since 1830 in the face of persecutions and ostracism (due in part

to their own immoral practices of polygamy one should note) proves conclusively, say the Mormon missionaries, that the Church of Jesus Christ of Latter-day Saints is the restoration of true, Biblical Christianity, and should be embraced as such.

Since the average person knows very little of church history, and even less of the backgrounds of Joseph Smith, Brigham Young and the early "Mormon saints," some of these things will go unchallenged. But if even a general knowledge of the massive contradictions and historical myth-making about the origins of Mormonism is known to a prospective convert, not to mention the Mormons' polytheistic theology, which by definition is not Christian, then the "saints" have a difficult time indeed defending the maze that is their history and theology. Usually when this occurs, they will depart, never to return.

The Reverend Gordon Fraser, who has spent some fifty years working as a missionary among the Navaho Indians in Arizona and Mexico, has had numerous encounters with Mormon missionaries and his judgment in this realm is most relevant.

The Mormons have striven for years to gain recognition as a Christian body. Until within a decade or so, their claim has been denied by even the most liberal groups of professing Christians. Lately, however, with the general lowering of Christian standards of thought and with the remarkable build-up in the public press and on the radio, the Mormons have achieved their goal in the thinking of the general public. But are the Mormons Christians? If the term covers all who use the name of Christ in their titles or in their teaching, we would have to allow the Mormons their claim, but we would have to include with them the Jehovah's Witnesses, Christian Scientists and most of the other metaphysical cults, as well as Unitarians, Universalists, Bahais and a host of so-called liberal adherents to the various Christian denominations, which were originally, completely orthodox.

All of these refer freely to Jesus Christ and use quotations from the Bible to support their views, but these, along with Mormons, deny what we consider to be the indispensable tenets of true . . . Christianity.

The Mormons are well trained in their methods, and nominal Christians are an easy prey to their arguments. We have yet to see, however, an intelligent and regenerate person who knows the Bible and its doctrines, succumb to Mormonism.

The Mormon missionaries who come to your door will be well-mannered, attractive young people. They will introduce themselves as "Christian missionaries," or will use some other innocuous term.

One team which has recently returned from Honduras announced themselves as members of the Central American Mission. Another team encountered recently merely asked:

"Could we step in and have a Christian word with you?"

They will avoid identifying themselves as Mormons of Latter-day Saints until they have gained an audience.

These young missionaries are given very careful training, both in the fine points of good sales approach and in the best methods of appealing to the members of the various churches. It is part of their training to attend services of the various churches, so as to be informed on matters of phraseology and doctrine.

We should insist that such visitors identify themselves. . . .

What Mr. Fraser says is, of course, a sound evaluation of Mormon practices, and we are forced to his conclusion when he says,

> Many Christians, uninformed as to the true nature of the Mormon
> teachings, will defend their Mormon neighbors as good, clean-living, pious
> and honest folks. They will point to the wonderful relief practices of the
> Mormon Church. They will extoll the thrift and industry of the Mormons
> as a whole. All these things we recognize and appreciate as valuable contri-
> butions to society. We cannot criticize these things. These virtues do not
> make one a Christian. Satan is delighted when his followers put up a good
> appearance. We insist that these virtues have nothing to do with one's ac-
> ceptance before God, if one has never yielded to God's claims concerning
> His Son, Jesus Christ. When Christians fail to demonstrate the above virtues,
> they are coming short of God's purpose, but these are the by-products of
> the Christian life (Gordon R. Fraser, *Is Mormonism Christian?*, Chicago, IL:
> Moody Press, 1977, pp. 7, 8, 117).

We must look then, beyond the appearances of Mormonism and its
missionaries; we must consider the fruit of its tree, not just its social benefits
and moral reform, but its doctrine, which, as has been noted, is as much fruit
from the tree of religion as is the practice of that religion.

In the case of the Mormons, their doctrinal fruit is corrupt, denying as
they do, the Christian doctrine of the Trinity, the Deity of our Lord and
salvation only by grace through justifying faith in Jesus Christ (Ephesians
2:8–10). The Jehovah's Witnesses and the Mormons share one thing in common—both are dedicated opponents of historic Christianity. Although they
utilize the name of Christ and the methods of Christianity where witnessing
and evangelism are concerned, the content of Christianity, which by necessity
revolves about the Person of Jesus Christ, is either ignored or redefined by
them. In the end, it is the gospel of "another Jesus, another spirit," and the
product of that supreme architect of religious deviltry, who delights in ar-
raying himself and his ministers as angels of light. Of him Jesus Christ said,
"He is a liar and a murderer from the beginning"—Satan, the god of this
age.

There is scarcely a mission field of the world that has not felt the impact
of these two major cult systems, and we would be foolish indeed, in discussing
the problem of missionary activities of the cults, to ignore their methodology
and their already fantastic accomplishments in a relatively short space of
time.

Much more could be written on this subject, but everything that needs
to be said could hardly be included in a chapter of this length. It might be
observed, however, that the cults do share some traits in common when it
comes to missionary methodology, and the primary ones are worth noting.

1. The cults do not generally identify themselves by their popular names
(Jehovah's Witnesses, Mormons, Swedenborgians, etc.). They prefer such
titles as Latter-day Saints, Bible Students, or The Church of the New Jerusalem, and generally reveal themselves in their historic connections only
when the prospect is on the way to indoctrination.

2. The literature of many cult systems is unmarked, so that it is difficult
to identify them because of the similarity of terminology employed in the
setting forth of their teachings.

3. Most cultists utilize terminology of historic Christianity and are masters of evangelical clichés, as Mr. Fraser has pointed out.

4. Their public meetings are seldom identified with the official name of the sponsoring group. The Seventh-day Adventists in particular, have been guilty of this, although they are not a non-Christian cult. But the fact that many are reluctant to identify themselves underscores some of their divisive methods of proselyting, which though regretted by some quarters of Adventist leadership, still continue on many mission fields around the world.

5. All major cult systems will use the Bible, quoting profusely from it, mostly out of context. In the case of Jehovah's Witnesses, they will even offer copies of their own translation (the Mormons have an "inspired version" also) to "aid a deeper understanding of the Scriptures."

6. Missionaries of the cults will also, when pressed, deny the historic doctrines of the Trinity, Deity of Jesus Christ and salvation by grace alone.

7. Cult missionaries will follow up major evangelistic campaigns, such as Billy Graham, as they did in England and elsewhere. Mormons and Jehovah's Witnesses specialize in this, and have even been found in counseling rooms after altar calls, attempting to proselytize the young converts.

These are some of the marks of the methods and content of some of the major cults on the world mission fields. There can be no doubt that they are effective and that the Church must rise to meet this challenge while there is yet time.

Chapter 18

THE JESUS OF THE CULTS

Since the earliest days of Christianity, both apostle and disciple alike have been confronted with the perversion of the revelation God has given us in the Person of Jesus Christ. This perversion has extended historically, not just to the teaching of our Lord, but more important, to the Person of Christ; for it is axiomatic that if the doctrine of Christ Himself, i.e., His Person, nature and work are perverted, so the identity of the life-giver is altered, then the life which He came to give is correspondingly negated. And it is at precisely this juncture that in this day and age, we come face to face with the phenomenon which the Apostle Paul described in 2 Corinthians chapter eleven as "the other Jesus."

The problem, then, is twofold, in that we must understand the nature of the "other Jesus," and then give the Biblical reasons why it is the obligation of Christians to identify him as a counterfeit and refute his other gospel.

There can be little doubt that the Christian of today then, can expect to encounter the very same, or at least, similar errors and perversions of the Gospel message that his ancestors before him did. He should not be discouraged when they appear to have more success in twisting the truth of God than the Christian has in presenting it.

The epistle to the Galatians reminds us that there are those who would "pervert the Gospel of Christ," and who represent "another gospel," which in reality is not another but a counterfeit of the original, designed by the master craftsman of all evils, our adversary, the devil.

It may seem like over-simplification and naiveté to some people to suggest that Satan is the prime mover and architect of the major cult systems, but a careful consideration of the Biblical evidence will allow no other conclusion.

In his Second Corinthian epistle, Paul penned one of the most solemn warnings recorded anywhere in the Bible, to which we have made previous reference. He addressed this warning to Christians who were in great danger of having their minds (not their soul's salvation) corrupted from the simplicity that is in Christ Jesus. He was afraid, he said, that if someone should come to Corinth preaching "another Jesus, another Spirit and another gospel," the Corinthians might well be swept along with it to the sterilization of their Christian life and witness for Christ. Paul went on to underscore this point by drawing a deadly parallel between true Christianity and pseudo-Christianity, that he likened to a carefully designed copy of the original revelation of God in Christ.

After revealing the existence of a counterfeit Jesus, Holy Spirit and gospel, Paul completed the parallel by showing that there are also counterfeit "apostles," and counterfeit "disciples" (workers), who transform themselves in appearance and demeanor to appear as ministers of Christ, but in reality, Paul states, they are representatives of Satan (2 Corinthians 11:13). He further informs us that this is not to be considered fantastic, unbelievable and incredible, for Satan himself is often manifested as "an angel of light." So we are not to be surprised when his ministers emulate their master and disguise themselves as ministers of righteousness (2 Corinthians 11:14, 15).

Now of course, Paul was speaking of those who could be readily identified as spiritual wolves in sheep's clothing the moment their teachings were compared with the true Gospel (Galatians 1:8, 9), not just anyone with whom we have a disagreement in the realm of theology.

Simply because Christians disagree on certain peripheral issues cannot be taken as a valid reason for asserting that such are dissenters and ministers of Satan, unless that dissent involves the Person and work of our Lord, in which case their unbelief would automatically invoke the apostolic judgment.

The Nature of the Other Jesus

The Person and work of Christ is indeed the very foundation of Christian faith. And if it is redefined and interpreted out of context and therefore contrary to its Biblical content, the whole message of the Gospel is radically altered and its value correspondingly diminished. The early apostle clearly saw this, as did John and Jude, hence their repeated emphasis upon maintaining the identity and ministry of the historical Jesus over against the counterfeits of that Person already beginning to arise in their own era.

The "other" Jesus of the false cults of that day (Gnosticism and Galatianism), threatened the church at Colosse, Ephesus and Crete, and invoked powerful apostolic condemnation and warning in the epistles of 1 John, Galatians and Colossians.

In order that we may better understand precisely how these Scriptures may be applied in our own day, we need only cite some contemporary illustrations of the "other" Jesus the Bible so graphically warns against, and the entire issue will come into clear perspective.

1. *The Jesus of Christian Science*

In the theological structure of the Christian Science religion as we have already seen, Gnosticism was revived and Mrs. Eddy became its twentieth century exponent. Mrs. Eddy declared concerning *her* Jesus:

> The Christian who believes in the First Commandment is a monotheist. Thus he virtually unites with the Jew's belief in one God, and recognizes that Jesus Christ is no God as Jesus Christ Himself declared, but is the Son of God (*Science and Health*, p. 152).

Mrs. Eddy spelled out her view so that no one could possibly misinterpret her when she wrote:

> The spiritual Christ was infallible; Jesus, as material manhood, was not Christ (*Misc. Writings*, p. 84).

Now a careful study of Matthew, chapter sixteen, will reveal that Jesus Christ acknowledged the confession of Peter to the effect that He *was* the Christ, the Son of the Living God. And it would be foolish to maintain that Jesus was not material manhood, in the light of the New Testament record that He was born of woman, subject to the limitations of our nature apart from sin, and physically expired upon the cross in our place. The Jesus of Mrs. Eddy is a divine ideal or principle, inherent within every man, and Jesus was its supreme manifestation. Since Mrs. Eddy denied the existence of the physical universe, she also denied the reality of human flesh and blood, maintaining that it was an illusion of mortal mind. Hence, neither Christ nor any man for that matter, possesses a real body of flesh and bones, and for her, Jesus Christ has not come in the flesh.

It seems almost unnecessary to refer to the fact that our Lord acknowledged the reality of flesh and blood when He declared to Peter: "Blessed art thou, Simon Bar-jona, for flesh and blood hath not revealed it unto thee, but my Father which is in heaven" (Matthew 16:17).

At this particular juncture, the words of the Apostle John take on new meaning when he declares:

> Every spirit that confesseth not that Jesus Christ is come in the flesh is not of God: and this is that spirit of antichrist, whereof ye have heard that it should come; and even now already is it in the world (1 John 4:3).

John's previous words then apply with great force to the Jesus of Christian Science and its prophetess, Mrs. Eddy:

> Who is a liar but he that denieth that Jesus is the Christ? He is antichrist, that denieth the Father and the Son (1 John 2:22).

We need not emphasize the point, for it is quite evident that the "other" Jesus of Christian Science is a gnostic Jesus, an idea, a principle—but not God Incarnate (John 1:14). Because of this, although Mrs. Eddy, her literature and Christian Scientists utilize the name of Jesus, theirs is not the Christ of the Scriptures, but an extremely clever counterfeit about whom the Holy Spirit graciously saw fit to warn the church.

2. *The Jesus of Jehovah's Witnesses*

The next example is quite different from the Jesus of Christian Science, but another Jesus, nonetheless. According to the theology of the Watchtower,

> . . . the true Scriptures speak of God's Son, the Word, as "a god." He is a "mighty god," but not the Almighty God, who is Jehovah (*The Truth Shall Make You Free*, p. 47).
> In other words, he was the first and direct creation of Jehovah God (*The Kingdom Is at Hand*, pp. 46, 47, 49).

The founder of Jehovah's Witnesses, Charles Taze Russell, described *his* Jesus as having been Michael the Archangel prior to his divesting himself of his angelic nature and appearing in the world as a perfect man (*Studies in the Scriptures*, Vol. 5, p. 84). For Jehovah's Witnesses, their Jesus is an angel who became a man. He is *a* god, but he is not God the Son, second Person of the Holy Trinity.

As the chapter on Jehovah's Witnesses amply demonstrated, the Scriptures refute this and flatly controvert the Watchtower's Christology by teaching that Jesus Christ is the Word, God the only begotten one (John 1:18, Greek), and no less than the great "I AM" of Exodus 3:14 (compare John 8:58) and the First and the Last of the apocalyptic-Isaiah contrast, well-known to any informed student of the Scriptures (compare Revelation 1:16, 17 with Isaiah 44:6).

As Mrs. Eddy's Christ is an abstract idea, and the Christ of Jehovah's Witnesses is a second god with an angelic background, he, too, qualifies as "another" Jesus in the context of the Pauline prophecy.

3. The Jesus of the Mormons

The teachings of the Mormon religion, which differs from both Christian Science and from Jehovah's Witnesses, claim that their god is one among many gods, as evidenced by their own literature:

> Each of these gods, including Jesus Christ and his Father, being in possession of not merely an organized spirit, but a glorious body of flesh and bones. . . (Key to the Science of Theology, p. 44, Parley Pratt [1973 ed.]).

Theologian Pratt held no unique view where Mormonism was concerned; in fact, the Mormons have a full pantheon of gods. Jesus, who before His incarnation was the spirit-brother of Lucifer, was also a polygamist, the husband of the Marys and Martha, who was rewarded for his faithfulness by becoming the ruler of this earth (see chapter 6 on Mormonism).

The Apostle Paul reminds us in his epistle to the Galatians that "God is one" (Galatians 3:20), and the numerous passages from the Old Testament, previously cited in the chapter on Mormonism, demonstrate the absolute falsity of the idea that there are a multiplicity of gods and an exaltation to godhood to which men can aspire. As for the concept of Jesus as a polygamist and a brother of Lucifer, this need not be dignified by further comment.

The Jesus of the Mormons is quite obviously "another" Jesus, with whom truly redeemed men have nothing in common, even though he be arrayed as an angel of light and with all the credentials of the angel Moroni's angelic proclamation to Joseph Smith, the prophet of the restored Christian religion!

It would be possible to go on listing the other cult systems, but it is apparent that other comment would be superfluous; the evidence is overpowering.

The Jesus of the Christian Scientists, the Mormons, the Jehovah's Witnesses, and of all the cult systems, is but a subtle caricature of the Christ of divine revelation. In cult theology, He becomes an abstraction (Christian Science, Unity, Metaphysics, New Thought), a second god (Jehovah's Witnesses, Mormonism, Theosophy, Rosacrucianism, Baha'ism), or a pantheistic manifestation of deity (Spiritism, The Great I Am); but He is still incontrovertibly "another Jesus," who represents another gospel and imparts another spirit, which by no conceivable stretch of the imagination could be called holy.

Herein lies the problem which Christians must face and come to grips with, and there are excellent reasons why it is not only our responsibility but our duty.

To Every Man an Answer

In the course of delivering numerous lectures on the subject of non-Christian cults and their relationship to the Christian Church, one of the most frequent questions addressed to me has been, "Why should Christians oppose and criticize the beliefs of others whether they be cults or other world religions?"

To answer this question we must first recognize that to oppose and criticize is neither unethical, bigoted, or un-Christian; rather it is the epitome of proper Christian conduct where a very vital part of the Christian witness is concerned. There are some good people who feel that it is beneath their dignity to engage in the criticism of the beliefs of others, and the society in which we live has done much to foster this belief. "Live and let live" is the motto of our civilization; don't buck the tide of uncritical tolerance, or as the saying goes, "bend with the wind or be broken." In addition to this type of reasoning there also has been promulgated a distinctly noncontroversial spirit mirrored in the fact that leading newspapers and periodicals, not to mention the mass media of communication, radio and TV, refuse to carry advertisements for debates on religious issues for fear of being thought un-American since it is now fashionable to equate criticism of another's religion with an un-American spirit!

We must remember, however, that controversy in itself has always been a stimulus to thought and in our own great country has provoked many needed reforms in numerous instances. We might also observe that there is the easily verifiable fact that the criticism of another's religious beliefs does not necessarily postulate personal antagonism toward those who entertain such beliefs. Hence it is possible for a Protestant to criticize Roman Catholicism or Judaism for example without being in the least antagonistic to members of either faith. Let us not forget that honest criticism, debate, and the exploration of controversial issues involves the basic right of freedom of speech within constitutional limits; and the New Testament itself, the very cradle of Christianity, reflects in a startling way the fact that the faith of Jesus Christ was built and nourished upon the controversy which it provoked. It was said of the early Christians that they "turned the world upside down" (Acts 17:6); indeed the message of the Cross itself is offensive and controversial by nature. Robert Ingersoll, the late great agnostic and renowned antagonist of Christianity, was wise enough to recognize this fact and stated in his famous lectures "If this religion is true, then there is only one Savior, only one narrow path to life. Christianity cannot live in peace with any other religion."

There are many reasons why books and chapters like this should be written, but we shall turn to the Bible itself for the basic reasons—believing that in God's Word, the source of our faith, will be found the evidence that its defense is very much His will.

Let us begin by noting the historical fact that Jesus Christ and His apostles warned repeatedly of false prophets and teachers.

Throughout His entire ministry our Lord was constantly on guard against those who attempted to ensnare Him with trick questions and supposed contradictions between what He taught and the teachings of Moses and the Prophets. Added to this, these professional interrogators masqueraded as religious, pious, and even tolerant zealots and professed that they were the descendants of Abraham, heir to the covenant and the servants of God. To these people our Lord addressed His most scathing denunciations, calling them among other things "whited sepulchres," "children of the devil," "dishonorers of God," "liars," "murderers" and "wolves." Since our Lord was both God and man, He alone could gaze through the centuries and see those who would arise following in the train of His contemporary antagonists and at least two very graphic prophecies of their characters and objectives are to be found in His discourses.

In the seventh chapter of the gospel according to Matthew, as previously noted in chapter 1 of this book, Christ enunciated a very definite warning (verses 15–23).

From this discourse we learn some very important things. We learn that there shall be false prophets; that they shall appear in sheep's clothing and that their inward or spiritual nature is that of wolves (verse 15). We are further told that we shall be able to recognize them by their fruits. We are informed that they will prophesy in His name; in His name cast out devils, and in His name perform miracles (verses 16, 22). With the full knowledge that they would do these things, our Lord then adds "I will profess unto them; I never knew you: . . . ye that work iniquity" (verse 23). There can be little doubt that He intended this as a warning for He prefaces His statements with a very strong Greek term "beware," literally "be wary of or take care, because of" false prophets. The designation "wolves in sheep's clothing" is therefore not that of some misguided and over zealous Christian apologist, but one that finds its authority in the words of God the Son and this is the reason why Christians are to listen to it.

Our Lord supplemented His discussion of these individuals when in the twenty-fourth chapter of Matthew while speaking of the circumstances surrounding His Second Advent Christ declared: "for there shall arise false Christs and false prophets, and shall shew great signs and wonders; insomuch that, if it were possible, they shall deceive the very elect" (verse 24).

Further comment on this point is not necessary; He designated them "false Christs" and "false prophets"; it was He who prophesied that they would show great signs and wonders, and it was He who warned that if it were possible, the subtlety of their evil would deceive the very elect, or the Church. Apparently our Savior thought it important enough to repeat for in verse twenty-five He says "Behold, I have told you before."

The Apostle Paul, utilizing the identical language of the Lord Jesus Christ, succinctly phrases a divine warning concerning these same people.

> For I have not shunned to declare unto you all the counsel of God. Take heed therefore unto yourselves, and to all the flock, over the which the Holy Spirit hath made you overseers, to feed the church of God, which he hath purchased with his own blood. For I know this, that after my de-

parting shall grievous wolves enter in among you, not sparing the flock. Also of your own selves shall men arise, speaking perverse things, to draw away disciples after them. Therefore watch, and remember, that by the space of three years I ceased not to warn every one night and day with tears (Acts 20:27–31).

It appears from this very pointed statement that Paul was not afraid "to declare unto you all the counsel of God." Indeed, the greatest of the apostles warns us to "take heed" and this is to involve not only ourselves but all Christians; and though it is addressed principally to pastors, it underlines the existence of "grievous wolves" about whom Paul says, "cease not to warn every one night and day with tears." Should not that which was important to him be as important to us for whom he intended it? It is of no small interest and importance that this charge of Paul to the Ephesian elders was taken very seriously by them for in Revelation, chapter 2, Christ commends the church at Ephesus for heeding Paul in that they "tested them who say they are apostles and are not and have found them out to be liars" (verse 2).

Paul, of course, made much mention of such persons elsewhere, describing them as "enemies of the cross of Christ" (Philippians 3:18), "false apostles and deceitful workers transforming themselves into the apostles of Christ" (2 Corinthians 11:13). He does not even hesitate to describe them as "satan's ministers" (2 Corinthians 11:14, 15). The first and second epistles to Timothy, also of Pauline authorship, reflect the same attitude: "Now the Spirit speaketh expressly, that in the latter times some shall depart from the faith, giving heed to seducing spirits, and doctrines of devils; speaking lies in hypocrisy; having their conscience seared with a hot iron" (1 Timothy 4:1–2).

The express speaking of the Spirit, of course, underscores the importance of the counsel given, and it is significant to observe that it is to take place in the "latter times" when men shall "depart from the faith," listen to "seducing spirits," and become captives of "the doctrines of demons." This is tremendously strong language in the original Greek and is followed by his counsel in the second epistle to, "preach the Word" and to "reprove, rebuke, and exhort with all longsuffering and doctrine" those who in the time to come "will not endure sound doctrine; but after their own lusts shall heap to themselves teachers who shall tickle their ears; and the truth shall be turned into fables" (2 Timothy 4:3–4, literal Greek).

It is more than a casual coincidence that the Apostle Peter acknowledges the authority of Christ and Paul by utilizing their very language: "But there were false prophets also among the people, even as there shall be false teachers among you, who privily shall bring in damnable heresies, even denying the Lord that bought them, and bring upon themselves swift destruction" (2 Peter 2:1).

For Peter, it appears "false prophets" were a distinct reality, "false teachers" not figments of overwrought fundamentalist imaginations, and "destructive heresies" which "denied the Lord that bought them," vivid dangers to be guarded against. As we approach the end of the New Testament we find John, always noted for his doctrine of love, balancing that doctrine magnificently with the teaching of divine judgment upon those whom he describes as "false prophets that are gone out into the world" (1 John 4:1) and "deceivers are entered into the world who confess not that Jesus Christ is come in the flesh. This is a deceiver and an antichrist" (2 John 7).

The next to the last book in the Bible, the comparatively small epistle of Jude, is likewise in full agreement with the verdict of our Lord and the other apostles:

> Certain men crept in unawares, who were before of old ordained to this condemnation, ungodly men, turning the grace of our God into lasciviousness, and denying the only Lord God, and our Lord Jesus Christ . . . These are spots in your feasts of charity . . . clouds they are without water, carried about of winds; trees whose fruit withereth, without fruit, twice dead, plucked up by the roots; raging waves of the sea, foaming out their own shame; wandering stars, to whom is reserved the blackness of darkness for ever (verses 4, 12, 13).

As we have noted, all of the quotations are in context, refer to the same individuals, and characterize them in an identical manner. The description is not pleasant, but it is a Biblical one originating with God the Holy Spirit, not with the so-called interpretational fancies or bigoted intolerances of uninformed extremists. God used these terms for people He describes in His Word; God warns the Church of Christ about their existence, their methods, their teachings, their subtleties, and their final judgment. The Church neglects, at her peril, such divine counsel.

There are naturally some who will not agree with this position; they will quote the advice of Gamaliel which he addressed to the Jews in the Book of Acts (5:38, 39); they, too, will say "let them alone; if the work is of man, it will perish; if it is of God we will be found to be opposing him." The only difficulty, as we have noted earlier, is that the context clearly indicates the advice was given by Gamaliel to the Jews and Gamaliel was not an inspired writer, an apostle or even a Christian. If his advice is to be followed and his criterion to be recognized, then the thriving growth of the various non-Christian cults, all of which deny the fundamentals of the Christian faith, must be acknowledged as the work of God! No consistent thinker of Christian orientation could long entertain such a warped conclusion without doing violence to a great portion of the New Testament.

There are also others who, in their attempt to excuse themselves from meeting the challenge of the Jesus of the cults, will refer to the ninth verse of Jude where Michael the archangel, when contending with the devil, refused to argue with him but rather referred him to the Lord for rebuke. Once again, however, the context reveals that Michael did not keep silence by choice but by necessity because as the Greek so clearly reveals "he did not dare bring against Satan a blasphemous judgment" for the simple reason that Satan was his superior in authority. The Greek word translated "durst" in our King James Bible carries the meaning of not doing something for fear of retaliation by a superior power (Greek: *etolmese*), so this line of reasoning also fails.

The reasons why we must answer as well as be prepared to evangelize such people are quite clear. The Church must do it because Christ and the apostles commanded her to do so, unpopular though it may be, and to this all true Christians should be unequivocally committed for no other reason than out of respect for our Lord. Certainly if our mothers, wives, children or country were attacked and misrepresented, our love for them would compel us to defend them. How much more then should love for our Redeemer so motivate us in the defense of Him and His Gospel.

The Jesus of the cults is a poor substitute for the incarnate God of the New Testament. Along with the equally important imperative of cult evangelism stands the very real need to give to everyone that asks of us "a reason for the hope that is within us" (1 Peter 3:15). That hope is the Jesus of Biblical theology and of history, and once we understand the true nature of the Jesus of the cults we can discharge our duty faithfully and by contrast unmask him and his creator for all to see. We may sum this up with the thought-provoking words of our Lord when with absolute finality He declared: "Behold, I have told you before" (Matthew 24:25).

Chapter 19

CULT EVANGELISM—MISSION FIELD ON THE DOORSTEP

The last one hundred years of American history have seen the evangelization of large segments of the American populace to a degree never imagined by any evangelist in the history of Christianity.

Beginning with the evangelical emphasis of Charles G. Finney, through the massive impact of D. L. Moody, Gypsy Smith, Billy Sunday, culminating in Billy Graham, American Christianity has enjoyed great spiritual privileges withheld from the world since the days of the Reformation and the Knox, Wesley and Whitefield revivals, so dear to the memory of church historians.

Yet there are many people today in both the clergy and the ranks of the laity, who are seriously reevaluating the meaning of evangelism and its importance, if not to the Church, at least to themselves. More and more, Christians are beginning to think in terms of *personal* evangelism as opposed to mass evangelism, primarily because all evangelism, since the earliest days of Christianity, that is, all *successful* evangelism of enduring worth, has been of a personal nature. While it is true that great evangelists draw crowds and preach to multitudes of people, they, too, are dependent upon the so-called "personal touch," as evidenced by the fact that Billy Graham has more than once attempted to remove the "tag line" from his Hour of Decision radio program "The Lord bless you real good," only to have such attempts reversed by the constituency that, despite its size, still desires the feeling of a personal relationship.

The follow-up work of every major evangelical crusade must be on a personal basis to be effective. A stamped envelope and a short memory course are no substitute for the personal workers, whose on-the-spot faithfulness, patience and perseverance builds up and edifies young converts after the first warm glow of the conversion experience has begun to abate.

This, of course, brings us to a consideration of the all-important question: What is evangelism? Is it merely mass rallies, where so-called "wholesale" decisions for Christ are made? Is it on the other hand, just the task of the local church to shoulder the responsibility of having a week or two of meetings for revival and evangelistic purposes each year? By evangelism, do we mean massive emphasis upon radio and television to communicate the good news of redemption? Or, is evangelism somehow or other bound up with *all* of these forms of expression, and yet, in essence, none of them? Is it perhaps possible that evangelism was intended, in its primary purpose, to be personal and individualistic to the degree that each Christian feels the responsibility to evangelize his neighbor, and that this is really the root of the whole matter from which the tree of church evangelism and mass evangelism, both in crusades and the mass media, are to draw their strength and spiritual stamina? To answer these questions, and to place evangelism in its proper perspective where the challenge of non-Christian cults is concerned, we must consider carefully the pattern laid out for us in the New Testament.

Holding Forth the Word of Life

If anything proceeds from the pages of the New Testament, it is the message that the early Christian Church labored under the magnificent obsession of the divine paradox. They were separate as individuals in each congregation, whether it be Ephesus, Corinth, Crete or Philippi. But in some mysterious sense, they were "one body" in Christ (Ephesians 4:4). Through acceptance of the divine Redeemer, God had shattered and broken down the walls of race, color and social status. There were no longer "Barbarian, Scythian, bond or free, but all were one in Christ" (Colossians 3:11).

Each of these New Testament Christians was admonished by the Holy Spirit to be an ambassador or representative for his Savior (2 Corinthians 5:20). The Apostle Paul set the supreme example of this in the New Testament Church by declaring that the primary responsibility of the Christian was to preach the Gospel (1 Corinthians 1), and it is precisely at this juncture, that, if we are willing, we can understand the meaning of New Testament evangelism.

The Greek word translated *gospel*, literally means "good news," as most Christians well know. But what many do not know is that the word translated *preach* comes from the Greek *evangelizomai*, which means "to publish" the Gospel or declare it abroad for all the world to hear.

The early Christians considered themselves evangelists in that sense (1 Corinthians 1:17), and in the writings of Paul, Peter, John and others, this great unalterable truth shines through. Christianity was not something just entrusted to clergymen, pastors, teachers or professional evangelists. It was a personal message entrusted to those who had experienced the power of its transforming properties in their own lives, and who went literally from house to house and turned the world upside down because they were not ashamed to proclaim it. The early Christians went forth two-by-two. They went forth in the power of the resurrected Christ. They went forth with a message—a message based upon experience shared by all and an experience which strengthened and comforted all. These were not people who were preoccupied with the things of the world, with contemporary political intrigues or the reigns of the Caesars, with the showplaces of Ephesus and the coliseums of Rome. These were people who were possessed by a Spirit totally removed from the spirit of the age in which they lived—a Spirit who commanded them to convict the world of sin because though they had been its victims, they had now become its conquerors because of the Redeemer.

The incredible zeal with which they proclaimed this message of the living Christ, the Gospel of Resurrection, the certainty of sin forgiven, the present possession of peace with God, exerted an awesome influence and power over the minds of those with whom they came in contact, almost without exception. The Philippian jailer abused Paul and Silas until he experienced the

Presence of their Master. Then he, too, with his whole house, believed the incredible. Sergius Paulus, beset though he was by a demonic medium who sought to pervert the Gospel and turn him away from the faith of Christ, was stunned by the authority of a man filled with the Holy Spirit, Saul, who was also called Paul, and whose amazement turned to faith and life eternal. Even those who resisted the magnificence of New Testament evangelism were frightened by its clarity and power, and felt even as Festus, who raved at the Apostle Paul, "Paul, thou art beside thyself; much learning doth make you mad" (Acts 26:24). Agrippa the king could not be dissuaded even by the remarks of Festus, but withdrew from the Presence of the Holy Spirit with the trembling admission, "Almost thou persuadest me to be a Christian" (Acts 26:28).

All of these evangelists had three things in common. They had experienced the Person of the Risen Christ and had passed out of death into life. Second, they were dominated by the Holy Spirit, alien to this world because the world does not know Him and cannot receive Him because the world is evil and He is God. Last, they obeyed the injunction of the apostles and as ambassadors for Christ fearlessly published the Good News that Light had come into the world, and that God had indeed appointed a day in which He would judge the world in righteousness by the man whom He had ordained and given assurance to all men by raising Him from among the dead.

It is not difficult to see why the Christians of the first century were able to spread Christianity throughout the earth without the aid of radio, television, traveling caravan, precision crusades or yearly evangelistic and revival meetings. Every day was an evangelistic campaign for them; every service a revival meeting; every road a path to someone who needed Christ; every house a dwelling place for those for whom He died. These were people who were evangelists in the full meaning of the term as God had intended and commanded it. They rose to the challenge with a supreme confidence and conviction born of experience and faith, which, despite their limitations and human frailties, made them worthy of the name, "saints." They could do all this because they had truly found Him, "of whom Moses in the law and in the prophets did write, Jesus of Nazareth" (John 1:45) . . . and they had believed Him that "Wherever two or three are gathered together in my name, there am I in the midst of them" (Matthew 18:20).

If we want to have evangelism in the true Biblical sense of the term, we must return to the content of the evangel and to the methods of the New Testament Church. We must utilize every modern method possible, but we must not allow them to overshadow or interfere with the great personal responsibility which rests upon every Christian. For, in that very real and personal sense it is true of us as it was of the Apostle Paul, "For Christ sent me not to baptize, but to preach the gospel" (1 Corinthians 1:17).

The Philippian Christians were admonished by the Apostle Paul to "shine as lights in the world, holding forth the word of life" (2:15, 16). This they could do only by being willing to shine in contrast to the darkness which surrounded them and by being willing to stand in the defense of the Gospel as they held forth the Word of Life.

We are told in the simplest terms that the Gospel is God's power unto salvation, but what *is* that Gospel?

The Apostle Paul states it for us in what might be called a capsule version when writing to the Corinthians he said:

> For I delivered unto you first of all that which I also received, how that Christ died for our sins according to the scriptures; and that he was buried, and that he rose again the third day according to the scriptures" (1 Corinthians 15:3, 4).

The very usage of the word Christ in the Pauline theology identifies the office of the Anointed One with that of the second Person of the Trinity, He who is God "over all, God blessed for ever. Amen" (Romans 9:5, Greek).

Paul does not, however, stop at this, but goes on to point out that Christ died for our sins, that is, in place of our sins, a clear statement of the substitutionary atonement of the Cross. Then he concludes with "He rose again the third day," which in the context of 1 Corinthians 15 can only refer to a bodily resurrection (Luke 24:39ff.).

We can see then, that the content of the Gospel is, at its very minimum, the Deity of Christ, the substitutionary atonement of the Cross and His bodily Resurrection from the grave. This good news, when enunciated and published fearlessly by believers, has the effect of convicting men of their sins and leading them to true repentance toward God and faith in the Lord Jesus Christ. James Packer in his stimulating book *Evangelism and the Sovereignty of God*, has put it this way:

> What was this Good News Paul preached? It was the news about Jesus of Nazareth. It was the news of the incarnation, the atonement, the kingdom, the cradle, the cross and the crown of the Son of God. It was the news of how God glorified His Servant, Jesus, by making Him Christ, the world's long-awaited Prince and Saviour. It was the news of how God made His Son man, and how as man, God made Him Priest and Prophet and King, and how as Priest, God also made Him a sacrifice for sins, and how as a Prophet, God also made Him a law-giver to His people, and how as King, God has also made Him Judge of all the world, and given Him prerogatives which in the Old Testament are exclusively Jehovah's own—namely to reign until every knee bows before Him, and to save all who call on His Name. In short, the good news was just this, that God has executed His eternal intention of glorifying His Son by exalting Him as the great Saviour for great sinners. Such was the Gospel which Paul was sent to preach; it was a message of some complexity, needing to be learned before it could be lived by, understood before it could be applied and needed therefore to be taught. Hence Paul as a preacher of it, had to become a teacher. He saw this as part of his calling; he speaks of "the Gospel whereunto I am appointed a preacher . . . and a teacher" (2 Timothy 1:10ff.).[1]

Evangelism then, has content, as well as zeal, courage and an attitude of constant prayer—distinct methods of propagation.

Techniques of Cult Evangelism

It is the testimony of the Word of God that He has raised up the Gentile nations and made available to them the Gospel of the Kingdom and its Mes-

---

[1]James I. Packer, *Evangelism and the Sovereignty of God*, Downers Grove, IL: InterVarsity Press, 1975, p. 47.

sianic King, which Israel rejected because of unbelief. The Scriptures declare that the purpose of God in doing this is to "provoke them to jealousy" (Romans 11:11) that they may perceive what they have lost and repent, that the natural olive branch may be grafted in again, whereas now, only the wild branch (Gentiles) shares the blessing of Messiah's covenant and coming Kingdom.

In the kingdom of the cults today, however, we are witnessing something akin to this and yet, despite its corrupt purposes, progressing at an alarming rate of speed. We see the various cult systems, specifically Jehovah's Witnesses, Mormonism, Unity, etc., utilizing the methods of Christianity and of New Testament propagation of the Christian message, wooing converts from professing Christian fellowships, Protestant as well as Roman Catholic! This bewildering proselytizing has caused consternation in many Protestant and Roman Catholic parishes across America and abroad and it is accelerating, not slowing down. We see the strange, but just, judgment of God upon the Christian Church because of its lethargy in that He is allowing the forces of darkness to succeed with the methods of light, while denying the source of light and life, the Gospel of Jesus Christ. In order that we may offset the ever-widening circle of cultic influence, Christians must first of all face the fact that we have been woefully delinquent in the exercise of our responsibility of personal evangelism. Second, many Christians have taken for granted the great doctrines of the Bible which they learned and accepted at their conversion and have not "studied, to show themselves approved by God, workmen who do not need to be ashamed, rightly dividing the word of truth." Third, the average Christian knows *what* he believes, insofar as being able to document the *why* of his belief from the Scripture, which he finds at times a frustrating and exasperating task. The clergy is largely at fault in this respect because they do not always emphasize the teaching ministry of the pulpit, but rather, settle for an evangelistic emphasis with very little doctrinal depth.

We took a survey in the Department of Biblical Studies at King's College. Of some three hundred students polled, less than ten had heard a sermon in the last four years in their respective churches on the doctrines of the Trinity, the Deity and Humanity of Jesus Christ, or the relationship of grace and faith to works. We have conducted similar surveys in colleges, seminaries and Bible institutes in many major cities throughout the country. The result has been almost identical. There *must* be something fundamentally wrong when important areas of doctrine such as these are neglected or glossed over lightly.

The various cult systems, particularly Jehovah's Witnesses and the Mormons, capitalize on conditions such as this. Many an embarrassed Christian rushes to the telephone when he has a Jehovah's Witness "minister" or Mormon "elder" in his living room, to get answers from a generally-overworked pastor, when a little consistent study of the Scriptures would have given him a tremendous sense of security and more important, provided him an opportunity to preach Christ in the true sense of personal evangelism to the cultists.

Throughout the world today, Christian missionaries are faced with proclaiming the unsearchable riches of the Gospel. And due to the tremendous amount of funds made available, comparatively speaking, for world missions in the last 100 years in the United States, a good many Christians have become lethargic and apathetic as to their own personal responsibility toward proclaiming the Gospel of Christ. Ministers are constantly discovering that their congregations are dwindling at prayer meetings, that even their Sunday evening services have been winnowed considerably by television and other extra-curricular social activities. Here then, lies part of the problem.

As we have shown in the preceding chapters, the non-Christian cult systems in America have grown tremendously in the last one hundred years. By a subtle utilization of a redefined terminology coupled with a surface knowledge of the Bible, and encouraged by the fact that a great many Christians are unable to answer their perversions (a fact which serves to confirm them even more definitely in those deviations), the zeal and missionary activities of the cults have tremendously increased. The only way to offset this is by a return to positive Christian evangelism on the fiercely personal basis of door-to-door and neighbor-to-neighbor effort whenever the opportunity presents itself. But over and beyond this, it is time that the Church of Jesus Christ begins to consider the cults themselves as a mission field—a mission field on the doorstep of the Church wherever she exists in the world, both at home and abroad

This is by no means an impossible task. The last thirty years of the writer's life has been spent largely in this field and has confirmed his opinion that cultists too can be reached with the Gospel. They are part of the world that God so loved that He sent His only begotten Son to redeem.

Precisely how we may implement the evangelization of cultists is an important and vital subject about which nothing has been written, comparatively speaking, in the last century and which today presents an ever-expanding challenge to the Christian. We, too, must obey, as did the Apostle Paul, the command to publish the Good News and to pick up our credentials as ambassadors for Christ and present them to those who would evangelize *us* with a gospel other than that which the New Testament proclaims.

The following techniques and observations the author feels would be useful in any genuine Christian effort to evangelize cultists, when they are offered, not as a panacea to the problem, but as a tested means toward the end of bringing cultists to personal faith in Jesus Christ. This is the object of all true evangelism in any century.

1. *The Human Element*
One of the first things which confronts a Christian as he attempts to evangelize a cultist, is the psychological barrier which exists in the minds of a great many persons, to the effect that cultists must be a special breed of individuals impervious to standard techniques of evangelism and generally well enough versed in the Bible to confuse, if not convince, the average Christian.

While there is an element of truth in both of these statements, it is generally traceable to experiences the Christian has had personally, either directly or indirectly, with cultists, or to those encounters with cultists in which the Christians did not fare too well. In fact, in not a few instances, they have been routed, frustrated and embarrassed. This generally tends toward reticence, lest there be a repeat performance.

The second explanation for this phenomenon is the seemingly implanted fear that cultists should not be permitted to enter the Christian's home, in the light of 2 John 10:

> If there come any unto you, and bring not this doctrine, receive him not into your house, neither bid him God speed.

Now in context, this passage is a sentence in a letter to the Elect Lady, in whose home a Christian Church quite obviously met, as the early church was prone to do, there being no cathedrals or modern churches such as we know them today. In this connection, a very common one (see Philemon 2), John warns her not to allow anyone to preach in church meetings or teach doctrines which do not honor Christ in every aspect of His Person, Nature and Work. It is clear that he is referring to false teachers being given a voice in the church, not to a cultist sitting in your living room! That the passage cannot be taken literally in that connection is quite evident, because if a twentieth century Christian's plumbing froze when the weather was twenty degrees below zero and his cellar was rapidly flooding with water, he would not dream of asking the plumber who came over at 2:00 A.M. to fix the pipes whether he "brought the doctrine of Christ" to his home. Rather, such a question would never enter his mind. Yet the plumber might be a Unitarian, Mormon or a Jehovah's Witness! Doubtless, Christians have had them in their homes, fixing their plumbing, electricity or oil burner and never once inquired of their views concerning the doctrine of Christ. Yet some Christians who utilize 2 John 10 as an excuse for not evangelizing cultists would never dream of using it if the cultist were a plumber!

Many pastors have instructed their flocks on the basis of this passage and other out-of-context quotations, to close the doors in the faces of cultists rather than to invite them in and, in the tradition of Christian evangelism, confront them with the claims of Christ. There is no authority in the Word of God for neglecting one's responsibility as an ambassador of Christ, and the cults do not constitute a special category of evangelism.

The Christian is probably right in assuming that the average cultist does have a working knowledge of the Bible. Most of them are quite diligent in their study, both of their own literature and that of the Scriptures. And it may be true that the well-trained cultist may appear to be impervious to the proclamation of the Gospel and its defense (when necessary). But that he is some special species of unbeliever in whose presence the Christian must remain mute and the Holy Spirit impotent, is a gross misconception and should be abandoned by all thinking Christians.

We must strive to keep foremost in our minds that cultists are precious souls for whom Jesus Christ offered Himself, and that they are human beings who have homes, families, friends, emotions, needs, ambitions, fears and frustrations which all men have in common. The cultist is special in only one sense, that he is already "deeply religious," and therefore, probably one of the most difficult persons in the world to reach with the Gospel of Christ.

He has rejected historic Christianity and entertains in most cases a hostility, if not active antagonism, to its message. The cultist, therefore, considers evangelical Christians his greatest potential, if not actual, adversaries. Hence, an attitude of tolerance and love should always be manifested by the Christian to relieve, where possible, this tension and the hostile feelings of the cult adherent. The technique of "setting the cultist at ease" does indeed take a great deal of patience, for the individual cultist firmly believes that he has found "the truth," and as such, often considers the Christian message to be inferior to his own revelation. This fact is generally reflected in his attitude of superiority and even genuine resentment when the Gospel is presented. This resentment may take many forms, but it always conforms to the general thrust that since he has found the truth, how can the Christian dare to attempt to convert *him*? Cultists believe they already have progressed far beyond the evangelical Christian stage or station on the "religious railroad track" through their special revelations and superior experiences with God.

According to one psychologist, cultists also transfer their antagonism for the theology of historic Christianity to those who propagate that message, thus identifying the belief with the individual and personalizing the controversy. If the Christian who is interested in evangelizing cultists would realize this fact at the outset of his conversation with cult adherents, he could then make a careful distinction between the theology of Christianity, which is the real source of the antagonism, and the personality of the individual Christian, thereby allowing the cultist to see the Christian as a redeemed personality, independent of his theological structure. This would make possible a form of objective discussion of Biblical truth, subject to the categories of analysis, logical consistency, context and exegesis.

While this may not necessarily undercut any portion of the cultist's theological system, it will break down or assist in breaking down the psychological conditioning of the cultist to the attitude that any person who disagrees with *his* interpretation of Christianity is automatically an object of antagonism.

Approaching the problem of cult evangelism, it must be remembered that cultists, in their respective systems of theology, are almost always by nature dependent upon either forms, ceremonies, rituals, good works, right-living or self-sacrifice as a means of pleasing God and obtaining justification. Fundamentally then, cultism is a form of self-salvation, emphasizing deliverance from sin through human effort or merit in cooperation with their concept of the personality of the Deity.

The Christian must therefore, in the light of this fact, point out from Scripture (since most cults recognize it as authoritative, or at least partially binding), the folly of self-justification, righteousness or human effort as a means of obtaining redemption. We should always remember that repentance, atonement, regeneration, resurrection and retribution in the Biblical sense is seldom part of the cultist's vocabulary, and *never* of his personal experience. The Christian must *define, apply* and *defend* the historic meanings of these terms, before it is possible to effectively proclaim the Gospel. In a word, one must begin at the beginning, repeat, emphasize and repeat. This is the sowing of seed that one day, by God's grace alone, will bear fruit to eternal life.

Adherents of the cults are constituted, psychologically speaking, so that they are, almost always, victims of what might be termed a mass delusion of grandeur coupled with a dogged sense of personal pride. The Scripture records that Satan fell from his first estate through measureless pride (Isaiah 14:12–14), so also today, he uses the same weaknesses of the human character as a tool in shaping cult adherents to his own ends. This pride is evident in most cultists, and contributes to the delusion that they are the possessors of the true faith that saves, guardians and defenders of that which is alone holy, and administrators of divine revelation to the mass of mankind who are enmeshed in a Christianity which all cultists agree has been perverted by theologians and philosophers, thus necessitating the true restoration of the Gospel through their efforts. It has been the writer's experience that almost all cultists suffer from the concept that his or her group will at last emerge victorious over all its adversaries, inherit an eternal kingdom and have the pleasure of viewing its enemies being either tormented or destroyed. Such cultists cling to an illusion of impending and imminent majesty or greatness, which, when linked with their intrinsic concepts of human ability and supposed merit before God, leads to mass delusion and spiritual darkness of the most terrible nature imaginable.

The task of the Christian evangelist then, is to reveal tactfully the true nature of man as Scripture portrays him. And in a spirit of deep concern with the practice of earnest prayer, reveal to the cultist God's view of fallen man and the certain destiny of those who follow in the pride-filled footsteps of Lucifer, "the god of this world" (2 Corinthians 4:4).

The nature of cultists is to be on the defensive, for they are acutely aware of the lack of unity and brotherly love clearly evidenced in many reputedly evangelical movements. They know that evangelicals are united, insofar as the cultist is concerned, only in their opposition to *him*. They, therefore, lay much stress upon the various divisions in orthodox circles, not to mention the lack of clarity where the cardinal doctrines of the Christian faith are concerned. They apparently never tire of stating, "at least we are united; you are divided, even in your own groups." It is this type of accusation which cuts the true Christian deeply. He must answer this charge by admitting differences of opinion on minor issues, but emphasizing solidarity on the fundamentals of the Gospel, which all cultists deny in one form or another.

The Christian must never forget, that a well-trained cultist can be a powerful opponent, adept at text-lifting, term-switching and surprise interpretations of "proof texts." He should be on guard constantly lest he be deceived into admitting something that will later be utilized against him and to the detriment of both the Gospel and his personal witness.

2. *Common Ground*

Before attempting to evangelize a cultist, the Christian should, whenever possible, find a common ground of understanding (preferably the inspiration and authority of the Scriptures, or the Personality of God), and work from that point onward. Christian workers must, in effect, become all things to all men that we might by all means save some (1 Corinthians 9:22). The

Christian cannot afford to have a superiority complex or reflect the idea that he is redeemed and the cultist is lost. Redemption of the soul is a priceless gift from God and should be coveted in all humility, not superiority, as just that—a gift—unearned and unmerited, and solely the result of Sovereign Grace.

The necessity of a common ground cannot be overemphasized for any sane approach to the problem of cult evangelism. Unless some place of agreement, some starting point be mutually accepted by both parties, the discussion can only lead to argument, charges, counter-charges, rank bitterness and, in the end, the loss of opportunity for further witness; and the soul of the cultist could be forfeited! Friendliness then, open and free manifestation of Christian love and a willingness to talk over the points of diversions, will go a long way toward allaying the suspicion of the average cultist and open further vistas for profitable and effective witnessing.

Throughout all of this, the Christian should be governed by increased activity in his prayer life, praying wherever possible in the presence of, and with, cultists, so that through the prayers that are uttered, the cultist may sense the relationship of the Christian to Him who is the Father of spirits, and our Father by faith in Jesus Christ.

3. Subliminal Seeding

The advertising industry of America has pioneered in motivational research and has taught us that ideas may be implanted in our minds beneath the level of consciousness or conscious awareness, and that they are dutifully recorded and do in no small measure influence our thinking and actions. Jingles sung on the radio and the television quite often motivate people to purchase the product about which the jingle chants.

Christians who wish to evangelize cultists can profit from the findings of such motivational research into subliminal suggestion to an amazing degree.

It is the conviction of this writer that the Word of God and prayer, addressed to Him through the Holy Spirit, is the most powerful motivating force in the universe, and can be subliminally utilized in cult evangelism by the implantation of seed thoughts about the Gospel of Christ, as well as the Gospel itself.

How this may be done is best illustrated by examples drawn from the writer's own experiences.

Jehovah's Witnesses are probably the most active and zealous of all the missionaries of cultism in America today. When called upon by Jehovah's Witnesses, the writer for many years employed the following approach with great success.

I would invite the Watchtower adherent or adherents into the living room, but before they had opportunity to speak concerning their literature, I would state that I never discussed religion or the Bible unless such a discussion was preceded by prayer, to which all present agreed. I would then quickly bow my head and address the Lord as Jehovah God. One must be particularly careful in dealing with Jehovah's Witnesses, to always address the Deity by the name Jehovah, or else the Witnesses may not pray or bow their heads. Instead, they will admire the bric-a-brac, thumb through their Bibles, reach for their briefcases and generally, keep occupied until you have completed your prayer. Should the reader be interested in knowing how I learned this, I must confess that on occasion—I peeked!

When the name of Jehovah is being used, the average Watchtower adherent will immediately bow his head, and after you have finished praying and *before* they can pray, begin the conversation by saying, "Now what was it that you wanted to discuss?"

Always keep in mind in dealing with Jehovah's Witnesses, that they come equipped with a portable arsenal in the form of a briefcase which contains the major publications of the Watchtower Society for their handy reference. At the outset you must insist that they use nothing but the Scriptures and that it must be a recognized translation (King James, Revised Standard Version, New International, New American Standard, etc.). You must further insist upon a discussion of cardinal doctrines, particularly concerning the Person, Nature and Work of Jesus Christ. Thus deprived of his Watchtower material and his Watchtower translations and circumscribed to the Person of Christ in discussion, even the best trained Jehovah's Witness is at a distinct disadvantage. On the other hand, the Christian who is indwelt by the Holy Spirit then has a definite advantage.

After the discussion had gone on for some time, and I had listened to as much of "Pastor" Russell's theology as I could tolerate for one evening, I would remind the Witnesses of the lateness of the hour and asked if we couldn't close with a word of prayer. I would then immediately bow my head and begin praying again.

Now what I have mentioned is, by itself, only an outline of how to conduct one's self in the presence of Jehovah's Witnesses, with one important exception. During my opening and closing prayers I would totally preach the Gospel, emphasizing the Deity of Christ, His death for our sins, the certainty of knowing that we have eternal life *now*, by faith in Him, and that salvation comes by grace alone, independent of human works. I would profusely quote the Scriptures, and in actuality be preaching a three-minute sermonette, subliminally implanting the true Gospel of Jesus Christ and, I might add, blissfully uninterrupted. For no one, not even the most zealous disciple of "Pastor" Russell, Joseph Smith or Brigham Young, can interrupt a prayer. I have seen such a methodology or technique of evangelism make a tremendous impact upon Jehovah's Witnesses and other cultists, because, for six minutes of the evening at least, the Christian has the opportunity to present the true Gospel of Christ without interruption.

We must believe that God's Word "will not return unto Him void, but shall accomplish what He has ordained and prosper in the thing whereunto He has sent it" (Isaiah 55:11).

4. *The Vocabulary of Redemption*
Non-Christian cultists of all varieties are prone to one psychological and spiritual insecurity. They are all aware of the fact that they do not *now* possess eternal life *or* peace with God. In fact, it is toward this end that they are vigorously pursuing the theology and practices of their respective systems.

There can never be a substitute, therefore, for an individual Christian's personal witness to what Christ has done for him. A word of caution, however, must be inserted at this juncture. As we know, cultists have their own vocabulary, so it will be necessary for the Christian to define carefully his terms when he speaks of conversion, its means and its effect upon his spirit, mind and life. The only really unanswerable argument is the argument of a transformed life, properly grounded in the authority of the Scriptures and motivated by love for God and for one's fellow man. Key terms which must be carefully defined are: the new birth or "born again"; justification; atonement; Deity and Resurrection of Christ; resurrection; forgiveness, grace and faith. It is inevitable that eternal retribution be discussed, because this is the very thing from which Christ died to save us.

The Scriptures admonish us to be "His witnesses," and in order to do this we must be willing to endure all things and be governed by patience, temperance, grace and love. Then regardless of how the truth of God be assailed, perverted or distorted, and no matter how much our own characters and motives are attacked, Christ will be honored by our conduct.

The vocabulary of redemption involves personal involvement, testimony to the effect of Christ's power both to redeem the soul and to transform the individual, his morals, his ethics, his life. And most of all, it involves the power to impart to him the peace of God which passes all understanding, the peace which Christ said would come only to those who made peace with God (Philippians 4:7).

5. The Secret of Perseverance

One of the most important techniques of cult evangelism is that of perseverance with cultists. Anyone who has ever worked extensively in the field of cults will readily testify that this takes a great deal of grace and understanding on the part of the Christian. Many times cultists will deliberately "bait" Christians (particularly Jehovah's Witnesses and the Mormons) in an attempt to provoke the Christian into losing his patience, thus justifying their own teachings. In order to avoid such pitfalls and to be able to endure the many forms of abuse and persecution which will come about when a Christian penetrates the theology of the cultist with the Sword of the Spirit, one must have discovered a secret which, when prayerfully understood and applied, can make the endurance of *anything*, for the sake of Christ, possible.

If one were attacked, severly assaulted and abused by a frightened blind man, it would be possible not only to forgive him, but even persevere to the end of loving him, despite his actions. For after all, both reason and logic argue, he *is* blind, and in a sense, not responsible for his actions.

We are forever in debt to the Apostle Paul, who pointed out in his second letter to the Corinthians that those who are outside of Christ have indeed been spiritually blinded by the god of this age. Satan has caused a cloak of delusion to descend over their minds and understandings, so that Christ's Gospel, which is the light of the world, cannot penetrate to them. The secret of perseverance is to know and to understand, regardless of what a cultist says or does, that he is doing it out of spiritual blindness. Since our warfare as Christians is not against flesh and blood (the cultist), but against the spiritual forces of darkness which rule this world (Satan and his emissaries), it is possible to love the cultist, endure his abuses, perversions and recriminations, while at the same time faithfully bearing witness for Christ. This technique of cult evangelism should never be minimized. And once it is properly appreciated, it can become a great asset to the Christian.

There are doubtless many, many more things which could be mentioned in connection with cult evangelism, such as the important fact that when dealing with the Gnostic cults (Christian Science, Unity, New Thought, etc.), distinct emphasis must be placed upon personal sin, which they all negate or deny; also the certainty of retribution as taught by the Lord Jesus Christ should be emphasized. We might also profitably note that, in dealing with religions which have had their origin outside the United States (Baha'ism, Theosophy, Zen, etc.), the Christian ought to have a working knowledge of what the doctrines of these cults are in relation to the historic Christian revelation. It is foolish to attempt to discuss Christian doctrines with those who do not accept the authority of the Scriptures, which is most certainly the case in regard to the three cults just mentioned.

Finally, evangelism, particularly cult evangelism, must never fail to emphasize that Christ and the disciples taught certain irrevocable doctrines as well as consistent ethics and morality.

It has been the experience of the author, based upon numerous personal contacts with cultists of all varieties, that there has yet to be born a cultist who can confuse, confound or in any way refute a Christian who has made doctrinal theology an integral part of his study of the Scriptures. Cults thrive upon ignorance and confusion where the doctrines of the Scriptures are concerned, but are powerless to shake Christians in their faith or effectively proselytize them when the Christian is well grounded in the basic teachings of the Bible and given over to a study of the great doctrinal truths of the Word of God. These mighty buttresses of Christian theology must no longer be taken for granted by Christian believers nor should pastors and teachers assume that the average Christian has sound knowledge concerning them. The rise of cultism to its present proportions indicates a great dearth of knowledge where doctrine is involved, and is a decided weakness in the battlements of orthodox theology, which the Church ignores, at the risk of innumerable souls.

Accepting then the fact that the poison of cultism can be effectively combated only by the antidote of sound doctrine, the next problem is the immunization of Christians against the teachings of the cults. The answer to this problem lies within the pages of God's Word; it involves study (2 Timothy 2:15) on the part of Christians, instruction on the part of the pastor and teacher (1 Timothy 4:1), coupled with a willingness to start at the beginning where sound doctrine is concerned, even as the risen Christ did with the doubting disciples, and to re-examine the reason *why* Christians believe what they believe. Particularly recommended for intensive study are the doctrines of Biblical inspiration, the Trinity, Deity of Christ, Personality and Work of the Holy Spirit, the Atonement, Justification by faith, works, the Bodily Resurrection of Christ and the resurrection of all mankind.

The great and true Trinitarian doctrine of God and the Deity of Jesus

Christ should be inculcated ceaselessly in Christian minds so that the Lord's people may never forget that Jesus Christ is the core of God's plan for the ages. The fact that He vicariously died and bodily arose, thus vindicating His claim to Deity through obedience to the righteous character of both His Father's will and law, both of which He perfectly fulfilled at Calvary, must be perpetually emphasized.

It is a well-known fact that no antidote for poison is effective unless it is administered in time and in the proper dosage prescribed by a competent physician. In like manner, Christian doctrine should not be taught in a dry, matter-of-fact way, as it so often is, but should be given in small doses over a long period. The treatment should begin at once, from the Sunday school level right through college and seminary where the need is urgent.

Christians must realize while the opportunity is yet ours that the teaching of sound doctrine does not predicate a dead orthodoxy. When properly understood, a living acceptance of and familiarity with doctrine form the giant pillars of truth upon which our faith rests, a familiarity which has always produced great leaders and effective workers for the proclamation of the Gospel of grace.

The evangelization of cultists is the task of the Christian Church of which each Christian is a member, a part of the Body of Christ. Until this is recognized, and Christians are urged and encouraged by their pastors and leaders to forsake the portals of Hollywood and the domain of the great god, Television, etc., for door-to-door publishing of the Good News of God's love in Jesus Christ for a lost world, the evangelization of cultists will continue to be one of the great tragedies of the Christian Church in our day. It is excellent that we support foreign missions and send the light of God's Gospel around the globe, but it is quite another thing for us to begin here, where the demand is personal, challenging and equally rewarding. This challenge is cult evangelism, the mission field on *your* doorstep.

Chapter 20

THE ROAD TO RECOVERY

In the preceding chapters of this volume, we have studied and evaluated in the light of the Word of God the major non-Christian cults or sects which have consistently challenged the missionary outreach of the Church of Jesus Christ. All the groups which were discussed are admitted rivals of historic Christianity. The question then quite logically arises, "What action can the church take, in both the ecumenical and independent wings of Christendom, to meet the challenge of contemporary American cults?" It is the purpose of this chapter to outline both a methodology and a plan whereby we may not only bring the inroads of the cults under control, but what is more important, to actually take positive steps to evangelize cultists, which of course is the primary task of the Christian Church. By traveling what might be called "the road to recovery," the Church may once again see the day when, by speaking the truth in love and with clarity, much of the ground lost to un-Christian cults in the last century may be regained. It should never be forgotten that whatever a specific cult offers to attract individuals is infinitesimal compared with what Jesus Christ offers to the soul who will cast all his care upon Him. The church has nothing to fear from the cults as long as she is faithful to her mission of both proclaiming and vigorously contending for the faith that was once for all delivered unto the saints (Jude 3).

It is the feeling of the writer that if the following suggestions were put into immediate practice, both in the United States and on the foreign mission fields, a constructive approach to the mounting problem of cults would emerge.

Project One—Research

In order to provide information of any type for the pastor, teacher, missionary, student or layman, it is vitally important that there be careful research into the background and theology of the major cult systems. There already exists a considerable amount of data which could be utilized, once it has been validated, codified and carefully weighed by mission agencies and field representatives of the major denominations and independent Christian groups. The average cultist is willing to listen to facts, particularly if they are at variance with what he has been taught, if only those facts, once he checks them, are shown to be accurate and reliable. We have seen more than a few Jehovah's Witnesses and Mormons, for instance, carefully reevaluate their religion as a result of careful research on the part of interested Christians.

Secondly, a statistical breakdown of the growth and development of the major cult systems at home and abroad must be worked out, so that those areas where they have grown most rapidly may be plotted and the factors contributing to that growth analyzed, in contrast to their lack of growth in other areas.

Thirdly, questionnaires must be sent out to key personnel in all Christian movements, seeking their reaction to the challenge of the cults in those areas under their jurisdiction. In this way, a broad perspective of cult methodology will be obtained.

Clipping services must also be utilized, for major population centers through the world are generally the targets of the major sects, and it is always helpful to know the coming and going of cult missionaries, as well as their planned area meetings (international conventions, missionary report sessions, special lectures, etc.).

Of course a research center dealing with cults is not a new proposal. The Christian Research Institute, of which I am the founder and director, was incorporated in 1960 to meet this need. It is our aim to collate and disseminate information to all Christian groups, ecumenical as well as independent, helping them to win those in the cults to Christ.

Through our facilities as a bureau of information on comparative religions, Christian leaders, missionaries, and workers throughout the world have ready access to information which is currently important. Through our newsletter we are able to provide much of the newest information to the general public. But the project is far too involved to be merely an independent effort. There must be cooperation and the free interchange of information between all concerned Christian groups, followed by financial support, in order that any research project of such scope and magnitude succeed in its objective.

Project Two—Computer Retrieval System

One of the newest ways for combatting the forces of the cults is through the use of computers. Christian Research Institute is proposing a plan which, if adopted, could revolutionize the field of apologetics. I propose that a computer information retrieval system be developed that can provide answers on the cults to practically anyone with access to a university or college library. This would be called the Christian Research Lending Library (SENT/EAST).

For example, many of the arguments that Jehovah's Witnesses bring forth against orthodoxy are mangled attempts to force the Greek text of the New Testament into their theological framework. What recourse does the average Christian have against such mistranslation if he does not have any knowledge of New Testament Greek? Through our projected computer network, individuals would be able to tap our resources via computer terminals. This person would be able to type his question at a terminal and receive an almost instantaneous reply complete with documentation.

There are around 60 million cultists and another 60 million Americans who dabble in the occult in the United States today and this is one way that they can be reached with very little struggle. This computer network will hopefully be used even in other countries. We will be able to take all of our research and information that we have been gathering for the last thirty years and make it available to anyone who needs it.

Of course, there are many things that are necessary to a viable program like this. We need the cooperation of all of the other organizations in this field in the United States and abroad. We need to share the information that is available in so many different locations.

A program like this is also very expensive, and although we visualize that participants in the program will contribute a share of the costs, donations and volunteers are needed to offset the enormous expense.

With the prayers and help of dedicated Christian laymen and leaders all over the country, a program such as SENT/EAST will energize the missionary forces as they seek to bring the gospel to those in the cults.

Project Three—Specialized Literature

Just as the function of project one would be the collecting, sorting and condensing of usable facts and information, so project three would be its logical outgrowth, the publication and distribution and also the translation of such material on an international scale. The value of tracts, pamphlets and books printed and disseminated at cost, both in the United States and on those mission fields where specific cults are rapidly growing, is incalculable, as any foreign missionary will readily testify.

Through the facilities of such organizations as the Christian Research Institute, Spiritual Counterfeits Project, Christian Apologetics: Research and Information Service, Saints Alive, the Institute for Contemporary Christianity, the American Tract Society, the New York Bible Society, The International Missionary Council, The Evangelical Foreign Missions Association and numerous other interested groups, practically all missionaries would have information available for distribution to indigenous churches and to Christian workers on their respective fields, so that no longer would it be possible for such organizations as Jehovah's Witnesses and the Mormons to capitalize upon the absence of literature accurately describing their faith and refuting their claims.

In South America alone, where the Mormons and the Jehovah's Witnesses, not to mention the indigenous animistic and spiritistic cults, exist in growing numbers and force of influence, preliminary surveys indicate that almost ninety per cent of those questioned not only desire, but earnestly request literature that will assist them in both refuting and evangelizing cults.

In the United States and Canada—where much headway is being made by cult systems—universities, colleges, seminaries, Bible institutes and local churches have consistently requested reliable literature from recognized denominational and independent sources. But since funding and support services are so unequal to the task, those organizations, including my own Christian Research Institute, who are working tirelessly to provide such information are deluged with more requests than can be handled. Special commissions should therefore be appointed, similar to that already sponsored by the World Council of Churches, so that independents and ecumenicists may pool their information, and erect a systematic defense against the proselyting of the cults. Though conservatives and liberals may disagree theologically, they suffer from the inroads of the cults individually, and yearly the ranks of American cultism are swelled by former Methodists, Episcopalians, Lutherans, Baptists, Congregationalists, etc., who attended both liberal and conservative churches until they were proselyted by the cults.

That there is a desperate need for literature and that it must be doctrinally oriented, no serious scholar in the field of cults will deny. But that such literature can be made available without the cooperation of interested churchmen, educators and lay readers, is quite dubious, if not impossible. The cults have capitalized upon the fact that the Christian Church has not made any really significant effort to halt their proselytizing techniques and to answer their propaganda directed against all forms of Christianity. This has been, in no small measure, a contributing factor to their success. It is true that research will produce and has already produced considerable amounts of useful information, but its printing and distribution is a fundamental concern, if we are to deal effectively with the issues which face us.

Project Four—Educational Reevaluation

Samuel Johnson, the great educator, once wrote, "The foundation of every state is the education of its youth," and we would do well to paraphrase this in the context of Christianity, "The future of the church is in the education of its leaders."

As a college professor, the writer has been deeply interested in the courses offered in Bible institutes, colleges and seminaries, as well as pre-theological schools, dealing with the subject of Comparative Religions, and particularly with non-Christian cults or sects. In this area, a very real problem exists, and it will do no good to let the matter rest with this observation. Rather, the facts, appalling as they may be, should be aired.

Since the advent of Christian missionary activities on an organized scale some 200 years ago, the proclamation of the Gospel message has faced many problems. Obstacles of language, culture, race, militant nationalism and the competition between missionaries of different doctrinal persuasions, have contributed a stormy atmosphere to world missions.

In addition to these difficulties, major non-Christian religions, such as Islam, Buddhism, Hinduism, Taoism, Shintoism, etc., have actively opposed Christian missionaries, so that progress has been slow in many areas, and in some instances, hardly recognizable.

Beyond this aspect, however, looms, as we have mentioned, the formidable obstacle of non-Christian American cults, many of which are now worldwide. Some of these movements have proselytized new converts on already established fields with startling success. Utilizing the methods reminiscent of early Christianity, the cults cater to the culture patterns of those they proselytize, provide literature in the language of the people, and one way or another, keep a certain emphasis on the Bible in the forefront of their work. In many instances they preach a militant "separation" from tobacco, alcohol and other practices classified as worldly and unspiritual. All these activities are bolstered by their so-called revelations (all of 19th century vintage), with an appeal to which they wage unceasing warfare against all religions, but against Christian denominations in particular. It is significant that they first approach known Christians. Seldom do they attempt to reach the unevangelized, which should be the first step in any genuine missionary program.

We are not to suggest that the activities of these movements be curtailed by law or that they should become the target of an evangelical barrage of abuse. Full freedom of worship and the right to promulgate one's convictions are historic planks in the platform of Protestant evangelism. Even such terms as "sect" or "cult" seem more appropriate in lands with a State Church than in open religious situations. But Christianity will need to preserve the distinction between truth and heresy if it is to have a future. Some groups, particularly Jehovah's Witnesses, by their demonstrated hostility to governmental authorities, have frequently jeopardized the reputation and efforts of others of genuine Christian persuasion. As a result, there has been great friction between their workers and Christian missionaries. It is difficult indeed for Christian missionaries to compete successfully with such divisive forces in a positive way and to evangelize missionaries of such zealous groups as the Mormons, Jehovah's Witnesses and other virulent indigenous groups.

Now we might ask at this juncture, "What is being done to train Christian missionaries abroad (and, for that matter, pastors, teachers and leaders in the United States) to deal with this growing problem. On the educational level, are Christian institutions taking seriously the needs at home and on the mission fields? Are there mandatory courses for future Christian leaders to aid them in both evangelizing and refuting cultists?"

The cults continually emphasize the Bible, but despite the prominence given the Scriptures, without exception they place themselves in the roles of infallible interpreters of the Word of God, their dogmatism rivaled only by Jesuit scholars. Instead of being the infallible rule of faith and practice, the Bible is relegated to a secondary position. This is accomplished almost subliminally, so that the convert is unaware that his primary authority is not really grounded in Scripture, but rather in the interpretation of Scripture put forth by the respective cult.

Though this fact is well-known among missionaries and Christian workers, it apparently has not filtered back to seminaries, Bible colleges and Bible institutes. It is a fact that at present less than five percent of all such institutions in the United States require as a prerequisite of graduation that a student take a course on comparative religions or non-Christian American cults, a fact which staggers the imagination when one can see the obvious inroads the cults have made both at home and abroad.

In a classic periodical article, Professor Gilbert Peterson, Chairman of the Department of Religious Education at the Philadelphia College of the Bible, made the following observations concerning the educational curricula of American Bible colleges, institutes and seminaries:

> Preparation is a word which is found to headline some newspapers, on the lips of statesmen, military leaders and educators as well as church leaders and mission board directors. It has taken on a significant meaning in our times as the threats of world leaders, nations and the varied ideologies of

men vie for prominence in the world around us. Christian educators need to stop from time to time, and evaluate the preparation men and women are receiving in the various Christian schools of higher learning. . . .

It is with a sense of great urgency that the graduates of Bible colleges, along with Christian young people from other educational backgrounds, face the task of living and witnessing to the truth of the Gospel in these troubled times. Each spring a new group of young people receive their diplomas or degrees to serve God as missionaries, both at home and on the foreign field.

In a recent survey conducted by the author, of over twenty-three Bible colleges in the United States and Canada, representing a total number of graduates in excess of 15,000, it was found that approximately twelve and one-half per cent of this number, or about 1900 individuals are presently serving on the foreign mission fields of the world. Our concern at present is not with the percentage of Bible college graduates going to the mission field, but rather, the preparation they receive in the area of formal cult apologetics before going to the mission field.

In the past ten years the outreach of cults and isms through the mediums of radio, the printed page and missionary endeavors, has reached enormous proportions. The rapidity of their growth is traceable in large measure to the dearth of information among Christians in regard to what is being promulgated by the various cults on the one hand, and a failure to act upon the Scriptural command to resist them on the other. In the survey, questionnaires were sent to over fifty Bible colleges. In the twenty-three schools replying, there is great diversity of requirements in the section of the curriculum dealing with apologetics, cults and unchristian religions. The course most often required of all graduates was "Cults and Isms." The course usually entailed the study of the history and development of several cults, their doctrinal position and a refutation of their position from the Scriptures. Apologetics was next in order of numbers of requirements. This course covers a systematic presentation of the reasons and evidences of the Christian faith. The course offered most often was Comparative Religions, with nine schools offering it as an elective, three requiring it for all mission majors, and four schools requiring it of all graduates. This course covers a comparative study of the major living religions of the world.

In order to meet the challenge of our day in preparing our young people to face the present religious world situation, we need to realize what is being offered to the students in our Bible colleges, institutes and seminaries by way of preparing them to serve Christ in the midst of the rise of cultism. The following is offered as a suggestion as to how we might structure this one area of the curriculum. This is of course, not a final pronouncement, rather, a recommendation for exploration of this difficult field.

There is no substitute for a thorough knowledge of the Word of God and the truth of God which it reveals. Courses in direct Bible study and doctrine provide one with the necessary foundation. In addition to this, a three-hour course in Apologetics is needed where the needs of men, the Christian answer to these needs, and the reasons for the uniqueness and truth of Christianity are presented.

It is not enough that one know only his own beliefs when faced by the average non-Christian and cultist, and therefore, following Apologetics there should be a three-hour course in Cults and Isms. This course, as previously suggested, would examine the historical and doctrinal development of such non-Christian groups as Jehovah's Witnesses, Christian Science, Mormon-

ism, Unity and the like. The course would include the Christian answer to
these systems and an evaluation of their terminologies, and an accurate,
consistent method of approaching them with evangelism as the goal.

A course such as comparative religions could be offered on an elective
basis, to give the student a broader view of non-Christian religions. When
a student goes to the mission field, a far more detailed study of the religion
of that particular field must be made by the missionary candidate, and can
be made in comparative religions. Therefore, specialized courses should be
offered in these fields. Also the training received in apologetics and cults
along the lines of definitive terminology and doctrinal evaluation will prove
extremely valuable.

At present, of the twenty-three Bible colleges reporting, ten offer a
course in Apologetics, with six requiring it of all students; eleven schools
offer a course in Cults, with seven requiring it of all students; sixteen schools
offer a course in Comparative Religions, with three requiring it of all mission majors and four requiring it of all students.

This means that a little more than one-fourth of the Bible colleges
replying already follow the suggested curriculum outlined or one very similar to it, and a little less than one-half of the reporting schools offer all
three courses (Apologetics, Cults and Comparative Religions) in their present curriculums.[1]

Mr. Peterson's remarks are very much to the point, for when it is remembered that only eleven schools out of twenty-three offered courses on
Cult Apologetics, and only seven out of those eleven required it for graduation, the situation is seen to be acute.

Now in the case of seminaries and Bible institutes in the United States,
a detailed study now in preparation indicates even at this early date that the
problem of non-Christian cults is not taken seriously by the majority.

Such information will not paint an encouraging picture to be sure, especially in the light of accelerated cult growth on our major mission fields.

Mission fields have the added problem of dealing with certain indigenous cults with strong nationalistic overtones, particularly in Africa and Asia.
These groups amalgamate some of the teachings of Christianity with the
older pagan religions, particularly animism and spiritism, and come equipped
complete with their own special revelations and messiahs. The situation is
particularly true in the Philippine Islands, Japan and Africa, where Christianity is caricatured as a "white man's religion," a Western import superimposed on native cultural and religious patterns. Such an approach by the
cults has been disastrously successful, particularly in South America, where
in Brazil we have seen a resurgence of spiritism on an unprecedented scale.
Time magazine even devoted its religious section once to comments by a
Roman Catholic missionary deploring the inroads of the spiritists into the
Roman Catholic Church. Unfortunately, the same can be said also in respect
to some Protestant agencies; so the problem is universal. In passing, it might
be noted that the Roman Catholic Church has recently begun detailed research in the area of non-Christian cults and sects, so effective have been the
methods of both American-based and indigenous cults in proselyting Roman
Catholic converts.

---

[1]*Religious Research Digest*, December, 1961, pp. 8–11.

On the basis of past performance, it is safe to prognosticate that within the next decade, all things remaining constant, the cults will intensify their propaganda activities to three or four times their present rate. The question is, will the Church of Jesus Christ rise to the occasion while time remains? The church must be prepared to defend the claims of Scripture interpreted by the Holy Spirit that it alone is "inspired by God and is profitable for doctrine, for reproof, for correction and for instruction in righteousness" (2 Timothy 3:16).

The Christian Church must also be ready to remind indigenous nationalistic sects that Christianity is an Eastern religion, that Christ was born, died and was resurrected in Asia, and ascended from the Mount of Olives; so it is anything but "a foreign religion." But if the cults are to be effectively dealt with at home and on the foreign mission fields of the world, then missionaries, pastors and particularly educators, who mold the curricula of Christian institutions, must press for strong curricula in those institutions. Christians must be taught not only what they believe, but why they believe it, that they may be able, as the Scripture admonishes us, "to be ready always to give an answer to every man that asketh you a reason of the hope that is in you with meekness and fear" (1 Peter 3:15).

The teachings of the major sects must be codified and indexed and a running commentary provided for all interested parties in the form of the publication of literature and perhaps a semi-annual journal. It will then be possible to understand the methodology of the cults at home and abroad, to note the areas of their doctrinal emphasis and growth and their use and abuse of Christian terminology. The Church of Jesus Christ, as we have noted, has nothing to fear from the zeal and competition of the cults, but she has much to fear from her own apathy and lethargy in this vital area of missionary concern. The means to evangelize and combat adherents of the cults can be made readily available to all interested parties. It remains for Christians of both ecumenical and independent persuasion to agree to cooperate in the dissemination of pertinent literature on this ever-growing field of mutual concern.

On every front the Church is faced with unrelenting and mounting pressures from anti-Christian forces. Our Lord has warned us, "The night cometh when no man can work" (John 9:4), but the publication of literature may yet give us some time to work in the twilight which precedes the sunset.

It will do us little good, however, to sponsor research and to publish and distribute literature, if at the fountainhead of all Christian work, the educational preparation of Christian leadership, we do not revise the curricula of numerous Bible institutes, colleges and seminaries to meet the needs, both in the United States and on the mission field. So it appears that education, as always, is of vital significance.

Project Five—Conferences on Cults

A final suggestion to help implement support for a unified approach to the challenge of the cults is the sponsoring of specialized conferences or lectures on the local church level, at Bible conferences and in schools and seminaries, by competent students of the major cult systems. I have used such conferences for years and other cult-watching organizations have followed the same successful pattern. These conferences continually stimulate a great deal of interest, showing as they would by contrast, the differences between the teachings of the cults and historic Christianity. If conducted in a dignified, scholarly, and yet popular manner, with question and answer periods following each lecture, such conferences would serve a dual purpose. They would both explain the divergent doctrines of the cults and, at the same time, strengthen the faith of Christians in the great fundamental teachings of Christianity. The author has been engaged in such a ministry for some years with considerable success, but much more yet remains to be done. For, as the Scripture reminds us, "The fields are white already to harvest, but the labourers are few. Pray ye therefore the Lord of the harvest, that He will send forth labourers" (John 4:35; Matthew 9:37, 38). Speakers are available from the Christian Research Institute in these areas and there are a few other organizations and individuals throughout the country that provide similar services. However, the need is much greater than the supply and it must be met quickly.

If the preceding suggestions were adopted and put into operation, it is the conviction of this writer that the major cult systems would soon feel the impact and receive the benefit of the unified Christian witness to the veracity of the faith which they have chosen to reject.

Through the use of good research material, properly disseminated and translated where possible into the language of the fields where the cults are most active, and aided by clipping services which would keep the research center informed of major cult efforts around the world, Christians of all denominations, as well as pastors, educators and missionaries would be kept abreast of the activities of the larger cult systems.

Concluding our observation then, the road to recovery will not be an easy one to travel, and will be fraught with problems and conflicts; but if we will begin to travel it, we will find at the end of it and along the way, those who have been delivered from the cults, those who have been dissuaded from joining them and those who have been both evangelized and strengthened by a determined effort of the Christian Church not only to proclaim the message of redeeming grace, but to defend the claims and the Gospel of her Savior. We can go a long way toward recovering the ground we have lost, but we must begin now.

APPENDIX SECTION

THE PUZZLE OF SEVENTH-DAY ADVENTISM

Preface

In a volume such as this dealing with the problem of non-Christian cults, the question might logically be asked, "Why include Seventh-day Adventism, especially since the writer has classified them in a full-length volume as a Christian denomination?"

The answer to this is that for over a century Adventism has borne a stigma of being called a non-Christian cult system. Whether or not this was justified in the early development of Adventism, I have already discussed at length in my earlier book, but it should be carefully remembered that the Adventism of today is different in not a few places from the Adventism of 1845, and with that change the necessity of reevaluation comes naturally.

Together with the Evangelical Foundation (founded by the late Dr. Donald Grey Barnhouse and publishers of *Eternity* magazine), I conducted a thorough reevaluation of the Seventh-day Adventists several years ago. The results of that reevaluation were presented comprehensively in my book, *The Truth About Seventh-day Adventism* (Grand Rapids, MI: Zondervan Publishing Company, 1960) and then later in the first editions of this volume.

It is my conviction that one cannot be a true Jehovah's Witness, Mormon, Christian Scientist, Unitarian, Spiritist, etc., and be a Christian in the Biblical sense of the term; but it is perfectly possible to be a Seventh-day Adventist and be a true follower of Jesus Christ despite certain heterodox concepts which will be discussed.

Such Christian leaders as Louis T. Talbot, M. R. DeHaan, John R. Rice, Anthony A. Hoekema, J. K. Van Baalen, Herbert Bird and John R. Gerstner have taken the position that Adventism is in fact a cult system; whereas, the late Donald Grey Barnhouse, myself, E. Schuyler English, and quite a few others have concluded the opposite.

Since the opposing view has had wide circulation over a long period of time, I felt it was necessary to include here Seventh-day Adventism as a proper counter-balance—presenting the other side of Adventism and representing the theology of Adventism as the Adventists themselves believe it and not as many critics have caricatured it.

This, of course, is not to be construed in any sense of the term as an endorsement of the entire theological structure of Seventh-day Adventism, a portion of which is definitely out of the mainstream of historic Christian theology and which I have taken pains to refute. But I believe it is only fair and ethical to consider both sides of an extremely difficult and provocative controversy which shows very little sign of abating in our day.

In fact, during the last ten years (since the early 1970s) the Seventh-day Adventist denomination has seen turbulence, both administratively and doctrinally, that is more extensive than any turmoil in the organization's history. Administratively, there have been a number of Adventist leaders and pastors who have been removed from their positions because of supposed or proven improper financial activities, including misappropriation of funds. On the United States government level, the IRS, SEC, FBI, and Justice Department have all initiated investigations and some Seventh-day Adventist conference administrators may even face trial for fraud. Doctrinally, the church has developed a large rift between those members and leaders who are solidly within the evangelical Christian camp and those members and leaders who, because of their emphasis on works-righteousness, legalism, and the prophetic status accorded to founder Ellen G. White, may well move the denomination over time outside of the evangelical camp and perhaps even into actual cultism.

Since I have always stressed the importance of doctrinal integrity in my evaluations of religious movements, the doctrinal upheaval in Adventism is of special concern. Consequently, on February 16, 1983, I wrote the General Conference of Seventh-day Adventists (Washington, D.C.), calling for the Conference's public and official statement reaffirming or denying the authority of the Adventist book, *Questions on Doctrine*, which was the representative Adventist publication on which I based my earlier evaluation and book. On April 29, 1983, W. Richard Lesher, vice-president of the General Conference, responded in a personal letter. His reply read, in part:

> You ask first if Seventh-day Adventists still stand behind the answers given to your questions in *Questions on Doctrine* as they did in 1957. The answer is yes. You have noted in your letter that some opposed the answers given then, and, to some extent, the same situation exists today. But certainly the great majority of Seventh-day Adventists are in harmony with the views expressed in *Questions on Doctrine*.
>
> Secondly, you addressed the question of the interpretation of Scripture in relation to the writings of Ellen White. As an attested agent of the prophetic gift we believe communication based on Ellen White's revelatory experience to be trustworthy and dependable. However, we do not believe that the writings of Ellen White exhaust the meaning of Scripture. We still hold with the statements on Ellen White included in *Questions on Doctrine*.

On the basis of the above letter, dialog with several Adventist leaders, and the continuing state of flux within Adventism itself, I must, for the time being, stand behind my original evaluation of Seventh-day Adventism as presented comprehensively in my first book on the subject and later in this volume. Only events not yet unfolded, but within the knowledge of the Lord himself, will determine whether my evaluation will need to be revised in the future. It is my prayer that the aberrational currents within contemporary Adventism will not prevail and that Adventism will continue to be a Christian and evangelical, albeit unique, Christian denomination.

It was Dr. Donald Barnhouse who said that simply because a person is a member of a specific denomination there is no reason to suppose that the entire denomination is represented by that person's theology, nor is it proper to assume that because there are heretical Baptists, Presbyterians, Methodists, Episcopalians, etc., that all such denominations are therefore heretical.

To expand upon this we might say that simply because a denomination is Christian in its profession does not guarantee that all members of that denomination are Christian by their confession and experience. Hence, it is our position that Seventh-day Adventism as a denomination is essentially Christian in a sense that all denominations and groups professing Christianity are Christian if they conform to the classical mission of Christianity as given in the Bible and the creeds and counsels of the Christian Church. But this does not mean that all Baptists, all Methodists, all Episcopalians, all Lutherans, or all Adventists are necessarily Christians. This is a matter between the individual and God and is to be viewed in the light of the revelation of Scripture and the testimony of the Holy Spirit.

This section on Seventh-day Adventism is an attempt to present for consideration facts which are little known in many areas and often distorted in others. It is an effort to examine, commend and criticize where necessary the theological structure of the Adventist denomination and is submitted with a prayerful hope that honest investigation, even if it does not agree with our preconceived notions, is to be encouraged and profited from, under the guidance of the Spirit of God.

The Historical Background of Seventh-day Adventism

Seventh-day Adventism sprang from the "Great second advent awakening" which shook the religious world just before the middle of the nineteenth century, when a reemphasis about the second advent of Jesus Christ was rampant in Britain and on the continent of Europe. Before long, many of the Old World views of prophetic interpretation crossed the Atlantic and penetrated American theological circles.

Based largely upon the apocalyptic books of Daniel and Revelation, the theology of the Advent Movement was discussed in the newspapers as well as in theological journals. New Testament eschatology competed with stock market quotations for front-page space, and the "seventy weeks," "twenty-three hundred days," and "the abomination of desolation" (Daniel 8, 9) were common subjects of conversation.

Following the chronology of Archbishop Ussher, and interpreting the 2300 days of Daniel as 2300 years, many Bible students of various denominations concluded that Christ would come back about the year 1843. Of this studious number was one William Miller, a Baptist minister and resident of Lower Hampton, New York. The great second advent movement which swept the United States in the 1840's stemmed largely from the activities of this William Miller, who confidently taught in the year 1818, that in "about" twenty-five years, i.e., 1843, Jesus Christ would come again. As Miller himself put it, "I was thus brought in 1818 at the close of my two-year study of the Scriptures to the solemn conclusion that in about twenty-five years from that

time all the affairs of our present state would be wound up."[1]
Miller further wrote:

> I believe the time can be known by all who desire to understand and
> to be ready for His coming. And I am fully convinced that some time be-
> tween March 21, 1843 and March 21, 1844, according to the Jewish mode
> of computation of time, Christ will come and bring all His saints with Him;
> and that then He will reward every man as His work shall be.[2]

At length his associates set October 22, 1844, as the final date when Jesus
Christ would return for His saints, visit judgment upon sin, and establish the
Kingdom of God upon earth.

One need only read the words of the Lord Jesus Christ to realize that
Miller was teaching in contradiction to the Word of God. Jesus said, "But of
that day and hour knoweth no man, no, not the angels of heaven, but my
Father only" (Matthew 24:36; also 24:42; 24:44; 25:13).

The gospel of Mark also shows that dates cannot be set, for in verse 33
of chapter 13 our Lord stated, "Take ye heed, watch and pray: for ye know
not when the time is." And almost His last words to His disciples are a rebuke
to those who set dates: "It is not for you to know the times or the seasons,
which the Father hath put in his own power" (Acts 1:7). Certainly this should
have been deterrent enough for William Miller and his associates, but sad to
say it was not.

Compare the two positions, Miller versus the Scriptures: God declared
that no man would know the time; Miller stated that he did know the time.
God said the times and seasons were within His own power; the Millerites
declared that they had the prophetic key to them. Jesus Christ stated, "No
man knows the day or the hour," but the Millerites set the exact day (October
22, 1844). And history bears a bitter record of their terrible disappointment.

Lest anyone reading the various accounts of the rise of "Millerism" in
the United States come to the conclusion that Miller and his followers were
"crackpots" or "uneducated tools of Satan," the following facts should be
known:[3] The great advent awakening movement which spanned the Atlantic
from Europe was bolstered by a tremendous wave of contemporary biblical
scholarship. Although Miller himself lacked academic theological training,
actually scores of prophetic scholars in Europe and the United States had
espoused Miller's views before he himself announced them. In reality, his
was only one more voice proclaiming the 1843/1844 fulfillment of Daniel
8:14, or the 2300 days period allegedly dating from 457 B.C. and ending in
1843–1844.

William Miller was born in Pittsfield, Massachusetts, on February 15,
1782, and while still a young child his family moved to Lower Hampton,
New York, close to the Vermont State border. Miller was raised by a deeply

---

[1]Francis D. Nichol, *The Midnight Cry* (Washington, D.C.: Review and Herald, 1944), p. 35.
[2]*Signs of the Times*, January 25, 1843.
[3]The various charges to the effect that the Millerites were fanatics who waited on rooftops
attired in white "ascension robes" anticipating the return of Christ; and further that in-
sanity swept the Millerite ranks in 1843–4 in the wake of the "Great Disappointment" are
purely mythological in character and have little basis in verifiable facts (see *The Midnight
Cry*, pp. 321–498).

religious mother, but despite her zeal for his conversion Miller became a deist. Only after a soul-searching experience which culminated in his conversion did he begin his preparation for the ministry in the Baptist church. A great many books have been written about William Miller and the Millerite movement, but to this writer's knowledge none of them proved Miller to be dishonest or deceptive in his prophetic interpretation of Scripture. Indeed, he enjoyed the reputation, among all who knew him, of being an honest, forthright Christian. One does not have to endorse the errors of Millerism, therefore, to respect the historical figure of William Miller. Regardless of his shortcomings, Miller was a deeply religious Christian who, had he had a more extensive understanding of the Scriptures, most probably would never have embarked upon his disastrous date-setting career.

Clearly it may be seen that although Miller popularized the 1843–1844 concept of Christ coming again, he was by no means alone. If we condemn him, we must also condemn a large number of internationally known scholars who were among the most highly educated men of their day. Yet they too had a blind spot in prophetic interpretation and endorsed this fallacious system of date-setting. Regardless of the number of scholars who confirmed his errors, however, the fact remains that Miller and the Millerite movement operated contrary to the express injunctions of Scripture. Both Miller and his followers lived to reap the reward of their foolhardy quest and to suffer crushing humiliation, ridicule and abject despair.

William Miller set the time for the return of the Lord between March 21, 1843, and March 21, 1844, reckoning according to the Jewish calendar.[4] As the first-named date approached, religious frenzy shook the Millerite world—the Lord was coming back!

Though the followers of Miller were zealous and sincere, stark disappointment awaited them as the Jewish year 1843 faded from time and the Lord did not come. When the dream closest to their hearts failed to materialize, they eagerly sought enlightenment from William Miller, who replied with characteristic honesty. Wrote Miller, in the very shadow of spiritual anguish:

> Were I to live my life over again, with the same evidence that I then had, to be honest with God and man I should have to do as I have done. Although opposers said it would not come, they produced no weighty arguments. It was evidently guess-work with them; and I then thought, and do now, that their denial was based more on an unwillingness for the Lord to come than on any arguments leading to such conclusion. I confess my error, and acknowledge my disappointment; yet I still believe that the Day of the Lord is near, even at the door; and I exhort you, my brethren, to be watchful and not let that day come upon you unawares.[5]

In the wake of this stunning declaration, the Millerites strove vainly to reconcile their interpretations of the prophetic Scripture with the stark truth that Christ had not returned. With one last gasp, so to speak, Miller reluctantly endorsed "The Seventh-month Movement," or the belief that Christ

[4]*Ibid.*, p. 169.
[5]Sylvester Bliss, *Memoirs of William Miller*, Boston, MA: n.p., 1853, p. 256.

would come on October 22, 1844, the tenth day of the seventh month according to the Karaite reckoning of the Jewish Sacred Calendar.[6] Once again the Millerites' hopes were lifted, and October 22, 1844, became the watchword for the return of the Lord Jesus Christ. The outcome can best be summed up in the words of Dr. Josiah Litch, a Millerite leader in Philadelphia, who wrote on October 24: "It is a cloudy and dark day here—the sheep are scattered—the Lord has not come yet."[7]

From Litch's statement, it is easy to piece together the psychological framework of the Millerites in the wake of these two disappointments. They were a shattered and disillusioned people—Christ had not come to cleanse the "sanctuary" (the earth), to usher in judgment, and to bring the world into subjugation to the "everlasting gospel." Instead, the sky was cloudy and dark, and the historical horizons were black with the failure of the Millerite movement. There was, of course, terrible confusion, of which God, Scripture tells us, is not the author (1 Corinthians 14:33).

The final phase of the movement, then, closed with the "Great Disappointment of 1844," but as the Millerites disbanded, there emerged other groups, such as the First-day Adventists. However, in our study we are concerned primarily with three segments which later fused to produce the Seventh-day Adventist denomination. William Miller, it should be noted, was *never* a Seventh-day Adventist and stated that he had "no confidence" in the "new theories" which emerged from the shambles of the Millerite movement. Dr. LeRoy Froom, professor of prophetic interpretation at the Seventh-day Adventist Theological Seminary, Takoma Park, Washington, D.C., in the fourth volume of his masterful series *The Prophetic Faith of Our Fathers*, pp. 828–29,[8] succinctly states what Miller's position was:

> Miller was outspokenly opposed to the various new theories that had developed following October 22, 1844, in an endeavor to explain the disappointment. He deplored the call to come out to the churches that had been given, and he never accepted the distinctive positions of the Sabbatarians. The doctrine of the unconscious sleep of the dead and the final destruction of the wicked was not, he maintained, part of the original Millerite position, but was introduced personally by George Storrs and Charles Fitch. He even came to deny the application of the parable in *The Midnight Cry* to the Seventh-month Movement and eventually went so far as to declare unequivocally that the movement was not "a fulfillment of prophecy in any sense."

Aside from chronological speculation, therefore, the theology of William Miller differed from Seventh-day Adventist theology in three distinct points: he denied the Seventh-day Sabbath, the doctrine of the sleep of the soul, and the final, utter destruction of the wicked—all doctrines held by the Seventh-day Adventist denomination. And he never embraced the "sanctuary" and "investigative judgment" theories developed by Seventh-day Adventists. For William Miller the era of chronological speculation was over, and he died shortly after the fiasco, a broken and disillusioned man who was,

[6]*The Midnight Cry*, p. 243.
[7]*Ibid.*, p. 256.
[8]Review and Herald Publishing Association, Takoma Park, Washington, D.C., 1950.

nevertheless, honest and forthright when in error or when repudiating error. I believe he now enjoys the presence of the Lord whose appearing he so anxiously awaited.

In order to understand the background of Seventh-day Adventist history and theology, let us look at the three segments of Millerism which eventually united to form the Seventh-day Adventist denomination. Each of these groups held a distinctive doctrine. The group headed by Hiram Edson in western New York proclaimed the doctrine of the sanctuary "as embracing a special or final ministry of Christ in the Holy of Holies in the *heavenly* sanctuary," thus giving new meaning to the message, "The Hour of God's Judgment has come." The second group, headed by Joseph Bates, whose main following was in Massachusetts and New Hampshire, advocated the observance of the seventh day Sabbath "as involved in the keeping of the commandments of God." The third group, in Maine, emphasized the "spirit of prophecy" or "the testimony of Jesus," which they believed was to be manifest in the "remnant" (Revelation 14:6–12; also Revelation 12:17; 19:10), or "the last segment of God's church of the centuries." Between the years of 1844 and 1847 the thinking of these groups crystallized and was actively declared and promulgated in the writings of their respective leaders, Hiram Edson, O. R. L. Crosier, Joseph Bates, James White and Ellen G. White.

At this point in our historical analysis of Seventh-day Adventism, we believe it will be profitable to briefly review "The Great Disappointment of 1844" and its relationship to the Seventh-day Adventist doctrines of the heavenly sanctuary and the investigative judgment. The entire superstructure of the Millerites' prophetic interpretation was based upon their view of the book of Daniel, chapters eight and nine, with particular emphasis upon Daniel 8:14 and 9:24–27. The Millerites believed that the prophecy of the seventy weeks of Daniel nine must date from the year 457 B.C., which, as recent archaeological evidence confirms,[9] was the exact date of the decree of King Artaxerxes to rebuild Jerusalem (Daniel 9:25). Tracing the seventy weeks of Daniel on the theory that, as the Hebrew indicated, it should be rendered "seventy weeks of years" or 490 years, the Millerites arrived at the date A.D. 33; that is from 457 B.C. to A.D. 33. Since this date reliably refers to Christ's crucifixion, Millerites then linked it to Daniel 8:14, "Unto two thousand and three hundred days; then shall the sanctuary be cleansed" with the seventy weeks of years prophecy, and the 2300 days became 2300 years. Thus if you subtract 490 years (adding of course, A.D. 1 to 33), the figure 1843 is arrived at. Many biblical scholars have historically shown that in Scripture a day frequently symbolizes a year; further, that the seventy weeks and 2300 days of Daniel could have begun on the same date. And that date, according to the Millerites, was 457 B.C. In *The Prophetic Faith of Our Fathers* (Washington, D.C.: Review and Herald Publishing Association, n.d., vols. 1–4), Dr. LeRoy Froom shows that many expositors had embraced the same method of interpretation, which is no argument for accepting it, but a strong argument for the *right* of the Millerites to do so.

[9]Siegfried H. Horn and Lynn H. Wood, *The Chronology of Ezra 7*, Washington, D.C.: Review and Herald Publishing Association, 1953.

As we have seen, when the Millerite calculations failed, all appeared to be lost; but a singular event took place the very next day in a cornfield near Port Gibson, New York, which changed the face of Adventist history and brought about a reinterpretation of the eighth and ninth chapters in the book of Daniel, an interpretation which is a keystone in the arch of the Seventh-day Adventist view of prophecy.

On October 23, 1844, the morning following the "Great Disappointment," Hiram Edson, a devout Adventist and follower of William Miller, was wending his way homeward with his friend, O. R. L. Crosier. In order to avoid the mocking gazes and taunts of their neighbors, they cut across a cornfield.

As they walked through the cornfield in deep silence and meditation, Hiram Edson stopped, became more deeply immersed in meditation, and then with upturned face indicative of a heartfelt prayer for spiritual light, he suddenly received a great spiritual "revelation." In the words of Dr. Froom,

> Suddenly there burst upon his mind the thought that there were two phases to Christ's ministry in the Heaven of Heavens, just as in the earthly sanctuary of old. In his own words, an overwhelming conviction came over him "that instead of our high priest coming out of the most holy of the heavenly sanctuary to come to this earth on the tenth day of the seventh month at the end of the twenty-three hundred days, He for the first time entered on that day the second apartment of that sanctuary, and that He had a work to perform in the most holy before coming to this earth."[10]

In that instant, according to Seventh-day Adventist history, Hiram Edson found the reason why the Millerites had been disappointed the day before. They had expected Christ to come to earth to cleanse the sanctuary, but the sanctuary was not the earth but was located in Heaven! Instead of coming to earth, therefore, Christ had passed from one "apartment" of the sanctuary into the other "apartment" to perform a closing work now known as the "investigative judgment." In the year 1846 this new interpretation of Daniel was convincingly put forth by O. R. L. Crosier,[11] who outlined and defended Hiram Edson's concept in a lengthy article in a special number of *The Day Star*, a Millerite publication in Cincinnati, Ohio. F. D. Nichol in *The Midnight Cry* refers to "a fragment" which Edson wrote about his experience in the cornfield. But as Dr. Froom has pointed out, Edson himself really believed that Christ had passed from the "holy place" to the "most holy" place in the heavenly sanctuary. The Old Testament tabernacle was divided by a veil into two apartments, the holy place and the most holy place. In the most holy place was the Ark of the Covenant. Into this apartment the high priest went once a year to sprinkle blood upon the mercy seat to make atonement for the sins of the people. In Christian theology, this blood symbolized

---

[10]*The Prophetic Faith of Our Fathers*, Vol. IV, p. 881. An extremely literalistic concept, which is refuted by Hebrews 9:12, 24 and Acts 1, which show that at His ascension Christ entered into the "holy places" not the "second apartment" of the heavenly sanctuary in 1844. Seventh-day Adventists have redefined their teaching in terms of "phases."

[11]Crosier later rejected this concept though it was endorsed by Ellen G. White and other prominent Adventist leaders. (See D. M. Canright, *Life of Mrs. E. G. White*, p. 107.)

prophetically the death of the Lord Jesus Christ, the Lamb of God, for the sins of all the world.

Transferring this Old Testament ceremonial to the New Testament, and making an extremely literalistic interpretation of the book of Hebrews, Edson and Crosier formulated the doctrine of "the heavenly sanctuary and investigative judgment." This concept is now understood to mean that in 1844 Christ entered the "second phase" of His ministry in the heavenly sanctuary, and ever since has been reviewing the cases of believers to determine their worthiness for eternal life. Further, He will come forth from the "second apartment," or finish the "second phase" of His ministry in the sanctuary, to usher in judgment upon the world at His great second advent. This in essence was the interpretation which shaped the later concept of the "heavenly sanctuary" and the "investigative judgment" in Seventh-day Adventist theology. Thus, good Millerite-Adventists were justified in endorsing the work of William Miller. They even maintained that God had allowed Miller to make mistakes for the greater blessing of the "little flock." In her *Early Writings* (Washington, D.C.: Review and Herald Publishing Association, n.d., p. 74), Ellen G. White made this assertion:

> I have seen that the 1843 chart was directed by the hand of the Lord, and that it should not be altered; that the figures were as He wanted them, that His hand was over and hid a mistake in some of the figures so that none could see it until His hand was removed.

In this context Mrs. White was distinctly referring to Fitch's prophetic chart utilized by the Millerites, which led them to the year 1843 instead of the date which she considered to be correct—October 22, 1844.

F. D. Nichol in *Ellen G. White and Her Critics* (Washington, D.C.: Review and Herald Publishing Association, n.d., pp. 332–334), attempts to explain Mrs. White's statement in the light of Acts 24, Mark 16, Exodus 8:15 and Exodus 10. Of course any are at liberty to accept his interpretation of the problem, which I do not. The fact remains, however, that the Millerites erred in their prophetic, chronological interpretation of the book of Daniel, and only the concept of Hiram Edson in the cornfield and the explanatory writings of O. R. L. Crosier buttressed by the "revelations" of Ellen G. White saved the day.

Although I do not accept Ellen White's explanation, or the interpretations of Edson, Crosier, Froom or Nichol, I would be at a loss to account for the growth and development of Seventh-day Adventism apart from the psychological framework of the "Great Disappointment of 1844." Therefore, I have carefully reviewed the doctrines which evolved from the Edson-Crosier-White pronouncements. The psychological factor is very important in Seventh-day Adventist history.

The second of the three Millerite-Adventist groups mentioned is also of great historical import. In Fairhaven, Massachusetts, following the "Great Disappointment of 1844," one Joseph Bates, a retired sea captain, issued a 48 page pamphlet entitled *The Seventh-day Sabbath a Perpetual Sign* (self-published, 1846). In it he argued for the Sabbath as a divine institution ordained in Eden, prefigured in Creation, and buttressed at Mt. Sinai. Some three years later Bates wrote a second pamphlet entitled, *A Seal of the Living God* (self-published, 1849), based largely upon Revelation 14:9–12. Bates' Sabbatarianism exerted a great influence upon what later became the Seventh-day Adventist denomination.

In Volume 4 of *The Prophetic Faith of Our Fathers* (pp. 957, 958), Dr. Froom sums it up:

> This became henceforth a characteristic and separating feature of Sabbatarian Adventist preaching. Bates here held that the message of Revelation 14 is the foundation of the full Advent message "Fear God and give glory to Him, for the hour of His judgment is come." This, he maintained, began to be fulfilled in the preaching of the Millerite movement. And the second angel's message on the fall of Babylon, with its climax in the call "Come out of her my people" was likewise initially sounded in 1843–1844 . . . They must not stop with the first two messages. There is a third inseparable in the series to be received and obeyed—namely, full obedience to God's holy commandments, including the observance of the Seventh day as a Sabbath. But that obedience is by faith. The Sabbath was next set forth as the "seal of God" as based on the sealing work of Revelation 7. On January 8, 1849, Bates issued his tract, "A Seal of the Living God." From the fact of John's declaration that the number of sealed was 144,000, Bates drew the conclusion that the "remnant" who keeps the commandments of God and have the testimony of Jesus Christ would number 144,000. So, to the concept of Christ entering the most holy place in the heavenly sanctuary on October 22, 1844, for the final work of judgment and the receiving of His kingdom, was added the Sabbath as involved in the third of this commission series of special "latter-day" messages. This concept of the "seal" was likewise built into the message of the Sabbath, as an added prophetic element. And this thought was similarly attested by Ellen White who wrote: "This seal is the Sabbath," and described the "most holy place" in which was the ark (Revelation 11:9), containing the Ten Commandments with a halo of light surrounding the fourth! Thus the Sabbath and the sanctuary became inseparably tied together.

The third group, which fused with the other two to form the Seventh-day Adventist Church, emphasized "the spirit of prophecy" (Revelation 19:10). This body of former Millerites accepted the interpretations of one Ellen G. Harmon of Portland, Maine. Ellen Harmon, later Mrs. James White, was recognized by this group as the possessor of the "Spirit of Prophecy," a restoration of the spiritual gift of prophecy (1 Corinthians 12) or counsel to the Seventh-day Adventist Church. Mrs. White had numerous visions which confirmed many Adventist doctrines. When the Edson-Crosier, Bates, and White adherents joined forces, the Seventh-day Adventist denomination was launched.

Although the name "Seventh-day Adventist" denomination was not officially assumed until 1860 at a conference held in Battle Creek, Michigan, nevertheless Seventh-day Adventism had been launched. In 1855, Adventist headquarters were established in Battle Creek and remained there until 1903, when they were transferred to Takoma Park, a Maryland suburb of Washington, D.C.

The three distinctive doctrines of Seventh-day Adventism—the Sabbath, the Sanctuary and the "Spirit of Prophecy"—will be discussed later. The Adventists had a definite theological platform which for many years remained almost constant. In recent years, however, there has been a definite movement toward a more explicit declaration of belief in the principles of the Christian faith and the tenets of Christian theology. In short, "clarification" and "redefinition" have characterized recent Seventh-day Adventist theological activities.

The Seventh-day Adventist denomination has approximately 2.8 million members in 20,000 churches worldwide. At 3.6 million, the Adventist "Sabbath School" enrollment is substantially larger than the church's general membership. There are just over 8,000 Seventh-day Adventist ministers worldwide. The Adventist publishing houses worldwide number 50, most of which republish American Review and Herald Publishing Association materials in the languages of their own countries. Hundreds of periodicals, books, and pamphlets on a variety of subjects are published each year. Over 5 million persons have enrolled in Adventist Bible correspondence courses since their inception. The Adventist *Voice of Prophecy* radio program is heard on 880 stations and is reaching people in some 75 languages. *Faith for Today*, their official TV program, is heard on 183 stations in the U.S. and many stations abroad. The *Signs of the Times* and *These Times*, their largest missionary magazines, have a combined circulation of 500,000 copies each month.

The Adventist school system, elementary, high school, college, graduate, and medical, has a worldwide reputation for academic excellency and innovation. Coupling Adventist doctrine and lifestyle with high educational standards has assured that Adventists and non-Adventists alike apply in great numbers to attend Adventist educational institutions, which number over 5,000 worldwide.

We cannot hope to cover the entire scope of Seventh-day Adventism's historical development in this brief résumé; but we see that from meager beginnings in the wake of the "Great Disappointment of 1844" and the collapse of the Millerite movement, the Seventh-day Adventist denomination has pressed forward and expanded until today it constitutes an important, albeit controversial, segment of American Protestantism.

Although this is but a background sketch, the reader can readily see that in Seventh-day Adventism, religious historians have an interesting subject for study, a subject from which many unusual theological speculations have emerged and continue to emerge.

Psychological Factors

One of the principal problems in understanding the Seventh-day Adventist movement is to discover the psychological motivation and basis of this thriving denomination of zealots.

I. *Early Handicaps*

From the beginning, the Adventists were regarded with grave suspicion by the great majority of evangelical Christians, principally because the Seventh-day Adventists were premillennial in their eschatology. That is, they believed that Christ would come before the millennium and so placed themselves squarely in opposition to the predominant postmillennial and amillennial schools of thought of that era. The "Great Disappointment of 1844" and the collapse of the Millerite movement naturally brought premillennialism into disrepute. Certain authors of the time considered premillennarians "peculiar" even to the point of condemning premillennialism outright and dubbed as "Adventist" all who held that view of eschatology. This is especially interesting when we consider that premillennialism is an accepted school of thought in eschatology today and that those who hold postmillennial and amillennial views are considered by the premillennarians to be peculiar.

Thus the Adventists started out with two great psychological handicaps: They had incurred disapproval of the group or the mainstream of Christianity, and the Millerites from which they sprang had been publicly humiliated by the failure of their chronological calculations. These two factors and the constant jeering by opposing schools of eschatology united the Seventh-day Adventists in a closely knit group, habitually on the defensive and suspicious of the motives and intentions of other Christians.

Moreover, the Adventists were drawn together by the "special truths" of the Advent message. They were convinced that they had a proclamation for the world—a great "last-day message." Later we shall describe how this attitude widened the chasm between Adventists and Christians of other denominations, so it is sufficient here to note that the Adventists considered themselves a special "remnant people" ordained by God to revive certain neglected truths of the Christian message. Filled with burning zeal to fulfill this mission, they laid themselves open to serious misunderstanding by Christians of other denominations who did not agree with them about the proper day of worship, the state of the dead, and investigative judgment.

Engaged in open conflict with Christians of virtually all denominations, the Adventists retreated into an "exclusivistic shell," despising what they termed "certain antinomian tendencies in contemporary Christian theology." They laid strong emphasis upon man's responsibility to the moral law of God, which eventually brought upon them the label, "Galatianists" or "legalists." Now, as we shall see, there can be little doubt that there was and still is legalism in Adventism, as in some other Christian churches; but when we consider these early psychological factors, certain of which still pertain today, their reactions are understandable, though hardly defensible.

Of course the aforementioned "neglected" truths made few friends for the Adventists with Christians of other denominations, mainly because these truths were frequently presented in such manner as to arouse opposition instead of inviting investigation. Seventh-day Adventism has woefully demonstrated many times the old but true adage, "Not what we say but how we say it makes or breaks a case."

II. *Identity Concealed*

In his book, *Answers to Objections* (Washington, D.C.: Review and Herald Publishing Association, 1952, pp. 421, 422), F. D. Nichol demonstrates how the psychological defense which Adventists erected in their early days has carried over into modern times. Nichol quotes the charge:

> When Seventh-day Adventist ministers go into a community to hold a series of lectures they conceal at first their denominational connection. They thus hope to draw into their audience people who would never have come if they knew Seventh-day Adventists were conducting the meetings. This is a form of deception. There is something the matter with a religious body that is afraid to identify itself as soon as it begins to carry on any activity in a community.

Nichol answers:

> Now it is a fact that during most of the history of the Seventh-day Adventist church, the very word Adventist has conveyed to the minds of most people a picture of a deluded band of fanatics sitting on housetops in ascension robes, awaiting the opening of the heavens. This story of ascension robes has become a part of American folklore and has been embalmed in impressive encyclopedias. And the ascension robe story is only part of the fanciful picture that has come to the minds of many when they have heard the word Adventist.
>
> The ascension robe story is a myth, and ninety-nine percent of related stories are likewise myths—as has now been proved—but that has not prevented people from believing them. The net result has been that many people have seen Seventh-day Adventists only through the distorting mists of slanderous myths. This is nothing new in religious history; witness, for example, the early history of the Quakers and the Baptists.
>
> It should not be difficult, therefore, for any reasonable person to see why Adventist ministers through the past years have sought first to cause people to see them simply as Christian preachers before announcing their Adventist connection. After all, we seek to be first, and before all else, Christian preachers of righteousness. Then we hope to build on the timely messages from Bible prophecy that may be described in the words of the Apostle Peter as "present truth" for these last days of earth's history.
>
> It has undoubtedly been true in years past that Adventists could not have gotten a crowd out to hear them in certain cities, at least, if they had revealed their identity at the outset. But we think that that proves not the weakness of the Adventist case, but the strength of distorted ideas founded on fanciful myths. The other side of the picture is that many people, after they have attended Adventist meetings for a time, frankly admit that they have changed their ideas about us and are glad that they first came to the meetings not knowing who was conducting them.
>
> In more recent years our activities have become so much better known that in many places the former distorted picture has been largely corrected. Accordingly, we are increasingly following the plan of announcing at the outset the Adventist sponsorship of the public meetings. That is what we like to do, and what we hope ere long to be able to do everywhere. We are not ashamed of our Adventism, far from it. . . . No, we don't want to boast, we simply want to proclaim to the world a message that we earnestly believe should be given at this time. And if, in order to secure an initial hearing, we must at first conceal the name, we do so for a brief period only with a view to a clear-cut announcement of our Adventist connections a little later in the meetings. Then those who have been coming may decline to come further, if they desire. They generally decide to stay!

Unhappily, as the literature of many objectors to Adventism reveals, it is they who have often been most active in spreading the distorting myths regarding us. And then they are wont to add, as though to prove conclusively their case against us, that we sometimes fail to reveal our Adventist connection at the outset of a series of evangelistic lectures! If they will help us to clear away completely the slanderous myths which folklore has often thrown around the name Adventist, we will be most happy to preface every one of our public meetings with the announcement of its Adventist sponsorship! In the meantime we shall, in such instances and areas as the situation necessitates, follow the precedent set by our Lord's instruction to His disciples as regards the time of disclosing our name.

Thus we see that some Adventist leaders, at least, maintain the premise that everyone's prejudice against them is based on myths and folklore, and on the fact that they deliberately disguise themselves until they can obtain a hearing and demonstrate that they are Christians. These practices have given rise to the charge of proselyting and it is not without foundation. In general, however, Nichol makes some very good points, though inadvertently he reveals only too clearly that he and many Adventists have been reared in this unhealthy climate of distrust, prejudice and suspicion.

Nichol declares:

> If they will help us to clear away completely the slanderous myths which folklore has often thrown around the name Adventist, we will be most happy to preface every one of our public meetings with the announcement of its Adventist sponsorship!

The only difficulty with Nichol's statement is that the burden of proof lies not upon the other denominations, but upon the Adventists themselves. By openly identifying themselves, they can refute these charges of deception and proselyting.

On p. 420, Nichol makes the mistake of using passages in the gospel of Matthew (8:4; 9:30; 16:20) where Christ enjoined secrecy, to prove that Adventists are only following Him when they conceal their identity, and he unfortunately tries to establish that such a behavior pattern on the part of Adventists is "honorable." Says Nichol,

> We have yet to hear any devout Christian expressing misgivings and doubts about the ministry of Christ or declaring that He was ashamed or afraid because He concealed His identity for a time. Evidently, then, this much at least may be established at the outset as being proved by these texts; concealing one's identity is not an insult or proof that one is either ashamed or afraid. There may be honorable and altogether reasonable grounds for such concealment.

Although Nichol's argument appears plausible, the cases are not parallel, for over against the incidents which he cites, the Lord Jesus did many miracles in public and taught openly in the Temple as He Himself declared before Caiaphas (John 18:20). But to compare the motives of Adventists with the motives of the Lord Jesus Christ is just a bit more than I am willing to concede.

True, there is much misinformation about Adventist history and theology, but not infrequently it can be traced to unfortunate statements in their own official publications. Although other denominations are likewise guilty, Adventists have largely been outside the mainstream of Christian fellowship and so are in an unenviable position. They must go the "second mile" in this respect.

It is evident, then, that because of the opposition and abuse suffered in their early days, and also because of the "special truths" of the Advent message and emphasis upon certain areas of theology, the Adventists have been at a distinct psychological disadvantage and so have tended to band together against other churches. Other denominations, of course, have encouraged this recluse-like behavior by endless repetition of some of the Millerite myths. These factors, therefore, must be soberly evaluated if we are to understand Seventh-day Adventism.

Adventist Theology and Classical Orthodoxy

For many years Seventh-day Adventists have been handicapped by the lack of a comprehensive volume which adequately defines their doctrinal position. Many publications clearly set forth certain aspects of Adventism, particularly the writings of F. D. Nichol, L. E. Froom and Ellen G. White, whose role is that of inspired commentator and "messenger" to the Adventist denomination.

Except for the brief statement of fundamentals in the Seventh-day Adventist Yearbook, the average Adventist has been somewhat at a loss to explain conflicting theological opinions within his denomination, and even expressions in the writings of Ellen G. White were in certain contexts so ambiguous as to frustrate even the most devout believer. As a result of this, in 1957 the General Conference of Seventh-day Adventists released the first definitive and comprehensive explanation of their faith, an authoritative volume entitled *Questions on Doctrine*.

This book truthfully presents the theology and doctrine which the leaders of Seventh-day Adventism affirm they have always held. Members of other denominations will find it a reliable source to consult when seeking to understand what the Adventists themselves describe as "the position of our denomination in the area of church doctrine and prophetic interpretation."[12]

There can be no doubt of the fact that there are conflicting statements in Adventist publications and diverse opinions about certain areas of Adventist theology and interpretation, some of which is quite the opposite of classical orthodox Christianity; but this situation is not peculiar to the Adventist since all Christian denominations have various "wings," in most instances quite vocal, which are a source of constant embarrassment because they represent their own particular interpretations of the denomination's theology as the viewpoint of the denomination itself.

It is, therefore, unfair to quote any one Adventist writer or a group of writers as representing "the position of our denomination in the area of church doctrine and prophetic interpretation" even though the writings of such persons may in a large area qualify as Adventist theology. One must

---

[12]*Questions on Doctrine*, p. 8.

consult in good faith what the denomination itself represents as its theology and assume that the Seventh-day Adventist theologians know better than non-Adventists the implications and conclusions which they are willing to admit as representative of their church's theology.

This section is divided into several parts, each of which contains statements of the official Adventist position of particular aspects of theology and is thoroughly documented from the primary source material provided in *Questions on Doctrine.* It is hoped that the reader will weigh carefully the declarations of the Seventh-day Adventist Church as represented by its general conference which alone is empowered to speak for the denomination. They have asserted initially, and reaffirmed currently, the authoritative force of *Questions on Doctrine* as accurately representative of Adventist doctrine. Until such time as there is clear, unequivocal, and equally authoritative evidence to the contrary, we must let the doctrine revealed in this book stand as Adventist doctrine. These doctrinal points we shall present and biblically evaluate below.

It is unnecessary to document at great length the fact that Seventh-day Adventism adheres tenaciously to the foundational doctrines of Christian theology as these have been held by the Christian Church throughout the centuries. Dr. Anthony Hoekema, who believes that Seventh-day Adventism is a non-Christian cult, makes this interesting admission, and since Dr. Hoekema is no friend of Adventism, his testimony on this point could hardly be called prejudiced:

> . . . I am of the conviction that Seventh-day Adventism is a cult and not an evangelical denomination. . . . It is recognized with gratitude that there are certain soundly Scriptural emphases in the teaching of Seventh-day Adventism. We are thankful for the Adventists' affirmation of the infallibility of the Bible, of the Trinity and of the full deity of Jesus Christ. We gratefully acknowledge their teachings on creation and providence, on the incarnation and resurrection of Christ, on the absolute necessity for regeneration, on sanctification by the Holy Spirit, and on Christ's literal return.[13]

It is puzzling to me, as a student of non-Christian cult systems, how any group can hold the above doctrines in their proper Biblical context which Dr. Hoekema admits the Adventist do and still be a non-Christian cult! However, we shall deal with this aspect of the critics of Adventism at the end of the chapter; therefore, suffice it to say that the Adventists do have a clean bill of health where the major doctrines of Christian theology are involved.

Lest there be any doubt on the subject, the following quotations taken from *Questions on Doctrine* are still upheld by the Seventh-day Adventist hierarchy as authoritative, and forthrightly declare the Seventh-day Adventist position in relation to historic Christianity as well as those areas where Adventism differs from the orthodox Christian position.

I. *Inspiration and Authority of the Scriptures*

1. "Seventh-day Adventists believe that all Scripture, both Old and New Testament, from Genesis to Revelation was 'given by inspiration of God'

---

[13]Anthony Hoekema, *The Four Major Cults*, Grand Rapids, MI: William B. Eerdmans Publishing Company, 1963, pp. 389, 403.

(2 Tim. 3:16), and constitutes the very word of God—the truth that 'liveth and abideth for ever' (1 Pet. 1:23). We recognize the Bible as the ultimate and final authority on what is truth" (p. 26).

2. "Seventh-day Adventists hold the Protestant position that the Bible and the Bible only is the sole rule of faith and practice for Christians. We believe that all theological beliefs must be measured by the living Word, judged by its truth, and whatsoever is unable to pass this test, or is found to be out of harmony with its message, is to be rejected" (p. 28).

3. "We believe in the authority, veracity, reliability, and truth of the Holy Scriptures. The same union of the divine and the human that is manifested in Christ, exists in the Bible. Its truths, revealed, are 'given by inspiration of God' (2 Tim. 3:16), yet are couched in the words of men" (pp. 27, 28).

II. *The Nature of Christ*

1. "Jesus Christ is very God, and He has existed with the Father from all eternity" (p. 22).

2. "Christ, the Word of God, became incarnate through the miraculous conception and the virgin birth; and He lived an absolutely sinless life here on earth" (p. 22).

3. "Christ is called the Second Adam. In purity and holiness, connected with God and beloved by God. He began where the first Adam began. Willingly He passed over the ground where Adam fell, and redeemed Adam's failure" (p. 650).

4. "In taking upon Himself man's nature in its fallen condition, Christ did not in the least participate in its sin. He was subject to the infirmities and weaknesses by which man is encompassed. . . . He was touched with the feeling of our infirmities, and was in all points tempted like as we are. And yet He 'knew no sin.' He was the Lamb 'without blemish and without spot.' . . . We should have no misgivings in regard to the perfect sinlessness of the human nature of Christ" (p. 651).

5. "In His human nature He maintained the purity of His divine character. . . . He was unsullied with corruption, a stranger to sin. . . . He was a mighty petitioner, not possessing the passions of our human, fallen natures, but compassed with like infirmities, tempted in all points like as we are" (pp. 658, 659).

6. "He was perfect, and undefiled by sin, He was without spot or blemish. . . . Jesus, coming to dwell in humanity, receives no pollution" (p. 660).

III. *The Atonement*

1. "Those who teach that a completed atonement was made on the cross view the term in its popular theological sense, but really what is meant by them is that on Calvary the all-sufficient atoning sacrifice of Christ was offered for our salvation. With this concept all true Christians readily and heartily agree. 'We are sanctified through the offering of the body of Jesus Christ, once for all' (Heb. 10:10). Those who view this aspect of the work of Christ as a completed atonement, apply this term *only* to what Christ accomplished on the cross. They do not include in their definition the application of the benefits of the atonement made on the cross to the individual sinner" (p. 342).

2. "Seventh-day Adventists do *not* believe that Christ made but partial

or incomplete sacrificial atonement on the cross" (p. 349).

3. "Most decidedly the all-sufficient atoning sacrifice of Jesus our Lord was *offered and completed* on the cross of Calvary. This was done for all mankind, for 'he is the propitiation . . . for the sins of the whole world' (1 John 2:2). This sacrificial work will actually benefit human hearts *only* as we surrender our lives to God and experience the miracle of the new birth. In this experience Jesus our High Priest, applies to us the benefits of His atoning sacrifice. Our sins are forgiven, we become the children of God by faith in Christ Jesus, and the peace of God dwells in our hearts" (p. 350).

4. "When, therefore, one hears an Adventist say, or reads in Adventist literature—even in the writings of Ellen G. White—that Christ is making atonement now, it should be understood that we mean simply that Christ is now making application of the benefits of the sacrificial atonement He made on the cross; that He is making it efficacious for us individually, according to our needs and requests. Mrs. White herself, as far back as 1857, clearly explained what she means when she writes of Christ's making atonement for us in His ministry:

" 'The great Sacrifice had been offered and had been accepted, and the Holy Spirit which descended on the day of Pentecost carried the minds of the disciples from the earthly sanctuary to the heavenly, where Jesus had entered by His own blood to shed upon His disciples the *benefits* of His atonement' " (pp. 354, 555).

5. *"When the Father beheld the sacrifice of His Son*, He bowed before it in recognition of its perfection. 'It is enough,' He said, 'the Atonement is complete' (p. 663).

IV. *The Resurrection*

1. "Jesus Christ arose literally and bodily from the grave. He ascended literally and bodily into heaven. He now serves as our advocate in priestly ministry and mediation before the Father" (p. 22).

2. "There shall be a resurrection both of the just and the unjust. The resurrection of the just will take place at the second coming of Christ; the resurrection of the unjust will take place a thousand years later, at the close of the millennium (John 5:28, 29; 1 Thess. 4:13–18; Rev. 20:5–10)" (p. 14).

V. *The Second Coming*

1. "[Jesus Christ] will return in a premillennial, personal, imminent second advent" (p. 22).

2. "As our denominational name indicates, the second coming of Christ is one of the cardinal doctrines of the Adventist faith. We give it such prominence in our beliefs because it occupies a pivotal place in Holy Scripture, not only in the New Testament, but also in the Old" (p. 449).

3. "Jesus will assuredly come the second time. . . . [His] second advent will be visible, audible, and personal. . . . Seventh-day Adventists believe on the evidence of Scripture that there will be one visible, personal, glorious second coming of Christ" (pp. 451, 452, 459).

VI. *The Plan of Salvation*

1. "The vicarious, atoning death of Jesus Christ, once for all, is all-sufficient for the redemption of a lost race. . . . Man was created sinless, but

by his subsequent fall entered a state of alienation and depravity. . . . Salvation through Christ is by grace alone, and through faith in His blood. . . . Entrance upon the new life in Christ is by regeneration, or the new birth. . . . Man is justified by faith . . . sanctified by the indwelling Christ through the Holy Spirit" (pp. 22, 23).

2. "Every person in order to obtain salvation must experience the new birth. This comprises an entire transformation of life and character by the recreative power of God through faith in the Lord Jesus Christ (John 3:16; Matt. 18:3; Acts 2:37–39)" (p. 12).

3. " . . . The law of ten commandments points out sin, the penalty of which is death. The law cannot save the transgressor from his sin, nor impart power to keep him from sinning. In infinite love and mercy, God provides a way whereby this may be done. He furnishes a substitute, even Christ the Righteous One, to die in man's stead, making 'him to be sin for us, who knew no sin; that we might be made the righteousness of God in him' (2 Cor. 5:21). That one is justified, not by obedience to the law, but by the grace that is in Christ Jesus. By accepting Christ, man is reconciled to God, justified by His blood for the sins of the past, and saved from the power of sin by His indwelling life" (p. 13).

4. "One who truly understands and accepts the teachings of the Seventh-day Adventist Church can assuredly know that he is born again, and that he is fully accepted by the Lord. He has in his soul the assurance of present salvation, and need be in no uncertainty whatsoever. In fact, he may know this so fully that he can truly 'rejoice in the Lord' (Phil. 4:4); and in 'the God of his salvation' (Psalm 24:5)" (p. 105).

5. "Nothing we can ever do will merit the favor of God. Salvation is of grace. It is grace that 'bringeth salvation' (Titus 2:11). It is 'through the grace of the Lord Jesus Christ we shall be saved' (Acts 15:11). We are not saved by 'works' (Rom. 4:6; Eph. 2:8; 2 Tim. 1:9), even though they be *good* works. . . . Neither can we be saved by 'law' (Rom. 8:3), nor by the 'deeds' or the 'works' of the law (Rom. 3:20; Gal. 3:2, 5, 10). . . . The law of God was never designed to save men. It is a looking glass, in which, when we gaze, we see our sinfulness. That is as far as the law of God can go with a sinful man. It can reveal his sin but is powerless to remove it, or to save him from its guilt and penalty and power" (pp. 108, 109).

VI. *The Spiritual Nature of Man*

1. "Some have maintained that man was created mortal, so far as his body was concerned, and that he possessed an immortal entity called either a 'soul' or a 'spirit.' Others have felt equally certain that man was not in any sense created immortal. They have been convinced that man was not in possession of an ethereal soul, or spirit, which survived death as a conscious entity, apart from the body. . . . We as Adventists believe that, in general, the Scriptures teach that the soul of man represents the whole man, and not a particular part independent of the other component parts of man's nature; and further, that the soul cannot exist apart from the body, for a man is a unit" (pp. 511, 515).

2. "We as Adventists have reached the definite conclusion that man rests in the tomb until the resurrection morning. Then, at the first resurrection (Rev. 20:4, 5), the resurrection of the just (Acts 24:15), the righteous come forth immortalized, at the call of Christ the Life-giver. And they then

enter into life everlasting, in their eternal home in the kingdom of glory. Such is our understanding" (p. 520).

VIII. *Punishment of the Wicked*

1. "In the expression 'eternal punishment,' just as in 'eternal redemption' and 'eternal judgment,' the Bible is referring to all eternity—not as of process, but as of *result*. It is not an endless process of punishment, but an effectual punishment, which will be final and forever" (p. 540).

2. "We reject the doctrine of eternal torment for the following major reasons: (1) Because everlasting life is a gift of God (Rom. 6:23). The wicked do not possess this—they 'shall not see life' (John 3:36); 'no murderer hath eternal life abiding in him' (1 John 3:15). (2) Because eternal torment would perpetuate and immortalize sin, suffering, and woe, and contradict, we believe, divine revelation, which envisions the time when these things shall be no more (Rev. 21:4). (3) Because it seems to us to provide a plague spot in the universe of God throughout eternity, and would seem to indicate that it is impossible for God Himself ever to abolish it. (4) Because in our thinking, it would detract from the attribute of love as seen in the character of God, and postulates the concept of a wrath which is never appeased. (5) Because the Scriptures teach that the atoning work of Christ is to 'put away sin' (Heb. 9:26)—first from the individual, and ultimately from the universe. The full fruition of Christ's sacrificial, atoning work will be seen not only in a redeemed people but in a restored heaven and earth (Eph. 1:14)" (p. 543).

IX. *The Sanctuary and the Investigative Judgment*

1. "*Does your teaching of the sanctuary service mean that the work of Christ on Calvary was not an all-sufficient, complete, once-for-all sacrifice—a sacrifice that obtains for us eternal redemption? Or was something subsequently necessary to make the sacrificial work of Christ effective for the salvation of man?*

"To the first part of the question our answer is an unequivocal No. The death of Christ on Calvary's cross provides the only sacrifice by which man can be saved. . . . This 'one sacrifice' (Heb. 10:12), or 'one offering' (verse 14), of Christ was 'for ever' (verse 12), and wrought 'eternal redemption' (Heb. 9:12) for man. The sacrifice was completely efficacious. It provided complete atonement for all mankind, and will never be repeated, for it was all-sufficient and covered the needs of every soul" (pp. 356, 357).

2. "The expression 'once' or 'once for all,' in connection with the sacrifice of Christ, is deeply significant. . . . 'He died to sin *once for all*' (Rom. 6:10); 'offering of the body of Jesus Christ *once for all*' (Heb. 10:10). He did this not by 'the blood of goats and calves' but by 'his own blood.' He entered *once for all* into the holy place (or, 'holiest'), 'thus securing an eternal redemption' for us (Heb. 9:12, R.S.V.).

"The Greek word here translated 'holy place' is *hagia*, and is in the plural form. A correct translation would be 'the holies,' or 'holy places,' as in Hebrews 9:24. This entrance, Scripture teaches, occurred at His ascension to glory (Acts 1), having already finished His sacrificial work on the cross. The word translated 'obtained,' in the Greek is from *heurisko*, and is rendered 'found,' 'procured,' 'gained,' or in R.S.V., 'secured' " (pp. 380, 381).

3. "Jesus our surety entered the 'holy places,' and appeared in the

presence of God for us. But it was not with the *hope* of obtaining something for us at that time, or at some future time. No! *He had already obtained it for us on the cross.* And now as our High Priest He ministers the virtues of His atoning sacrifice to us" (p. 381).

4. "The time of the cleansing of the sanctuary, synchronizing with the period of the proclamation of the message of Revelation 14, is a time of investigative judgment; first, with reference to the dead, and second, with reference to the living. This investigative judgment determines who of the myriads sleeping in the dust of the earth are worthy of a part in the first resurrection, and who of its living multitudes are worthy of translation (1 Peter 4:17, 18; Dan. 7:9, 10; Rev. 14:6, 7; Luke 20:35)" (p. 15).

5. "The great judgment scene of heaven will clearly reveal those who have been growing in grace and developing Christ-like characters. Some who have professed to be God's people, but who have disregarded His counsel, will in amazement say to the Lord, 'Have we not prophesied in thy name? and in thy name have cast out devils? and in thy name done many wonderful works?' His reply to such will be brief but emphatic: 'I never knew you. Depart from me, ye that work iniquity' (Matt. 7:22, 23)" (p. 417).

6. "In view of the principles here set forth, it seems to us abundantly clear that the acceptance of Christ at conversion does not seal a person's destiny. His life record after conversion is also important. A man may go back on his repentance, or by careless inattention let slip the very life he has espoused. Nor can it be said that a man's record is closed when he comes to the end of his days. He is responsible for his influence during life, and is just as surely responsible for his evil influence after he is dead" (p. 420).

7. "It is our understanding that Christ as High Priest, concludes His intercessory ministry in heaven in a work of judgment. He begins His great work of judgment in the investigative phase. At the conclusion of the investigation the *sentence* of judgment is pronounced. Then as judge Christ descends to *execute* or carry into effect, that sentence. . . . When God's final sentence of judgment is consummated the redeemed will be singing the song of Moses and the Lamb" (p. 422).

8. "The blotting of names out of the book of life is, we believe, a work of the investigative judgment. A complete and thorough check of all the candidates for eternal life will need to be completed before Christ comes in the clouds of heaven, for when He appears, the decisions for life and death are already made. The dead in Christ are called to life, and the living followers of Christ are translated (1 Thess. 4:15–17)—the entire citizenry of the everlasting kingdom. There's no time subsequent to the second advent for such decisions" (pp. 438, 439).

X. *The Scapegoat Teaching*

1. "Two goats were obviously required, and used, on the Day of Atonement, because there is a *twofold responsibility for sin*—first, my responsibility as the *perpetrator*, agent, or medium; and second, Satan's responsibility as the *instigator*, or tempter, in whose heart sin was first conceived.

"Now, concerning my sin, Christ died for *my* sins (Rom. 5:8). . . . He assumed *my* responsibilities, and His blood alone cleanses *me* from all sin. . . . The atonement for *my* sin is made solely by the shed blood of Christ.

"And concerning Satan's sin, and his responsibility as instigator and tempter, no salvation is provided for him. He must be punished for his responsibility. There is no savior, or substitute, to bear his punishment. He must himself 'atone' for his sin in causing men to transgress, in the same way that a master criminal suffers on the gallows or in the electric chair for his responsibility in the crimes that he has caused others to commit. *It is in this sense only that we can understand the words of Leviticus 16:10 concerning the scapegoat, 'To make an atonement with him.'*

"Under criminal law, the instigator, or mastermind, may be punished more severely than his agents. . . . Satan is the responsible mastermind in the great crime of sin, and his responsibility will return upon his head. *The crushing weight of his responsibility in the sins of the whole world—of the wicked as well as the righteous—must be rolled back upon him.* Simple justice demands that while Christ suffers for my guilt, *Satan must also be punished as the instigator of sin*" (pp. 397, 399).

2. "Satan makes no atonement for our sins. But Satan will ultimately have to bear the retributive punishment for his responsibility in the sins of all men, both righteous and wicked. Seventh-day Adventists, therefore, repudiate *in toto* any idea, suggestions, or implication that Satan is in any sense or degree our sin bearer. The thought is abhorrent to us, and appallingly sacrilegious. Such a concept is a dreadful disparagement of the efficacy of Christ and His salvation, and vitiates the whole glorious provision of salvation solely through our Savior.

"Satan's death a thousand times over could never make him a savior in any sense whatsoever. He is the archsinner of the universe, the author and instigator of sin. . . . Only Christ, the Creator, the one and only God man, could make a substitutionary atonement for men's transgressions. And this Christ did completely, perfectly, and once for all, on Golgotha" (pp. 399, 400).

XI. *The Sabbath and the Mark of the Beast*

1. "We believe that the Sabbath was instituted in Eden before sin entered, that it was honored of God, set apart by divine appointment, and given to mankind as a perpetual memorial of a finished creation. It was based upon the fact that God Himself had rested from His work of creation, had blessed His Sabbath, or rest day, and had sanctified it, or set it apart for man (Gen. 2:1–3; Mark 2:27)" (p. 149).

2. "We believe that the restoration of the Sabbath is indicated in the Bible prophecy of Revelation 14:9–12. Sincerely believing this, we regard the observance of the Sabbath as a test of our loyalty to Christ as Creator and Redeemer.

"Seventh-day Adventists do not rely upon their Sabbathkeeping as a means of salvation or of winning merit before God. We are saved by grace alone. Hence our Sabbath observance, as also our loyalty to every other command of God, is an expression of our love for our Creator and Redeemer. . . .

"We are saved through the righteousness of Jesus Christ received as a gift of grace, and grace alone. Our Lord's sacrifice on Calvary is mankind's only hope. But having been saved, we rejoice that the righteous requirements of the law are fulfilled in the experience of the Christian 'who walks not after the flesh but after the spirit,' and who by the grace of God lives in harmony with the revealed will of God" (pp. 153, 190).

3. *"Do Seventh-day Adventists teach in their authorized literature that those who worship on Sunday and who repudiate in its entirety the Seventh-day Adventist teaching as a consequence have the mark of apostasy, or 'the mark of the beast'? Does not*

Mrs. White teach that those who now keep Sunday already have the mark of the beast'?

"Our doctrinal positions are based upon the Bible and not upon Mrs. White's writings. But since her name has been introduced into the question, an explicit statement from her pen should set the record straight. The following was penned by her in 1899: 'No one has yet received the mark of the beast. Testing time has not yet come. There are true Christians in every church, not excepting the Roman Catholic Church. None are condemned until they have had the light and seen the obligation of the fourth commandment. But *when the decree shall go forth enforcing the counterfeit sabbath,* and the loud cry of the third angel shall warn men against the worship of the beast and his image, the line will be clearly drawn between the false and the true. *Then those who still continue in transgression will receive the mark of the beast'* " (p. 183).

4. "To your inquiry, then, as to whether Mrs. White maintained that all those who do not see and *observe* the seventh day as the Sabbath *now* have the 'mark of apostasy,' the answer is definitely no" (p. 184).

5. "We hold the firm conviction that millions of devout Christians of all faiths throughout all past centuries, as well as those today who are sincerely trusting in Christ their Savior for salvation and are following Him according to their best light, are unquestionably saved" (p. 184).

XII. *The Question of Unclean Foods*

1. "It is true we refrain from eating certain articles, . . . but not because the law of Moses had any binding claims upon us. Far from it. We stand fast in the liberty with which God has set us free" (p. 623).

2. "Our health teaching is not a matter of religious taboo; in fact it is much more than careful selection in diet. It is, to us, the following of a well-balanced health program. We feel it to be our Christian duty to preserve our bodies in the best of health for the service and glory of God. We believe that our bodies are the temples of the Holy Spirit (1 Cor. 3:16; 2 Cor. 6:16), and that whether therefore we eat, or drink, or whatsoever we do we should 'do all to the glory of God' (1 Cor. 10:31)" (p. 634).

XIII. *The "Remnant Church"*

1. "*It is alleged that Seventh-day Adventists teach that they alone constitute the finally completed 'remnant church' mentioned in the book of Revelation. . . . Do Adventists maintain that they alone are the only true witnesses of the living God in our age. . . ?*

"The answer to this threefold question will depend quite largely on the definition given to the word 'remnant.' If, as is implied in the second part, 'remnant' is taken to mean the church invisible, our answer to the first part is an unqualified no. Seventh-day Adventists have never sought to equate their church with the church invisible—'Those in every denomination who remain faithful to the Scriptures' " (p. 186).

2. "It is in a spirit of deep humility that we apply this scripture to the Advent Movement and its work, for we recognize the tremendous implications of such an interpretation. While we believe that Revelation 12:17 points to us as a people of prophecy, it is in no spirit of pride that we thus apply the scripture. To us it is the logical conclusion of our system of prophetic interpretation" (p. 191).

3. "But the fact that we thus apply this scripture does not imply in any way that we believe we are the only true Christians in the world, or that we are the only ones who will be saved" (pp. 191, 192).

4. "Seventh-day Adventists firmly believe that God has a precious remnant, a multitude of earnest, sincere believers, in every church. . ." (p. 192).

5. "We believe the majority of God's children are still scattered in this way throughout the world. And of course, the majority of those in Christian churches still conscientiously observe Sunday. We ourselves cannot do so, for we believe that God is calling for a reformation in this matter. But we respect and love those of our fellow Christians who do not interpret God's Word just as we do" (pp. 192, 193).

6. "We fully recognize the heartening fact that the host of the true followers of Christ are scattered all through the various churches of Christendom, including the Roman Catholic Church. These God clearly recognizes as His own. *Such do not form a part of the 'Babylon' portrayed in the Apocalypse*" (p. 197).

Author's Note

1. *The Concept of Christ's Sinful Human Nature*
Since almost all critics of Seventh-day Adventism contend that Seventh-day Adventists believe Christ possessed a sinful human nature during the incarnation, a word should be said to clarify this point. These charges are often based on an article in *Signs of the Times*, March 1927, and a statement in *Bible Readings for the Home Circle*, edition of 1944. Regarding the first reference, a critical article states:

> My . . . quotation is from L. A. Wilcox, for many years an editor of *The Signs of the Times*, which according to the latest figures given by the Adventists has been published by them for 82 years. Certainly a statement by an editor of that publication may be considered official. I'm sure that anything that Mr. Wilcox wrote did not just happen to get in. In March 1927 he wrote, "In His (Christ's) veins was the incubus of a tainted heredity like a caged lion ever seeking to break forth and destroy. Temptation attacked Him where by heredity He was weakest, attacked Him in unexpected times and ways. In spite of bad blood and an inherited meanness, He conquered."
>
> And again in the December 1928 issue of *Signs of the Times* this editor Mr. Wilcox stated: "Jesus took humanity with all its liabilities, with all its dreadful risks of yielding to temptation."[14]

First, L. A. Wilcox was never on the editorial staff of *Signs of the Times*. Moreover, Mr. L. A. Wilcox, who wrote the article, in a letter dated April 26, 1957, stated:

> The writer of the *Signs* article was a very young man in 1927 and not by any means always felicitous in his phraseology. I know, for I was the writer. The first sentence quoted is crude and shocking and theologically inaccurate, and I was properly spanked for it by Adventist officials, which proves that this article cannot be truly represented as "official" or "authoritative."

It is no more than fair to point out that no man has taught more

---

[14]*The King's Business*, April, 1957.

earnestly or fervently than I as an Adventist minister, the deity of the Lord Jesus Christ, the sinlessness of Christ, salvation by grace, righteousness by faith, the finished work of Calvary, a Christ-centered religion, than I—with the "Amen" of Seventh-day Adventist leadership.

Virtually every critic of Seventh-Day Adventism, including the author quoted above, also uses a statement quoted from *Bible Readings for the Home Circle* (1944 edition, p. 174)—even though in 1945 the statement was expunged by Adventists because it was not in line with official Adventist theology.

A further quotation often seized upon is taken from the book *Desire of the Ages*, by Ellen G. White. On page 117 she says, "Our Savior took humanity, with all its liabilities. He took the nature of man, with the possibility of yielding to temptation." Mrs. White also speaks of "fallen nature." Understandably, not having read all she has written on the subject, these critics conclude that she means that Christ possessed a sinful, carnal, or degenerate human nature. However, Mrs. White's writings clearly indicate that when she speaks of the fallen nature of Christ, she means the physical properties of the race, which degenerated since the time of Adam who was created perfect without the ravages of sin upon either his physical or spiritual being. Adam did not age before the fall, but Christ was born into the world a true man and with the curse of sin operative upon the physical properties of the human race. For thirty-three years He endured the aging process. He could not have reached the age of thirty-three without organic changes taking place in His body, and were He not subject to the physical decline of the race, he would not have been a true man, "made under the law" (Galatians 4:4). Mrs. White's position has been held by many eminent scholars who have never been accused of being either heretics or non-Christians. Why, then, should she and the Adventists be condemned for holding this view? For centuries Christians have argued about the human nature of Christ. Some have believed that He could have sinned, but did not. Others, including this writer, that He could not have sinned. However, it is a theological issue not likely to be resolved by trite phrases and dogmatic pronouncements.

It is true that various Adventist publications, in the past and present, sometimes have contradicted each other. However, at its release and up through this year (see, for example, the quote presented earlier from the April 29, 1983, Adventist letter to me), *Questions on Doctrine* presents the *official* position of the Adventist denomination regarding Christ's sinless nature. It is to that position that I can say "Amen."

Dr. Anthony Hoekema in his volume, *The Four Major Cults*, falls into the same error as E. B. Jones, Louis Talbot, and other critics of Seventh-day Adventism, and ignores totally the fact that Wilcox publicly and in print (1957) repudiated his position. This fact they all know but seem determined to ignore since Wilcox's statement suits so well their assumption that despite official Adventist statements on doctrine, they, the critics, know more than the Adventists do about their own faith!

2. *The Incomplete Atonement Concept*

It is also often charged that inherent in SDA theology is the unbiblical teaching that "the atonement was not finished on the cross of Calvary." Certain Seventh-day Adventist sources are cited to bolster these charges. For instance, Uriah Smith, a prominent Adventist of the past, stated in his book *Looking Unto Jesus*, "Christ did not make the atonement when He shed His blood upon the cross." Other earlier writers such as J. H. Waggoner have expressed the same thought. He said, "There is a clear distinction between the death of Christ and the atonement" (fn. *The Atonement in the Light of Nature and Revelation*, p. 181). Even some later writers like C. H. Watson have been influenced by these early exponents of Adventism.

However, a little investigation of these writings would show that Smith and Waggoner wrote eighty years ago. As demonstrated elsewhere in this book, this concept has been repudiated by the SDA denomination. The current position of the Seventh-day Adventist denomination—not the opinions of a few scattered writers over a hundred year period—should be considered in judging this charge of "incomplete atonement."

Current Adventist writings teach that the atonement was completed on the cross; and no less an Adventist than Ellen G. White, writing in the *Review and Herald*, September 21, 1901, stated: "Christ planted the cross between Heaven and earth and when the Father beheld the sacrifice of His Son, He bowed before it in recognition of His perfection. 'It is enough,' He said. 'The atonement is completed.' " In the same periodical, under the date of August 16, 1899, Mrs. White stated, "No language could convey the rejoicing of heaven or God's expression of satisfaction and delight in His only begotten Son that He saw the completion of the atonement."

Many more quotations could be cited, but critics usually overlook the greater number of statements relative to the completeness of the atonement which are readily available in past and present Seventh-day Adventist literature.

Nothing could be clearer than the Adventist declaration that:

> When . . . one hears an Adventist say or reads in Adventist literature—*even in the writings of Ellen G. White—that Christ is making atonement now, it should be understood that we mean simply that Christ is now making application of the benefits of the sacrificial atonement He made on the cross; that He is making it efficacious for us individually, according to our needs and requests.* Mrs. White herself, as far back as 1857, clearly explained what she means when she writes of Christ's making atonement for us in His ministry:
>
> "The great Sacrifice had been offered and had been accepted, and the Holy Spirit which descended on the day of Pentecost carried the minds of the disciples from the earthly sanctuary to the Heavenly, where Jesus entered by His own blood to shed upon His disciples the benefits of His atonement."[15]

Is Seventh-day Adventism a Non-Christian Cult?

We earlier mentioned Dr. Anthony Hoekema's book *The Four Major Cults* in which he classifies Seventh-day Adventism as a non-Christian cult system. It is necessary for me to take exception with Dr. Hoekema in this area because, in my opinion, the reasons which Dr. Hoekema gives cannot be jus-

---

[15]*Questions on Doctrine*, pp. 354, 355.

tified by the Word of God, historical theology, or present-day practices in denominational Christianity as a whole. To illustrate this point, Dr. Hoekema stated, "I am of the conviction that Seventh-day Adventism is a cult and not an evangelical denomination. In support of this evaluation I propose to show that the traits which we have found to be distinctive of the cults do apply to this movement" (p. 389).

Dr. Hoekema then proceeds to list his reasons:

1. An extra-scriptural source of authority (Ellen G. White).
2. The denial of justification by grace alone.
   a. The investigative judgment.
   b. The keeping of the Sabbath.
3. The devaluation of Christ.
4. The group as the exclusive community of the saved.

It is Dr. Hoekema's contention that Ellen White is an extra-Biblical authority in that her counsels are taken to be manifestations of the gift of prophecy (1 Corinthians). But granting that the Adventists are entitled to believe that this gift was manifested in Mrs. White as evidence of the charismata (a fact Dr. Hoekema could hardly honestly challenge since the gifts of the Spirit have been and are still manifested in the Christian Church), why does he not take into consideration the repeated emphasis of Adventist writers concerning their official pronouncement, *Questions on Doctrine*, to the effect that they do not consider Mrs. White to be an extra-Biblical authority, but that her writings are only authoritative in those areas where they are in agreement with the Word of God which is the final standard for judging all the gifts of the Spirit?

If the Adventists put Mrs. White's writings on a par with Holy Scripture, if they interpreted the Bible in the light of her writings, and not the reverse, if they willingly admitted this and owned it as their position, then his criticism would be justified, but they do not do so. Dr. Hoekema has apparently ignored what the Adventists say they believe concerning Mrs. White in favor of what he thinks they mean as a result of his deduction from certain of their publications. It is far safer to accept at face value the published statements of a denomination representing its theology, particularly if, as in the case of *Questions on Doctrine*, they are answering direct questions bearing on the subject, than it is to rely upon one's own preconceived interpretations, as Dr. Hoekema has apparently done in this instance.

It is a serious charge to maintain that any professing Christian group denies justification by grace alone as the basis of eternal salvation; and, if the Adventists were guilty of this, surely there would be ground for considering them as a cultic system. However, literally scores of times in their book *Questions on Doctrine* and in various other publications, the Adventists affirm that salvation comes only by the grace of God through faith in Jesus Christ's sacrifice upon the cross.

Why it is necessary again for Dr. Hoekema to question the sincerity of the Adventists in this area and yet accept at face value their other statements concerning their faith in the Scriptures, the Trinity, the full Deity of Jesus Christ, creation, providence, incarnation, the resurrection of Jesus Christ, the absolute necessity for regeneration, sanctification by the Holy Spirit and Christ's literal return, is a puzzling inconsistency in his presentation. (See *The Four Major Cults*, p. 403.)

Dr. Hoekema insists that the investigative judgment and the keeping of the seventh-day Sabbath are part of the reasons why he classifies Seventh-day Adventists as cultists, but, in doing this, he makes his Calvinistic interpretation of theology the criterion while ignoring the claims of the Arminian school and of semi-Arminian and semi-Calvinistic theologians, many of whom take strong exception to Dr. Hoekema's pronounced Calvinism. On the basis that Dr. Hoekema would call the Adventist a cult, the same charge could be leveled against all devoted Calvinists who consider the *Institutes* and Calvin's *Commentaries* every bit as much illumination and guides in the study of the Scriptures as the Adventists do where Mrs. White's writings are concerned. In addition to this, the Seventh-day Baptists are Arminian in their theology and keep the seventh-day Sabbath. Are they, too, a non-Christian cult? They certainly have some of Dr. Hoekema's qualifications.

Underscoring his Calvinistic oppositions, Dr. Hoekema writes:

> Adventists further teach that it is possible for a person through subsequent sinful deeds and attitudes to lose the justification he once received. This teaching implies that one can only be sure of retaining his justification if he continues to do the right kind of deeds and to maintain the right attitudes throughout the rest of his life (p. 390).

This point on the investigative judgment is clear evidence of Arminianism in which Dr. Hoekema finds sufficient ground to justify the cult label being applied to Adventists. But why just to Adventists? Why not to Pentecostals, Methodists, Anglicans, Episcopalians, Lutherans and others who accept the same Arminian premises, though they have not carried them out to the literalism that the Adventists have in the investigative judgment?

Relative to Sabbatarianism, the fourteenth chapter of Romans justifies the keeping of the seventh-day Sabbath or any other day by any Christian who believes he is keeping it unto the Lord. It can become legalistic as Sunday can become legalistic, but merely because the seventh day is honored instead of the first is no ground for the description of "cult."

Dr. Hoekema on page 394 of his volume affirms that:

> Seventh-day Adventists do not . . . deny the full deity of Jesus Christ or the doctrine of the Trinity. . . . Seventh-day Adventists today affirm Christ's complete equality with the Father, and the pre-existence of the Son from eternity. . . . Adventists also accept the doctrine of the Trinity, and that of the personality and full deity of the Holy Spirit.
>
> As far as the work of Christ is concerned, Seventh-day Adventists teach the vicarious, substitutionary atonement of Christ. Yet there remains some ambiguity in their teachings on the question of whether the atonement has been finished on the cross, since Mrs. White says on more than one occasion that Christ is making atonement for us today and frequently refers to a "final atonement" after the one completed on the cross. . . .

Dr. Hoekema follows this up by listing five reasons for his feeling that the Adventists "devalue" Christ. Three of these points involve Arminianism concerning which Dr. Hoekema has an admitted prejudice; the fourth concerns the Sabbath, which is a matter of Christian liberty, unless one presupposes Calvin's interpretation; the fifth reiterates the old accusation that the Seventh-day Adventists believe that "the sins of all men will be laid on Satan just before Christ returns, and that only in this way will sin finally be 'eradicated' or 'blotted out' of the universe" (pp. 395, 396).

Once again, Dr. Hoekema defeats his own case by admitting that the Adventists are soundly orthodox in their Christology, hardly a devaluation of Christ!

The implications and deductions which he draws from their Arminianism cannot be considered as evidence against the Adventists, since not only they, but the entire Arminian school of theological interpretation could argue vigorously for the principles which the Adventists lay down.

Finally, the Adventists themselves have repeatedly affirmed that Christ alone vicariously bears the sins of the world and that Satan only bears "his responsibility" for tempting the world to sin.

A careful reading of the book *Questions on Doctrine*, which Dr. Hoekema lists in his bibliography in *The Four Major Cults*, would have answered his question regarding Mrs. White's usage of the term "making atonement now" and "final atonement."

The Adventists declare forthrightly that whenever terms of this nature are used they understand them to refer to the benefits of the atonement of Christ being shed abroad through the ministry of the Holy Spirit and disown completely any implication or suggestion that the atonement of Christ was not completed upon the cross.

Dr. Hoekema in company with other critics of Adventism has not hesitated to draw upon repudiated sources to underscore the claim that the Adventists devalue Christ. On page 114 of *The Four Major Cults* Dr. Hoekema states:

> One of the best known is the statement by L. A. Wilcox to the effect that Christ conquered over sin "in spite of bad blood and an inherited meanness." Though the discussion of this matter in *Questions on Doctrine* implies that the denomination would now repudiate this statement, nowhere in the book are we definitely told that this has been done.

In my book *The Truth About Seventh-day Adventism* conclusive proof was introduced of the total repudiation of that statement by Wilcox himself. Dr. Hoekema lists the book in his bibliography but unfortunately omits reference to Wilcox's repudiation, in order to utilize Wilcox's statement. This is not a fair representation of what the Adventist denomination has taught or teaches in this area.

These then are a few of the problems which face the interested student of the puzzle of Seventh-day Adventism, and they must be fairly considered before hastily classifying Adventism as a non-Christian cult.

Ellen G. White and the Spirit of Prophecy

In most religious movements, one extraordinary and gifted personality dominates the scene, and so it was with Seventh-day Adventism. This dominant personality was and is today, through her writings, Ellen G. White. She was one of the most fascinating and controversial personages ever to appear upon the horizon of religious history. Her memory and work have been praised by Adventists and damned by many of their enemies since the early years of the movement. Born Ellen Gould Harmon at Gorham, Maine, in 1827, and reared a devout Methodist in the city of Portland, Mrs. White was early recognized as an unusual person, for she bore witness to certain "revelations" which she believed she had received from heaven.

When Ellen was thirteen, the Harmon family came under the influence of the Millerite movement. William Miller delivered a series of addresses in the Casco Street Christian Church in Portland in 1841 and 1842. At the age of seventeen, Ellen embraced the Adventist faith of the Millerites.[16] Although deeply stirred by Miller's sincerity and his chronological calculations, the Harmon family remained in fellowship with the Chestnut Street Methodist Church of Portland, which in 1843 disfellowshiped them because they believed in the premillennial second advent of Jesus Christ.

Despite her youth, Ellen Harmon passed through trying times, emotionally, physically and spiritually, between 1837 and 1843. In the words of Dr. Froom, "She rebelled against the dismal prospects resulting from an early accident, and its attendant invalidism.[17] In 1840, at a Methodist camp meeting at Buxton, Maine, Ellen Harmon found wonderful deliverance and "her burden rolled from her shoulders," for she experienced great joy in learning that she was truly a child of God, which she publicly confessed afterward by requesting baptism by immersion. Many points still perplexed her, among them the doctrine of the eternal punishment of the wicked, which in subsequent years she surrendered to as well as the concept of conditional immortality and the sleep of the soul while awaiting the resurrection. In December 1844, after *The Great Disappointment,*" while visiting a friend in Portland, Ellen Harmon experienced what she termed her first vision which portrayed the "vindication" of the Advent faith. In that vision she claimed to see the Adventists triumphant over their critics—pressing upward to heaven in the face of insuperable obstacles.

For many years controversy has raged about Mrs. White and her "revelations," and there are conflicting opinions within and without Adventism regarding her "revelations" and "inspiration," their extent and nature. The position of Ellen White in Adventist teaching, then, is most significant and must be understood if we are to get a proper picture of this people. The writings and counsels of Ellen Harmon (later Ellen G. White by her marriage to James White, a prominent Adventist leader), are termed the "Spirit of prophecy," an expression taken from Revelation 19:10. Adventists believe that in the last days special counsels from God are to be revealed, which neither add to nor contradict Scripture, and that these counsels are primarily for the Seventh-day Adventist denomination. And while following these counsels, they claim they always test them by the Word of God. Finally, they believe that the visions of Mrs. White, and her counsels to their denomination are the "Spirit of prophecy" for their church.

---

[16]Ellen G. White, *Life Sketches,* Washingotn, D.C.: Review and Herald Publishing Association, n.d., pp. 64–68.
[17]*The Prophetic Faith. . . ,* Vol. 4, p. 978.

There is a circular reasoning involved in defending Mrs. White. Adventists say that the writers of the Bible did the same thing in quoting (without credit) pagan sources as did Mrs. White. If they are permitted to do so, then she should be permitted to do so. That only holds, however, if one assumes that Mrs. White is to be considered as one of the writers of the Bible! That is giving her a rank official Adventist spokesmen won't give her!

Through the years, some over-zealous Adventist writers have given the impression that everything Mrs. White said or wrote, even in private letters, was inspired and infallible. This is decidedly *not* the official position. The Adventist denomination readily admits that not everything Mrs. White said or wrote was either inspired or infallible, although some individual Adventists still cling to that idea. Until the Adventists officially repudiate the doctrinal statements of *Questions on Doctrine* and officially espouse the errant doctrinal statements of some Adventists and Adventist factions, we can use *Questions on Doctrine* as representative of the denomination's official views. This we have done below.

I. *Seventh-day Adventist Statements—Life and Ministry of Ellen G. White*
(Page numbers are in Questions on Doctrine, unless otherwise indicated.)

1. "We do not regard the writings of Ellen G. White as an addition to the sacred canon of Scripture. We do not think of them as of universal application as is the Bible, but particularly for the Seventh-day Adventist Church. We do not regard them in the same sense as the Holy Scriptures, which stand alone and unique as the standard by which all other writings must be judged" (p. 89).

2. "Seventh-day Adventists uniformly believe that the canon of Scripture closed with the Book of Revelation. We hold that all other writings and teachings, from whatever source, are to be judged by, and are subject to, the Bible, which is the spring and norm of the Christian faith" (pp. 89, 90).

3. "I recommend to you, dear reader, the Word of God as the rule of your faith and practice. By that Word we are to be judged" (p. 90).

4. "The Spirit was not given—nor can it ever be bestowed—to supersede the Bible; for the Scriptures explicitly state that the Word of God is the standard by which all teaching and experience must be tested" (p. 90).

5. "We have never considered Ellen G. White to be in the same category as the writers of the canon of Scripture" (p. 90).

6. "It is in . . . the category of messengers [other than the Biblical writers] that we consider Ellen G. White to be. Among Seventh-day Adventists she was recognized as one who possessed the gift of the spirit of prophecy, though she herself never assumed the title of prophetess" (p. 91).

7. "Seventh-day Adventists regard her writings as containing inspired counsel concerning personal religion and the conduct of our denominational work. . . . That portion of her writings, however, that might be classified as predictions, actually forms but a small segment. And even when she deals with what is coming on the earth, her statements are only amplifications of clear Bible prophecy" (p. 92).

8. "In His Word, God has committed to men the knowledge necessary for salvation. The Holy Scriptures are to be accepted as an authoritative, infallible revelation of His will. They are the standard of character, the

revealer of doctrines, and the test of experience" (pp. 92, 93, quoting Ellen G. White).

9. "While Adventists hold the writings of Ellen G. White in highest esteem, yet these are not the source of our expositions. We base our teachings on the Scripture, the only foundation of all true Christian doctrine. However, it is our belief that the Holy Spirit opened to her mind important events and called her to give certain instructions for these last days. And inasmuch as these instructions, in our understanding, are in harmony with the Word of God, which Word alone is able to make us wise unto salvation, we as a denomination accept them as inspired counsels from the Lord. But we have never equated them with Scripture as some falsely charge. Mrs. White herself stated explicitly the relation of her writings to the Bible: 'Little heed is given to the Bible, and the Lord has given a lesser light to lead men and women to the greater light' " (*Review and Herald*, Jan. 20, 1903; *Questions on Doctrine*, p. 93).

10. "While Seventh-day Adventists recognize the Scripture canon closed nearly two thousand years ago and that there have been no additions to this compilation of sacred books, yet we believe that the spirit of God, who inspired the Divine Word known to us as the Bible, has pledged to reveal Himself to the Church and through the different gifts of the Spirit. . . . It is not our understanding that these gifts of the Spirit take the place of the Word of God, nor does their acceptance make unnecessary the Scripture of truth. On the contrary, the acceptance of God's Word will lead God's people to a recognition and a manifestation of the Spirit. Such manifestations will, of course, be in harmony with the Word of God. We know that some earnest Christians have the impression that these gifts ceased with the apostolic church. But Adventists believe that the closing of the Scripture canon did not terminate Heaven's communication with men through the gifts of the Spirit, but rather that Christ by the Ministry of His Spirit guides His people, edifying and strengthening them, and especially so in these last challenging days of human history" (pp. 93–95).

11. "The Spirit of prophecy is intimately related to the gift of prophecy, the one being the Spirit which indited the prophecy, the other the evidence of the gift bestowed. They go together, each inseparably connected with the other. The gift is the manifestation of that which the Spirit of God bestows upon him whom, according to His own good purpose and plan, He selects as the one through whom such spiritual guidance is to come. Briefly then, this is the Adventist understanding of Ellen G. White's writings. They have been for a hundred years, to use her own expression, 'a lesser light' leading sincere men and women to 'the greater light' " (p. 96).

12. "Concerning the matter of church fellowship, we would say that while we revere the writings of Ellen G. White, . . . we do not make acceptance of her writings as a matter for church discipline. She herself was explicit on this point. Speaking of those who did not fully understand the gift, she said: 'Such should not be deprived of the benefits and privileges of the church, if their Christian course is otherwise correct, and they have formed a good Christian character' " (*Testimonies*, Vol. I, p. 328; *Questions on Doctrine*, pp. 96, 97).

13. "We therefore do not test the world in any manner by these gifts. Nor do we in our intercourse with other religious bodies who are striving to walk in the fear of God, in any way make these a test of Christian character" (J. N. Andrews in *Review and Herald*, Feb. 15, 1870; *Questions on Doctrine*, p. 97).

14. "James White, thrice General conference president, speaking of the work of Ellen G. White, expressly declares that Adventists believe that God called her 'to do a special work at this time, among this people. They do not, however, make a belief in this work a test of Christian fellowship'" (*Review and Herald*, June 13, 1871; *Questions on Doctrine*, p. 97).

15. "In the practice of the church it has not been customary to disfellowship one because he did not recognize the doctrine of spiritual gifts. . . . A member of the church should not be excluded from membership because of his inability to recognize clearly the doctrine of spiritual gifts and its application to the second advent movement" (p. 98).

It may be seen from these quotations that Seventh-day Adventists hold to the restoration of the "gift of prophecy" in the last days of the Christian Church, and that they believe this restoration occurred in the life and ministry of Ellen G. White. The Adventists differ from other churches, then, in that while they hold the Bible to be the unique, complete, infallible, inerrant Word of God, they maintain that in specific contexts Ellen White's writings are to be accepted by Adventists as "testimonies" from the Spirit of God to guide their denominational activities.

Dr. Wilbur M. Smith has summed up the objections of most evangelicals where Seventh-day Adventism emphasis upon Mrs. White and the Spirit of prophecy is involved when he recently observed Mrs. White's place in the new Seventh-day Adventist Bible Commentary.

> I do not know any other denomination in all of Christendom today that has given such recognition, so slavishly and exclusively to its founder or principal theologian as has this commentary to the writings of Ellen White. At the conclusion of every chapter in this work is a section headed, "Ellen G. White Comments." For example, on Genesis 28, the blessing conferred upon Jacob, there are less than three pp. of comment, but at the end, forty references to the various works of Ellen White. In addition, at the end of the first volume of this commentary is a section again headed, "Ellen G. White Comments," containing eighty columns of material quoted from her writings. There is no section devoted to anyone else, Calvin, Luther, Wesley, or anyone else.
>
> The Preface to this commentary contains the statement: "At the close of each chapter is a cross reference or index to those passages in Ellen G. White's writings that comment on the various texts in that chapter." And the second sentence following reads: "The Advent movement has grown strong through the study of the Bible; and it can be said with equal truth that the movement has been safely guided in that study by the light shining from the Spirit of prophecy." I would say that the writers of this commentary believe that "the Spirit of prophecy" has rested *exclusively* upon Ellen G. White, for no one else is so classified in this work.[18]

Dr. Smith is correct in his evaluation of the place of Ellen G. White's writings in the denomination. Seventh-day Adventists are of necessity committed to her visions and counsel because they believe that the Spirit of prophecy rested upon her and upon no other person of their group.

This writer rejects this concept of inspiration but one should carefully note that, for Adventists, "inspiration" in connection with Mrs. White's writ-

---

[18]In a letter to the author.

ings has a rather different meaning from the inspiration of the Bible. Adventists freely admit that the Bible is *objectively* the Word of God, the final authority in all matters of faith and morals. But the writings of Mrs. White cannot be so regarded, and they are the first to say so. Apparently, they have adopted a qualified view of inspiration as related to her writings—"a lesser light to lead men and women to the greater light"—which emphasizes subjective interpretation as the criterion for determining specifically where in Mrs. White's writings the "Spirit of prophecy" has decisively spoken. There is no doubt in my mind that the Adventists are defending a situation which is at best paradoxical and at times contradictory. But this position, as a matter of religious liberty, they are *entitled* to hold so long as they do not make faith in Mrs. White's writings a test of fellowship between themselves and other denominations, and do not attempt to compel other Christians to accept the "testimonies" of Mrs. White as indispensable to a deeper, richer experience of Christian consecration and living.

If Seventh-day Adventists did indeed claim for Mrs. White inspiration in *every* area of her writings, then we might well be cautious about having fellowship with them. However, this they do not do, as I have amply demonstrated from official denominational sources. Since they do not consider Mrs. White's teachings the source of their expositions of faith, the claim that one has only to refute Ellen G. White and her writings, in order to refute Seventh-day Adventism, falls by its own weight.

II. *Mrs. White and Her Critics*

Through the years a great deal of literature has appeared, criticizing the life and works of Ellen G. White. These criticisms have ranged from the mild judgment that Mrs. White was a sincere but emotionally disturbed mystic, to the charge that she was a "false prophetess" who sought material gain and deliberately plagiarized much of her writing. In the interest of honest investigation and truth, and since it is impossible in a book of this size to analyze all the conflicting data, we shall present some highlights of the controversy, and let the reader determine the validity of these charges.

The inspiration for 90 percent of the *destructive* personal criticisms leveled against Mrs. White is found in the writings of Dudley M. Canright, an ex-Adventist leader of great ability, and a one-time personal friend of Ellen G. White, her husband James, and a great number of prominent Adventist leaders. Canright, one of the most able of the Seventh-day Adventist writers and debaters of his day, left the movement because he lost faith in the inspiration of Mrs. White and in many doctrines then held by the Adventist Church. While it is true that Canright thrice ceased to preach, his credentials as a minister were never revoked. He finally resigned from the Seventh-day Adventist ministry in 1887 to become a Baptist minister. By Canright's own admission, his personality conflicts with Ellen G. White and her advisers were largely responsible for his turning away from the active ministry at the times mentioned. He, however, apparently maintained close personal relations with James White, Mrs. White's husband, and other prominent Seventh-day Adventist leaders as evident from the correspondence quoted below. Canright rebelled violently against Arianism (the denial of the Deity of Christ) and extreme legalism, which existed among some of the early Seventh-day Adventists; and his convictions led him later to write two volumes (*Seventh-day Adventism Renounced,* and *Life of Mrs. E. G. White*), which systematically and scathingly denounced Seventh-day Adventism theologically and impugned the personal motives and integrity of Mrs. White.

In these two volumes, D. M. Canright laid the foundation for all future destructive criticism of Seventh-day Adventism, and careful research has confirmed the impression that nearly all subsequent similar publications are little more than repetitions of the destructive areas of Canright's writings, buttressed by standard theological arguments. This is especially true of the writings of a former Seventh-day Adventist missionary printer, E. B. Jones, now editor of a small news sheet, *Guardians of the Faith,* who has issued a number of vitriolic pamphlets against Seventh-day Adventism, all of which are drawn almost exclusively from Canright and other critics, and are for the most part outdated and in some cases both scholastically and ethically unreliable. It can be seen, therefore, that what D. M. Canright has written about Ellen G. White is of prime importance as firsthand evidence, and no Seventh-day Adventist apologist, regardless of the scope of his knowledge of Adventism or the breadth of his scholastic learning, can gainsay all that Canright has written.

In the March 22, 1887, issue of the *Review and Herald,* his former brethren wrote of Elder Canright:

> We have felt exceedingly sad to part in our religious connection with one whom we have long esteemed as a dear brother. . . . In leaving us he has taken a much more manly and commendable course than most of those who have withdrawn from us, coming voluntarily to our leading brethren and frankly stating the condition of mind he was in. He did this before his own church in our presence and so far as we know has taken no unfair underhanded means to injure us in any way. He goes from our midst with no immoral stain upon his character. He chooses associations more pleasant to himself. This is every man's personal privilege if he chooses to take it.

Writing to Canright on May 22, 1881, from Battle Creek, Michigan, James White, Ellen's husband, stated, "It is time there was a change in the offices of the General Conference. I trust that if we are true and faithful, the Lord will be pleased that we should constitute two of that Board." In another letter to Canright, dated July 13, 1881, James White said, "Brother Canright, I feel more interest in you than in any other man because I know your worth when the Lord is with you as a laborer." It is apparent, therefore, that Canright was in good standing with the Adventists, despite his later renunciation of Mrs. White's testimonies and the "special truths" of the Adventist message.

In 1951 a carefully documented volume of almost 700 pages was issued by the Review and Herald Publishing Association of Washington, D.C. The author was Francis D. Nichol, leading apologist of the Seventh-day Adventist denomination. This volume, entitled, *Ellen G. White and Her Critics,* attempts a point-for-point refutation of many of the charges made by D. M. Canright in his *Life of Mrs. E. G. White.* Nichol has dug deep into early Adventist history—even beyond Canright's day, but after reading both Nichol and Canright, I have concluded that there is much to be said on both sides. But Canright, we believe, has the edge because he can say, "I was there," or "Mrs. White said . . ." and contradictory contemporary statements are not to be found where many of Canright's charges are concerned.

My own conclusion is that in some areas (particularly theology) Canright's statements are irrefutable, especially with regard to his personal relationships with Mrs. White and the leading members of the Adventist denomination. It is also significant to note that many charges which are based on personal experiences and have been well documented have never been refuted.

By this I do not mean that all of Canright's writing is to be trusted, for many of his criticisms of Mrs. White's activities have been neatly undercut by contemporary evidence unearthed by F. D. Nichol and others. Where Nichol is concerned, "methinks he doth protest too much," and he often goes to extremes to defend Mrs. White. This in my judgment has hurt his case and has proved nothing except that he is a devoted disciple of Mrs. White and therefore strongly biased. Nichol is none the less the most able Adventist apologist.

III. *The Verdict of the Evidence*

After considering all the evidence obtainable, of which the foregoing is only a part, this writer is convinced that Ellen G. White was a highly impressionable woman, strongly influenced by her associates. That she sincerely believed the Lord spoke to her, none can fairly question, but the evidence set forth in this book gives good reason, we believe, to doubt the inspiration of her counsels, whether Seventh-day Adventists will concede this or not.

My personal evaluation of the visions of Ellen G. White is best summed up in the following statement from a friendly critic. In 1847, at the outset of her work, one of Mrs. White's cousins stated:

> I cannot endorse Sister Ellen's visions as of Divine inspiration, as you and she think them to be; yet I do not suspect the least shade of dishonesty in either of you in this matter. I may, perhaps, express to you my belief in the latter without harm—it will, doubtless, result either in your good or mine. At the same time I admit the possibility of my being mistaken. I think that what she and you regard as visions from the Lord are only religious reveries in which her imagination runs without control upon themes in which she is most deeply interested. While so absorbed in these reveries she is lost to everything around her. Reveries are of two kinds: Sinful and religious. In either case, the sentiments in the main are obtained from previous teaching, or study. I do not by any means think that her visions are from the Devil.[19]

If Seventh-day Adventists are to defend their claim for Mrs. White's inspiration, they must explain a number of contradictions in her writings. They would do better to admit, we believe, that she was very human, capable of errors in judgment, and subject to lapses of memory.

---

[19]Reproduced in *A Word to the Little Flock*, p. 29 (1847) by Elder James White.

It is my considered opinion that Ellen G. White had an extremely complex personality and plagiarized materials because she believed the Lord had shown her that what the sources said was the truth. She simply appropriated material and gave it out. Her actions cannot be excused, but they can be understood as the actions of a Christian who made mistakes. She was both mortal and a sinner like anyone else. I think those around her aided and abetted her in her "cover-up." Also, I think the White Estate continued the cover-up after her death for many years. No objective person, in possession of all the facts, can doubt that.

The difference between her and, for example, the Jehovah's Witnesses, is not the crime itself. That was wrong. The difference is in the nature of the person we are talking about. Was Jehovah's Witness founder Charles Russell a Christian? Did he hold to the foundations of the gospel? Did he promulgate the things of Christianity and stand in their defense? No. Did Ellen White? Yes. Therefore, although she committed the same crime he did, she cannot be judged on the same basis as Charles Russell. She was a Christian who committed a sin. Christians can and do commit sins.

A biblical false prophet was not a believer. A biblical false prophet was a servant of the devil attempting to lead people away from the truth. Mrs. White, in my opinion, made false statements. She misused what she claimed was the prophetic gift she had. But one cannot say that she was just like a biblical false prophet. Of course, technically, all would agree that the person who prophesies in the name of God and turns out to be wrong, has prophesied falsely. But Mrs. White is not a biblical false prophet because she was a true Christian, even though what she did was sinful.

Mrs. White was definitely influenced in some of her writings by time and circumstances, and also by the powerful personalities who surrounded her. Some Adventists maintain that this would in no way prevent her conveying messages from the Lord. However, as I see it, anyone who attempts to prove her divinely inspired or infallible (no informed Adventist holds the latter) must first dispose of the evidence here presented, as well as other evidence which space does not admit. F. D. Nichol in *Ellen G. White and Her Critics*, makes a masterful attempt to answer some of these problems, but not all of them can be answered with a good conscience or an airtight defense of Mrs. White and her actions. It does not detract from her stature as a sincere Christian or from the quality of her contribution to insist upon an honest and systematic evaluation of her statements by thinking Adventists, to ascertain just how far Adventists may rightfully maintain that the Lord has "spoken" through Mrs. White. Non-Adventists, of course, reject the claims made for Mrs. White and her writings and hope that Adventists will some day amend their questionable view of "Ellen G. White and the Spirit of Prophecy."

After reading the publications of the Seventh-day Adventist denomination and almost all the writings of Ellen G. White, including her *Testimonies*, the writer believes that Mrs. White was truly a regenerate Christian woman who loved the Lord Jesus Christ and dedicated herself unstintingly to the task of bearing witness for Him as she felt led. It should be clearly understood that some tenets of Christian theology as historically understood and the interpretations of Mrs. White do not agree; indeed, they are at loggerheads. Nevertheless, Ellen G. White was true to the cardinal doctrines of the Christian faith regarding the salvation of the soul and the believer's life in Christ. We must disagree with Mrs. White's interpretation of the sanctuary, the investigative judgment, and the scapegoat; we challenge her stress upon the Sabbath, health reform, the unconscious state of the dead, and the final destruction of the wicked, etc. But no one can dispute the fact that her writings conform to the basic principles of the historic Gospel, for they most certainly do. However, we must not assume as many Adventists do that Mrs. White's writings are free from theological and exegetical errors *for they are not.* Although I believe that the influence of Mrs. White's counsels on the Advent denomination parallels the influence of J. N. Darby of the Plymouth Brethren and A. B. Simpson of the Christian and Missionary Alliance, the claim that she possessed a "gift of prophecy" akin to that described in 1 Corinthians 14 as believed by the Seventh-day Adventist Church, I cannot accept.

Many critics of Seventh-day Adventism have assumed, mostly from the writings of professional detractors, that Mrs. White was a fearsome ogre who devoured all who opposed her, and they have never ceased making the false claim that Seventh-day Adventists believe that Mrs. White is infallible, despite the often published authoritative statement to the contrary. Although Seventh-day Adventists do hold Mrs. White and her writings in great esteem, they maintain that the Bible is their only "rule of faith and practice." Christians of all denominations may heatedly disagree with the Seventh-day Adventist attitude toward Mrs. White, but all that she wrote on such subjects as salvation or Christian living characterizes her as a Christian in every sense of the term.

Farther on in this discussion, we shall look at Mrs. White's relations with the Adventist denomination, particularly in the field of theology. Enough has been presented here, however, to show that she was a most interesting personality, far different from the "Sister White" idealized beyond reality in certain Seventh-day Adventist publications.

Dudley M. Canright, the chief critic of Seventh-day Adventism, has, I feel, rendered good service in this respect. He has presented the human side of Mrs. White, from the standpoint of a firsthand friendship which lasted through the formative years of the Seventh-day Adventist denomination. Despite his criticisms of Seventh-day Adventism and Mrs. White, Canright himself never ceased to believe that, despite what he believed to be her errors in theology and her mistaken concept of visions, she was a regenerate Christian. With his brother, Canright attended the funeral of Mrs. White in 1915. His brother describes the occasion thus: "We joined the passing throng, and again stood by the bier. My brother rested his hand upon the side of the casket, and with tears rolling down his cheeks, he said brokenly. 'There is a noble Christian woman gone!' "[20]

The controversy between Seventh-day Adventist historians and personal

---

[20]W. A. Spicer, *Our Day in the Light of Prophecy,* Washington, D.C.: Review and Herald Publishing Association, n.d., p. 127.

recollections of D. M. Canright will probably never be settled this side of Heaven, but beyond question, Canright has left an indelible mark upon the history of both the denomination and Ellen G. White, a woman of great moral fortitude and indomitable conviction. Her influence will doubtless affect the religious world through the Seventh-day Adventist denomination for many years to come.

The Sleep of the Soul and the Destruction of the Wicked

The doctrine of conditional immortality, commonly called "soul sleep" outside Adventist circles, and its necessary corollary, annihilation, have been cardinal teachings from the beginning of the Seventh-day Adventist Church. They must be dealt with from an exegetical standpoint if the theology underlying the basic premise is to be understood. These positions, incidentally, are held today by the Advent Christian Church, an affiliate of the National Association of Evangelicals, and by outstanding Bible scholars in not a few denominations.

The purpose here is essentially to review the historic position of the Christian Church from the days of the apostles to the present, and to examine the teaching of the Scriptures on these subjects. Many noted Christians of the past believed in conditional immortality, among them Martin Luther, William Tyndale, and John Wycliffe, all of whom were competent Greek scholars. Luther even stated that he could not support the doctrine of immortality of the soul, which he called one of the "endless monstrosities in the Roman dunghill of decretals.[21] Tyndale declared that:

> in putting them [the souls of the departed dead] in Heaven, hell and purgatory you destroy the arguments wherewith Christ and Paul doth prove the resurrection . . . and again, if the souls be in Heaven, tell me why they be not in as good case as the angels be? And then what cause is there for their resurrection?[22]

However, in his *Commentary on Genesis*, Luther later categorically stated, "In the interim [between death and resurrection], the soul does *not* sleep but is awake and enjoys the vision of angels and of God, and has converse with them."[23]

However, neither preponderance of one opinion nor the opinions of a few great thinkers can validate theological speculation or interpretation. The Christian Church does not base its belief in the conscious bliss of departed saints on the opinions of individuals, no mater how prominent or learned, but upon the historic, Biblical foundation of the Christian faith.

I. *Textual Analysis*

The Seventh-day Adventist doctrine of the sleep of the soul is best expressed in their own words: "We as Adventists believe that, in general, the

---

[21]Weimar edition of Luther's *Works*, Vol. VII, pp. 131, 132.
[22]*An Answer to Sir Thomas More's Dialogue*, Parker's 1850 reprint, Book 4, chapter iv, pp. 180, 181.
[23]*Works, op. cit.*, vol. 25, p. 321.

Scriptures teach that the soul of man represents the whole man, and not a particular part independent of the other component parts of man's nature; and further, that the soul cannot exist apart from the body, for man is a unit. . . . We, as Adventists, have reached the definite conclusion that man rests in the tomb until the resurrection morning. Then, at the first resurrection (Revelation 20:4, 5), the resurrection of the just (Acts 24:15), the righteous come forth immortalized at the call of Christ, the Lifegiver, and *they then enter into life everlasting* in their eternal home in the kingdom of glory. Such is our understanding.[24]

The key to the preceding statements, of course, is the last phrase of the second paragraph, "They *then* enter into life everlasting, in their eternal home in the kingdom of glory." Now, the majority of Christians through the centuries have held that this proposition contradicts the teaching of the Word of God contained in the following passages:

1. *1 John 5:11–13*: "And this is the record, that God hath given to us eternal life, and this life is in his Son. He that hath the Son hath life; and he that hath not the Son of God hath not life. These things have I written unto you that believe on the name of the Son of God; that ye may know that ye have eternal life, and that ye may believe on the name of the Son of God." In the grammar and context of this passage eternal life (*eionion zoes*) is the present possession of every believer in the Lord Jesus Christ, and if the term *eternal life* does not include *conscious fellowship* then the whole New Testament meaning is destroyed. The Holy Spirit used the present indicative active of the verb *echo*, expressing present, continuous action. Thus we see that the believer, having been regenerated by the Holy Spirit, *already* possesses never-ending life as a continuing *quality* of conscious existence.

2. *John 11:25, 26*: "Jesus said unto her, I am the resurrection and the life: he that believeth in me, though he were dead, yet shall he live: and whosoever liveth and believeth in me shall never die. Believest thou this?" The context here indicates that the Lord Jesus Christ was consoling Martha upon the death of her brother Lazarus. Therefore, the words "life" and "dead" must refer to that particular occasion. To attempt to wrest the meanings of these terms from their expressed context, and to teach that the end of the age is primarily in view or somehow close, is a violation of the grammar and context.

All thorough students of the Word of God, including the Adventists, recognize that in any study of the doctrines of eternal life and immortality, it is vitally essential to apply the hermeneutic principle (comparing all texts on a given subject) of interpretation, and the application of this principle, we believe, leads to the following facts. The root meanings for the words "death" and "life" in the New Testament usage ("death" *thanatos*, in its verb form *apothnesko*, and "life" *zoe* or its verb form *zac*) are respectively "separation or to separate," from communion or fellowship. The Scriptures describe two types of death, physical and spiritual, the former being the separation of the body from the soul, and the latter being the separation of the soul from God as the result of sin. Also, two kinds of life are spoken of in the

---

[24]*Questions on Doctrine*, pp. 515, 520.

New Testament: physical life (*bios*), which is the union or communion of body and soul; and spiritual life (*zoe*), which is the communion or fellowship of the soul with God. These terms we equate with the Greek of the New Testament, and they are essential to an understanding of Christ's words to Martha.

He was assuring her that despite the physical evidence of death, Jesus, the eternal Word of God made flesh, was Himself the source of life. And, *as such*, He was able to give life, even though death had actually occurred. Let us therefore take His words literally.

Christ's primary purpose was to comfort Martha. And what better comfort could He give than the knowledge that her family's limited concept of life as dependent upon the resurrection was depriving her of the joyous knowledge that the Prince of Life gives to the believer eternal life, unaffected by physical death.

Now let us look carefully at this context with no violation to hermeneutics or grammar, and this great truth becomes clear. John 11:20 tells us that as soon as Martha heard that Jesus was coming to Bethany, she went out to meet Him. In verse 21 she greets Him thus: "Lord, if thou hadst been here, my brother had not died." In answer to her obvious affliction and grief, Jesus, with divine compassion, stated, "Thy brother shall rise again." Verse 24 indicates, however, that Martha thought He was referring to the resurrection of the dead which will take place at "the last day."

To dispel her confused and grief-instilling concept of life (spiritual life), Jesus gives comfort beyond measure: "I am the resurrection and the life," He declares; "he that believes in me, even though he were dead, yet shall he live, and the one living and believing in me shall never die."

Now it is apparent from the context of verse 25 that Jesus was referring to Martha's brother Lazarus, one who believed in Him and had physically died. Christ's promise is, "yet shall *he* live." But going beyond this, Jesus lifts the veil and reveals that, in the realm of the physically alive, whoever believes in Him shall never experience the greatest of all terrors, spiritual death.

The Greek is extremely powerful in verse 26 for our Lord deliberately used the double negative, a construction which intensifies with great emphasis that to which it is applied. Jesus *could not* grammatically have been more emphatic in stating that the believer, who is alive both physically and spiritually, can never experience loss of communion of fellowship as a spiritual entity, though his body may "become" dead.

We see, further, that Seventh-day Adventists have no warrant for the idea that death is a state of unconsciousness. The New Testament frequently indicates that the unregenerate man is already "dead," but not even the Adventists would say that he was extinct or unconscious! Some instances of this are: Matthew 8:22, "Let the dead bury their dead"; John 5:25, "The hour is coming and now is, when the dead shall hear the voice of the Son of God, and they that hear shall live"; and Ephesians 2:1, "You hath he quickened, who were dead in trespasses and sins."

Admittedly in the New Testament, death is compared with sleep, but this is recognized by Bible scholars generally as a grammatical metaphor. One does not develop a doctrine from a figure of speech, as conditional immortalists apparently have done, but upon the sound principles of Biblical hermeneutics, contextual analysis, and linguistic exegesis. The application of these principles leads to the one conclusion which the Scripture unreservedly teaches, that *eternal life* is vastly different from "immortality"; although immortality *will* be bestowed upon the believer at the resurrection, *in this life* he already possesses "eternal life," a spiritual quality of existence which will at length be united with the physical quality of incorruptibility which the Bible speaks of as immortality, and "we shall be like him, for we shall see him as he is" (1 Corinthians 12; 1 John 3:2). A study of these words in any Greek lexicon, and of their use in the New Testament, will show that immortality and eternal life are neither identical nor synonymous. For certain Adventist writers therefore to treat these terms as interchangeable is clearly a linguistic impossibility.

3. *2 Timothy 1:10*: The Apostle Paul writes that God's eternal purpose "is now made manifest by the appearing of our Savior Jesus Christ, who hath abolished death, and hath brought *life* and *immortality* to light through the gospel." In this verse "life" (*zoen*) and "immortality" (*aphtharsian*) are clearly distinguished. Life has been bestowed upon the believer at the moment of regeneration by faith in Jesus Christ (1 John 5:11, 12); immortality is a future gift, to be bestowed upon the believer's body at the second advent of our Lord, or as Paul expressed it, "This corruptible must put on incorruption (*aphtharsian*), and this mortal must put on immortality" (*athanasian*).

Again in Romans 2:7, the Apostle clearly distinguishes between "eternal life" as a conscious quality of spiritual existence bestowed upon the believer as a gift; and "immortality," which, in this connection in the New Testament refers to the resurrection bodies of the saints or to the nature of God Himself. Thus, God's Word clearly indicates the difference between "life" as spiritual existence, and "immortality," incorruptibility in a body like that of our risen Lord.

4. *Philippians 1:21–23*: "For to me to live is Christ, and to die is gain. But if I live in the flesh, this is the fruit of my labour: yet what I shall choose I wot not. For I am in a strait betwixt two, having a desire to depart, and to be with Christ; which is far better: nevertheless to abide in the flesh is more needful for you."

Seventh-day Adventists say here:

> Of course it will be better to be with Christ, but why, it must be asked, should we conclude that the apostle expects immediately upon death to go at once into the presence of Christ? *The Bible does not say so.* It merely states his desire to depart and be with Christ. One might reason that the *implication* is to the effect that being with Christ would be immediately on his departure. But it must be admitted that such is not a necessary implication, and it certainly is not a definite statement of the text. In this particular passage Paul does not tell us *when* he will be with his Lord. In other places he uses an expression similar to one in this passage. For instance, he says, "The time of my departure is at hand" (2 Tim. 4:6). The Greek word used in these two texts, *analuō*, is not used very often in the Greek New Testament, but the word has the meaning "to be loosened like an anchor." It is a metaphor drawn from the loosened moorings preparatory to setting sail.[25]

---

[25] *Questions on Doctrine*, pp. 527, 528.

Now, of all the texts in the New Testament on the state of the believer after the death of his body, this one alone gives us Paul's mind on the subject, so we need to pay strict attention to what he says. In the main, Seventh-day Adventists support their arguments with Old Testament passages, most of which, I maintain, are taken out of context while ignoring metaphorical usages, implications or deductions. To treat literally such words as "sleep," "death" and "destroy," is I feel, unwarranted. However, in the New Testament, when faced with a positive statement like this one by the Apostle Paul, it seems that they refuse to be literal and insist upon metaphors, deductions and implications. They seem unwilling to accept the Apostle's statement at face value. The noted Adventist author F. D. Nichol, in his book *Answers to Objections*, states that if Philippians 1:21–23 were the only passage about the condition of man in death, he would be forced to acknowledge the accepted Orthodox position. Nichol then attempts to strengthen his argument by taking texts out of context to "prove" that Paul does not *mean* what he most decidedly *says*. With this thought in mind, let us examine the context and grammar of the Apostle's statement for it answers the Seventh-day Adventist contention.

In verse 21 Paul states that to continue to live *is* Christ and to die "is gain." Since Paul was ordained to preach the Word of God to the Gentiles while enjoying fellowship with the living Christ, what would he gain by death or unconsciousness? According to the Adventist idea, fellowship with Christ would end and Paul would merely go to sleep until the resurrection. This argument violates both context and grammar.

Verse 23 is grammatically uncomplicated. It is a series of coordinate statements tied together by the conjunctions *kai* and *de*. The phrase "to depart and be with Christ, which is far better" (*eis to analusai kai sun christo einai*) is grammatically devastating to the Seventh-day Adventist position. The preposition *eis* plus the definite article *to* shows "true purpose or end in view"—the strong desire which causes Paul's dilemma. Both infinitives (*analusai* and *einai*) have one construction—they are used with one definite article—so are *one* thought, *one* grammatical expression: literally, "my desire is to the 'to depart and to be with Christ.' " In simple English, Paul's one desire has a twofold object: departure and being *with* Christ! If departure did not mean his immediately being with Christ, another construction would have been employed. It therefore seems impossible that soul sleep was in the mind of the Apostle since he desired to depart *from* his body and to spiritually enjoy the presence of his Lord. The Second Advent could not have been in view in this passage for the context indicates that Paul expected death—and instantaneous reunion with Christ—*then, not* at the resurrection. There would have been no need of his staying to instruct the Philippians (vs. 24) if he were speaking of the Second Advent, for they would all be glorified together and no longer in need of His presence to strengthen them. Most translators and recognized Greek authorities contend that Philippians 1:21–23 teaches the historic position of the Christian Church, i.e., the conscious presence of the believer with Christ at the death of the body.

As quoted above, the Adventists, in common with all conditionalists, say, but "Why . . . should we conclude from this remark that the Apostle expects, immediately upon death, to go at once into the presence of Christ? The Bible does not say so. It merely states his desire to depart and to be with Christ." We answer that the context of the chapter, the grammatical construction of the verse, and every grammar book on New Testament Greek usage teaches that from the construction utilized the Apostle expected to go *at once* into the presence of his Lord. Nevertheless the Adventists insist, "The Bible does not say so. It merely states his desire to depart and to be with Christ." This statement is not accurate, it is not exegetically sound, and it will not stand the test of contextual criticism. It is only an attempt, I believe, to justify a doctrine that is *not* supported by the Word of God.

In reply to the Adventist statement, "In this particular passage Paul does not tell us *when* he will be with his Lord," we point out that the Apostle categorically states that his desire *is* "to depart." If this departure did not mean immediate presence with Christ, he would have used a different grammatical construction as previously noted; but as it stands, it can have *no other meaning*. In the face of these facts, Seventh-day Adventists disregard the preponderance of historical scholarship in favor of the doctrine of "soul sleep."

5. *1 Thessalonians 4:13–18*: "I would not have you to be ignorant, brethren, concerning them which are asleep, that ye sorrow not, even as others which have no hope. For if we believe that Jesus died and rose again, even so them also which sleep in Jesus will God bring with him. For this we say unto you by the word of the Lord, that we which are alive and remain unto the coming of the Lord shall not prevent them which are asleep. For the Lord himself shall descend from heaven with a shout, with the voice of the archangel, and with the trump of God: and the dead in Christ shall rise first: then we which are alive and remain shall be caught up together with them in the clouds, to meet the Lord in the air: and so shall we ever be with the Lord. Wherefore comfort one another with these words."

This final passage, I believe, refutes the SDA teaching on the intermediate state of the dead, and is marked by explicit emphasis of construction in the Greek and cannot be ignored by any serious student of the language.

The key is the preposition *sun* which carries the primary meaning of "together with." In verse 14 the Holy Spirit tells us that God intends to bring with Him (*sun auto*), that is, with Jesus at His Second Advent, believing Christians who have experienced physical death. The physical state of their bodies is described as "sleep," a common metaphor in the New Testament. In every instance where the word "sleep" is used to describe death, it always refers to the *body* and cannot be applied to the soul, especially since "sleep" is never used with reference to the soul. This fact Seventh-day Adventists seem to overlook.

The second use of *sun* is in verse 17 which tells us that believers who survive to the coming of the Lord will be caught up together with them (*sun autois*), that is, with the dead in Christ (*oi nekroi en Christo*) to meet the Lord in the air. Here again, *sun* has no meaning other than "together with"; a fact most difficult for Seventh-day Adventists to explain.

The last use of the preposition *sun* is also in verse 17, "and so shall we ever be with the Lord" (*sun kurio*). It is quite obvious, therefore, that at the

Second Advent of Christ those who at death departed to be spiritually with the Lord (Philippians 1:21–23) *return* with Him or "together with" Him to claim their resurrected, immortal bodies. Simultaneously, their corrupting bodies in the graves, spoken of as "asleep," are instantly metamorphosed or changed and reunited with the returning personalities. This fact is consistently emphasized by continual use of the preposition *sun*, "together with." Since the preposition *sun* means "together with" both times in verse 17, grammatically it cannot mean something altogether different in the same context and parallel usage of verse 14. Therefore, if at Christ's advent our bodies are to go with Him physically (verse 16), it is obvious that the saints who preceded us in death have been with Him from the moment of death, since they accompany Him in His return (verse 14).

A final grammatical point is the Holy Spirit's use of *nekroi* which throughout the New Testament refers primarily to the physical body of man, and only metaphorically to the soul. We see, then, that the corpses (*nekroi*) of the physically dead saints are to be raised and united with their returning souls (verse 14). Not once does the context or grammar indicate that the souls of departed believers are "asleep." Instead, it categorically states that they are "with Jesus" or returning "together with" Jesus.

The great hope of the believer, then, is the joy of personal union with the Lord, and this union, the Apostle Paul tells us, takes place at the death of the body. That this has been the position of the large majority of the Christian Church since the times of the apostles, the Adventists have never denied. In 1 Thessalonians 4, the Apostle Paul was giving comfort to people who were mourning for departed loved ones; and his words carry the undeniable conclusion that they are not "dead" in the usual pagan sense. Although physically dead, they are spiritually alive and with Christ, and are awaiting the day when they will return "together with him" (verse 14) to claim their inheritance of completion, physical immortality or incorruptibility.

II. *"Soul" and "Spirit"*

For a fuller treatment of Adventist teaching on soul sleep, we must discuss briefly the Bible use of "soul" and "spirit." In the Old Testament, the words "soul" and "spirit" are the Hebrew *nephesh* and *ruach*. In the New Testament they are the Greek *psuche* and *pneuma*. Although in the Old Testament *nephesh* and *ruach* frequently refer only to the *principle* of life in both men and animals, in many other places they mean the intellectual and spiritual nature of man. Such verses as Isaiah 57:16, Zechariah 12:1, Isaiah 55:3 and Genesis 35:18,[26] belie the Adventists' criterion for determining the spir-

---

[26]"For I will not contend for ever, neither will I be always wroth: for the spirit should fail before me, and the souls which I have made" (Isaiah 57:16); "The burden of the word of the Lord for Israel, saith the Lord, which stretcheth forth the heavens, and layeth the foundation of the earth, and formeth the spirit of man within him" (Zechariah 12:1); "Incline your ear, and come unto me: hear, and your soul shall live; and I will make an everlasting covenant with you, even the sure mercies of David" (Isaiah 55:3); "And it came to pass, as her soul was in departing, (for she died) that she called his name Benoni: but his father called him Benjamin" (Genesis 35:18).

itual nature of man. On page 522 of *Questions on Doctrine*, the Adventists list eight Scripture passages about death to show that at the death of the body, the intellect, will, and spirit of man (*nephesh* and *ruach*) lapse into unconsciousness pending the resurrection. However, seven of these are from the Old Testament and each refers to the *body*. Adventists lean strongly on the book of Ecclesiastes, especially 9:5, 6, to substantiate their doctrine. But Ecclesiastes 12:7 tells us that upon the death of the body, "the spirit [*ruach*] shall return unto God." Unlike the mere principle of life in the animals, man possesses a cognizant, immaterial nature created in God's image.[27]

It is a basic Christian principle, which Adventists share, that the Old Testament must be interpreted by the New Testament, and not the reverse. However, where conditional immortality is involved, Adventists do not follow this principle. The New Testament teaches that the immaterial nature of man (soul and spirit) is separate from the body (Matthew 10:28; Luke 8:55; 1 Thessalonians 5:23; Hebrews 4:12; Revelation 16:3);[28] that it is independent of man's material form and departs from that form at death to go either into the presence of the Lord (Philippians 1:23) or into a place of punishment (Luke 16). In Acts 7:59, Stephen committed his spirit (*pneuma*) into the hands of the Lord Jesus Christ. This establishes the fact that the immaterial nature of man is independent of his body. At the same time, the Scripture tells us, "He [Stephen] fell asleep" in death; that is, his physical body took on the appearance of "sleep." But he as a unit did not die; he merely experienced separation of the soul from the body and he went to be with the Lord, into whose hands he had committed his spiritual nature.

In Luke 23:46 the Lord Jesus Christ said, "Father, into thy hands I commend my spirit." This verse would be meaningless if it applied only to the "breath of Jesus." The classic example of the penitent thief, who in his last moments believed on the Lord Jesus Christ, is proof that eternal life is a *quality including conscious existence*. It does not terminate with the death of the physical but continues in never-ending personal fellowship with our Lord. "Today shalt thou be with me in paradise," is the guarantee of the Son of God that those who trust Him will never be separated from His presence and fellowship. Seventh-day Adventists, in company with other Conditionalists, attempt to explain this by reading the text, "Verily, verily, I say unto thee today, thou shalt be with me in paradise." The reason is that Christ's statement calls in serious question their doctrine of soul sleep. Moreover,

---

[27]It is almost universally agreed among Biblical scholars that Ecclesiastes portrays Solomon's apostasy and is therefore questionable for determining doctrine. It sketches man's life "under the sun" and reveals the hopelessness of the soul apart from God.

[28]"And fear not them which kill the body, but are not able to kill the soul: but rather fear him which is able to destroy both soul and body in hell" (Matthew 10:28); "And her spirit came again, and she rose straightway: and he commanded to give her meat" (Luke 8:55); "and the very God of peace sanctify you wholly; and I pray God your whole spirit and soul and body be preserved blameless unto the coming of our Lord Jesus Christ" (1 Thessalonians 5:23); "For the word of God is quick, and powerful and sharper than any twoedged sword, piercing even to the dividing asunder of soul and spirit, and of the joints and marrow, and is a discerner of the thoughts and intents of the heart" (Hebrews 4:12); "And the second angel poured out his vial upon the sea; and it became as the blood of a dead man: and every living soul died in the sea" (Revelation 16:3).

Adventists seem to overlook the important fact that wherever Jesus used the words, "verily, verily, I say unto you," He never qualified them because qualification was unnecessary. It would have been redundant for Jesus to say, "Verily, verily, I say unto you, that is, *today* I am saying unto you. . . ." By this type of interpretation, the Adventists violate the plain sense of one of Christ's favorite expressions of emphasis.

In Matthew 17:3, we see Moses and Elijah with Christ on the Mount of Transfiguration. We know that Moses died (Deuteronomy 34:5), and Elijah was translated (2 Kings 2:11). However, it *was* Moses who was communing with our Lord. Since the Scripture nowhere states that Moses had been raised from the dead for this occasion (Adventists attempt to teach this from the book of Jude, where such an assertion is *not* made), it is evident that the soul of Moses appeared to our Lord. Thus conscious existence is a necessary predicate of the intermediate state.

It is the strong conviction of mine, based upon Scripture, that the doctrine of soul sleep cannot stand in the light of God's revelation. Perhaps the reader will think that there has been too much space given to the meanings of words and the grammar of the Greek New Testament. However, this is most essential because the crux of Adventist argument, it seems to me, is a denial of the meaning of terms in their context. For example, they say:

> There is nothing in the word *psuche* [soul] itself that even remotely implies a conscious entity that is able to survive the death of the body. And there is nothing in the Bible use of the word indicating that the Bible writers held any such belief. . . . There is nothing inherent in the word *pneuma* [spirit] by which it may be taken to mean some supposed conscious entity of man capable of existing apart from the body, nor does the usage of the word *with respect to man* in the New Testament in any way imply such a concept. . . . A careful study of all the adjectives used in Scripture to qualify the word "spirit" as applied to man, indicates that *not one* even remotely approaches the idea of immortality as one of the qualities of the human "spirit."[29]

In Matthew 10:28, Jesus Christ apparently believed and taught that the soul was more than "body and breath" as Seventh-day Adventism teaches, for He said, "Fear not them which kill the body, but are not able to kill the soul!"

Seventh-day Adventist writers charge that orthodox theologians have been overly dogmatic about the nature of man while Adventists have maintained a guarded reserve. But Adventists have been equally dogmatic in denouncing the orthodox position. To be dogmatic one should have a sound, scholarly basis for his dogmatism, and such a basis exegetically speaking is conspicuously absent from the historic position of conditional immortalists. As mentioned above, Adventists generally confuse "immortality" with "eternal life." We quite agree that "a careful study of all the adjectives used in Scripture to qualify the word 'spirit' as applied to man, indicates that *not one* even remotely approaches the idea of immortality," as our Adventist brethren have stated. But as we have shown, "immortality" refers *only* to the resur-

---

[29]*Questions on Doctrine*, pp. 514, 517, 518.

rection body of the saints and to the nature of God Himself. Therefore, since the saints are to be clothed with their resurrection bodies at the Second Advent, they do not *now* possess "immortality." For Adventists to confuse "immortality" with "eternal life" and then to argue that "immortality" *means* "eternal life" and is never applied to the spirit, is logical and theological error.

The question of soul sleep, however, should cause no serious division between Christians since it does not affect the foundational doctrines of the Christian faith or the salvation of the soul. It is merely an area of theological debate and has no direct bearing upon any of the great doctrines of the Bible. The ground of fellowship is not the condition of man in death but faith in the Lord Jesus Christ and the love He commanded us to have one for another (John 13:34, 35). Seventh-day Adventists are welcome to hold this doctrine, but when one is faced with such concrete Old Testament instances as Samuel's appearance to Saul (1 Samuel 28:18, 19) and such New Testament accounts as those given by the Apostle Paul (2 Corinthians 5:8), "To be absent from the body is to be at home with the Lord," or (Philippians 1:23) ". . . to depart and be with Christ, which is far better," it is difficult to see how our Adventist brethren can long substantiate their claim for the "sleep of the soul."

III. *Hell and Punishment in New Testament Greek*

The grammar of the Greek New Testament teaches unquestionably the doctrine of Hell and eternal punishment. Nowhere is this more pointedly brought out than in the following passages:

1. *Matthew 5:22 and 10:28*: "Whosoever shall say, Thou fool, shall be in danger of hell fire." "Fear him which is able to destroy both soul and body in hell."

In both passages the Greek word *gehenna* portrays a place of punishment for the unsaved. *Gehenna* originally meant the Valley of Hinnom, a garbage dump which smoldered perpetually outside Jerusalem. The rabbis believed that punishment after death could be likened to Gehenna and often threatened their people with punishment after death. The Lord Jesus Christ, however, pointed out to the unbelieving Jews that those who rejected Him could look forward to everlasting Gehenna. In Matthew 10:28, He coupled *gehenna* with *apolesai*, which Thayer's Greek lexicon defines as "to be delivered up to eternal misery." *Gehenna*, then, symbolizes eternal separation and conscious punishment for the spiritual nature of the unregenerate man. This eternity of punishment is also taught in the Old Testament; e.g., "Their worm shall not die, neither shall their fire be quenched" (Isaiah 66:24).

2. *2 Thessalonians 1:8, 9*: "In flaming fire taking vengeance on them that know not God, and that obey not the gospel of our Lord Jesus Christ: who shall be punished with everlasting destruction from the presence of the Lord and from the glory of his power."

From the context, especially verse 8, "everlasting destruction" is to be that of "flaming fire," visited upon those who "obey not the gospel of our Lord Jesus Christ." The heart of the problem here is the meaning of the word "destruction," which the Adventists claim is reduction to a state of nonexistence (*Questions on Doctrine*, p. 14). As a matter of fact, the Greek word *olethros* used here has the clear meaning of "ruining." (For this and the following lexical studies, any standard New Testament Greek lexicon or grammar bears out the meanings presented here.) We see then, that everlasting destruction or "ruination" is the lot of those who know not God. Many people who are not well versed in Greek try to make "destruction" synonymous with "annihilation." This does violence to New Testament Greek, which supports no such concept. A common illustration will show the fallacy of this idea.

In the course of her work a housewife changes light bulbs and sometimes one drops to the floor and breaks. Of course the bulb has been "destroyed," but no one would say that it had been annihilated, for there is a difference between the *function* of an object and its *nature*. The function of the bulb is to give forth light. When broken, its function is destroyed, but the glass remains, although in fragments, and so does the metal base. Although the bulb has been "ruined" or "destroyed," it certainly has not been "reduced to nothing."

The Bible teaches that unregenerate men will suffer the eternal wrath of God and must undergo destruction and ruin of their original function which was "to glorify God and to enjoy Him forever." But the human spirit, created in the image of God (Genesis 1:26, 27), remains intact, a spiritual entity of eternal existence, capable of enduring eternally the righteous and just Judge.

3. *Revelation 20:10*: "The devil who deceived them was cast into the lake of fire and brimstone where the beast and the false prophet are, and they will be tormented day and night into the everlasting of the everlasting" (literal translation).

The root meaning of the Greek word *basanizo* is "to torment, to be harassed, to torture or to vex with grievous pain," and is used throughout the New Testament to denote great conscious pain and misery, never annihilation or cessation of consciousness. The reader who wishes to pursue this point may look up the following verses where this word is used: Matthew 8:6, 29; Mark 5:7; Luke 8:28; Revelation 14:10, 11. In each place, *basanizo* means conscious "torment." In Revelation 14:10, 11, speaking of the followers of the Beast, unmistakably it means torment or punishment, everlasting or never-ceasing.

In Revelation 20:10, Satan, the beast and the false prophet are described as tormented (*basanis thesontai*) "day and night into the everlasting of the everlasting." So if language means anything at all, in these contexts alone the theory of the annihilation or, as the Adventists say, the final destruction of the wicked is itself annihilated.

4. *John 3:36*: "He that believeth on the Son hath everlasting life, and he that believeth not the Son shall not see life, but the wrath of God abideth on him."

Our fourth and final grammatical point relative to the doctrine of annihilation is made by coupling Romans 2:8, 9 and Revelation 14:10 with John 3:36. Jesus tells us that the one who believes in the Lord Jesus Christ already *has* everlasting life (present tense); and then, of one who "believes not the Son," he states that he "shall not *see* life, but the wrath of God abides on him." The Greek word *menei*, here translated *abide*, appears several times in the New Testament. It carries the idea of continuous action (see John 1:33; 2:12; 8:31; 15:9). Thus, in John 3:36 the Holy Spirit says that the wrath of God continually abides on the one who "believeth not the Son." Comparing this with Romans 2:8, 9, we see that those who do not obey the truth but do evil are the objects of God's wrath, which Revelation 14:10, 11 describes as eternal. "The same shall drink of the wine of the wrath of God . . . and the smoke of their torment ascendeth up for ever and ever: and they have no rest day nor night."

Orges, translated "wrath," appears in each of the verses cited, so there can be no doubt that the same subject is being discussed. It is apparent then that, far from the comparatively blissful prospect of total annihilation, those who "have not the Son of God have not life,"[30] and "the wrath of God continues upon them."[31] God's wrath even now hangs like the sword of Damocles over the heads of those who deny Jesus Christ. It will strike when the rebellious soul goes into eternity and appears before the bar of God's eternal justice.

Seventh-day Adventists should not be ostracized because they cling to this doctrine, since they believe that an undetermined period of punishment will elapse before the actual ultimate destruction of the wicked with Satan and his hosts.

Dr. Francis Pieper, the great Lutheran scholar and author of the monumental *Christian Dogmatics*, states my views in essence when he says:

> Holy Scripture teaches the truth of an eternal damnation so clearly and emphatically that one cannot deny it without, at the same time, rejecting the authority of Scripture. Scripture parallels the eternal salvation of the believers and the eternal damnation of the unbelievers. Whoever therefore denies the one must, to be consistent, deny the other (Matthew 25:46). We find the same juxtaposition and antithesis in other passages of Scripture. This parallelism proves that the term *eternity* in the sense of limited duration as sometimes used in Holy Writ, is inapplicable here. We must take the predicate eternal in its proper or strict sense, a sense of *sine fine* in all Scripture texts which use it to describe the duration and the penalties of the wicked in yonder life (see 2 Thessalonians 1:9; Matthew 18:8; Mark 3:29). . . . The objections raised in all ages to the endlessness of the infernal punishment are understandable; for the thought of a neverending agony of rational beings fully realizing their distressing plight is so appalling that it exceeds comprehension. But all objections are based on the false principle that it is proper and reasonable to make our human sentiments and judgments the measure of God's essence and activity.
>
> This is the case in particular with those who contend that an everlasting punishment of a part of mankind does not agree with the unity of God's world plan, or that it is compatible neither with divine love nor with divine justice, who accordingly substitute for eternal damnation eventual salvation

---

[30] I.e., personal communion or fellowship with Christ. Spiritual death is the opposite of eternal life in that the soul is deprived of such communion or fellowship and is conscious of it.

[31] Death (spiritual), far from being unconsciousness, is eternal *conscious* endurance of God's just wrath.

by gradual improvement in the next life, or an immediate or later annihilation of the wicked. Against such views we must maintain the general principle that God's essence, attributes and actions exceed our comprehension, that we can therefore not know *a priori* but only from God's revelation in His Word what agrees or conflicts with God's essence and attributes. The nature of eternal damnation consists in eternal banishment from the sight of God or, in other words, in being forever excluded from communion with God. . . . To illustrate the terrible agony setting in with this banishment from the sight of God, the dogmatician points to the agony of the fish removed from its element. But there is this difference; the fish which is removed from its element soon dies, whereas the man who is banished from communion with God must by God's judgment live on, "is guilty of eternal judgment," Mark 3:29.[32]

Seventh-day Adventists would do well to heed Dr. Pieper's observation as well as the testimony of the Christian Church generally for the last two thousand years. But most important, they should heed the teaching of the Word of God that the soul of man, whether regenerate or unregenerate, exists after the death of the body. The justice of God makes everlasting punishment for the unregenerate and everlasting life for the saved to be two sides of one coin—God's justice and God's love. We believe the Bible clearly teaches that there is neither authority nor warrant for the doctrines of conditional immortality and annihilation. God grant in the fullness of His wisdom that none of His children will persist in setting up their standards as the criterion to determine His perfect righteousness. It is my opinion that Seventh-day Adventists have done just this; first by predicating that a God of love *would not* eternally punish a conscious being, and second by attempting to force the Scriptures into their frame of thought while seeming to ignore context, hermeneutics and exegesis. Their fellow Christians can only pray that they may soon be led to embrace the historic position of the church, which is the antithesis of the sleep of the soul and the annihilation of the wicked.

The Sabbath, the Lord's Day, and the Mark of the Beast

Certainly the most distinctive doctrine promulgated by the Seventh-day Adventist denomination, and one of the two from which they derive their name, is the Seventh-day Sabbath. How Adventists came to hold the Sabbath as the true day of worship, and why they continue to champion it and jealously urge it upon all who worship on Sunday, provides the key to understanding their psychological and theological motivations.

I. *The Sabbath or the Lord's Day?*

Seventh-day Adventists from the beginning have always attempted to equate the Sabbath with the Lord's Day. Their principal method for accom-

---

[32]Francis Pieper, *Christian Dogmatics*, Grand Rapids, MI: Zondervan Publishing House, n.d. (reprint), vol. 3, pp. 544, 555.

plishing this is to link Mark 2:28 with Revelation 1:10, and thus to undercut one of the strongest arguments against their postion, i.e., the Lord's Day as opposed to Sabbath observance.

They reason that since "the Son of Man is Lord also of the Sabbath" (Mark 2:27, 28), when John says he "was in the Spirit on the Lord's day" (Revelation 1:10), the Sabbath and the Lord's Day must be the same! The weakness of their position is that they base their argument on an English translation instead of on the Greek original. When one reads the second chapter of Mark and the first chapter of Revelation in Greek, he sees that there is no such interpretation inherent in the grammatical structure. The Greek of Mark 2:28 clearly indicates that Christ did not mean that the Sabbath was His *possession* (which the Adventists would like to establish); rather, He was saying that as Lord of all He could do as He pleased on the Sabbath. The Greek is most explicit here.

Nothing could be clearer from both the context and the grammar. In Revelation 1:10, the Greek is not the genitive of possession, which it would have to be in order to make *te-kuriake* (the Lord's) agree with *hemera* (day). John did not mean that the Lord's Day was the Lord's possession, but rather that it was the day dedicated to Him by the early church, not in accordance with Mosaic law, but in obedience to our Lord's commandment of love.

We may certainly assume that if the Sabbath had meant so much to the writers of the New Testament; and if, as Adventists insist, it was so widely observed during the early centuries of the Christian Church, John and the other writers of Scripture would have equated it with the Lord's Day, the first day of the week. Scripture and history testify that they did not, and Adventists have, therefore, little Scriptural justification for their Sabbatarianism.

A. *Testimony of the Fathers*

The Church Fathers provide a mass of evidence that the first day of the week, not the seventh, is the Lord's Day. Some of this evidence is here submitted for the reader's consideration. In company with the overwhelming majority of historians and scholars, we believe that not only the New Testament but the following citations refute Sabbatarianism. We have yet to see any systematic answer to what the Christian Church always believed.

1. *Ignatius, Bishop of Antioch,* in the year 110, wrote: "If, then, those who walk in the ancient practices attain to newness of hope, no longer observing the Sabbath, but fashioning their lives after the Lord's Day on which our life also arose through Him, that we may be found disciples of Jesus Christ, our only teacher."

2. *Justin Martyr* (100–165): "And on the day called Sunday, all who live in cities or in the country gather together in one place and memoirs of the apostles or the writings of the prophets are read, as long as time permits. . . . Sunday is the day on which we all hold our common assembly because it is the first day on which God, having wrought a change in the darkness in matter, made the world; and Jesus Christ our Saviour on the same day rose from the dead."

3. *The Epistle of Barnabas* (between 120 and 150): " 'Your new moons and your sabbaths I cannot endure' (Isaiah 1:13). You perceive how He speaks: Your present sabbaths are not acceptable to me but that which I had made in giving rest to all things, I shall make a beginning of the eighth day, that is a beginning of another world. Wherefore also, we keep the eighth day with joyfulness, a day also in which Jesus rose from the dead."

4. *Irenaeus, Bishop of Lyons* (about 178): "The mystery of the Lord's resurrection may not be celebrated on any other day than the Lord's Day."

5. *Bardaisān* (born 154): "Wherever we be, all of us are called by the one name of the Messiah, namely Christians and upon one day which is the first day of the week we assemble ourselves together and on the appointed days we abstain from food."

6. *Cyprian, Bishop of Carthage* (200–258): "The Lord's Day is both the first and the eighth day."

7. *Eusebius* (about 315): "The churches throughout the rest of the world observe the practice that has prevailed from the Apostolic tradition until the present time so that it would not be proper to terminate our fast on any other day but the resurrection day of our Saviour. Hence, there were synods and convocations of our bishops on this question and they unanimously drew up an ecclesiastical decree which they communicated to churches in all places— that the mystery of the Lord's resurrection should be celebrated on no other than the Lord's day."

8. *Peter, Bishop of Alexandria* (about 300): "We keep the Lord's Day as a day of joy because of Him who arose thereon."

9. *Didache of the Apostles* (about 70–75): "On the Lord's own day, gather yourselves together and break bread and give thanks."

10. *The Epistle of Pliny* (about 112, addressed to the Emperor Trajan): "They [the Christians] affirmed . . . that the whole of their crime or error was that they had been wont to meet together on a fixed day before daylight and to repeat among themselves in turn a hymn to Christ as to a god and to bind themselves by an oath (*sacramentum*) . . .; these things duly done, it had been their custom to disperse and to meet again to take food—of an ordinary and harmless kind. Even this they had ceased to do after my edict, by which, in accordance with your instructions, I had forbidden the existence of societies."

Thus it appears that from apostolic and patristic times, the Christian Church observed the Lord's Day or the first day of the week; further, the Jewish Sabbath, in the words of Clement of Alexandria (about 194) was "nothing more than a working day."

In their zeal to establish the authority of the Sabbath, Adventists either reject contrary evidence as unauthentic (and so conflict with the preponderance of scholastic opinion), or they ignore the testimony of the early church. Although they seem unaffected by the evidence, the fact remains that the Christian Church has both apostolic and historical support for observing the Lord's Day in place of the Sabbath.

B. *"Authoritative Quotations"*

Recently the Adventist radio program *Voice of Prophecy* circulated a 31 page pamphlet entitled, *Authoritative Quotations on the Sabbath and Sunday.* In it they quoted "leading" Protestant sources to "prove" that Sunday usurped the Sabbath and is a pagan institution imposed by Constantine in 321.

However, many of the sources quoted actually establish what the Adventists flatly deny; i.e., that the seventh-day Sabbath is *not* the Lord's Day or the first day of the week, but is, in fact, the seventh day as its name indicates.

Since the Adventists are willing to quote these authorities to buttress their position in one area, surely they will give consideration to contradictory statements by these same authorites in another:

1. "The Lord's Day did not succeed in the place of the Sabbath. . . . The Lord's Day was merely an ecclesiastical institution. . . . The primitive Christians did all manner of work upon the Lord's Day" (Bishop Jeremy Taylor, *Ductor Dubitantium*, Part 1, Book 2, Chap. 2, Rule 6, Secs. 51, 59).

2. "The observance of the Lord's Day [Sunday] is founded not on any command of God, but on the authority of the church" (*Augsburg Confession of Faith*, quoted in *Catholic Sabbath Manual*, Part 2, Chap. 1, Sec. 10).

3. "But they err in teaching that Sunday has taken the place of the Old Testament Sabbath and therefore must be kept as the Seventh day had to be kept by the children of Israel" (J. T. Mueller, *Sabbath or Sunday*, pp. 15, 16).

4. "They [the Catholics] allege the Sabbath changed into Sunday, the Lord's Day, contrary to the Decalogue as it appears, neither is there any example more boasted than the changing of the Sabbath Day" (Martin Luther, *Augsburg Confession of Faith*, Art. 28, Para. 9).

5. "Although it [Sunday] was in primitive times and differently called the Lord's day or Sunday, yet it was never denominated the Sabbath; a name constantly appropriate to Saturday, or the Seventh day both by sacred and ecclesiastical writers" (Charles Buck, *A Theological Dictionary*, 1830, p. 537).

6. "The notion of a formal substitution by apostolic authority of the Lord's Day [meaning Sunday] for the Jewish Sabbath (or the first for the seventh day) . . . the transference to it perhaps in a spiritualized form of the Sabbath obligation established by promulgation of the fourth commandment has no basis whatever, either in Holy Scripture or in Christian antiquity" (Sir William Smith and Samuel Cheetham, *A Dictionary of Christian Antiquities*, Vol. II, p. 182, article on the Sabbath).

7. "The view that the Christian's Lord's Day or Sunday is but the Christian Sabbath deliberately transferred from the seventh to the first day of the week does not indeed find categoric expression till a much later period. . . . The Council of Laodicea (A.D. 364) . . . forbids Christians from Judaizing and resting on the Sabbath Day, preferring the Lord's Day and so far as possible resting as Christians" (*Encyclopedia Britannica*, 1899 ed., vol. 23, p. 654).

Thus the Adventists have in effect destroyed their argument by appealing to authorities which state unequivocally that the first day of the week is the Lord's Day and that it was observed by the early Christian Church from the time of the Apostles.

It should also be carefully noted that in their "Authoritative Quotations" the Adventists overlook the fact that nearly all the authorities argue forcefully for the Lord's Day as the first day of the week, and state that legal observance of the Sabbath terminated at the cross (Colossians 2:16, 17). The Adventists also, in their compilation of quotations, appeal even to the Church of Jesus Christ of Latter-day Saints (Mormon), and to Fulton Ousler, a Roman Catholic lay writer. The Mormons are a non-Christian cult, a fact which the Adventists admit; and Ousler, a layman, hardly represents the position of Rome.

On page 13 of this same pamphlet, the Adventists make misleading use of the ellipsis. The following is a direct quotation as it appears:

> Sunday (*dies-solis*, of the Roman calendar, day of the sun, because dedicated to the sun), was adopted by the early Christians as a day of worship. The sun of Latin adoration they interpreted as the "sun of righteousness." . . . No regulations for its observance are laid down in the New Testament, nor, indeed, is its observance even enjoined. Schaff-Herzog *Encyclopedia of Religious Knowledge*, 1891 ed., Volume 4, Article on Sunday.

Now here is the paragraph as it appears in the *Encyclopedia*:

> Sunday (*dies-solis*, of the Roman Calendar, day of the sun because dedicated to the sun), was adopted by the early Christians as a day of worship. The sun of Latin adoration they interpreted as "the sun of righteousness." SUNDAY WAS EMPHATICALLY THE WEEKLY FEAST OF THE RESURRECTION OF CHRIST, AS THE JEWISH SABBATH WAS THE FEAST OF THE CREATION. IT WAS CALLED THE "LORD'S DAY," AND UPON IT THE PRIMITIVE CHURCH ASSEMBLED TO BREAK BREAD (Acts 20:7, 1 Corinthians 16:2). No regulations for its observance are laid down in the New Testament, nor, indeed, is its observance even enjoined; YET CHRISTIAN FEELING LED TO THE UNIVERSAL ADOPTION OF THE DAY, IN IMITATION OF APOSTOLIC PRECEDENCE. IN THE SECOND CENTURY ITS OBSERVANCE WAS UNIVERSAL. (Sentences in capital letters were omitted by the writer of the Adventist pamphlet on p. 22. This mutilation of authoritative sources first occurs in *The Present Truth*, Vol. I, No. 9, published in the 1880s. So our Adventist brethren apparently failed to check the quotation's validity.)

Such use of the ellipsis is not uncommon in certain Seventh-day Adventists' writings in connection with the Sabbath, the Lord's Day, etc., and we regret that they resort to it in order to substantiate their position.

In this pamphlet they quote Martin Luther, despite the well-known fact that Luther violently opposed Sabbatarianism. His refutation of his Sabbatarian colleague, Dr. Carlstadt, is a monument to his apologetic genius. Thus, to quote Luther in order to support the doctrine of the Seventh day suggests that Adventists are not familiar with Luther's theology.

We admire the boldness of our Adventist brethren in their claims for the Sabbath, but their boldness is misplaced and leads to a distorted concept of the value of the law of God; for when a person believes and teaches that "the fourth commandment is the greatest commandment in the Decalogue," it is apparent that he has no understanding of the spirit of the law. Volume IV of the *International Standard Bible Encyclopedia* represents the reasons why the Christian Church observes the Lord's Day in preference to the Sabbath, and also clearly states (pp. 2629–34) the Seventh-day Adventist position.[33] On page 2633 the Adventists contend: "According to church history the seventh day Sabbath was observed by the early church, and no other day was observed as a Sabbath during the first two or three centuries."

This sentence epitomizes the Adventist propensity for overstating their case; i.e., attempting to read "Sabbath" into "Lord's Day," which all leading authorities confute as we have seen.

II. *Primary Anti-Sabbatarian Texts*

In more than one place, the New Testament comments unfavorably upon the practice of any type of legalistic day keeping. In fact, from the ascension of Christ on, the New Testament and early church observed the first day of the week or the Lord's Day (Revelation 1:10), as we have endeavored to show. Besides the passages which contrast the Lord's Day with the Sabbath, the Apostle Paul, Hebrew of the Hebrews and Pharisee of the Pharisees, the outstanding New Testament authority, apart from our Lord, on the Law of Moses, declared that the Sabbath as "the law" was fulfilled at the cross and was not binding upon the Christian (Colossians 2:16, 17). Since the subject is so vast in scope, the reader is referred to the bibliography, especially to Dr. Louis Sperry Chafer's *Grace*, and Norman C. Deck's *The Lord's Day or the Sabbath, Which?* These contain excellent refutations of Sabbatarianism. D. M. Canright in *Seventh-day Adventism Renounced* also dealt exhaustively and ably with the Sabbath subject.

To narrow the issue down to simple analysis, we shall review the major New Testament texts, which in context and in the light of syntactical analysis refute the Sabbatarian concept, and substantiate the historic position of the Christian Church since the days of the Apostles and the Fathers.

A. *Colossians 2:13–17*

Of all of the statements in the New Testament, these verses most strongly refute the Sabbatarian claim for observance of the Jewish Sabbath. Let us listen to the inspired counsel of Paul, not only the greatest of the apostles, but a Pharisee whose passion for fulfilling the law outdoes that of the most zealous Seventh-day Adventist:

> And you, who were dead in trespasses and the uncircumcision of your flesh, God made alive together with him, having forgiven us all our trespasses; having canceled the bond which stood against us with its legal demands; this he set aside, nailing it to the cross. He disarmed the principalities and powers and made a public example of them, triumphing over them in him. Therefore let no one pass judgment on you in questions of food and drink or with regard to a festival or a new moon or a sabbath. These are only a shadow of what is to come; but the substance belongs to Christ (Colossians 2:13–17, RSV).

This translation, one of the best from the Greek text today, contains tremendously important teaching.

---

[33]Bible Question Column in *Signs of the Times*, Jan. 8, in 1952.

First, we who were dead have been made alive in Christ, and have been forgiven all trespasses and sins. We are free from the condemnation of the law in all its aspects, because Christ took our condemnation on the cross. As already observed, there are not two laws, moral and ceremonial, but one law containing many commandments, all perfectly fulfilled by the life and death of the Lord Jesus Christ.

"Therefore," the Apostle Paul boldly declares, "let no one pass judgment on you in question of food and drink or with regard to a festival or a new moon or a sabbath. These are only a shadow of what is to come; but the substance belongs to Christ."

In the face of this clear teaching, Sabbatarians revert to their dual-law theory and argue that Paul is referring only to observance of the Jewish ceremonial law, not to the Sabbath which, they insist, is a moral precept because it is one of the Ten Commandments. We have seen, however, that the Ten Commandments are but a fragment of the moral law encompassed by the commandment, "Thou shalt love thy neighbor as thyself" (Leviticus 19:18; Romans 13:9).

Sabbatarians, however, overlook the mass of contradictory evidence and appeal to certain commentators who do not analyze the uses of the word "sabbath," or exegete the New Testament passages where the word occurs. Such commentators are Albert Barnes, *Notes on the New Testament*; Jamieson, Fausset and Brown, *Critical and Explanatory Commentary*; and Adam Clark in his *Commentary*. If a commentator's opinion is not in accord with sound exegesis, it is *only an opinion*, and the commentators named above make no grammatical or textual analysis of the second chapter of Colossians!

Many New Testament commentators try to retain the moral force of the Sabbath (although all of these transfer it to the first day of the week) because it is the subject of the fourth commandment. For this serious theological error there is no warrant in the New Testament. Sabbatarians fail to mention that all the commentators whom they cite repudiate the Sabbath, and most of them teach that the true Sabbath was the Lord's Day (Revelation 1:10), carried over by the early church from apostolic tradition as a memorial to redemption, or the recreation of mankind through the regenerative power of the Holy Spirit. Adventists are therefore without historical or exegetical support when they make the Lord's Day the same as the Sabbath.

With regard to this passage, Adventists maintain that since the word in Colossians 2:16 (*sabbaton*) is in the plural, it means the ceremonial Sabbaths, not the weekly Sabbath, which they contend is still in effect. However, their argument seems to be that Colossians 2:16, 17 refers to sabbaths and feast days which were shadows of things to come, and thus part of ceremonial laws, but that the seventh-day Sabbath is not a shadow of redemption but a memorial of creation and part of the moral law. The leading modern translations, following the best New Testament scholars, render Colossians 2:16 as "a sabbath" or "a sabbath day" not "sabbath days" as in the King James Version. Their reason for doing this is well stated by W. E. Vine who wrote:

> *Sabbaton* or *sabbata*, the latter the plural form, was transliterated from the Aramaic word which was mistaken for a plural: hence the singular *sabbaton* was formed from it. . . . In the epistles the only direct mentions are

in Colossians 2:16 "a sabbath day" (RV), which rightly has the singular . . . where it is listed among things that were "a shadow of things to come"; i.e., of the age introduced at Pentecost and in Hebrews 4:4–11 where the perpetual *sabbatismos* is appointed for believers: . . . . For the first three centuries of the Christian era the first day of the week was never confounded with the Sabbath; the confusion of the Jewish and Christian institutions was due to declension from apostolic teaching.[34]

Supplementing Dr. Vine's statement is the comment of M. R. Vincent who declared:

Sabbath days (*sabbaton*), the weekly festivals revised correctly as *day*, the plural being used for the singular. See Luke 4:31 and Acts 20:7. The plural is only once used in the New Testament of more than a single day (Acts 17:2). In the Old Testament, the same enumeration of sacred seasons occurs in I Chronicles 23:31; II Chronicles 2:4; II Chronicles 31:3; Ezekiel 45:17; Hosea 2:11.[35]

As Dr. Vincent points out, the revisers' rendering of *sabbaton* in the singular accords with the use of the word throughout the New Testament. It is significant that in 59 of 60 occurrences in the New Testament, Adventists affirm that they refer to the *weekly* Sabbath; but in the 60th occurrence they maintain it does *not*, although *all* grammatical authorities contradict them.

With regard to Albert Barnes, whom the Adventists delight to quote because he agrees with their interpretation of Colossians 2, his comments are demolished by Dean Henry Alford, a truly great Biblical exegete whom the Adventists also frequently quote. Wrote Dean Alford concerning Colossians 2:

Let no one therefore judge you (pronounce judgment of right or wrong over you, sit in judgment on you) . . . in respect of feasts or new moon, or sabbaths (i.e. yearly, monthly, or weekly celebrations). (The relative may refer either to the aggregate of the observances mentioned, or to the *last* mentioned, i.e. the Sabbath. Or it may refer to *all*.)[36]

After making significant comments on the grammar, Dean Alford went even further in his insistence that in verse 17, grammatically speaking, the Apostle Paul contrasts *all* the Jewish laws with their fulfillment in Christ, the former being a shadow, pointing forward to the real substance (*soma*), which was Christ.

Alford summed up his comments thus:

The blessings of the Christian covenant: these are the substance, and the Jewish ordinances the mere type of resemblance, as the shadow is of the living man. . . . We may observe, that if the ordinance of the Sabbath had been, *in any form* of lasting obligation on the Christian church, it would have been quite impossible for the Apostle to have spoken thus. The fact of an obligatory rest of one day, whether the seventh or the first, *would have*

---

[34]W. E. Vine, *An Expository Dictionary of New Testament Words*, Old Tappan, NJ: Fleming H. Revell Company, 1940, pp. 311–313.
[35]M. R. Vincent, *Word Studies in the New Testament*, MacDill AFB, FL: MacDonald Publishing Company, n.d., vol. 2, p. 494.
[36]D. H. Alford, *The New Testament for English Readers*, Grand Rapids, MI: William B. Eerdmans Publishing Company, n.d., pp. 1299, 1300.

been directly in the teeth of his assertion here: the holding of such would have been still to retain the shadow, while we possess the substance. And no answer can be given to this by the transparent special-pleading, that he is speaking only of that which was *Jewish* in such observances: the whole argument being *general*, and the axiom of verse 17 universally applicable.[37]

We see, then, that from a grammatical standpoint if the Adventists insist that Colossians 2:16 refers only to ceremonial sabbaths, they run against the use of the word for weekly sabbaths in the New Testament; and, as Alford points out, if "sabbaths" be allowed, it must include all Sabbaths, weekly, monthly or yearly. On the other hand, if Adventists admit the correction of the revisers and render Colossians 2:16 "a sabbath day," its use in the New Testament still refers almost exclusively (see Acts 17:2) to the weekly Sabbath, which Adventists maintain is permanent, although Paul deliberately classes it with the ordinances which Christ by His death nailed to the cross! (Colossians 2:14).

Dr. J. B. Lightfoot, an acknowledged authority on New Testament Greek, makes this interesting observation:

> The word *sabbata* is derived from the Aramaic *shabbatha* (as distinguished from the Hebrew), and accordingly preserves the Aramaic termination of *a*. Hence it was naturally declined as a plural noun, *sabbata, sabbaton*. The New Testament *sabbata* is only once used distinctively as more than a single day, and there the plurality of meaning is brought out by the attached numeral (Acts 17:2).[38]

It is apparent therefore that the use of "sabbath" in the New Testament refutes the Adventist contention that in Colossians 2 it means Sabbaths other than the weekly Sabbath of the Decalogue. Since it is impossible to retain the "shadow" while possessing the "substance" (Colossians 2:17), the Jewish Sabbath and the handwriting of ordinances "which was contrary to us" found their complete fulfillment in the person and work of the Lord Jesus Christ.

Seventh-day Adventists are also deprived of the support of Albert Barnes, because he admits that if Paul had *"used the word in the singular number, 'the sabbath,' it would then of course have been clear that he meant to teach that that commandment had ceased to be binding and that a sabbath was no longer to be observed."*[39]

Since Barnes makes this admission, and since modern conservative scholarship establishes the singular rendering of "sabbath" in the New Testament (see RSV, *et al.*), Adventists find even less support for their position.

We conclude our comments on this passage of Scripture by observing that in Numbers 28 and 29, which list the very "ordinances" referred to in Colossians 2:16, 17, the Sabbath is grouped with burnt offerings and new moons (Numbers 28:1–15). Since these offerings and feasts have passed away as the shadow (*skia*), fulfilled in the substance (*soma*) of the cross of Christ, how can the seventh-day Sabbath be retained? In the light of this Scripture

[37]*Ibid.*, p. 1300.
[38]D. H. Alford, *Commentary on Colossians*, Grand Rapids, MI: William B. Eerdmans Publishing Company, n.d., p. 225.
[39]*The New Testament for English Readers, op. cit.*, p. 229.

alone, I contend that the argument for Sabbath observance collapses, and the Christian stands under "the perfect law of liberty" which enables him to fulfill "the righteousness of the law" by the imperative of love.

B. *Galatians 4:9–11*

> But now that you have come to know God, or rather to be known by God, how can you turn back again to the weak and beggarly elemental spirits, whose slaves you want to be once more? You observe days, and months, and seasons, and years! I am afraid I have labored over you in vain (RSV).

Paul's epistle to the Galatians was primarily a massive theological effort to bolster the young church against the Judaizers who added to the gospel of grace "another gospel" (1:6), and sought to "pervert the gospel of Christ" (1:7).

Though steeped in Jewish lore and the law of Moses, Paul steadfastly opposed the Judaizers. The entire epistle to the Galatians is an apologetic against those who would seek to bring the Christian "under the law." After mentioning the errors into which the Galatian church had fallen, Paul, evidently with great disgust, remarks, "You observe days, and months, and seasons, and years! I am afraid I have labored over you in vain" (4:10, 11, RSV). In the Greek the expression "days, and month, and seasons, and years," matches both the Septuagint translation of the ordinances in Numbers 28 and 29, of which all Sabbaths are a principal part, and the ordinances mentioned in Colossians 2. Paul was familiar with the Septuagint and quoted it, and the law, including the weekly Sabbaths, was so cherished by the Judaizers of his day that its legalistic observance called forth his strong words. Adventists insist that Paul meant ceremonial feasts and yearly Sabbaths, not the weekly Sabbath; but Paul's language and the Septuagint translation of Numbers 28 and 29 refute their objections. It is one thing to interpret your way out of a verse when your interpretation is feasible; it is another to ignore grammar, context, and comparative textual analysis (hermeneutics) as our Adventist friends and others appear to do. To substantiate their interpretation of Paul's statements they do not practice exegesis (taking out of), but eisegesis (reading into) the texts.

After studying Seventh-day Adventist literature, it is my opinion that the overwhelming majority of Seventh-day Adventists do not actually consider themselves "under the law." I believe they fail to realize that by trying to enjoin Sabbath observance upon other members of the Body of Christ, they are in serious danger of transgressing the gospel of grace. To them Paul says,

> Tell me, you who desire to be under the law, do you not hear the law? . . . Now before faith came, we were confined under the law, kept under restraint until faith should be revealed. So that the law was our custodian until Christ came, that we might be justified by faith. But now that faith has come, we are no longer under a custodian; for in Christ Jesus you are all sons of God, through faith (Galatians 4:21; 3:23–26, RSV).

Bearing in mind that "the law" in its larger connotation includes the entire Pentateuch, it is apparent from Paul's language that one is "under the law" when he attempts to observe any part of it, because the Christian has been freed from the law. Seventh-day Adventists are doubtless Christians, saved by grace, but we do not find Scriptural warrant for their attempt to enjoin the Sabbath upon their fellow believers.

C. *Romans 13:8–10*

Owe no one anything, except to love one another; for he who loves his neighbor has fulfilled the law. The commandments, "You shall not commit adultery, You shall not kill, You shall not steal, You shall not covet," and *any other commandment*, are summed up in this sentence, "You shall love your neighbor as yourself." Love does no wrong to a neighbor; therefore love is the fulfilling of the law.

It is really unnecessary to comment extensively upon the foregoing verses since they speak so plainly for themselves.

The Greek word *pleroma*, translated respectively "fulfilled" and "fulfilling" in Romans 13:8, 10, RSV, appears 90 times in the New Testament and has the same basic meaning. The Apostle Paul surely understood this term; since the Adventists confess the divine inspiration of the Scriptures, they must concede that the Holy Spirit guided his pen. Quoting from the Decalogue upon which the Adventists rely for perpetual Sabbathkeeping, Paul declares, "The commandments . . . are summed up in this sentence, 'You shall love your neighbor as yourself.' Love does no wrong to a neighbor; therefore love is the *fulfilling* of the law." In verse eight the apostle declares, "He who loves his neighbor has *fulfilled* the law"; and since he quotes from the Decalogue as part of the law, the fourth commandment is also fulfilled, not by rigid observance of a given day, but by loving one's neighbor as oneself! Since it is impossible in the Christian context to love one's neighbor at all, apart from loving God as the prerequisite, the issue is clear. The false teaching that love of one's neighbor does not fulfill all the law of God comes from a failure to realize that our love for God and neighbor stems from God's initiating act of love in Christ. This law of love is first enunciated in Leviticus 19:18, which our Lord coupled with the commandment to "love the Lord thy God" (Deuteronomy 6:4), and stated that observance of those two commandments fulfilled "all the law and the prophets."

While our Adventist brethren may seek to escape the implications of Colossians 2:14–17, and to explain away Galatians 4:9–11, in the present passage the Holy Spirit twice declares that love *fulfills* the law. They cannot exempt the Sabbath from this context without destroying the unity of the "Eternal Ten," hence their dilemma.

In Galatians Paul also declares, "The whole law is fulfilled in one word. 'You shall love your neighbor as yourself' " (5:14, RSV). So we see that Paul's theology rested upon the imperative of love. Therefore, it is my conviction that the Holy Spirit, not the Christian Church, is the authority for the nullification of all sabbathkeeping. How any student of New Testament Greek could read the unmistakable language of the apostle and then exclude the Sabbath commandment from his argument, passes my understanding.

D. *Romans 14:4–6, 10, 12, 13*

> Who are you to pass judgment on the servant of another? It is before his own master that he stands or falls. And he will be upheld, for the Master is able to make him stand. One man esteems one day as better than another, while another man esteems all days alike. Let every one be fully convinced in his own mind. He who observes the day, observes it in honor of the Lord. He also who eats, eats in honor of the Lord, since he gives thanks to God; while he who abstains, abstains in honor of the Lord and gives thanks to God. . . . Why do you pass judgment on your brother? Or you, why do you despise your brother? For we shall all stand before the judgment seat of God; . . . so each of us shall give account of himself to God. Then let us no more pass judgment on one another, but rather decide never to put a stumbling-block or hindrance in the way of a brother (RSV).

In this writer's opinion, and according to Romans 14, the Seventh-day Adventist is entitled to observe the seventh-day Sabbath if he feels that this is what God desires. Further than this, the Holy Spirit adjures us not to "pass judgment" on our fellow Christians regarding such matters as observance of days and diet. I believe that Seventh-day Adventists, Seventh-day Baptists, and Sabbatarians of other religious groups have the right to worship on the seventh day in the liberty wherein Christ has made us free. It is wrong and un-Christian to discriminate against Sabbatarians merely because they "esteem" the Sabbath above the first day of the week, or the Lord's Day. I suggest it is no more legalistic for them to observe the seventh day out of conviction than it is for the Christian Church to observe the first day. It is a matter of liberty and conscience.

If Seventh-day Adventists, however, would follow the Biblical teaching of Romans 14 with regard to those who wish to observe Sunday, we would not have the conflict which has been generated by their dogmatic insistence that all should worship on the Sabbath. The sad fact is, however, that all Sabbatarians transgress the very counsels given by the Apostle Paul when he asks,

> Who are you to pass judgment on the servant of another? It is before his own master that he stands or falls. And he will be upheld, for the Master is able to make him stand. . . . Why do you pass judgment on your brother? Or . . . why do you despise your brother? For we shall all stand before the judgment seat of God; . . . so each of us shall give account of himself to God. Then let us no more pass judgment on one another, but rather decide never to put a stumbling-block or hindrance in the way of a brother (Romans 14:4–13).

Of course Seventh-day Adventists feel that they are called upon to perpetuate or promulgate certain truths which they believe are to be found in the Word of God, and which they believe are to be emphasized in "these last days." Furthermore, the counsels of Ellen G. White, they believe, emphasize the importance of these truths. Granting their basic premise that God has indeed spoken to them concerning Sabbath observance, it is easy to see the source of their zeal. But I feel that there is good evidence that the "spirit of prophecy" is not what they claim; and their "special truths" have, to say the least, questionable theological origins. Non-adventists reject the claims that they make for Mrs. White, and merely because Adventists accept her counsel is no reason for other Christians to feel bound to do so. We repeat—the faith the Adventists place in "the spirit of prophecy" which has endorsed their "special truths," sincere though they may be, does not entitle them to contradict the counsel of the Holy Spirit as revealed in the Word of God. This I believe they have done. I could cite scores of references from contemporary Adventist writers who do indeed pass judgment upon their Christian brothers and upon the Christian Church at large, because the latter do not observe the seventh-day Sabbath. It is my opinion in these cases that they neglect the counsel of the Holy Spirit: "One man esteems one day as better than another, while another man esteems all days alike. Let everyone be fully convinced in his own mind. He who observes the day, observes it in honor of the Lord. . . . Happy is he who has no reason to judge himself for what he approves . . . for whatever does not proceed from faith is sin" (Romans 14:5, 6, 22, 23, RSV).

By contending that other members of the Body of Christ should recognize "the spirit of prophecy," Seventh-day Adventists appear to juxtapose the "spirit of prophecy" with the Holy Spirit who says: "Then let us not pass judgment on one another but rather decide never to put a stumbling-block or hindrance in the way of a brother" (verse 13).

There can be little doubt that the great majority of Christians who worship on Sunday would never have discriminated against the Seventh-day Adventists, had the latter not insisted upon "passing judgment" on first-day observance as opposed to Sabbathkeeping. Although motivated by the best intentions and sincere in faith, Adventists have nevertheless put a stumbling-block or hindrance in the way of fellow Christians by their rigid Sabbatarianism. It is indeed unfortunate that such a source of strife exists among Christians.

The fourteenth chapter of Romans is a masterpiece on the subject of Christian liberty, not only in diet but in worship, and in the context of all Paul's writings on the subject it appears that Adventists ignore the plain teaching of Scripture about the observance of days. We ask, should they not be more charitable in the light of 1 Corinthians 13? They will thus avoid opposition from their fellow Christians.

These four passages from the writings of Paul reflect the position of the historic Christian Church from the times of the Fathers and the reformers to the leading exegetical commentators of our day. The reader should remember that Adventist arguments, although buttressed by selected Bible passages (sometimes cited out of context), must be studied in the clear light of these four passages which contain the comprehensive New Testament teaching on Sabbatarianism. The early Christian Church met upon the *first* day of the week (1 Corinthians 16:2). The disciples received the Holy Spirit on the *first* day of the week; collections were taken for the saints on the *first* day of the week, and historic evidence establishes that the *first* day of the week was the Lord's Day, the memorial of the new creation in Christ Jesus which completely fulfilled the law in Christ.

No amount of argument by Adventists can alter these facts, and if we believe the Apostle Paul was inspired by the Holy Spirit it is apparent that we must reject Sabbatarianism. We do not judge Seventh-day Adventists for their Sabbath observance, and they in turn should extend the same charity to their fellow Christians. Only in the recognition of the principles of Romans 14 can true unity in the Body of Christ be realized. There can be no legislation of moral choice on the basis of "special revelation." This we believe is the case in Seventh-day Adventism, for it was Ellen G. White's "Vision" confirming Joseph Bates' "Seal of the Living God" concept as set forth in his pamphlet on the Sabbath that established Sabbatarianism in Seventh-day Adventism. The Bible must be the supreme court of appeal and authority; and the verdict of this court, it appears to me, invalidates the contentions of our Adventist friends.

Author's Note on "The Mark of the Beast"

The subjects of the Seventh-day Sabbath and the Mark of the Beast already have been covered in sufficient detail. However, it is often charged that Adventists teach that salvation depends upon observance of the seventh day as Sabbath, and that the mark of the beast (Revelation 13:16, 17) rests upon all Sunday-keepers. For this reason, the record should be examined.

One ex-Adventist layman writes that there are "characteristic false doctrines of the sect . . . the obligation of seventh-day Sabbath observance on the part of all professing Christians, the 'mark of the beast' for Sunday-keepers." Now if this charge were correct, we too would doubt the possibility of fellowship with Adventists. But such is not the case. Ellen G. White on a number of occasions pointedly denied what is claimed to be the position of the Adventist denomination on this point. Wrote Mrs. White:

> No one has yet received the mark of the beast. The testing time is not yet come. There are true Christians in every church, not excepting the Roman Catholic communion. None are condemned until they have had the light and have seen the obligation of the fourth commandment. . . . Sunday-keeping is not yet the mark of the beast, and will not be until the decree goes forth causing men to worship this idol sabbath.[40]

In addition to this quotation, the Adventists have stated:

> When Sunday observance shall be enforced by law, and the world shall be enlightened concerning the obligation of the true Sabbath, then whoever shall transgress the command of God, to obey a precept which has no higher authority than that of Rome, will thereby honor popery above God.[41]

To sum up, the Adventists declare,

> God surely does not hold men accountable for truth that has not yet come to their knowledge and understanding. . . . We hold the firm conviction that millions of devout Christians of all faiths throughout all past cen-

---

[40]*Questions on Doctrine*, pp. 183, 184.
[41]*Ibid.*, p. 178.

turies, as well as those today who are sincerely trusting in Christ their Saviour for salvation and are following Him according to their best light, are unquestionably saved. Thousands of such went to the stake as martyrs for Christ and for their faith. Moreover, untold numbers of godly Roman Catholics will surely be included. God reads the heart and deals with the intent and understanding. . . . Seventh-day Adventists interpret the prophecies relating to the beast and the reception of his work as something that will come into sharp focus just before the return of our Lord in glory. It is our understanding that this issue will then become a worldwide test.[42]

The statement, then, that Seventh-day Adventist believe that anyone who is a Sunday-keeper *has* the mark of the beast or the mark of apostasy, is made without regard to the facts. Why do these critics attempt to make it appear that Adventists believe that their fellow Christians are lost? The authoritative statements of this denomination are available for all to read. Doubtless some Seventh-day Adventist writers have gone contrary to the teaching of the denomination, but to indict the entire denomination for the excesses of a few is neither ethical nor Christian.

The Sanctuary, the Investigative Judgment, and the Scapegoat

The foundation of Seventh-day Adventism is its view of prophecy which is of the historic school of interpretation, a school which maintains that prophecy is to be understood in the light of consecutive fulfillment in history. The exaggeration of this idea led William Miller and his followers to teach that the 2300 days of Daniel 8:14 were actually 2300 years. Figuring from 457 B.C., the now verified time of the decree to rebuild Jerusalem (Daniel 9:24), the Millerites thought that 1843 would be the date for the second advent of Jesus Christ. Miller and his followers, among whom were James and Ellen G. White and other prominent Seventh-day Adventists, understood "the sanctuary" of Daniel 8:14 to be the earth which would be cleansed by Christ at the "great and terrible Day of the Lord," which they interpreted as the Second Advent of Christ. We have seen, however, that the Millerites were bitterly disappointed; and when Christ did not appear, Miller himself renounced the system and all resultant movements, including Seventh-day Adventism. But the early Seventh-day Adventists, relying upon the "vision" of Elder Hiram Edson, transferred the location of the sanctuary from the earth to Heaven, and taught that in 1844 Christ went instead into the second apartment of the sanctuary in Heaven (which contemporary Seventh-day Adventists term *the second phase* of His ministry), there to review the cases of those deemed to be worthy of eternal life. This phase of our Lord's ministry the Seventh-day Adventists call the "investigative judgment." This unique theory is intended, I believe, to discipline Christians by the threat of impending judgment and condemnation upon those whose cases are decided upon unfavorably by our Lord. When concluded, the Investigative Judgment will usher in the Second Advent of Jesus Christ, according to the Seventh-day Adventist theology, and the devil, prefigured by the second or scapegoat

---

[42]*Ibid.*, pp. 178, 184, 185.

of Leviticus 16 (Azazel), will bear away unto eternal destruction or annihilation his responsibility for causing sin to enter the universe.

James White, a stalwart Seventh-day Adventist leader, when first confronted with the doctrine of the Investigative Judgment, opposed it *in toto*, giving in substance the very arguments put forth by all subsequent ex-Seventh-day Adventists. And it was only after considerable time that James White finally acceded to the doctrine of the Investigative Judgment. There are many critics of Seventh-day Adventism who, when approaching the Sanctuary, Investigative Judgment and Scapegoat concepts, deride and mock the early Adventists and their descendants for accepting such unsupported, extra-Biblical theories, but derision is not the answer, and it should be remembered that Adventists hold these doctrines in sincerity. Therefore, if they are ever to be persuaded of the mistaken nature of their faith, in these areas at least, only the facts of Scripture and the guidance of the Holy Spirit will bring it about.

The view of Hiram Edson is, so far as this writer is concerned, an attempt to escape the terrible calamity which befell the Millerite movement and the disappointment and embarrassment that must have followed the failure of the Millerite prophecies and their interpretations of the Book of Daniel. We shall confine ourselves in this short analysis, to the salient points of the theological issues raised by these special teachings or doctrines of the Advent message. In the matter of prophetic interpretation, this writer is convinced that the Holy Spirit has wisely veiled from the prying eyes and intellect of man many great truths which will doubtless be revealed toward the end of the age. It is not for us to judge whether the pretorist, historicist, or futurist schools of interpretation are correct, and we ought not to overly concern ourselves with when Christ is coming, whether before, during or after the Great Tribulation. Rather, we ought to be concerned *that* He is coming, because His coming is indeed "the blessed hope of the Christian Church" (Titus 2:13), which hope Adventists and non-Adventists alike who share the Christian message and faith, anticipate with joy.

I. *The Sanctuary*

Since the Seventh-day Adventists believe that the sanctuary to be cleansed is in Heaven (Daniel 8:14), which the Millerites identified as the earth (a regrettable early mistake), we might ask, What is the purpose of the heavenly sanctuary and its cleansing? What are the Adventists really teaching?

The book of Hebrews definitely sets forth a "heavenly sanctuary" of which Christ is the minister (Hebrews 8:1, 2), and the writer of the epistle repeatedly contrasts the Lord Jesus Christ, our risen high priest, with the Aaronic priesthood. He shows that, as a priest after the order of Melchizedek, Christ derives His authority after the power of "an endless life" (Hebrews 7:16), and that He was born *high priest and offering* on Calvary.[43] And this Adventists also emphasize.

---

[43]Hebrews 7:2, 4–7, 14, 16, 22, 25, 26; 8:1, 2, 6–8, 10; 9:2–12, 14, 23, 24; 26–28; 10:1–10, 12, 19–21.

It is futile, therefore, to argue that the word "sanctuary" does not apply to Heaven or something of a heavenly nature, since the Scriptures teach that it does. But the Adventists' error is that they draw from the Scriptures interpretations which cannot be substantiated by exegesis but rest largely upon inference and deduction, drawn from theological applications of their own design.

In their Sanctuary teaching, the Adventists do indeed declare, in the words of Ellen G. White:

> As anciently the sins of the people were by faith, placed upon the sin offering and through its blood transferred in figure to the earthly sanctuary, so in the new covenant the sins of the repentant are by faith placed upon Christ and transferred in fact to the heavenly sanctuary. And as the typical cleansing of the earthly was accomplished by the removal of the sins by which it had been polluted, so the actual cleansing of the heavenly is to be accomplished by the removal or blotting out of the sins that are there recorded.[44]

Here we have the very heart of Seventh-day Adventist teaching relative to the expiation of sin, which is that the sins of believers have been transferred, deposited or recorded in the heavenly sanctuary, and are now being dealt with in the Investigative Judgment.

Let us again listen to Mrs. White:

> In the sin offerings presented during the year, a substitute had been accepted in the sinner's stead; but the blood of the victim had not made full atonement for the sin. It had only provided a means by which the sin was transferred to the sanctuary. By the offering of the blood the sinner acknowledged the authority of the law, confessed the guilt of his transgression, and expressed his faith in Him who was to take away the sin of the world; but he was not entirely released from the condemnation of the law. On the day of atonement the high priest having taken an offering for the congregation went into the most holy place with the blood and sprinkled it upon the mercy seat above the table of the law. Thus the claims of the law which demanded the life of the sinner were satisfied. Then in his character of mediator the priest took the sins upon himself and leaving the sanctuary he bore with him the burden of Israel's guilt. At the door of the tabernacle he laid his hands upon the head of the scapegoat, confessed over him all the iniquities of the children of Israel and all their transgressions and all their sins, putting them upon the head of the goat. And as the goat bearing these sins was sent away, they were with him regarded as forever separated from the people.

Mrs. White further stated, "Not until the goat had been thus sent away did the people regard themselves as freed from the burden of their sins.[45]

The Adventist teaching, then, is that Christ as our high priest transferred the sins of believers (i.e., the *record* of sins in Adventist thinking) to the heavenly sanctuary which will be finally cleansed at the conclusion of the great day of atonement, the Investigative Judgment having been concluded.

---

[44]*The Great Controversy, op. cit.*, pp. 421, 422.
[45]Ellen G. White, *Patriarchs and Prophets*, Washington, D.C.: Review and Herald Publishing Association, n.d., pp. 355, 356.

Then the cases of all the righteous having been decided, their sins will be blotted out, followed by the return of the Lord Jesus Christ in glory. Mrs. White made it clear that the sin transferred to the sanctuary in Heaven would remain there until the conclusion of the Investigative Judgment and the subsequent cleansing of the santuary.

> The blood of Christ, while it was to release the repentant sinner from the condemnation of the law, was not to cancel the sin; it would stand on record in the sanctuary until the final atonement; so then the type, the blood of the sin offering removed the sin from the penitent but it rested in the sanctuary until the day of atonement.[46]

To substantiate this particular position, Adventists quote Acts 3:19 in the King James Version: "Repent ye therefore and be converted that your sins may be blotted out *when* the times of refreshing shall come from the presence of the Lord."

The chief difficulty with the Adventist contention is that the Greek of Acts 3:19 does *not* substantiate their teaching that the blotting out of sins will take place as a *separate* event from the forgiveness of sins. According to modern translations (the Revised, the American Standard and the Revised Standard Versions), the text should read "Repent therefore and turn again *that* your sins may be blotted out, *that* times of refreshing may come from the presence of the Lord." Peter was urging his listeners to repent, turn from their sins, in order to receive the forgiveness that comes only from the presence of the Lord. This text gives our Adventist brethren no support for their "heavenly sanctuary, investigative judgment" teaching.

II. *Investigative Judgment*

The Bible explicitly declares that when one accepts Christ as Lord, God freely forgives all his sins and ushers him from spiritual death to spiritual life solely on the merits of the perfect life and death of the Lord Jesus Christ. To this Adventists fully agree, and this makes their teaching on investigative judgment inconsistent. In John 5:24 the Greek deals a devastating blow to the Seventh-day Adventist concept of investigative judgment: "He that hears my word and believes him that sent me has everlasting life and shall not come under *judgment* but is passed from death to life" (literal translation).

Christians, therefore, need not anticipate any investigative judgment for their sins. True, we shall all appear before the judgment seat of Christ to receive the deeds done in the body (2 Corinthians 5:10), but this has nothing to do with any investigative judgment. It is a judgment for rewards. Several judgments are mentioned in the Bible, but it is my opinion that not one passage substantiates the "investigative judgment" theory—for theory it truly is, relying upon out-of-context quotations and supported by the "spirit of prophecy." They are welcome to this dogma, but faithfulness to New Testament teaching forbids the idea that "the blood of Christ, while it was to release the repentant sinner from the condemnation of the law, was not to cancel the sin; it would be on record in the sanctuary until the final atone-

---

[46]*Ibid.*, p. 357.

ment," or "blotting out." The Scriptures clearly teach, "If we confess our sins he is faithful and just to forgive us our sins and to cleanse us from *all* unrighteousness" (1 John 1:9). Further evidence of the completeness of the forgiveness of God and the cleansing power of the blood of Christ is found in the first chapter of the book of Hebrews, where the Holy Spirit informs us that Christ as "the image of God," "upholds all things by the word of his power" and that on Calvary He by Himself purged our sins (Hebrews 1:3).

For the word translated "purged" or "purification" the Holy Spirit chose the Greek word *katharismon*, from which we derive *cathartic*. Hence it is said of the Lord Jesus and His sacrifice that He alone, "by himself," gave to our sinful spiritual natures the complete cathartic of forgiveness and purification on the cross. Christians may now rejoice that the Lord Jesus Christ is not engaged in weighing our frailties and failures, for "He knoweth our frame, he remembereth that we are dust" (Psalm 103:14). We cannot, therefore, accept the Adventist teaching on the investigative judgment since we are convinced that it has no warrant in Scripture. We must reject what we believe to be their un-Biblical concept that the sins of believers remain in the sanctuary until the day of blotting out of sins.

Our Adventist brethren, in teaching this doctrine, are overlooking the fact that "the Lord knoweth them that are his" (2 Timothy 2:19) and it was no less an authority than the Lord Jesus Christ who declared, "I know my sheep" (John 10:14). The Apostle Paul declares that "Christ died for the ungodly . . . while we were yet sinners Christ died for us . . . when we were enemies we were reconciled to God by the death of his Son" (Romans 5:6, 8, 10). This does not balance with the Seventh-day Adventist teaching of the heavenly sanctuary, the transfer of sins and the investigative judgment. In his epistle to the Colossians the Apostle Paul further declared, "Having made peace through the blood of his cross . . . you that were sometime alienated and enemies in your mind by wicked works, yet now hath he reconciled in the body of his flesh through death, to present you holy and unblameable and unreprovable in his sight" (1:20–22). Once again the Holy Spirit declares that we are *now* reconciled through the death of Christ, *having been forgiven all* our trespasses through the blood of the cross (Colossians 2:13).

Seventh-day Adventists, relying upon Daniel 8:14, Daniel 7:9, 10, Revelation 14:7 and 11:18, which refer to "judgment," and "books," attempt to "prove" that the investigative judgment is meant, but examination of each of these texts in context reveals the paucity of the claim. None of these texts has anything to do with any judgment *now* going on. Neither the grammar nor context supports such a contention. One can only base this interpretation on the Adventist premise that the historicist school of prophetic interpretation is the only accurate one, and by accepting the Adventist definition of the sanctuary and judgment. It is significant that non-Adventist Biblical scholars have never allowed these so-called "investigative judgment" interpretations, because there is no Scriptural warrant for them apart from implication and inference.

As mentioned previously, James White at first categorically denied the teaching of the investigative judgment and gave good reasons for his rejection. Although he later embraced this doctrine his objections are still valid:

It is not necessary that the final sentence should be given before the first resurrection as some have taught; for the names of the saints are written in Heaven and Jesus and the angels will certainly know who to raise and gather to the New Jerusalem. . . . The event that will introduce the judgment day will be the coming of the Son of Man to raise the sleeping saints and to change those that are alive at that time.[47]

Relative to the time for the beginning of the great judgment, James White quoted, "I charge thee therefore before God and the Lord Jesus Christ, who shall judge the quick and the dead at [not before] his appearing in his kingdom" (2 Timothy 4:1).[48]

Asked when he expected the judgment of Daniel 7 to take place, James White stated,

Daniel in the night vision saw that judgment was given to the saints of the most high, but not to mortal saints. Not until the ancient of days comes will the little horn cease prevailing which will not be until he is destroyed by the brightness of Christ's coming.[49]

We see, then, that James White at the beginning rejected the investigative judgment with good reasons. But two more of his statements are quite revealing: He wrote,

The advent angel, Revelation 14:6, 7, saying with a loud voice, "Fear God and give glory to him for the hour of his judgment is come" *does not prove* that the day of judgment came in 1840 or in 1844, nor that it will come prior to the second advent. . . . Some have contended that the day of judgment was prior to the second advent. This view is certainly without foundation in the Word of God.[50]

At that time, James White was on good Biblical ground, but he later forsook this position for the theories and prophetic speculation promulgated by his wife and other influential Adventist leaders. The Lord Jesus Christ Himself placed the judgment after His second advent when He said, "When the Son of man shall come in his glory, and all the holy angels with him, then shall he sit upon the throne of his glory: and before him shall be gathered all nations" (Matthew 25:31, 32). One need only read the following passages to see that the judgments of God upon believers and unbelievers are future events. Notice the language employed:

1. "The quick and the dead" "at his appearing and his kingdom" (Acts 10:42; 1 Peter 4:5; 2 Timothy 4:1).

2. "When the Son of Man shall come in his glory . . . he shall set the sheep on his right hand, but the goats on the left" (Matthew 25:31–46).

3. The wheat and the tares: "so shall it be in the end of the world" (Matthew 13:24–30, 36–43).

4. "For we must all appear before the judgment seat of Christ that everyone may receive the things done in the body . . . whether it be good or bad" (2 Corinthians 5:10).

---

[47]*A Word to the Little Flock* (1847), p. 24.
[48]James White in the *Advent Review*, August 1850; the brackets are his.
[49]*Ibid.*
[50]*Ibid.*

5. "So that every one of us shall give account of himself to God" (Romans 14:10–12).

6. "Every man's work shall be made manifest: for the day shall declare it" (1 Corinthians 3:13).

In addition to these verses which unmistakably indicate future judgment, the writer to the Hebrews declares, "As it is appointed unto men once to die, but after this the judgment" (Hebrews 9:27). This, to any non-Adventist, is conclusive evidence that there is no investigative judgment now going on for believers to fear.

Hebrews 4:13 also exposes the faulty concept of investigative judgment: "Neither is there any creature that is not manifest in his sight: but all things are naked and opened unto the eyes of him with whom we have to do." Since our Lord knows the disposition of "cases" allegedly being reviewed in Heaven, what need is there for "investigative judgment"? We believe the Scriptures decidedly do not warrant such a doctrine.

Concluding our comments on the investigative judgment, note that rewards for believers will be meted out *after* the second coming of our Lord, or at "the resurrection of the just," for the resurrection of life (John 5:29; Luke 14:14). Even the Adventists concur in believing that the judgment of the wicked will *not* take place until the end of the millennial age (Revelation 20:11, 12; Matthew 25:31–46). Once again the investigative judgment theory conflicts with the Biblical teaching on judgment regarding both believer and unbeliever. To this writer's mind, the great error of the sanctuary and investigative judgment teachings is the premise that sins confessed by Christians are not fully dealt with until the conclusion of the investigative judgment, a position Scripture will *not* allow.

Adventists, in the opinion of conservative Biblical scholars, not to mention the liberal wing of Protestantism, are only speculating with their sanctuary and investigative judgment theories. Actually, most are agreed that they have created doctrines to compensate for errors in prophetic interpretation. But the very doctrines intended to solve their theological problems have in turn only increased their dilemma—a dilemma which they have yet to solve! Romans 8:1 declares, "There is therefore now no condemnation [i.e. *judgment*, Greek] to them who are in Christ Jesus"; and here every Christian's case must rest. We can never be indicted again for our sins nor convicted for them, because Christ has fully paid the penalty. For those who believe in Jesus Christ there is *no* judgment for the *penalty* of sin, i.e., eternal separation from God. However, as 2 Corinthians 5:10 teaches, we shall be judged for how we live as Christians. Seventh-day Adventists, we believe, needlessly subscribe to a doctrine which neither solves their difficulties nor engenders peace of mind. Holding as they do to the doctrine of the investigative judgment, it is extremely difficult for us to understand how they can experience the joy of salvation and the knowledge of sins forgiven. This is, however, true of so-called Arminian theology on the whole, which teaches that eternal life, given by God to the believer, is conditioned by the sustained faith of the believer in the grace of God.

There is, however, clarification and summary of the doctrine of investigative judgment in *Questions on Doctrine*.

It is our understanding that Christ, as high priest, concludes His intercessory ministry in heaven in a work of judgment. He begins His great work of judgment in the *investigative* phase. At the conclusion of the investigation, the *sentence* of judgment is pronounced. Then as judge, Christ descends to *execute*, or carry into effect, that sentence. For sublime grandeur, nothing in the prophetic word can compare with the description of our Lord as He descends the skies, not as a priest, but as King of kings and Lord of lords. And with Him are all the angels of Heaven. He commands the dead, and that great unnumbered host of those that are asleep in Christ spring forth into immortality. At the same time those among the living who are truly God's children are caught up together with the redeemed of all ages to meet their Saviour in the air, and to be forever with the Lord. . . .

As we have suggested, Seventh-day Adventists believe that at the second coming of Christ the eternal destiny of all men will have been irrevocably fixed by the decisions of a court of judgment. Such a judgment obviously would take place while men are still living on the earth. Men might be quite unaware of what is going on in heaven. It is hardly to be supposed that God would fail to warn men of such an impending judgment and its results. Seventh-day Adventists believe prophecy does foretell such a judgment, and indeed point out the very time at which it was to begin. . . .

When the high priest in the typical service had concluded his work in the earthly sanctuary on the Day of Atonement, he came to the door of the sanctuary. Then the final act with the second goat, Azazel, took place. In like manner, when our Lord completes His ministry in the heavenly sanctuary, He, too, will come forth. When He does this, the day of salvation will have closed forever. Every soul will have made his decision for or against the divine Son of God. Then upon Satan, the instigator of sin, is rolled back his responsibility for having initiated and introduced iniquity into the universe. *But he* [Satan] *in no sense vicariously atones for the sins of God's people.* All this Christ fully bore, and vicariously atoned for, on Calvary's cross.[51]

It is apparent, then, that for Adventists the investigative judgment is something very real, and they believe that the final blotting out of their sins depends upon the results of that judgment, culminating in the final destruction (annihilation) of the wicked and Satan, typified by the scapegoat of Leviticus 16.

III. *The Scapegoat*

Perhaps no doctrine of Seventh-day Adventism has been more misunderstood than the teaching concerning the scapegoat (Leviticus 16). Because of certain unfortunate choices of words by a few Adventist writers, the impression has been given that Adventist regard Satan as a partial sin-bearer for the people of God. This may be accounted for by the fact that in the early days of Adventism they built much of their theology on the typology of the Mosaic sanctuary, using almost exclusively the phraseology of the King James Version. Hence they got into difficulty when dealing with such involved Old Testament concepts as the scapegoat (Leviticus 16). Not a few scholars, however, support the Seventh-day Adventist concept that Azazel represents Satan. Be that as it may, the important thing is the place of the

---

[51]*Questions on Doctrine*, pp. 422, 423, 444.

scapegoat with regard to the atonement of Christ. Do Seventh-day Adventists believe that Satan eventually becomes their vicarious sin-bearer? Not at all! This writer is convinced that the Adventist concept of the scapegoat in connection with the day of atonement, the sanctuary and the investigative judgment is a bizarre combination of prophetic interpretation and typology; but it is by no means the soul-destroying doctrine that many people think it is. Let the Adventists speak for themselves:

> We take our stand without qualification on the gospel platform that the death of Jesus Christ provides the *sole* propitiation for our sins (1 John 2:2; 4:10); that there is salvation through no other means or medium, and no other name by which we may be saved (Acts 4:12); and that the shed blood of Jesus Christ *alone* brings remission for our sins (Matthew 26:28). That is foundational.
>
> When Satan tempted our first parents to take and eat of the forbidden fruit, he as well as they had inescapable responsibility in that act—he the instigator, and they the perpetrators. And similarly, through the ages—in all sin, Satan is involved in responsibility, as the originator and instigator, or tempter (John 8:44; Rom. 6:16; 1 John 3:8).
>
> Now concerning my sin, Christ died for *my* sins (Romans 5:8). He was wounded for *my* transgressions and for *my* iniquities (Isaiah 53). He assumed *my* responsibilities, and His blood alone cleanses *me* from all sin (1 John 1:7). The atonement for *my* sin is made solely by the shed blood of Christ.
>
> Concerning Satan's sin, and his responsibility as instigator and tempter, no salvation is provided for him. He must be punished for his responsibility. . . . He must himself "atone" for his sin in causing men to transgress, in the same way that a master criminal suffers on the gallows or in the electric chair for his responsibility in the crimes that he has caused others to commit. It is in this sense only that we can understand the words of Leviticus 16:10 concerning the scapegoat, to make atonement with him.
>
> Satan is the responsible mastermind in the great crime of sin, and his responsibility will return upon his own head. The crushing weight of his responsibility in the sins of the whole world—of the wicked as well as of the righteous—must be rolled back upon him. Simple justice demands that while Christ suffers for my guilt, Satan must also be punished as the instigator of sin.
>
> Satan makes no atonement for our sins. But Satan will ultimately have to bear the retributive punishment for his responsibility in the sins of all men, both righteous and wicked.
>
> Seventh-day Adventists therefore repudiate *in toto* any idea, suggestion, or implication that Satan is in any sense or degree our sin bearer. The thought is abhorrent to us, and appallingly sacrilegious.
>
> Only Christ, the Creator, the one and only God-man, could make a substitutionary atonement for men's transgressions. And this Christ did completely, perfectly, and once for all, on Golgotha.[52]

To be sure, the Seventh-day Adventists have a unique concept of the scapegoat, but in the light of their clearly worded explanation, no critic could any longer with honesty indict them for heresy where the atonement of our Lord is concerned. The Adventists have stated unequivocally that Jesus Christ is their sole propitiation for sin and that Satan has no part whatsoever in the

---

[52]*Questions on Doctrine*, pp. 396, 398–400.

expiation of sin. This writer agrees that Satan is the master criminal of the universe and that it is axiomatic, therefore, that he should suffer as the instigator of angelic and human rebellion. There are, of course, many interpretations of Leviticus 16 set forth by learned scholars, the great majority of whom are most certainly not Adventists; so at best the question is quite open. The *Abingdon Bible Commentary* (Methodist) relative to Leviticus 16 and the scapegoats states,

> On the goats lots are to be cast, one for Jehovah and the other for Azazel. The translation "Dismissal" in the Revised Version margin here (cf. removal in ASV margin) is inadmissible being based on a false etymology. What the word meant is unknown but it should be retained as a proper name of a wilderness demon.

To this statement could be added the opinions of Samuel Zwemer, E. W. Hengstenberg, J. B. Rotherham and J. Russell Howden, the last of whom wrote in the *Sunday School Times* of January 15, 1927,

> The goat for Azazel as it is sometimes misleadingly translated, typifies God's challenge to Satan. Of the two goats, one was for Jehovah signifying God's acceptance of the sin offering; the other was for Azazel. This is probably to be understood as a person being parallel with Jehovah in the preceding clause. So Azazel is probably a *synonym* for Satan.

Although Seventh-day Adventists have no exegetical support for their sanctuary and investigative judgment theories, one thing is certain: they have more than substantial scholastic support for assigning the title "Satan" to Azazel in Leviticus 16 concerning the scapegoat, but where the Scripture does not speak specifically it is far wiser to withhold comment. Many critics, in their zeal to shred Seventh-day Adventism and classify it as "a dangerous non-Christian cult," lay much stress upon the scapegoat teaching. In the light of current Adventist statements concerning their concept of the scapegoat, the misunderstandings of the past have at last been brought out into the open, clarified, and presented in a plausible manner.

Much, much more could be written concerning the Seventh-day Adventist concepts of the sanctuary, investigative judgment and the scapegoat, since they are inseparably linked together. But such writers as W. W. Fletcher (*The Reasons for My Faith*) and other ex-Seventh-day Adventists have exhaustively refuted the position of their former affiliation. The reader is urged to consider the bibliography for additional information on this subject. The saving grace of the entire situation is that the Adventists fortunately deny the logical conclusions to which their doctrines must lead them; i.e., a negation of the full validity of the atonement of Christ which validity they absolutely affirm, and embrace with considerable fervor—a paradoxical situation at best!

Author's Note

We could wish that some of the earlier unrepresentative Seventh-day Adventist statements on the scapegoat teaching had not been made, or better yet, that they were not still circulated in some quarters. However, to ignore their honest current declarations is, I believe, fundamentally unfair. It appears to me to be little more than blind prejudice. One review of the book, *Questions on Doctrine*, contains an error frequently found in critical writings. Imputing to their account a position the Adventists do not hold, the review then proceeds to destroy it as if, in the final analysis, it had both exposed and refuted a pernicious error. While it is true that the Seventh-day Adventists do believe that Azazel, in Leviticus 16, does represent Satan, their interpretation of it is far removed from this reviewer's straw man. After quoting the Seventh-day Adventist statement: "Seventh-day Adventists repudiate *in toto* any idea . . . that Satan is in any sense our sin bearer," this review states "but then two entire chapters are devoted to proving that Satan did bear our sin." It goes on to describe the Adventist position as "repulsive blasphemy" and "unholy twisting of the Scripture. If the Seventh-day Adventist were sound in everything but this and still held this one gross error, we would still have to consider them as an unscriptural cult."[53]

Now with some other portions of this review we are in agreement. But many of the statements show a marked predisposition toward removing various statements from context and placing them together to prove contradiction without respect to their setting. It ignores all the Seventh-day Adventist statements which contradict these out-of-context criticisms. The very chapter alluded to clearly shows that Adventists repudiate the meaning the reviewer has attached to the scapegoat concept. As we have noted, it is regrettable that this teaching has been so stated in some Adventist writings as to give the impression that the scapegoat represents Satan in the vicarious role of sin-bearer, but the Adventists have clarified this beyond reasonable doubt in the large majority of their publications.

Questions on Doctrine clarifies the concept of the scapegoat in Seventh-day Adventist theology. For Adventists, when the Lord Jesus Christ returns He will place upon Satan the full responsibility for his role of instigator and tempter to sin. Since Satan caused angels and man to rebel against their Creator, Adventists reason that Azazel, the scapegoat of Leviticus 16, is a type of Satan receiving the punishment due him. However, as we have seen, Adventists repudiate the idea that Satan is their vicarious sin-bearer in any sense. They point out, and rightly so, that in Leviticus 16 only the first goat was slain as the vicarious offering. The second goat was not killed but was sent into the wilderness to die. Satan similarly bears the weight of guilt and final punishment culminating in the annihilation as the master criminal who has promulgated sin during the period of God's grace toward lost men. To quote the Adventists:

> Satan's death a thousand times over, could never make him a savior in any sense whatsoever. He is the archsinner of the universe, the author and instigator of sin. . . . Only Christ, the Creator, the one and only God-man, could make a substitutionary atonement for men's transgressions. And this Christ did completely, perfectly and once for all on Golgotha.[54]

---

[53]*The King's Business*, March 1958, pp. 22, 23.
[54]*Questions on Doctrine*, p. 400.

Law, Grace and Salvation

In order to understand the Adventist view of law and grace, especially in relation to eternal salvation, we must consider the Adventist antipathy toward antinomianism.

The very word "antinomian" (*anti*, against, and *nomos*, law) describes the conflict between those who believe that not only were the Ten Commandments abrogated at Calvary but even the principles underlying them were "abolished" so that the Christian is not bound by them; and those who believe that the Decalogue is as binding today as when it was given at Sinai.

From the beginning of church history, the great majority of evangelical Christians have been as strongly opposed to antinomianism as are the Adventists. Unfortunately, however, the latter have tended to label antinomian anyone who disagrees with their definition of "the law of God." Consequently this has created a great problem in semantics which has disrupted the lines of communication, so to speak, between Adventists and other Christians. Although we believe in obeying the laws of God, and in good works as the evidence of saving faith, we strenuously object to "commandment keeping," to the extent of supposed spiritual superiority. A principal cause of their legalistic tendencies then is the Adventists' abhorrence of antinomianism.

By virtue of the fact that they obey the Fourth Commandment as well as the other nine, Adventists maintain that they alone are God's commandment-keeping church. To be sure, theologians have differed over the nature and extent of the moral law of God, and doubtless the controversy will continue until our Lord comes again. Any group, however, which feels they are the only ones that keep God's commands is likely to foment schism in the Body of Christ.

From their beginning, Adventists have concentrated upon "the law of God," and in *Questions on Doctrine* they devote 34 pages to the exposition of this subject. Although the Adventists repudiate legalism, that is, the doctrine that keeping the law merits salvation, a legalistic spirit does exist in some of their teaching. For example, although denying that the ceremonial law is binding upon Christians, they quote from it to defend their classifying certain foods as "unclean." Although Adventists reject antinomianism, in their desire to avoid the abuses of grace they actually abuse grace by magnifying the letter of the law. How Adventists arrived at this position has been well explained by D. M. Canright (*Seventh-day Adventism Renounced* [chapter 17]). In one place, Canright sets forth a series of propositions which, in some areas, are exegetically irrefutable, and with which I am in full agreement.

Now let us examine the Adventist claim that the law is binding upon the Christian, as stated in their Fundamental Beliefs, *Questions on Doctrine*, and wherever their writings touch on this subject.

I. *The Principle of Law*

To begin with, we agree to the proposition that the principle underlying the moral laws of God is indeed eternal, and consistent with His character. However, we must distinguish between the principle of the law of God, and the expression of that principle in specific statutes such as those in the Pentateuch. Because Adventists do not seem to make this distinction, it appears to this writer that they relate law to grace, which is an unhealthy practice. They claim that "the Law" was in effect in Eden and during all the centuries thence to Sinai. Wherever the Bible speaks of "commandments" or "law," most Adventists apparently assume that it means the Decalogue. We must, however, clearly differentiate between the *principle* of the law of God and the *function* of the law of God as revealed in the Pentateuch. Not only the Adventists but many historic Protestant groups have failed to make this distinction, and therefore have been guilty of carrying over into the New Covenant some of the legalistic Jewish functions of the law.

A. *The Dual Law Theory*

In *Questions on Doctrine*, the Adventists distinguish between "the moral law of God—the Decalogue—and the ceremonial law," setting forth the distinctions in two columns.[55] In column one is the Decalogue which was spoken by God, written by Him on tables of stone, given to Moses and deposited in the Ark. It dealt with moral precepts, revealed sin, and is in effect today. They insist that Christians must "keep the whole law" (James 2:10), and that we shall be judged by this law (James 2:12). They believe that the Decalogue is established in the life of a Christian by faith in Christ (Romans 3:31), and that Christ magnified the law (Isaiah 42:21), which Paul described as "spiritual" (Romans 7:14).

In column two, Adventists analyze the law of ceremonial ordinances, which were abolished at the cross. They contrast this with "the moral law of God—the Decalogue," stating that the latter was not abolished because it was separate from the ceremonial law. Concerning the ceremonial law, Adventists teach that it was spoken and written by Moses, and given to the Levites who deposited it by the side of the Ark, and that it governed ceremony and ritual. This law prescribed offerings for sins but the apostles gave no commandment to keep it, and the Christian is not bound by it nor can he be blessed by it. Indeed, they say, "the Christian who keeps this law loses his liberty"; it "was abolished by Christ," and was "the law of a carnal commandment" containing nothing of a moral nature, the Decalogue being "the moral law of God."

Now although there are both moral and ceremonial aspects of the law in the Pentateuch, as well as civil and judicial, nowhere does the Bible state that there is any such juxtaposition of ceremonial with moral law. In fact, the whole Bible teaches that "the law was given through Moses" (John 1:17) and that it is essentially a *unit*, a fact which the Adventists have overlooked. We make this observation after comparing the application of the term "law" in the Old and New Testaments.

To illustrate: As noted above, the Adventists claim that the law of Moses and the Decalogue are separate, the one being ceremonial, the other "the moral law of God." Therefore, although the ceremonial law was abolished at the cross, the moral law remains in effect; and so they insist in "commandment-keeping," not to *earn* salvation, but as it works out in the practice

---

[55]Pages 130, 131.

of many, to *retain* salvation. If, however, the ceremonial law and the Decalogue are inextricably bound together, and if both are referred to as "the law," the distinction which the Adventists and others make between them is fictitious. To prove this is to nullify their interpretation concerning "the moral law." Let us examine the Scriptures to see whether such a distinction as they propose can be sustained.

The highest authority on this subject is the Lord Jesus Christ. When speaking of "the law," He alluded to both moral and ceremonial precepts; e.g., Mark 10:19 (moral); and Luke 5:12–14 (ceremonial). The Gospels abound with similar references to "the law," without distinguishing between the moral and the ceremonial, and certainly not teaching that they are separate codes.

We do not mean that the law has no moral and ceremonial aspects, for it has, but they are only aspects, not separate codes or units. They are parts of the one law which "was our schoolmaster to bring us unto Christ, that we might be justified by faith" (Galatians 3:24). The Apostle Paul, certainly an authority on "the law," dogmatically affirms that the role of the schoolmaster has *ceased* and that the Christian is "dead to the law." Note, also, that the word "schoolmaster" is in the singular, which destroys the Adventist notion that there is more than one law. If the moral law were separate from the ceremonial law, instead of both being aspects of one law, Paul would have had to write that the *laws* were our *schoolmasters* to bring us to Christ, and that now "we are no longer under *schoolmasters*." But he knew and taught that the law was a unit and that it was perfectly fulfilled as such in the life of our Lord and on the cross of Calvary.

By His perfect life, the Lord Jesus met all the requirements of the moral aspect of the law. By His death, He fulfilled all the ceremonial ordinances which prefigured His incarnation and sacrifice. He himself said,

> Think not that I am come to destroy the law, or the prophets: I am come not to destroy, but to fulfill. For verily I say unto you, Till heaven and earth pass, one jot or one tittle shall in no wise pass from the law, till all be fulfilled (Matthew 5:17, 18).

Which law did Christ fulfill? If He fufilled only the ceremonial law as the dual law theory states, the moral law is yet to be satisfied. But "Christ is the *end* of the law for righteousness to every one that believeth" (Romans 10:4); and as we have shown, there are no distinct codes such as moral and ceremonial law. The distinction is arbitrary and contradicts the declaration of Scripture that the believer lives by a higher principle: "The law of the Spirit of life in Christ Jesus hath made me free from the law of sin and death" (Romans 8:2).

In order to maintain the dual law theory against the Biblical declaration that the one law has divisions or aspects, Adventists must explain why, in at least 20 passages in the New Testament, a dozen of them in the words of Jesus Christ, the Holy Spirit teaches that there are not two laws, but one; that this law is not only in the five books of Moses but in the Prophets and the Psalms as well. Christ looked upon moral, ceremonial and prophetic precepts as parts of the one law which pointed to His life, ministry, death, and resurrection, as He said to His disciples that first Easter day, "These are the words which I spake unto you, while I was yet with you, that all things must be fulfilled, which were written in the law of Moses, and in the prophets, and in the psalms concerning me" (Luke 24:44).

A study of the relevant biblical passages (including John 8:17 cf. Deut. 19:15; John 10:34 cf. Ps. 82:6; John 12:34 cf. Ps. 72:17; John 15:25 cf. Ps. 35:19; and John 19:7 cf. Lev. 24:16) should convince any objective reader that the law is a single gigantic structure comprised of several aspects: moral, ceremonial, civil, judicial, and prophetic. This whole structure was referred to by Christ and the apostles under the heading of "the law," and which structure was completely fulfilled in the life and death of the Lord Jesus Christ who instituted the universal principle of divine love as the fulfillment of every aspect and function of the law. Our Lord said.

> Therefore all things whatsoever ye would that men should do to you, do ye even so to them: for *this is the law* and the prophets. . . . Thou shalt love the Lord thy God with all they heart, and with all thy soul, and with all thy mind. This is the first and great commandment. And the second is like unto it. Thou shalt love thy neighbor as thyself. On these two commandments hang *all the law* and the prophets (Matthew 7:12; 22:37–40).

Instead of the Adventist belief that the law must be "kept" as a sign of obedience to God, Christ here teaches that the Christian obeys God when he obeys the supreme commandment of love. This teaching is reiterated by the greatest of the apostles, who wrote to the Galatians, "All the law is fulfilled in one word, even in this: Thou shalt love thy neighbor as thyself" (Galatians 5:14). Obviously, if we love our neighbors as ourselves, we do so because we love God with all our hearts, souls, and minds. If we do not so love God, we cannot love our neighbors as ourselves. Thus on this "great commandment" rests the law in all its aspects.

Note the language of these passages, for they indicate the strong emphasis given by our Lord. In Matthew 22:40 Christ uses the Greek word "*holos,*" translated 65 times in the New Testament as "all," 43 times as "whole," twice as "every whit," once "altogether," and once "throughout." With these renditions all lexicons agree, so there can be no linguistic doubt that the all-inclusive principle which binds and seals all aspects of the law into a unit, to be fulfilled in the life of a believer because it has been fulfilled by the Savior, is once again declared to be "love."

The Apostle Paul uses an entirely different word to sum up the unifying principle of the law and the only principle which the Scriptures say fulfills it. This is the Greek word *pas.*

In the New Testament *pas* is translated 748 times as "all," 170 times as "all things," 117 times as "every," 41 times as "all men," 31 times as "whosoever," 28 times as "everyone," 12 times as "whole," and 11 times as "every man." We see then how the Holy Spirit rendered linguistically impossible any escape from the clear declaration that the principle of love indeed *fulfills* all the precepts of the law in their *entirety* since the two terms used most frequently in the New Testament to describe inclusiveness were utilized by both Christ and Paul to enunciate this vital issue.

Finally, notice Paul's powerful admonition to the believers at Rome:

Owe no man any thing but to love one another: for he that loveth another *hath* fulfilled the law. For this, Thou shalt not commit adultery, Thou shalt not kill, Thou shalt not steal, Thou shalt not bear false witness, Thou shalt not covet; *and if there be any other commandment*, it is briefly comprehended in this saying, namely, Thou shalt love thy neighbor as thyself. Love worketh no ill to his neighbor: therefore love is the fulfilling of the law (Romans 13:8–10).

In this context the greatest authority on the law in the New Testament, next to Jesus Christ, used the very emphatic Greek word *etera* which is translated 42 times in the New Testament as "other." Unquestionably the Apostle Paul not only considered the law a unit of which the Decalogue is only a part (quoting five of the Ten Commandments), but he indicated the rest of the law—ceremonial, civil, and judicial—by the word "other." Thus if one is to be a true "commandment-keeper," he has only to obey the divine principle of love, and God looks upon this as fulfillment of "the law." The Holy Spirit does not specify the moral, ceremonial, or civil law. He emphatically states that love is the fulfillment of "the law"—a tremendously important statement, to say the least!

It is significant that in the thirteenth chapter of Romans, after quoting five of the ten commandments which the Adventists steadfastly affirm constitute "the moral law," the apostle conspicuously omits what the Adventists maintain is God's great "seal"—the Sabbath. In fact, the words "any other commandment" must include even the Sabbath in the law of love. Nowhere is this more decidedly emphasized than in the usage of a peculiar term which appears but twice in the New Testament; here in Romans 13:9, and again in Ephesians 1:10. The term in question is the Greek "*anakephalaioutai*" which in both instances means "to sum up, to repeat summarily, and so to condense into a summary . . . to bring together."

We see then that the Apostle Paul, under the inspiration of the Holy Spirit, taught in both Romans 13:9 and Ephesians 1:10 that as God in the fulness of time intended to "gather together" (KJV) or "sum up" (RSV), those whom He had chosen in Christ, in like manner He has forever condensed or summed up, comprehended or gathered together, the law in all its aspects and divisions under the all-embracing principle of love. By not adhering strictly to the established laws of sound Biblical interpretations, Seventh-day Adventists seem to have overlooked this fact in the New Testament. In the course of our study of Seventh-day Adventist literature, we have been impressed by the fact that some Adventists will cite texts largely out of their context and grammatical structure in what appears to be an attempt to enforce an arbitrary theory of two laws (moral and ceremonial) upon the believer in the age of grace. In so doing, they violate that principle which the Apostle Paul states "sums up or condenses" all of the commandments of the entire law, perfectly fulfilling them under the one heading, "the great commandment," upon which, our Lord declared, "hang all the law and the prophets," the imperative of love.

On page 131 of *Questions on Doctrine* it is stated that the ceremonial law is now "abolished" (Ephesians 2:15); and, "the Christian who keeps this law is not blessed," but "loses his liberty" (Galatians 5:1, 3). Nevertheless, Adventists religiously observe some ceremonial laws, especially with regard to "unclean food." Now, although they deny that their rejection of "unclean" food is based on Mosaic prohibitions, all their literature on the subject appeals to the very law which they insist has been "abolished." Under the covenant of law, nowhere but in the Mosaic ceremonial aspects of the law are people forbidden to eat oysters, clams, lobsters, crabs, reptiles, rabbits, and swine's flesh, but the Adventists still claim the validity of such prohibition. We wish that they would be consistent in following their dual law theory and abandon their "unclean foods" restriction which binds them to what even they admit is an abolished ceremonial teaching; a teaching which they also declare can cause the Christian to "lose his liberty" and miss the blessing of God. Writing on this subject of unclean foods with apostolic authority and in the power of the Holy Spirit, the Apostle Paul unequivocally declared, "Therefore let no one pass judgment on you in questions of food and drink." And he warns Timothy that in the latter days some persons will "enjoin abstinence from foods which God created to be received with thanksgiving by those who believe and know the truth. For everything created by God is good, and nothing is to be rejected if it is received with thanksgiving, for then it is consecrated by the Word of God and prayer." Finally he sums it up thus:

> I know and am persuaded in the Lord Jesus that nothing is unclean in itself; but it is unclean for any one who thinks it unclean. . . . For the kingdom of God does not mean food and drink but righteousness and peace and joy in the Holy Spirit; he who thus serves Christ is acceptable to God and approved by men (Romans 14:14a, 17, 18).

From these texts it is apparent that Adventists limit their own liberty in Christ by voluntary bondage to ceremonial precepts, and it is the dual law theory which has largely caused their confusion and the consequent error of law-keeping.

For this teaching, which lapses so easily into legalism, we find no Biblical authority since it is demonstrably true that the law of Moses and the Decalogue are a unit described throughout Scripture as *"the"* law." The fact that the Decalogue was written on stones (Exodus 31:18), and the law of Moses written in a book (Exodus 24:4, 7; Deuteronomy 31:24), in no way proves that one is moral and the other ceremonial. As we have seen, the law of Moses, written in a book, and deposited by the Levites by the side of the Ark, deals not only with ceremonial ritual matters, but with those moral precepts contained in the Decalogue itself. One could not be fulfilled, as Christ prophesied and accomplished, and the other left unfulfilled, for then God's sacrificial plan would not have been consummated at Calvary.

B. *"Law" in the New Testament*

When New Testament writers spoke of "the law," they usually meant all five books of Moses, which contain moral, ceremonial and civil ordinances. It was national and applied only to Israel and to anyone who became an Israelite. Nowhere in Scripture is it applied to anyone else. Although the Gentiles, as Paul says, "have not the law," its great moral principle applied to them, so that the Gentiles "do by nature that which is contained in the law" but they did not come under law as given to Israel.

Acts 15:23–32 describes how the leaders of the Christian Church at Jerusalem, all Jews, were very careful not to impose the demands of the law upon the Gentiles. For them, the complete "law"—moral, ceremonial and civil—had been fulfilled, and the one law to observe now was to love God and your neighbor. St. Augustine remarked "Love God, and do as you please," for if we truly love God with heart, soul, mind and strength, we do only those things which please Him. This is "the law" of the New Testament, the only guide for the Christian. We are "no longer under the law, but under grace," and the function of the "schoolmaster" (Galatians 3:24) has forever and irrevocably ceased.

Let us see how these first Christian leaders solved the problem of "the law":

> And they wrote letters by them after this manner; the apostles and elders and brethren send greetings unto the brethren which are of the Gentiles in Antioch and Syria and Cilicia. Forasmuch as we have heard, that certain which went out from us have troubled you with words, subverting your souls, saying, Ye must be circumcised, and keep the law: to whom we gave no such commandment: It seemed good unto us, being assembled with one accord to send chosen men unto you. . . . We have sent therefore, Judas and Silas. . . . For it seemed good to the Holy Ghost, and to us, to lay upon you no greater burden than these necessary things; that ye abstain from meats offered to idols, and from blood, and from things strangled, and from fornication: from which if ye keep yourselves, ye shall do well. Fare ye well (Acts 15:23–25, 27–29).

Since "the law" includes the precepts of the Pentateuch and certain sections of the Psalms and Prophets, this message to the Gentiles contradicts all dual law teachers who insist that we must for any purpose "keep the law." We know from a comparison of the New Testament with the Old that the Decalogue of itself is not the entire moral law of God, as our Adventist brethren often insist, for there are many other commandments which are neither *inferred, implied* nor *contained* in the Decalogue, but which are just as moral as anything appearing in Exodus 20. Although nine of the Ten Commandments are enunciated in the New Testament, we have seen that they are "comprehended, summed up or condensed" in the words of Paul, in the great commandment of love (Romans 13, Galatians 5). So the Adventists have no argument against the total fulfillment of all the law by the life and death of our Savior.

In Acts 15:24, the leaders of the church in Jerusalem reiterate this principle in their letter to the Gentiles in Antioch, Syria and Cilicia: "Certain which went out from us have troubled you with words, subverting your souls, saying, Ye must be circumcised, and keep the law: to whom we gave no such commandment."

Now although Seventh-day Adventists affirm that law-keeping cannot merit salvation, nevertheless they teach that by breaking the law one forfeits salvation. They invoke a principle which was fulfilled in the life and death of Christ; and in so doing they place themselves in direct opposition to the great law of love enunciated by Christ and the apostles, and are in effect putting "a yoke upon the neck of the disciples, which neither our fathers nor we were able to bear" (Acts 15:10). To those who invoke the law as the criterion of obedience in the Christian life, the Word of God replies, "We gave no such commandment" (Acts 15:24).

Paul's phrase "any other commandment" in Romans 13:9, of course, includes abstinence from meats offered to idols, blood, things strangled and fornication, for love of God would enjoin discernment and obedience in all these things.

To support their argument that a Christian must obey the commandments, Adventists and other Christian bodies cite such passages as the following:

> If ye love me, keep my commandments. He that hath my commandments, and keepeth them, he it is that loveth me (John 14:15, 21). And hereby we do know that we know him, if we keep his commandments. He that saith, I know him, and keepeth not his commandments, is a liar, and the truth is not in him. . . . And whatsoever we ask, we receive of him, because we keep his commandments, and do those things that are pleasing in his sight. . . . He that keepeth his commandments dwelleth in him, and he in him. And hereby we know that he abideth in us, by the Spirit which he hath given us. . . . By this we know that we love the children of God, when we love God, and keep his commandments. For this is the love of God, that we keep his commandments: and his commandments are not grievous (1 John 2:3, 4; 3:22, 24; 5:2, 3).

We, too, yield to the authority of those verses; but the fallacy of the position lies in the concept that the word "commandments" always refers to the Ten Commandments, which they maintain are "the moral law of God." This claim cannot be substantiated from Scripture, in fact, it is contradicted by the Bible. Let us see how the Lord Jesus and the Apostle John applied the words "commandments" and "law." First, consider the conversation of our Lord with the lawyer in Luke 10:25–28:

> And, behold, a certain lawyer stood up, and tempted him, saying, Master, what shall I do to inherit eternal life?
> He said unto him, What is written in the law? how readest thou?
> And he answering said, Thou shalt love the Lord thy God with all thy heart, and with all thy soul, and with all thy strength, and with all thy mind; and thy neighbor as thyself.
> And he said unto him, Thou hast answered right: this do, and thou shalt live.

Clearly, the Lord Jesus did not subscribe to the Seventh-day Adventist view that "commandment-keeping means keeping all of the Ten Commandments," none of which He mentions in this passage. Christ did not say, "Keep the Ten Commandments, especially the fourth one, and thou shalt live." He said, in effect, "Obey the law of love upon which all the law and the prophets rest, and thou shalt live." This refutes the Adventist claim that when Jesus spoke of commandments he meant *only* the Decalogue.

Among those who listened to our Lord's discourse in the Upper Room was the Apostle John, who records the "new commandment . . . That you love one another as I have loved you" (John 13:34). To this commandment John refers in the passages quoted from his first epistle. Nowhere does he mention the Decalogue or any part of the moral law of God. Instead, he writes:

> This is his commandment, That we should believe on the name of his Son Jesus Christ, and love one another, as he gave us commandment. . . . And this commandment have we from him, That he who loveth God love his brother also (1 John 3:23; 4:21).

And in his second epistle he says,

> I beseech thee, lady, not as though I wrote a new commandment unto thee, but that which we had from the beginning, that we love one another. And this is love, that we walk after his commandments. This is the commandment, That, as ye have heard from the beginning, ye should walk in it" (2 John 5, 6).

What then does John mean when he speaks of "commandment" or "commandments"? In his own words he means:

> . . . That which we had from the beginning, that we love one another. And this is love, that we walk after his commandments. This is the commandment, That, as ye have heard from the beginning, ye should walk in it (2 John 5, 6).

How different from ironclad obedience to what many, including Adventists, sometimes call "The Eternal Ten"! By "the righteousness of the law" and fulfillment of the law, Christ and all the New Testament writers mean *not* the Ten Commandments but the eternal law of *love*. The motivating power of the universe, love, is to motivate obedience to God. By loving Him and one another, we fulfill all moral law. The chief function of the law was to reveal sin and to "slay" the soul, that righteousness might come by faith, and it was given for the unregenerate, *not* the redeemed: "Knowing this, that the law is not made for a righteous man, but for the lawless and disobedient, for the ungodly and for sinners, for unholy and profane, for murderers of fathers and murderers of mothers, for manslayers" (1 Timothy 1:9).

C. *The Charge of Pharisaism*

By believing they are God's commandment-keeping church, Adventists have exposed themselves to the charge of Pharisaism. Because they monopolize such passages as the following, they give the impression of claiming to be the only people on earth: (1) "Which keep the commandments of God"; (2) "They that keep the commandments of God, and the faith of Jesus"; and, (3) "Blessed are *they that do his commandments*,[56] that they may have the right to the tree of life, and may enter in through the gates into the city" (Revelation 12:17; 14:12; 22:14).

We admire the desire of our Adventist brethren to obey the command-

---

[56] All the oldest and best Greek manuscripts of Revelation 22:14 read "They that wash their robes," so the verse gives no support whatever for "commandment-keeping." This fact well-informed Adventists recognize, but a large segment still attempt to utilize certain faulty and incorrect English translations to "prove" their position.

ments of God; but, we ask, what commandments? If they answer, "The Decalogue," we reject their effort to bring us under bondage, for we "are not under the law, but under grace" (Romans 6:14). If some fail to recognize that "the law" of the New Testament is love for God and for one another, and that it fulfills and supersedes all previous embodiments of divine principle, then the issue is clear. Such people speak like "a noisy gong or a clanging cymbal," because they do not give supremacy to the "new" and "great commandment."

Concluding this section on the principle of law, we may sum up our position briefly:

The Adventist insistence that there are two separate codes of laws, the moral and the ceremonial, and that the former is in effect today and the latter was abolished at the cross, finds, we believe, no exegetical or theological basis in Scripture. We have also shown that they select numerous texts out of context and juxtapose them in order to validate their contention. We have seen that the greatest of all commandments is not included in the Decalogue or "moral law." And yet upon this great commandment, love for the Lord and for one's neighbor, "hang all the law and the prophets." The nineteenth chapter of Leviticus alone is sufficient to refute the dual law theory, for it contains *moral, ceremonial* and *civil* laws sometimes all appearing in the same verse, and yet Leviticus is called by Christ, "the law," as are the other four books of Moses.

The Adventist contention that since the Ten Commandments were spoken by God, inscribed on stone and placed within the Ark, they are superior to the law written by Moses in a book and placed by the side of the Ark, is fallacious. This is true because the book placed by the side of the Ark actually contains *more* moral law than does the Decalogue itself. It is therefore, superior to the Decalogue, at least in scope.

The Bible refutes the Adventist contention that the law was in force in Eden and that it was known to Adam, Noah, Abraham and the patriarchs. Not one verse of Scripture can be cited free from inference, deduction and implication, that teaches such a doctrine. The Word of God frequently states,

> *The law* was given by Moses. . . . Did not Moses give you *the law*. . . . If therefore perfection were by the Levitical priesthood, for under it the people received *the law*. . . . The covenant, that was confirmed before of God in Christ, *the law*, which was 430 years after, cannot disannul. . . . The Lord our God made a covenant with us in Horeb. The Lord made not this covenant with our fathers, but with us (John 1:17; 7:19; Hebrews 7:11; Galatians 3:17; Deuteronomy 5:2, 3).

The Adventists' contentions, therefore, concerning the eternal nature of the Decalogue and the time of its application to man, are mere conjecture. Although we admit that the principle of the law was, in effect, written upon the hearts of men by the Holy Spirit, so that they were judged by it (Romans 2), there is a vast difference between the principle of the law and the embodiment of that principle in a given code (Sinaitic-Mosaic), which the Adventists fail to recognize.

Finally, the Old Testament Scriptures all teach the unity of the law.

Christ endorsed it, and the Apostles pointed out that its chief purpose was to condemn man and show him his need of redemption that he might come to Christ, the author and fulfiller of *all* the law. We who are "led of the Spirit are not under the law" (Galatians 5:18); for "love is the fulfilling of the law" (Romans 13:10). This love energizes us to "walk not after the flesh, but after the Spirit" that in us "the righteousness of the law might be fulfilled" (Romans 8:4). In Jeremiah 31:31–34 the prophet states that under the new covenant God would write His law "in their inward parts, and write it in their hearts." In 2 Corinthians 3:3 the Apostle Paul declares that Christians are "the epistle of Christ . . . written not with ink, but with the Spirit of the living God; not in tables of stone, but in fleshy tables of the heart." The motive for obedience to this law is the imperative of Love—"We love him because he first loved us" (1 John 4:19).

The great foundational moral law of the universe is therefore declared to be unchanging love. This is vastly different from the national or Mosaic law given only to Israel. That law was designed to be fulfilled, even though it was based upon the eternal principles of the moral character of God (Colossians 2:14–17). And when its fulfillment did take place and the character of God was imputed to the believer and imparted to his life by the power of the indwelling Spirit, the entire Mosaic system passed away; but the eternal principle, its foundation, remained, and is operative today as the law of love, the supreme "commandment" and the only "law" under which the Christian is to live.

The concept of law in Seventh-day Adventism, then, leads them to the un-Biblical and at times legalistic position that although they are "under grace," by failing to "keep the commandments" they are in danger of coming "under law" again.

The Word of God, however, describes the Christian under grace as "dead to the law" and "alive unto God" (Galatians 2:19), and nowhere is it taught that one can "come alive" again so that the function of the law is resumed.

II. *The Relationship of Grace to Salvation*

Although Adventists lay great stress on "commandment-keeping" and "obedience to the moral law of God as contained in the Ten Commandments," they devote a large portion of their writings to the New Testament doctrine of grace. As we saw earlier, Seventh-day Adventists believe in salvation by grace alone, and vehemently deny that "law" plays any part as a basis for redemption. In their own words,

> Salvation is not now, and never has been, by law or by works; salvation is only by the grace of Christ. Moreover, there never was a time in the plan of God when salvation was by human works or effort. Nothing men can do, or have done, can in any way *merit* salvation.
>
> While works are not a *means* of salvation, good works are the inevitable *result* of salvation. However, these good works are possible only for the child of God whose life is inwrought by the Spirit of God. . . . One thing is certain, man cannot be saved by any effort of his own. We profoundly believe that no works of the law, no deeds of the law, no effort however commendable, and no good works—whether they be many or few, sacrificial or not—can

in any way justify the sinner (Titus 3:5; Rom. 3:20). Salvation is wholly of grace; it is the gift of God (Rom. 4:4, 5; Eph. 2:8).[57]

These and many similar clear-cut statements in current authoritative Seventh-day Adventist literature reveal that, despite the "dual law theory" and the peculiar concept that the law is still operative in the life of the believer, Adventists confess the basis of their salvation to be grace, and grace alone, the only basis upon which God deigns to save the fallen children of Adam.

In Chapter 14 of *Questions on Doctrine*, Adventists spell out their allegiance to divine grace as the only channel of salvation: "According to Seventh-day Adventist belief, there is, and can be, no salvation through the law, or by human works of the law, but only through the saving grace of God."[58]

Christians who are familiar with historical theology know that the Adventists position on law, though tinged with legalism, has its roots in the basic Arminian position that one receives salvation as a free gift of God; but, once he has received this gift, the believer is responsible for its maintenance and duration, and the chief means of accomplishing this is "commandment-keeping" or "obedience to *all* the laws of God."

Since Adventists are basically Arminian, we may logically deduce that, in a sense, their salvation rests upon legal grounds. But the saving factor in the dilemma is that by life and by worldwide witness, Adventists, like other so-called Arminians, give true evidence that they have experienced the "new birth," which is by grace alone, through faith in our Lord and His sacrifice upon the cross. One would be callous and uncharitable indeed not to accept their profession of dependence upon Christ alone for redemption, even though there is inconsistency in their theological system.

Some Christians make a great issue of the teaching of "eternal security," and perhaps rightly so because it is an important truth. However, no matter how strongly we may feel about it, our conviction does not entitle us to judge the motives and spiritual condition of other believers in this respect. This is our principal reason for taking the position that Seventh-day Adventists are Christians who believe the historic gospel message. They cannot rightly be called non-Christian cultists or "judaizers," since they are sound on the great New Testament doctrines including grace and redemption through the vicarious offering of Jesus Christ "once for all" (Hebrews 10:10) and give evidence of "life in Christ."

For many centuries, there has been much controversy over the juxtaposition of the principles of law and grace in the Scripture. If evangelicals today were asked, "Do you believe that grace and law are in direct opposition?" the answer in most cases would be a strong affirmative. Through the years, confusion has been caused by the abuse of both principles by two groups of equally sincere Christians. One group believes that all law has ceased; the other that the Ten Commandments are still God's standard of righteousness and must be obeyed or salvation is forfeit. What both groups have failed to grasp is that the great conflict is not between law and grace as

---

[57]*Questions on Doctrine*, pp. 141, 142.
[58]*Ibid.*, p. 135.

such; rather, it centers around a proper understanding of their relationship and respective functions.

We have established that love is the ground and source of the doctrine of grace, but the law was necessary to expose the sinfulness of sin and the depth of man's moral depravity. When law becomes the ground of salvation or of restraining the Christian from practicing sin, it intrudes upon the province of grace. When a Christian is not controlled by love, grace is abused and its purpose is nullified. All law is fulfilled by love, as our Savior and the apostles taught, but the Christian can never please God if he obeys for fear of the law. Life under law binds the soul, for the tendency is for man to obey not because he wants to please God but because he fears God's judgment. Under grace, love works upon the regenerate heart, and what was legalistic duty under law becomes gracious obedience under grace. Actually, grace and love demand more than the law, which to the Pharisees required only outward obedience. Grace commands us to "do the will of God from the heart" (Ephesians 6:6). Seventh-day Adventists declare that they obey the law not out of fear but out of love for God, but it is to be regretted that in a large proportion of their literature on the subject, they declare that the keeping of the law is necessary to *maintain* salvation, and thus they introduce the motive of fear instead of the Biblical imperative of love.

The Apostle John defined the issue when he wrote, "The law was given by Moses, but grace and truth came by Jesus Christ" (John 1:17). As a governing principle, a measure of righteousness, a schoolmaster and an instrument of death, the law was supplanted by grace—the unmerited favor of God. All believers in the Lord Jesus Christ, having passed from death to life through the sacrifice of the Son of God, possess the divine nature and righteousness. Because He first loved us, we are compelled and impelled to love and serve Him. In obedience to the great law of love, the Christian fulfills the *righteousness* of the law (not the law itself; this Christ alone did); and by the transforming power of the indwelling Holy Spirit he will "walk not after the flesh, but after the Spirit" (Romans 8:4).

Seventh-day Adventists believe, we repeat, that they are saved by grace. However, they are often prone to believe that their remaining saved depends on "commandment-keeping."

III. *The Author of Salvation*

Because He took our sins upon Himself, in obedience to His Father's will, the Lord Jesus "became the author of eternal salvation unto all them that obey him" (Hebrews 5:8–10). This truth Seventh-day Adventists believe. They strongly assert their belief in the Deity of the Lord Jesus Christ, His equality with the Father, and His perfect, sinless human nature, and expound these truths in detail. However, they teach that before His incarnation the Lord Jesus Christ bore the title of Michael the archangel. This interpretation differs greatly from that of Jehovah's Witnesses who believe that Christ was a created being and that "He was a god, but not the almighty God who is Jehovah."[59] The Adventists make this very clear:

---

[59]*Let God Be True*, Brooklyn, NY: Watchtower Bible and Tract Society, 1952, p. 100.

We emphatically reject the idea . . . and the position held by the Jehovah's Witnesses. We do not believe that Christ is a created being. We as a people have not considered the identification of Michael of sufficient prominence to dwell upon it at length either in our literature or in our preaching. . . . We believe that the term Michael is but one of the many titles applied to the Son of God, the second person of the Godhead. But such a view does not in any way conflict with our belief in His full deity and eternal pre-existence, nor does it in the least disparage His person and work.[60]

Although a number of authoritative commentators support the Adventist view, the New Testament, I believe, does not warrant this conclusion. Most of the evidence that the Adventists submit is from the Book of Daniel, the rest from the Apocalypse. By comparing such designations as "angel of Jehovah," "angel of the Lord," "Prince," and "Michael," the Adventists conclude that Michael is another title for the Lord Jesus Christ. But Seventh-day Adventists maintain that although he is called "the arch angel" (*arch-angelos* or "first messenger"), he is *not* a created being since, in the Old Testament, "angel of Jehovah" is a term of Deity. In the light of this, we do not judge them because of their view of Michael, but call the reader's attention to the ninth verse of the book of Jude, which says, "Yet Michael the archangel, when contending with the devil he disputed about the body of Moses, *durst not* bring against him a railing accusation, but said, The Lord rebuke thee."

The word translated *durst* in the King James Bible is the archaic past tense of "dare"; so Michael "did not dare" bring against Satan a railing or blasphemous (*blasphemos*) judgment. The Greek word for "dare" is *tolmao* and appears 16 times in the New Testament, and in the negative always means "not daring through fear of retaliation." Thus if Michael was Christ, according to the Seventh-day Adventists, "He did not dare" to rebuke Satan for fear of retaliation.

Adventists agree that 15 times in the New Testament "*tolmao*" carries the meaning indicated. But, since its use in Jude 9 refutes their notion that Michael is a title of Christ, they *reverse* its meaning here! As the Adventists know, none of the commentators to whom they appeal has grammatically analyzed or diagrammed the passage in the Greek or for that matter commented upon exclusive usage of *tolmao* in the Scripture of the New Testament. The agreement of such commentation therefore gives no validity whatever to the Adventists' misuse of *tolmao*. The preincarnate Christ, the *Logos*, having the nature of God (John 1:1), certainly would not refer the creature Satan to God the Father for rebuke. While He was on earth, Christ the Creator rebuked Satan many times. Would He then fear him during His preincarnate life? Scripture contradicts this.

The Adventist explanation is:

> The devil, the prince of evil, could rightly be said to deserve a railing accusation, but to such a thing Michael would not stoop. To say that Michael *could not*, in the sense that He did not have the power or the authority to do so, would not be true. It is not that Michael *could not*, in the sense of being restricted, but rather that He *would not* take such an attitude.[61]

[60]*Questions on Doctrine*, p. 71.
[61]*Questions on Doctrine*, p. 80.

This statement appears to be an attempt to escape the fact that the word "dare" (*tolmao*) in the New Testament always connotes fear, including its use in Jude 9. The text teaches that because Michael did not have the authority to rebuke Satan, "he did not dare" to do so through fear of superior retaliation. There is no implication that Michael's position was so high that he "would not stoop." The context, grammar and root meaning of *tolmao* contradict the Adventists' attempt to make this text support their view of Michael. All authorities on Greek grammar agree that the Adventist interpretation violates the classic and New Testament usage of *tolmao*.

Thus the Adventist statement about Michael is neither linguistically nor Scripturally accurate. Although they repudiate the Jehovah's Witnesses' position, they wrest this passage from its true meaning and read into it their own theory concerning Michael as Christ.

In conclusion, I am convinced of the sincerity of the Adventists' claim to regeneration, and allegiance to the New Testament principle of saving grace. I appreciate their high regard for the law of God and their desire to obey it. I cannot agree, however, with their insistence upon linking "commandment-keeping" to observance of the ceremonial law, especially with regard to "unclean" foods. I feel, moreover, that they err in saying that Michael is a title of Christ, and I believe that I have shown that they violate the linguistic and Scriptural meaning of Jude 9.

Author's Note

One of the chief critics of Seventh-day Adventism is a vocal ex-Adventist printer of Minneapolis, a man who has written much against his former church. Writing in *The Sword of the Lord*, August 2, 1957, he bitterly assailed Seventh-day Adventists as willful deceivers. Since his writings are repeatedly quoted by most of the other critics we shall discuss his charge, but in the interest of brevity we shall confine ourselves to one of his chief areas of criticism, law and salvation in Seventh-day Adventist theology.

This critic quotes the books, *Steps to Christ*, by Mrs. Ellen G. White, in the following manner: "The condition of eternal life is now just what it has always been . . . perfect obedience to the law of God."

He then maintains that Seventh-day Adventism teaches this, and on the surface it appears that he has proved his point; namely that to Adventists, salvation is a combination of grace, faith in Christ, plus the keeping of the law. A closer look at the statement in the context from which the critic removed it, however, serves to refute this position. Wrote Mrs. White in the very same context:

> We do not earn salvation by our obedience for salvation is the free gift of God to receive by faith. But obedience is the fruit of faith . . . here is the true test. If we abide in Christ and the love of God dwells in us, our feelings, our thoughts, our actions will be in harmony with the will of God as expressed in the precepts of His Holy law. . . . Righteousness is defined by the standard of God's holy law as expressed in the ten precepts given on Sinai. That so-called faith in Christ which professes to release men from the obligation of obedience to God is not faith but presumption. "By grace are ye

saved through faith." But "faith if it has not works is dead." Jesus said of Himself before He came to earth, "I delight to do thy will O my God. Yea, thy law is within my heart." And just before He ascended again to Heaven, He declared, "I have kept my Father's commandments and abide in his love." The Scripture says, "Hereby we do know that we know him, if we keep his commandments. He that saith he abides in him ought also himself to walk even as he walked," because "Christ also suffered for us, leaving us an example, that ye should follow his steps."

The condition of eternal life is now just what it always has been—just what it was in Paradise before the fall of our first parents—perfect obedience to the law of God, perfect righteousness. Since we are sinful, unholy, we cannot perfectly obey a holy law. We have no righteousness of our own with which to meet the claims of the law of God. But Christ has made a way of escape for us. He lived on earth amid trials and temptations such as we have to meet. He lived a sinless life. He died for us and now He offers to take our sins and give us His righteousness. If you give yourself to Him and accept Him as your Saviour, then sinful as your life may have been for His sake you are counted righteous. Christ's character stands in place of your character and you are accepted before God just as if you had not sinned.

So we have nothing in ourselves of which to boast. We have no ground for self exaltation. Our only ground of hope is in the righteousness of Christ imputed to us by His Spirit working in and through us.[62]

In the light of Mrs. White's complete statement on this subject, we see that our critic omitted her principal thesis, that we are saved by grace. There are not a few instances of similar carelessness on the part of the writer of this article. The result is that his work is largely discredited and discounted by those who know the proper methods of research.

Seventh-day Adventists are well aware of the law and grace problem and in *Questions on Doctrine* they state:

There has been regrettable misunderstanding as to our teaching on grace, law, and works, and their interrelationships. According to Seventh-day Adventist belief, there is, and can be, no salvation through the law, or by human works of the law, but only through the saving grace of God. This principle, to us, is basic.[63]

Further the Adventists state:

Salvation is not now, and never has been, by law or works; salvation is only by the grace of Christ. Moreover, there never was a time in the plan of God when salvation was by human works or effort. Nothing men can do, or have done, can in any way *merit* salvation.

While works are not a *means* of salvation, good works are the inevitable *result* of salvation. . . . One thing is certain, man cannot be saved by any effort of his own. We profoundly believe that no works of the law, no deeds of the law, no effort however commendable, and no good works—whether they be many or few, sacrificial or not—can in any way justify the sinner (Titus 3:5; Rom. 3:20). Salvation is wholly of grace; it is the gift of God (Rom. 4:4, 5; Eph. 2:8).[64]

---

[62]Ellen G. White, *Steps to Christ*, Washington, D.C.: Review and Herald Publishing Association, 1945, pp. 36–49.
[63]*Questions on Doctrine*, p. 135.
[64]*Questions on Doctrine*, pp. 141, 142.

Ellen G. White, certainly an authoritative voice in Adventism, summarized it thus:

Christ is pleading for the church in the heavenly courts above, pleading for those for whom he paid the redemption price of his own lifeblood. Centuries, ages, can never diminish the efficacy of this atoning sacrifice. The message of the gospel of His grace was to be given to the church in clear and distinct lines, that the world should no longer say that Seventh-day Adventists talk the law, but do not teach or believe Christ.[65]

---

[65]Ellen G. White, *Testimonies to Ministers*, Mountain View, CA: Pacific Press, n.d., p. 92.

UNITARIANISM

The Unitarian Universalist Church is more properly designated by Biblical Christians as a non-Christian cult. Today its membership, almost entirely in the United States, is around 150,000. This figure is below that of the group shortly after the Unitarians and the Universalists merged in 1959, but is still greater than any other period of its history. With its liberal and humanistic attitudes, beliefs, and practices, it is little wonder that it enjoys popularity in liberal America.

The central theme of Unitarianism is that there is but one God, a solitary entity, who has revealed Himself through various men and in the Bible, which is considered to be one among a number of divine books. The writings of Buddha, Mohammed, Confucius, Lao and the Vedas and Upanishads are sources of revelation, none of which are infallible, but all of which contribute something to the religious growth and development of mankind. Unitarianism generally affirms that salvation is progressive, and that it is essentially a matter of character development, joined with faith in God and attendant good works, which are counted as means toward an end of final redemption.

To understand Unitarianism, the background of history must be utilized to the fullest.

Unitarians generally like to trace their history to apostolic times, especially to the Council of Nicaea (A.D. 325) where the great Arian heresy enunciated a semi-unitarian theme by denying the New Testament doctrine of the full Deity of Jesus Christ.

Unitarians, however, are notoriously poor historians, and it was not until the fourteenth century that the dogmas now designated as Unitarian markedly gained any popular support. Of a certainty, some poorly-informed thinkers in the early church adhered to various principles now claimed by Unitarians; but none of the leading theologians of the Christian Church ever held to Unitarian teachings, nor do they today. For it is impossible to remain in fellowship with the Christian Church and to maintain a Unitarian interpretation of Christian theology.

Unitarians, although they have managed to gain recognition in local church councils in certain areas of the United States (due primarily to a laxity in doctrine on the part of such groups), are refused membership as a body in the National Association of Evangelicals and are denied status as a Christian denomination by conservative Protestants, Catholics, and Orthodox bodies. The term, "Unitarian," and the term, "Christian," are mutually exclusive by definition, historically and theologically.

The first Unitarian writer of note was Martin Cellarium (1499–1564), a friend of Martin Luther, who advanced Unitarian views in 1527. This bold presentation was followed in succession by the anti-Trinitarian positions of Ludwig Haetzer, 1529, Michael Servetus, 1531, who was martyred for his views at Geneva in 1553, and culminated in the work of Fausto Sozini, better known to history as Socinus (1539–1604). Socinus, an Italian by birth, was a nephew of Lelio Sozini, an associate of John Calvin and Philip Melanchthon, whose theology at times wavered, but apparently remained orthodox enough for him to escape martyrdom and to remain in fellowship with Reformed theologians.

In contrast to his Uncle Lelio, Socinus became an anti-Trinitarian, denying the Trinity and the true Deity of Jesus Christ, as do all Unitarians to this day.

Socinianism found strong roots in Hungary, Poland, and Transylvania and eventually spread to Holland, then to England and finally to the United States.

Early in the history of America, the Unitarian faith made itself known through the work of such preachers as Jonathan Mayhew, 1720–1766, pastor of the West Church in Boston, Joseph Priestley, 1794, Hosea Ballou, 1771–1852; William Ellery Channing, 1803, and Ralph Waldo Emerson, 1838, to mention just a few Unitarians of note.

During the course of its American development, Unitarianism passed through three distinct stages. The first period was 1800–1835. Throughout this era, Unitarianism was subject, in a large measure, to English philosophic rationalism, a semi-supernaturalism and the practice of general philanthropy. The second period of development, 1835–1885, found the Unitarians strongly influenced by German idealism and rationalistic theology flavored by a definite leaning toward mysticism. By 1865 the National Unitarian Conference was organized, and a definite theology was evolved, in which the Unitarians envisioned themselves as disciples of Christ.

The third period of Unitarian illusion began in 1885 and continues on to this day. This period of growth has seen an acceptance of evolution, the empirical methods in religion, higher criticism, the higher recognition of the Universal religion and "an ethical attempt to realize the higher affirmations of Christianity."

These aims were confirmed at the International Congress held by the Unitarians in 1900, and have not undergone any major changes to this day. As was previously noted, the Unitarians merged with the Universalists and have publicly announced that they are not altogether sure whether they can classify themselves as Christians. In fact, some of their leaders have not hesitated to disclaim the title of "Christian," where Unitarian theology is concerned.

The Theology of Unitarianism

As its name implies, Unitarianism unequivocally denies the Christian doctrine of the Trinity and by necessity, the Deity of Jesus Christ. During the year 1955, *Look* magazine sent out a questionnaire to the major religions of the United States, asking specific questions in the context of generally accepted terminology in the realm of Christian theology. This collection of articles is now available in book form.*

The Unitarian Church selected as its spokesman, the Rev. Carl M. Chorowsky, minister of the first Unitarian Church of Fairfield, Connecticut. Dr. Chorowsky answered the questions of *Look* magazine with great candor, and with a refreshing directness seldom found in the major, non-Christian cults. His answers are of great value, because they stand as an official statement of Unitarian theology. Dr. Chorowsky is the author of the following statements, taken from the March 8, 1955, issue of *Look* magazine, in an article entitled, "What is a Unitarian?"

1. *The Doctrine of God and the Person of Christ.*

In general, a Unitarian is a religious person whose ethic derives primarily from that of Jesus, who believed in One God, not the Trinity. . . . Unitarians hold that the orthodox Christian world has forsaken the real, human Jesus of the Gospel, and has substituted a Christ of dogmatism, metaphysics and pagan philosophy. Because Unitarians refuse to acknowledge Jesus as their Lord and God, they are excluded from the National Council of the Churches of Christ.

Further evidence of the Unitarian attitude toward Jesus Christ is found in another of Dr. Chorowsky's statements.

Unitarians repudiate the doctrine and dogma of the Virgin Birth. . . . Unitarians do not believe that Jesus is the Messiah, either of Jewish hope or of Christian fantasy. They do not believe He is "God Incarnate," or the Second Person of the Trinity, as the final arbitrator at the end of time, who shall come to judge the quick and the dead.

2. *The Doctrines of Sin and Redemption.*

Unitarians recognize evil and man's responsibility for much of it. . . . Because of the total depravity of man, supposedly, God sent His only begotten Son to the world to die for sinful men. Such doctrine Unitarians find offensive, un-Biblical, even immoral. It is certainly inconsistent with the nature of God or the dignity of man, whom the Eternal One created in the image of God, to love with an everlasting love.

Relative to the doctrine of eternal salvation, Dr. Chorowsky declared:

Unitarians believe in salvation of a character. . . . God's help is not likely to come to those who cast all their burdens on the Lord. There is practical wisdom in the saying, "God helps those who help themselves," . . . if by heaven, you mean an abode of eternal light, where the saved and redeemed enjoy everlasting bliss, and if by hell, you mean the devil's eternal darkness, where the wicked suffer unending torment—then Unitarianism emphatically repudiates such beliefs.

Unitarianism and the Bible

"Do Unitarians believe the Bible is divinely inspired and infallible?" This was one of the key questions addressed to the Unitarian Church, and re-

---

*Rosten, Leo, *Religions of America*, (New York City: Simon & Schuster, 1975).

ceived the following reply from Dr. Chorowsky:

> No. The doctrine of revelation of the absolute and indisputable authority of the Bible is alien to Unitarian faith and teaching.

It is not necessary to point out that this view of the Scripture is the same view held by reformed Judaism, Christian Science, Unity and a host of other non-Christian cults, all of whom are content to utilize the Scriptures, but in a manner never intended by the authors.

Theological Analysis

To sum up the basic issues of Unitarianism, past and present, three important tenets should be carefully noted by the reader.

First, Unitarianism, while it rejects the authority of the Bible in spiritual, moral and doctrinal matters, paradoxically quotes the Bible repeatedly, and mostly out of context at that, in an attempt to substantiate many of its own teachings.

This fact can be shown easily by perusing any standard Unitarian work, where it will be found that practically every author, without exception, quotes the very Book his religion denies, to establish or to make a point concerning that religion!

Dr. Chorowsky himself makes the mistake, in his answers to *Look* magazine, relative to the question "Do Unitarians believe in the divinity of Jesus?"

In that particular instance, in his answer he quotes Scripture, although completely out of context, to establish his contention. The question quite naturally arises in the logical mind, Why quote the Bible at all, if you reject nearly every one of the cardinal doctrines it teaches? This, there can be no doubt, Unitarianism does. If Unitarians were truly honest, they would abandon the Scriptures, for it is either reliable or it is not. Why pick and choose whatever parts suit your theology, while denying the hundreds of affirmations within its pages that it is God's Word to man?

The answer must be obvious—Unitarians dare not abandon the Bible outright, though in effect they have, because it is a tried and true badge of religious prestige, useful in attracting the unregenerate man, who has a general respect for the Bible even though he doesn't live up to it or accept the Savior revealed within its pages. Unitarianism displays a mock reverence for Scripture and for Jesus of Nazareth, although it is clear that it wants no part of His intrinsic Deity, Atoning Death, Bodily Resurrection or triumphant Second Advent.

The Unitarians, it appears, will heap honors upon Christ, but they will not obey His express command:

> The Father loveth the Son, and . . . hath committed all judgment unto the Son: that all men should honour the Son, even as they honour the Father (John 5:20–23).

Second, Unitarianism claims to be a form of Christianity, but at the same time it denies the historic doctrines of the Christian Church (the Trinity, Deity of Christ, Virgin Birth, Vicarious Atonement, Bodily Resurrection and Glorious Return of our Lord). All of these are described as "dogmatisms, metaphysics and pagan philosophy," to quote the official view given by Dr. Chorowsky to *Look* magazine, and which view is also available in numerous official publications.

Dr. Chorowsky further claims that God's plan of redemption as portrayed in the Bible is "offensive, un-Biblical and even immoral." This is strange reasoning indeed, coming from those who claim to practice a scientific emperical method of gaining knowledge, and who venerate the great gods—Reason, Logic and Rationalism.

It may be true, and doubtless is in the case of Unitarians, that the redemption of man on the cross by virtue of Christ's atoning sacrifice is "offensive and even immoral." But it could hardly be called "un-Biblical!" In fact, Dr. Chorowsky could easily have verified this by consulting any standard concordance to the Bible.

The fact of the matter is that Christ's vicarious death is referred to not less than 100 times in the New Testament alone, by every major writer (see Matthew 26:28; Mark 14:24; Luke 22:20; John 6:50–55; 1 Corinthians 11:25; Colossians 1:20; 1 Peter 1:18, 19; Revelation 1:5).

In addition to this, the Bible in countless instances refers directly to the Deity, Virgin Birth, Bodily Resurrection and Second Coming of Jesus Christ, in direct contradiction to Unitarian teachings.

Christianity is more than a way of life, a code of ethics and a pseudo-Christian vocabulary. Christianity is, in its very essence, the Person, Nature and Work of our Lord Jesus, the Eternal Word and Incarnate Son of God, the recognition of whom as personal Savior and Lord is absolutely essential, the Bible teaches, for entrance into the kingdom of God (John 1:12; 3:3; 5:24; 6:37, 47; 14:6; Acts 4:12).

Only the sinner comes to Christ, for He alone of the religious figures of history, could say "Come unto me, all ye that labour and are heavy laden, and I will give you rest" (Matthew 11:28).

This rest, of which our Lord spoke, comes only to those who are willing to cast themselves wholly on the mercy of God. Or, to put it most pointedly, those who would live to please Him, must first please Him to live.

Dr. Chorowsky and the Apostle Peter are at direct variance in this all-important matter of human salvation. For according to Dr. Chorowsky, "God's help is not likely to come to those who cast their burdens on the Lord." The Apostle Peter reminds us, however, that above all things we are to cast "all your care upon him, for he careth for you" (1 Peter 5:7). If, as in the words of the writer of the epistle to the Hebrews, Jesus Christ is indeed "the same yesterday, today and for ever" (13:8), and if with the God of the Bible "there is no variableness, neither shadow or turning" (James 1:17), the Unitarian program of "salvation by character" linked by human effort, "God helps those who help themselves," cannot stand the test.

Unitarianism quite literally puts the cart (a moral and ethical life) before the horse (repentance toward God and faith in the Lord Jesus Christ), and is therefore rightly confused, seeing that Unitarians cannot find peace with either God or their fellow man, since "there is no peace, saith the Lord, unto the wicked" (Isaiah 48:22).

In the third chapter of the gospel of John, following Jesus' discourse with Nicodemus, we read:

And this is the condemnation, that light is come into the world, and men loved darkness rather than light, because their deeds were evil (verse 19).

This is the real reason why Unitarians do not receive Jesus Christ as their Savior; because despite their affirmation of the necessity of a moral and ethical life and faith in God, good works and the golden rule, etc., by rejecting the historic Christ of Scripture, the God-man of Revelation, they have indeed demonstrated irrevocably their love of darkness, rather than light, because their deeds are evil. There is no greater evil than to reject the Infinite Love on the cross, Love Incarnate, Jesus Christ who "bears in His own body on the tree, our sins."

Jesus Christ was manifested, the Scripture informs us, to bring to ruination the works of the devil and to ruin him who had the authority of death (Hebrews 2:14). It is a foolish thing, indeed, to change the glory of the Immortal God for corruptible things, and to lay up for one's self treasure on earth where the moth and the rust do indeed corrupt and where the thieves break through and steal.

Unitarians are, in effect, doing this very thing. How then, shall they escape the judgment of Him who is called the Eternal Word, the fullness of God in human form?

Third, Unitarianism desires to escape biblical teaching that God has indeed committed all judgment unto His Son (John 5:22, 23). The obvious reason for this is, that the doctrine of everlasting punishment which Christ will administer at His Second Advent in power, the end of the ages, is a spiritual thorn in the flesh of contemporary Unitarianism.

Dr. Chorowsky and Unitarians in general "emphatically repudiate eternal darkness, where the wicked suffer unending torment."

In this connection, both Peter and Jude declare eternal darkness to indeed be the fate of all who reject Jesus Christ, "God manifest in the flesh" (1 Timothy 3:16). And both are agreed that "the mists of darkness" are reserved for such souls "for ever" (2 Peter 2:17; Jude 13). The usage of the Greek *ionion* (everlasting) is quite forceful here and cannot be ignored by any thorough student of the Scriptures.

In the light of these facts, the future of Unitarians could hardly be described as bright.

Unitarianism is a product of the deification of Reason, the rejection of Biblical authority and an indescribably fierce pride in one's ability to save himself from the awful penalty of sin. It is one thing for Unitarianism to exercise its prerogative of denial where the foundations of Christianity are involved. But it is quite another to use the Christian Scriptures and abuse numerous contexts therein in order to implement such denials. This is why not a few Christian thinkers have been led to observe that while Unitarianism may be a religion which attempts to exalt reason and rationalism, it is one in which logical consistency is conspicuously absent.

THE ROSICRUCIAN FELLOWSHIP

"May the roses bloom upon your cross," intones the mystical and authoritative voice of the leader, and the echoed response, "And on yours also," from the disciples, probationers and students making up a typical Rosicrucian Fellowship Center, signals the beginning of another excursion into the metaphysical labyrinths of the 600 year old cultic movement which today, with its several factions, is known collectively as the Rosicrucian Fellowship.

Of all the cult systems under discussion in this book, the Rosicrucians most certainly qualify, along with the spiritists, Theosophists and Swedenborgians, as the most mystically inclined. More than any of the others, they are also devoted to a detailed system of doctrine composed of so many strains of other cult viruses, as to be almost beyond the point of comprehension, much less analysis.

Rosicrucianism is not only an eclectic theological system which mixes pagan mythology with Judaism, and Christianity with traces of Hinduism and Buddhism throughout, but it is a system of thinking which seeks to synthesize the basic truths of all religions and absorb them into a master system.

In the literature of Rosicrucianism one will find enormous deposits of symbolism, anthropology, transmigration and even some spiritism.

There is a great similarity in some areas to the vocabulary of Theosophy and to the concept that man progresses through many reincarnations, each of which purges him of his preceding sins.

In Rosicrucian theology there exists seven worlds with seven sections or divisions presided over on the highest level by a "universal spirit." All nature, for that matter, all creation, is unified and bears a direct relationship to the cross which represents man's evolutionary past as well as his future destiny. In Rosicrucian theology the cross loses what the Bible describes as its "reproach" and no Rosicrucian stands ready to "go forth therefore unto him without the camp, bearing his reproach" (Hebrews 13:13).

The cross in Rosicrucianism is the mystical symbol of man's evolutionary development—past, present and future—and has no true significance as the symbol of what it cost God to redeem the sons of men (Revelation 1:5).

Prominent still, though it has been redefined, the cross stands at the center of Rosicrucianism circled with roses. This creates the concept of the rosy cross.

Man progresses by the mystical number seven, for at seven he possesses a vital body, at fourteen a desire body, at twenty-one a full formation of the mind, though the so-called "dense body" is present at birth.

The mission of the Lord Jesus Christ in Rosicrucian theology was to manifest Himself for the aid of mankind in the evolutionary struggle. Rosicrucian theology relegates Him to the highest manifestation or initiate of the Son. And He, along with Buddha and other great leaders, was revealed to facilitate human progress. Sovereign over all the manifestations is the highest initiate from Saturn. This is designated the Father. The Holy Spirit is known as the highest initiate of the moon. However, neither the Holy Spirit nor the Son have any activity in vicarious atonement or spiritual regeneration which consummates in personal redemption apart from psychic reincarnation.

As one travels through the mazes of Rosicrucian terminology and theology, one encounters the fabulous three heavens which are attained through suffering, silence, thought and eventually the reincarnation wheel. A silver chord allegedly connects the physical or dense body with the spiritual body, and at death the chord is broken, releasing the higher nature from the physical. We are told in Rosicrucian literature that Plato was a believer in Rosicrucianism due to his emphasis upon the world soul, and that countless others were secret initiates of Rosicrucian truths. Even the lost continent of Atlantis and the mysterious Lemuran race are included in Rosicrucian speculation. In fact, there is very little that Rosicrucianism does not seek to enfold within its mythological-magical lore, yet everything Christian that it touches suffers violence at its hands.

By the time the average reader of Rosicrucian literature extricates himself or herself from the various Periods (Sun, Moon, Saturn, etc.), ethers, bodies and multiple hypotheses of Rosicrucian philosophy, he is pretty generally impressed with the enormous amount of data the Rosicrucians have amassed as a substitute for the revelations of the Bible. Most always, he is confused by the fact that Rosicrucian terminology and concepts do have a distinct Christian flavor and sound. But somehow or other, the taste is distinctly different!

The Rosicrucians have a pantheistic world view. By this they believe that in some way, all of reality is a part of or an expression of the essence or nature of God. God is all. This pantheism colors every aspect of Rosicrucian belief. Because of this, it has much in common with other pantheistic cults such as Unity, Christian Science, Theosophy and The Mighty I Am.

It is not our intention in this Appendix to occupy ourselves at great length with the theology of Rosicrucianism which will generate, in the minds of most Christians, a great deal of heat, and very little, if any, light. But since the cult is effective in the Southwestern and Western parts of the United States and is penetrating the Eastern seaboard and Midwest with steady effectiveness, as evidenced by the establishment of Rosicrucian fellowship centers in key cities throughout the Midwest and the East, some mention should be made of its history and its theological structure as it affects the Christian doctrine of God, the Person, Nature and Work of Jesus Christ and the destiny of mankind.

Historical Synopsis

The founder of present day Rosicrucianism was Christianus Rosenkreutz (1378–1484), a German scholar who roundly opposed Roman Catholicism and claimed to be the revealer of the mysteries of the rose cross. From its inception, Rosicrucianism put emphasis upon the occult and the mystical relationship of Christianity to all the great religions of the world. It was by admission a secret society. It flourished in a day when secret societies were in vogue, and "a century after its origin, Rosicrucianism underwent a recrudescence in connection with Free Masonry, which not only deemed Rosicrucianism genuine, but even borrowed usages and customs from the writings of those who had satirized the fraternity" (Samuel Macauley Jackson, ed., *The New Schaff-Herzog Encyclopedia of Religious Knowledge*, Grand Rapids, MI: Baker Book House, 1977 reprint, vol. 10, p. 97).

In a world which was trying to analyze the meaning of comets, alchemy and Eastern occultism, Rosicrucianism proved to be an attractive alternative to orthodoxy. It was careful to utilize an orthodox Christian vocabulary, however, and to speak out vehemently against Roman Catholicism, Alchemy and dogmatic theology of any type, although it zealously promoted some of the principles of the Protestant Reformation, the theology of which, it might be noted, is the antithesis of Rosicrucian teaching!

Today there are more than 500 Rosicrucian centers throughout the world, and the headquarters of the largest faction of the movement (AMORC) to all intents and purposes, is in San Jose, California. The writer visited there in 1961 and obtained valuable information about the methods of the Rosicrucians in propagating their beliefs, as well as additional data about some of the more "spiritual" teachings.

Of all the modern Rosicrucian writers, the best known is the late Max Heindel.

In this age of ecumenicity, the Rosicrucians play heavily upon the notes of "universal brotherhood," publish millions of copies of their magazines (*The Rosicrucian Digest* and *Rosicrucian Forum*), and maintain the "supreme temple of North and South America," which is located in San Jose, California, in Rosicrucian Park.

This group of Rosicrucians, identified by the letters AMORC, deny being either a religion or a church. They identify themselves as a brotherhood or organization which is attempting to help mankind to master its destiny. AMORC, the largest Rosicrucian faction, has a membership of around 50,000 and accounts for over 90% of worldwide Rosicrucian membership.

Rosicrucians collectively probably number fewer than 60,000 worldwide, but due to a heavy advertising campaign, the zealous propagation of their brotherhood and destiny publications, Rosicrucianism is, in our time, a successful non-Christian cult, which uses the terminology of Christianity whenever possible (and profitable) to lead the untutored mind into the mazes of a philosophical religion so complex that those who know it best are content to admit readily the limitations of their own understanding.

Rosicrucianism and Christianity

1. *The Nature of God.*
It is a historic affirmation of Rosicrucianism that God is an impersonal being, composed of seven spirits, which manifest themselves as a "triune

godhead," or, Father, Son and Holy Spirit. Lest there be any doubt on the subject, Heindel, in one of his many books, declares:

> ... The seven spirits before the throne ... collectively, they are God, and make up the triune godhead ... the Father is the highest initiate among the humanity of the Saturn. ... The Son is the highest initiate of the Sun ... the Holy Spirit (Jehovah) is the highest initiate of the Moon. ...[1]

In such a semantic jungle, the nature of God, the holy Trinity, or Triune Deity of Biblical revelation undergoes total, if not complete, mutilation. It becomes a type of occult pantheism, culminating in an impersonal spirit-being, who is "collectively" God.

The Rosicrucians believe that the Trinity portrays aspects of God:

> ... the only begotten, the Word of whom John speaks, is the second aspect of the Supreme Being. This word, and it alone, is begotten of His Father, first aspect before all worlds. ... Therefore, the Only Begotten is the exalted Being which ranks above all else in the universe, save only the Power aspect, which created it.[2]

For the Rosicrucians, the Holy Spirit is Jehovah, the third aspect of the triune Godhead. But in the sense of Christian theology, these definitions are meaningless, since the Bible declares unequivocally that God is the Father, the Son and the Holy Spirit, three divine Persons, all sharing the same nature and attributes, coexistent, coequal and coeternal, and, above all else, personal. The Lord Himself declared:

> I AM THAT I AM ... Thus shalt thou say to the children of Israel, I AM hath sent me unto you (Exodus 3:14).

The Christian doctrine of the Trinity then, cannot be equated with the Rosicrucian caricature of it, although it is significant that the Rosicrucians do usually bend over backward as it were, in an attempt to make their pantheistic theology sound Christian, thus identifying it with the predominant form of religion in the United States, which is the Christian religion. They are equally at home among the Buddhists, Hindus or Mohammedans, and can adapt their theology much like chameleons adapt the color of their skins, to the protective coloration of the theological climate in which they find themselves. Such passages as Matthew 28:19; John 14:16 and 26; Luke 1:35; John 1:1 and 14; Colossians 2:9 and Acts 5:3, 4, etc., demonstrate the Christian doctrine of the Trinity beyond reasonable doubt.

2. *The Nature and Work of Jesus Christ.*

As Rosicrucianism stands opposed to the historic Christian doctrine of the Trinity, so also it opposes the true divinity of the Lord Jesus. Rosicrucianism teaches that Jesus Christ was not Jesus nor the only begotten Son of God. Instead, Jesus was a man, the highest luminary possible. The Christ-spirit was a manifestation of the cosmic Christ and the only begotten is "an exalted being which ranks above all else in the universe, save only the Power aspect which created it."[3]

---

[1] *The Rosicrucian Cosmo-Conception*, San Jose, CA: AMORC, n.d. pp. 376, 252.
[2] *Ibid.*, p. 374.
[3] *Ibid.*, p. 374.

It is obvious then, that as Christian Science divides Jesus and Christ, into Jesus, an apparent manifestation of manhood indwelled by a Christ-consciousness or idea, so Rosicrucianism employs the same type of spiritual schizophrenia and ends, as does Christian Science and all the Gnostic cults, with a divided Messiah.

In the philosophy of Rosicrucianism, "the Christ-spirit which entered the body of Jesus when Jesus Himself vacated it, was a ray from the cosmic Christ. We may follow Jesus back in His previous incarnations and can trace His growth to the present day."[4]

Jesus Christ, in the theology of the Rosicrucians, "was a spirit belonging to our human evolution, and so was Gautama Buddha,"—a theology which makes no allowance for the incarnation of the only God in the Person of the man from Nazareth (John 1:1, 14, 18).

Christianity and Rosicrucianism can never be reconciled because the former declares the absolute and unique Deity of the central figure of all history, and the latter relegates Him to a pantheon of incarnate deities or spirits. Our Lord vigorously denied such inferences when He stated, concerning His own mission: "All that ever came before me are thieves and robbers: but the sheep did not hear them" (John 10:8).

The Christ of Holy Scripture cannot be divided and subdivided into pantheistic and Gnostic segments. He refuses to be considered one of many equally good ways, or a mere aspect of the truth. Instead, it is His declaration that He is the Life itself, and as such, the only Way and the Truth. It is folly of the highest order to attempt to equate the Christ of revelation with the Christ of Rosicrucianism. For Heindel's Christ, and the Christ of the "brotherhood," is in reality, "another Jesus" (2 Corinthians 11:4), the creation of a fertile imagination and a broad intellect (Heindel) projected into the twentieth century, infused with occult and mystical teachings, and lightly coated with Biblical terminology. He is a clever counterfeit, but nevertheless, he is a counterfeit!

It is unnecessary to point out the Rosicrucian concept of the atonement, since for them it is not vicarious, in the sense that Christ paid the penalty for all sin. The primary reason is that they do not believe that Jesus was *the* Christ.

It is the teaching of Holy Scripture that there is but one God (Deuteronomy 6:4; Galatians 3:20), and that to know Him and Jesus Christ whom He has sent, is to possess life eternal (John 17). The Rosicrucian Fellowship does not know Him; it does not accept His vicarious sacrifice for all sin (Isaiah 53), and substitutes reincarnation for resurrection, teaching that man passes through stages of incarnations, through various spheres of progressive perfection, all a product of cosmic evolution.

The History and Destiny of Mankind

We conclude this brief survey of the Rosicrucian Fellowship by noting that its concept of mankind is also un-Biblical. In the thinking of Rosicru-

---

[4] *The Rosicrucian Philosophy, Max Heindel,,* p. 181.

cians, there have been various epics or stages of the development of man upon the earth. For instance, blacks were known as the Lemurian, or the third of these epics. He was followed by the red race, the yellow race and the white race. The white race, according to the Rosicrucians, were originally Semetic and were the fifth of the Atlantean race.

Along with this type of occult anthropology, the Rosicrucians would have us believe that Atlantis, a mythical lost continent, brought forth this race, which were the ancestors of those destined to become the fathers of the Aryan race of our day.

For Rosicrucianism, man is evolving into a divine being, and in fact, he is a divine being of sorts, a type of demi-god, in the grand cosmic evolutionary scale.

With such a view of man, the Rosicrucians can indeed forge ahead to build an international world brotherhood, because, in their theology, cosmic evolution and the law of progression point ever onward and upward to the eventual salvation of all mankind.

The reader might take into consideration in this connection, the words of the Apostle Paul who dimmed the Rosicrucian illumination of occult anthropology when he declared that "the first man (was) Adam" (1 Corinthians 15:45).

This is a terse judgment of the concept of progressive races, some of which, according to Rosicrucianism, antidate Adam. Under the inspiration of the Holy Spirit, the Apostle declares that there was only *one* human race, and the father of it is Adam, and that in this man Adam, all have died (Romans 5:12; 1 Corinthians 15:22) because of sin, Rosicrucians not excepted. All the occult mumbo-jumbo, secret symbols and rosy crosses in creation therefore cannot put "Humpty" Adam together again. There has been only one remedy for sin in all history, and that is divine grace, expressed prophetically before the cross, and experientially after the cross. There can be no substitute for the commands of God, and the Rosicrucian Fellowship would do well to hearken to the words of Him who left as His heritage to mankind, a blood-spattered cross, not one shrouded with roses. It was His promise to His followers that, "Because I live, you will live also." This is the Christ of historic Christianity, and it is His word, not ours that will be the judge of all men, including the Rosicrucians "in that day" (2 Timothy 1:12, 18).

THE CHURCH OF THE NEW JERUSALEM— SWEDENBORGIANISM

It is virtually impossible to study the field of cult systems without coming to grips with the theology of the Church of the New Jerusalem, which, although small in number in America (around 8,000 members in two different conferences), wields a considerable influence in intellectual church circles. This is true both in the United States and abroad. In foreign countries, particularly in England and in the Scandanavian nations, this particular cult has declined in growth over the last few years, with a worldwide membership of around 50,000.

Whereas most if not all of the major cult systems are the products of individuals who could scarcely be called intellectuals, the Church of the New Jerusalem had as its founder, one of the most gifted and respected intellectuals of any age—Emanuel Swedenborg.

Swedenborg was born in Stockholm, Sweden, on January 29, 1688. He died in London on March 29, 1772, in his eighty-fifth year. The son of the Reverend Jasper Swedenborg, noted Lutheran minister and court chaplain to the king of Sweden, he was later to become a professor and dean of the University of Upsala. Swedenborg indeed sprang from noble roots, and at an early age distinguished himself as a mathematician, mining expert, engineer and inventor. So enormous were his contributions to his homeland, particularly in the area of high finance and in mining, that in 1808, thirty-six years after his death, his remains were removed from their crypt in the Lutheran church in Princes Square, Radcliffe Highway, London, and transported by the Swedish navy to their final resting place in a cathedral in Upsala. Some two years after this, the king of Sweden and his family, in the presence of numerous dignitaries and churchmen, dedicated a memorial to him, which action had been unanimously voted by the Swedish parliament.

Swedenborg received his education at Upsala and then traveled for the next four years in Germany, Holland, England and France. He occupied his spare time between studies with various inventions.

William White, in his life story of Swedenborg, stated that, as a result of his inventive genius, Swedenborg produced "a new stove, a magazine air gun, methods of salt manufacture . . . and drew plans for a flying machine and the construction of docks" (p. 29, also see *Transactions of the International Swedenborg Congress*, 1910, p. 5).

To add to his achievements during this particular period of inventive genius, Swedenborg was working on what he called a sort of ship in which a man can go below the surface of the sea and do great damage to the fleet of an enemy.

At the close of his journeys abroad, Swedenborg wrote various books and attracted the attention of his sovereign, King Charles XII, who recognized his genius and appointed him a professor in the Swedish College of Mines. Following the death of the King in 1718, Swedenborg became a member of the Swedish Diet. In his capacity as Royal Assessor of Mines, he traveled extensively throughout Europe, broadening his background and already tremendous grasp of philosophy, art, theology and metaphysics. This he dutifully recorded in his *Diary of Travel*, a type of John Gunther approach to the Europe of the eighteenth century.

Swedenborg was the associate of kings, princes, scholars, mathematicians, engineers, astronomers and theologians. Few men have ever attained the degree of acceptance and prominence which he enjoyed during his long life, a recognition which extended to multiple fields of interest, and was a lasting tribute to his intellectual breadth and brilliance.

The year 1745 marks the turning point in Swedenborg's career as a world figure in many fields of endeavor, for it was then that he maintained that he received a divine summons to become "both a seer and a revelator of the things of the spiritual world, and simultaneously of the spiritual truth and doctrine which underlies the literal and symbolic sense of the sacred Scriptures." Between the years 1743 and 1749 Swedenborg maintained that he experienced heavenly visions and periods of great temptation, which culminated in a prodigious writing program, producing such works as *Arcana Coelestia; The Earths in the Universe; The White Horse of the Apocalypse; The Apocalypse Explained; The Last Judgment; The New Jerusalem and Its Heavenly Doctrines* and *The Apocalypse Revealed.*

Swedenborg went on to publish *The Angelic Wisdom Respecting the Divine Love and Wisdom,* 1763; *The Angelic Wisdom Respecting the Divine Providence,* 1764; *The Delights of Wisdom Concerning Conjugial Love,* 1768; *A Re-fixed Position Concerning the Doctrine of the New Church, Signified by the New Jerusalem in Revelation,* 1769; and his final work, *The True Christian Religion Containing the Universal Theology of the New Church, or Universal Theology and the New Church,* 1771. This was, quite literally, a compendium of his entire theological structure.

One authority on Swedenborg also points out that,

> He wrote books on algebra, giving the first account in Swedish of the differential in integral calculus; on a mode of finding the longitude at sea by the moon; on decimal money and measures; on the motion and position of the earth and planets; on the depth of the sea and the greater force of the tides in the ancient world; on docks, sluices and salt works; on chemistry and on atomic geometry. . . . After some philosophical writing, dissatisfied with his results, he studied anatomy and physiology and wrote books thereon. . . . At the age of fifty-four, Swedenborg was probably one of the most learned men alive, taking learning as meaning acquaintance with the universe as then known. One small indication of this is the fact that the then president of our royal society, Sir Hans Sloan, invited him to become a corresponding member.
>
> Then a curious thing happened. In 1743 he had spiritual illumination, with tremblings, voices, lights, etc. and began to have access to the spiritual world, or to think that he had. During the years 1749 to 1756 he published

in London his *Arcana Coelestia,* in four volumes quarto, and later, other works containing the exposition of his doctrines, which were mainly concerned with the spiritual interpretation of the Scriptures, and particularly, of Genesis and Exodus. Much of this seems fanciful, but the thought is always systematic, and no one can reasonably say that Swedenborg was insane. Moreover, he was shrewd in worldly affairs, affable in society, and discussed politics and finance in the Swedish Diet like a man of the world. For a score of years after, he began to write and publish his theological works, which number about forty volumes.

But this exposition of Scripture, received, as he believed, direct from the Lord, and considered by him to be the important part of his work, is less interesting to us than his spiritual experiences, which are mostly described in his spiritual diary, from whence he copied extracts occasionally into his theological works. These experiences were admittedly of such a character, that in an ordinary man they would have sufficed to qualify him for an asylum. Swedenborg talked, or thought he talked, with Luther, Calvin, St. Augustine, St. Paul—arguing theological questions with them and disagreeing violently with the last-named, and many others including "one who, it was given me to understand, was Cicero."

All this, although probably not hallucinatory, is at least perilous stuff, and the Swedenborgians have done wisely not to base much on it. He wrote automatically, heard clairaudiently, and saw writings and the very words of the writings, even with the eyes shut. But there are a few incidents on record which are evidential, and these may reasonably give us pause before deciding for a subjective explanation of this seer's experiences.[1]

I shall allude in a few moments to this passage. But enough has been shown to establish beyond reasonable doubt that Swedenborg was a unique individual whose mind and influence reached into many quarters in the age in which he lived. Frank Sewall best summed it up when he wrote:

> Like many leaders of the world's thought, Swedenborg has required the vistas of the years by which to be seen in his real significance. Immanuel Kant concealed his indebtedness to him under the persiflage of the "Dreams of the Spirit-Seer"; Goethe is more outspoken in his gratitude and his *Faust* is full of the Swedenborg world-view. Swedenborg's trinal monism, the doctrine that the one embraces in itself the three essential degrees, end, cause, effect: the grand man, or the human form of society; the spiritual, as being the real, world; the spiritual meaning as the true and essential meaning of the Scriptures; God as divine Man, visible and adorable in the glorified humanity of Jesus Christ; the doctrine of the world as a vast system of tremulations set in motion by its center, the infinite divine love, and transmitted through successive spiritual and natural spheres and atmospheres; of the kingdom of heaven as a kingdom of uses—these ideas are permeating all the newer developments of philosophic and religious thought. Early theological prejudice is giving way to profound respect; the time seems near when Swedenborg's own prophecy, from the words of Seneca, will be realized: "There will come those who will judge without offense or favor."[2]

[1] J. Arthur Hill, *Spiritualism: Its History, Phenomena, and Doctrine*, New York: George Doran, 1919, pp. 42–44.
[2] Frank Sewall in *The New Schaff-Herzog Encyclopedia of Religious Knowledge*, Samuel M. Jackson, ed., Grand Rapids, MI: Baker Book House, 1977 reprint, vol. 11, p. 188.

I cannot agree with Mr. Sewall relative to any idea of accepting Swedenborg's basic theological system, which I shall review shortly. But that his place in the intellectual hall of man is secure, no objective person can deny. Swedenborg's theological position, however, in the realms of non-Christian cultism, constitutes quite another area of concern. For genius though he was, his concept of the Bible, the writings of the Apostle Paul and numerous other books of the Old and New Testaments, places him well outside the pale of Christian theology. This is true not only concerning the Canon, but concerning such doctrines as the Nature of God, the Holy Trinity, the Atonement of Jesus Christ, and the doctrines of Salvation and Resurrection. We cannot ignore the person of Emanuel Swedenborg; in fact, as the years pass, through the church which he inspired and the reputation which he earned, he is becoming a growing influence to be reckoned with and carefully examined in the light of historic Christianity.

No less an authority than the noted scholar, Conrad J. Bergendoff, writing in the *Encyclopedia of Religion* edited by Virgilius Ferm, declared of Swedenborg's theology and background:

> Swedenborg's student days included impressions from Rudbeck at Upsala, Newton, Boyle, Halley, Locke in England, Polhem in Sweden, the Cartesian philosophy and the Cambridge Neo-platonists.
>
> The *Principia* (1734) explained the universe in mechanistic terms. A mystical view pervaded the *Oeconomia regni animalis* (1736); the world was now less a machine, more an organism. The *anima* receives illumination from the central source of life and light when the *mens* controls man's physical nature. Between the physical and spiritual world there is a close correspondence, each natural phenomena shadowing a spiritual reality . . . this idea was extended to the mystical correspondence between words and their inner meaning—a basis for his later spiritual interpretation of Scripture, which was a means whereby the divine was communicated to the mind of man.
>
> In Amsterdam, 1736, Swedenborg had an experience of photism; in Amsterdam, 1744, and in London, 1745, he experienced visions which he interpreted as revelations of the Creator-Redeemer. Henceforth he proclaimed the truth received by direct vision, though the biblical imagery of *De Cultu Amore Dei* (1745) concealed much the same cosmology and psychology as the earlier works. Even his visions were more confirmation than a source of his speculations.
>
> The theology of Swedenborg is systematically presented in *The True Christian Religion* (1771). The orthodox doctrines of the Trinity and the Atonement were repudiated. Redemption consists of the Incarnate God overcoming the increasing powers of hell. Man's freedom enables him to choose and follow the good. On death he enters the realm of the spirits, when he either ascends to the heavenly sphere, becoming an angel, or descends to hell, becoming an evil spirit. Following a spiritual mode of interpreting Scripture which he held to be inspired, Swedenborg considered the Judgment to have come in 1757 and Christ's Second Coming as a victory over rebellious spirits. The heavenly world corresponds to the human, and even marriage finds transcendent meaning in heavenly marriage of kindred souls. . . . The orthodox churches must give way to the New Church (which

dates from the completion of *The True Christian Religion*, 1771) when men will be correctly instructed in the truth of God.[3]

The organization of The Church of the New Jerusalem took place in London, in 1788, although it is generally traced back by its membership to the Second Coming of Christ, which, according to Swedenborg, took place when he received "the key to the interpretation of Scripture." There can be little doubt that Swedenborg's revelation of what he termed the spiritual meaning of Scripture did indeed become the doctrinal basis of the church formed in his honor.

The first general conference of the church met in 1789. It was organized in 1821 the "General Conference of the Ministers and Other Members of the New Church Signified by the New Jerusalem in the Apocalypse, or Revelation of John."

This particularly British convention in 1926 numbered seventy societies, with 7,100 members.

The Swedenborg Society since the year 1810 has published a voluminous amount of literature, specializing in translations of Swedenborg's works. Branches of the church are today to be found in Africa, South America, Russia, Italy, Sweden and many other countries.

In the United States, the church was organized in Baltimore, Maryland, in 1792. Its name is "The General Convention of the New Jerusalem in the United States," the name taken in 1817. The churches are essentially autonomous, but are bound together in a cooperative type of association governed by a general convention, which meets annually. Under the powers of the convention, the education and ordination of pastors for the establishment of missions, orders of worship and church government, etc., are carried out.

The Church of the New Jerusalem has had its internal controversies, however, particularly in 1890 when the Pennsylvania association, which might be termed "fundamentalist Swedenborgians," insisted upon the virtual canonization of Swedenborg's writings, and withdrew when they could not force this upon the convention. In 1897 this group became known as "The General Church of the New Jerusalem," which has a presiding bishop, a cathedral and an educational institution, located in Bryn Athyn, Pennsylvania.

The Church of the New Jerusalem is, therefore, inextricably bound to the teachings of Swedenborg and his interpretations of the Bible. Women may join the church at the age of eighteen and men at the age of twenty-one, but only after studying the writings of Swedenborg for some six months. The Christian sacraments of baptism and communion are copied in the church, as are the marriage and burial services. The official liturgy (resembling in practically every detail the Anglican *Book of Prayer*) and the church government are Episcopal, with but minor alterations.

Such is the background of Swedenborgianism, seen in the perspective of history. In the realm of theology, however, a somewhat different picture emerges.

---

[3]Conrad Bergendoff in *Enclyclopedia of Religion*, Vergilius Ferm, ed., New York: Philosophical Library, 1945, p. 752.

The Occult Theology of Swedenborg

As has been noted in the preceding history, Swedenborg considered himself, from 1745 until his death, the seer of a new revelation from God which superseded the interpretational powers of the apostles, church fathers and the reformers. This is a singular fact which emphasizes that modesty was not one of his strong points. Mr. Hill has already mentioned a point which can be easily documented, namely Swedenborg's preoccupation with dreams, visions and alleged messages and conversations with spirits and the spirit world. It is of no small significance that Sir Arthur Conan Doyle, the great advocate of Spiritism, and every spiritist, historian and theologian of note, claim Swedenborg as a medium who practiced clairvoyance and other phenomena associated with Spiritism. Swedenborg never denied such practices, and therefore, whether his followers wish to concede it or not, he was most certainly, in a large area of his theological and metaphysical practices and thought, a thoroughgoing spiritist. One instance of Swedenborg's clairvoyance should be noted in order to underscore this fact:

> In September, 1759, Swedenborg was one of a party of sixteen guests at the home of Mr. William Castel at Gottenburg, three hundred miles from Stockholm. He had arrived from England at four o'clock P.M.
> About six o'clock Swedenborg went out and returned to the company, quite pale and alarmed. He said a dangerous fire had just broken out in Stockholm at the Sodermalm (Gottenburg is about fifty German miles from Stockholm), and that it was spreading very fast. He said that the house of one of his friends, whom he named, was already in ashes, and that his own was in danger. At eight o'clock, after he had been out again, he joyfully exclaimed, "Thank God! The fire is extinguished the third door from my house!" This news occasioned great commotion throughout the whole city. . . .
> It was announced to the governor that same evening. Sunday morning, Swedenborg was summoned to the governor, who questioned him concerning the disaster. Swedenborg described the fire precisely, how it had begun and in what manner it ceased, and how long it had continued. On the same day the news spread throughout the city, and as the governor thought it worthy of attention, the consternation was considerably increased; because many were troubled because of their friends and property. . . . On Monday evening a messenger arrived at Gottenburg, who was dispatched by the Board of Trade during the term of the fire. In the letters brought by him the fire was described in precisely the manner stated by Swedenborg. On Tuesday morning a royal courier arrived at the governor's with a melancholy intelligence of the fire, of the losses it had occasioned, and of the houses which had been damaged and ruined, not in the least differing from that which Swedenborg had given at the very time when it happened; for the fire was extinguished at eight o'clock.[4]

This remarkable piece of clairvoyance is in company with Swedenborg's actual communication with a deceased Dutch ambassador. This "ghost" had informed Swedenborg that his wife should not pay for a silver service as

[4]See Borowsky's, *Darstellung Des Lebens und Charakters*, Immanuel Kant, Konigsberg. 1804, pp. 211–225. Trans. in *Dreams of a Spirit Seer*, pp. 158, 159, appen. Letter from Kant to Charlotte Von Knobloch. See also Tafels, *Documents Concerning Swedenborg*, Vol. II, Part One, p. 628.

demanded by a goldsmith, for he declared he had paid the smith several months earlier. The receipt of the transaction was in a bureau in a room upstairs in the house which the widow then occupied. The lady insisted that the bureau had been thoroughly searched, but Swedenborg informed her that her husband had a secret drawer behind the left drawer of the bureau where the receipt would be found. Upon complying with Swedenborg's instructions, the widow found the receipt precisely as he had described it. Jung Stilling in his *Theory of Pneumotology*, page 92, recounts this, as does Kant in *Dreams of a Spirit Seer*, appendix, pages 157 and 158. The gentleman who "received the proof from Swedenborg" was an intimate friend of Stilling.

Such evidence of Swedenborg's communication with the spirit world in direct violation of the express commands of Scripture (Leviticus 19:31; 20:6) would be sufficient to make any thoughtful Christian suspicious of his theological system, even before examining it thoroughly. But happily, an exhaustive analysis of his voluminous works is not necessary to reveal the fact that Swedenborg was far from being a Christian, and certainly was not a Christian theologian.

The following quotations drawn from his basic writings reveal his thinking in certain key areas of Christian theology and are reproduced for the purpose of contrast with the teachings of Scripture.

Doctrines

I. *The Holy Scriptures—the Word of God*

Which are the books of the Word? That the books of the Word are all those which have the internal sense; but that those books which have not the internal sense are not the Word. The books of the Word in the Old Testament are: The five books of Moses, the book of Joshua, the book of the Judges, the two books of Samuel, the two books of the Kings, the Psalms of David, the prophets Isaiah and Jeremiah, Ezekiel, Daniel, Hosea, Joel, Amos, Obadiah, Jonah, Micah, Nahum, Habakkuk, Zephaniah, Haggai, Zechariah and Malachi. In the New Testament, the four evangelists, Matthew, Mark, Luke and John and The Apocalypse. The rest have not the internal sense . . . The book of Job is an ancient book, which indeed contains internal sense, but not in series . . . (Emanuel Swedenborg, *Miscellaneous Theological Works*, New York: Philosophical Library, 1916, p. 312).

II. *The Trinity of God*

1. That many of the false tenets . . . as likewise concerning the person of Christ, together with all the heresy from the first ages down to the present day, have flowed from no other source than from a doctrine founded upon the idea of three Gods. We have not room to demonstrate within the limits of this epitomy, but that assertion shall be shown and proved at large in the work itself (C. O. Sigstedt, *The Swedenborg Epic*, New York: Twayne, 1952, p. 177).

2. From the Nicene Trinity and the Athanasian Trinity together a faith arose by which the whole Christian Church has been perverted. That both the Nicene and Athanasian trinities are a Trinity of Gods can be seen from the creeds (*Ibid.*).

3. After this they proceeded to deliberate about the Holy Spirit; and previous thereto they laid open the idea generally received concerning God the Father, the Son and the Holy Spirit which is, that God the Father is seated on high with the Son at His right hand, that by them is sent forth the Holy Spirit to enlighten and instruct mankind. But instantly a voice was heard from heaven saying, "We cannot endure an idea formed on such a conception. . . . There is not a mediating God distinct from Him (Jehovah); much less is there a third God distinct from two others, as one person is distinct from two others, as one person is distinct from another person; wherefore, let the former idea which is vexing and frivolous be removed, and let this which is just and right be received, then you will see clearly. . . . One God cannot come forth and proceed from another, by another, but what is divine may come forth and proceed from one God? Is not the Divine Essence one and indivisible, and inasmuch as the Divine Essence is God, is not God therefore one indivisible? On hearing these words, they that sat on the seats unanimously agreed in this conclusion, that the Holy Spirit is not a distinct person of Himself, consequently not a distinct God of Himself; but that by the Holy Spirit is meant the divine sanctity, coming forth and proceeding from the one and only omnipresent God, who is the Lord (*Miscellaneous Theological Works, op. cit.*, pp. 249, 250).

III. *Vicarious Atonement*

1. "Who does not know that God is essential compassion and mercy . . . and who does not hereby see that it is a contradiction to assert that mercy itself or goodness itself can heal man from anger, become his enemy, turn himself away from him and determine on his damnation, and still continue to be the same divine being or God? Such things can scarcely be attributed to a good man, but only to a wicked man, thus not to an angel of heaven, but only to an angel of hell; wherefore, it is abominable to ascribe them to God. That they have been ascribed to Him appears evident from the declaration of many fathers, churches and councils from the first ages unto the present day; also from the inferences which have necessarily followed from first principles and to their derivatives, or from causes and to their effects, as from a head into the members; such as, that He required to be reconciled; that He is reconciled through the love He bears toward the Son, and by His intercession and mediation; that He required to be appeased by the view of the extreme sufferings of His Son; so to be brought back to mercy and constrained as it were, to show it, and thus from an enemy to be made a friend, and to adopt those who were the children of wrath, as the children of grace. That the notion that God can impute the righteousness and merits of His Son to an unrighteous man, who supplicates it from faith alone, is also a mere human invention, as will be seen in the last analysis of this work" (*Ibid.*, pp. 202, 203).

2. "This I can affirm, that whenever the angels hear anyone say, that God determined in anger on the damnation of the human race, and as an enemy was reconciled by His Son, as by another God begotten from Himself, they are affected in a manner similar to those who from an uneasiness in their bowels and stomach are excited to vomiting; on which occasion they say, What can be more insane than to affirm such things to God?" (*Ibid.*).

3. "That no other salvation is believed this day than such as is instantaneous, from an immediate act of mercy is evident from hence . . . for if the cooperation is taken away which is effective through the exercise of

charity by man as of himself, the spontaneous cooperation which is said to follow faith of itself, becomes passive action, which is nonsense, and a contradiction of terms; for supposing this to be the case, what need would there be of anything more than such momentary and immediate prayer as this: 'Save me, O God, for the sake of the sufferings of Thy Son, who has washed me from my sins in His own blood, and presents me pure, righteous and holy before thy throne?' . . . And this ejaculation of the mouth might avail even at the hour of death, if not sooner, as a seed of justification. But nevertheless, instantaneous salvation, by an immediate act of mercy, is to this day a fiery, flying serpent in the church, and that thereby religion is abolished, security introduced and damnation imputed to the Lord, may be seen . . . in the work concerning Divine Providence, published at Amsterdam in the year 1764" (*Ibid.*, pp. 204, 205).

4. "Hence may be seen the import of the Lord's words in Mark, 'He that believeth and is baptized shall be saved, but he that believeth not shall be damned' (Mark 16:16).

"Here, to believe, signifies to acknowledge the Lord and to receive divine truths from him by means of the Word, and to be baptized, is to be regenerated by the Lord by means of those truths . . . hence it is evident what is signified by these words of the Lord, 'Except a man be gotten of water and of the spirit, he cannot enter into the kingdom of God'; namely, that unless man is regenerated by the truths of faith, and by a life according to them, he cannot be saved . . . that all regeneration is effected by the truths of faith and by a life according to them . . . Let those therefore who are baptized remember that baptism itself confers upon its subjects neither faith nor salvation, but testifies that they will receive faith and that they will be saved if they are regenerated" (*Ibid.*, pp. 110, 111).[5]

IV. *The Destiny of Man*

1. "Man is so created that, as to his internal, he cannot die . . . this internal exists in every man who is born: his external is that by which he brings into effect the things which belong to his faith and love. The internal of man is the spirit, and the external is the body. The external, or the body, is suited to the performance of uses in the natural world, and is rejected or put off, at death, but the internal, which is called the spirit, and which is suited to the performance of uses in the spiritual world, never dies. After death, this internal exists as a good spirit and an angel, if the man has been good during his abode in this world, but if during that time he has lived in evil, he is, after death, an evil spirit. . . . The spirit of man after the dissolution of the body appears in the spiritual world in a human form in every respect, as in the natural world . . . except that he is not encompassed with the gross body which he had in the world. This he leaves when he dies, nor does he ever resume it. This continuation of life is meant by the resurrection. The reason why men believe that they shall not rise again before the Last Judgment, when, as they suppose, the whole creation will be destroyed, is that they do not understand the Word, and because sensual men place

---

[5]It is generally recognized as poor Biblical scholarship to *base* any doctrine upon a passage of questionable authenticity such as Mark 16:16. The testimony of some of the best and most ancient New Testament manuscripts is that the last portion of Mark was interpolated *after* the original composition of the gospel. Swedenborg and his "ghosts" should have stayed with Biblical texts of undisputed veracity!

all their life in the body and imagine that unless the body be re-animated, the man be no more" (*Ibid.*, pp. 117, 118).

Some Answers to Swedenborg

Swedenborg is consistently and energetically refuted by the epistles of Paul, particularly, the Book of Romans, chapters five through eight, which Swedenborg detested with abject horror. By attempting to circumscribe the New Testament revelation of Christianity to the gospels and the Book of Revelation, Swedenborg revealed the essential weakness of his theological system. He was apparently well aware of the fact that Pauline theology, if accepted at face value, would vitiate almost en toto his own. So he began with the basic assumption that *he* was right, and that the Apostle Paul was wrong! In some of his visions and dreams, he stated that he actually argued with Paul, Luther, Calvin and others. And, as ego triumphed, these great thinkers all retreated before Swedenborg's new revelations.

However, one factor must never be forgotten, and that is the statement that the New Testament is the criterion for measuring all subsequent revelations, and whatever is found to be contrary to it, must be and always has been, rejected by the Christian Church.

Swedenborg would have done well to remember that the interpretations of dreams and visions, and the things of the dimension of the spirit "belong to God" (Genesis 40:8), and that we are constantly admonished to accept no other gospel, even if it be revealed by an "angel from heaven" (Galatians 1:8, 9), two points he apparently overlooked. The Apostle Peter, ever consistent with Paul, urges the Christian Church to always remember that "prophecy came not at any time by the will of man, but holy men of God spoke as they were moved by the Holy Ghost" (2 Peter 1:21). But since Swedenborg did not believe in the person of the Holy Spirit, it is easy to understand how he could reject such divine counsel.

True to the pattern of most non-Christian cults and cult leaders, Swedenborg vigorously attacked the Christian doctrine of the Trinity. Apparently he was unaware of the fact that he was involved in contradiction when he asserted that Jesus Christ was Jehovah, while at the same time he denied the tri-unity of Jehovah, so clearly taught in both the Old and New Testaments (see Genesis 1:26; Isaiah 6:8; Zechariah 12:10; Luke 1:35; Matthew 3:16, 17; Matthew 28:19, etc.).

Dr. Charles Hodge, the great Princeton theologian, recognized the dangers of Swedenborg's theology and summed them up in his own terse manner when he wrote:

> Concerning God, he taught that He was not only essence but form, and that that form was human. He called God "the eternal God-Man." There are two kinds of bodies, material and spiritual. Every man, besides his external material body has another, which is internal and spiritual. The latter has all the organs of the former, so that it can see, hear, and feel. At death the outer body is laid aside, and the soul thereafter acts through the ethereal or spiritual vestment. This is the only resurrection which Swedenborg admitted. There is no rising again of the bodies laid in the grave. As however

the spiritual corresponds to the material, those who know each other in this world will enjoy mutual recognition in the world to come. This feature of his anthropology is connected with his doctrine concerning God. For as the soul from its nature forms for itself a body for action . . . so the essence of God forms for itself a spiritual body for external manifestation.

As there is but one divine essence, Swedenborg maintained that there can be but one divine person. The Church doctrine of the Trinity he regarded as tritheistic. He admitted a Trinity of principle, but not of person. As soul and body in man are one person, and from them proceeds the activity which operates without, so in God the divine and human are the Father and the Son, as one person, and the Holy Spirit is their efficiency or sanctifying influence.

Concerning man, Swedenborg taught that he was created in the image of God, and was a creature of a very exalted nature. The Scriptural account of the fall he understood allegorically of the apostasy of the Church. Men, however, he admits, are sinful, and are even born with a bias to evil, but they have not lost their ability to do good. They consequently need redemption. They are susceptible of being delivered from evil not only because they retain their moral liberty, but also because in virtue of the inward spiritual body they are capable of intercourse with spiritual beings. . . . Swedenborg reports many instances in which he conversed with God and angels, good and bad. By angels, he meant men who had departed this life. He did not admit the existence of any created intelligence other than man.

Christ he held to be Jehovah, the only living and true God, the creator, preserver, and ruler of the world. As this divine person was God and man from eternity, his incarnation, or manifestation in the flesh, consisted in his assuming a material body with its physical life in the womb of the Virgin Mary. This was the body which grew, suffered, and died. In the case of ordinary men the material body is left forever in the grave, but in the case of Christ the outward body was gradually refined and glorified, until it was lost in that which is spiritual and eternal. This idea of a twofold body in Christ is not by any means peculiar to Swedenborg. . . .

Christ's redemptive work does not consist in his bearing our sins upon the tree, or in making satisfaction to the justice of God for our offenses. All idea of such satisfaction Swedenborg rejects. The work of salvation is entirely subjective. Justification is pardon granted on repentance. The people of God are made inwardly righteous, and being thus holy are admitted to the presence of God and holy spirits in heaven (Charles Hodge, *Systematic Theology*, Grand Rapids, MI: William B. Eerdmans Publishing Company, reprint 1977, vol. 2, pp. 421-423).

Dr. Hodge's evaluation is, of course, accurate, and Swedenborg's denial of the person of the Holy Spirit, as previously mentioned, places him and his followers not only outside historic Christian theology, but in diametric opposition to the express declaration of the Word of God.

The Apostle Peter, in dealing with the sin of Ananias and Sapphira, most explicitly declared that the Holy Spirit was a person to whom men could lie, as did they, and that in perpetrating this sin, its magnitude could only be realized when it was understood that "thou hast not lied unto men, but unto God" (Acts 5:4, 5).

Numerous other incidents in the New Testament can be used to document the person of the Holy Spirit, and Swedenborg's denial of the vicarious nature of the atonement needs no serious refutation in the light of such passages as Isaiah 53, Matthew 20:28, Mark 10:45 and 1 Peter 2:24.

In his epistle to the Romans, chapter five, the Apostle Paul underscores the role of our Lord as the "second Adam," who died for us when we were "yet sinners," and his entire fifteenth chapter of his first epistle to the Corinthians is devoted to proving the resurrection of the body, citing Christ as the archetype of that resurrection (see also Colossians 1:15–18; 1 Thessalonians 4:13–17; 2 Thessalonians 1). Far from Swedenborg's concept that Christ's body was not raised in mortal flesh and bones, and that man will not participate in this resurrection, the redeemed to immortality and the unregenerate to eternal judgment, the Bible is replete with references to just such a historical and still future event. The Book of Revelation, of which he was so fond, refutes his position entirely by teaching the very thing Swedenborg denied, namely, that there will be a resurrection of both the just and the unjust (Revelation 20:1–14), an event declared to be in conjunction with "the appearing of the glory of the great God and our Saviour, Jesus Christ" (Titus 2:13).

Quite to the contrary then where Swedenborg's theology is involved, Jesus Christ's Second Coming did not take place in the eighteenth century. The New Jerusalem has not descended out of heaven from God. Our resurrection has not taken place, and judgment has neither begun nor consummated. Swedenborg, despite his acknowledged brilliance and abilities, is found in far too many places to be in opposition to the teachings of the Word of God, and demonstrates in a most unique way an analysis of this type of mind. Oddly enough, this type was described by the Apostle Paul, whom Swedenborg could not abide:

> For Christ sent me not to baptize, but to preach the gospel: not with wisdom of words, lest the cross of Christ should be made of none effect. For the preaching of the cross is to them that perish foolishness; but unto us which are saved it is the power of God. For it is written, I will destroy the wisdom of the wise, and will bring to nothing the understanding of the prudent. Where is the wise? where is the scribe? where is the disputer of this world? hath not God made foolish the wisdom of this world? For after that in the wisdom of God the world by wisdom knew not God, it pleased God by the foolishness of preaching to save them that believe. For the Jews require a sign, and the Greeks seek after wisdom: But we preach Christ crucified, unto the Jews a stumblingblock, and unto the Greeks foolishness; But unto them which are called, both Jews and Greeks, Christ the power of God, and the wisdom of God. Because the foolishness of God is wiser than men; and the weakness of God is stronger than men. For ye see your calling, brethren, how that not many wise men after the flesh, not many mighty, not many noble, are called: But God hath chosen the foolish things of the world to confound the wise; and God hath chosen the weak things of the world to confound the things which are mighty; And base things of the world, and things which are despised, hath God chosen, yea, and things which are not, to bring to nought things that are: That no flesh should glory in his presence. But of him are ye in Christ Jesus, who of God is made unto us wisdom, and righteousness, and sanctification, and redemption: That, according as it is written, He that glorieth, let him glory in the Lord (1 Corinthians 1:17–31).

It would be possible to go on at some length in a refutation of Swedenborg's theology, but the issues, we believe, are clearly discernible, as is the verdict of Scripture. Swedenborg was a rationalist, and paradoxically, a mystic. He was one who absorbed the introspective and subjective philosophy of René Descàrtes, and the empiricism of John Locke, which he combined with the transcendentalism of Immanuel Kant, thus forming a mold into which Christian theology was poured, and what would not go into the mold (selected Old Testament works, the Pauline epistles, Acts, James, Peter, Jude, etc.), he simply discarded. What emerged was a deeply speculative philosophical system of theology, couched in a redefined Christian terminology, and buttressed with mystical visions, trances and dreams. These, when apparently confirmed by clairvoyant experiences, such as the Stockholm fire episode previously narrated, gave some credence to his claims and still continue to deceive many so-called intelligent persons today.

In his counsel to the church at Colosse, the Apostle Paul uttered a warning which the followers of Swedenborg in particular might well take cognizance of:

> Beware lest any man spoil you through philosophy and vain deceit, after the tradition of men, after the rudiments of the world, and not after Christ. For in him dwelleth all the fulness of the Godhead bodily (Colossians 2:8, 9).

The great tragedy of Emanuel Swedenborg is that he would not submit himself and his great mind to the discipline of the Holy Spirit and the Scriptures. Because of this, and because of his deliberated preoccupation with spiritism and the occult, in direct disobedience to the express teachings of God, he was despoiled, even as Paul had warned. He was deceived by dreams and visions and the machinations of him whom the Scriptures describe as the "spirit that now worketh in the children of disobedience" (Ephesians 2:2b).

BIBLIOGRAPHY

GENERAL REFERENCES

Adair, James R., and Ted Miller, eds. *Escape From Darkness.* Wheaton: Victor Books, 1982.

Atkins, G. *Modern Religious Cults and Movements.* New York: Fleming H. Revell Co., 1923.

Bach, Marcus. *They Have Found a Faith.* New York: Bobbs-Merrill, 1946.

Bjornstad, James. *Counterfeits at Your Door.* Ventura: Gospel Light Publications, 1979.

Boa, Kenneth. *Cults, World Religions and You.* Wheaton: Victor Books, 1977.

Braden, Charles S. *These Also Believe.* New York: Macmillan, 1951.

Clark, Elmer T. *The Small Sects in America.* (rev. ed.) Nashville: Abingdon Press, 1949.

Davies, Horton. *The Challenge of the Sects.* Philadelphia: Westminster Press, 1961.

Enroth, Ronald, et al. *A Guide to Cults and New Religions.* Downers Grove: InterVarsity Press, 1983.

Ferguson, Charles. *New Books of Revelation.* Garden City, N.J.: Doubleday-Doran, 1929; *Confusion of Tongues.* 1928.

Ferm, Vergilius. *Religion in the Twentieth Century.* New York: Philosophical Library, 1948.

Gerstner, John H. *The Theology of the Major Sects.* Grand Rapids: Baker Book House, 1960.

Gruss, Edmond C. *Cults and the Occult.* Grand Rapids: Baker Book House, 1982.

Hesselgrave, David J., ed. *Dynamic Religious Movements.* Grand Rapids: Baker Book House, 1978.

Hoekma, Anthony A. *The Four Major Cults.* Grand Rapids: Wm. B. Eerdmans Publishing Co., 1963.

Larson, Bob. *Larson's Book of Cults.* Wheaton: Tyndale House Publishers, Inc., 1982.

Lewis, Gordon R. *Confronting the Cults.* Grand Rapids: Baker Book House, 1966.

Martin, Walter R. *The Christian and the Cults.* Grand Rapids: Zondervan Publishing House, 1956; *The Rise of the Cults,* 1955.

_____. *Walter Martin's Cults Reference Bible.* Santa Ana: Vision House Publishers, 1981.

Mathison, Richard R. *Faiths, Cults and Sects of America.* Indianapolis: Bobbs-Merrill, 1960.

Mayer, F. E. *Religious Bodies of America.* St. Louis: Concordia, 1954.

Mead, Frank S. *Handbook of Denominations in the United States.* (rev. ed.) Nashville: Abingdon, 1956.

Melton, J. Gordon. *The Encyclopedia of American Religions.* (2 vols.) Wilmington, N.C.: McGrath Publishing Co., 1978.

Neve, J. L. *Churches and Sects in Christendom.* Minneapolis: Augsburg, 1952.

Passantino, Robert and Gretchen. *Answer to the Cultist at Your Door.* Eugene: Harvest House Publishers, 1981.

Petersen, William J. *Those Curious New Cults.* New Canaan, Conn.: Keats Publishers Inc., 1973, 1975.

Rosten, Leo, ed. *Religions In America.* New York: Simon and Schuster, 1962, 1963.

Sanders, J. Oswald, and Wright, J. Stafford. *Some Modern Religions.* London: Tyndale Press, 1956.

Schaff, Philip, and Herzog, Johann. *The New Schaff-Herzog Encyclopedia of Religious Knowledge.* (15 vols.) Grand Rapids: Baker Book House.

Sire, James W. *Scripture Twisting.* Downers Grove: InterVarsity Press, 1980.

Spittler, Russell P. *Cults and Isms.* Grand Rapids: Baker Book House, 1962.

Strong, James. *Strong's Exhaustive Concordance of the Bible.* New York: Abingdon-Cokesbury Press.

Van Baalen, Jan Karel. *Chaos of the Cults.* Grand Rapids: Wm. B. Eerdmans Publishing Co., 1962, 4th ed., rev.

Wyrick, Herbert M. *Seven Religious Isms.* Grand Rapids: Zondervan, 1940.

AUTHORITY OF THE SCRIPTURES

Allis, Oswald T. *The Old Testament: Its Claims and Its Critics.* Nutley, N.J.: Presbyterian and Reformed Publishing Co., 1972.

Archer, Gleason L. *Encyclopedia of Bible Difficulties.* Grand Rapids: Zondervan Publishing House, 1982.

Bruce, Frederick Fyvie. *The Books and the Parchment: Some Chapters on the Transmission of the Bible.* Revised Edition. Westwood, N.J.: Fleming H. Revell Co., 1953.

_____. *The New Testament Documents: Are They Reliable?* Grand Rapids: Wm. B. Eerdmans Publishing, 1953.

Geisler, Norman L. *Christian Apologetics.* Grand Rapids: Baker Book House, 1976.

_____. *Decide for Yourself: How History Views the Bible.* Grand Rapids: Zondervan Publishing House, 1982.

_____. and Nix, William E. *From God to Us.* Chicago: Moody Press, 1974.

_____. *A General Introduction to the Bible.* Chicago: Moody Press, 1968.

Laird, R. *Inspiration and Canonicity of the Bible.*

Grand Rapids: Zondervan Publishing House, 1966.

Lewis, Clive Staples. *The Case for Christianity*. New York: Macmillan Publishing Co., 1956.

Lewis, Gordon R. *Testing Christianity's Truth Claims: Approaches to Christian Apologetics*. Chicago: Moody Press, 1976.

McDowell, Josh. *Evidence That Demands a Verdict: Historical Evidence for the Christian Faith*. Arrowhead Springs: Campus Crusade for Christ, Inc., 1972.

———. *More Evidence That Demands a Verdict: Historical Evidences for the Christian Scriptures*. Arrowhead Springs: Campus Crusade for Christ, 1975.

———. *More Than a Carpenter*. Wheaton: Tyndale House Publishers, 1980.

Montgomery, John W. *History and Christianity*. Downers Grove: InterVarsity Press, 1965.

Pinnock, Clark H. *Reason Enough: A Case for the Christian Faith*. Downers Grove: InterVarsity Press, 1980.

———. *Set Forth Your Case: An Examination of Christianity's Credentials*. Chicago: Moody Press, 1971.

Unger, Merrill Frederick. *Archaeology and the New Testament*. Grand Rapids: Zondervan Publishing House, 1962.

———. *Archaeology and the Old Testament*. Grand Rapids: Zondervan Publishing House, 1966.

JEHOVAH'S WITNESSES

I. GENERAL

Ball, Francis K. *The Elements of Greek*. New York: Macmillan, 1950.

Bergman, Jerry. *Jehovah's Witnesses and Blood Transfusions*. Costa Mesa: CARIS, 1979.

———. *Jehovah's Witnesses and Mental Illness*. Costa Mesa: CARIS, 1983.

Bowser, Arthur. *What Every Jehovah's Witness Should Know*. Denver: B/P Publications, 1975.

Breese, Dave. *Know the Marks of the Cults*. Wheaton: Victor Books.

Bullions, Peter. *Principles of Greek Grammar*. New York: Farmer, Bruce and Company.

Carnell, E. J. *An Introduction to Christian Apologetics*. Grand Rapids: Wm. B. Eerdmans Publishing Co., 1950.

Cline, Ted. *Questions for Jehovah's Witnesses*. Ventura: Gospel Light Publishers, 1975.

Cole, Marley. *Jehovah's Witnesses, The New World Society*. New York: Vantage Press, 1955.

Cooper, Lee. "Publish or Perish: Negro Jehovah's Witnesses' Adaptation in the Ghetto." In *Religious Movements in Contemporary America*. Irving Zaretsky and Mark P. Leone, eds. Princeton, N.J.: Princeton University Press, 1974.

Countess, Robert H. *The Jehovah's Witnesses' New Testament*. Phillipsburg, N.J.: Presbyterian and Reformed Publishing Co., 1982.

Davies, Horton. *Christian Deviations*. Philosophical Library, 1954.

Dencher, Ted. *The Watch Tower Versus the Bible*. Chicago: Moody Press, 1961.

———. *Why I Left Jehovah's Witnesses*. Ft. Washington: Christian Literature Crusade, 1966.

Deissman, Adolf. *Light From the Ancient East*. New York: Harpers, 1951.

Finnegan, Jack. *Light From the Ancient Past*. Princeton, N.J.: Princeton Press, 1946.

Gaebelein, Arno C. *The Hope of the Ages*. Our Hope.

Gaebelein, Frank E. *Exploring the Bible*. Van Kampen Press, 1950.

Gerstner, John H. *The Theology of the Major Sects*. Grand Rapids: Baker Book House, 1963.

Gruss, Edmond C. *Apostles of Denial*. Nutley, N.J.: Presbyterian and Reformed Publishing Company, 1970.

———. *The Jehovah's Witnesses and Prophetic Speculation*. Nutley, N.J.: Presbyterian and Reformed Publishing Co., 1972.

———., ed. *We Left Jehovah's Witnesses: A Non-Prophet Organization*. Nutley, N.J.: Presbyterian and Reformed Publishing Company, 1972.

Hamilton, Floyd E. *The Basis of Christian Faith*. New York: Harper, 1949.

Hoekema, Anthony A. *Jehovah's Witnesses*. Grand Rapids: Wm. B. Eerdmans Publishing Co., 1972.

———. *The Four Major Cults*. Grand Rapids: Wm. B. Eerdmans Publishing Co., 1963.

Irvine, William C. *Heresies Exposed*. Neptune, N.J.: Loizeaux, 1955.

Kauper, Paul G. *Religion and the Constitution*. Louisiana: Louisiana State University Press, 1964.

Knoch, Adolf E. *Concordat Version, New Testament* (Greek Translation). Los Angeles: Concordat Publishing Concern, 1931.

Knox, Ronald. *Translation of the Bible*. 3 vols. New York: Sheed & Ward, 1953.

Lewis, Gordon R. *The Bible, the Christian and Jehovah's Witnesses*. Philadelphia: Presbyterian and Reformed Publishing Co., 1966.

Machen, J. G. *The Origin of Paul's Religion*. Grand Rapids: Wm. B. Eerdmans Publishing Co., 1950.

———. *The Virgin Birth of Christ*. Grand Rapids: Wm. B. Eerdmans Publishing Co., 1950.

MacMillan, A. H. *Faith on the March*. Englewood Cliffs, N.J.: Prentice Hall, 1957.

Magnani, Duane, and Barrett, Arthur. *Dialogue With Jehovah's Witnesses* (2 vols.). Clayton, Calif.: Witness Inc., 1983.

Martin, Walter, and Klann, Norman. *Jehovah of the Watchtower*. Minneapolis: Bethany House Publishers, 1981.

Mayer, F. E. *Jehovah's Witnesses*. St. Louis: Concordia Publishing House, 1943.

Metzger, Bruce M. "The Jehovah's Witnesses and Jesus Christ." *Theology Today*, April 1953, pp. 65 ff.

Moulton, J. H. *A Grammar of New Testament Greek.* (3rd. ed.) Edinburgh: Tavil T. Clark.

Newman, John Henry. *The Arians of the Fourth Century.* Longmans Green, 1911.

———. *St. Athanasius.* (Vol. 1, 2), Longmans Green, 1911.

———. *Basic Writings of St. Augustine.* Random House, 1950.

Pegis. *Basic Writings of St. Thomas Aquinas.* Random House, 1950.

Ross, Rev. J. J. *Some Facts and More Facts About the Self-styled Pastor, Charles T. Russell.*

Sanders, J. Oswald. *Heresies Ancient and Modern.* Edinburgh: Marshall, Morgan & Scott, 1954.

Schnell, W. J. *Into the Light of Christianity.* Grand Rapids: Baker Book House, 1958.

———. *Thirty Years a Watchtower Slave.* Grand Rapids: Baker Book House, 1956.

Souter, Alexander. *The New Testament in Greek.* Oxford, 1947.

Spittler, Russell P. *Cults and Isms.* Grand Rapids: Baker Book House, 1962.

Stroup, Herbert Hewitt. *The Jehovah's Witnesses.* New York: Columbus University Press, 1945.

Thiessen, Henry. *An Introduction to the New Testament.* Grand Rapids: Wm. B. Eerdmans Publishing Co., 1948.

Thomas, F. W. *Masters of Deception: An Expose of the Jehovah's Witnesses.* Grand Rapids: Baker Book House, 1970.

Van Baalen, Jan Karel. *Chaos of the Cults.* Grand Rapids: Wm. B. Eerdmans Publishing Co., 1962, 4th ed., rev.

Van Buskirk, Michael. *The Scholastic Dishonesty of the Watchtower.* Costa Mesa: CARIS, 1976.

Warfield, Benjamin B. *Christological Studies.* Princeton Press, 1950.

Watters, Randall. *Thus Saith . . . the Governing Body of Jehovah's Witnesses.* Manhattan Beach: Bethel Ministries, 1982.

Westcott and Hort. *The New Testament in the Original Greek.* New York: Macmillan, 1885, 1943.

Whalen, William J. *Armageddon Around the Corner.* New York: The John Day Co., 1962.

Wilson, Robert Dick. *A Scientific Investigation of the Old Testament.* Philadelphia: Sunday School Times.

Wright, J. Stafford. *Some Modern Religions.* Chicago: InterVarsity Press, 1956.

Wulfken, George W. *Let There Be Light* (published by the author).

Yonge, C. D. *An English Greek Lexicon.* London, 1859.

Young, E. J. *An Introduction to the Old Testament.* (rev. ed.) Grand Rapids: Wm. B. Eerdmans Publishing Co., 1958.

Young, G. Douglas. *Grammar of the Hebrew Language.* Grand Rapids: Zondervan Publishing House, 1951.

Young, Robert. *Annalytical Concordance to the Bible.* New York: Funk & Wagnalls Co., 1919.

MAGAZINE AND NEWSPAPER ARTICLES

Stewart, E. D. "The Life of Charles Taze Russell," *Overland Monthly,* Los Angeles, 1917, pp. 126–132.

Davidson, Bill. "Jehovah's Travelling Salesman," *Readers Digest,* 50:77–80, Jan., 1947.

The Brooklyn Daily Eagle. Back issues, 1912, 1913, 1916.

The Brooklyn Eagle. Back issue, 1942.

The Daily Standard Union, Wednesday, November 1, 1916, page 5.

The Brooklyn Daily Times. November 1, 1916, page 4.

The New York Times. Back issues, 1916.

II. WATCH TOWER BIBLE AND TRACT SOCIETY PUBLICATIONS

Awake (magazine).

The Emphatic Diaglott. Interlinear Greek-English Translation of the New Testament.

Let God Be True. (rev. ed.) 1952.

Make Sure of All Things. 1953.

The New World Translation of the Hebrew Scriptures. (rev. ed) 1951.

The New World Translation of the Hebrew Scriptures. vol. I, 1953.

Russell, Charles T. *Studies in the Scriptures.* vols. I–VII.

The Watchtower (magazine).

Rutherford, J. F. *The Harp of God; Creation; Religion; The Kingdom; Salvation; Deliverance; Children; Enemies; Light; Government; Why Serve Jehovah?; Jehovah's Witnesses—Why Persecuted?; Religious Intolerance—Why?,* etc.

Rutherford, J. F. Pamphlets (most now out of print). International Bible Students Association—

A Great Battle in the Ecclesiastical Heavens. 1915. 64 pages.

Can the Living Talk With the Dead? 1920, 128 pages.

Talking With the Dead. 1920, 155 pages.

Prohibition and the League of Nations. 1920, 59 pages.

Millions Now Living Will Never Die. 1920, 128 pages.

Comfort for the Jews. 1925, 128 pages.

Restoration. 1927, 127 pages.

The Lost Days. 1928, 61 pages.

The Kingdom, The Hope of This World. 1931, 62 pages.

Liberty. 1932.

What is Truth? 1932.

What You Need. 1932.

Where Are the Dead? 1932.

Who Is God? 1932.

Health and Life. 1932.

Hereafter. 1932.

Home and Happiness. 1932.

Keys of Heaven. 1932.

The Kingdom. 1932.

Causes of Death. 1932.

Final War. 1932.

Good News. 1932.
The Crisis. 1933.
Dividing the People. 1933.
Escape to the Kingdom. 1933.
Intolerance. 1933.
Angels. 1934.
Beyond the Grave. 1934.
Favored People. 1934.
His Vengeance. 1934.
His Works. 1934.
Righteous Ruler. 1934.
Supremacy. 1934.
World Recovery. 1934.
Who Shall Rule the World? 1935.
Government. 1935.
Loyalty. 1935.
Universal War Near. 1935.
Choosing Riches or Ruin. 1936.
Protection. 1936.
Armageddon. 1937.
Safety Comfort. 1937.
Uncovered. 1937.
Face the Facts. 1938.
Warning. 1938.
Fascism or Freedom. 1939.
Government and Peace. 1939.
Judge Rutherford Uncovers the Fifth Column. 1940.
Refugees. 1940.
God and the State. 1941.
Books and pamphlets published by the Dawn Bible Student Association—
Our Most Holy Faith, a collection of writings and sermons of "Pastor Charles Taze Russell, 1948, 719 pages.
Armageddon. 31 pages.
Divine Healing. 31 pages.
Born of the Spirit. 32 pages.
Hope Beyond the Grave. 96 pages.
Does God Answer Prayer? 30 pages.
When a Man Dies. 46 pages.
What Can a Man Pay? 32 pages.
His Chosen People. 62 pages.
Hope For a Fear Filled World. 30 pages.
The Day of Judgment. 32 pages.
Spiritualism. 32 pages.
Our Lord's Return. 48 pages.
The Truth About Hell. 63 pages.
Father, Son, and Holy Spirit. 32 pages.
God and Reason. 96 pages.
Jesus the World Saviour. 32 pages.
God's Plan. 47 pages.
When "Pastor" Russell Died. 70 pages.
Creation.

CHRISTIAN SCIENCE

I. WRITINGS BY MARY BAKER EDDY

Science and Health, With Key to the Scriptures.
Miscellaneous Writings.
Manual of the Mother Church.
Christ and Christmas.
Retrospection and Introspection.
Unity of Good.

Pulpit and Press.
Rudimental Divine Science.
No and Yes.
Christian Science Versus Pantheism.
Message to the Mother Church, June, 1900.
Message to the Mother Church, June, 1901.
Message to the Mother Church, June, 1902.
Christian Healing.
The Peoples' Idea of God.
Poems.
The First Church of Christ, Scientist, and Miscellany.
Christian Science Hymnal, with five hymns written by Mary Baker Eddy, Christian Science Publishing Society, 1909.

II. ADDITIONAL GENERAL BIBLIOGRAPHY

A Complete Concordance to the Writings of Mary Baker Eddy Other Than Science and Health.
A Complete Concordance to Science and Health, With Key to the Scriptures.
The Christian Science Journal.
The Christian Science Sentinel.
The Christian Science Monitor.
Armstrong, Joseph. The Mother Church. C.S.P.S., 1937.
Bates, Ernest Sutherland, and Dittemore, John V. Mary Baker Eddy—The Truth and The Tradition. Alfred A. Knopf. 1932.
Beasley, Norman. The Cross and The Crown, The History of Christian Science. Duell, Sloan & Pearce, 1952, 1963.
The Blight That Failed. Charles Scribner's Sons, 1929.
Boa, Kenneth. Cults, World Religions and You. Wheaton: Victor Books, 1977.
Boltzly, Rev. Oliver D. The Death Pot in Christian Science. The Lutheran Literary Board, 1935.
Braden, Charles S. Spirits in Rebellion. Dallas: Southern Methodist University Press, 1963.
Dakin, Edwin Franden. Mrs. Eddy. Charles Scribner's Sons, 1929.
Dickey, Adam. Memoirs of Mary Baker Eddy. England: Robert G. Carter, 1927.
Douglass, R. C. Christian Science, A Defense.
Dresser, Horatio W., ed. The Quimby Manuscripts. New York: Thomas Y. Crowell Co., 1921.
Gray, James M. The Antidote to Christian Science. Chicago: Moody Press.
Gruss, Edmond C. Cults and Occult. Grand Rapids: Baker Book House, 1982.
Hadden, Robert A. Christian Science and the Christian Scriptures Compared and Contrasted. American Prophetic League, 1952.
Haldeman, Isaac Massey. Christian Science in Light of Holy Scripture. New York: Fleming H. Revell Co., 1909.
Hanna, Septimus J. Christian Science History. C.S.P.S., 1899.
Haushalter, Walter M. Mrs. Eddy Purloins From Hegel. Boston: A. A. Beauchamp, 1936.
Hawkins, Ann Ballew. Phineas Parkhurst Quimby.

Published by the author, 1951.

Hoekema, Anthony A. *Christian Science.* Grand Rapids: Wm. B. Eerdmans Publishing Co., 1974.

Johnston, Julia Michael. *Mary Baker Eddy, Her Mission and Triumph.* C.S.P.S., 1946.

Judah, J. Stillson. *The History and Philosophy of the Metaphysical Movements in America.* Philadelphia: The Westminster Press, 1967.

Martin, Walter. *Walter Martin Speaks Out on the Cults.* Ventura: Vision House Publishers. 1983.

———, and Klann, Norman H. *The Christian Science Myth.* Grand Rapids: Zondervan Publishing House, 1956.

Meekan, M. *Mrs. Eddy and the Late Suit in Equity.* Concord, 1908.

Miller, Elliot. "Christian Science." In *Walter Martin's Cults Reference Bible.* Walter Martin, ed. Santa Ana: Vision House Publishers, 1981.

Milmine, Georgine. *The Life of Mary Baker G. Eddy and the History of Christian Science.* New York: Doubleday, Page & Co., 1909. Grand Rapids: Baker Book House, 1971 repr.

Moore, Rev. A. Lincoln, *Christian Science—Its Manifold Attraction.* Theodore E. Schulte Publishing Co., 1906.

Paget, Stephen, M.D. *The Faith and Works of Christian Science.* London, 1909.

Peabody, Frederick W. *The Religio-Medical Masquerade.* Fleming H. Revell, 1910.

Phillips, Jane. *Mary Baker Eddy's Early Writings Compared With the Quimby Manuscripts.* Pasadena: Toujours Publishing Co., 1931.

Powell, Lyman P. *Mary Baker Eddy.* Macmillan, 1930.

Ramsay, E. Mary. *Christian Science and Its Discoverer.* C.S.P.S., 1935.

Riddle, T. Wilkinson. *Christian Science in the Light of Holy Scripture.* London: Marshall, Morgan and Scott, 1931.

Riley, Woodbridge; Peabody, W. Frederick; and Humiston, Charles E. *The Faith, the Falsity and the Failure of Christian Science.* Fleming H. Revell, 1925.

Sheldon, Henry C. *Christian Science So-Called.* The Abingdon Press, 1913.

Smith, Clifford P. *Historical Sketches.* C.S.P.S., 1941.

Snowden, James H. *The Truth About Christian Science.* Westminster Press, 1920.

Stewart, Herbert. *Christian Science—True or False.* Belfast: Graham L. Healy, Ltd.

Tenney, Rev. Herbert Melville. *Christian Science, Its Truths and Errors.* The Burrows Brothers Co., 1888.

Tomlinson, Irving C. *Twelve Years With Mary Baker Eddy.* C.S.P.S., 1945.

Twain, Mark. *Christian Science.* Harper. 1907.

Wilbur, Sibyl. *The Life of Mary Baker Eddy.* C.S.P.S., 1923.

Williamson, Margaret. *The Mother Church Extension.* C.S.P.S., 1939.

Wittmer, George W. *Christian Science in the Light of the Bible.* St. Louis: Concordia Publishing House, 1949.

Woodbury, Josephine C. *War in Heaven.* Boston: S. Usher Printer, 1897.

Christian Science Wartime Activities, 1939–1947. C.S.P.S.

Legal Aspects of Christian Science, 1899. C.S.P.S.

III. NEWSPAPER AND MAGAZINE ARTICLES

Arena magazine, Selected copy regarding Mrs. Eddy and Christian Science.

Buckley, Dr. J. M. "Dr. J. M. Buckley on Christian Science," *North American Review,* July, 1901.

Cabot, M.D., Richard C. "100 Christian Science Cures," *McClures* magazine, Aug., 1908.

"The Deadly Parallel," *New York Times,* July 10, 1904.

Fishbein, M.D., Morris. "Mary Baker Eddy," *Plain Talk,* Vol. 1, No. 2, Nov., 1927, pp. 21–26.

McClures magazine, Selected copy regarding Mrs. Eddy and Christian Science.

The New York Herald Tribune, Article and editorial on Christian Science, Dec. 12 and 13, 1951.

The New York Times, Selected material on Christian Science.

The New York World, Selected material on Christian Science.

Woodbury, Josephine C. "Quimbyism or the Paternity of Christian Science," *Arena,* May, 1899.

Wright, Livingston. "How Reverend Wiggin Rewrote Mrs. Eddy's Book," *New York World.*

MORMONISM

Anderson, Edward H. *A Brief History of the Church of Jesus Christ Latter Day Saints.* Jackson County, Mo.: Zion's Printing and Publishing Company, 1928.

Anderson, Einar. *Mormonism.* Chicago: Moody Press, 1956.

Arbaugh, G. B. *Gods, Sex, and the Saints.* Rock Island: Augusta Press, 1957.

Arrington, Leonard J., and Bitton, Davis. *The Mormon Experience.* New York: Alfred A. Knopf, Inc., 1979.

Bales, James D. *The Book of Mormon?* Rosemead: Old Paths Book Club, 1958.

Baskin, R. N. *Reminiscences of Early Utah.* 1914.

Beadle. J. H. *Polygamy or the Mysteries and Crimes of Mormonism.* Philadelphia: The National Publishing Company, 1882.

Bennett, Wallace Foster. *Why I am a Mormon.* New York: T. Nelson, 1958.

Brewer, David L. *Utah Elites and Utah Racial Norms.* Salt Lake City: Modern Microfilm Company.

Brodie, Fawn M. *No Man Knows My History—The Life of Joseph Smith, the Mormon Prophet.*

New York: Alfred A. Knopf, Inc., 1957; enlarged ed., 1971.

Brooks, Juanita (ed.) *On the Mormon Frontier. The Diary of Hosea Stout.* Salt Lake City: University of Utah Press.

Budvarson, Arthur, *The Book of Mormonism—True or False?* Grand Rapids: Zondervan Publishing House, 1941.

Call, Lamoni. *2000 Changes in the Book of Mormon.* Salt Lake City: Modern Microfilm Company.

Cannon, Frank J. *Under the Prophet in Utah.* Boston: C. M. Clark, 1911.

Cannon, Frank J. *Brigham Young and His Mormon Empire.* New York: Fleming H. Revell Company, 1913.

Clark, J. A. *Gleanings by the Way.* 1842.

Codman, Jr. *The Mormon Country.* U.S. Publishing Company, 1874.

Corrill, John. *A Brief History of the Church of Christ of Latter-day Saints.*

Cowan, Marvin W. *Mormon Claims Answered.* Salt Lake City: Marvin W. Cowan, 1975.

Draper, Maurice I. *Christ's Church Restored.* Independence: Herald Publishing House, 1948.

Erickson, Ephraim E. *The Psychological and Ethical Aspects of Mormon Group Life.* Chicago: University of Chicago Press, 1922.

Evans, R. H. *One Hundred Years of Mormonism.* Salt Lake City: Deseret News, 1905.

Etenhouser, R., and Phillips, A. B. *Three Bibles Compared.* Independence: Herald Publishing House, 1954

Folk, Edger E. *The Mormon Monster.* New York: Fleming H. Revell, 1900.

Fraser, Gordon H. *Is Mormonism Christian?* Chicago: Moody Colportage Library, 1957.

Gibbs, Josiah F. *The Mountain Meadows Massacre.* Salt Lake City: Salt Lake Tribune, 1910.

Goodspeed, Edgar J. *The New Testament—An American Translation.* Chicago: University of Chicago Press, 1923.

Hanson, Klaus: *Quest for Empire.* East Lansing: Michigan State University Press.

Hickman, William A. *Brighams Destroying Angel.* New York: G. A. Crofutt, 1872.

Hield, Charles R. *Baptism for the Dead.* Independence: Herald Publishing House, 1953.

History of the Mormons or Latter-Day saints. Auburn-Derby and Miller, 1852.

Hoekema, Anthony A. *Mormonism.* Grand Rapids: Wm. B. Eerdmans Publishing Co., 1974.

Hougey, Hal. *Archeology and the Book of Mormon.* Pacific Press, 1973.

Hougey, Hal. *Truth About the 'Lehi Tree of Life' Stone.* Pacific Press, 1973.

Howe, E. D. *Mormonism Unveiled.* 1834.

Hunter, Milton R. *The Gospel Through the Ages.* Melchizedik Priesthood Course of Study. Salt Lake City. 1945-46.

Ivins, Stanley S. *The Mose Thatcher Case.* Salt Lake City: Modern Microfilm Company.

Jenson, Andrew. *Latter-day Saint Biographical Encyclopedia.* Salt Lake City: A. Jenson, 1901–1936.

Jenson, Andrew. *Plural Marriage.* (Reprint from the Historical Record, Vol. 6) May, 1887.

Jonas, Larry, *Mormon Claims Examined.* Salt Lake City: Modern Microfilm Company.

Kidder, Daniel P. *Mormonism and the Mormons,* New York: G. Lane & P. P. Sanford, 1842.

Lamb, M. T. *The Golden Bible.* New York: Ward and Drummond, 1887.

Lee, John Doyle. *A Mormon Chronicle.* San Marino: Huntington Library, 1955.

Lewis, William. *The Church of Jesus Christ: How Shall I Know It?* Independence: Herald Publishing House.

Linn, William Alexander. *The Story of the Mormons.* New York: Macmillan, 1902.

Lyford, C. *The Mormon Problem.* New York: Hunt and Eaton, 1866.

Martin, Stuart. *The Mystery of Mormonism.* New York: E. P. Dutton and Company.

Martin, Walter R. *The Maze of Mormonism.* Santa Ana: Vision House Publishers, 1978.

McConkie, Bruce R. *Mormon Doctrine.* Salt Lake City: Bookcraft, 1958; enlarged ed., 1966; rev. 1978.

———. *What the Mormons Think of Christ.* Salt Lake City.

McElveen, Floyd C. *The Mormon Illusion.* Ventura: Regal Books, 2nd ed., rev., 1979.

Meyer, Edward. *Ursprung und Geshichte der Mormonen mit Exkursen ueber Anfange des Islams und des Christentums.* 1912.

Mulder, Wm. *Among the Mormons.* New York: Knopf, 1958.

Nelson, Dee Jay. *The Joseph Smith Papyri—A Translation and Preliminary Survey.* Salt Lake City: Modern Microfilm Company.

Nutting, J. D. *The Little Encyclopedia of Mormonism.* Cleveland: Utah Gospel Mission, 1927.

O'Dey, Thomas F. *The Mormons.* Chicago: University of Chicago Press, 1957.

Peck, Reed. *Reed Peck Manuscript.* Salt Lake City: Modern Microfilm Company.

Penrose, Charles W. *Mormon Doctrine Plain and Simple or Leaves From the Tree.* Salt Lake: G. Q. Cannon, 1897.

Petersen, LaMar. *Problems in Mormon Text.* Salt Lake City: Modern Microfilm Company.

Petersen, Mark E. *Race Problems as They Affect the Church.* Salt Lake City: Modern Microfilm Company.

Pratt, Orson. *Pamphlets by Orson Pratt.* Liverpool: R. James, 1851.

Pratt, Parley P. *Key to the Science of Theology.* Liverpool: F. D. Richards, 1855.

Reiser, A. H., and Merkley, Marian G. *What It Means to Be a Latter-Day Saint: Course of Study for the First Intermediates Dept.* Salt Lake City, 1946.

Richards, Le Grand. *A Marvelous Work and a Wonder.* Salt Lake City: Deseret Book Company, 1950.

Rosten, Leo, *A Guide to the Religions of America.*

New York: Simon and Schuster, 1963.

Rushton, John W. *The Apostasy and the Restoration*. Independence: Herald Publishing House.

Sackett, Charles C. *What's Going On in There?* Thousand Oaks: Ex-Mormons for Jesus, 2nd ed., rev., 1982.

Schindler, Harold. *Orrin Porter Rockwell: Man of God, Son of Thunder*. Salt Lake City: University of Utah Press.

Shields, Stephen L. *Divergent Paths of the Restoration*. Bountiful, Utah: Restoration Research, 3rd ed., rev., 1982.

Shook, Charles A. *The True Origin of the Book of Mormon*. Cincinnati, 1914.

Smith, Elbert A. *Differences that Persist Between the Reorganized Church of Christ Latter Day Saints and the Utah Mormon Church*. Independence: Herald Publishing House, 1943.

Smith, Ethan: *View of the Hebrews*. Poutney: Smith & Shute, 1823.

Smith, Joseph, Jr. *A Book of Commandments for the Government of the Church of Christ*. (Reprinted by the Salt Lake Tribune, 1884).

Smith, Joseph, Jr. *The Book of Mormon*. Salt Lake City: The Church of Jesus Christ Latter Day Saints, 1952.

Smith, Joseph Fielding, comp. *Teachings of the Prophet Joseph Smith*. Salt Lake City: Deseret Book Company, 1976.

Smith, Lucy Mack. *Biographical Sketches of Joseph Smith*. Liverpool: S. W. Richards, 1853.

Snowden, James H. *The Truth About Mormonism*. New York: George H. Durant Company, 1926.

Spalding, F. S. *Why Egyptologists Reject the Book of Abraham*. Salt Lake City: The Arrow Press.

Spencer, Orson. *Letters Exhibiting the Most Prominent Doctrines of the Church of Jesus Christ of Latter-day Saints*. Liverpool: O. Spencer, 1848.

Starks, Arthur E. *A Complete Concordance to the Book of Mormon*. Independence: Herald Publishing House, 1950.

Stenhouse, T. B. *The Rocky Mountain Saints*. New York: B. Appleton Company, 1873.

Stewart, George. *Priesthood and Church Welfare*. Deseret Book Company, 1939.

Swartzell, William: *Mormonism Exposed*. 1840.

Talmage, James E. *The Articles of Faith*. Salt Lake City: The Church of Jesus Christ Latter Day Saints, 1952.

Tanner, Jerald. *The Negro in Mormon Theology*. Salt Lake City: Modern Microfilm Company.

———. *Changes in Joseph Smith's History*. Salt Lake City: Modern Microfilm Company.

———. *Changes in the Pearl of Great Price*. Salt Lake City: Modern Microfilm Company.

———. *Changes in the Key to Theology*. Salt Lake City: Modern Microfilm Company.

Tanner, Jerald and Sandra. *The Case Against Mormonism*, Vol. I. Salt Lake City: Modern Microfilm Company.

———. *The Changing World of Mormonism*. Chicago: Moody Press, 1980; rev. ed., 1981.

———. *Joseph Smith and Polygamy*. Salt Lake City: Modern Microfilm Company.

———. *Joseph Smith's Curse Upon The Negro*. Salt Lake City: Modern Microfilm Company.

———. *Joseph Smith's Strange Account of the First Vision*. Salt Lake City: Modern Microfilm Company.

———. *Mormonism—Shadow or Reality?* Salt Lake City: Modern Microfilm Co., 1972; rev. ed., 1982.

———. *The Mormon Kingdom*. Salt Lake City: Modern Microfilm Company.

———. *The Mormon Papyri Question*. Salt Lake City: Modern Microfilm Company.

———. *Revealing Statements by the Three Witnesses to the Book of Mormon*. Salt Lake City: Modern Microfilm Company.

———. *3,914 Changes in the Book of Mormon*. Salt Lake City: Modern Microfilm Company.

Taylor, Samuel W. *Rocky Mountain Empire: The Latter-day Saints Today*. New York: Macmillan, 1978.

Thayer, Joseph Henry. *Greek-English Lexicon*. Grand Rapids: Zondervan Publishing House, 1973.

Tope, Wallace W. *On the Frontlines*. La Canada-Flintridge, Calif.: Frontline Ministries, 1980; rev. ed., 1981.

Tucker, Pomeroy. *Origin, Rise and Progress of Mormonism*. 1867.

Tullis, F. LaMond., ed. *Mormonism: A Faith for All Cultures*. Provo: Brigham Young University Press, 1978.

Turner, Wallace. *The Mormon Establishment*. Boston: Houghton Mifflin, 1966.

Van Wagoner, Richard S., and Walker, Steven C. *A Book of Mormons*. Salt Lake City: Signature Books, 1982.

Walters, Wesley P. *New Light on Mormon Origins from the Palmyra (NY) Revival*. La Mesa: Utah Christian Tract Society, 1973.

Wardle, James D. *Selected Changes in the Book of Mormon*. Salt Lake City: Modern Microfilm Company.

Weldon, Roy. *Other Sheep: Book of Mormon Evidences*. Independence: Herald Publishing House, 1956.

Whitmer, John. *John Whitmer's History*. Salt Lake City: Modern Microfilm Company.

Widtsoe, John A. *Priesthood and Church Government*. Deseret Book Company, 1939.

Witte, Robert C. *Where Does it Say That?* Safety Harbor, Fla.: Ex-Mormons for Jesus, 1982, rev. ed.

Young, Eliza. *Wife No. 19: A Life in Bondage*. 1876.

Young, Brigham. *Journal of Discourses*. 1901.

SPIRITISM

Boa, Kenneth. *Cults, World Religions, and You*. Wheaton: Scripture Press, 1977.

Braden, Charles S. *These Also Believe*. New York: Macmillan, 1960.

——. *The World's Religions.* New York: Abingdon Press, 1954.

Butterworth, George W. *Spiritualism and Religion.* New York: Macmillan, 1944.

Doyle, A. Conan. *The History of Spiritualism.* 2 vols.; *Phineas Speaks: Direct Communications in the Family Circle.* London, 1927.

Ferm, Vergilius. *Encyclopedia of Religion.* New York: Philosophical Library, 1945.

Fodor, Nandor. *Encyclopaedia of Psychic Science.* Secaucus, N.J.: The Citadel Press, 1966.

Gray, James M. *Spiritism and the Fallen Angels.* London: Fleming H. Revell, 1920.

Gruss, Edmond C. *Cults and the Occult.* Grand Rapids: Baker Book House, 1982.

Harding, Emma. *Modern American Spiritualism—A Twenty Year Record of the Communion of the World and Spirits.* New York, 1870.

Hill, Arthur J. *Spiritualim—Its History, Phenomena and Doctrine.* New York: George H. Doran & Co., 1919.

Hull, Moses. *Encyclopedia of Biblical Spiritualism.* Chicago: Moses Hull & Co., 1895.

Koch, Kurt E. *Christian Counseling and Occultism.* Grand Rapids: Kregel Publications, 1973 (21st ed.).

Larson, Bob. *Larson's Book of Cults.* Wheaton: Tyndale House Publishers, 1982.

Lewis, Gordon R. *Confronting the Cults.* Grand Rapids: Baker Book House, 1966.

McCabe, Joseph. *Spiritualism—A Popular History From 1847.* London, 1920.

McKight, Marcus. *Spiritualism.* London, 1950.

Melton, J. Gordon, *The Encyclopedia of American Religions* (vol. 2). Wilmington, N.C.: McGrath Publishing Company, 1978.

Petersen, William J. *Those Curious New Cults.* New Canaan, Conn.: Keats Publishing Company, 1975.

Schofield, A. T. *Modern Spiritism—Its Science and Religion.*

Spittler, Russell P. *Cults and Isms.* Grand Rapids: Baker Book House, 1962.

Stoddard, Jane T. *The Case Against Spiritualism.* New York: Houghton and Stoughton, 1919.

Unger, Merrill F. *Demons in the World Today.* Wheaton: Tyndale House Publishers, 1971.

Wade, Alda Madison. *Evidences of Immortality.* Boston: The Christopher Publishing House, 1956.

Walton, George S. *The Drama of Life After Death.* New York: A. H. Holt & Co., 1932.

Wilson, Clifford A., and Weldon, John. *Occult Shock and Psychic Forces.* San Diego: Master Books, 1980.

Zaretsky, Irving I., and Mark P. Leone, eds. *Religious Movements in Contemporary America.* Princeton: Princeton University Press, 1974.

PAMPHLETS—

Biederwolf, William E. *Spiritualism Divine? Devilish? or Deception?* Grand Rapids: Wm. B. Eerdmans Publishing Co., 1952.

Froom, Leroy Edwin, *Spiritualism Today.* Washington, D.C.: Review and Herald, 1963.

Wright, The Rev. J. Stanford. *Spiritualism.* London: The Church Book Room Press, 1959.

THE THEOSOPHICAL SOCIETY

Besant, Anne. *The Ancient Wisdom,* An Outline of Theosophic Teaching. London, 1897; *An Autobiography.* London, 1893.

Blavatsky, Helena P. *Isis Unveiled.* Wheaton: Theosophical Publishing House, 1972.

——. *The Key to Theosophy—An Abridgement.* Wheaton: Theosophical Publishing House, 1972.

——. *The Secret Doctrine.* London, 1893.

——. *Theosophical Glossary.* Los Angeles: The Theosophical Co., 1892, 1973 repr.

Braden, Charles S. *These Also Believe.* New York: Macmillan, 1960.

Butt, Baseden G. *Madam Blavatsky.* London, 1926.

Ellwood, Robert S. Jr. *Alternative Altars.* Chicago: University of Chicago Press, Ltd., 1979.

Judah, J. Stillson. *The History and Philosophy of the Metaphysical Movements in America.* Philadelphia: The Westminster Press, 1967.

Kuhn, Alvin B. *Theosophy, A Modern Revival of Ancient Wisdom.* New York: H. Holt & Co., 1930.

Leadbeater, Charles W. *Textbook of Theosophy.* Chicago: The Theosophical Press, 1925.

McNiele, E. R. *From Theosophy to Christian Faith.* London. Longmans Green & Company, 1919.

Olcott, Henry S. *Old Diary Leaves.* An Authentic History of the Theosophical Society. Madras Theosophical Publishing Society, 1935.

Rogers, L. W. *Elementary Theosophy.* (6th ed.) Wheaton: The Theosophical Press, 1956.

Sheldon, H. C. *Theosophy and New Thought.* New York, 1916.

Sinnett, Alfred Percy. *The Theosophical Movement 1875–1925*—A History and a Survey. New York: E. P. Dutton, 1925.

Sloan, Ellen M. *Modern Theosophy, Whence, What, Whither?* St. Paul: The Way Press, 1922.

Symonds, John. *Madame Blavatsky, Medium and Magician.* London: Odhams Press, 1959.

Williams, Gertrude Leavenworth. *Priestess of the Occult, Madam Blavatsky.* New York: A. A. Knopf, 1946.

Wilson, Colin. *The Occult—A History.* New York: Random House, 1971.

ZEN BUDDHISM

Arvon, Henri. *Buddhism.* New York: Walker and Company, 1962.

Barrett, William. *Zen Buddhism,* Selected Writings of D. T. Suzuki. Doubleday, 1956.

Chen-Chi-Chang: *The Practice of Zen.* Harper, 1959.

Conze, Edward. *Buddhism, Its Essence and Development*. New York: Harper & Row, 1951.

David-Neel, Aléxandra. *Buddhism, Its Doctrines and Its Methods*. New York: Avon Books, 1977.

Eerdmans Handbook to the World's Religions. Grand Rapids: Wm. B. Eerdmans Publishing Co., 1982.

Guenther, Herbert V. *Buddhist Philosophy in Theory and Practice*. Middlesex: Penguin Books, 1971.

Humphreys, Christmas. *Zen Buddhism*. London: Allen and Unwin, 1957.

Kapleau, Philip, ed. *The Three Pillars of Zen*. Boston: Beacon Press, 1965.

Layman, Emma McCloy. *Buddhism in America*. Chicago: Nelson-Hall, 1976.

Linssen, Robert. *Living Zen*. New York: Grove Press, 1958.

Melton, J. Gordon. *Encyclopedia of American Religions* (vol. 2). Wilmington, N.C.: McGrath Publishing Co., 1978.

Ogata, Sohaku. *Zen for the West*. New York: Apollo, Williams, Morrow, 1962.

Robinson, Richard H. *The Buddhist Religion*. Belmont, Calif.: Dickenson Publishing, 1970.

Suzuki, D. T. *Essays in Zen Buddhism*. 3 vols. London, 1949–51.

———. *An Introduction to Zen Buddhism*. New York: Philosophical Library, 1949.

———. *Manual of Zen Buddhism*. New York: Grove Press, 1960.

Watts, Alan. *The Spirit of Zen*. New York: Grove Press, 1958.

———. *The Way of Zen*. New York: Pantheon Books, 1959.

———. *The Way of Liberation in Zen Buddhism*. San Francisco: American Academy of Asian Studies, 1955.

Yamamoto, J. Isamu. *Beyond Buddhism*. Downers Grove: InterVarsity Press, 1982.

ROSICRUCIANISM

Braden, Charles S. "Rosicrucianism." In *Encyclopedia Brittanica* (vol. 9). Chicago: Benton Publishing, 1964, 19th ed.

Clymer, R. S. *The Boor of Rosicrucae*. 3 vols. Quakerstown, Pa.: The Philosophical Publishing Co.

Gruss, Edmond C. *Cults and Occult*. Grand Rapids: Baker Book House, 1982.

Howe, Ellic. "Rosicrucians." In *Man, Myth & Magic* (vol. 18). Richard Cavendish, ed. New York: Marshall Cavendish Corp., 1970.

Heindel, Max. *The Rosicrucian Cosmo-Conception*. Oceanside: The Rosicrucian Fellowship, 1922.

———. *The Rosicrucian Philosophy*. Oceanside: The Rosicrucian Fellowship, 1922.

Lewis, H. Spencer. *Rosicrucian Questions and Answers With Complete History of the Rosicrucian Order*. San Jose: Supreme Grand Lodge of A.M.O.R.C., 1981, 15th ed.

———. *The Secret Doctrines of Jesus*. The Rosicru-

cian Press, Ltd., 1965, 10th ed.

Melton, J. Gordon. *The Encyclopedia of American Religions* (vol. 2). Wilmington, N.C.: McGrath Publishing Co., 1978.

Van Baalen, Jan Karel. *Chaos of the Cults*. Grand Rapids: Wm. B. Eerdmans Publishing Co., 1962, 4th ed., rev.

Wilson, Colin. *The Occult—A History*. New York: Random House, 1971.

SWEDENBORGIANISM

Barrett, B. F. *The Science of Correspondences Elucidated*. Germantown, Pa.: Swedenborg Publishing Assoc., 1909.

Ferm, Vergilius, ed. *Encyclopedia of Religion*. New York: Philosophical Library, 1945.

Jackson, Samuel Macauley, ed. *The New Schaff-Herzog Encyclopedia of Religious Knowledge*. Grand Rapids: Baker Book House, 1977 reprint.

Judah, J. Stillson. *The History and Philosophy of the Metaphysical Movements in America*. Philadelphia: The Westminster Press, 1967.

Larson, Bob. *Larson's Book of Cults*. Wheaton: Tyndale House Publishers, Inc., 1982.

Robertson, Irvine, *What the Cults Believe*. Chicago: Moody Press, 1981.

Sigstedt, Cyriel O. *The Swedenborg Epic, the Life and Works of Emmanuel Swedenborg*. New York: Twayne, 1952.

Smyth, Julian K., and Wunsch, William. *The Gist of Swedenborg*. Philadelphia: J. B. Lipincott, 1920.

Spittler, Russell P. *Cults and Isms*. Grand Rapids: Baker Book House, 1962.

Swedenborg, Emmanuel. *The Complete Works*. Boston: Houghton Mifflin Co., 1907.

Trobridge, G. *Swedenborg: Life and Teachings*. New York: Swedenborg Foundation, 1938.

Vrooman, Hiram. *Science and Theology Co-ordinated*. Chicago: Swedenborg Philosophical Center. (pamphlet)

THE BAHAI FAITH

I. MAGAZINE ARTICLES

Bach, Marcus. "Bahai, A Second Look," *Christian Century*, April 10, 1957.

"We Love All Religions," *Time* magazine, April 26, 1963.

II. PUBLICATIONS OF BAHAI PUBLISHING TRUST, WILMETTEL.

Abdu'l-Bahá. *Some Questions Answered*. (Emphasis on Christianity)

Bahá'u'lláh. *Gleanings From the Writings of Baha'u'llah*. 1952.

Bahá'u'lláh and Abdu'l-Bahá. *Baha'i World Faith. Principles of the Baha'i Faith*.

Sears, William. *Release the Sun*.

Shoghi, Effendi. *Promised Day to Come*.

Townshend, George. *The Promise of All Ages*.

Willoughby, John. *All Things Made New*.

III. GENERAL

Enroth, Ronald, et al. *A Guide to Cults and New Religions.* Downers Grove: InterVarsity Press, 1983.

Esslemont, J. E. *Bahá'u'lláh and the New Era.* 1923. Reprint. Wilmette: Baha'i Publishing Trust, 1970.

Gruss, Edmond C. *Cults and Occult.* Grand Rapids: Baker Book House, 1982.

Martin, Walter. *Walter Martin Speaks Out on the Cults.* Ventura: Vision House Publishers, 1983.

Miller, Elliot. "The Baha'i Faith." In *Walter Martin's Cults Reference Bible.* Walter Martin, ed. Santa Ana: Vision House Publishers, 1981.

Miller, William McElwee. *What Is the Baha'i Faith?* Grand Rapids: Wm. B. Eerdmans Publishing Co., 1977.

Van Baalen, Jan Karel. *Chaos of the Cults.* Grand Rapids: Wm. B. Eerdmans Publishing Co., 1962, 4th ed., rev.

THE UNITY SCHOOL OF CHRISTIANITY

Braden, Charles S. *Spirits in Rebellion.* Dallas: Southern Methodist University Press, 1963.

Cady, H. Emilie. *God a Present Help.* Unity School of Christianity, 1942.

———. *Lessons in Truth.* Lees Summit, Mo.: Unity School of Christianity, 1962.

Ferguson, Charles W. *The New Books of Revelation.* Garden City: Doubleday and Sons, 1929.

Fillmore, Charles. *Christian Healing.* Unity School of Christianity, 1954 (first published, 1909, 25th printing).

———. *Keep a True Lent.* 1954.

———. *Twelve Powers of Man.* 1943.

———. *Mysteries of Genesis.* 1936.

———. *What Practical Christianity Stands For.* 1939.

Fillmore, Charles and Cora. *Teach Us to Pray.* Kansas City: Unity School of Christianity, 1945.

Fillmore, Lowell, *New Ways to Solve Old Problems.* (2nd ed.) Kansas City: Unity School of Christianity, 1939.

Fillmore, Myrtle, *Healing Letters.* Lees Summit, Mo.: Unity School of Christianity, 1954 (first published, 1936, 8th printing).

Foulks, Francis W. *Effectual Prayer.* Kansas City: Unity School of Christianity, 1949.

Freeman, James Dilett. *The Household of Faith.* Lees Summit, Mo.: Unity School of Christianity, 1951.

———. *The Story of Unity.* Lees Summit, Mo.: Unity School of Christianity, 1954.

Gruss, Edmond C. *Cults and Occult.* Grand Rapids: Baker Book House, 1982.

Metaphysical Bible Dictionary. Lees Summit, Mo.: Unity School of Christianity.

Miller, Elliot. "Unity School of Christianity." In *Walter Martin's Cults Reference Bible.* Walter Martin, ed. Santa Ana: Vision House Publishers, 1981.

Metaphysical Bible Dictionary. Lees Summit, Mo.: Unity School of Christianity, 1962.

Quimby, Phineas P. *The Quimby Manuscripts.* Edited by Horatio W. Dresser. New York: Julian Press, 1961.

Shanklin, Octavia A. *Selected Studies.* Unity School of Christianity, 1953.

Teener, James W. "The Challenge of Unity." *Crossroads Magazine.* July 6, 1952, pp. 9–11.

Unity Statement of Faith, Unity School of Christianity.

Van Baalen, Jan Karel. *Chaos of the Cults.* Grand Rapids: Wm. B. Eerdmans Publishing Co., 1962, 4th ed., rev.

Wilson, Ernest C. *Have We Lived Before?* Unity School of Christianity, 1953.

ARMSTRONGISM

I. MAGAZINES

Ambassador Report. P.O. Box 4068, Pasadena 91106.

Campbell, Roger. "Herbert W. Armstrong: Does He Really have the 'Plain Truth'?" *Moody Monthly, October, 1972*

Campbell, Robert. "Herbert W. Armstrong: Mr. Confusion," *The Kings Business,* February, 1962.

Darby, Knuteson and Campbell. *The Delusions of Herbert W. Armstrong.* A reprint of *The Discerner,* January-March, 1962.

Hopkins, Joseph Martin. (No title) *Christianity Today,* December 17, 1971.

Eternity. "Mr. Jones, meet Herbert W. Armstrong," October, 1972.

Tarr, Leslie. "Herbert W. Armstrong: Does he really have the 'Plain Truth'?" *Moody Monthly,* September, 1972.

II. BOOKS

Anderson, Stanley E. *Armstrongism's 300 Errors Exposed by 1300 Bible Verses.* Nashville: Church Growth Publications, 1973.

Benware, Paul N. *Ambassadors of Armstrongism: An Analysis of the History and Teachings of the Worldwide Church of God.* Philadelphia: Presbyterian and Reformed Publishing Co., 1975.

Buchner, J.L.F. *Armstrongism Bibliography.* Sydney, Australia: the author, 1983.

Chambers, Roger R. *The Plain Truth About Armstrongism.* Grand Rapids: Baker Book House, 1972.

De Loach, Charles F. *The Armstrong Error.* Plainfield: Logos International, 1971.

Grant, Robert G. *The Plain Truth About the Armstrong Cult.* (No imprint)

Hopkins, Joseph M. *The Armstrong Empire.* Grand Rapids: Wm. B. Eerdmans Publishing Co., 1974.

Kirban, Salem, *The Plain Truth About the Plain Truth.* Huntington Valley, Pa.: Salem Kirban, Inc. 1970.

Larson, Egon. *Strange Cults and Sects.* New York: Hart Publishing Co., 1972.

Leyendecker, Ruth and Wayne, with Roger F. Campbell. "We Escaped From Armstrongism." In James R. Adair and Ted Miller, eds. *We Found Our Way Out.* Grand Rapids: Baker Book House, 1965.

Lowe, Harry W., Radio Church of God: *How its teachings differ from those of Seventh-Day Adventists.* Mountain View, Calif.: Pacific Press Publishing Association, 1970.

Marson, Richard A. *The Marson Report Concerning Herbert W. Armstrong.* Seattle: The Ashley-Calvin Press, 1970.

Ord, David R. *The Jet-Set Galatians.* Exeter, Devon, U.K.: The Paternoster Press, 1982.

Piepkorn, Arthur C. *Profiles in Belief* (vol. 4). San Francisco: Harper & Row Publishers, Inc., 1979.

Petersen, William J. *Those Curious New Cults.* New Canaan, Conn.: Keats Publishing, 1973.

Smith, Noel. *Herbert W. Armstrong and His World of Tomorrow.* Springfield: Bible Baptist Tribune, 1964.

Smith, Paul B. *Other Gospels.* Denver: Gospel Advance Press, 1970.

Sumner, Robert L. *Herbert W. Armstrong: False Prophet.* Murfreesboro, Tenn.: Sword of the Lord Foundation, 1961.

Wilson, Paul. *The Armstrong Heresy: A Brief Examination.* Denver: Wilson Foundation, n.d.

UNIFICATION CHURCH

Bjornstad, James. *Sun Myung Moon and the Unification Church.* Minneapolis: Bethany House Publishers, 1976.

Durham, Deanna. *Life Among the Moonies: Three Years in the Unification Church.* Plainfield: Logos International, 1981.

Edwards, Christopher. *Crazy for God.* Englewood Cliffs: Prentice-Hall, Inc., 1979.

Elkins, Chris. *Heavenly Deception.* Wheaton: Tyndale House Publishers, Inc., 1980.

———. *What Do You Say to a Moonie?* Wheaton: Tyndale House Publishers, Inc., 1981.

Kemperman, Steve. *Lord of the Second Advent.* Ventura: Regal Books/Gospel Light, 1981.

Martin, Walter. *The New Cults.* Ventura: Vision House/Gospel Light, 1981.

Passantino, Robert and Gretchen. *Answers to the Cultist at Your Door.* Eugene: Harvest House Publishers, 1981.

Yamamoto, J. Isamu. *The Puppet Master.* Downers Grove: InterVarsity Press, 1977.

SCIENTOLOGY

Alexander, Brooks, and Halverson, Dean C., eds., *Scientology: The Technology of Enlightenment.* Berkeley: Spiritual Counterfeits Project, 1982.

Cooper, Paulette. *Scandal of Scientology.* New York: Tower Publishers, 1971.

Evans, Chris. *The Cults of Unreason.* New York: Dell Publishing Co. Inc., 1973.

"Federal Prosecutors Unveil the Astonishing Intrigues of the Scientology Church." *People,* August 14, 1978.

Foster, Sir John G. *Enquiry into the Practice and Effects of Scientology.* London: Her Majesty's Stationery Office (report to the British government).

Gardner, Martin. *Fads and Fallacies in the Name of Science.* New York: Dover Publications, 1957.

Kaufman, Robert. *Inside Scientology.* New York: Olympia Publications, 1972.

Martin, Walter. "Scientology." Ventura: Vision House/Gospel Light, 1976 (cassette tape).

Methvin, Eugene H. "Scientology: Anatomy of a Frightening Cult." *Readers Digest,* May, 1980.

———. "Scientology: The Sickness Spreads." *Readers Digest,* September, 1981.

Scientology: An In-Depth Profile of a New Force in Clearwater. Clearwater, Fla.: St. Petersburg Times, 1980.

Smith, Ralph Lee. "Scientology—Menace to Mental Health." *Today's Health,* December, 1968.

Wallis, Claudia. "Mystery of the Vanished Ruler." *Time* magazine, January 31, 1983.

EASTERN RELIGIONS

HINDUISM

Anderson, Sir Norman, ed. *The World's Religions.* rev. ed. Grand Rapids: William B. Eerdmans Publishing Co., 1975.

Anderson, J.N.D. *Christianity and Comparative Religion.* Downers Grove: InterVarsity Press, 1970.

Mangalwadi, Vishal. *The World of Gurus.* New Delhi: Vikas Publishing House, 1977.

Bouquet, A. C. *Hinduism.* rev. ed. London: Hutchinson University Library, 1962.

Zaehner, R. C. *Hinduism.* 2d. ed. Oxford: Oxford University Press, 1966.

HARE KRISHNAS

Levine, Faye. *The Strange World of the Hare Krishnas.* New York: Fawcett Publications, 1974.

Judah, J. Stillson. *Hare Krishna and the Counterculture.* New York: John Wiley and Sons, 1974.

Yamamoto, J. Isamu. *Hare Krishna Hare Krishna.* Downers Grove: InterVarsity Press, 1978.

Miller, Elliot. "Inside ISKCON." *Forward,* Vol. 4, no. 1, p. 1.

Miller, Elliot. "Inside ISKCON Part 2." *Forward,* Vol. 4, no. 2, p. 3.

TRANSCENDENTAL MEDITATION

Weldon, John, and Levitt, Zola. *The Transcendental Explosion.* Irvine: Harvest House Publishers, 1976.

Haddon, David, and Hamilton, Vail. *TM Wants*

You! Grand Rapids: Baker Book House, 1976.
Bjornstad, James. *The Transcendental Mirage.* Minneapolis: Bethany House Publishers, 1976.
Lewis, Gordon R. *What Everyone Should Know About Transcendental Meditation.* Glendale: G/L Regal Books, 1975.
Spiritual Counterfeits Project. *TM in Court.* Berkeley: Spiritual Counterfeits Project, 1978.

ISLAM

Abdul-Haqq, Adijah Akbar. *Sharing Your Faith with a Muslim.* Minneapolis: Bethany House Publishers, 1980.
Accad, F. E. *Theological Principles in the Towrah, the Zabur, the Injil, and the Qur'an.* Booklet. Colorado Springs: Navigators, n.d.
Bavinck, J. H. *The Church Between Temple and Mosque.* Grand Rapids: Wm. B. Eerdmans Publishing Co., 1981 (reprint).
Christian Witness Among Muslims. Ghana, W. Africa: Africa Christian Press, 1971.
Clair-Tisdall, Rev. W. St. *A Manual of the Leading Muhammadan Objections of Christianity.* London: Society for Promoting Christian Knowledge, 1904.
_____, *The Sources of Islam.* Edinburgh: T. & T. Clark, n.d.
Cragg, Kenneth. *The Call of the Minaret.* New York: Oxford University Press, 1964.
Dayton, Edward, et al. *Unreached Peoples '80.* Elgin: David C. Cook Publishing Co., 1980.
Elder, John. *The Biblical Approach to the Muslim.* Fort Washington: Worldwide Evangelism Crusade, 1974.
Fry, C. George, and King, James R. *Islam: A Survey of the Muslim Faith.* Grand Rapids: Baker Book House, 1980.
Gilchrist, John. *Christianity and Islam Series.* Booklets. Durban, Republic of South Africa: Jesus to the Muslims, 1980.
Glasser, Carol A. *Muslim Awareness Seminar.* Booklet. Monrovia: Samuel Zwemer Institute, 1981.
_____. *Quran and Bible Series.* Booklets. Durban, Republic of South Africa: Jesus to the Muslims, 1981.
Goldsack, W. *The Origins of the Qur'an.* London: Christian Literature Society, 1907.
Goldsmith, Martin. *Islam and Christian Witness.* Downers Grove: InterVarsity Press, 1982.
Handbook for Christians Working with Iranians in North America. Altadena, Calif.: Samuel Zwemer Institute, 1980.
Hanna, Mark. *The True Path.* Colorado Springs: International Doorways Publishers, 1975.
Hirji-Walji, Hass, and Strong, Jaryl. *Escape from Islam.* Wheaton: Tyndale House Publishers, Inc., 1978.
Jeffery, Arthur, ed. *Material for the History of the Text of the Qur'an: The Old Codices.* New York: AMS, Inc., 1975.

Jones, L. Bevan. *Christianity Explained to Muslims.* Calcutta: Baptist Mission Press, 1937.
_____. *The People of the Mosque.* London: Student Christian Movement Press, 1932.
Kateregga, Badru D., and Shenk, David W. *Islam and Christianity.* Grand Rapids: Wm. B. Eerdmans Publishing Co., 1980.
Kershaw, R. Max. *How to Share the Good News with Your Muslim Friend.* Colorado Springs: Fellowship of Faith for Muslims, 1978.
Marsh, Charles R. *Share Your Faith With a Muslim.* Chicago: Moody Press, 1975.
McCurry, Don M., ed. *Sharing the Gospel With Iranians.* Altadena, Calif.: Samuel Zwemer Institute, 1982.
_____. *The Gospel and Islam: A 1978 Compendium.* Monrovia: Missions Advanced Research Communications Center, 1978.
Muslim/Christian Cross-Cultural Dating & Marriage. Altadena, Calif.: Samuel Zwemer Institute, 1981.
Parrinder, Geoffrey. *Jesus in the Qur'an.* New York: Oxford University Press, 1977.
Parshall, Phil. *New Paths in Muslim Evangelism.* Grand Rapids: Baker Book House, 1980.
Pfander, C. G. *The Mizanu'l Haqq: Balance of Truth.* London: Religious Tract Society, rev. 1910 (Clair-Tisdall).
Register, Ray G. *Dialogue and Interfaith with Muslims.* Kinsport: Moody Books, Inc., 1979.
Sell, Canon. *Outlines of Islam.* London: Christian Literature Society for India, 1912.
Spencer, H. *Islam and the Gospel of God.* Delhi: S.T.C.K., 1956.
Vander Werff, Lyle L. *Christian Mission to Muslims; The Record. Anglican and Reformed Approaches in India and the Near East, 1860–1938.* South Pasadena: William Carey Library, 1977.
Wilson, Christy J. *Today's Tentmakers. Self-support—An Alternative Model for Worldwide Witness.* Wheaton: Tyndale House Publishers, Inc., 1979.
Your Muslim Guest: A Practical Guide in Friendship and Witness for Christians Who Meet Muslims in North America. Toronto: Fellowship of Faith for Muslims, 1975.
Zwemer, Samuel. *Islam: A Challenge to Faith.* New York: Student Volunteer Movement for Foreign Missions, 1907.

SEVENTH-DAY ADVENTISM

I. WRITINGS OF ELLEN G. WHITE

Review and Herald Publishing Association, Takoma Park, Maryland: *The Adventist Home; Child Guidance; Christ's Object Lessons; Counsels on Diets and Foods; Early Writings; Education; Evangelism; Messages to Young People; The Ministry of Healing; Steps to Christ.*
Pacific Press Publishing Association, Mountain View, Calif.: *The Acts of the Apostles; Christian Experience and Teachings; The Desire of the Ages; The Great Controversy; Index to the Writings of*

Ellen G. White; Patriarchs and Prophets; Prophets and Kings; Testimonies for the Church, vols. 1–9; Testimonies to Ministers; Thoughts From the Mount of Blessings.

II. SEVENTH-DAY ADVENTIST PUBLICATIONS

Anderson, R. A. The Shepherd Evangelist. Review and Herald.
———. Unfolding the Revelation. Pacific Press.
Andreason, M. L. The Book of Hebrews. Review and Herald.
———. God's Holy Day. Review and Herald.
———. The Sabbath. Review and Herald.
———. The Sanctuary Service. Review and Herald.
———. What Can a Man Believe? Pacific Press.
The Bible Made Plain, a series of short Bible Studies for the home circle upon the fundamentals of the Christian faith. Review and Herald.
Bible Readings for the Home, compilation. Review and Herald, 1956.
Bible Reading for the Home Circle. Review and Herald.
Bollman, Calvin P. Sunday, Origin of Its Observance in the Christian Church. Review and Herald.
Branson, W. H. In Defense of the Faith. Review and Herald.
Bunch, Taylor G. Behold the Man. Southern Publishing Assoc.
———. The Ten Commandments. Review and Herald.
Christian, Lewis Harrison. The Fruitage of Spiritual Gifts: The Influence and Guidance of Ellen G. White in the Advent Movement. Washington, D.C.: Review and Herald, 1947.
Church Manual. Takoma Park, Md: General Conference of Seventh-day Adventists.
Cottrell, Raymond F. Perfection in Christ. Washington, D.C.: Review and Herald, 1965.
———. The True Sabbath. Southern Publishing Assoc.
Daniels, A. G. The Abiding Gift of Prophecy. Pacific Press.
———. Christ Our Righteousness. Takoma Park, Md: The Ministerial Association of Seventh-day Adventists.
Dixon, Louis J. Law or Grace. Southern Publishing Assoc.
Everson, Charles T. The Rich Man and Lazarus. Southern Publishing Assoc.
———. Who Are the Angels? Review and Herald.
Froom, Leroy E. The Coming of the Comforter. Review and Herald.
———. Finding the Lost Prophetic Witness. Review and Herald.
———. The Prophetic Faith of Our Fathers. vols. 1–4. Review and Herald.
General Conference Young Peoples Department of Missionary Volunteers pamphlet. Studies in Bible Doctrine. Senior Missionary Volunteer. Review and Herald.
Genesis—John. Review and Herald.

Haskell, S. N. Bible Hand Book. Review and Herald.
Haynes, Carlyle B. The Christian Sabbath, Is It Saturday or Sunday? Southern Publishing Assoc.
———. From Sabbath to Sunday. Review and Herald.
———. The Gift of Prophecy. Southern Publishing Assoc.
———. Life, Death and Immortality. Southern Publishing Assoc.
———. Seventh-day Adventists, Their Work and Teachings. Review and Herald
———. When a Man Dies. Review and Herald.
Horn, Sigfried H., and Wood, Lynn H. The Chronology of Ezra Seven. Review and Herald.
How to Handle Objections, prepared by the publishing department of The Secretaries of the Southern Union Conference. Southern Publishing Assoc.
Jamison, T. Housel. A Prophet Among You. Pacific Press.
Johns, Varner J. The Secret Rapture and the Antichrist. Pacific Press.
Lickey, Arthur E. Fundamentals of the Everlasting Gospel. Review and Herald.
Marsh, F. L. Evolution, Creation and Science. Review and Herald.
Maxwell, Arthur S. The Coming King. Pacific Press.
———. Your Friends the Adventists. Pacific Press.
The Ministry (magazine).
Moseley, Calvin Edwin. The Lord's Day. Southern Publishing Assoc.
Nichol, Francis D. Answers to Objections. Review and Herald.
———. The Certainty of My Faith. Review and Herald.
———. Ellen G. White and Her Critics. Review and Herald.
———. The Midnight Cry. Review and Herald.
Odom, Robert L. The Final Crisis and Deliverance. Southern Publishing Assoc.
———. How Did Sunday Get Its Name? Southern Publishing Assoc.
———. Sunday in Roman Paganism. Review and Herald.
Problems in Bible Translation. Takoma Park, Md: General Conference, Seventh-day Adventists.
Reed, W. E. The Bible, the Spirit of Prophecy and the Church. Review and Herald.
Review and Herald (magazine).
Richards, H.M.S. Hard Nuts Cracked. Southern Publishing Assoc.
Robinson, D. E. The Story of Our Health Message. Southern Publishing House.
Sabbath-School Quarterly (magazine).
The Seventh-day Adventist Bible Commentary. vols. 1–5.
Seventh-day Adventist Church Directory, United States and Canada. Review and Herald.
Seventh-day Adventist Year Book, 1957. Review and Herald.

Signs of the Times (magazine).

Smith, Uriah. *Daniel and the Revelation.* vols. 1 and 2. Review and Herald.

Spalding, Arthur W. *Sister White.* Review and Herald.

Spicer, W. A. *Our Day in the Light of Prophecy.* Review and Herald.

Straw, W. E. *Origin of Sunday Observance.* Review and Herald.

These Times (magazine).

Walker, Allen. *The Law and the Sabbath.* Southern Publishing Assoc.

Werner, A. J. *Fundamentals of Bible Doctrine.* Review and Herald.

Wheeler, Ruth. *His Messenger.* Review and Herald.

Wilcox, F. M. *The Coming Crisis.* Review and Herald.

_____. *The Lord's Day, the Test of the Ages.* Pacific Press.

_____. *Questions Answered.* Pacific Press.

III. GENERAL

The Advent Herald (Millerite).

The Advent Shield and Review (Millerite). 1844.

Auchincloss, Douglas. "Peace With the Adventists," *Time* magazine, Dec. 31, 1956. pp. 48–49.

Baer, James E. "The Seventh-day Adventists," Series: "The Bible and Modern Religions," *Interpretation,* Journal of Theology, Jan., 1956.

Barnhouse, Donald Grey. "Are Seventh-day Adventists Christian?" *Eternity* magazine, Sept., 1956.

Biederwolf, Wm. Edward. *Seventh-day Adventism, the Result of a Predicament.* Grand Rapids: Wm. B. Eerdmans Publishing Co.

Bird, Herbert S. *Theology of Seventh-day Adventism.* Grand Rapids: Wm. B. Eerdmans Publishing Co., 1961.

Bliss, Sylvester. *Memoirs of William Miller.* Boston, 1853.

Booth, A. E. *Seventh-day Adventism, What Is It?* vol. 12, article on William Miller.

Buswell, J. Oliver. *The Length of Creative Days.* Monograph. New York: Shelton College, 1950.

Canright, D. M. *Hard Nuts for Seventh-day Adventists* (tract).

_____. *Life of Mrs. E. G. White.* Nashville: B. C. Goodpasture, 1948.

_____. *Seventh-day Adventism Renounced.* Grand Rapids: Baker Book House, 1961 (reprinted from 1889).

Chafer, Louis Sperry. *Grace.* Van Kampen Press, 1947.

Davies, Horton. *Christian Deviations.* New York: Philosophical Library. Chapter on Seventh-day Adventism.

Deck, Norman C. *The Lord's Day or the Sabbath, Which?* Sydney, Australia: Bridge Printery, Ltd.

Dictionary of American Biography. New York: Charles Scribner's Sons.

Douty, Norman F. *Another Look at Seventh-day Adventism.* Grand Rapids: Baker Book House, 1962.

Dugger, A. F. *The Bible Sabbath Defended.* Stanbury, Mo.: The Church of God Publishing House.

Dungan, D. R. *Sabbath or Lord's Day, Which?* Nashville: Harbinger Book Club.

Feinberg, Charles L. *The Sabbath and the Lord's Day.* Van Kampen Press.

Fletcher, W. W. *The Reasons for My Faith.* Sydney, Australia: William Brooks & Co., Ltd.

Hoekema, Anthony. *The Four Major Cults.* Grand Rapids: Wm. B. Eerdmans Publishing Co., 1963.

Hulbert, Terry C. "Seventh-day Adventism Weighed in the Balances," *The Discerner Magazine,* Oct.-Dec., 1956. (This issue is a refutation of Seventh-day Adventism.)

Ironside, H. A. *What Think Ye of Christ?* New York: Loizeaux.

Irvine, Wm. C. *Heresies Exposed.* New York: Loizeaux.

Jones, E. B. *The Answer and the Reasons,* eye-opening information regarding Seventh-day Adventism. Oak Park: Designed Products.

_____. *Free Indeed,* the author's testimony concerning his deliverance from Seventh-day Adventism. Designed Products.

_____. *Forty Bible-Supported Reasons Why You Should Not Be a Seventh-day Adventist.* Designed Products.

Martin, Walter. *The Truth about Seventh-day Adventism.* Grand Rapids: Zondervan Publishing House, 1960.

Miller, William. *Apology and Defense.* Aug., 1845 (pamphlet); *A Few Evidences of the Time of the Second Coming of Christ* (Mss. 1831).

Paxton, Geoffrey J. *The Shaking of Adventism.* Grand Rapids: Baker Book House, 1977.

Pickering, Ernest. "Can We Fellowship With Seventh-day Adventists?" *The Voice* of the Independent Fundamental Churches of America, Oct., 1956.

Pollock, A. J. *Seventh-day Adventism Briefly Tested by Scripture.* London: The Central Bible Truth Depot.

Putnam, C. E. *Legalism and the Seventh-day Question, Can Sinai Law and Grace Coexist?* Chicago: The Bible Institute Colportage Assoc.

Rowell, J. B. *Seventh-day Adventism Examined.* Norwalk, Calif.: Challenge Publishing Co.

"Seventh-day Adventists and the Date of Creation," editorial, *The Examiner* magazine, March-April, 1952.

Smith, Oswald J. *Who Are the False Prophets?* Toronto: The People's Press.

_____. *Who Are the Seventh-day Adventists and What Do They Teach?* Hugh Warren, Wesley Press and Publishing House.

Talbot, Louis T. *What's Wrong With Seventh-day Adventism?* Grand Rapids: Dunham.

IV. MAGAZINE ARTICLES

Bibliotheca Sacra, April, 1956.

Christianity Today
"What of Seventh-day Adventism?" by Harold Lindsell, Part I, March 31, 1958. Part II, April 14, 1958. "Another Look at Adventism" by Herbert S. Bird, April 28, 1958. "A Seventh-day Adventist Speaks Back" by Frank H. Yost, July 21, 1958.

Eternity, September, 1956.

Eternity, June, 1958.

Jones, E. B. "The Historical Background of Seventh-day Adventism," "Seventh-day Adventism and the Gospel of Grace," etc. *The Sunday School Times,* 1954.

———. "Seventh-day Adventists Counterfeit Gospel," *Christian Victory* magazine, Feb., 1952.

King's Business, The, April, 1957.

King's Business, The, March, 1958.

Martin, Walter R. "Are Seventh-day Adventists Evangelical?" *Christian Life* magazine, Oct., 1956.

———. "Seventh-day Adventism Today," *Our Hope* magazine, Nov., 1956.

Signs of the Times, January 8, 1952.

Sword of the Lord, The, August 2, 1957.

UNITARIANISM

Braden, Charles S. *The World's Religions.* New York: Abingdon Press, 1954.

DeWolf, Harold F. *Present Trends in Christian Thought.* New York: Association Press, 1960.

Ferm, Vergilius. *Encyclopedia of Religion.* New York: Philosophical Library, 1945.

Kegley, Charles W., and Bretall, Robert W. *The Theology of Paul Tillich.* (The Library of Living Theology) New York: Macmillan, 1961.

Kimmel, William, and Clive, Geoffry. *Dimensions of Faith.* New York: Twayne Publishers, 1959.

Larson, Bob. *Larson's Book of Cults.* Wheaton: Tyndale House Publishers, 1982.

Machen, John G. *Christianity and Liberalism.* New York: Macmillan, 1923; *What Is Faith?* 1935.

MacKintosh, Hugh Ross. *Types of Modern Theology From Schleiermacher to Barth.* New York: Charles Scribners' and Sons, 1937.

Nash, Arnold S. *Protestant Thought in the Twentieth Century.* New York: Macmillan, 1951.

Piepkorn, Arthur C. *Profiles in Belief* (vol. 4). San Francisco: Harper & Row Publishers, Inc., 1979.

Rosten, Leo. *Religions in America.* New York: Simon and Schuster, 1963.

Scholefield, Harry, ed. *Unitarian Universalist Pocket Guide.* Boston: Beacon Press, 1963; *A Pocket Guide to Unitarianism.* 1954.

Spittler, Russell P. *Cults and Isms.* Grand Rapids: Baker Book House, 1962.

Wilbur, Earl Morse. *A History of Unitarianism.* Cambridge: Harvard University Press.

INDEX